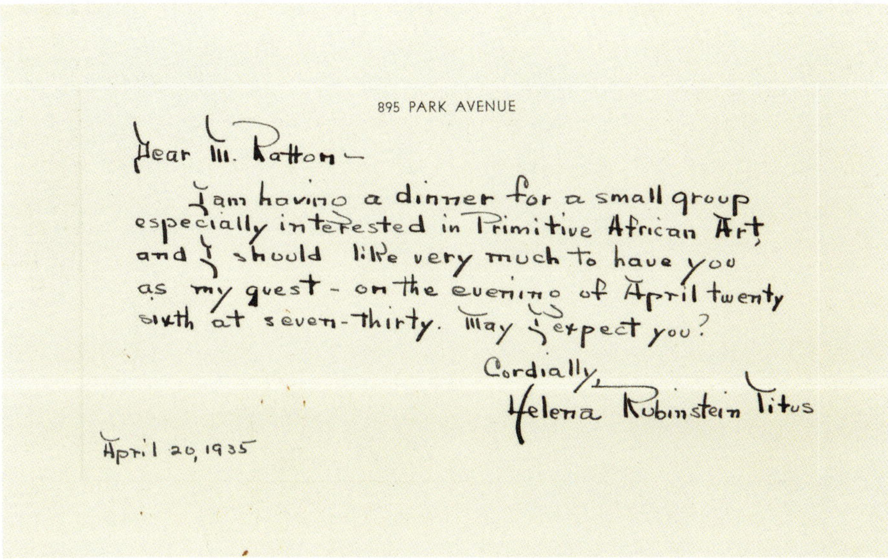

895 PARK AVENUE

Dear M. Ratton –

I am having a dinner for a small group especially interested in Primitive African Art, and I should like very much to have you as my guest – on the evening of April twenty sixth at seven-thirty. May I expect you?

Cordially,

Helena Rubinstein Titus

April 20, 1935

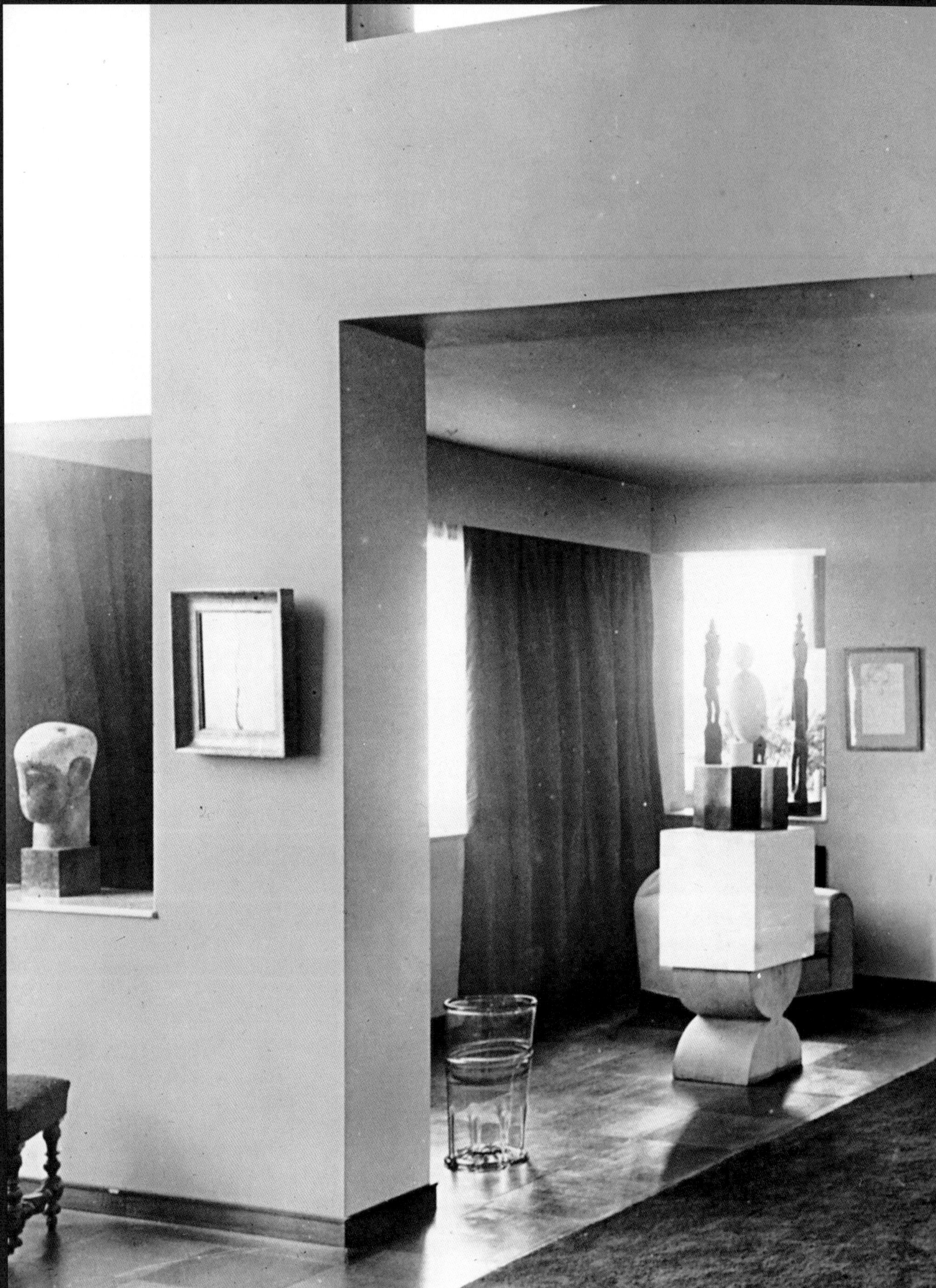

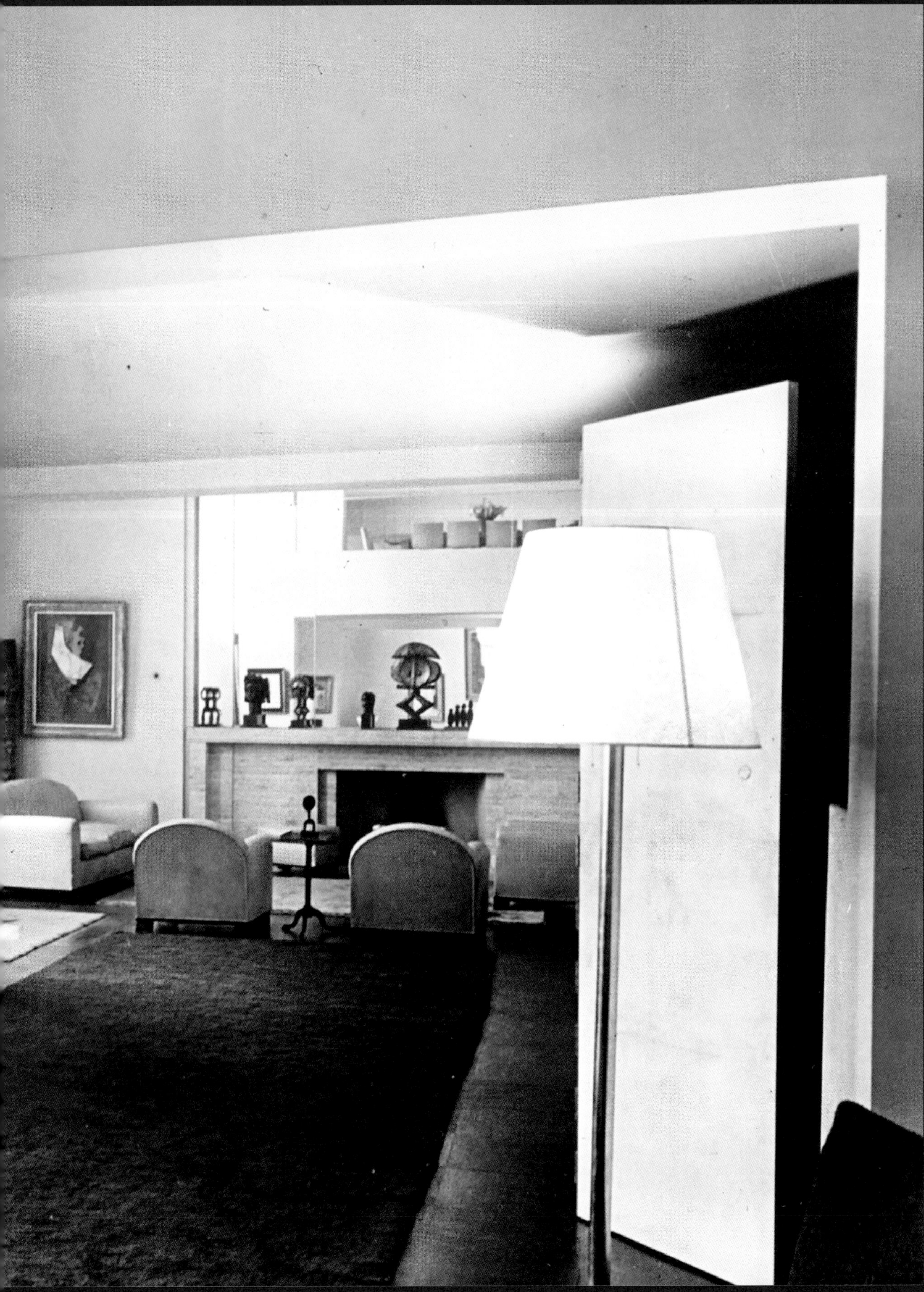

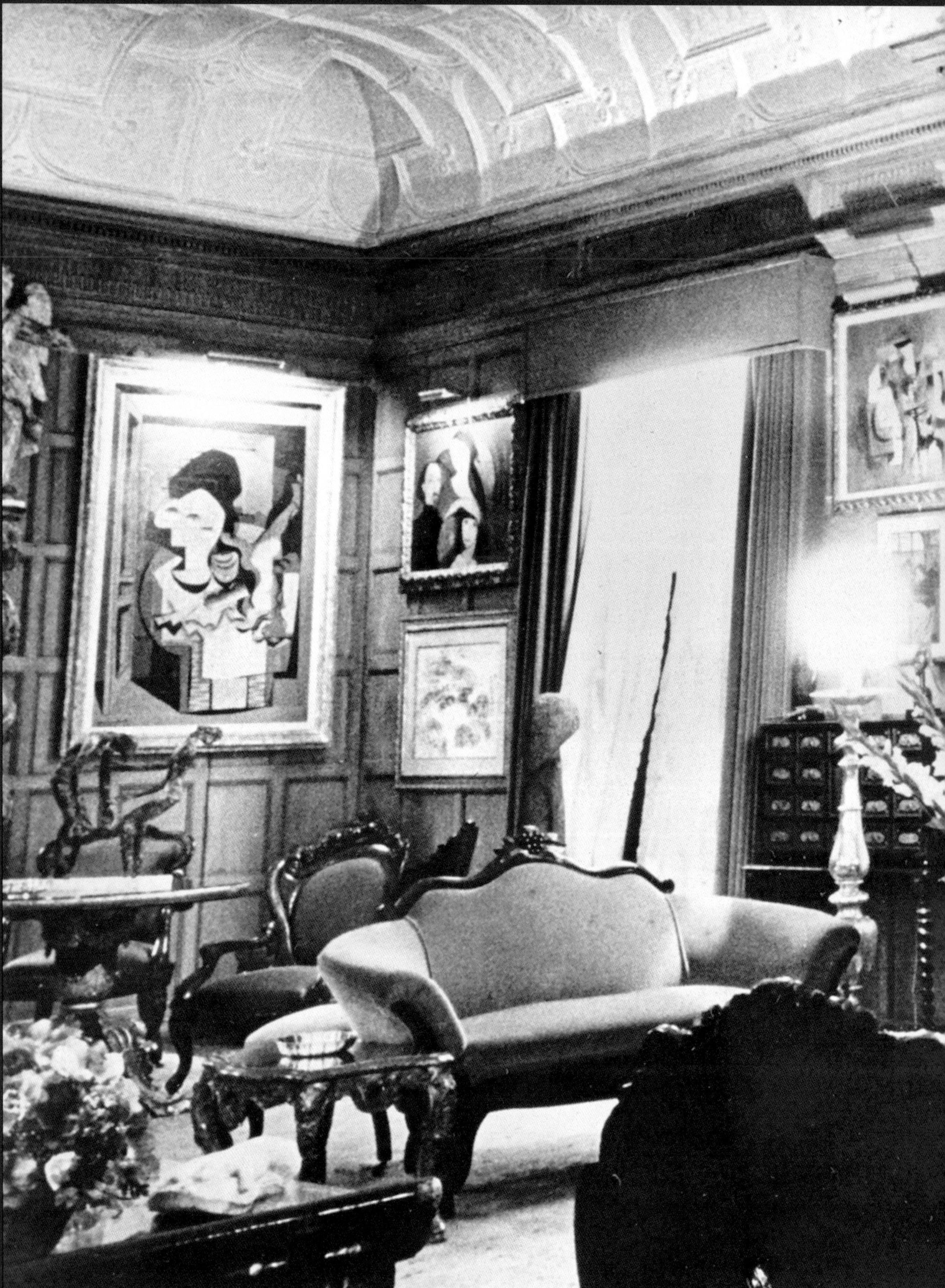

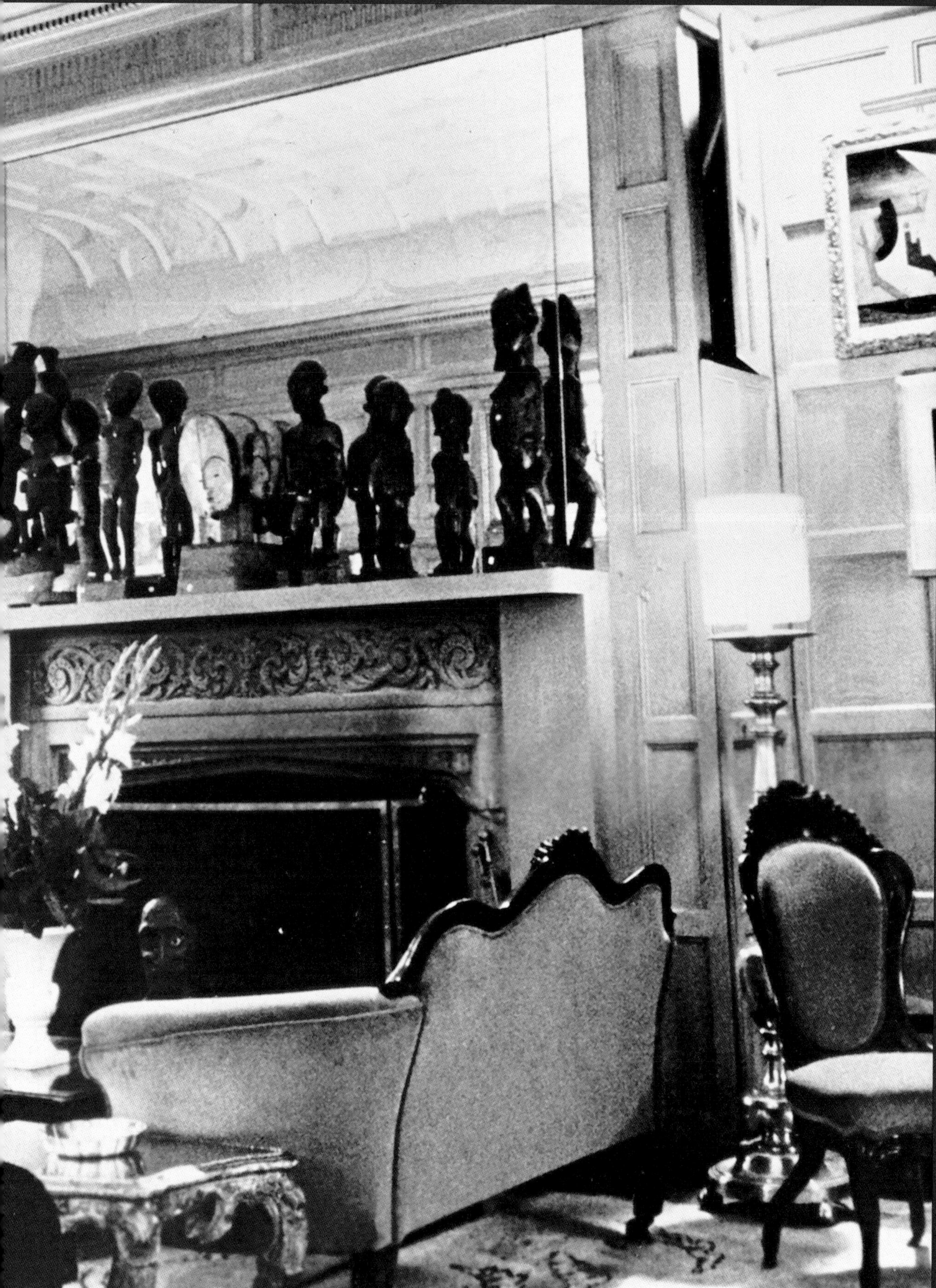

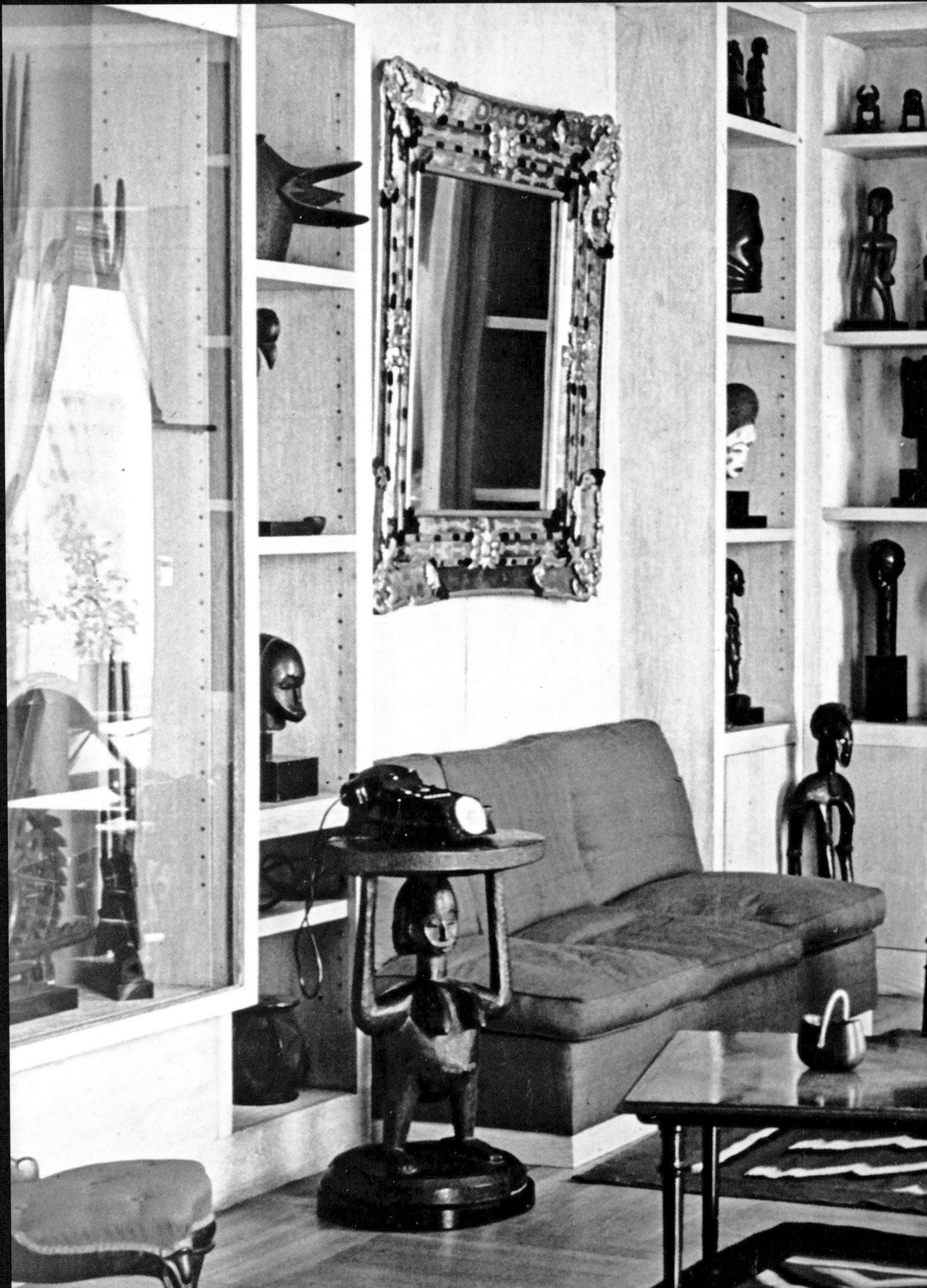

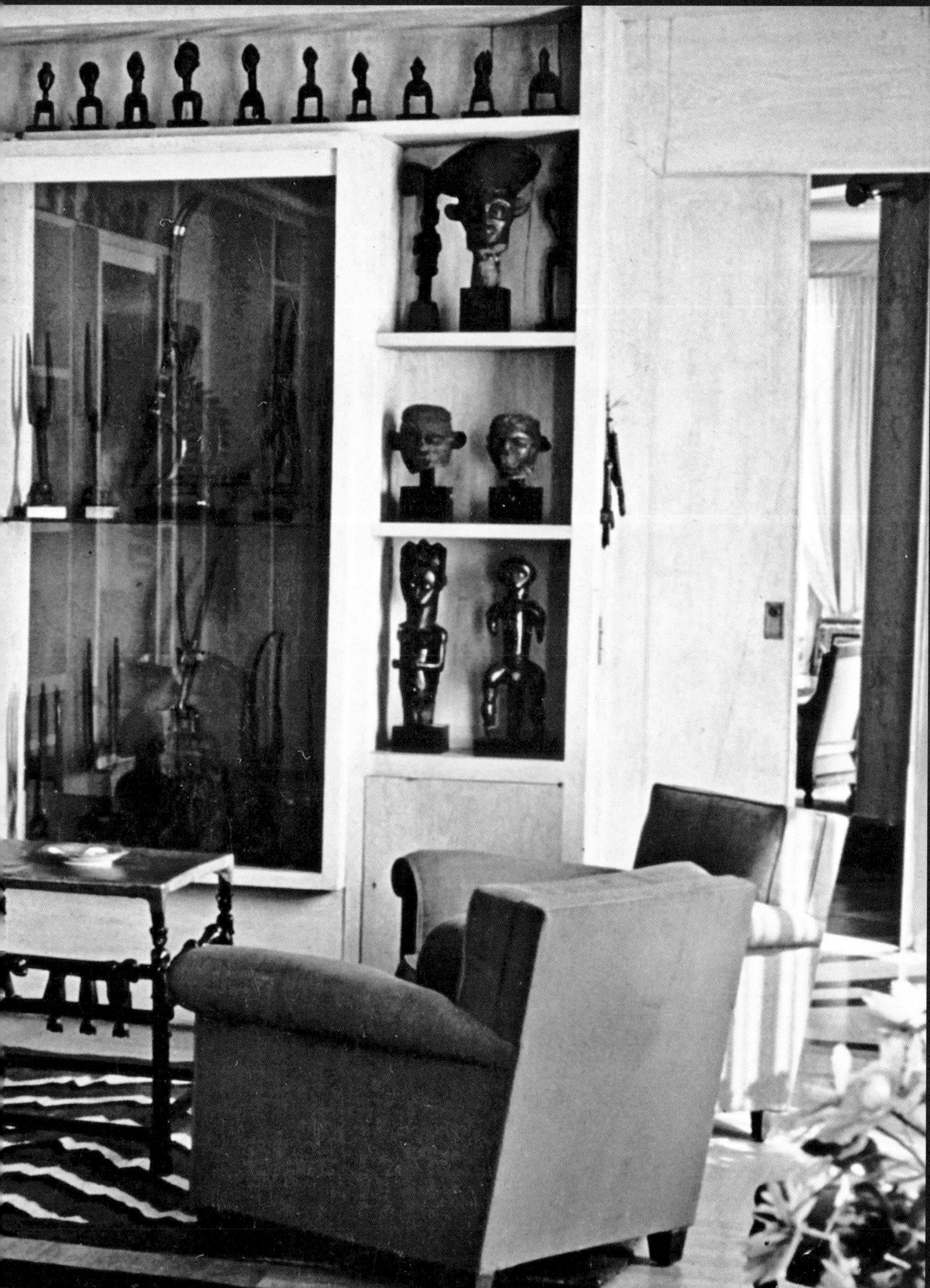

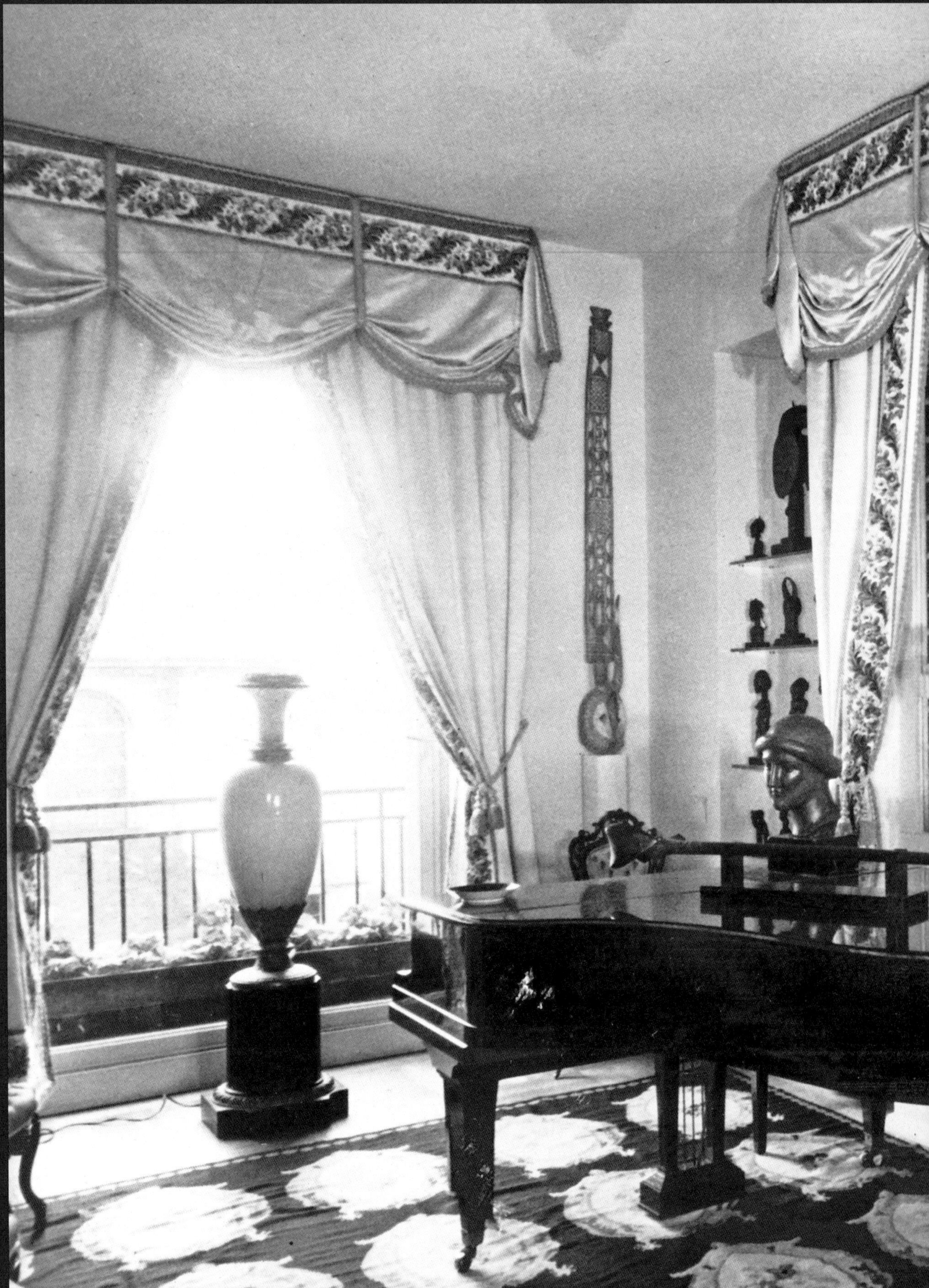

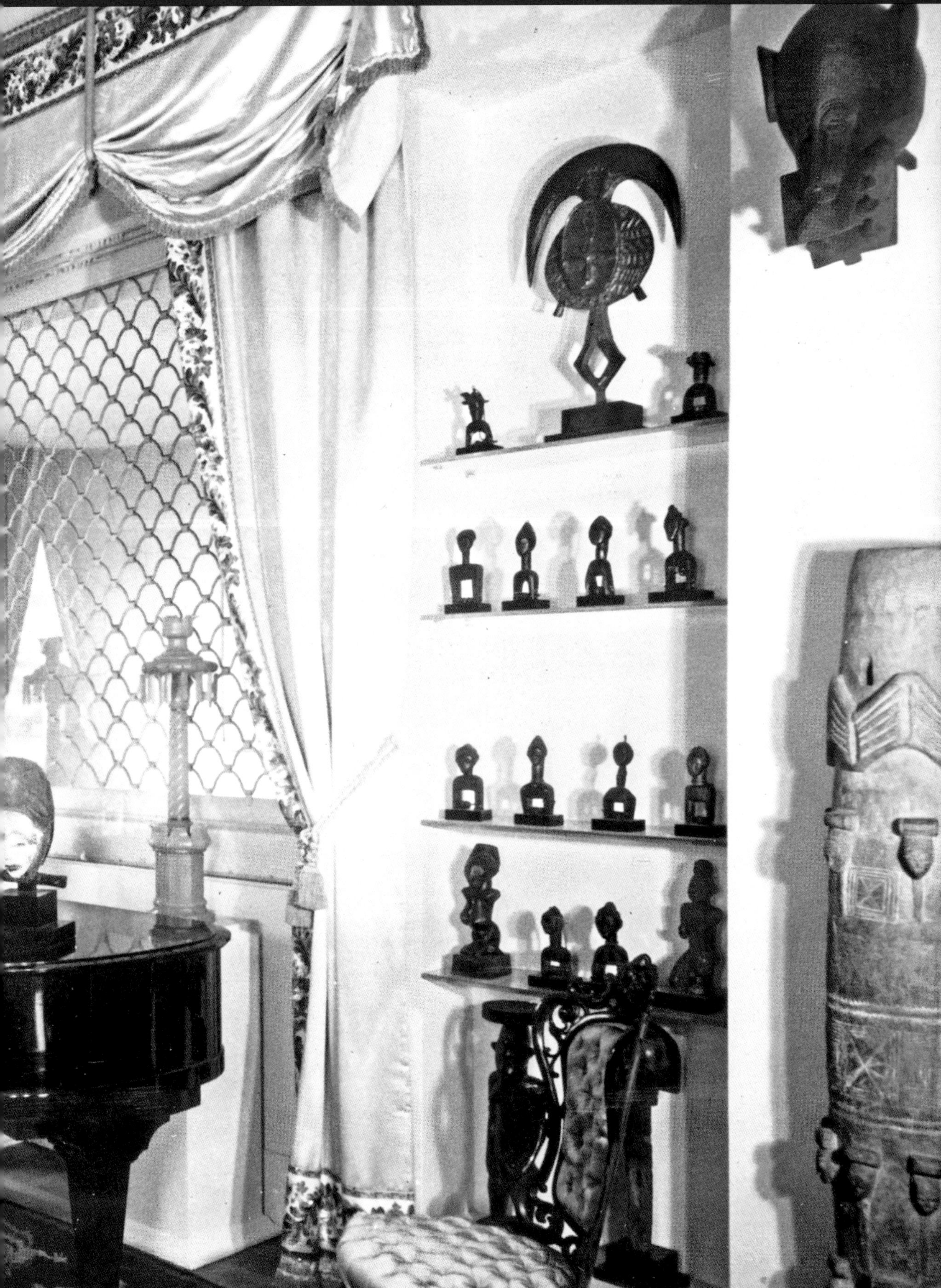

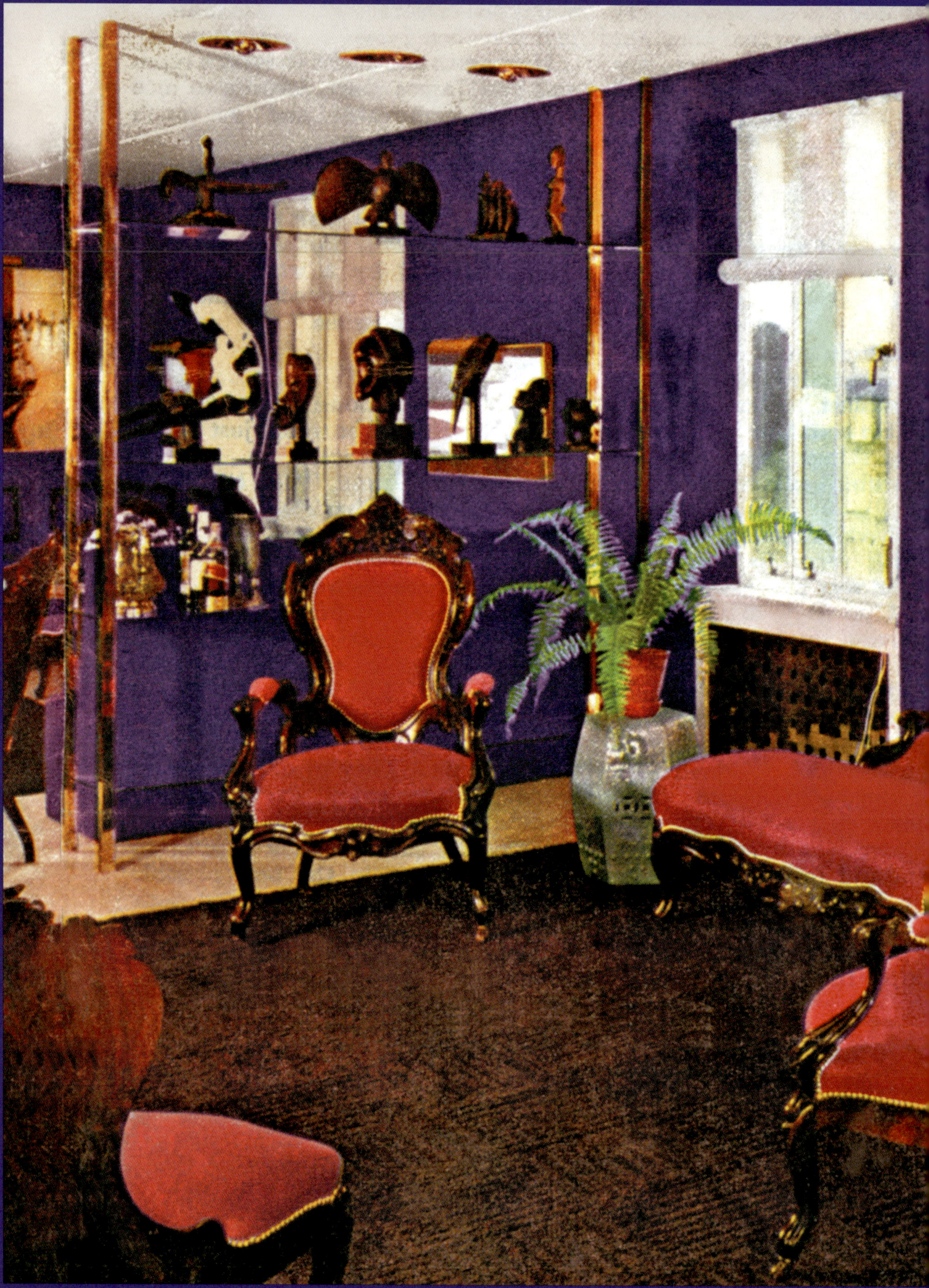

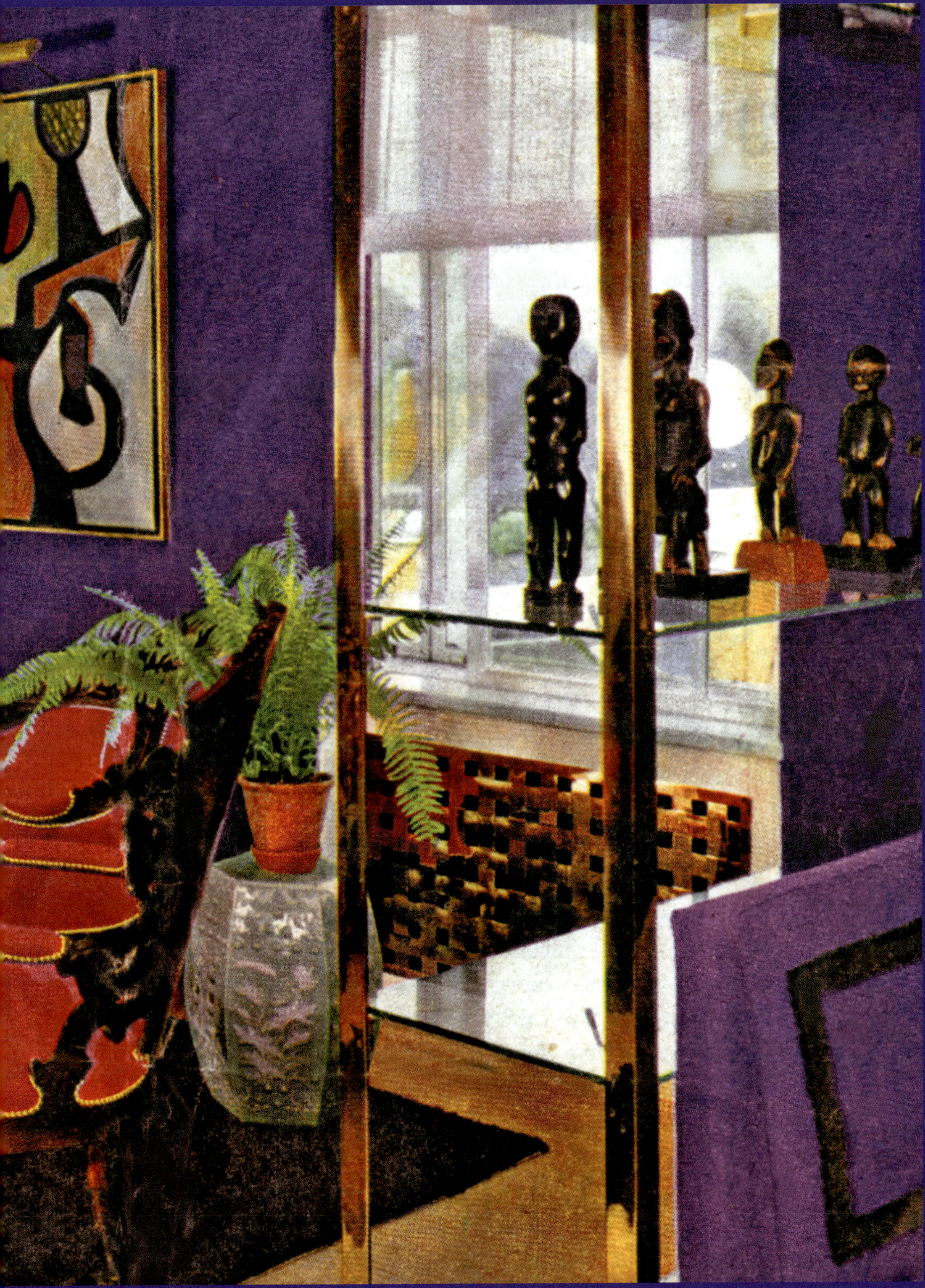

Cover
Protection mask Dan-Ngere (lot 10), Paris,
Marc Ladreit de Lacharrière collection

Madame next to a Yoruba *Gelede* mask, New York, 1957

P. 1
Dinner invitation from Helena Rubinstein Titus to Charles Ratton during the *African Negro Art* exhibition in New York, April 20, 1935, Guy Ladrière collection

P. 2-3
The drawing-room at 216, Boulevard Raspail, Paris, after 1932

P. 4-5
The drawing-room at 625, Park Avenue, New York, c. 1950

P. 6-7
The "African Room," 24, Quai de Béthune, Paris, c. 1960

P. 8-9
The music room, 24, Quai de Béthune, Paris, 1950

P. 10-11
The apartment in Knightsbridge, London, c. 1961

In the captions the lot number identifying each object refers to the Parke-Bernet auction catalog of April 21 and 29, 1966; when followed by an asterisk it refers to the Parke-Bernet auction catalog of October 15, 1966.

HELENA RUBINSTEIN

Madame's Collection

Edited by Hélène Joubert

SKIRA

MUSÉE DU QUAI BRANLY - JACQUES CHIRAC

Following Marc Ladreit de Lacharrière's exceptional donation to the national collections in February 2018, what used to be called the *Mezzanine Ouest* space is henceforth known as the *Galerie Marc Ladreit de Lacharrière*.

From September 2020, a permanent display of works from the donation will be on show in the northern section of the *Galerie Marc Ladreit de Lacharrière*. The southern part of the gallery will hold temporary exhibitions on themes relating to the history of non-Western art or illustrating intriguing perspectives on these arts by artists or major collectors.

Marc Ladreit de Lacharrière has been pleased to act as patron for these projects, which resonate with his donation. The "Marc Ladreit de Lacharrière fund for the awareness and promotion of African and Oceanic civilizations" established on this occasion will thus improve our knowledge of cultures and works all too often neglected by history.

Le musée du quai Branly – Jacques Chirac est placé sous la double tutelle du ministère de la Culture et du ministère de l'Enseignement supérieur, de la Recherche et de l'Innovation.

This book is published on the occasion of the exhibition ***Helena Rubinstein. Madame's Collection*** presented at the Galerie Marc Ladreit de Lacharrière of the Musée du Quai Branly – Jacques Chirac from November 19, 2019 to June 28, 2020

This exhibition is made possible thanks to the support of Marc Ladreit de Lacharrière

Curatorship
Hélène Joubert, Head of the African Heritage Unit, Musée du Quai Branly – Jacques Chirac

Scenography
Vaste

Graphic Design
Cécilia Génard

Lighting design
Vaste

Production

Direction of Cultural Development, Musée du Quai Branly – Jacques Chirac

Director of Cultural Development
Christine Drouin

Exhibition

Head of the Exhibitions Department
Isabelle Lainé

Production
Domitille Chaudieu

Exhibition Registrar
Quiterie d'Ariès

Heads of Display Projects
Anne-Cécile Maineray and Marion Forissier

Audio-visual Production
Marc Henry, Johann Demarigny and Gabriel de Swarte

Image Production
Audrey Lagrue

Catalog co-published with Skira Paris

Musée du Quai Branly – Jacques Chirac

Head of the Publishing Department
Delphine Halgand

Deputy Head of the Publishing Department
Sophie Chambonnière

Editorial Coordination
Maryse Vaissière

Image production
Audrey Lagrue

Skira Paris

Senior Editor
Nathalie Prat-Couadau

Editorial Coordination
María Laura Ribadeneira

Editorial Assistant
Louis Moisan

Graphic design and layout
Sophie Dupriez

Translations
David Radzinowicz

Copy-editing
Mark Nathan

Color Separation
Litho Art New, Turin

With the kind participation of the Helena Rubinstein brand (Archives Helena Rubinstein, L'Oréal)

List of Authors

Yaëlle Biro
Associate Curator for the Arts of Africa, Metropolitan Museum of Art, New York

Susan Elizabeth Gagliardi
Associate Professor of African Art History at Emory University, Atlanta

Bertrand Goy
African Art Historian

Charlotte Grand-Dufay
African Art Historian

Catherine Grenier
Director of the Fondation Giacometti and President of the Institut Giacometti

Hélène Joubert
Head of the African Heritage Unit, Musée du Quai Branly – Jacques Chirac

Susan Kloman
Christie's International Head of the African and Oceanic Art Department

David Nash
Director of the Mitchell-Innes & Nash Gallery, New York

Suzanne Slesin
Publisher and Editorial Director of Pointed Leaf Press, New York. Author of *Over the Top. Helena Rubinstein. Extraordinary Style, Beauty, Art, Fashion, Design*, Pointed Leaf Press, 2003

Julie Verlaine
Lecturer in Contemporary History, Junior member of the Institut Universitaire de France

Lenders

Bahamas
Jean-Louis Danis

United States
Detroit, Detroit Institute of Arts

Newark, Newark Museum

New York, The Arman Marital Trust, Corice Arman Trustee

New York, Brooklyn Museum

New York, The Metropolitan Museum of Art

Saint Louis, James C. Jamieson III collection, with kind permission from Schweizer Premodern, New York

Tenafly, Malcolm collection with kind permission from Schweizer Premodern, New York

Washington D.C., National Museum of African Art – Smithsonian Institution

Célestin Clamra

Private collection, courtesy Donald Morris Gallery

Private collections with kind permission from Schweizer Premodern, New York

The Jerome Kenney Family

Diane and Bryan Leyden

Laura and James J. Ross

Suzanne Slesin

Gordon Sze, MD

France
Paris, Fondation Dapper

Paris, Liliane and Michel Durand-Dessert

Paris, Nicolas Hug

Paris, Marc Ladreit de Lacharrière

Paris, Q. Laurens

Paris, Marceau Rivière

Paris, Jean-François Schmitt

Alain Elcabas

As well as those who prefer to remain anonymous

The curator would like to thank most warmly all those who have helped to make this project possible and all those who have showed their interest in it, since even the smallest snippet of information has often proved invaluable in this reconstruction of a few aspects of Madame's wonderful collection:

Pierre Amrouche
Gassia Armenian
Jean-Baptiste Bacquart
Carlo Bella
Guy Bennett
Ari Birnbaum
Yaëlle Biro
Joaquin Blanco
Najwa Borro
Kay Breslow
Aude Breusse
Marie-Thérèse Brincard
April Calahan
Vittorio Carini
David Cassera
Bruno Claessens
Célestin Clamra
Christa Clarke
Jean-Louis Danis
Sylphide de Daranyi
Bernard Dulon
Lance Entwistle
Christiane Falgayrettes-Leveau
John Fishel
Michèle Fitoussi
Valérie Franklin
Sarah Frioux-Salgas
Theodor Froelich
Susan Elizabeth Gagliardi
Nicolas Garnier
Jacques Germain
Deborah Glasser
Bertrand Goy
Charlotte Grand-Dufay
Michel Grandsard
Allan Green
Catherine Grenier
Alexander Grogan
Bernard de Grunne
Kathryn Gunsch
Alice Gumy
Barbara Harding
Marie-Pierre Hontebeyrie
Charles-Wesley Hourdé
Nicolas Hug
Anne-Sophie Jest
David Joralemon
Carol B. Kenney
Mason Klein
Susan Kloman
Rolf Korek
Christine Kreamer
Marc Ladreit de Lacharrière
Dominique Lachewsky
Guy Ladrière
Sandrine Ladrière
Alisa LaGamma
Sacha Lainovic
Quentin Laurens
Yves Le Fur
Hélène and Philippe Leloup
Marie-Victoire Leloup
Diane and Brian Leyden
Sonia and Albert Loeb
Daniella Luxembourg
Jennifer MacCarthy
Dr Marian Malcolm
Elena Martinez-Jacquet
Anthony Meyer
Steven Morris
David Nash
Paz Nuñez-Regueiro
Michael Oliver
Philippe Peltier
Constantine Petridis
Fabienne de Pierrebourg
Lydia Puccinelli
Nii Quarcoopome
Lucas Ratton
Philippe Ratton
Marceau Rivière
Nicolas Rolland
Nancy Rosoff
Laura and James J. Ross
Jean Roudillon
Marguerite de Sabran
Sefa Saglam
Elisabeth Sandager
Elena Savenkova
Jean-François Schmitt
Andrew Schoelkopf
Alain Schoffel
Judith Schoffel
Heinrich Schweizer
Molly Seegers
Henricus Simonis
Suzanne Slesin and Michael Steinberg
Dorota Sniezek
Dalton Somaré
Gordon Sze
Darienne Turner
Robert Vallois
Julie Verlaine
Susan Vogel
Francis Wahl
Roslyn Walker
Margaret Weber
Ilse and Gunter Zink

In particular the team of the Direction of Cultural Development of the Musée du Quai Branly – Jacques Chirac:

Hélène Fulgence
Christine Drouin
Agathe Moroval
Isabelle Lainé
Domitille Chaudieu
Quiterie d'Ariès
Sophie Chambonnière
Maryse Vaissière

The curator would also like to express her gratitude to the internship students under her supervision who have also provided valuable assistance over the two years spent preparing this project:

Julien Jourand
Justin Kalinowski
Margaux Lefèvre
Romane Mélingue
Clémence Vallée

Foreword

Stéphane Martin
President of the Musée du Quai Branly – Jacques Chirac

Since opening in June 2006, the Musée du Quai Branly – Jacques Chirac has been regularly remodeled to adapt the exhibition space designed by Jean Nouvel to its changing demands. A few years ago, the central mezzanine was transformed into the Atelier Martine Aublet, where modular showcases serve as a venue for small-scale exhibitions on a wide range of topics. The first exhibition to be held in the new Marc Ladreit de Lacharrière gallery, *Helena Rubinstein: Madame's Collection* continues this policy.

To open up fresh aesthetic and scientific perspectives and to set up dialogs between all the artworks that share its space, the gallery—which, due to its location in the building, the museum calls the "west mezzanine"—has been completely refurbished. From September 2020, the exceptional pieces generously donated by Marc Ladreit de Lacharrière to the national collection will be placed on permanent display in cases specially designed for the purpose by Jean Nouvel. Moreover, the other section of the gallery will stage annual temporary exhibitions reflecting the history of interest in non-Western art, a process exemplified by the explorations of Helena Rubinstein.

As is widely known, "Madame" — as she liked to be called, in an echo of Gabrielle Chanel's "Mademoiselle" — acquired a vast quantity of works, furniture, and artifacts of every type, in the process becoming a legendary patron and arbiter of taste. The most remarkable and innovative components of this astonishing collection, dispersed in 1966 at a historic series of auctions, were its African holdings, with the remainder being made up of Oceanic, Indonesian, and pre-Hispanic art.

It is the history of this collection, its content, and above all its spirit, that *Helena Rubinstein: Madame's Collection* reconstructs. The aim, as well as the approach, of the exhibition is entirely novel. Paradoxically, until now, the story of Helena Rubinstein's collection of non-Western art has had to be read between the lines: clues can be gleaned from a handful of texts, but the main sources are the countless features the international press devoted to the interiors that Madame occupied.

In a long-term investigation, Hélène Joubert, head of the African heritage unit, hunted down, identified, and scientifically documented half of the nearly four hundred pieces in the collection. Sixty-five of them are showcased here in the exhibition, including the famous "Bangwa Queen", photographed by Man Ray and shown in 1935 at the Museum of Modern Art in New York at the legendary *African Negro Art* exhibition. These works conjure up an evocative portrait of Helena Rubinstein, creating an authentic and intimate image of a personality whose global fame simultaneously functioned as a mask, mirror, and doppelganger.

I would like to warmly congratulate Hélène Joubert on her rigorous and pioneering endeavors. Her efforts will make a genuine contribution to the cultural history of the 20th century. She has benefited from the insight of many eminent experts, dealers, and collectors, all of whom are hereby thanked for their aid.

Naturally we extend our gratitude to the numerous institutions and individuals who have kindly loaned pieces. I am thinking in particular of the Fondation Dapper, the Smithsonian Institution's National Museum of African Art in Washington DC, the Metropolitan Museum of Art and the Brooklyn Museum in New York, the Detroit Institute of Arts, and also of L'Oréal for permitting access to its photographic archive. Finally, we are delighted to acknowledge the generosity of Suzanne Slesin, who kindly lent the museum a rare album of photographs that eloquently evoke the incomparable, magical qualities of Madame's world.

Recollections of the Helena Rubinstein sale of African and Oceanic Art

David Nash

Helena Rubinstein – also known as Princess Gourielli – was the founder of the highly successful, international cosmetics empire which bore her name. When she died in 1965 at the age of 94, her estate contained a very large quantity and an enormous variety of artworks spread over several residences. There was the grand, cluttered apartment on Park Avenue in New York, a house in London and a wonderful light-filled penthouse apartment in a mansion on the Île Saint Louis in Paris. It was in Paris that Helena Rubinstein kept the finest sculptures from her African art collection.

Over the course of fifty years of acquisitions, Madame Rubinstein filled all her homes with an astonishingly varied personal collection. For her New York apartment she commissioned Salvador Dalí to paint three murals in her dining room, which was filled with quite uncomfortable and overly-baroque Venetian furniture. In her bedroom was her famous Lucite bed [ill. 2] above which hung an extraordinary early painting by de Kooning. The walls were covered with paintings and drawings by both famous and unknown artists, mostly Europeans, with a subsection of works by her fellow Polish refugees such as Elie Nadelman. "Madame" liked to buy in quantity and had a very good nose for a bargain. There were thus 15 bronze and white marble sculptures by Nadelman, around 50 Agni terracotta sculptures from the Ivory Coast and 25 Bakota reliquary figures in brass, copper and wood. Her collection of modern art, particularly modern paintings, was large and very varied; the stars were two remarkable sculptures by Constantin Brancusi: "Bird in Space," a brilliant, soaring bronze rocket, and the famous white marble, *Négresse Blanche* [ill. 3]. There were paintings and drawings by Matisse, Picasso, Chagall, Laurencin, van Dongen, de la Fresnaye and other well-known avant-garde artists in Paris between the wars. Many of these works were acquired directly from the artists themselves.

ill. 1

Helena Rubinstein among her collection of African and modern art (works by Constantin Brancusi, Joan Miró, Amedeo Modigliani, Elie Nadelman, Serge Poliakoff, and Pierre-Auguste Renoir), 24, Quai de Béthune, Paris, c. 1960

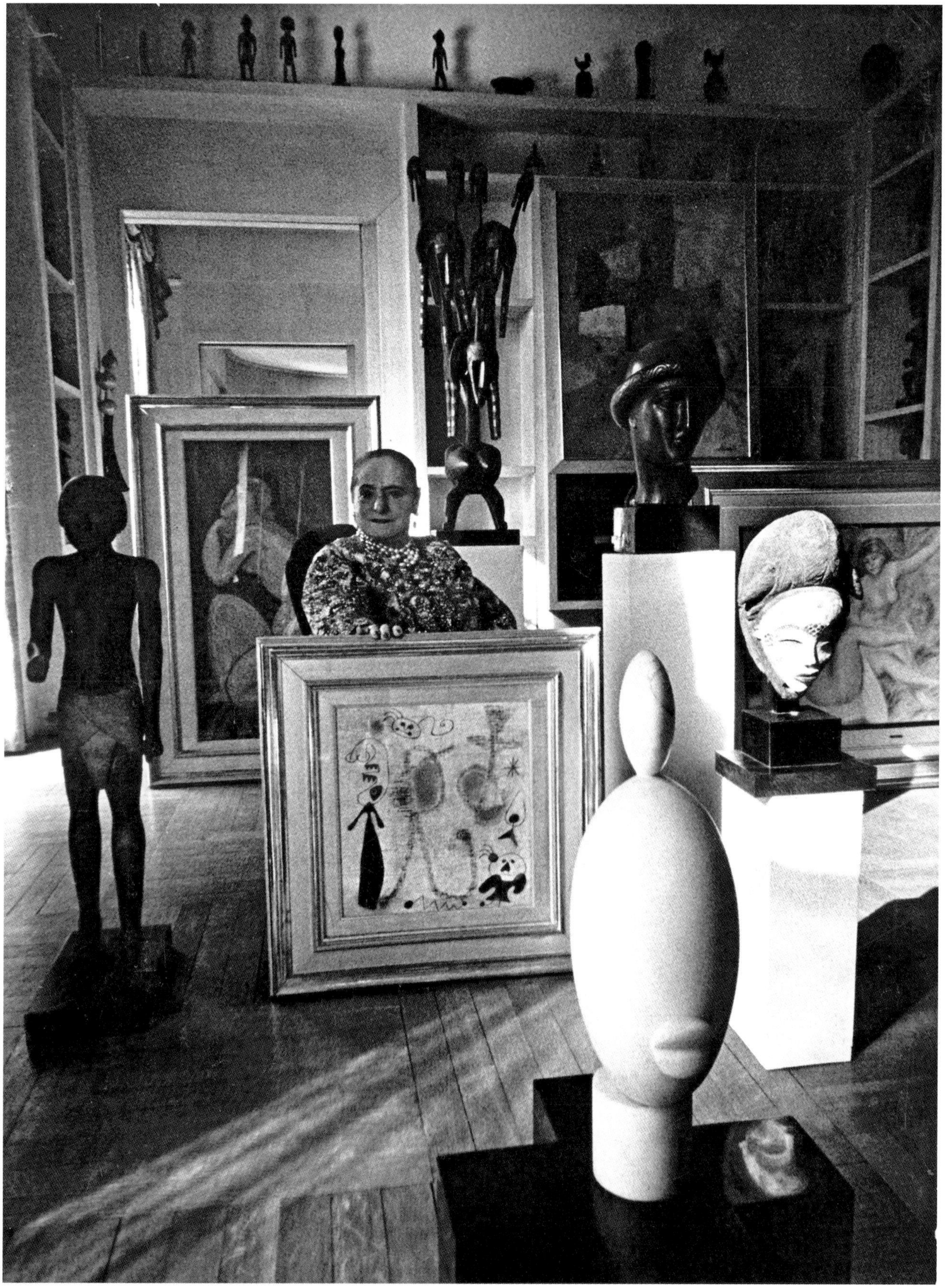

However, it was Helena Rubinstein's collection of African and Oceanic art which made this estate unique. The international auction market for twentieth century French artists was well established by the time of Rubinstein's death but this was not at all the case with "Primitive Art." Madame was an American citizen and taxpayer and her estate had to be settled in the United States. The executors of her estate wanted her art collection to be sold at auction in New York and, after some deliberation, they chose Parke-Bernet Galleries to undertake the task. They were confident that the auction gallery could handle the sale of works by the European masters but had concerns about its ability to put such a large quantity of African art up for auction without flooding the market and diluting prices.

When I first came to New York to work as a representative for Sotheby's in 1963, there was a thriving market for African and Oceanic works of art, but it was almost entirely conducted by dealers, museums, and collectors. It was a small and quite self-contained world in which most of the players knew each other; dealers played a very significant role in educating and advising their clients who went on to form some of the great collections that are now housed in museums in the United States. The Museum of Primitive Art, financed by Nelson Rockefeller and directed by Robert Goldwater, had just opened its doors five years earlier.

In 1964 Sotheby & Co acquired the Parke-Bernet Galleries, the leading fine arts auctioneers in New York, and merged the two firms. Sotheby's had a policy of dividing auctions into specialized areas and the department of Antiquities and Primitive Art at that time was being run in London by a young man named Bruce Chatwin. Bruce was a friend as well as being a colleague, and I shared his interest in Primitive Art and classical antiquities. At his suggestion and with his help, I began to organize specialized sales in New York similar to those held in London, where the department had a long and distinguished history of selling African and Oceanic art to a clientele of mainly European dealers. Collecting and dealing in this field had been established in Great Britain for more than 100 years and several British museums had large collections of objects from Africa and the South Pacific brought back by explorers, missionaries, whalers and colonial officers. Paris, where Helena Rubinstein made most of her purchases, had a similarly long-standing market and amazing museum collections.

In contrast, collecting African and Oceanic art in the United States only began to gather speed in the years after the Second World War. Very few museums had collections in this field prior to 1950, although the Museum of Modern Art organized a brilliant exhibition of masterpieces of African art under the curatorship of James Johnson Sweeney in 1935. Rubinstein was a significant lender to this exhibition. Of the 600 pieces that Sweeney assembled for the exhibition, at least 90% were lent by French collectors.

As soon as the estate's executors had signed the contract with Parke-Bernet Galleries, work began on cataloging every piece in the collection spread over the three locations. Chatwin was the principal cataloger of the African objects, a huge responsibility for a (very talented) man who was then only 26. As his transatlantic counterpart, I spent a full week in the Paris apartment with him identifying and examining the entire range of objects; our task would have been easier if Madame had kept thorough records of her purchases but unfortunately she did not. Chatwin had access to advice from a well-known French American dealer named Henri Kamer who volunteered not only the use

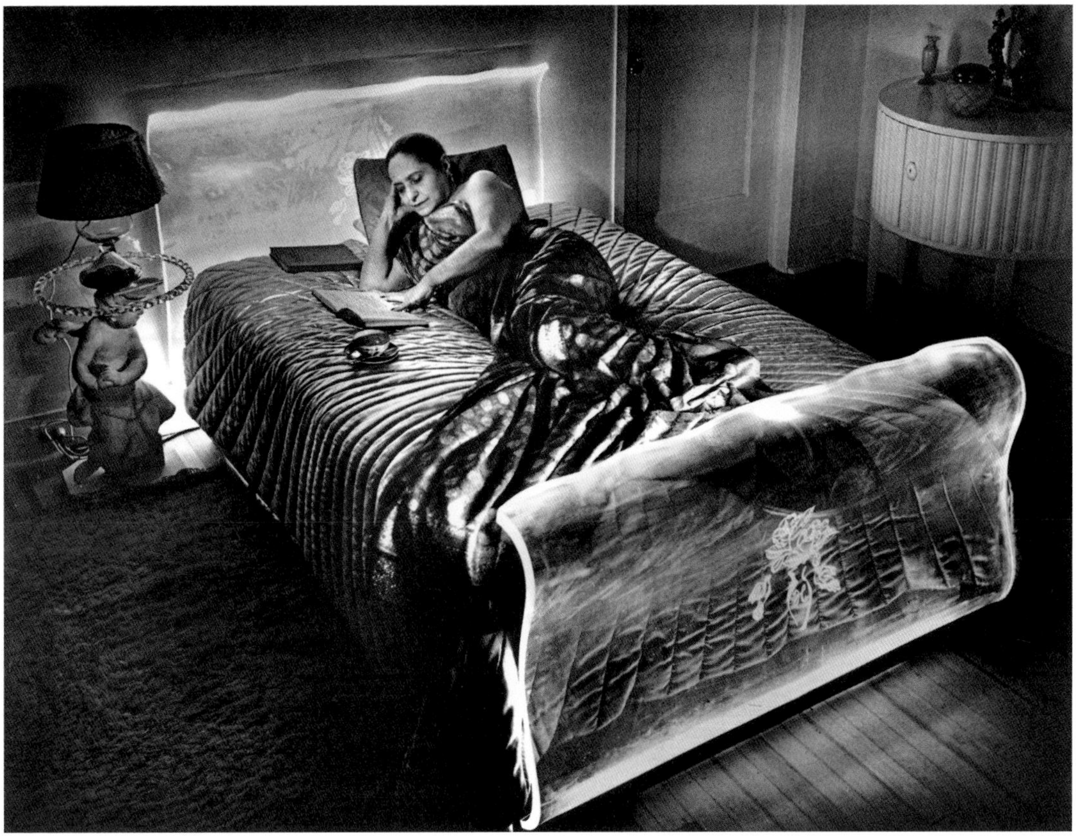

of his library but also the benefit of his connections with the government officials who were responsible for authorizing the export of the collection from France. In return for a gift to the French nation of several crucial pieces from the collection, the major part of the collection was given an export permit and was shipped to New York at the end of 1965.

Helena Rubinstein's collection was vast and very diverse. A series of six catalogs was published to cover all the different specialties. In an effort to avoid flooding the market with too many similar pieces of African art, this part of the sale was divided into two sessions held a week apart, on April 21 and 29, 1966. In retrospect, this was unnecessary as almost every lot in the auction was sold with vigorous bidding and many new buyers emerging to compete for the objects. The two sessions were held as evening sales which was highly unusual at the time for anything other than distinguished collections of paintings. This showed a far-sighted recognition of the importance of this field and promoted its exposure to a newer, wider audience.

ILL. 2
Helena Rubinstein in her bed made of lucite, 625 Park Avenue, New York, 1941, photograph by Herbert Gehr

The week of auctions began with the sale of the finest works from Madame's Impressionist and Modern art collection. In fact, this group of works was of rather uneven quality; the sale started with eight very uninteresting little canvasses by Renoir

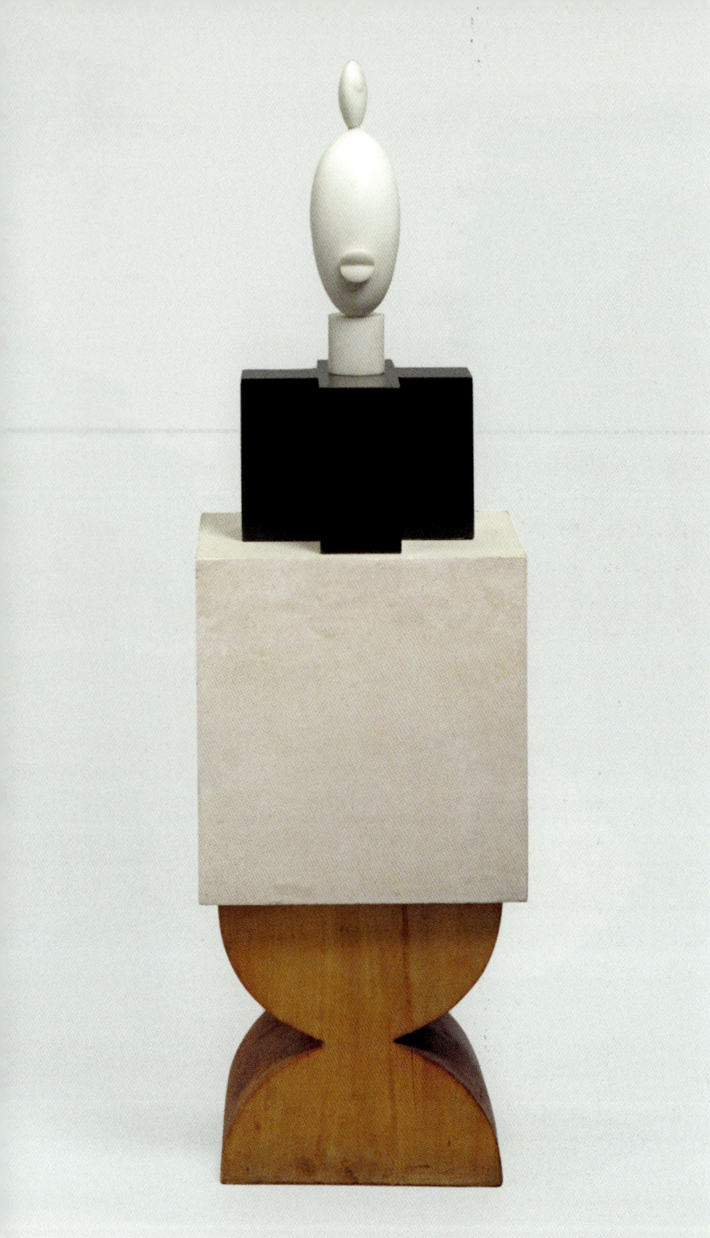

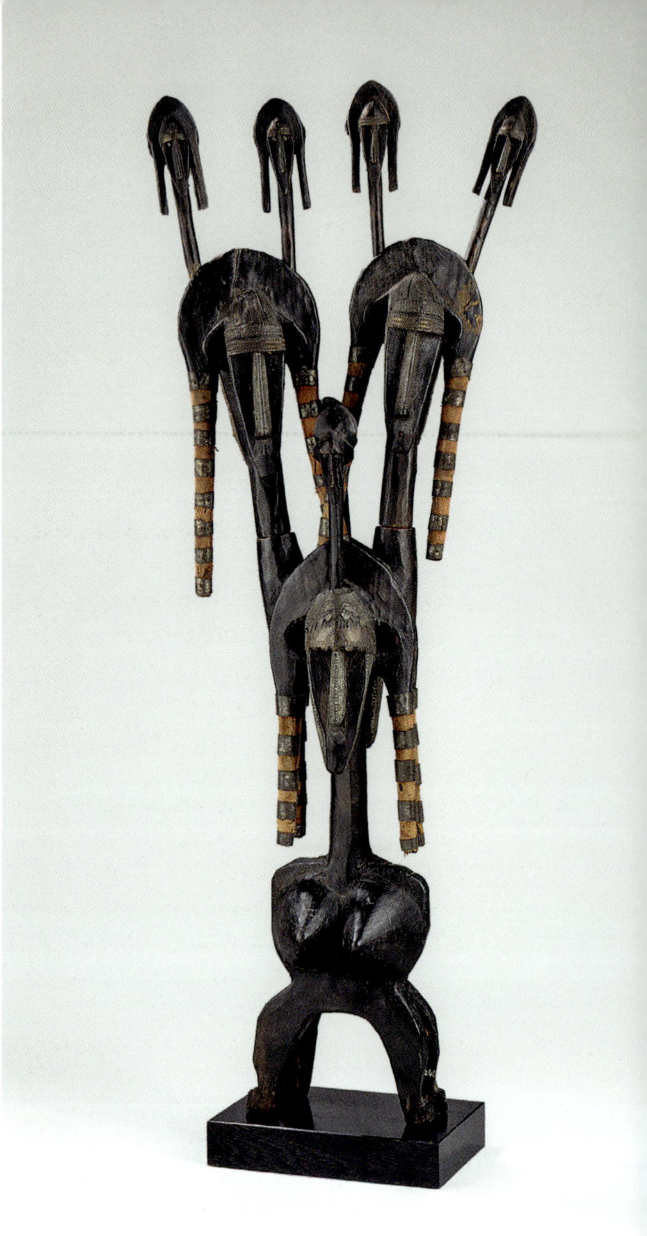

followed by second-rate paintings by Degas, Monet and Sisley. However, when it came to the twentieth century, there was a dramatic improvement. Lot 13 was the famous *L'Oiseau dans l'Espace* by Constantin Brancusi which sold for $140,000, a record at the time. This was acquired by the American collector Taft Schreiber and is now in the National Gallery in Washington DC. Rubinstein's second Brancusi *La Négresse Blanche II* [ill. 3], a black and white marble sculpture, which he produced in 1930 and which owes a considerable debt to African art, was acquired by the Art Institute of Chicago for $92,000.

The following evening, April 21, the first session of the African art sale began. Parke-Bernet's large saleroom was packed with so many potential bidders that only standing room remained for anyone who wanted to be close to the action. At the last minute, the galleries' technicians arranged for an overflow room next door to be connected to the main room by a closed-circuit television. By virtue of the glamour associated with the name of Helena Rubinstein, what was once a relatively obscure collecting field became the subject of international attention.

The sale was conducted by the chief auctioneer, John Marion, who was dressed for the occasion in formal evening attire. Most of the estimates (which, in those less regulated times, were not published) for the 260 lots in the two sales were very modest; only a handful exceeded $1,000! Among the most expensively estimated lots were an elaborate Bambara Marionette [lot 64, ill. 4] which sold to a Scandinavian collector for $24,000 against an estimate of $12-15,000, and a tall, elegant Poro Senufo figure [lot 95, ill. 10] which sold for $27,000 against the same estimate. The latter was bought on behalf of a client by Sidney Janis, the renowned pioneering twentieth-century art dealer. For the most part, the buyers were Americans. A distinguished collector from Pennsylvania, Jay C. Leff, bought several lots as did the Museum of Primitive Art who engaged the services of Pierre Matisse to bid for them. The Baltimore Museum and the Detroit Institute of Art also made purchases.

Eight days later, the same crowd gathered again in the packed saleroom for the second session of Helena Rubinstein's African art collection. The auction began with a series of 30 terra cotta funerary sculptures which she had bought as a "job lot" from a certain Dr Lheureux. There was considerable concern that the market could not absorb such a large quantity of similar pieces. Again, the estimates were modest with most of them around $500. However, every lot was sold, a single American private collector buying nearly half of them at quite substantial prices.

The star lot in this second session was the famous Bangwa Figure of a Woman [lot 189, ill. 107], one of the few African sculptures to show a figure in movement. The "African Queen," as it was popularly known, was one of eight sculptures lent by Rubinstein for J. J. Sweeney's *African Negro Art* exhibition at the Museum of Modern Art in 1935, where it was famously photographed with a nude model by Man Ray [ill. 22]. It was bought by a California dealer named Harry Franklin for $29,000, far surpassing the estimate of $12-18,000. This proved to be the highest price for any piece in the two sales. As a footnote, when the Franklin collection was sold at Sotheby's in April 1990, this piece went for $3,400,000!

Fifteen Bakota reliquary figures followed next in the auction. They all sold within the range of their (modest) estimates or higher, with the highest price rising to $7,750 [lot 92, ill. 113]. Almost fifty years later, this same reliquary figure was auctioned in Paris by the heirs of William Rubin, the former paintings curator at the Museum of Modern Art, for EUR 5,500,000. Its provenance was embellished by the fact that it was included in Rubin's landmark exhibition at the Museum of Modern Art in 1984-5 called *Primitivism in 20th Century Art: Affinity of the Tribal and the Modern.*

The first session of the sale focused primarily on art from West Africa much of which had been acquired in Paris in the 1930s from a scholar and art historian named F-H. Lem. Lem had collected many of these pieces directly in the field in 1934-35 with the intention of creating a museum in Dakar but was eventually obliged to sell the collection to Helena Rubinstein.

By contrast, the second session of the sale mainly contained pieces from Central Africa. Fifteen remarkable sculptures from the Fang tribe were the next lots to come up

ill. 3
Constantin Brancusi
La Négresse Blanche II
1928
White and black marble, stone, wood
49.5 × 14.5 × 19 cm (sculpture)
Chicago, The Art Institute of Chicago

ill. 4 [lot 64]
Marionnette
Bamana, Mali, San region
Late 19th–early 20th cent.
Wood, metal, fibers
H. 146.7 cm
Bloomington, Sidney and Lois Eskenazi Museum of Art

for sale. Several of them were still glistening from the palm oil with which they had been ritually anointed. The finest and most expressive reliquary head [LOT 213, ILL. 5] had been lent by Rubinstein to the 1935 exhibition at the Museum of Modern Art. The estimate for this masterpiece was $28-32,000 and it was a notable disappointment when it only went for $24,000. Curiously, the Fang pieces were virtually the only group of objects to sell below their estimates.

In October 1966, a small catalog containing 100 lots of African and Oceanic art was published by Parke-Bernet Galleries. This represented the third tranche of the Helena Rubinstein collection and consisted of items which had been deemed not good enough to offer in the first highly publicized sale. It included another ten Bakota reliquary figures

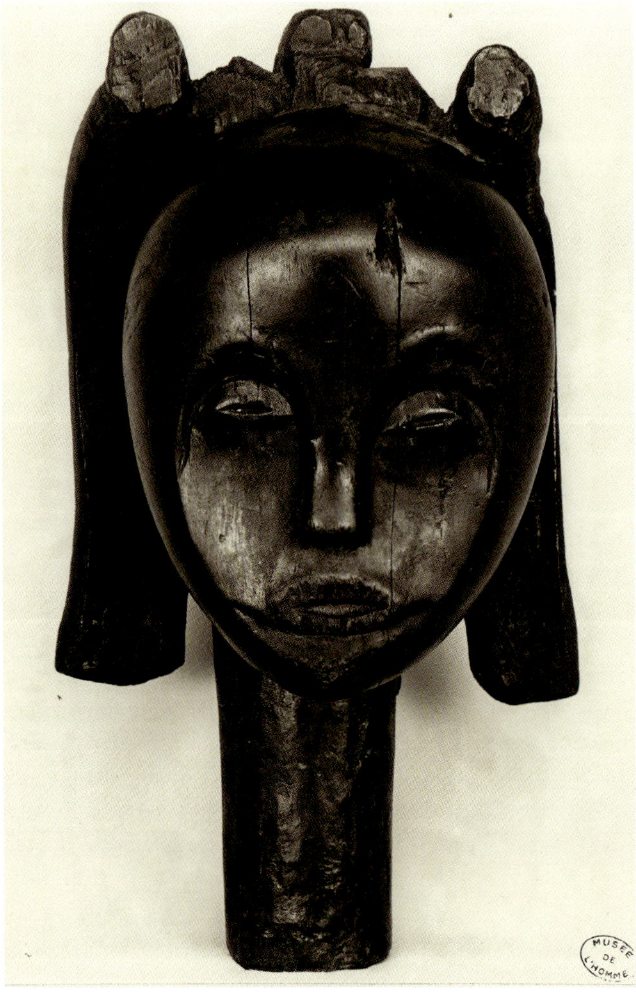

ILL. 5

"Ancestor figure, head" [Fang ancestor head, reliquary guardian, Gabon] Photograph by Walker Evans, taken from the *African Negro Art* portfolio, New York, Museum of Modern Art, 1935 (cat. 78)

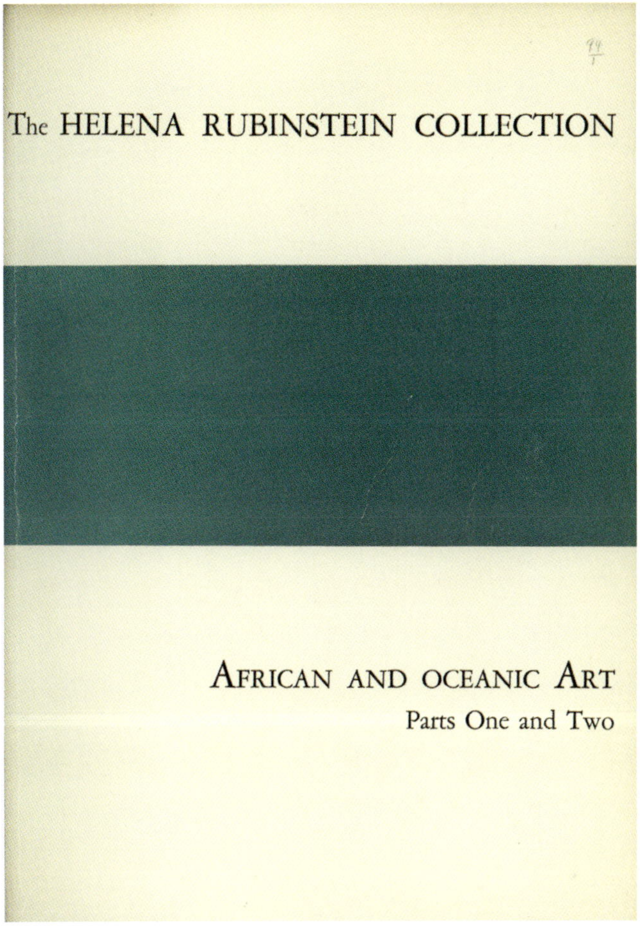

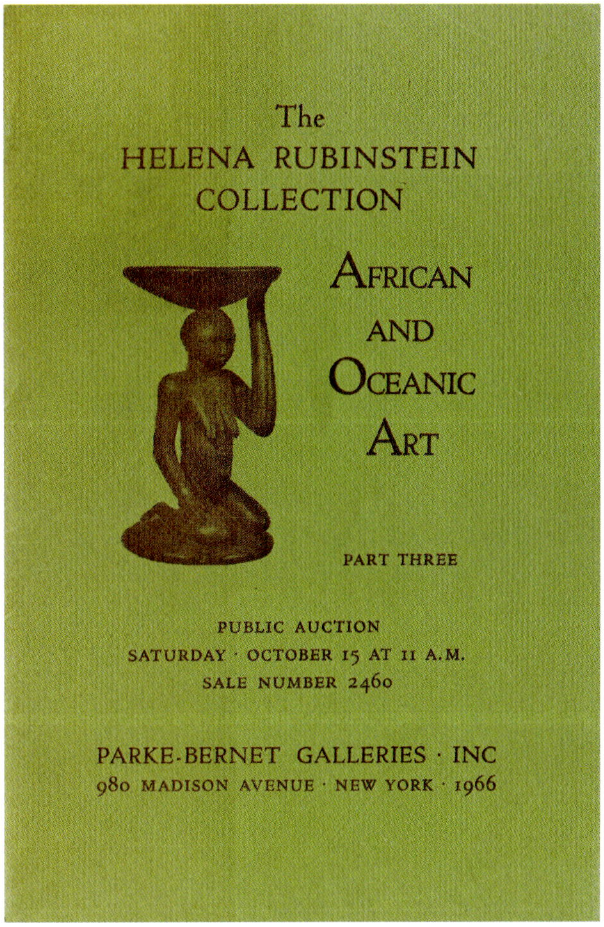

Ill. 6

Cover for the sale catalog of the Helena Rubinstein "African and Oceanic Art, Parts One and Two" collection, Parke-Bernet Galleries, October 21 and 29, 1966 (cat. 66)

Ill. 7

Cover for the sale catalog of the Helena Rubinstein "African and Oceanic Art, Part Three" collection, Parke-Bernet Galleries, October 15, 1966 (cat. 67)

Following pages
Ill. 8

Advertisement for the sale of the Helena Rubinstein collection, published in *L'Œil*, no. 135, March 1966

and a further twenty-one Agni terracotta figures. Unsurprisingly, hidden from the limelight and the extravagant promotion of the week of sales in April, the prices were very modest indeed. The Agni terracottas sold at half the prices they had reached in April and the Bakota reliquary figures sold for even less. Nevertheless, the final overall results were surprisingly strong; over 350 lots of African and Oceanic art were all sold for a total of $470,000, close to the high estimate of $500,000. Parke-Bernet Galleries were very proud of this achievement in a little-known market. This sale was so widely reported in the international press that a dealer jokingly said to me that his business was finished as every village in Africa would now have a priced copy of the catalog!

Helena Rubinstein and "Primitive Arts"

Madame's collection: Africa at its heart

Hélène Joubert

Assembled over the course of her life, "Madame's" collection, half real, half mythical, mirrored her own self-construction.[1] Ever expanding and ever in motion, its history is difficult to retrace. Its contents were first cataloged in preparation for the auctions staged in New York by Parke-Bernet between October 1965 and October 1966, a year after its owner's death. The seven catalogs[2] for these sales are the last record of the collection before it was dissipated.[3] For the non-Western arts—from Africa chiefly, and, to a lesser extent, Oceanic, Amerindian, and Indonesian art—two catalogs, the first of which (Parts One and Two) is copiously illustrated, were produced before the sale scattered the collection far and wide. Reunited and listed one last time, this extraordinary corpus comprises three hundred and sixty-one lots among the many thousands in a collection that also included modern art (paintings, sculptures, drawings, prints), antiques, furniture, decorative arts, folk art, Russian icons, and jewelry—everything, with the exception of Madame's legendary wardrobe,[4] which was divided among her family and her employees. For the non-European arts, this sell-off—both an apotheosis and a turning-point—set records that could be termed unexpected: in particular, the Bamana puppet, [lot 64, ill. 4], the Senufo statue, [lot 95, ill. 10] and the Bangwa "queen", lot 189 [ill. 107]..

A rare example in this domain of a collection by a woman, one might well ask how it grew to be so exceptional. Fluctuating over time, and also including less significant objects that Helena Rubinstein would give away as generous presents, by the 1950s it seems to have run to more than six hundred items.[5] An exhaustive, formal inventory was never drawn up during its owner's lifetime. During her first interview with Patrick O'Higgins, however, Rubinstein herself alluded to the need for it to be cataloged. A partial start was probably made,[6] notably by F.-H. Lem,[7] though no actual register was

ill. 9
Helena Rubinstein with two of her Bamana masks from Mali (lots 53 and 54), 24, Quai de Béthune, Paris, 1963

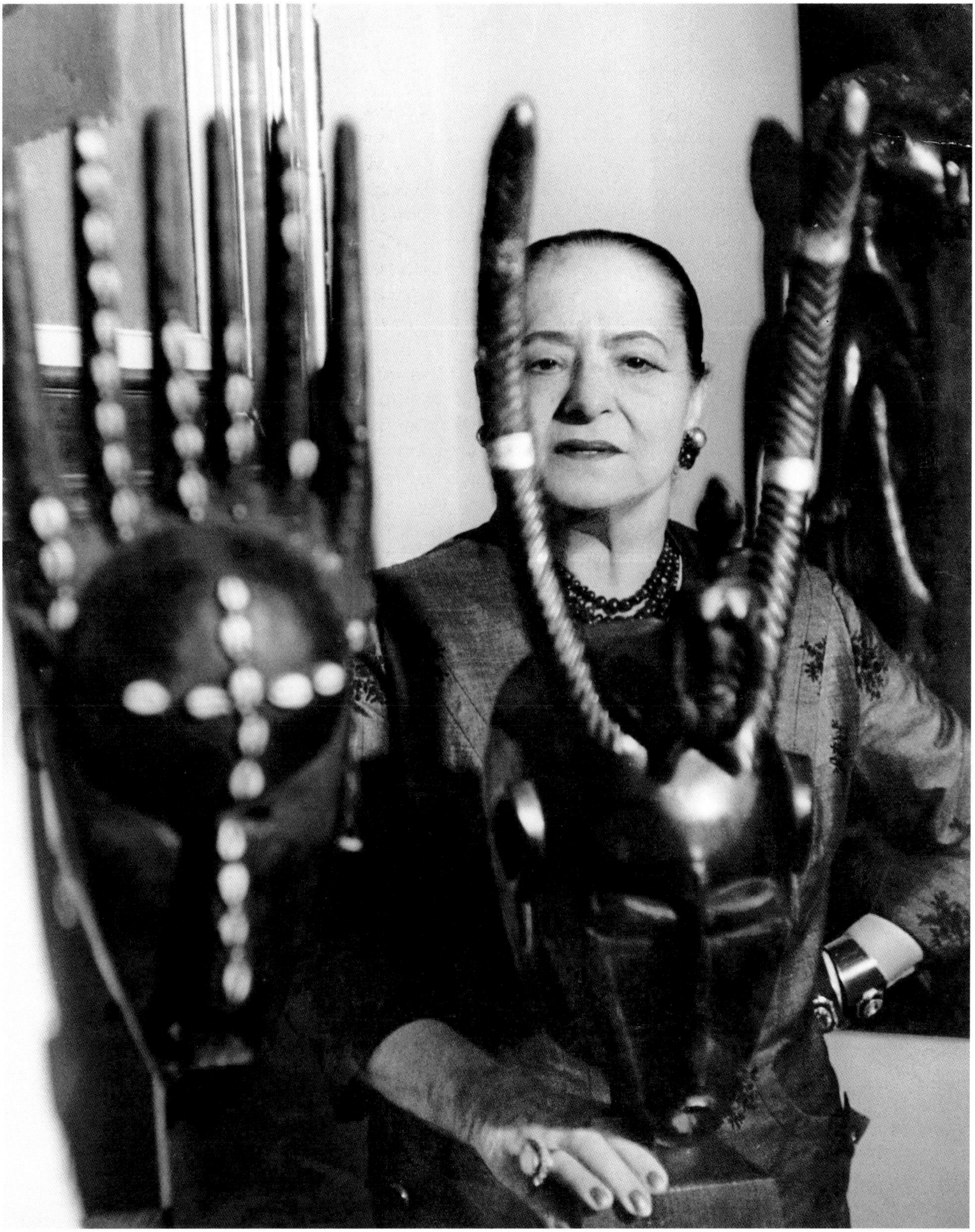

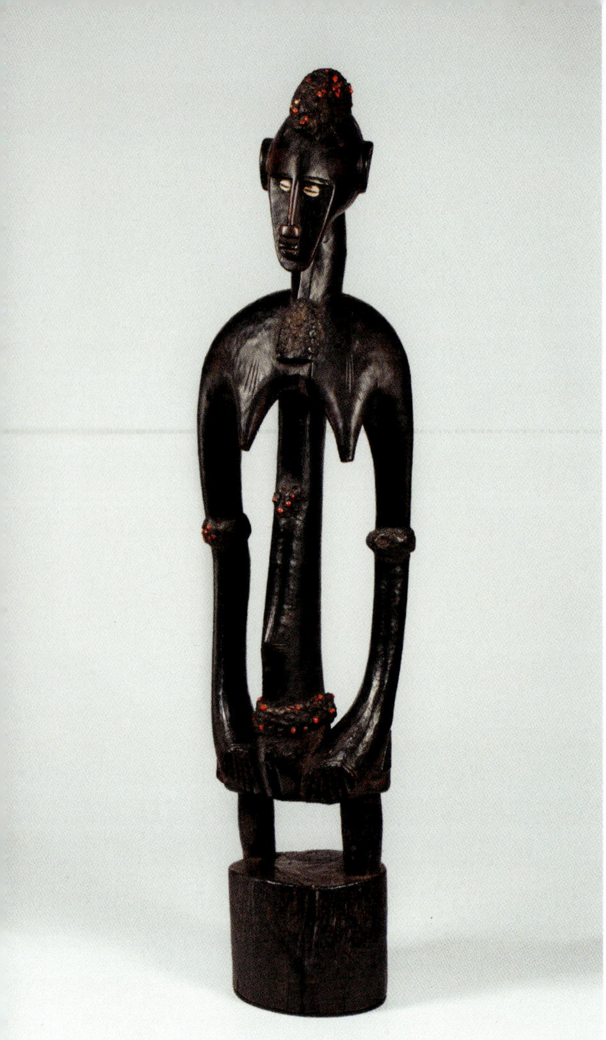

ever compiled. Madame was an outstanding negotiator, and, since all her purchases were made in cash [ill. 23], whatever the amount, no accounting records were kept.[8]

Back in time: sources and initiations

Broad in her artistic tastes, Helena Rubinstein forged an eclectic, opulent, and flamboyant personal style. Appearing regularly in the press, many photos of her various apartments filled with works of art in Paris,[9] New York,[10] and London,[11]—spaces she both lived and entertained in—became iconic. Though inseparable from the explosively colorful worlds that emerged from the dazzling impression left by the sets and costumes for the Ballets Russes performed in London in 1907, the austerity and unfamiliarity of the dark African wood carvings afford a glimpse of the hidden face of an atypical collector bewitched by every kind of beauty. Admiring the canons of classical antique beauty no less than modernity and the arts of her time, Helena Rubinstein managed to associate the *"arts nègres,"* as they were termed at the time, with her image as an active and enlightened woman. Her enthusiasm for African "Negro arts" surprised her friends and acquaintances from beyond avant-garde circles, causing much amusement for Madame, though she took pains to make sure it never jeopardized her business dealings.[12]

Ill. 10 [lot 95]

Deble *statue*
Senufo, master of Folona
Sikasso region,
northern Ivory Coast
19th-early 20th cent.
Wood, cowries, *abrus precatorius*, latex
H. 90.5 cm
Private collection

Ill. 11

View down the corridor
from the music room,
24, Quai de Béthune, Paris,
c. 1954–55, colorized
photograph from
an album composed
by Jean Vincent (cat. 91)

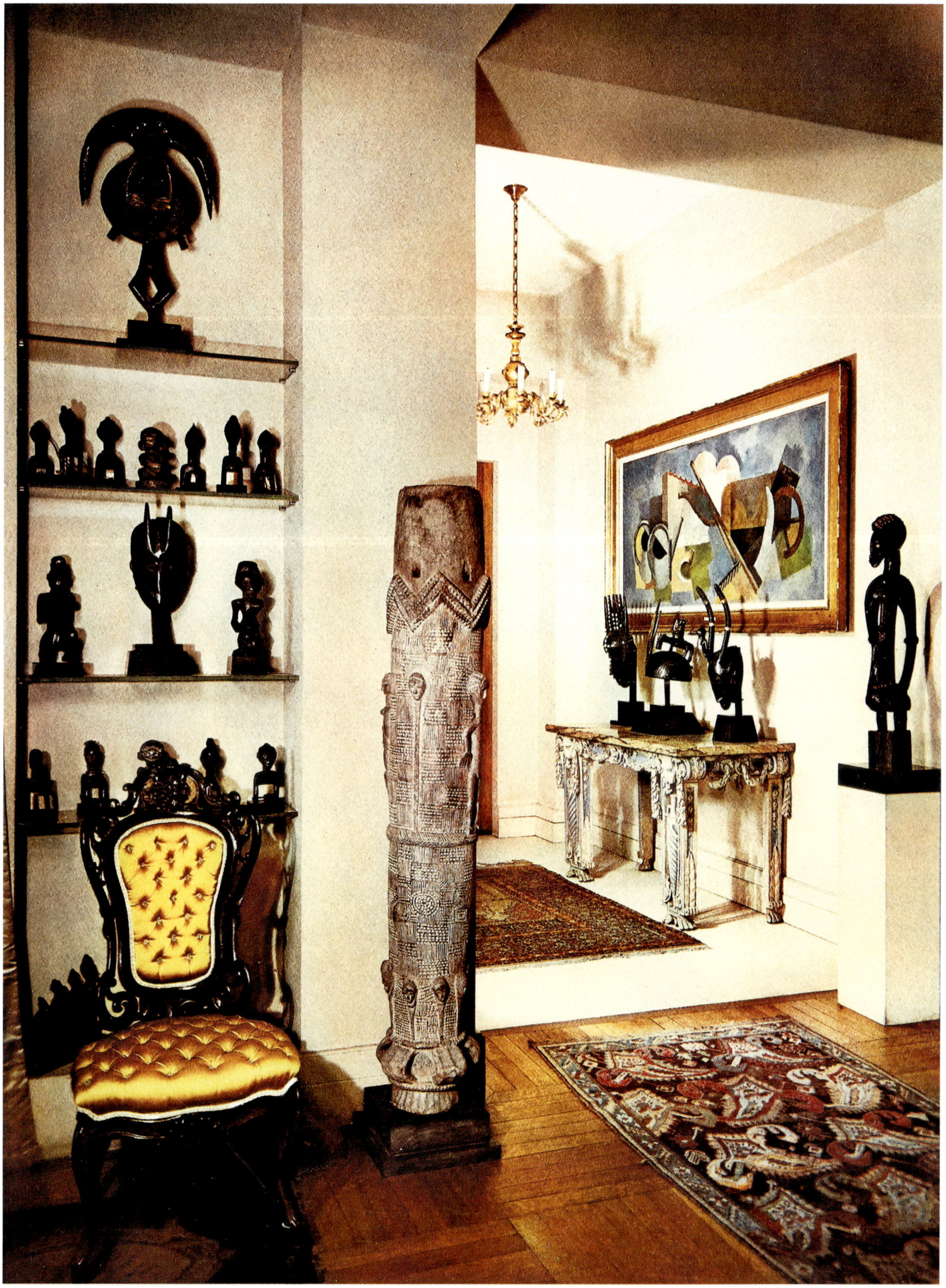

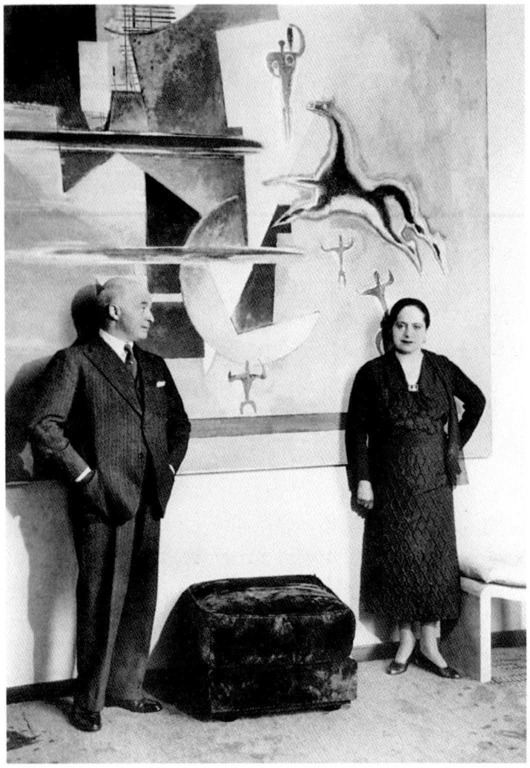

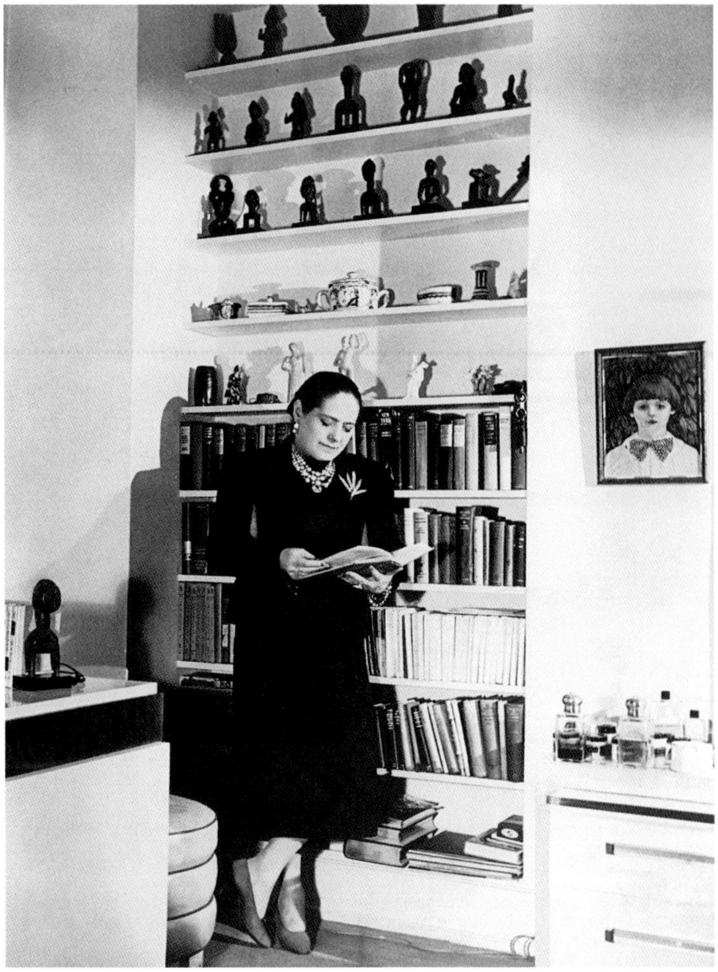

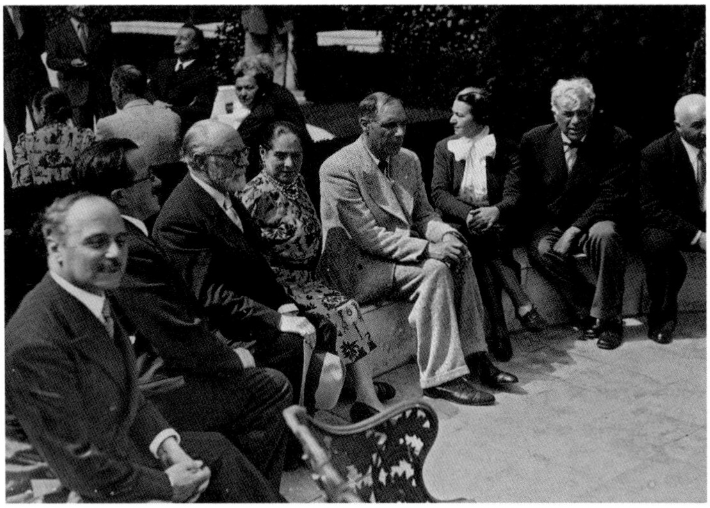

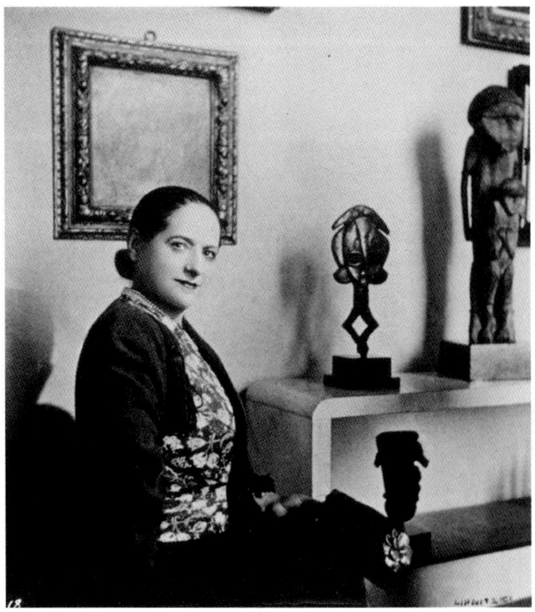

Her unbridled curiosity went beyond mere exotic beauty to embrace pieces that others regarded as ugly, asymmetrical, uneven and deeply lined—while she found them expressive, moving and powerful. Her legendary eagle eye was extraordinarily attuned to details and to the marks left by time, in keeping with a personal and professional world dedicated to a tireless quest for beauty and which rejected the tyranny of aging. Selling less dreams than hopes, by the end of a life that had contained so many she considered even death with implacable curiosity: "It should be [...] an interesting experience."[13] When did this non-conformist passion for African arts take root? How did it develop with such breadth and quality? What were the stages in the process? As Madame used to say: "A good story is always better than the truth,"[14] and she was convinced on the one hand that, "no-one likes to remember the truth"[15] and on the other hand that "it is useless to look back"[16].

Here we will use the collector's own memories as they were confided or appear in her many interviews, as well as a handful of masterly biographies—including one authorized and "written" by herself[17]—with a measure of circumspection.

Though a devotee of "embroidering" and of playing fast and loose with dates, she could, contrariwise, take refuge in silence, heeding a piece of advice from her mother given to her as a young girl. It is hard to unearth the key moments in this story among the traces left by a woman so totally committed to her freedom. In a subtle and lively biography of fourteen years spent in her service[18] between 1951 and her death on April 1, 1965, her private secretary, the charming Patrick O'Higgins noted at their first interview Madame's unique way of juggling apparently irreconcilable styles. "Her life was intimately linked with her possessions. These were rich, avant-garde, schmaltzy; but they meshed perfectly with her personality as did the clothes she wore and the jewels she studded herself with."[19]

It is undeniable that her earliest mentor in the art world, Edward William Titus,[20] who later became her first husband,[21] played an essential role in her burgeoning interest in avant-garde currents, providing her with the culture, self-confidence, and contacts she lacked.

In 1907, Helena Rubinstein arrived in London, then an epicenter of the world of taste and beauty around which her life revolved. In 1908, after a period of training, notably in Paris,[22] and enjoying a meteoric rise, she moved into a house on Roehampton Lane called "Solna." Her neighbor proved to be none other than Jacob Epstein, a renowned sculptor of Polish descent, a friend of her husband's and a major art collector, with whom she learned how to look at modern art, and even more so at African artifacts. "How wisely he had advised me. He had always favored the unusual, and when I followed such sound advice as his, as well as my own 'inner eye,' my purchases were invariably good."[23] She remarks how, every time she had to go to Paris, Epstein would lend her sale catalogs of African collections, noting the finest pieces on which he wanted her to bid. As she confessed: "My enthusiasm often went beyond his suggestions, but prices were low then[24] and the range of objects extraordinary."[25] It is not known exactly when this relationship began. O'Higgins recalls remarks dating back to the year his employment began and to one of his first appointments with Madame in early 1951: "Jacob Epstein started me off when I first lived in London round about 1908."[26]

Jacob Epstein's collection was a paragon of its type: sold off from 1961 onward,[27] following the artist's death two years earlier, it ran to almost a thousand objects. While in some respects it recalled the Helena Rubinstein collection, its breadth was still more encyclopedic, embracing the ancient cultures of India, China, Egypt, the Cyclades, and

Above left
Ill. 12
Louis Marcoussis and Helena Rubinstein in front of a work by the painter, *Voyage*, 216, Boulevard Raspail, Paris, before 1934

Above right
Ill. 13
Madame in the dressing-room cum study in her bedroom, 895 Park Avenue, New York, c. 1934; behind her, loom pulleys arranged on the library shelves

Below left
Ill. 14
André Dezarrois, Henri Laugier, Helena Rubinstein, Henri Laurens, Marie Cuttoli, and Georges Braque at the ceremony for the award of the Helena Rubinstein Modern Art Prize given to Henri Laurens, on the terrace at 24, Quai de Béthune, Paris, June 1937

Below right
Ill. 15
Helena Rubinstein, in front of some objects from her collection at 216, Boulevard Raspail, Paris, c. 1930, photograph by Boris Lipnitzki. On the table a Kota reliquary guardian (lot 81*) and a Sentani figure (lot 259) in front of a Bamun pipe

Greece. However, most of the objects came from Africa, Oceania, Alaska, and Pre-Columbian America. It is in the field of African art that the typological and cultural axes of Epstein's pieces intersect with those of the Rubinstein collection: Sapi stone figures, female helmet masks from Guinea/Liberia, Dan, We, Yaure, Baule, and Senufo anthropomorphic and zoomorphic masks, Baule statuary, loom pulleys, Agni terracotta statuettes from Ivory Coast, Fang and Kota reliquary guardians from Gabon, Kuba and Luba functional items from the Democratic Republic of Congo, staffs of office and seats from Central Africa. More comprehensive, the Epstein collection also boasted objects from the British colonies, Ghana and Nigeria, and South Africa, items virtually absent from the Rubinstein collection. It seems to have been during a six-month stay in Paris during the first decade of the 20th century[28] that Jacob Epstein met personalities such as Pablo Picasso, Amedeo Modigliani, Manuel Ortiz de Zárate, Constantin Brancusi, Guillaume Apollinaire, Maurice de Vlaminck, and Henri Matisse, as well as the art dealers Paul Guillaume[29] and Joseph Brummer.[30]

Helena Rubinstein, who had set up in Paris in 1909, and who had the same friends and tastes as Epstein and frequented like him the same Paris addresses as the avant-garde art dealers, must have followed in his footsteps, crossing paths over the years with Daniel-Henry Kahnweiler and knocking on the doors of Anthony Morris,[31] the Percier gallery, Charles Vignier, Charles Ratton,[32] Pierre Loeb[33] and Pierre Vérité, as successive acquisitions demonstrate. With Misia Sert, a friend, inspiration, and initiator of her initial sorties into the Paris intellectual and artistic avant-garde world, she recognized, as she did with Jacob Epstein, that: "She had an eye... she had an eye for the unusual."[34]

The flea market at Clignancourt was a treasure trove for this love of eclectic objects, particularly for the famous opaline vases purchased from the "Marquise." Much later, in August 1964, Madame made a final pilgrimage to Paris for one last glimpse of the haunts that had left such a mark on her life.[35]

The years 1908–14 spent shuttling between Great Britain and France and rubbing shoulders with an upmarket Bohemian crowd were crucial for the construction of Helena Rubinstein's social image.[36] In 1909, she opened a beauty salon in Paris, at 255, Rue du Faubourg-Saint-Honoré,[37] keeping an apartment above the premises in which she was to live both before[38] and after WWI.[39] Practically no document of interest concerning our topic survives from this period of encounters and growth. The first tangible traces come from the other side of the Atlantic, where she emigrated as soon as hostilities broke out.

In a photograph dated 1915 of the interior of her New York living-room at 15 East 49th Street, a table appears covered with artifacts: the foreground seems to feature a Fang head with round metal eyes.[40] This image[41] attests to the presence of African works in her possession at a relatively early date, even if in her beauty salons she preferred to display neoclassical works by Elie Nadelman, an entire exhibition of which she had acquired in London in 1911.[42] African pieces—Ashanti stools, a couple of Baule statues—could be observed in the company of Nadelman's works and portraits in the salon at 715 Fifth Avenue which she opened in 1936[43]. There were often vitrines in her beauty salons, in which she liked to place eclectic objects, just as she was wont to do in her own interiors. It is hard to tell whether she spent much time among New York art dealers, but she may have known Joseph Brummer (†1947) and his brother Ernest, who, setting up on Park Avenue after the former's death, was a good friend and business associate of Charles Ratton's.

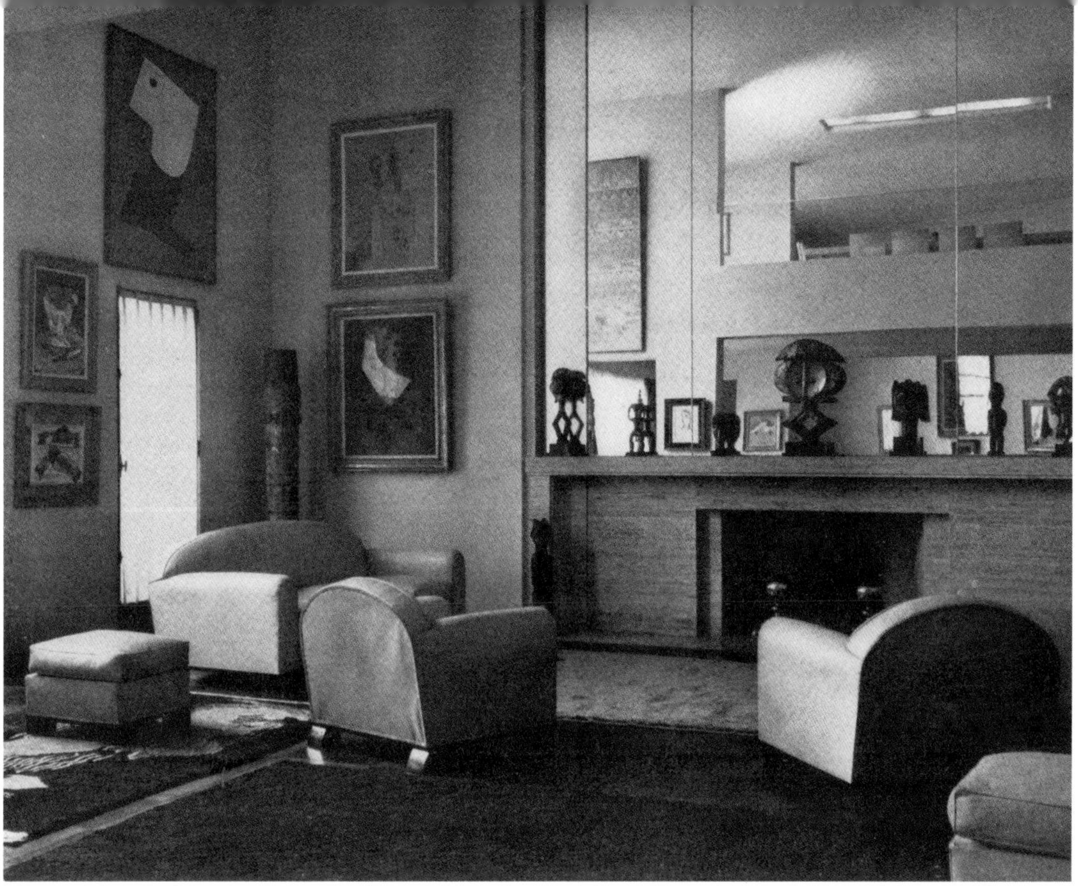

In Paris she kept her collection of non-European arts in the domestic sphere. Having once stood in her apartment on Boulevard Raspail and then on Quai de Béthune, Brancusi's famous sculpture *Bird in Space* (1927) formed a towering eye-catcher in her beauty salon at 52, Rue du Faubourg-Saint-Honoré, which did not feature any African pieces.

Helena Rubinstein is first mentioned as a collector of African art in Marya Mannès' article of 1929. Among the illustrations accompanying the text are a Kota reliquary guardian[44] and the black Punu mask,[45] but no documents reproducing the other three objects survive, nor are they included in the 1966 sales catalogs. Clearly, some mystery still envelops the hidden part of the iceberg of this fabulous collection.[46]

The 1930s and beyond: a great collector constructs her own world

On a personal level, the 1930s proved critical for Rubinstein. A double masterstroke had already placed her fortune on a secure footing: first, in 1928, she had sold her company's American branch to Lehman Brothers at the top of the market; then, the following year, she bought it back for a song in the aftermath of the Wall Street Crash. 1931 proved a pivotal year: a debut book,[47] published in 1930, became a bestseller and business was going swimmingly. Her health, on the other hand, failed to keep pace. Struggling to recover from surgery she had undergone in Vienna, she persisted in alternating between Paris and New York, even managing to enrich her collections in glorious fashion at landmark sales in the French capital. It was at this time that, during a sojourn in Paris with her husband and the journalist Grace Davidson, she bought Brancusi's *White Negress*.

Ill. 16

The drawing-room in the apartment at 216, Boulevard Raspail, Paris, c. 1932; on the mantelpiece a Kota reliquary guardian (lot 192), and in a corner, a drum (lot 32*)

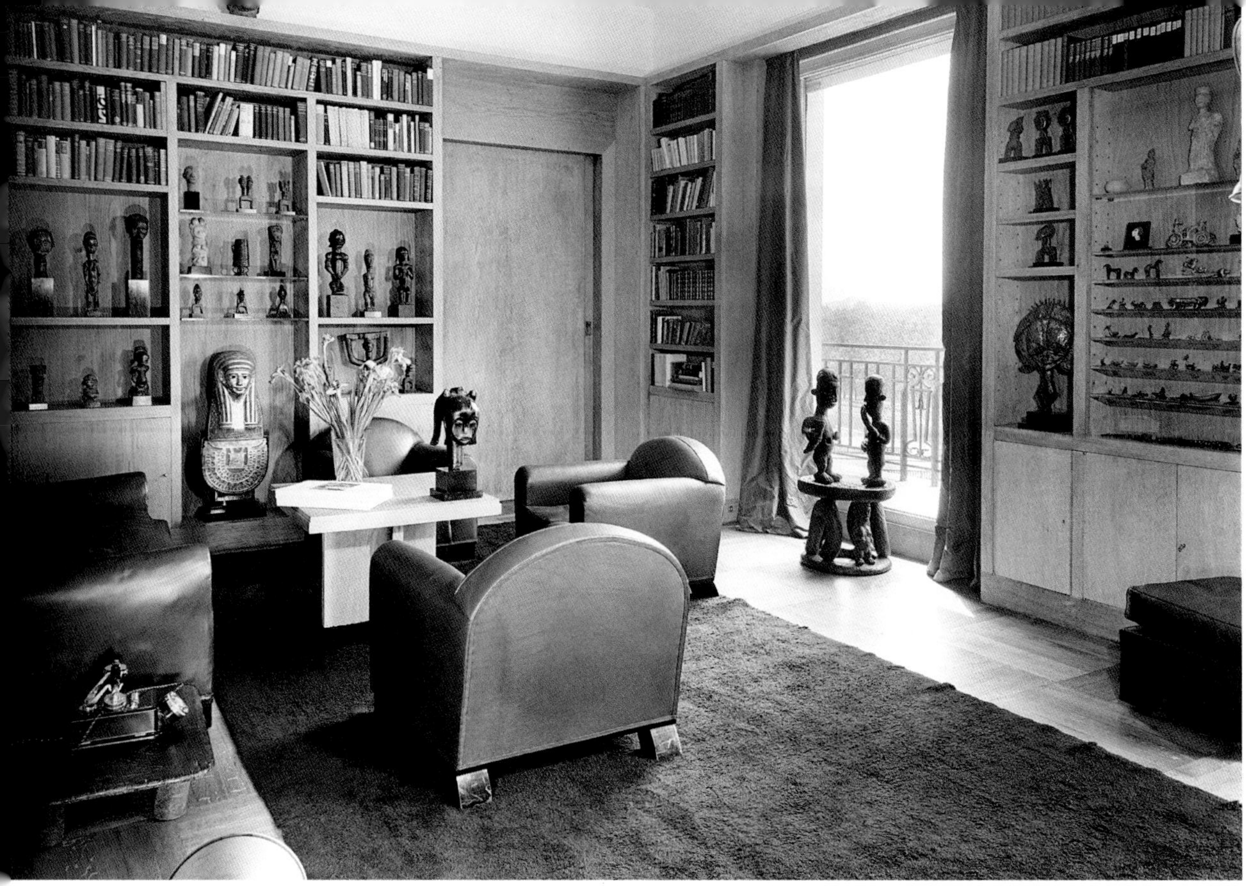

Likewise, around this period, wounded by rumors spread by mean-spirited friends, she decided to separate from Titus and file for divorce, before at length repairing to a clinic in Germany to convalesce in 1932.

These years also marked a turning point in the constitution of the collection. In private remarks she pinpoints two decisive incidents: "My big collection came later, in the thirties when Hitler started being difficult. There was this German Jew who managed to get out of Berlin with a wagonload of African stuff. He was broke. I helped him out. Pfft! That's how to collect... By the wagonload."[48] Betokening an assertion of power and her self-confidence and opportunism, as well as a desire to be provocative, there lurks a mysterious truth behind this statement. In fact, this memory of a watershed moment—with the picture it conjures up of important objects subjected to a wholesale handover against the backdrop of aiding a Jew during the war—is partly anchored in reality. The hypothesis is that it refers to the acquisition of the collection of objects gathered together by F.-H. Lem, a Jew of Polish descent, who, after the 1929 crash and marrying in the 1930s,[49] found himself posted to West Africa. During the course of his stay from 1934–35, he collected 225 objects in Mali, northern Ivory Coast, and Burkina-Faso, documenting them as much as possible at the time with a view to arranging for them to be housed by the museum at the IFAN (French Institute of Black Africa) in Dakar[50]. Since this plan came to naught, he returned to France with the results of his prospecting.[51] Following this acquisition, in August 1937 Helena Rubinstein was able to display in her apartment on the Quai de Béthune a seminal collection from the French-speaking area of West Africa

ILL. 17

First version of the African room with shelves lined with a mix of books and artifacts, 24, Quai de Béthune, Paris, 1937, photograph by Dora Maar

known as the "Soudan français."[52] She also financed Lem's publication on the subject, featuring essentially the collection she herself acquired[53] on the cessation of hostilities in 1948–49.[54] F.-H. Lem continued to go under the title of "curator of the collections of Princess Gourielli"[55]—with a rather vague remit (management? conservation? acquisitions?)—until at least 1954.[56] He was also responsible, in the early 1950s, for the purchase by Helena Rubinstein of fifty-six Agni terracotta pieces from Dr. Lheureux.[57] Lem was thus instrumental in facilitating two major additions to the Rubinstein collection, with the ensemble of sculptures from the Sudan and the Agni terracottas, which he helped to publicize with exhibitions and publications.[58]

For the dramatic ascendency of the Rubinstein collection, the years 1930–31 were crucial. Though no earlier photographic records exist, it is certain that by this time it was of considerable size, already propelling Madame to the rank of a great collector[59]. If her collection, or at least her interest in the "Negro arts," had been sparked—timidly at first, as she freely confessed—in 1908, it only became visible in photographs, sales archives, exhibitions, and publications in the early 1930s.

It is possible that by this date, having been relocated on several occasions, probably during WWI, the focus of the collection may have shifted somewhat. Perhaps Helena Rubinstein was initially interested only in smaller articles, such as Akan gold weights, combs, heddle pulleys from Ivory Coast, figurative sculpture, and anthropomorphic masks—all objects that overlapped with her concern with the face and the body.[60] Fifteen auctions of "primitive art" (Africa, Oceania, America) were organized at Drouot's by André Portier between April 1927 and June 1930. In them we find traces of objects later owned by Madame that probably marked her first forays into public sales.

On July 2, 1931, lots 19 (a Fang with long arms, 3,200 francs[61]) and 27 (a tall Kongo-Portuguese figurative staff, 320 francs[62]) from the sale of the famous Breton-Éluard collection were paid for by "M. Titus," though they actually joined the Epstein collection. The two lots were, in fact, purchased on behalf of the sculptor[63] who was to keep them until his death.[64] Though discrepancies between her reminiscences (see note 24) and reality are legion, this incident confirms what Rubinstein herself observed about her relationship with Epstein. The Fang statue was one of the most expensive pieces in the sale. Shortly after the auction, Helena Rubinstein acquired a statue from the Nyas Islands (lot 173 in the Breton-Éluard sale; **lot 256** in the 1966 sale[65] **[ill. 152]**) and a Maori post (lot 142 in the Breton-Éluard sale; **lot 253** at the 1966 sale). These two pieces, acquired by Paul Chadourne [66] at the Breton-Éluard sale, enjoyed pride of place in the apartment on Boulevard Raspail.

Events unfolded in similar fashion at the sale of the Georges de Miré collection on December 16, 1931, with Maître Bellier wielding the hammer and Charles Ratton and Louis Carré acting as consultants. Madame was present in person. She made purchases for sums ranging from 125 to 3,000 francs: 12 Akan weights (lots 4 and 10b), a Dan female mask decorated with feathers (lot 18), a Baule mask, the base of whose face ends in a bird's beak (lot 22), two Baule statuettes (lots 25 and 26), a heddle pulley (lot 30), a drum (lot 33), a Bamun bronze pipe bowl (lot 44), a Kota reliquary guardian dubbed a "fetish mask" (lot 57), a Kuba cup (lot 80b), a vase from Peru (lot 139), and a Pre-Columbian mask (lot 157). Some of these objects, reproduced in the catalog (lot 26) or not (lots 4, 10b, 18, 22, 44), have vanished without trace, and do not appear in the 1966 auction catalogs. Some persuasive hypotheses can be arrived at, however, thanks to the almost perfect agreement between all the available evidence (dimensions, descriptions): the Baule

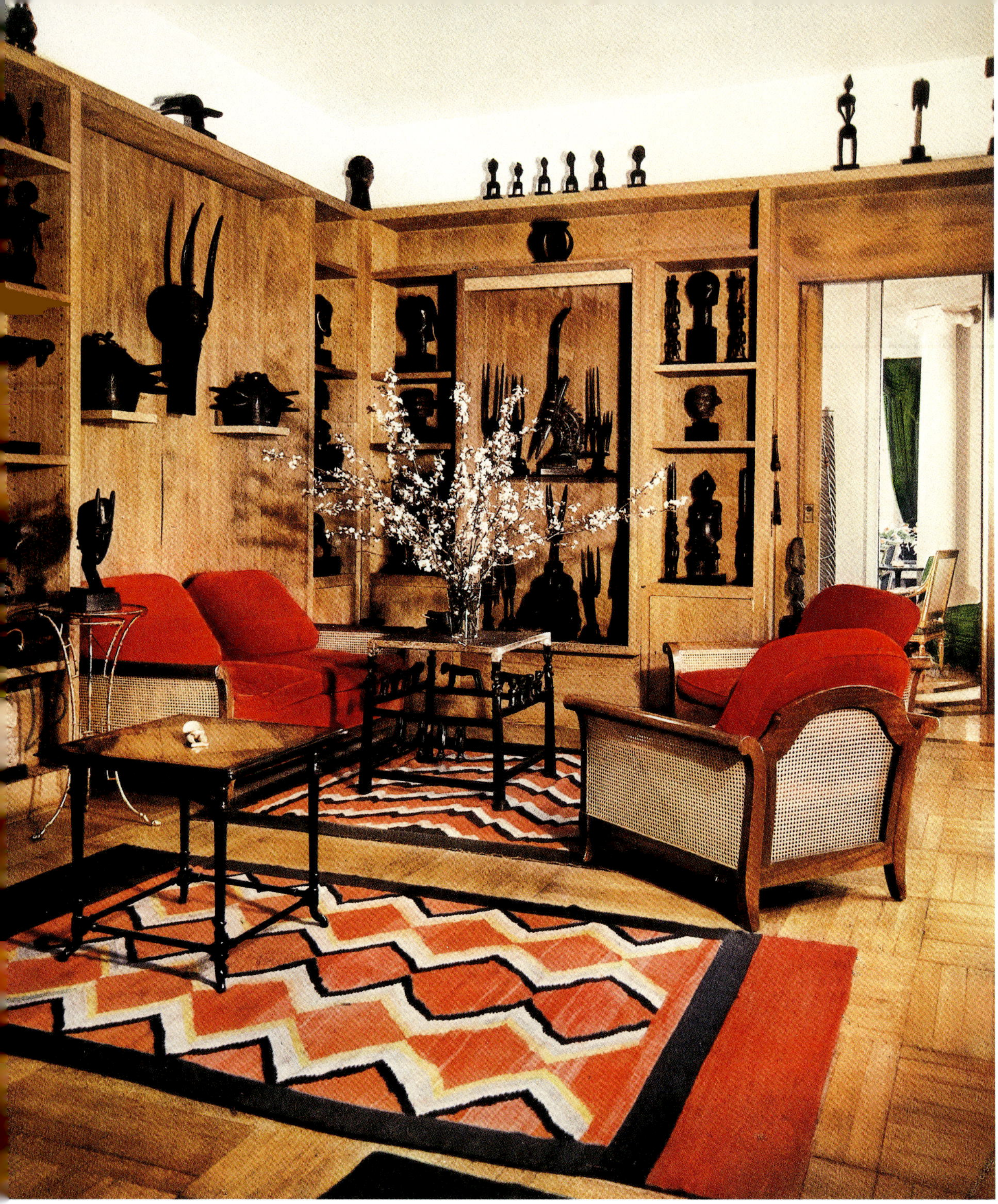

ILL. 18

The African room,
24, Quai de Béthune, Paris,
c. 1954–55, colorized
photograph taken from
the album composed
by Jean Vincent (cat. 91);
African seats are used as
coffee tables

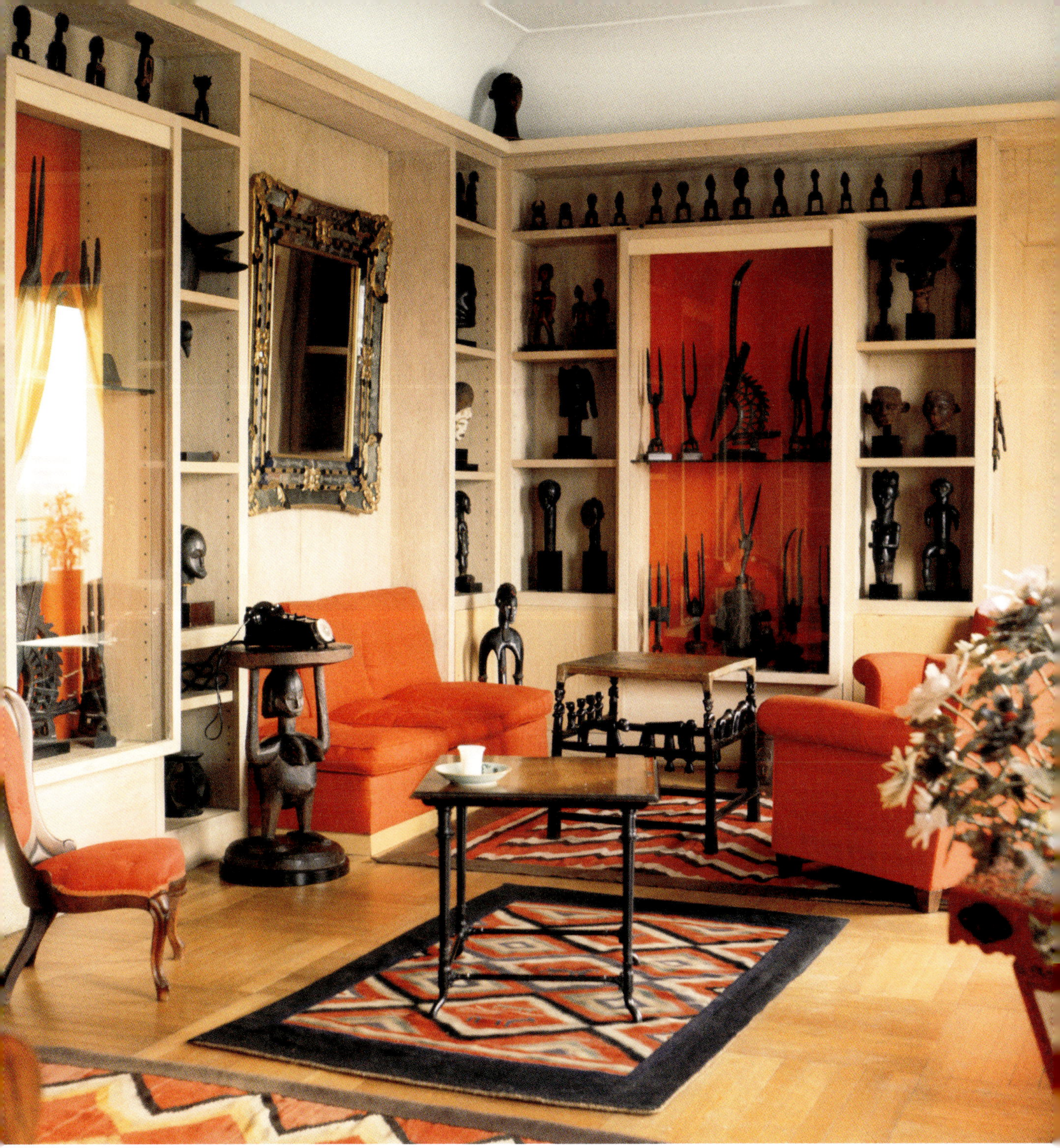

Ill. 19

The African room,
24, Quai de Béthune, Paris,
1962, photograph by
Giancarlo Botti; artworks
now filling all the shelving
space available

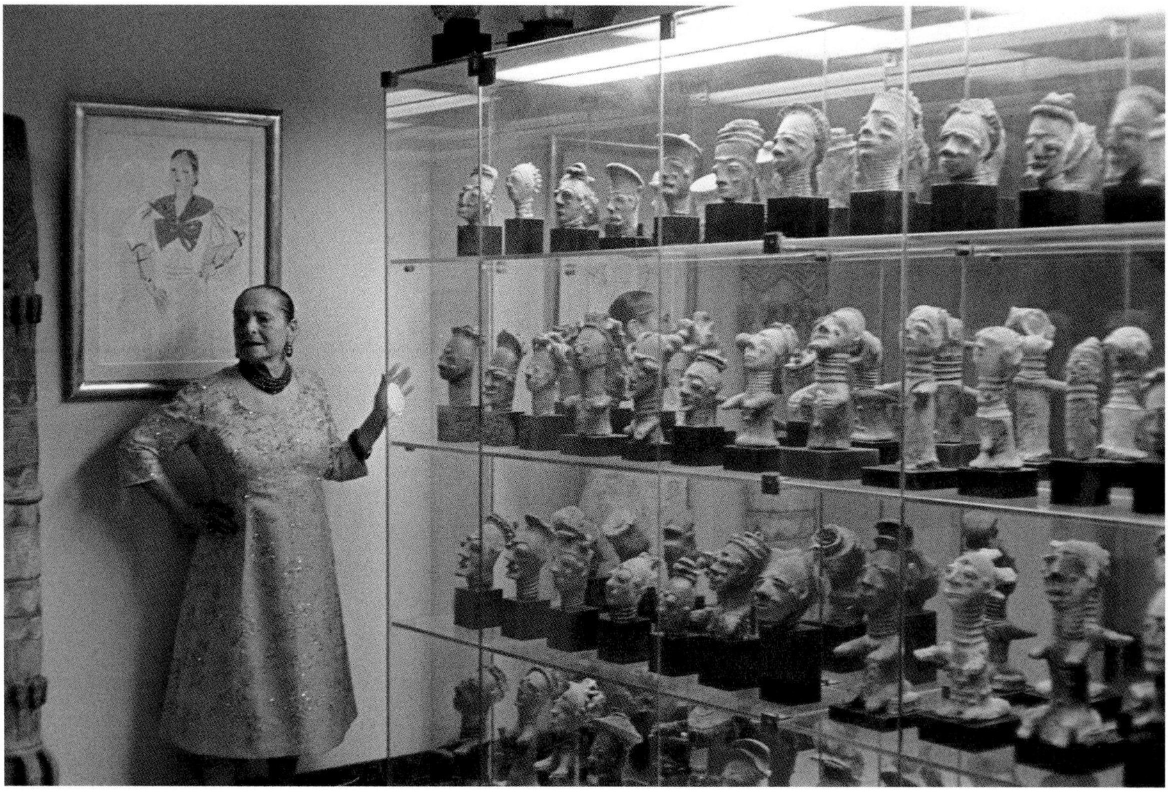

statue (lot 25 from the De Miré sale) is LOT 40 in the 1966 sale [ill. 76]; the heddle pulley (lot 30) is LOT 36 at the 1966 sale (National Museum of African Art, Washington, inv. NMAFA 96.7.1); the drum (lot 33) is LOT 47 at the 1966 sale (The Metropolitan Museum, New York, inv. 1995.64.10); the Kota reliquary figure (lot 57) is the famous LOT 192 in the 1966 sale [ill. 113]; the cup from the Kasai (lot 80) is lot 230 in the 1966 sale (Phoebe Hearst Museum, Berkeley University, inv. 5.5289); the Pre-Columbian vase (lot 139) was donated after the sale to the Museum of Ethnography in the Trocadéro, Paris [ill. 133]. Above all, Helena Rubinstein acquired and paid for the Fang statue (lot 46), the record item at the sale (29,325 francs), apparently at Epstein's behest—a fact that once again contradicts her claim that he would only buy at rock-bottom prices. It is surprising that she did not try to withhold this splendid "Black Venus"—a veritable jewel of African art, today part of the Dapper Foundation's collection in Paris (inv. 3132)—for herself.

Her connections with museums in France date back to the same period, as is clear from the aforementioned donation, in 1931, of a piece of Pre-Columbian pottery to the Museum of Ethnography in the Trocadéro, which probably related to her links with Georges-Henri Rivière.[67] For the International Colonial Exhibition organized in 1931, and later for the opening of the indigenous art gallery at the Musée des Colonies et de la France Extérieure (1932–33), she agreed to the loan of a "*pahouine*" head (Fang, Gabon), which was returned on January 16, 1932.[68] A receipt dated September 7, 1932, for articles loaned by a private collector mentions Helena Rubinstein at the address, 216, Boulevard Raspail.[69]

ILL. 20
Helena Rubinstein in front of the showcase containing Agni heads from the collection of Dr. Lheureux, 24, Quai de Béthune, Paris, 1962, photograph by Giancarlo Botti

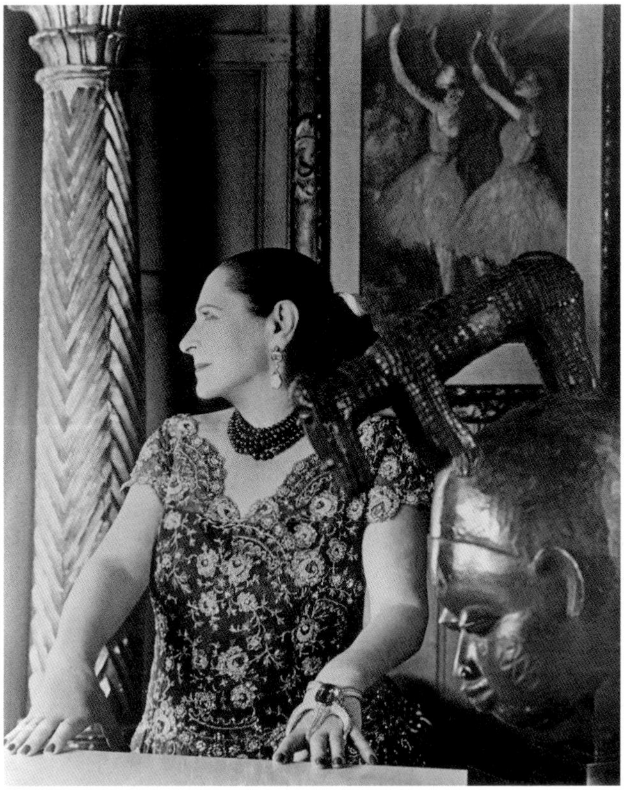

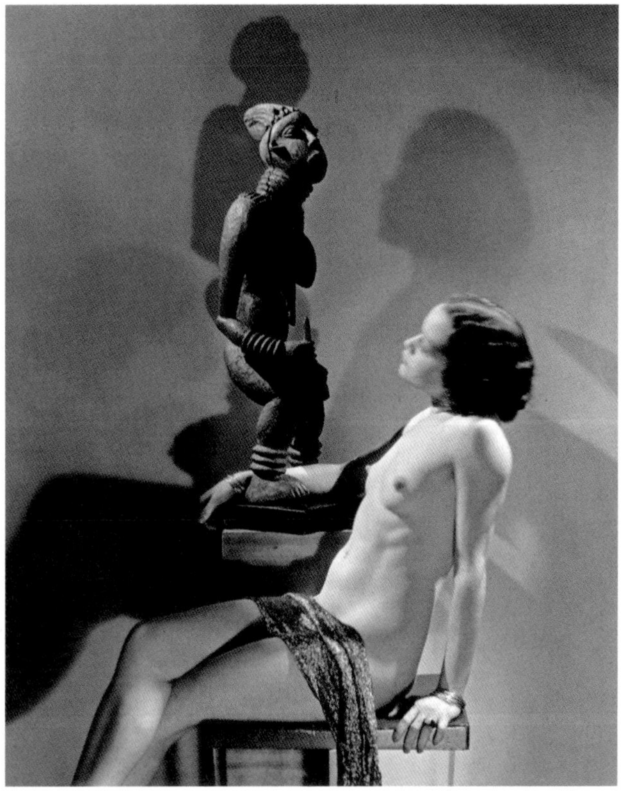

Madame is virtually the only woman among all these great dealers, such as Paul Guillaume and Charles Ratton, Louis Carré, Anthony Morris, Pierre Loeb, the Percier gallery (André Level), Raphaël Stora, and likewise among the collectors, like Paul Chadourne, Joseph Gaillard-Groleas, author of the "Cantique africain," Georges Salles, Louis Marcoussis—a close friend of Helena Rubinstein's—and Tristan Tzara.

Did she ever find time to visit the sprawling exhibition at the Théâtre Pigalle in 1930?[70] A number of objects on show found their way into her collection: Louis Marcoussis's famous Bamana seated statue,[71] a Senufo loom pulley of an extremely rare type, then the property of Stephen Chauvet,[72] a Yoruba *oshe Shango*, belonging at this time to Félix Fénéon, which she was to see again at the MOMA in 1935, and which she was to purchase on the conclusion of the sale on June 11–13, 1947, the two Bamileke heads [ill. 103 and 104], ornaments for a large drum, one of which is today in the Metropolitan Museum, New York,[73] the Bamileke seat now in the High Museum, Atlanta, the Easter Island statue [ill. 130], at present in a private collection,[74] all four belonging to Pierre Loeb, Ernst Ascher's magnificent Fang head [ill. 5],[75] another Fang head belonging to Paul Guillaume,[76] a Fang statue, property of the modern American painter, Patrick Henry Bruce, whose whereabouts are unknown today,[77] the much-vaunted Kota reliquary guardian figure belonging to Georges de Miré [ill. 113] and acquired by Helena Rubinstein in 1931, which after the 1966 sale [78] came into the hands of William Rubin, and finally a Kongo magic statue of large size owned by Paul Chadourne [ill. 47].[79] Eleven major African pieces and one Pacific item featured in this historic exhibition were eventually to enter the Rubinstein collection.

ill. 21

Madame in a Dior dress wearing her "starfish" bracelet, next to a Yoruba *Gelede* mask (lot 179), 625 Park Avenue, New York, 1957

ill. 22

Man Ray
Black and White, photograph of the Bangwa "queen" (lot 189) and of the model Ady, 1934

In 1935, Helena Rubinstein, who had until then been remarkable by her absence from the groundbreaking publications[80] and major events[81] involving these pioneer dealers and collectors—including her mentor, Jacob Epstein—came to front of stage as a collector by lending nineteen objects[82] to the *African Negro Art* show held at the Metropolitan Museum, New York. On April 26, 1935, she organized a dinner for a "coterie of admirers of primitive African art" at 895, Park Avenue, to which she invited Charles Ratton. One can picture around the table Frank Crowninshield, editor-in-chief of *Vogue US* and one of Ratton's regular customers, who also collected heddle pulleys, and whose Yoruba *gelede* mask surmounted by a saurian[83] she acquired and posed with [ill. 21], Mrs. Edith Isaacs, a New York-based collector of weapons from the Congo, and perhaps a few other collectors from the city who were participating in an event chiefly centered around French collections and European museums.[84] It may have been at this soirée that Helena Rubinstein brought up the subject of purchasing the large Dengese statue lent by Charles Ratton [ill. 123] that was later to join her collection.[85]

The question remains as to how Helena Rubinstein was able to manage all these acquisitions, given the diversity of their origins, even if Louis Marcoussis, who died in 1941, Pierre Loeb, Paul Chadourne, and Charles Ratton appear to have shared their address books with her.

Thus, in the early 1930s, Madame acquired the famous Bangwa[86] "queen,"[87] collected in 1897–98 by Gustav Conrau, which Charles Ratton had only recently obtained from the German dealer Arthur Speyer, who had himself "extracted" it from the collections of the Ethnographical Museum in Berlin in 1926 by purchase or exchange. A dynamic embodiment of African femininity, this statue was photographed in 1934 together with a living model by Man Ray [ill. 22], who had already taken a picture destined to become famous entitled *Black and White* in which the face of a white woman contrasts with a dark-colored Bassa mask.

In the earliest display of the African room on the Quai de Béthune, the Bangwa statue[88] figures at the rear of the central niche in the wall on the right on entering, practically obscured behind the large club chairs that had furnished the apartment on Boulevard Raspail which Helena Rubinstein had hurriedly abandoned after her separation from Edward Titus, while the other walls are lined with bookcases groaning under the weight of books. Rearranged after the war, this room was converted into a permanent exhibition space dedicated exclusively to African objects [ill. 18 and 19].

After 1939, Madame acquired several Kota[89] reliquary guardian figures which appear in Charles Ratton's photographs of the Ali Baba's cave-inspired apartment belonging to "Père Morris" [ill. 45]. Probably around the same years she also acquired the Luluwa statuette [ill. 120],[90] which until 1938 formed part of E. Gustave de Hondt's magnificent collection in Brussels. On June 11 and 13, 1947, on the occasion of the auction at Drouot's of the renowned Félix Fénéon collection, "Africa, Oceania, the Americas," probably through Charles Ratton who worked as a consultant on the sale, she bought a Yoruba *oshe Shango*.[91]

A nomadic collector with a nomadic collection

It might be said that, once set up in the treasure trove of the "African room" on Quai de Béthune, as well as along the corridors leading to the countless rooms of the apartment, the objects in the collection, now frequently photographed, had found a more or less definitive location that gradually offered a distillation of Helena Rubinstein's

Above left
Ill. 23
Madame in Hong Kong paying cash for some Far Eastern antiquities, 1957, photograph by Brian Brake

Above right
Ill. 24
Madame traveling by boat with her artifacts. A Guro mask and a Fang mask (lot 220); photograph taken setting off from Le Havre to New York, February 15, 1934

Below left
Ill. 25
Madame showing one of her Dan masks to the actress Pier Angeli, 625, Park Avenue, New York, 1961

Below right
Ill. 26
Madame adjusting the position of a heddle pulley and some Senufo, Baule, and Bamana statuettes, Knightsbridge, London, after 1959, photograph by Francis Thompson

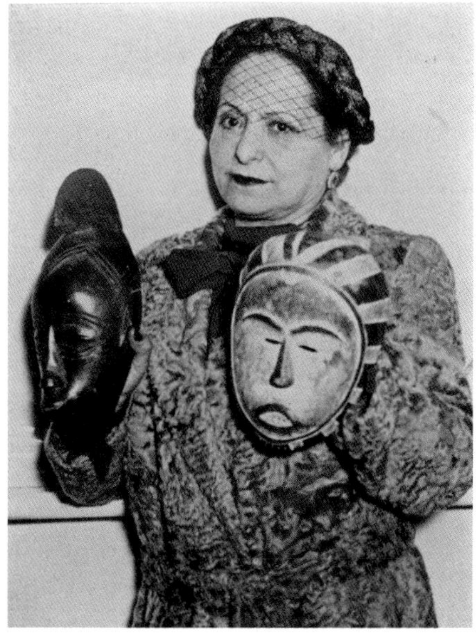

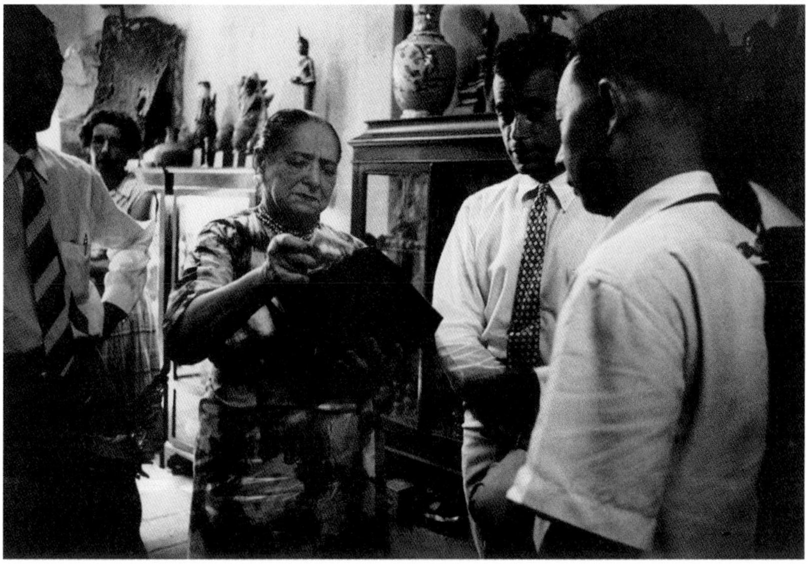

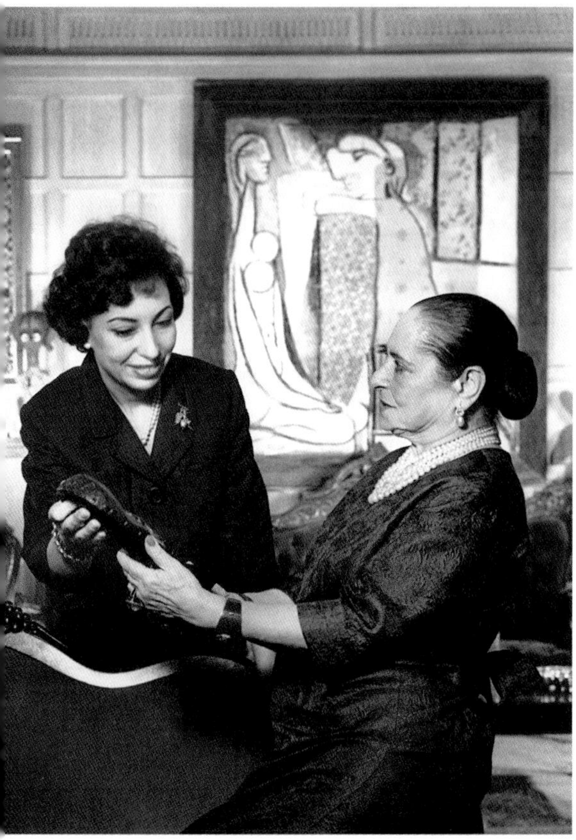

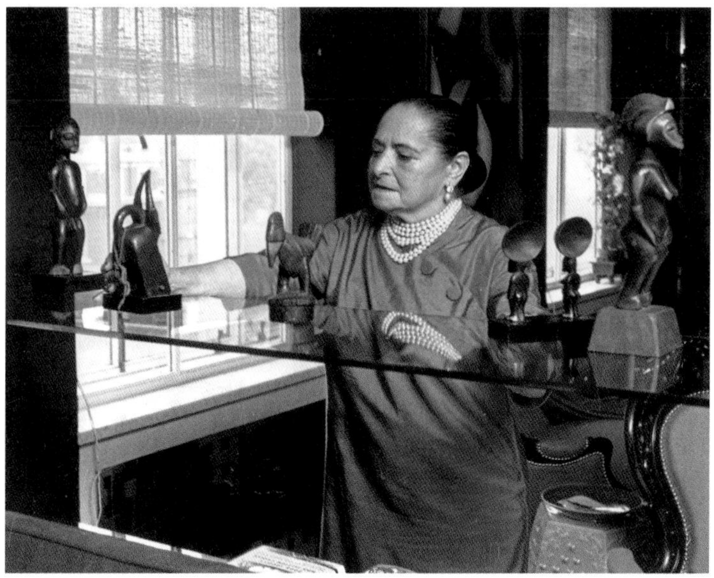

personality. Objects reproduced in the 1966 auction catalogs can be identified from the famous 1951 shoot, in which she appears in the guise of a lady of the manor [ill. 90]. The artifacts, whether as individuals or in sequence (the Baule and Senufo statues together; the pulleys in the same place; the Kota together; the Ejagham heads in the corners, on the top shelf of the display units lining the walls), seem to have found their rightful place, rather like in a museum storehouse. Subsequently, the Agni heads were to be gathered together in a big showcase against the wall [ill. 20 and 68]. At this time the muted presence and random arrangement of the African art objects in the New York apartment, in which portraits of Madame and modern painting predominate, imply quite different priorities.

According to the scant elements at our disposal, the collection was assembled and laid out essentially between 1930 and 1950.[92] After the 1950s, however, its development becomes difficult to track: Helena Rubinstein certainly continued her practice of buying in bulk and on impulse, but the fundamentals were already in place. The core of this admirable ensemble that proved such a comfort to this extraordinary collector in difficult times remained unchanged.

Her early years of personal and professional success were refracted through this attachment to her collection. Thus, on a trip to Hollywood in 1934, Madame took along seventy of her African sculptures [ill. 24]—out of a total then estimated at four hundred—delivering lectures that praised the: "strange charm and beauty of expression [of masks... that] played an important part in the religious and social life of the tribes which created them."[93] As she resolutely declared before a predominantly female audience respectful of her professional attainments: "they are recognized as having a true aesthetic value and a peculiar beauty all their own, entirely different, but no less interesting than the more long-accepted standards of Greek sculptural beauty."[94] Publicity material for the lectures was accompanied by a photograph of the elegantly gloved collector in front of her collection at 216, Boulevard Raspail, in which she poses with a somber mask from Ivory Coast, which "[...] was worn thousands of years ago by primitive priests in a dance of the Masks in the [...] belief that it would frighten away evil spirits or attract good ones,"[95] in an image that perfectly captures the personality of this striking, modern, unusual, and militant woman.

Marya Mannes's analysis in 1929 of five objects from the collection served as a basis for commentaries, informed for the period, which went beyond mere cultural identification to deal with context and use. [96] This then fledgling area of science adhered to simplistic constructs (savannah/forest) that allowed for an initial classification of what was in fact a world of extremely diverse forms. Appearing in numerous exhibitions and publications, [97] Helena Rubinstein's collection mirrored in real time the progress of a field of knowledge developed by ethnologists, art historians, dealers, and art lovers exclusively from the West whose characteristics it assimilated—for instance, highlighting the essential role in African societies of lineage, since this squared with its own values.

On course for eternity: 1966, Madame's curtain call[98]

At the three sales in April and October 1966, all the objects Helena Rubinstein had collected with her perceptive and stylish eye, having lived together for more than thirty years, were finally to fall prey to the law that states that nothing remains together forever. Their owner had made no provision whatsoever to ensure that the collection might be handed down intact. An inventory and valuation of the Paris collection was undertaken by Jean Roudillon before being handled by Parke-Bernet in New York, then in the process of being bought out by Sotheby's, were contacted to arrange a sale.[99]

Once export permits had been obtained from the French Ministry of Culture for the most valuable pieces in a collection then domiciled in Paris, it was studied and documented by Bruce Chatwin (1940–1989),[100] the cataloger of the sale, and his future wife, Elisabeth Chatwin, in New York. Photographed for the majority, the two hundred and sixty-one lots in the first two sales (April 21 and 29, 1966) were generously illustrated, while only ten of the hundred lots in the third sale (October 10, 1966) were accompanied by a photograph.[101] The man who carried out the substantial task of cataloging three hundred and sixty-one lots was an exceptional individual with an eye honed in various artistic fields. The exercise—Bruce Chatwin's final Sotheby's consignment before his fancy took him on to the study of archaeology and later to the famous journeys that he turned into stories which won him international fame during his lifetime[102]—proved, by his own admission, exhausting.[103]

With its record bids for the Bangwa[104] "queen", the Senufo *deble*, and the oft-quoted Bamana marionette, this collection—snapped up by dealers from the United States[105] and Paris, by collectors,[106] and by people close to[107] Helena Rubinstein or acquaintances,[108] and scattering in directions that can only be imperfectly reconstructed today—acquired additional resonance thanks to the international celebrity of the woman who had assembled it.

Thus, the Fang female bust, lot 209, acquired in New York by a French dealer, returned to France to find a home with the great sculptor, Henri Laurens, the first winner of the prize Helena Rubinstein had created in the winter of 1937 [ill. 14]. Laurens's son, who had kept this icon of art, recalled how the sculptor would stand it at the end of the family dining-room table at mealtimes and would regularly gaze at the bust in silence, entering into an unspoken dialog that those present took as a lesson. Acquired by a French dealer with the aid of Charles Ratton,[109] André Breton's statue from the Nyas Islands [lot 256, ill. 152] entered the Pavillon des Sessions in the Louvre thanks to a donation by Alain Schoffel at the time the *Arts premiers* were being reevaluated under President Jacques Chirac, a process that initiated plans for the Musée du Quai Branly.

Spectators, accessories, or actors in the theater of human life? Above and beyond how they might have been looked at by those who selected and treasured them during their existence as collectibles, these ritual or functional objects all absorbed particles of the energy inspirited in them since they were taken from their native land. Companions to an experience in which the ordinary meets the extraordinary, collected, then scattered, and then rediscovered through the power of desire, they open a window onto the spiritual side of all those who cherished them and who were, in return, shaped by them.

Frederic-Henri Lem's mid-twentieth-century case for African art and its study

Susan Elizabeth Gagliardi

Art enthusiast Frédéric-Henri Lem reports that during a 1934-35 stay in *Soudan français* (French Sudan)—then a French colony and today the West African nation-state of Mali—he assembled a collection of nearly 225 objects[1]. Lem explains that he sought to combine aesthetic evaluation of the objects with ethnographic information gathered in the places where the objects were produced[2]. He adds that he selected the sculptures in the collection from more than 1000 works that dealers, makers, or other people in French Sudan had offered him[3]. Lem also notes that in 1936, he offered the group of objects he amassed to the French colonial administration for exhibition in Paris and subsequent transfer to the museum of the *Institut français d'Afrique Noire* (IFAN), the Musée d'IFAN, in Dakar, Senegal.[4] But the transfer never happened. By the time Lem published *Sculptures soudanaises* and its English translation *Sudanese Sculpture* in 1948 and 1949 respectively, cosmetics magnate Helena Rubinstein had acquired for her own collection many of the objects Lem had gathered and illustrated in the book.[5]

The collection Lem assembled, and the information about it that he published, reflects and reinforces views of African art prevalent in France in the 1930s and 1940s. Yet in his publications, Lem also attempts to explain how his approach to African art and its documentation differed from the approaches of other European admirers of African art at the time. Lem highlights his ability to determine the aesthetic quality and character of objects as well as his attention to the accuracy of his documentation. While Lem may have addressed European and North American audiences in his texts, his publications demonstrate that he also sought to maintain some West African art and cultural knowledge within West Africa. Lem expresses disappointment at the dispersal in Europe of his collection. He explains that had the museum in Dakar acquired the

Ill. 27

Excerpt of the article "Magie soudanaise" by F.-H. Lem, published in *Soleils*, Paris: Arts et métiers graphiques, 1947, p. 86

Ill. 28 and 29

Cover and title page of F.-H. Lem, *Sculptures sudanaises*, Paris: Arts et métiers graphiques, 1948

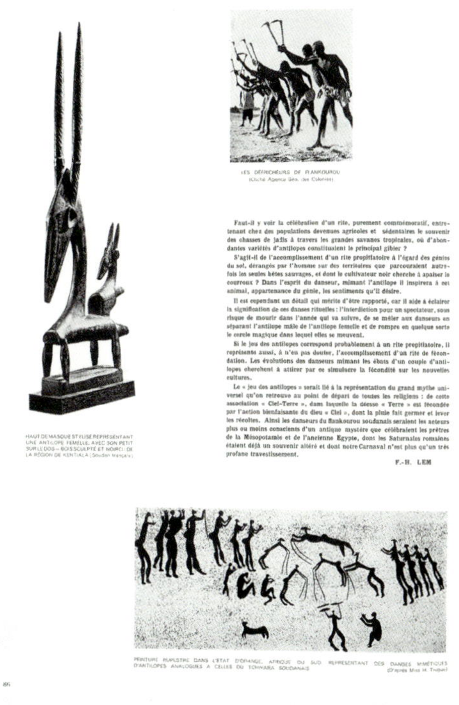

LES DÉFRICHEURS DE FLANKOUROU
(Cliché Agence Gén. des Colonies)

Faut-il y voir la célébration d'un rite, purement commémoratif, entretenant chez des populations devenues agricoles et sédentaires le souvenir des chasses de jadis à travers les grandes savanes tropicales, où d'abondantes variétés d'antilopes constituaient le principal gibier ?

S'agit-il de l'accomplissement d'un rite propitiatoire à l'égard des génies du sol, dérangés par l'homme sur des territoires que parcouraient autrefois les seules bêtes sauvages, et dont le cultivateur noir cherche à apaiser le courroux ? Dans l'esprit du danseur, mimant l'antilope il inspirera à cet animal, appartenance du génie, les sentiments qu'il désire.

Il est cependant un détail qui mérite d'être rapporté, car il aide à éclairer la signification de ces danses rituelles : l'interdiction pour un spectateur, sous risque de mourir dans l'année qui va suivre, de se mêler aux danseurs en séparant l'antilope mâle de l'antilope femelle et de rompre en quelque sorte le cercle magique dans lequel elles se meuvent.

Si le jeu des antilopes correspond probablement à un rite propitiatoire, il représente aussi, à n'en pas douter, l'accomplissement d'un rite de fécondation. Les évolutions des danseurs mimant les ébats d'un couple d'antilopes cherchent à attirer par ce simulacre la fécondité sur les nouvelles cultures.

Le « jeu des antilopes » serait lié à la représentation du grand mythe universel qu'on retrouve au point de départ de toutes les religions : de cette association « Ciel-Terre », dans laquelle la déesse « Terre » est fécondée par l'action bienfaisante du dieu « Ciel », dont la pluie fait germer et lever les récoltes. Ainsi les danseurs du flankourou soudanais seraient les acteurs plus ou moins conscients d'un antique mystère que célébraient les prêtres de la Mésopotamie et de l'ancienne Egypte, dont les Saturnales romaines étaient déjà un souvenir altéré et dont notre Carnaval n'est plus qu'un très profane travestissement.

F.-H. LEM

HAUT DE MASQUE STYLISÉ REPRÉSENTANT UNE ANTILOPE FEMELLE, AVEC SON PETIT SUR LE DOS — BOIS SCULPTÉ ET NOIRCI, DE LA RÉGION DE KENTIALA (Soudan français)

PEINTURE RUPESTRE DANS L'ÉTAT D'ORANGE, AFRIQUE DU SUD, REPRÉSENTANT DES DANSES MIMÉTIQUES D'ANTILOPES ANALOGUES À CELLES DU TCHWARA SOUDANAIS (D'après Miss H. Tongue)

86

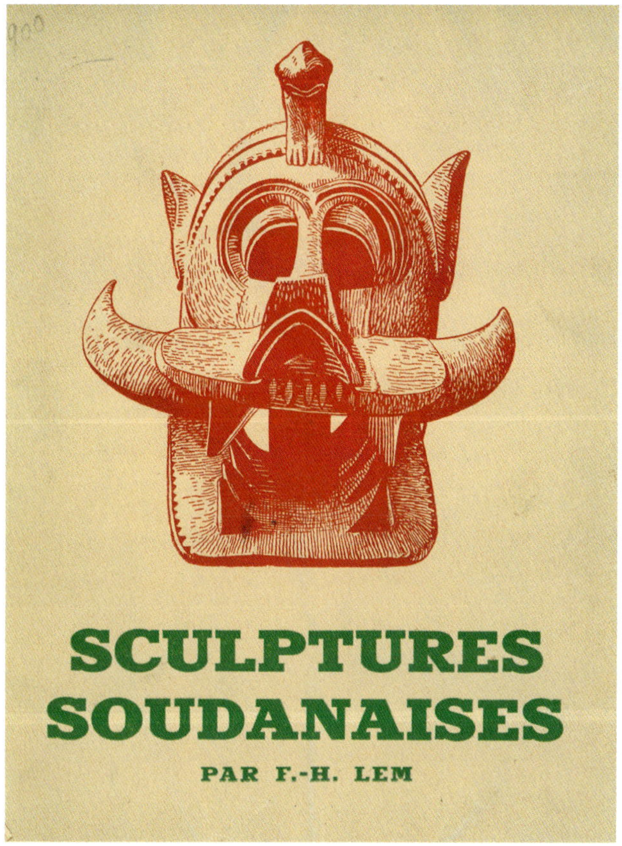

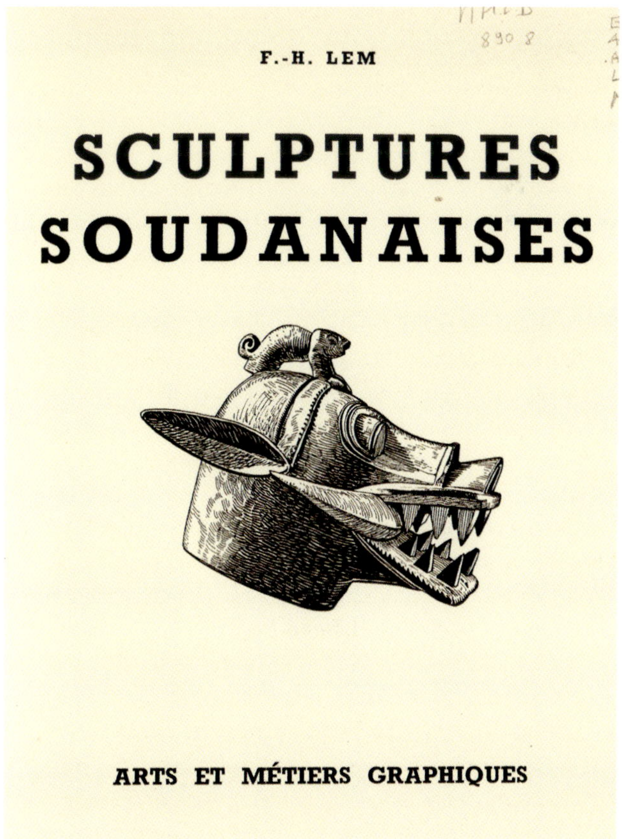

objects, then it "would... have called forth many gifts and the return to Africa of some of the beautiful things which lie hidden from everyone in cupboards or on the shelves of Parisian high-brows."[6]

Pour un musée d'Art Africain ("[The case] for an African Art museum")

Prior to the outbreak of World War II in the late 1930s, Lem worked to promote the collection of objects he had assembled as well as his conviction that the collection belonged in a museum dedicated to African art. *Les Annales Coloniales* published Lem's essay, "Pour un musée d'art africain", in three parts in late September and early October 1938. Lem asserts that at the time, no museum in the world had yet dedicated itself to the presentation of objects from Africa as art rather than as ethnographic artifacts. Certain art museums had by that time hosted short-term exhibitions or other focused installations to show museumgoers objects from Africa as art on a temporary basis. According to Lem, the museum in Dakar was well positioned to feature African art on a permanent basis and thus distinguish itself from other museums, such as France's Musée de l'Homme, located in Paris's Trocadero, the Musée des Colonies in Vincennes, the Ethnologisches Museum in Berlin, the British Museum in London, or the Musée du Congo Belge in Tervuren.[7]

The third installment of Lem's three-part essay makes clear the motivation for the text. Lem informs readers that he acquired more than 200 old, rare works during what he characterized as a "recent" trip to West Africa, apparently a reference to the stay that he dates to 1934-35 in his later publication. Lem describes the collection he gathered in West Africa as first-rate. He also explains that he offered the collection to the director of the *Agence d'information et de documentation coloniales* for an exhibition to promote colonial enterprise in France and then for incorporation into the collection of the Musée d'IFAN. As Lem recounts it, the officer declined the offer, noting that the museums at the Trocadero and in Vincennes were better situated to constitute the collections than the museum in Dakar.[8]

Lem insists in his essay that neither institution in France devoted itself to the study of African art, thus suggesting that neither entity was well placed to oversee the creation of the world's first museum of African art.[9] He further informs the reader that he would likely not be able to keep the collection he amassed together and that he does not have the means to exhibit the works or to publish them.[10] But a decade later, following the end of World War II, Lem produced *Sculptures soudanaises* and its English translation. The book features images of and information about nearly sixty objects, including some forty works that Lem indicates he acquired in West Africa. For the works he gathered, Lem provides names of the regions or places where he obtained the works. He also offers his assessment of each work's origin. The publication of such details may intrigue early-twenty-first-century art scholars and other enthusiasts eager to recover specific details about the historical arts of Africa. Closer examination of the information Lem provides reveals ambiguities in details that may seem precise at first glance.

Understanding of African art in France in the 1930s and 1940s

Throughout his three-part essay of 1938, Lem identifies characteristics of objects he regarded as high-quality art. He indicates that the category includes *bois sculpté* (carved wood). He also attempts to maintain that the best examples of African art reflect

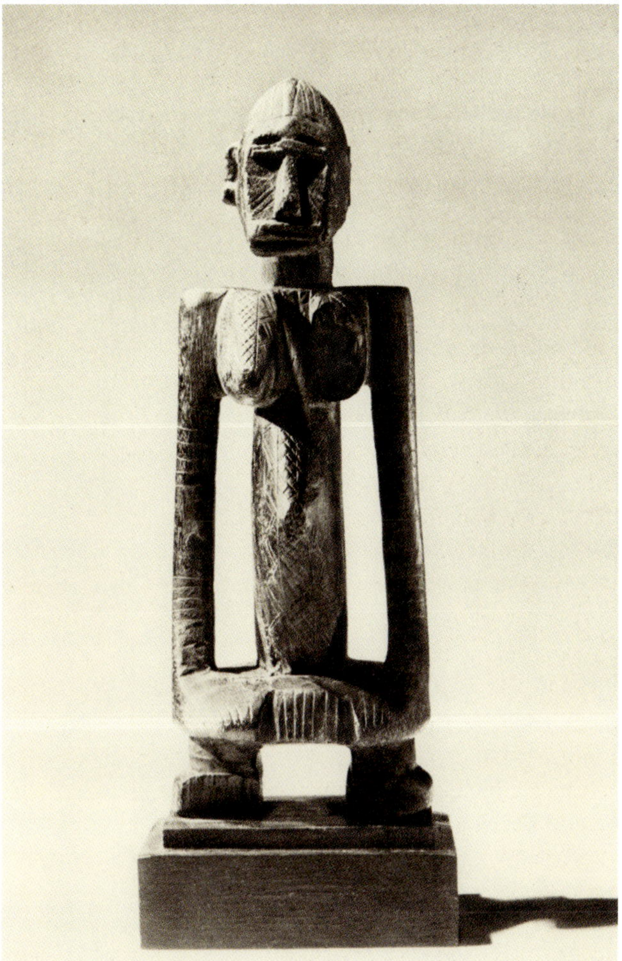

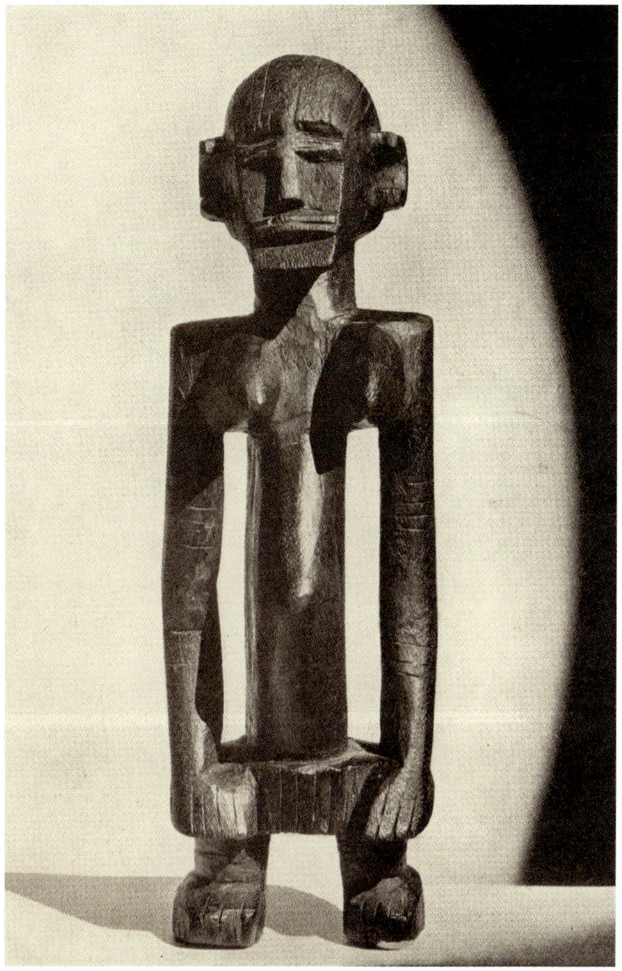

Ill. 30

"Statuette with socle, in very hard wood, in poker-work, with its natural patina", F.-H. Lem, *Sudanese Sculpture*, Paris: Arts et métiers graphiques, 1949, pl. 40 and pl. 41

Ill. 31

"Bell power object", in Carl Kjersmeier *Centre de style de la sculpture nègre africaine*, vol. I: Afrique occidentale française, Paris: A. Morencé, Copenhagen: Illums Bog-Afdeling, 1935, pl. 32

old traditions and customs.[11] He acknowledges a long history of interaction and exchange among people in West Africa prior to European colonization, and he recognizes that objects move about the continent.[12] He concludes that art reflects the uniqueness of each distinct group of people, which he calls a "tribe".[13] But he also refers to different castes, separate subgroups, and multiple style centers within a larger group, thus signaling complexity.[14]

Lem's reference to "tribes" and his efforts to explain differences within each distinct group hint at the dynamism often eclipsed by use of the term tribe. Few scholars in the early twenty-first century use the term for groups of people on the African continent because its meaning does not correspond with current knowledge. The term suggests a bounded group of people with its own distinctive art, culture, geography, language, religion, political structure, and social organization, a notion common during the colonial period. Scholars have recognized for decades that there have never been isolated and homogeneous cultural or ethnic groups on the African continent.[15]

While Lem briefly references histories of interaction and exchange in his texts, the concept of discrete groups, each with its own art style, remains prominent in his imagination. Lem concludes that the art he considers "Sudanese Art"—with a capital *A*—"varies in its tendencies according to the region or the particular mentality of the tribes."[16] His formulation implies that each group produces unique art, even if the group encompasses different castes, subgroups, or style centers. He focuses his analysis on art he categorizes as Dogon, Mossi, Bambara [Bamana], Senufo, and Bobo, each label corresponding to the name of a cultural or ethnic group. But Lem also attempts to recognize dynamic exchange within and among such groups. Under the section of his book entitled, "The Sculptures of the Senufo," Lem includes information about a nearly ten-inch-tall figurative sculpture [ill. 30], thereby suggesting Senufo origins for the work. Lem's caption introduces other possibilities. He writes, "[Carl] Kjersmeier reproduces a similar piece, which he assumes to be of Bobo origin [ill. 31]." Lem also adds, "This sculpture presents all the characteristics of the art of the Mande smiths and probably comes from the region of Segu [Ségou]. It should rather be classified among the Bambara [Bamana] sculptures."[17] While Lem presents the sculpture with other works he recognizes as Senufo, he acknowledges that Kjersmeier provides a different attribution for a formally similar work. Lem then proposes yet another attribution for the object even as he includes it in a list of Senufo sculptures.[18]

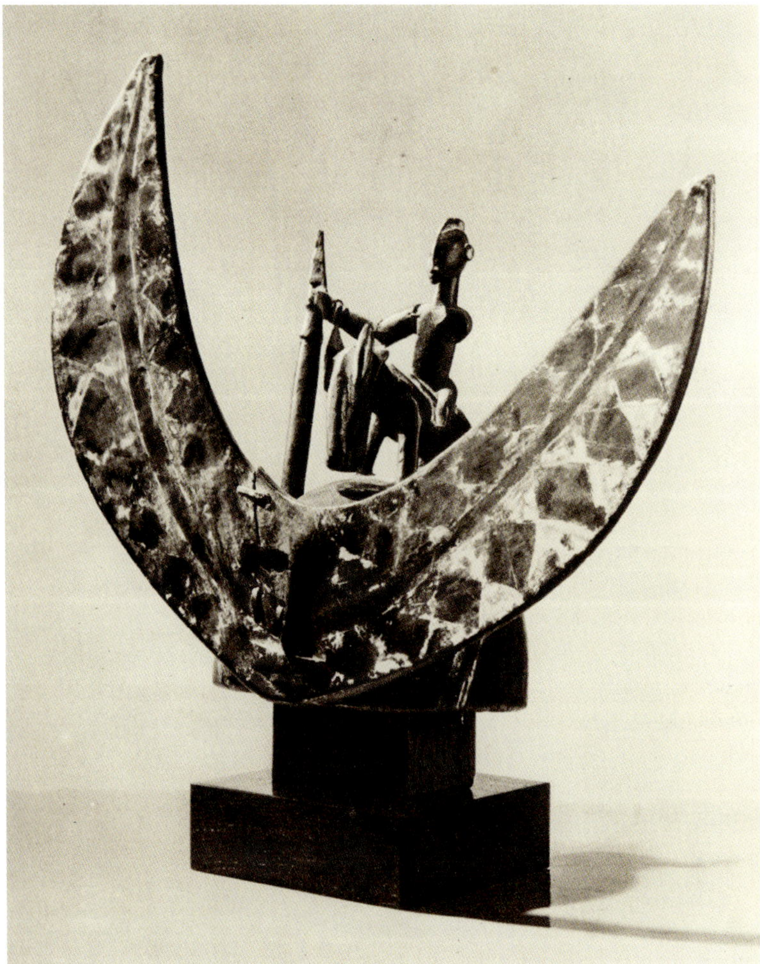

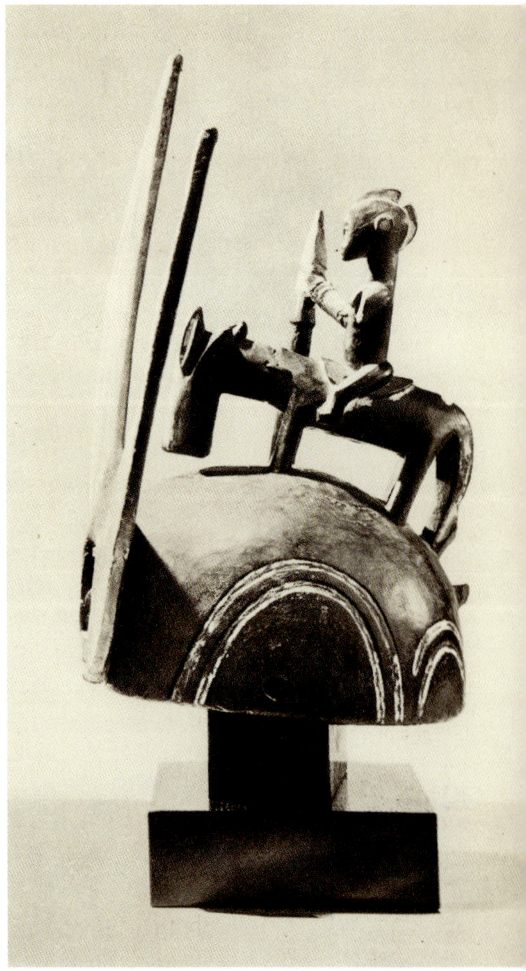

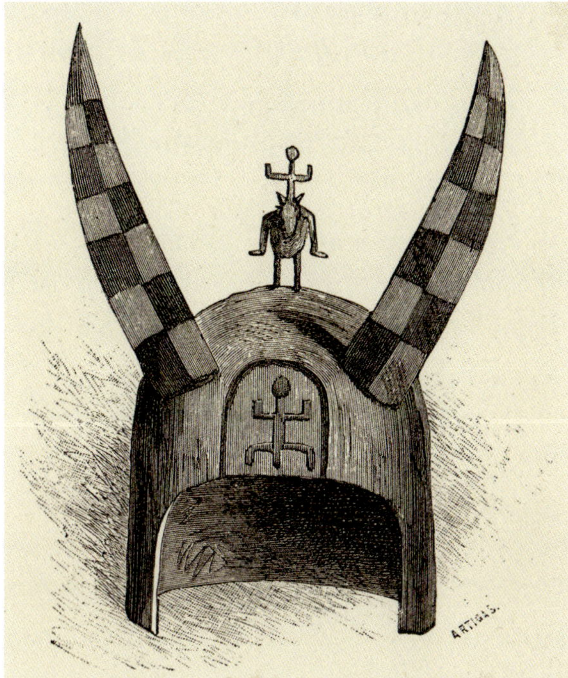

Another label that Lem provides for an object did not stick for long. Lem recognizes as Bamana a helmet now in the collection of the Newark Museum in the United States [ill. 32 and 33]. He posits that "Macina [Fulfulde] carvers influenced by the art of the Cliff [probably a reference to the Bandiagara Escarpment]" created the helmet.[19] In the early 1960s, Robert Goldwater offered a different attribution, identifying the same object as Senufo.[20] When Parke-Bernet Galleries included the work in its April 1966 sale of objects then in Rubinstein's collection, the auction house compared the object to one shown in illustrations created in France to accompany Louis-Gustave Binger's 1892 account of his travels through West Africa from 1887 to 1889 [ill. 34].[21] The auction house explains that Binger "observed similar masks in the Siené [Senufo] region."[22] Yet Binger's text is not so clear. Binger reports that he saw a man wearing a distinctive helmet, and his account follows from a general description of Senufo burials.[23] But Binger also reports that he observed the helmet-wearing man in the town of Katon. According to Binger, the town's inhabitants included Senufo as well as Jula populations.[24] If the man wearing the helmet was a resident of Katon, he may have identified or been identified as Senufo or Jula. However, the identity of the person wearing the helmet does not necessarily reveal anything about the identity of the person who made it.[25]

Lem's publications include other assessments that were consistent with European and North American views of African arts at the time. For example, he characterizes African art as "ancient" and laments what he considered a decline in the quality of artistic production as a result of European colonization.[26] But he also recognizes change, asserting that "this art [of the French Sudan] has nothing static in it, neither of space or time."[27] And he explains that "so far as chronology is concerned, to fix the age of an object and to determine the period of style to which it belongs, everything is rather uncertain."[28] Still concerned about the possibility of losing "ancient" forms, Lem insisted that communities needed to retain "prototypes [of objects] indispensable [sic] for maintaining the tradition."[29] He notes that he commissioned copies of the objects he

Left
ill. 32 and 33
"Upper-part of mask, on a socle. Hard wood blackened by fire with part in poker-work, white and blue on black ground", F.-H. Lem, *Sudanese Sculpture*, Paris: Arts et métiers graphiques, 1949, pl. 36 and pl. 37

Right
ill. 34
"Katon helmet", Louis-Gustave Binger, *Du Niger au golfe de Guinée par le pays de Kong et le Mossi (1887-1889)*, Paris: Hachette, 1892, p. 225

recognized as prototypes and then acquired. He explains that he left the copies of the prototypes with "the owners of the original works."[30] Lem asserts that his attention to the preservation of copies of prototypes within West Africa distinguished him from the German explorer Leo Frobenius, who led object-collecting missions in different areas of the African continent in the first decades of the twentieth century. According to Lem, Frobenius "systematically emptied some districts [of prototypes] in the course of his missions in Africa."[31]

Interest in original or authentic works

Lem often estimates the relative age of objects photographed in his book published in the late 1940s. He recognizes several objects as "recent." He characterizes most objects as "old." He reserves the terms "very old" or "very ancient" for a smaller selection of objects, including the helmet that he identifies as Bamana but that Goldwater and Parke-Bernet Galleries later recognize as Senufo. Another object he considers as "very old" is a nearly three-foot-tall figurative sculpture he reports he found in the Folona region [ill. 35]. Lem writes that the "very old carving" was "covered by the course of time with a beautiful satin-like patina," raising the possibility that his assessment of the object's patina may have contributed to his assessment of the object's age.[32] Writing about a crest mask that Lem classifies as Bamana [ill. 36] and regards as "old" rather than "very old," Lem's description still implies local use and age. He highlights its "natural patina." He also explains "the tips of the horns [on the object] are mutilated."[33] Such examples suggest that Lem considered indications of wear or age important criteria for evaluating an object.

According to Lem, the "original character of Sudanese Art" was dwindling by the early twentieth century, and such art risked disappearance. He claims that European colonization as well as the influence and exchange that came with it prompted a decline in West African artistic production.[34] Lem also acknowledges the development of thriving markets in West Africa for the sale of objects to foreign patrons.[35] By the 1930s, Lem was not the only European observer who mentioned vibrant markets for the sale of African art to foreigners in West Africa. Reflecting on his travels to West Africa in the early 1930s, Kjersmeier refers to the sale of sculptures as souvenirs in northern Ivory Coast.[36] Belgian art historian Albert Maesen, who conducted research on Senufo arts in northern Ivory Coast in 1939, described centers for the production of tourist art and other sculpture.[37]

Writing about art he recognizes as Senufo, Lem notes that headpieces decorated with avian figures [ill. 37 and 38] "are turned out in quantities for export and are sold to tourists." He adds that one "often finds [such works] in the best collections."[38] When Lem provides specific information about two face masks featuring bird imagery that he identifies as Senufo and claims he "found," he indicates that the works are "old." In the section of each caption that Lem dedicates to describing a particular object's more general function, he connects each object to "ritual dances."[39] However, Lem does not identify exact sources for his statements about the functional aspects of the two face masks or other objects, making it difficult to determine if the descriptions apply to the specific objects he acquired or more broadly to the particular object type. Nevertheless, Lem's age determinations and functional descriptions raise the possibility that he wanted the reader to view the two face masks with bird imagery he acquired as "original" or "authentic," and thus different from sculptures created for export or for tourists and also rare.[40]

Interestingly, Lem refers to another face mask pictured in his book as a commissioned copy rather than an original. Lem's text does not make it clear if Lem acquired the object in West Africa or if another person did. When Lem published his book in French and its English translation, the face mask was housed in an unnamed private collection in Paris. Lem includes the face mask in his list of Senufo sculptures, although present-day connoisseurs may recognize the style as Marka. Lem specifies that the work is an "exact copy of a mask from San, executed by a smith of the region." He also characterizes it as a "recent piece." But his description of the functional use of the work characterizes it as a "ritual mask... used by the dancers of a young men's association, grouped according to age." He also invites the reader to compare it to "funerary Egyptian masks," signaling his interest in making broad connections among forms from disparate regions of the world.[41] Perhaps Lem himself commissioned the face mask from a smith in the San region or someone Lem knew ordered it. While other captions in his book refer clearly to the author's acquisition of particular objects, the caption for the face masks does not.

Attention to place

Lem's publications suggest he sought to identify and understand different geographic locations linked to individual objects. While he recognizes that other European authors had aimed to understand how place connects to West African arts, Lem asserts that authors often relied on "superficial information and... inexact references," leading them to faulty conclusions about "authenticity, special style, and extent of originality."[42] The geographic locations for individual objects that Lem provides in his book point to his desire to provide specific place-based information. Consequently, details Lem offers in his book may appeal to connoisseurs and other researchers seeking specificity in their analyses of so-called historical arts of Africa.

Yet a closer look at the details Lem provides demonstrates the uneven quality of his information. Lem refers to towns or regions, and he variously identifies them as the names of locations where he acquired objects or to areas linked to a particular style. Lem provides few details about where exactly he found objects, how he obtained them, or with whom he interacted to acquire them. Similarly, he offers little explanation about how exactly he assessed the geographic origins of an object or determined contexts for the objects' use. The apparent specificity of the information he provides combined with its actual vagueness may lead to conclusions that Lem's book does not necessarily support.

Referring to a sculpture that he describes as a "seated female figure," Lem indicates that he obtained it "in the Folona, region of Sikasso." In the section of his caption reserved for functional description, he characterizes the sculpture as a "doll belonging to a little girl [ill. 39]."[43] Lem's description of the object as a "doll" echoes a more general statement he presents in the main essay of his book. Commenting on a decline in certain uses for objects in the region he recognizes as Senufo, Lem notes that young women in the region once received sculptures that assured women's fertility throughout their lives. He adds that the practice is waning and that sculptures in the same form "now appear to be nothing more than dolls which... girls treat much as they would other toys."[44] Perhaps the figure he obtained in an area near the city of Sikasso known as the Folona was a girl's doll when Lem acquired it.[45] But the information he provides is unclear, in part because it appears in the section of the caption for the object that Lem consistently uses to describe the general function of an object. And his assessment of

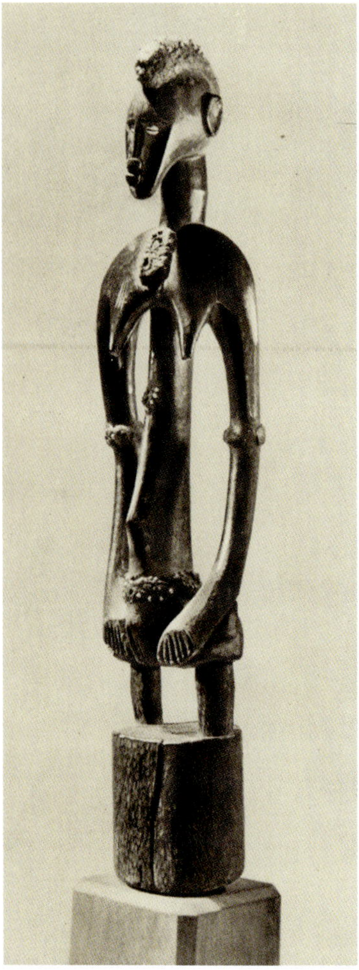
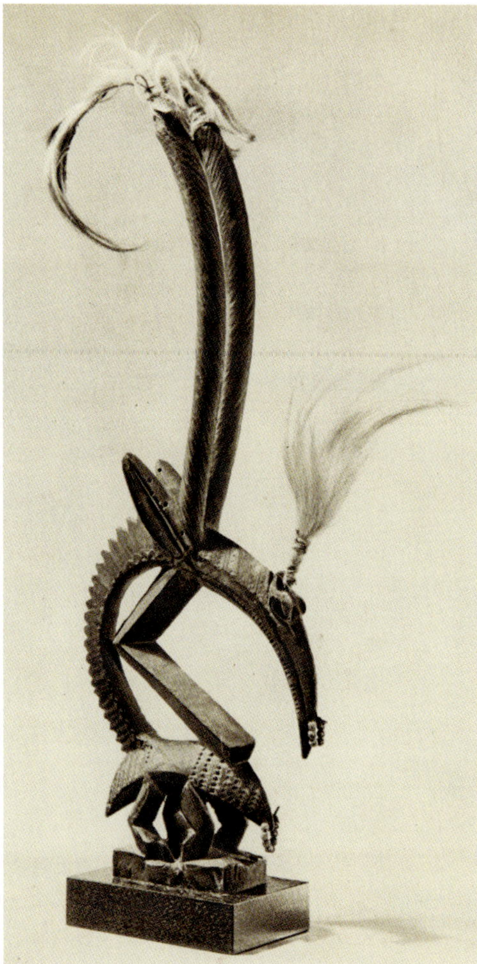
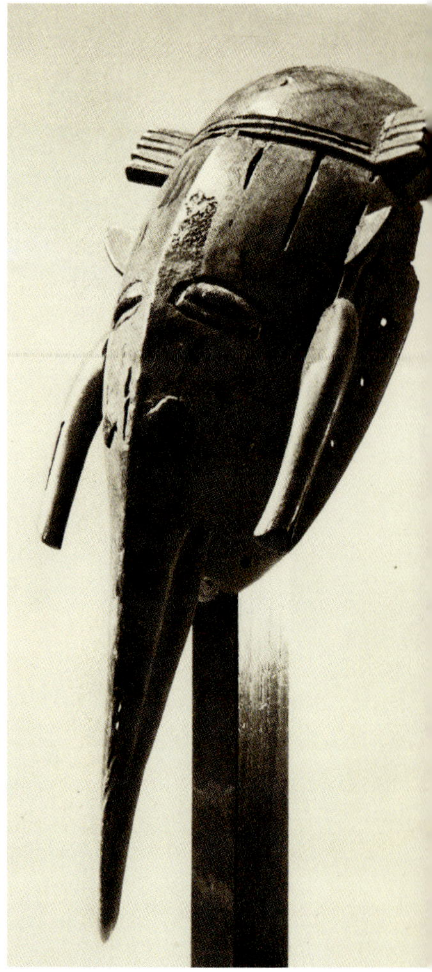

the particular object as "old" indicates that he may have thought it was originally created to safeguard a woman's fertility before a girl may have used it as a doll. Such mismatch between Lem's desire for specificity and his use of more general statements throughout his book reminds us of the impossibility for any observer at any time to provide completely objective information.[45]

One other aspect of Lem's attention to place requires consideration because of its distinctiveness in the 1930s and 1940s, when collections of African art and cultural knowledge were growing in Europe and North America. Lem appears to have recognized the importance of investing in repositories of West African art and cultural knowledge in West Africa. He argued that establishment in West Africa of the world's first museum dedicated to African art would appeal to tourists and also honor the "original qualities" of local populations.[47] He wrote about his efforts to transfer the collection he assembled to such a museum.[48] The bibliographies in Lem's French and English books also refer to an unpublished study that he deposited at IFAN in Dakar.[49] And the information he provides for the last plate of his book indicates that he collected the door illustrated in the plate.[50] The caption further specifies that the door was in the collection of the Maison des Artisans in the city of Bamako, then in French Sudan, at the time of the book's publication.

Ill. 35

"Statue, fixed on a socle, in hard wood, coloured in black and adorned with coloured seeds and cowries fixed by latex", F.-H. Lem, *Sudanese Sculpture*, Paris: Arts et métiers graphiques, 1949, pl. 45

Ill. 36

"Upper-part of mask, with socle, in soft wood, in its natural patina, in poker-work, adorned with coloured beads and hair tufts", F.-H. Lem, *Sudanese Sculpture*, Paris: Arts et métiers graphiques, 1949, pl. 25

Ill. 37

"Mask, fixed on a socle, hard wood coloured in black", F.-H. Lem, *Sudanese Sculpture*, Paris: Arts et métiers graphiques, 1949, pl. 50

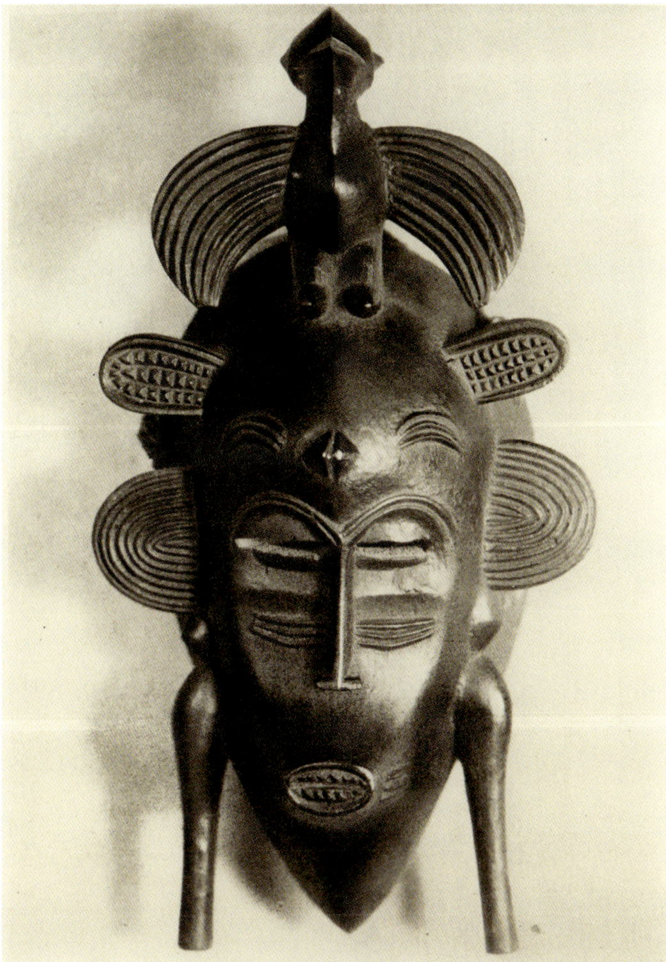

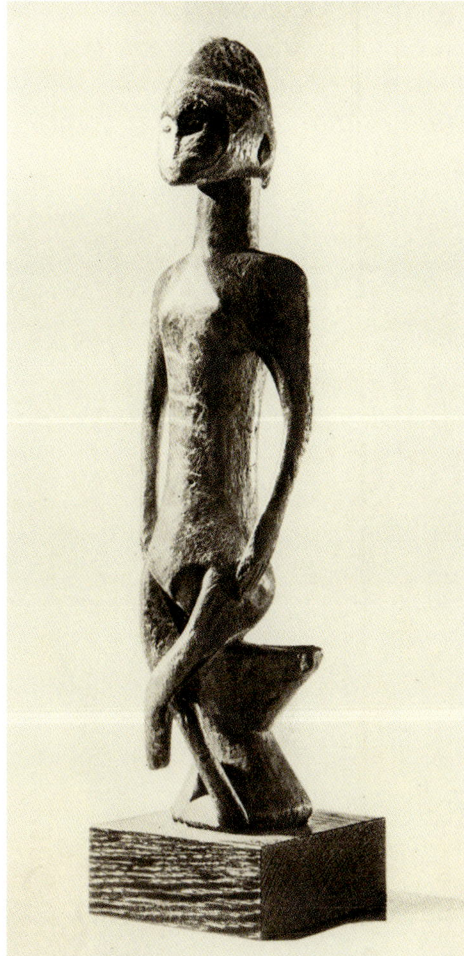

The enigmatic F.-H. Lem (1902–1991)

Bertrand Goy

Ill. 38

"Mask in hard wood, coloured in black, partly coloured red background faded by usage", F.-H. Lem, *Sudanese Sculpture*, Paris: Arts et métiers graphiques, 1949, pl. 52

Ill. 39

"Statuette, with socle, in soft wood, coloured in black with partly coloured red background, faded by usage", F.-H. Lem, *Sudanese Sculpture*, Paris: Arts et métiers graphiques, 1949, pl. 47

Félix-Henri Lem was born in a little village in the Puy-de-Dôme on August 1, 1902, his life practically coinciding with the twentieth century. A multifaceted yet discreet figure, even the French National Library fails to record his first name. However, F.-H. Lem's signature appears at the bottom of countless publications in fields as diverse as "Colonial Careers" and "Géricault's Sojourn in Italy." In 1935, Lem was appointed civil service officer in the French Upper Volta (now Burkina Faso) and then for the next two years in the Sikasso region, in what is today Mali. Unusually discerning among collectors of the period, his early interest in art led him to amass a large collection of Senufo sculpture from Kénédougou and examples of Mossi art from Yatenga. Admirers of African art know him for his study *Sculptures soudanaises*, published in 1948, which has the signal advantage of mentioning the places where he collected his pieces, later owned by Princess Gourielli. Upon his return to France in the summer of 1937, wounded by the refusal of the Intercolonial Service to accept the donation of his collection to the brand-new IFAN museum in Dakar, Lem asked Paul Chadourne, journalist, man of the world, and art broker, to arrange for the transfer of a significant proportion of his nearly two hundred pieces to Helena Rubinstein. With assistance from the painter Louis Marcoussis, a compatriot of the businesswoman and her close friend, the transaction was concluded by late August. After the war, Lem worked for some of the foremost specialized journals of the time, gradually turning away from Africa and its culture to devote himself to painting, spanning from the Italian Renaissance to the Second School of Paris.

Equatorial African treasures from the Rubinstein collection

Charlotte Grand-Dufay

Helena Rubinstein first encountered the international avant-garde art scene in Paris in 1912. She was introduced to what was then called *"art nègre,"* which came into vogue following the First Exhibition of Black and Oceanic Art held at the Devambez Gallery in 1919, by sculptor Jacob Epstein (1880–1959). Carl Einstein's theoretical study *Negerplastik* (1915[1]) had provided ethnographic objects with a new status as works of art in their own right. This conceptual shift was followed by the incipient ranking of such works at the Pigalle Gallery exhibition in Paris in 1930. Against the background of the ascension of African art, between 1931 and 1935 Helena Rubinstein acquired Georges de Miré's famous Kota piece before going on to enthusiastically buy up other treasures from equatorial Africa, with a preference for Fang and Kota carvings, already acknowledged as being among the most "classical" expressions of African art.

The catalogs of the two Helena Rubinstein auction sales of April 21–29 and October 15, 1966, are a treasure trove of information, with every artifact being illustrated in black and white, from the front and/or the side. Today the collection is scattered about the United States and Europe, with pieces in international private and public collections.

Fang statuary

The Rubinstein collection boasted thirteen Fang masterpieces: five *eyema byeri* statues, seven *añgokh-nlo-byeri* heads, and a drum. The reliquary figures, once referred to as "Pahouin idols," are placed on *nsekh byeri* chests made of sewn bark containing skulls of lineage or clan elders, which serve as genealogical reference points for the community's social life and matrimonial alliances. The ancestor cult, in promoting wealth, hunting, warfare, and female fertility, forms the core of traditions intrinsic to social organization and to the initiation of boys. The *byeri* is placed in the custody of a

ill. 40 [lot 217]
Male figure,
byeri guardian reliquary
Ntumu Fang, Gabon, Cameroon
19th–early 20th cent.
Wood, bone
67.9 × 13 × 17.1 cm
New Orleans Museum of Arts

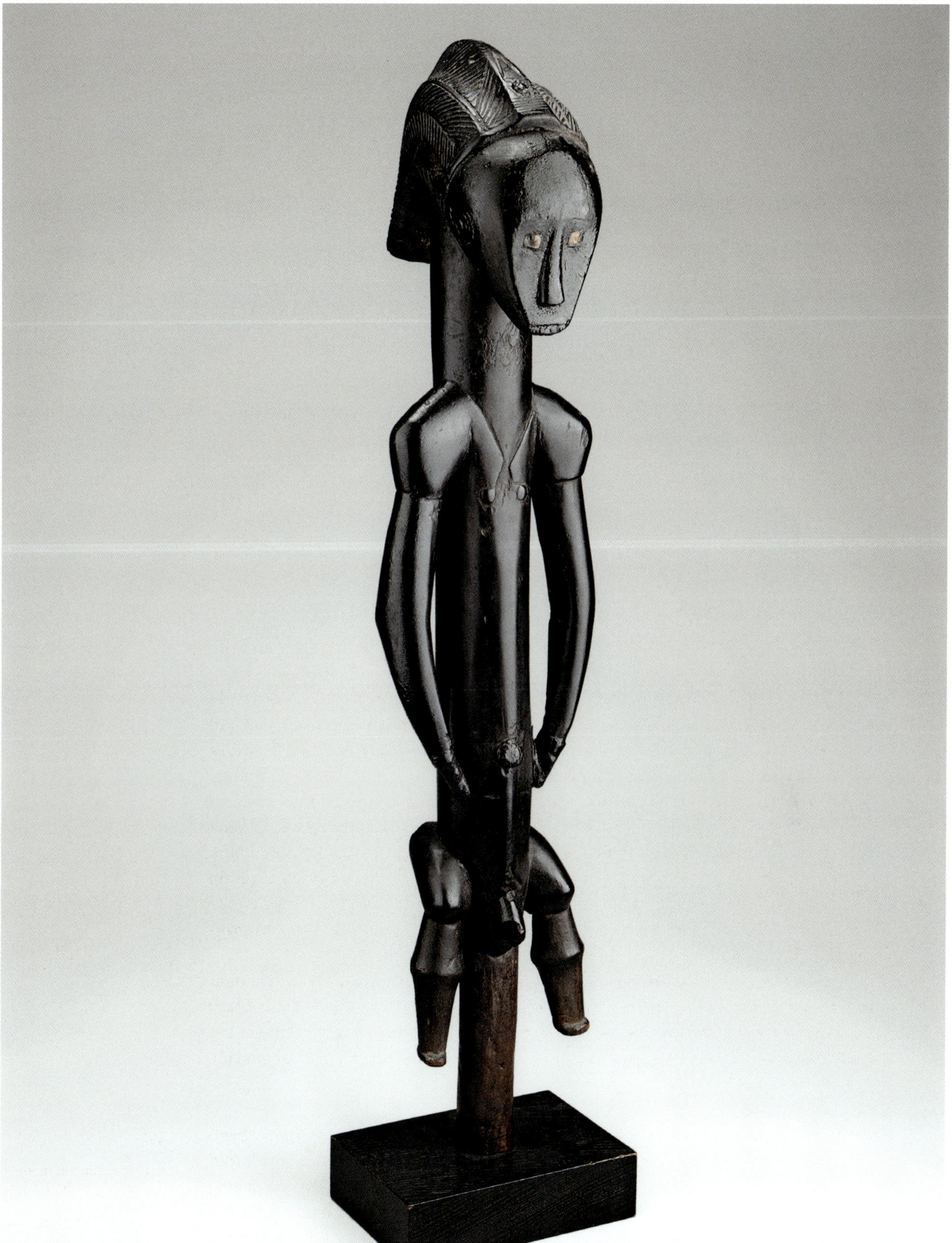

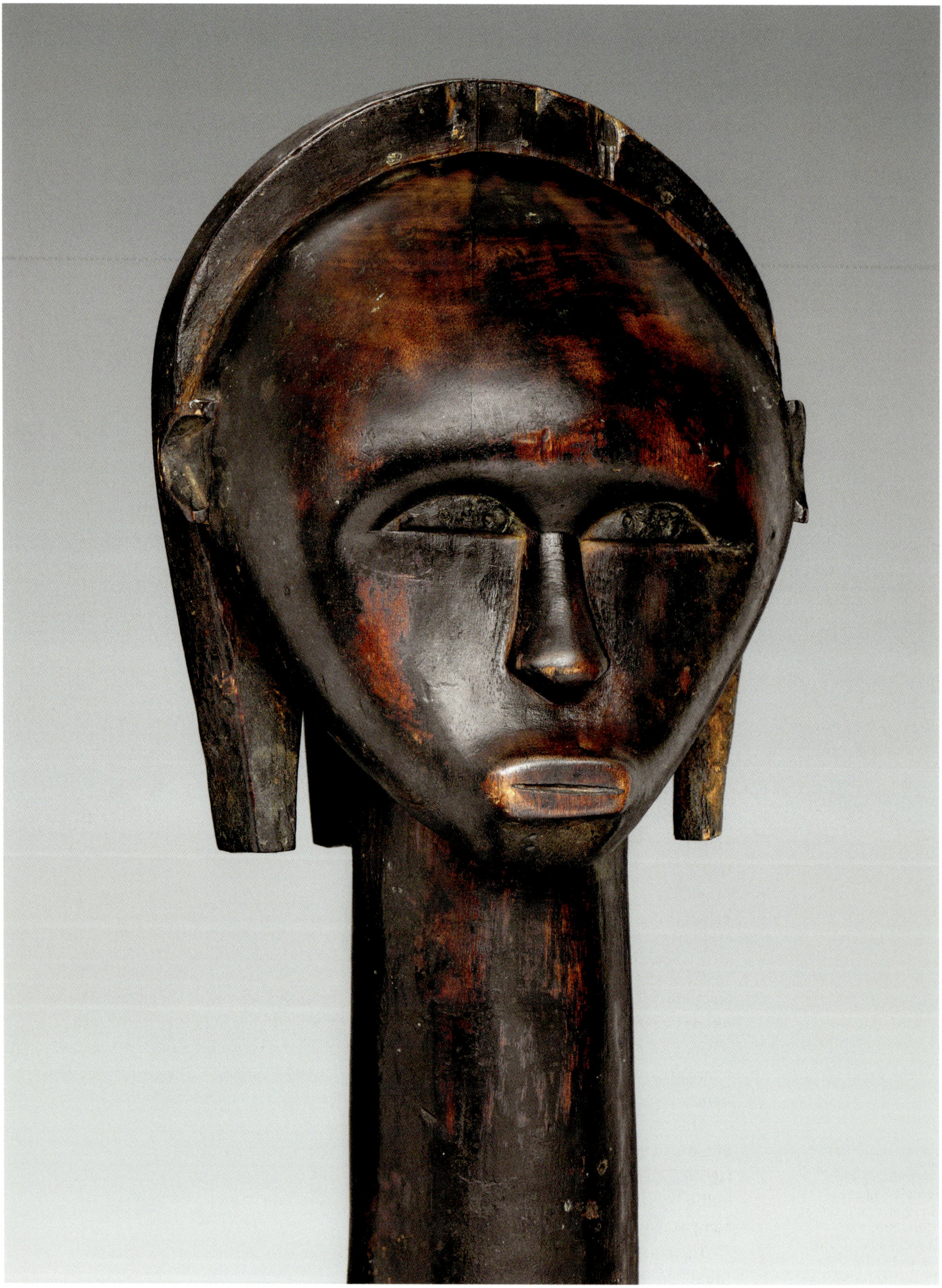

headman who keeps it from being seen by the womenfolk. Sketches by the Protestant pastor Fernand Grébert[2] indicate that the standing statues seem to have coexisted with the heads.

The *byeri* LOT 209 [ILL. 114], originates from the small group of the Mvae, Fang of the valley of the River Ntem in the north of Gabon, identified in 1913 by Günter Tessmann.[3] Representing an ancestor meditating in a hieratic attitude, the carving's imposing head is crowned by a characteristic hairstyle in three bunches. The prominent forehead echoes the large coffee-bean shaped eyes underscored with pupils made of beads, a fine nose, and a downwardly curving mouth. The neck is sturdy, the shoulders rounded, while the thick-set, "barrel-shaped" trunk presents high, voluminous breasts. Separate, the arms are attached, while the fanning fingers hold a small dish. The abdomen is adorned with scarifications to form a frieze of incised triangles with a half-moon. With its damaged face and broken right shoulder, this byeri features on the cover of the special *L'Art Nègre* issue of *Présence africaine* (1951). The only female statue in the "Masters of the Ntem series, traces of a break at the level of the thighs suggest that the statue must once have been complete."[4]

The *byeri* LOT 217, [ILL. 40], belongs to the Ntumu style of the Southern Fang in the Oyem valley. Male, with an elongated structure, it resembles a column sculpture with a stretched, cylindrical neck-cum-trunk extending into the fixing handle. The hair is dressed into three thin braids pulled to the back of the head. The vast, spherical forehead overtops a concave face extending into globular eyes, a long, flattened nose, and a thin-lipped mouth. The simian arms hang outwards from the body, while the tiny legs terminate in stylized feet. The moist patina intended to protect the wood has kept it safe from attack by wood-boring insects and resisted the equatorial climate. Oil was employed to purify these ancestor figures and maintain their power of intercession. This *byeri* is similar to one owned by Jacob Epstein wearing three torques.[5]

The *byeri* LOT 210, identified as Ntumu,[6] is a male figure with a child's head, capped with three flat braids falling diagonally across the neck. The prominent forehead presents almond-shaped eyes, a short nose, and a rectangular mouth with filed teeth. The cylindrical body is thick-set, the arms muscular, the thighs stocky; the hands and feet are stylized. Hermaphrodite and high-waisted, it displays small breasts carved in relief and a discreet penis. It can be compared to a *byeri* formerly in the collection of Félix Fénéon[7] and to another with broken legs once belonging to Jacob Epstein (priv. coll., Switzerland).

A representative of the classic Betsi sub-style—the Betsi form part of the Southern Fang—LOT 211, shows a seated ancestor, his feet joined with his weight on his heels. The head is covered with flat braids, long down the sides and short at the neck; the bulging forehead overtops eyes carved in relief and a snub nose. The powerful neck surmounts a large, round-shouldered body. The muscle-bound arms standing out from the body bend upwards and end in severed hands.

The *byeri* of the Betsi-Okak sub-style, LOT 212, is a seated male effigy whose long, outspread legs balance on tiptoe. According to the interpretation by James W. Fernandez (1966), it depicts an old man-child with a heart-shaped face, stretched-out mouth, and bulbous eyes. With its forearms broken and sporting a torque, this byeri is immediately comparable to one in the Vérité collection.[8]

The small Betsi drum LOT 218, is surmounted by a bust with folded arms, holding a ritual flute connected to the *so* initiation. Beneath a bulging forehead, the eyes in the

ILL. 41 [LOT 219]
Añgokh-nlo-byeri
female head
Southern Fang, Gabon
19th–20th cent.
Wood, kaolin, pigment
49.5 × 16.5 × 11.4 cm
Detroit Institute of Arts

slightly incurved face are inlaid with metal. The elegant braided hairstyle in "fins" resembles that of a small Fang head.[9] Decorated with parallel copper strips, this pretty drum appeared in a showcase at Louis Carré's Villa Guibert during the *Sculptures et Objets* exhibition organized in 1933.[10]

The seven wooden female heads *añgokh-nlo-byeri* (head of the ancestor *byeri*), adorned with different hairstyles, belong to the style of the Fang of the South, in northern Gabon; they are perched on a rather long neck [ill. 41]. Lots 207 and 213 are the two heads that were on display at the Museum of Modern Art in New York in 1935. Once belonging to Paul Guillaume, the first possesses an imposing head with a lacquered patina, topped by a set of broad, stiff braids falling to the rear; the large, prominent forehead overhangs circular brass eyes emphasized with nails. The fact that the nose and mouth have been damaged by rodents in no way affects its high aesthetic quality.

The second [ill. 5]—formerly in the Ernst Ascher collection—is the Fang jewel of the collection. Of considerable age (c. 1750), it is absolutely perfect: ovoid in shape, the rounded forehead dominates a heart-shaped face with coffee-bean eyes, a flattened nose, and a protruding mouth. The majestic hairstyle consists of three wide, smooth braids, starting from the top of the skull and arranged gracefully over the back of the head. An icon of African art, like the small Ntumu head lot 214, it was exhibited at the Pigalle Gallery in 1930. Interest is focused on its tiara headdress tilted back over straight hair. The immense forehead overhangs eyes in relief and a fine nose, while the mouth sinks into the chin.

With its head perched on its long fixing handle, lot 215 [ill. 115], has been described as the authentic portrait of a tortured face, owing to the skull bones showing through at the temples and the scarified lines on the forehead. To the front, the headdress is finely chiseled, while, on the back, one of the braids is decorated with a frieze of cowries.[11]

Kota reliquary Figures

The Kota preserve the bones of their ancestors in baskets protected by a "guardian"—a wooden figure covered with brass and copper strips, known as a *mbulu-ngulu*. One of the most famous styles since the discovery of *art nègre*, the abstraction and two-dimensional sculptural treatment of Kota art has long proved fascinating; it is "without equivalent in the art of any other part of the world at any time."[12]

Helena Rubinstein owned twenty-two Kota reliquary figures. Seven mentioned in the second sales catalog are not illustrated; half are decorated with lamellae and belong to the Obamba of the Upper Ogooué valley, between Franceville and Okondja (Gabon). Its owner considered the reliquary lot 192, [ill. 44 and 113], as the star of her collection. Of impressive size, this example of the Kota Shamaye style has a foliated almond-shaped face with studded, bulbous eyes; a ridge down the middle divides a face of plain veneer. The hairstyle, represented by a crescent, is ornamented with five vertical bands of cowries. Placed horizontally, the pendants are decorated with crosspieces. The large rhombus, its upper edges incurved, is lined with a repoussé veneer. Known as "William Rubin's Kota," this reliquary was reproduced on an Air France advertising poster in 1963 [ill. 42].

Rather different, lots 194 and 82 (second catalog) are reliquary figures that are both convex and concave; the "heart" face with oblique eyes extending to the temples, the short nose, the pointed chin, and the side bunches ending in a ducktail are the essential characteristics. The lozenge-shaped support is minute.

Above left
ill. 42
"Afrique" Air France poster by Jacques-Nathan Garamond, 1963

Above right
ill. 43 [lot 196]
Ancestor figure, reliquary guardian
Kota, Gabon
19th–20th cent.
Wood, brass, copper
H. 49.5 cm
Private collection

Below left
ill. 44
"Ancestor figure" [Kota reliquary guardian figure, Gabon], photograph by Walker Evans from the *African Negro Art* portfolio, New York, Museum of Modern Art, 1935 (cat. 80)

Below right
ill. 45
The interior of the apartment owned by Anthony Morris, known as "Père Morris", 1939, photograph by Charles Ratton; top left, a reliquary guardian from the Helena Rubinstein collection (lot 194)

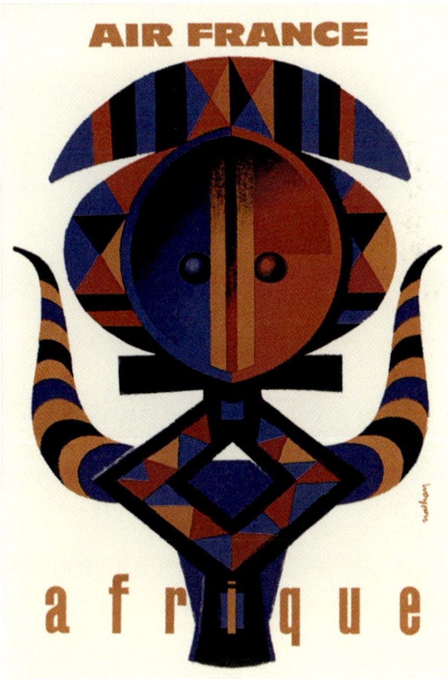
AIR FRANCE
afrique

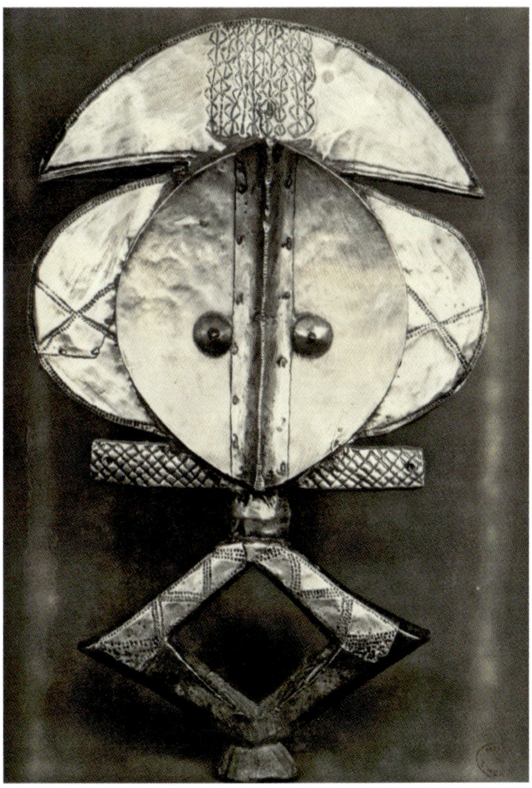

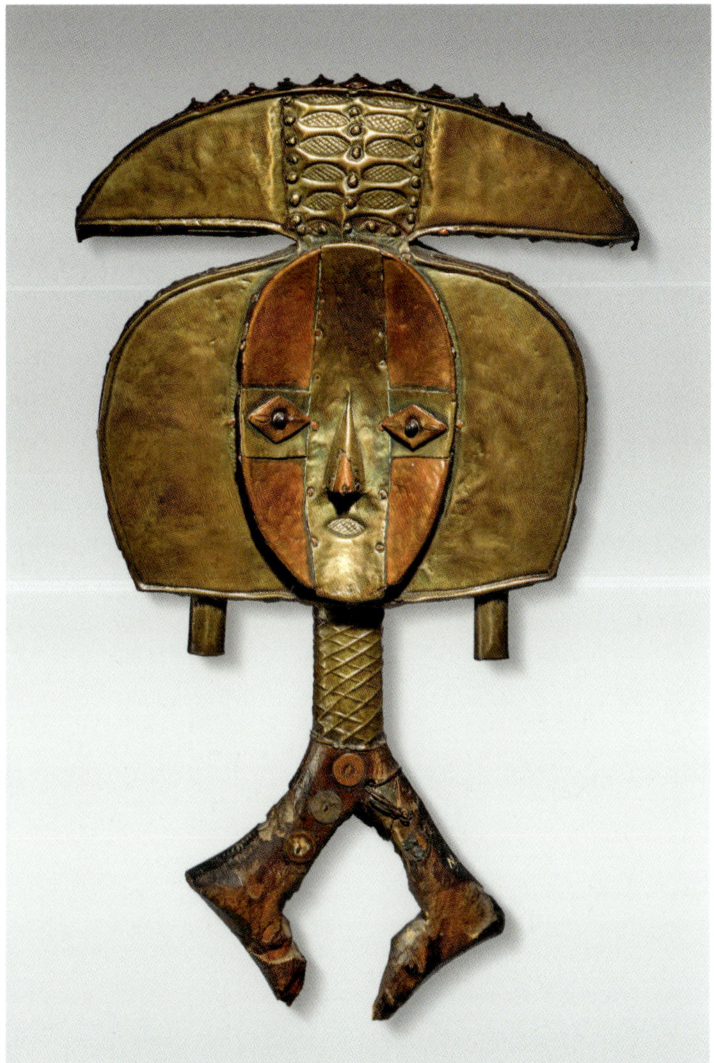

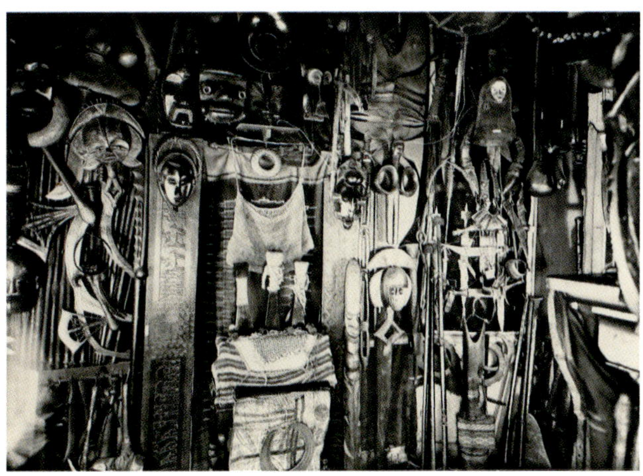

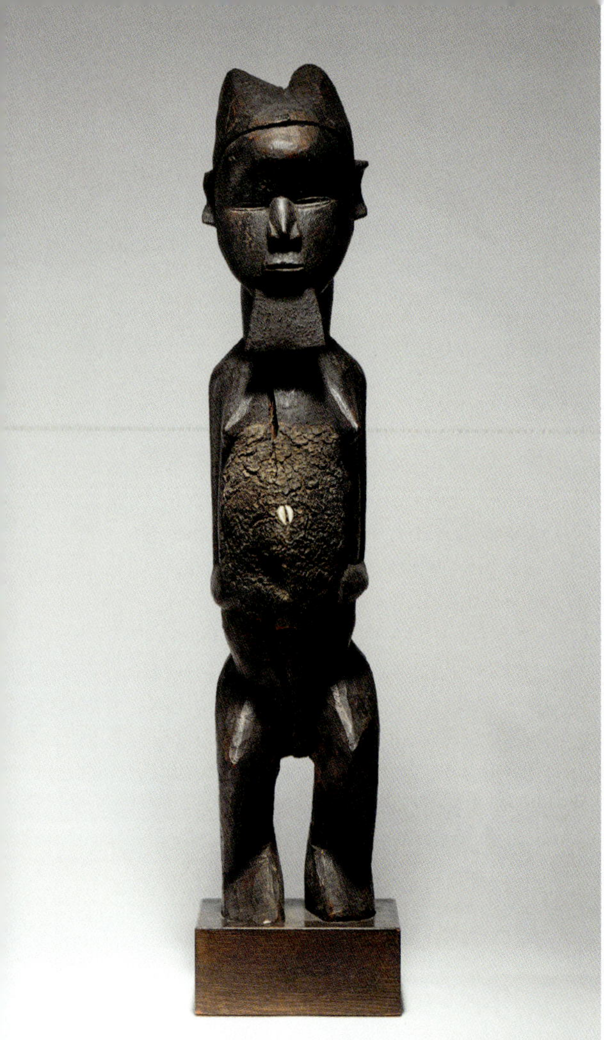

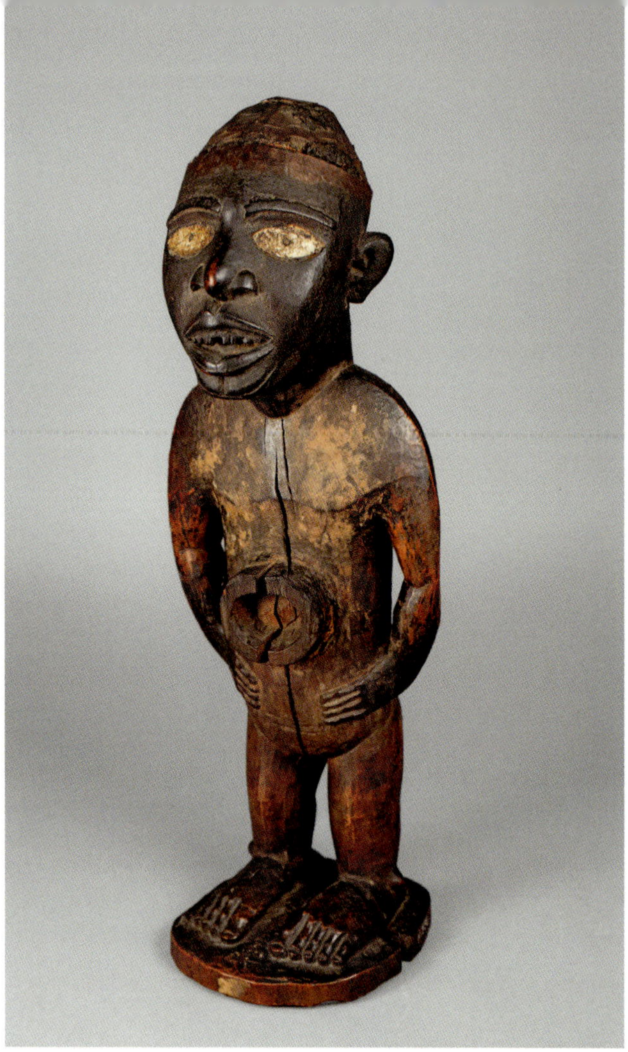

The crescent of lot 194 presents eight pointed barbs standing for the feathers of the ancient *mbulu-ngulu*, while the pupils are represented by nails. A photograph by Charles Ratton [ill. 45] shows this Kota reliquary[13] on a wall in the Père Morris gallery. Lot 82 is a piece comparable to the mbulu-ngulu in the Musée du Quai Branly – Jacques Chirac.[14]

Covered in strips of red copper, the *mbulu-ngulu*, lot 195 [ill. 112], is remarkable for its thickness, the simplicity of its decoration, the quality of its patina, and the perfection of its proportions. The small face is rounded, while the pendants are chunky. It appears on the cover of the book by Alain and Françoise Chaffin[15] and today belongs to Alain Schoffel.

Presenting a cross pattern in yellow brass, the Kota reliquary lot 196 [ill. 43], is the only one in the Rubinstein collection to be plated with plain red copper. The diamond-shaped eyes are set off with nails. The center of the crescent is emblazoned with two friezes of ovals arranged crosswise and surrounded by cabochons, while three copper studs decorate the support. The reverse of the *mbulu-ngulu* shows an abstract, elongated diamond-shaped face, with arched eyebrows and eyes marked by slits reminiscent of Kwele masks.

ill. 46 [lot 245]
Hermaphrodite figure
Teke, Democratic Republic of the Congo
19th–20th cent.
Wood, organic materials, cowries
H. 69.9 cm
Private collection

ill. 47 [lot 234]
Nkisi figure
Democratic Republic of the Congo
19th–20th cent.
Wood
H. 53 cm
Berkeley University, Phoebe Hearst Museum

The reliquary figures lots 197 and 198 are characterized by an elegant crest welded to the bunches at the side and, as on the neck, incised with crosspieces. The strips are set at an angle along the two cross-shaped bands on the face, with a pattern of dots representing the mouth. Only lot 197 presents a nose set at the end of a vertical ridge, a semi-circular décor of dots at eye level, and a sheaf pattern at the base of the crescent. This Kota reliquary, whose lozenge is damaged, also appears on a wall in the Père Moris gallery; it is comparable to those in the Musée du Quai Branly – Jacques Chirac[16] and the Henri Kamer collection.[17]

Exceptionally, the Janus lot 200 [ill. 111], presents two concave, oval female faces with lamellae. The recto is decorated with a broad band of red copper and a diamond-shaped frieze of dotted lines on the head crest; the mouth is represented by a dotted line. The verso presents a cross pattern, a crest carpeted with small crosses, and oblique-type pendants. Very ancient, this *mbulu-viti* represents the mother goddess who reigns over the dead.[18] It appears in a photograph showing an accumulation of Kota reliquaries by Arman.

The rounded side sections of the extremely elegant Kota reliquary lot 201, meet and are adorned with friezes of triangular, oblique, and half-moon designs that recall the motifs on the copper-covered Kota stool in the Musée Barbier-Mueller in Geneva.[19] Fitted with oblique pendants, a tapered crest on a stalk and cabochons, the oval, almost flat face presents a plain veneer. The almond eyes echo a triangular nose and a hollowed-out mouth. This *mbulu-ngulu* is by the same master as the one in the Barnes Foundation.[20]

The 52 cm tall death's-head reliquary lot 202 [ill. 109], comes from the workshop of the "Master of the Sebé," a tributary of the Ogooué River. Both concave and convex, it is characterized by a transversal crested hairstyle and a heart-shaped face beneath a bulging forehead; the concave portion of the face is delimited by eyebrow arches over large circular eyes in flattened copper strips set off with nails. Bunches to the side of the head are decorated with a double frieze of dotted lines, while the cylindrical pendants are arranged at an angle. The verso of the reliquary displays an elongated lozenge. It is comparable to five other *mbulu-ngulu*.[21]

White and black

A Fang helmet mask covered with whitish clay displaying four similar faces of different sizes, lot 221, [ill. 116], presents a scooped-out face decorated with linear scarification across the forehead and nose. The eyes are incised and the prognathic mouth is represented by a rectangular slit. The rounded chin has been pierced with holes to hang a fiber parure. Associated with the *ngil*—a fearsome secret society—the role of this *ñgontang* mask was to use its four pairs of eyes to uncover evil sorcerers. It features among the twenty-four photographs in Guillaume Apollinaire and Paul Guillaume's album *Sculptures nègres*.[22]

One of the very oldest, the Punu-Lumbu *okuyi* mask lot 191 [ill. 49], is a fine specimen.[23] Sporting a central bun with two short tufts, it is remarkable for its ivory patina, the twelve scarifications on the forehead, the plaits on the side of the neck, and the handle under its chin. This white mask now belongs to the Kreeger Museum in Washington, as does the black Tsangui mask lot 190 [ill. 48]. Presenting bulbous clumps on the side, the headdress in the shape of a judge's toque is covered with human hair. The ovoid face with its coffee-bean eyes is adorned with scarification lines running from the sides of the slender nose to the ears. Of excellent workmanship, this mask can

Following pages
Ill. 48 [lot 190]
Okuyi mask
Punu-Lumbu, Gabon
19th–early 20th cent.
Wood, hair
H. 29.8 cm
Washington,
The Kreeger Museum

Ill. 49 [lot 191]
Okuyi mask
Punu-Lumbu, Gabon
19th–early 20th cent.
Wood, kaolin, pigment
H. 31.7 cm
Washington,
The Kreeger Museum

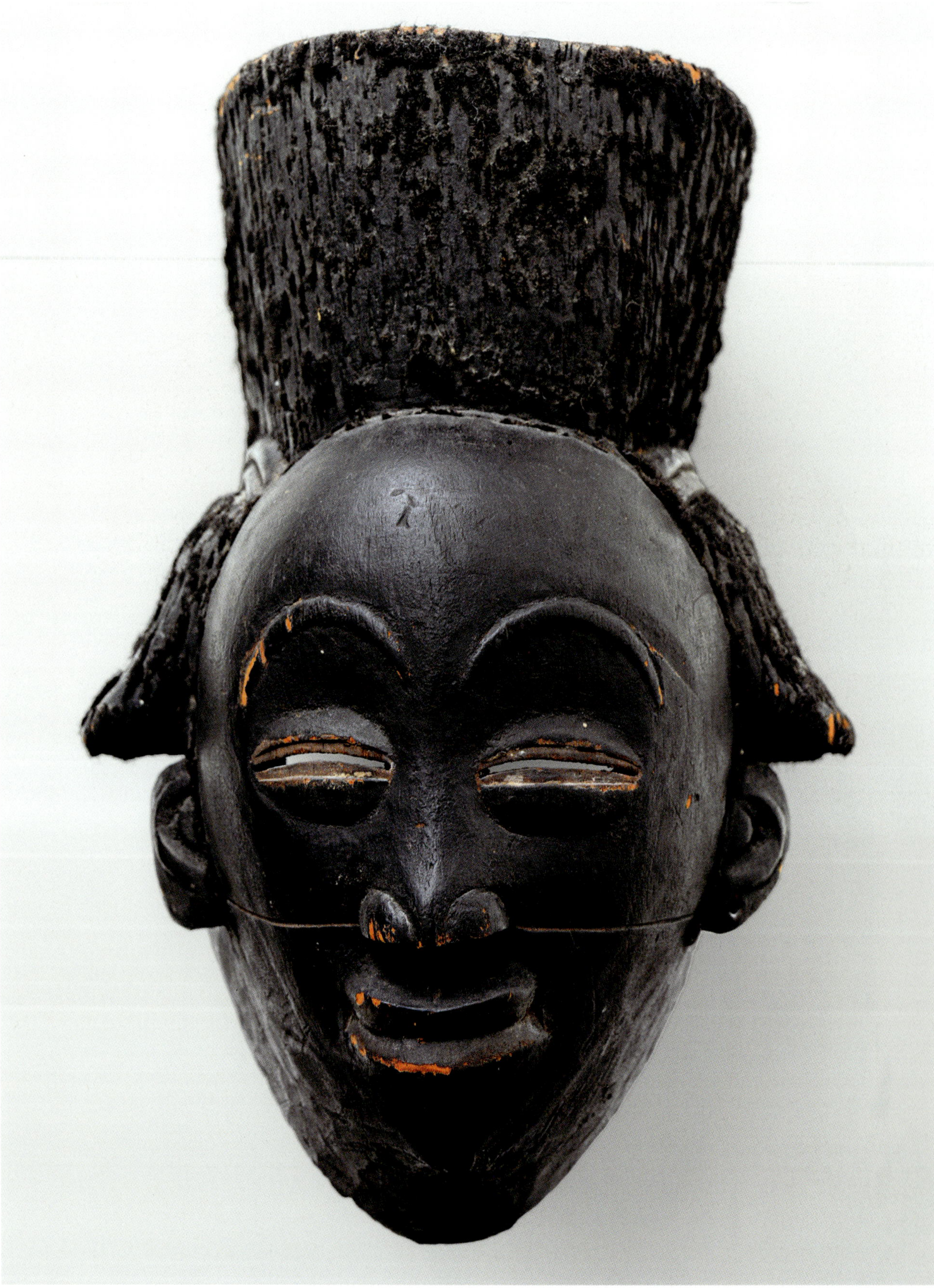

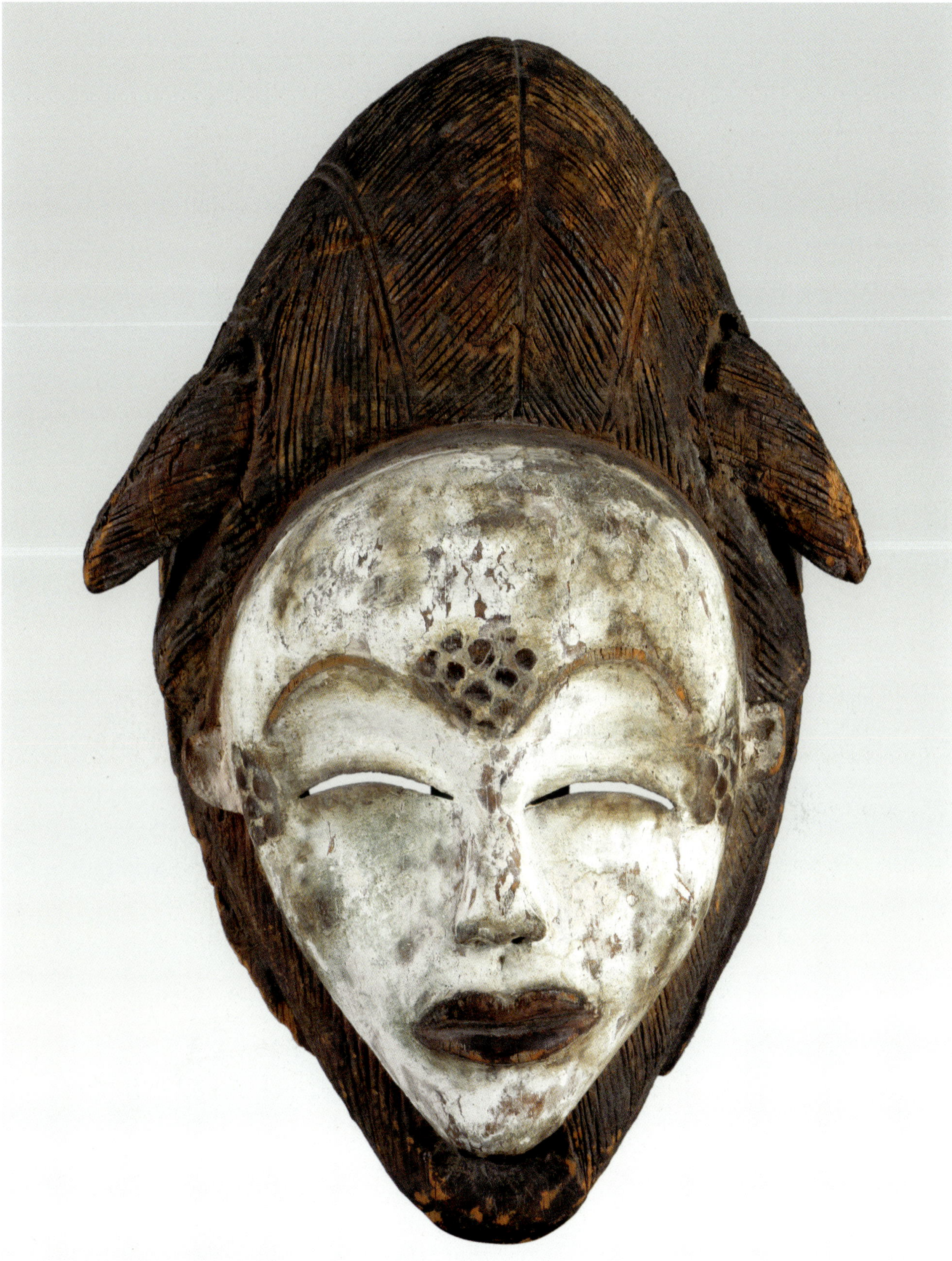

be compared with those in the Musée Dapper, Paris (formerly. Charles Ratton coll.), and in the Centre Pompidou, Paris (formerly, Alberto Magnelli coll.).

Statues from South Gabon-Congo

The Lumbu statuette **lot 237, [ill. 121]**, from South Gabon-Congo is of consummate perfection. It depicts a kneeling girl holding a bottle in one hand. Dressed like a visor, her hair overhangs a fine-featured face with huge eyes encrusted with slivers of glass and studded with nails. Beneath youthful breasts, the belly is adorned with four spirals that meet at a diagonal—a Yombe pattern that refers to the original four clans of the Loango kingdom. This statuette recalls the amulets that constitute the summit of Lumbu art.[24] Of considerable height and covered with a coating of plaster stuck with a cowry, the Teke statue **lot 245 [ill. 46]**, stands with bent legs, the thin arms held close to the stomach and the breasts pointed. The face topped with two bunches and a trapezoidal beard is free of scarification. Coated in a dark patina, this consecrated statue presents similarities with the Teke piece **lot 246**; the latter, smaller but wearing a torque, was shown at the Musée du Quai Branly in the *Fleuve Congo* exhibition.

Nkisi from the Democratic Republic of the Congo

The *nkisi* power figure lot 233 **[ill. 122]**, represents a naked man, showing respect by kneeling as if preparing to be "knighted." The body is well-proportioned and the broken arms bent, while the head sports a Kongo cap. Asymmetrical, this original figure portrays a notable in ecstasy with wide-open eyes.

Standing hands on hips, the *nkisi* **lot 234, [ill. 47]**, carries on its abdomen a load with a mirror. The short legs with "rake-shaped" feet are spread wide apart; each adorned with a round anklet. The head is characterized by large eyes inlaid with mirror glass and touched off in black, a long nose, and a cavernous rhomboid mouth baring filed teeth. The upturned eyes invoke the power of the "other world" for an act of judgment or healing. The statue in the Yombe style **lot 89** (second catalog), represents a broad-shouldered man standing and bending over slightly. His chest is pierced by an iron blade and he wears a cap on his head. With realistically treated features and wide-open eyes, his forehead is adorned with nine small scarification marks. The arms are folded back beneath a spherical load covered in a grainy patina. The legs are spread apart with the imposing feet, whose nails are marked out in relief, each standing on a base—a Kongo characteristic.

The carved Ndengese (Dengese) bust **lot 232**, wears a finely braided hat; the necklaces and bracelets refer to an important personage, holding out large hands with thumbs spread apart. The disproportionate body is severed at the level of the hips. Spiral scarifications on the temples and upper arms refer to the allegory of the origins of the Kongo. This bust resembles those in the collections of the Tervuren and Zurich museums.[26]

The three Bembe biteki statuettes **lots 235, 236, and 238**, with mirror-glass eyes —a constant in Bembe art—are idealized portraits and are used during therapeutic consultations or rites for the dead. The first two depict seated dignitaries with hands on knees and displaying similar scarifications (two opposed arcs of a circle on the stomach). The powerfully-shouldered bearded man sits on a cubic seat—a mark of power; the large-breasted woman is seated cross-legged. The third statuette depicts a standing warrior with his hair dressed in a crest, carrying a knife and a piece of wood.

Realistic in its handling, the Lulua *bwanga bwa* female half-figure LOT 228, has a huge head, with a hairstyle tapering to a point at the top of the skull; the forehead and cheeks show half-moon scarifications. While sizable copper nails indicate the big eyes, the tall, ringed neck surmounts a long, slender bust with thin arms bent at right angles, and a navel in the shape of a bird's beak. This power object was used in the *cibola* (maternity) initiation cycle; the pointed base was inserted into a clay pot or basket filled with soil and other substances.[27]

The two Luba caryatid seats LOTS 86 AND 87 (second catalog), are prestige objects, the latter figuring on the green cover of the second catalog of the Rubinstein sale [ILL. 7]. Both were made by the same sculptor (Luvua workshop); one of the stools has only one arm, while the other presents two to support the top. The folded legs stand open to display genitals on a level with the plinth. Suggestive in posture, it represents woman as intermediary between the power of the king seated on his throne and that of the ancestors and "genii."[28]

Helena Rubinstein possessed the eye of an African art enthusiast and collected "real art objects," whose qualities were enhanced by the Japanese sculptor and cabinet-maker Kichizo Inagaki. Seventeen of her masterpieces featured in the exhibition *African Negro Art* at the Museum of Modern Art, New York, in 1935. In addition to numerous Kota and Fang reliquaries, it also boasted other treasures, such as the white and black Fang, Punu-Lumbu, and Tsangui masks, as well as Lumbu, Teke, Luluwa, and Nedengese statuary.

Bearing the imprint of the preeminent first and second-generation *art nègre* dealers such as Paul Guillaume and Charles Ratton, the legendary Rubinstein collection reflects all the formal and stylistic diversity of equatorial Africa.

Masks, mirrors, and *mise en scène*. The collection and the image

Yaëlle Biro

Helena Rubinstein looks straight into Man Ray's lens [ill. 53]. Among the many photographs of the great patron, this face-on view is rare. The few rows of pearls around her neck contrast with the heavy, conspicuous necklaces she usually sported. In the apparent simplicity of this pose Rubinstein seems to be knowingly exposing herself to the gaze of the photographer and the viewer. Her face, however, is not without artifice: the eyes are deeply underscored in black, the lips emblazoned in dark red, and her skin coated with a thick layer of white foundation. Face or mask? Controlling every aspect of her image, "Madame" is here clearly intent on covering her tracks...

As well as commissioning photographs of interiors, artifacts, and portraits from exponents such as Man Ray, Cecil Beaton, and Dora Maar, in the course of her career Helena Rubinstein made adroit use of the photographic tool. As both a manufacturer and retailer of beauty products, and adopting her own name as a brand, she soon realized that her image was to be inextricably linked to her business. Transforming her beautician salons into comfortable lounges and, conversely, her apartments into social and public spaces, she exploited mirror effects—literally and figuratively. Blending diverse styles and making art, fashion, design, and science appear inseparable, she disseminated an ideal of the independent modern woman with decided tastes.

Often photographed, her collection of African and Oceanic pieces played a central role in defining her identity. Omnipresent in views of her residences and some of her salons, where they were handled as well as admired, and, above all, skillfully arranged around her in portraits, such artifacts formed part of the visual discourse Rubinstein spent a number of decades constructing.

Above left
Ill. 50
Augusta Rubinstein and her daughters: standing, Manka, Helena (or Regina?), and Ceska; seated, Erna; Krakow, studio Wilhelm Kleinberg, 1889-1890

Above right
Ill. 51
Helena Rubinstein wearing a Paul Poiret outfit with turban, c. 1920–30, photograph by Boris Lipnitzki

Below left
Ill. 52
Madame in the drawing-room in her apartment at 895 Park Avenue, New York, 1934, photograph by George Maillard Kesslere (cat. 89)

Below right
Ill. 53
Helena Rubinstein, c. 1924, photograph by Man Ray (cat. 90)

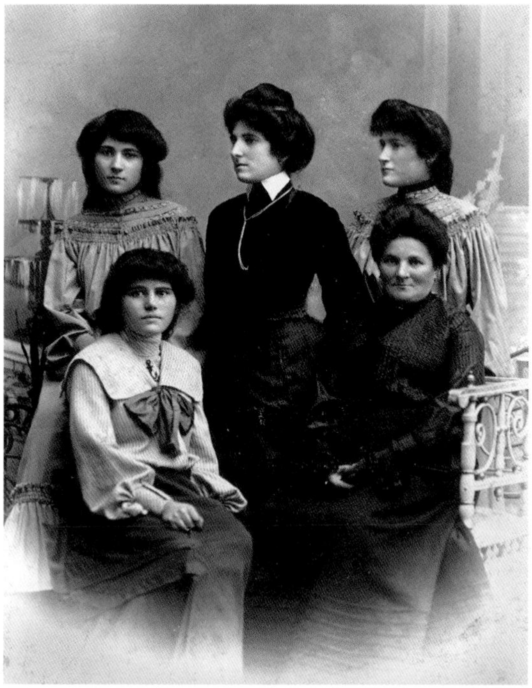

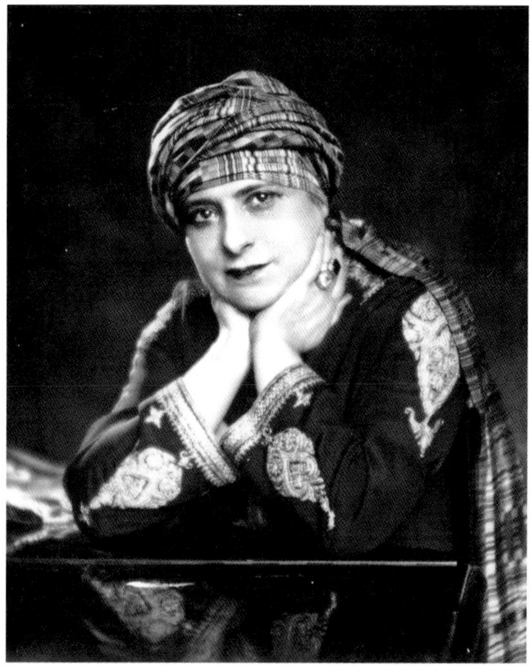

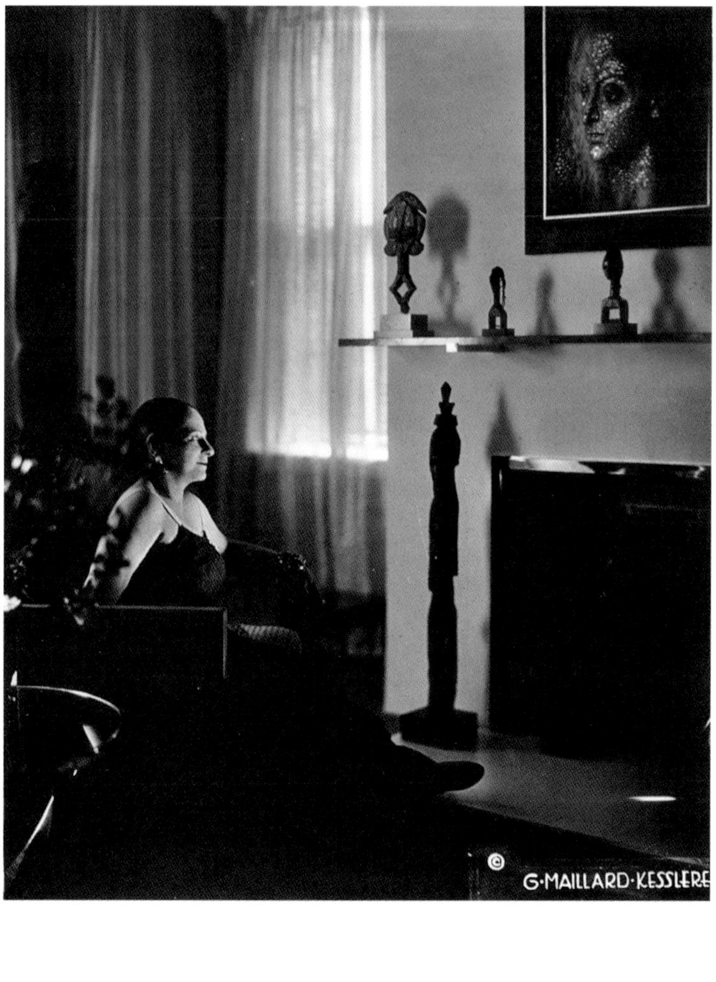
© G·MAILLARD·KESSLERE

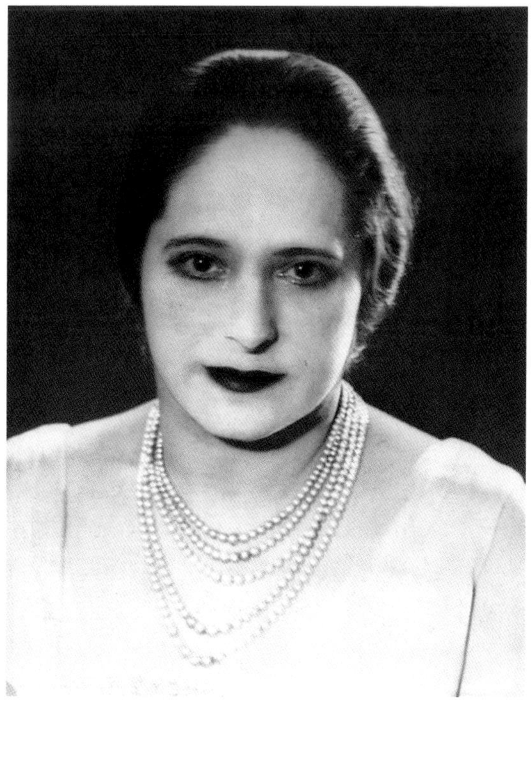

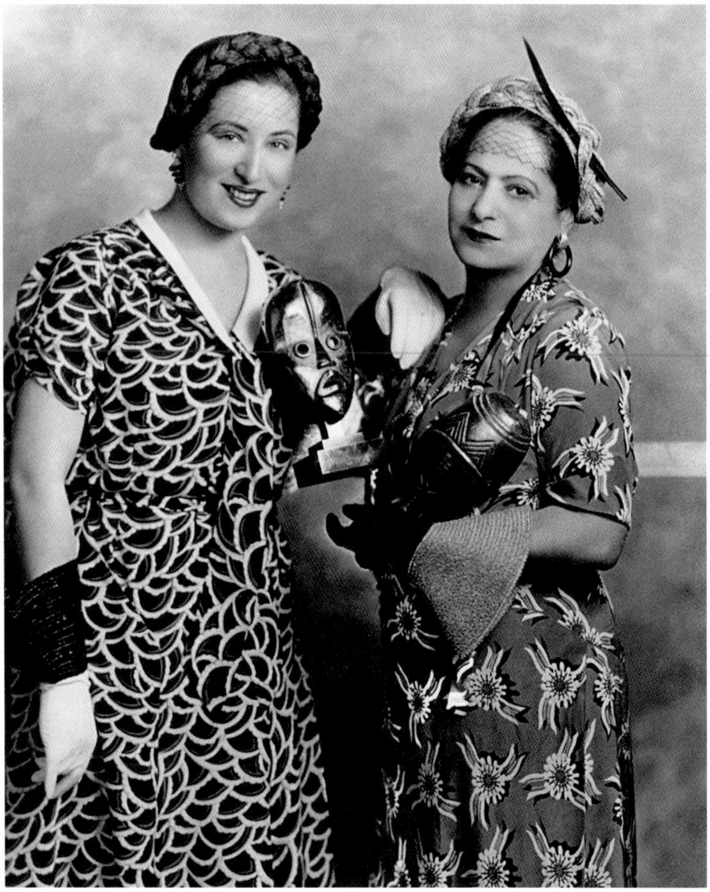

Multiple viewpoints

Enhancing both her own image and the kaleidoscopic views she created in her interiors and with her collection, Helena Rubinstein had already become aware of the power of photography in her youth. From her early years in Poland, and then in Austria and Australia, her portraits all skillfully exploit the lens.

A rare photograph from 1889-1890[1] [ill. 50], when she was only seventeen or eighteen, testifies to what the American curator Mason Klein[2] called "her natural affinity with the camera." Leading with her right profile and despite her modest stature, she dominates the family group, her keen fashion sense making her stand out from her mother and sisters. This portrait proved to be the first in a long series. Like the notorious Countess of Castiglione in the 19th century, who, over the course of countless photographic shoots, forged an imaginary self-portrait,[3] Rubinstein was a collector of her own image. While the Countess of Castiglione's sequences were the fruit of her close collaboration with a single photographer, Pierre-Louis Pierson, Rubinstein preferred multiple viewpoints. The result was a composite involving many artists that fused images of Rubinstein as a woman of the world, an art lover, and an entrepreneur.

Rubinstein thus liked to view herself through the eyes of artists, be they painters or photographers. Hailing from several continents and extending over many decades, the list of artists is impressive. From George Maillard Kesslere [ill. 52], who snapped the

ill. 54

Helena Rubinstein and her niece Mala holding African masks, early 1930s, photograph Studio Granere beautiful people of New York in the 1920s and 1930s, to the Franco-Ukrainian Boris Lipnitzki [ill. 51], who, best-known for his fashion and celebrity shots, had settled in Paris in the 1920s; from Dora Maar, who opened a photographic studio together with Pierre Kefer in Neuilly-sur-Seine in the early 1930s, to the British-born Francis Thompson in the 1960s, it seems as if images of the collector were captured by practically every photographer of the age. Each photograph is the visual and concrete expression of the links Rubinstein forged with the artistic community and the fashion world. And if Rubinstein did not press the shutter herself, they are pictures that blur the line between artist and model. Her desire to have her image reproduced in every form can then be viewed as the manifestation of her own creativity.

It is then worthwhile to compare the many photographs and her activity as a collector in the wider sense. "Madame" collected her image just as she collected objects. Moreover, the wealth of photographic archives in both private and institutional hands show the diverse ways in which the African and Oceanic works in her possession played a prominent role in the images she devised. Filling photographs of her private sphere and her commercial premises alike, they are gathered round her in portraits that show her holding them, or with her face partially concealed behind them in a game of mask and duplication. Through this process, artifacts from Africa and Oceania joined a narrative pointedly at odds with their original context, forming part of a discourse characteristic of the period that combined physical and aesthetic appropriation with a pattern of mutual legitimization not unconnected with the reception of modern art.

Interiors and backdrops

Helena Rubinstein's lifestyle was predicated on multiplicity. Just as the medium of photography allowed her to duplicate and circulate images, as a collector, she moved her collection about so as to increase the number of backdrops and settings in which it appeared. From her palatial apartments with their countless floors, suites, and rooms in Paris and New York, to her beauty salons in other global capitals, the possibilities were endless. Several members of her entourage remained on hand to regularly transport her artworks from place to place, and to make sure that any residence on either continent would always be ready to receive her. This perpetual motion is reflected in the photographs. A paradox then arises: though the sheer mass of photographs of the artworks should make it possible to obtain a clear image of the collection, any serious attempt at visual cross-referencing simply exacerbates the vertiginous sense of oscillation and concludes with an elusive concatenation of registers.

In Rubinstein's sumptuous apartment in a building she had rebuilt by the architect Louis Süe between 1934 and 1937 at 24, Quai de Béthune on Paris's Ile Saint-Louis there was always one room dedicated to African art. The many photographs of this space reflect not only the growth of the collection, but also the ebb and flow of furniture and fittings. The walls of this "African room," as it was dubbed, were gradually lined from floor to ceiling with shelves [ill. 18 and 19]. Initially intended for books, they were little by little adapted to house a wide range of African pieces, from the famous and imposing "Bangwa Queen" to delicate loom pulleys from the Ivory Coast. The dizzying sense of accumulation and displacement is amplified by the fact that the interior decoration of the apartments also changed frequently over the years, to the point of becoming unrecognizable from one period to the next [ill. 55 and 56].

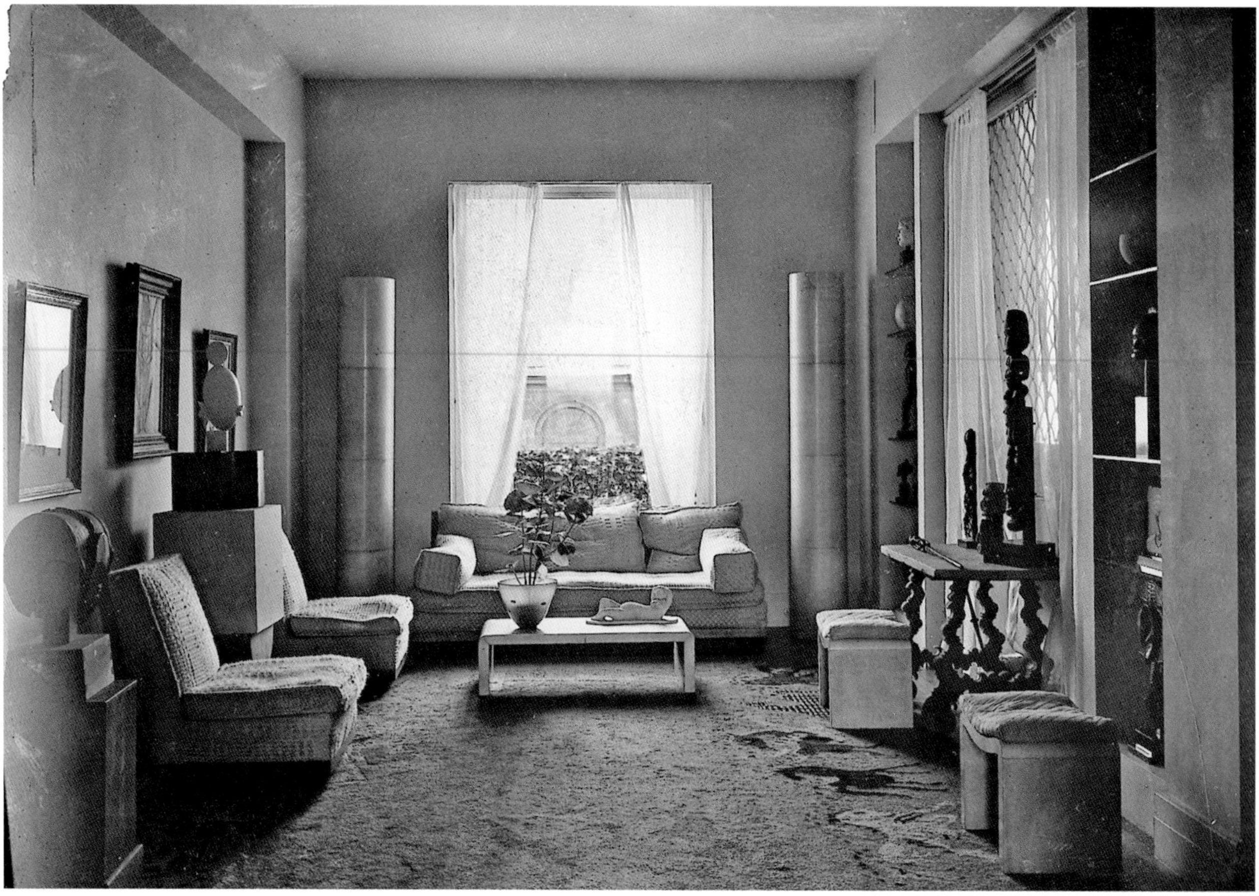

Several photographs present Rubinstein amid works in the "African room," the interior space, the objects, and the collector forming a kaleidoscopic portrait. While "Madame" generally preferred to be photographed from an angle that disguised her small stature, a few pictures show her as if engulfed by the artifacts [ill. 90]. Posing in a gown whose whiteness contrasts with the somber shades of the living room and surrounded by a mass of artworks, she is shown gazing at the sculptures with her hand on one of them. If sometimes she seems subordinate to the African pieces, they can also be viewed as an extension of her persona—a kind of "imaginary incorporation" characteristic of collections and collectors, as Brigitte Derlon and Monique Jeudy-Ballini theorized.[4] The researchers quote as an example a telling remark by the painter Henri Cueco: "Perhaps all these artworks surrounding me are of the same nature as myself, they amplify, inflate, extend me, so as to protect and perpetuate me."[5] As if fused with its artifacts, Helena Rubinstein also appears aggrandized by her collection.

Cueco's observation takes on a new pertinence when applied to the African and Oceanic arts in the colonial context of the first half of the 20th century. A reflection of the zeitgeist, the assimilation of such objects to Rubinstein's persona is far from anodyne. Reducing the distance between near and far—and, in the words of art historian Sabine

ILL. 55

One of the rooms (future music room) in 24, Quai de Béthune, Paris, 1937, photograph by Dora Maar

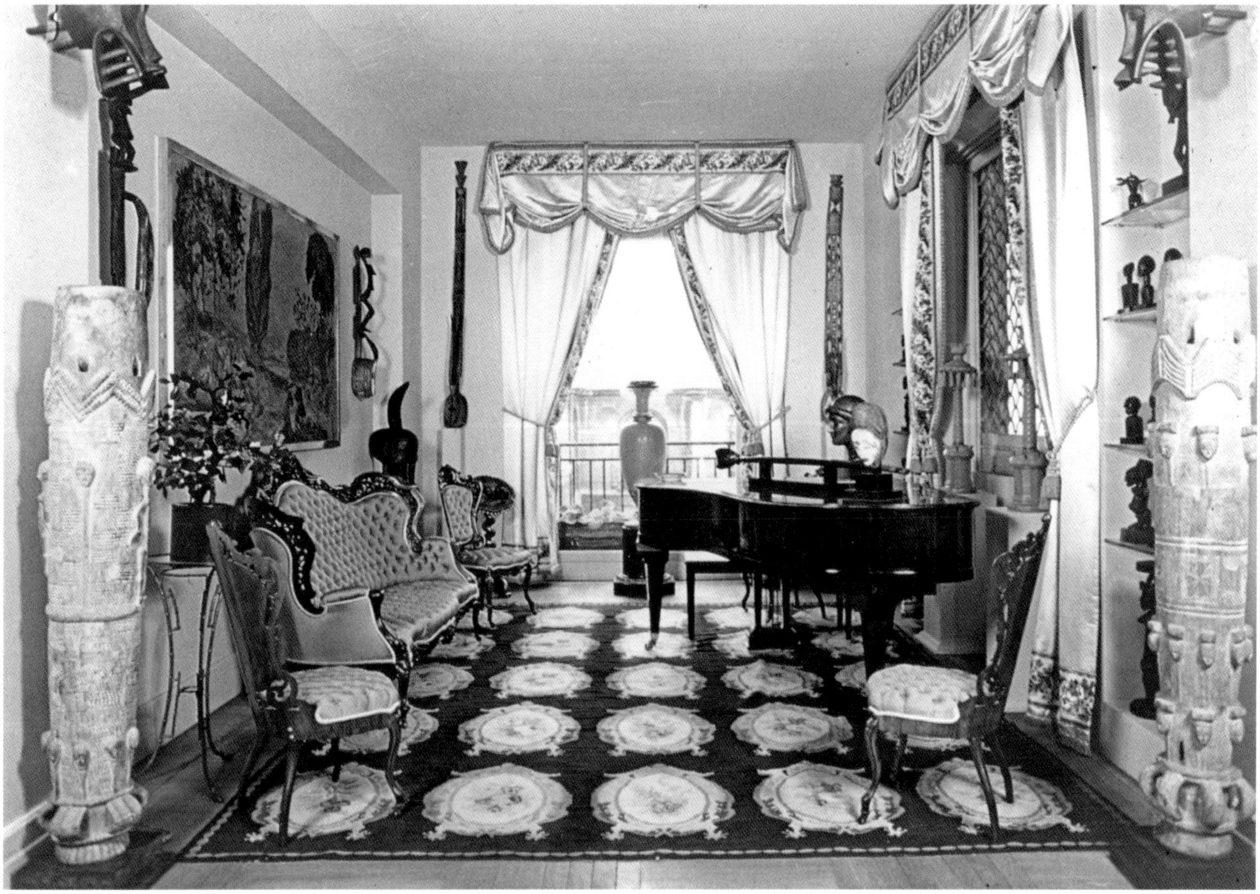

du Crest, in creating the "self with the other"[6]—the collector thus epitomizes the characteristic phenomenon of appropriation and transformation of art from what was then the colonies.

Face, mask, and duplication: transformation and reinvention

Helena Rubinstein developed her beauty brand at a time when women's emancipation stood at a crossroads that more than ever offered women the opportunity to reinvent themselves.[7] As a cosmetics pioneer, "Madame" was naturally interested in the female face and in a new definition of beauty. It can come as little surprise that this trend was also reflected in her collection, as well as in the photographic strategies put in place to represent it. Two themes in particular systematically emerge from her "portraits with objects": on the one hand, the visual interplay between face and mask, and on the other, the parallel with the famous 1926 photograph by Man Ray, *Black and White*.

ill. 56
The music room at 24, Quai de Béthune, Paris, c. 1950

Duplication has been an integral part of the Helena Rubinstein brand since its inception. Starting with the logo showing two affronted stylized faces, similar themes appeared over the decades in many advertisements [ill. 58]. The concepts of doubling

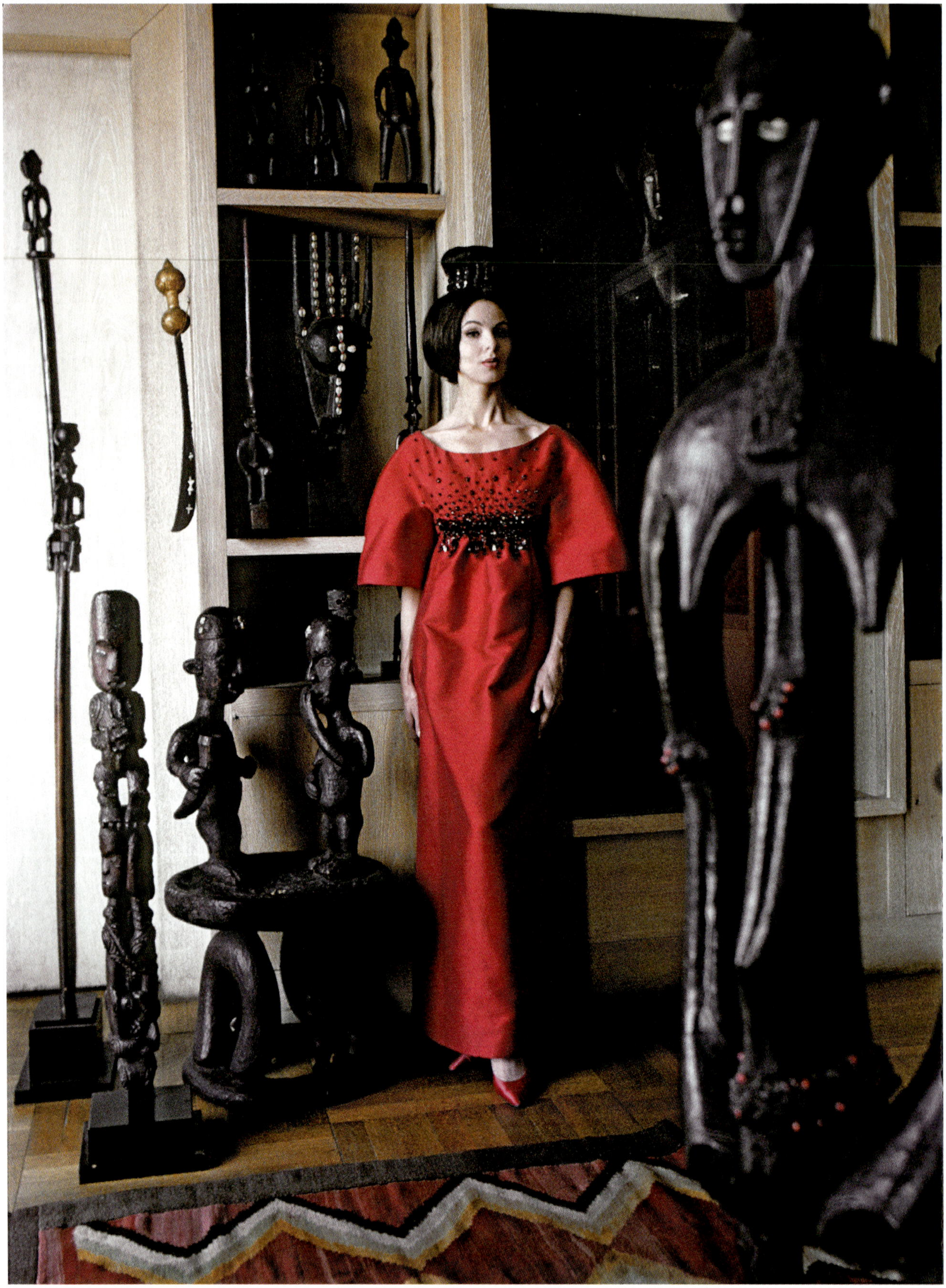

and the mask are closely linked, as is suggested by art historian Herbert Cole in the title of his book, *I Am Not Myself. The Art of African Masquerade.*[8] Like masks, make-up and cosmetics offer the possibility to "become (an)other." It is a connection Rubinstein implicitly understood. Among the works in her collection, one object in particular frequently appears in photographs: a *mukudj* mask in the Punu style made by a sculptor from Gabon.

With a surface covered with a thick layer of kaolin, its lips are highlighted in red, as are the indicators of beauty, such as the traces of scarification on the temples and forehead. As a foil to the face, a towering arrangement of fine braids of black hair offers balance to the composition. It can be imagined what Rubinstein saw in this piece: a particularly refined example of a face made up, and, as a consequence, transformed. It is also possible to draw a parallel with the thick coat of make-up worn by the collector in the portrait by Man Ray that exalts criteria of beauty close to her own.

Signaling its importance to Rubinstein, this mask was the only African artifact photographed on its own in a color album of works from her collection that she presented to her second husband, Prince Artchil Gourielli, in 1955 [ill. 59]. In the many photographs in which this mask is juxtaposed with a black marble head carved by Elie Nadelman, one of her favorite artists, it takes on other meanings. European black head and white African mask: perhaps Rubinstein sought to emphasize a form of universal beauty that would transcend origin and skin color? Or was she simply interested in the multitude of shapes a face can take? Pushing this to an extreme, a photograph of around 1950 [ill. 1] inserts these two works into a composition centered on Rubinstein, alongside an Egyptian figure, an imposing Bamana marionette with eight faces, figures painted by Miró, Renoir, and Modigliani, and Brancusi's famous sculpture, *White Negress II*—a particularly apt title in this context. In the way of the many-headed hydra, this complex composition lays bare the points of intersection and friction between modernity and exoticism, and brings out the diversity of ways in which beauty can be expressed.

There also lurk underlying references to Man Ray's photograph *Black and White*, published in Vogue in 1926, which had already reached the status of a modernist icon in the 1930s. Art historian Wendy Grossman has drawn attention to the tensions inherent in this image, to its "ambiguous and provocative" character, simultaneously channeling the modernist impulse in favor of universalism and equality, a reflection on questions of gender and race, and formalist game-playing.[9] All these elements reemerge in photographs depicting Rubinstein and masks in her collection from the 1930s to the 1960s. Grossman points out how, in addition to nods to Man Ray's picture, a portrait by fashion photographer George Maillard Kesslere of around 1935 [ill. 146] transforms the Ivorian style mask Rubinstein holds (with hands gloved in Chanel!) into a fashion accessory,[10] recalling the role of African art in this field during the first half of the 20th century. Here, Rubinstein plays the role of an expert rather than a model, while the mask is presented as a commercial object likely to arouse the interest of a collector.[11] The publication of this photograph in a New York magazine in 1935 to coincide with the major exhibition *African Negro Art* organized at the Museum of Modern Art attests to the informed use of advertising tools by the businesswoman, who deftly combined her status as an art lover with her position of an empress of beauty.[12]

ill. 57

A model posing in the African room at 24, Quai de Béthune, Paris, photograph by Carlo Bavagnoli published in *Life*, August 30, 1963

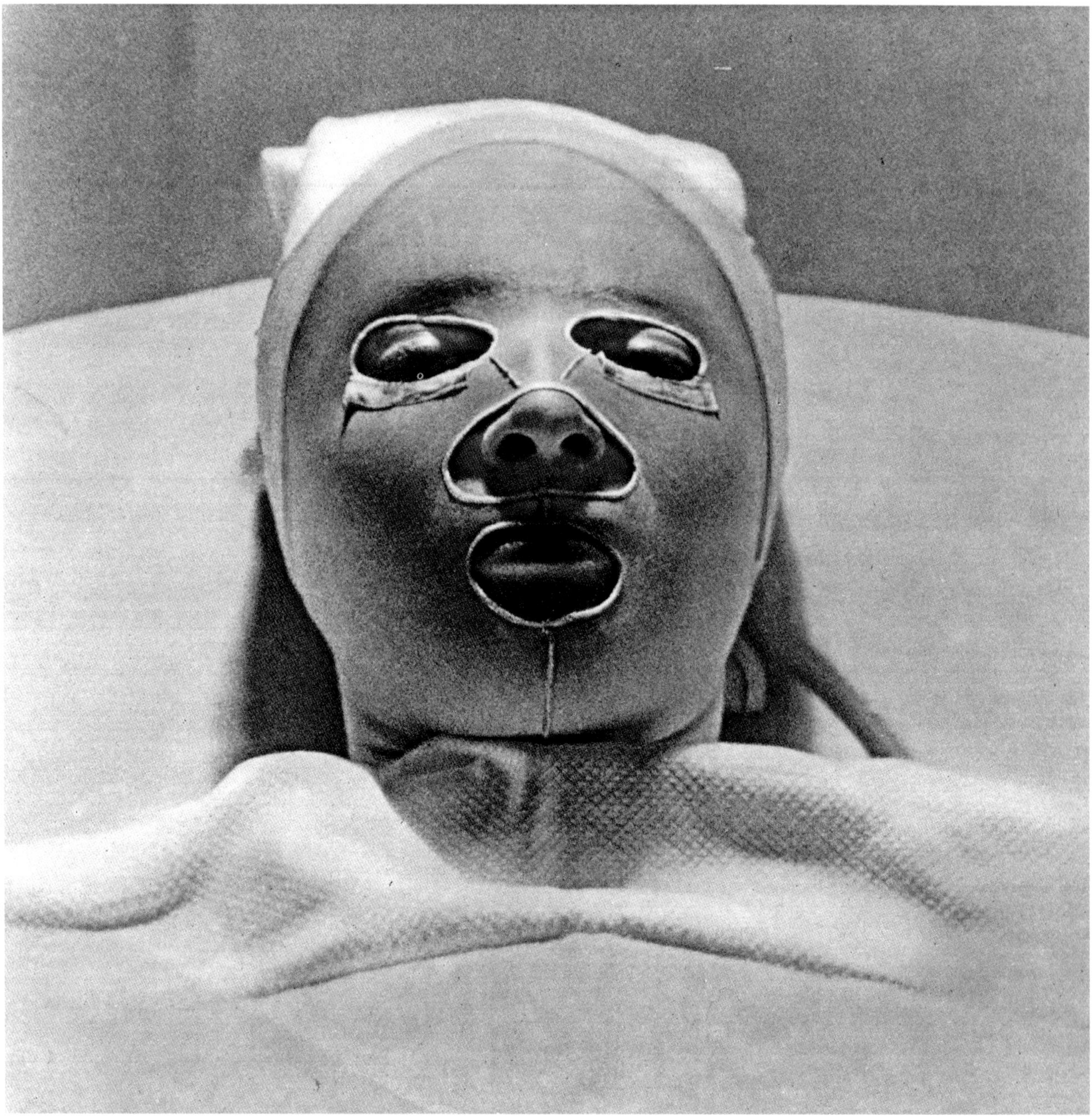

Ill. 58

The "Beautilift" treatment
by Helena Rubinstein,
1937, photograph
by Alfred Eisenstaedt

Ill. 59

Helena Rubinstein's
Punu mask (lot 191)
photographed c. 1954–55,
colorized photograph
taken from the album
composed by
Jean Vincent (cat. 91)

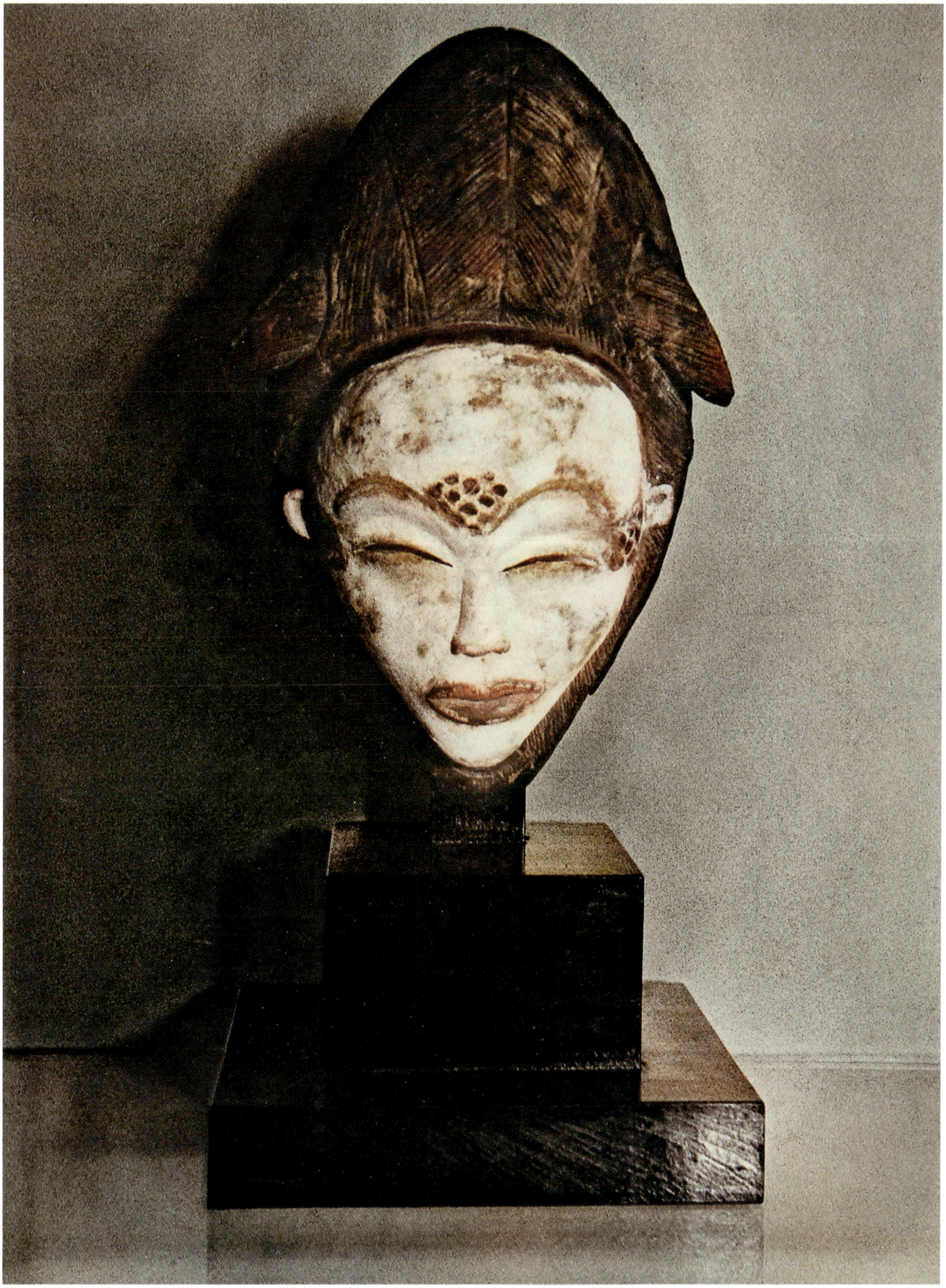

Fashion, artifice and reality

Similarly reflected in the photographs, the strategy consisting in using her activity as a collector to promote her professional interests is a recurring one. Rubinstein combines trade, art, beauty, artifice, and reality, whether by displaying flesh and blood models in the windows of her institutes, or by filling them with artworks from her collection, or co-opting her living space for photography shoots and catwalk shows. From the 1930s to the 1960s, her apartments in Paris, London, and New York were regularly used for fashion reportages published in *Vogue* or *Life Magazine*. Whereas some photographs, such as Edward Steichen's portrait of the actress Merle Oberon [ill. 60], once again hark back to Man Ray's *Black and White*, others, in a less subtle and more exoticizing idiom, highlight the contrast between the sophisticated gowns and the nudity of the African figures surrounding them [ill. 57]. The caption to a photo for Life Magazine dated 1963 taken in the "African room" on Quai de Béthune dismissively underscores the contrast: "Goya-esque gown from Simonetta-Fabiani is crowned with Alexandre hairdo. Sculpture is African."

Portraits *in absentia*

Rubinstein's African works, while not invariably occupying the center of her interiors or the images in which they appear, are often perceptible as an undercurrent. A view of one of her New York beauty salons shows a miscellany of pieces by European and African artists: two female statuettes in the Baule style from Ivory Coast rub shoulders with the low-relief, *Two Nudes*, by Elie Nadelman; two stools in the Akan style from Ghana echo, are paired on the one hand with a drawing by Amedeo Modigliani representing a caryatid, and on the other, with the chairs of an unfussy modernism that furnish the space: meanwhile, a portrait of Rubinstein painted by the Russian artist Pavel Tchelitchew peers down on the company. Though the actual beauty care was provided by others, for clients at the chic institute on Fifth Avenue the queen of cosmetics remained omnipresent. Like her portraits, Helena Rubinstein's artifacts from Africa and the Pacific embody her presence. The *nec plus ultra* of this game of presence and absence is a series of no less than eighty-eight photographs by Dora Maar.[13] A woman as well as an artist, Maar intrigued Rubinstein on two fronts. In all probability commissioned by the businesswoman in 1937,[14] shortly after moving into the mansion on the Quai de Béthune, Maar's piece focused at once on the apartment's luxury and on more functional concerns (there are several photographs of radiators), placing the emphasis on the furnishings and the spectacular view over the Seine.

If functionality tends to predominate, several pictures convey Dora Maar's poetic vision. The photographer's taste for mirror effects and unusual perspectives echoes Rubinstein's [ill. 61]. Hazy in atmosphere and tinged with Surrealism, one image juxtaposes, in front of a large mirror, a seashell standing on a shiny table with an ancient steatite woman's head from the Esie region in Nigeria placed atop a tall column. While the image is cropped by a heavy curtain blocking the view, the mirror reflects a glimpse of the large Art Deco staircase designed by Louis Süe on the other side of the room. Draped in semi-darkness the woman's head is turned outwards, apparently threatening to tumble out of the frame. The apartment's space is thus simultaneously revealed and concealed. Imbued with mystery and femininity, the language adopted here elevates the photograph from mere commission into the realm of art. It thus opens an intermediate space between the near and the far, between the natural and the artificial, the visible and the invisible to become a portrait *in absentia*.

ill. 60
Actress Merle Oberon in the apartment at 895 Park Avenue, New York, photograph by Edward Steichen published in *Vogue* (US edition), April 1935; in the background, a Fang head (lot 213)

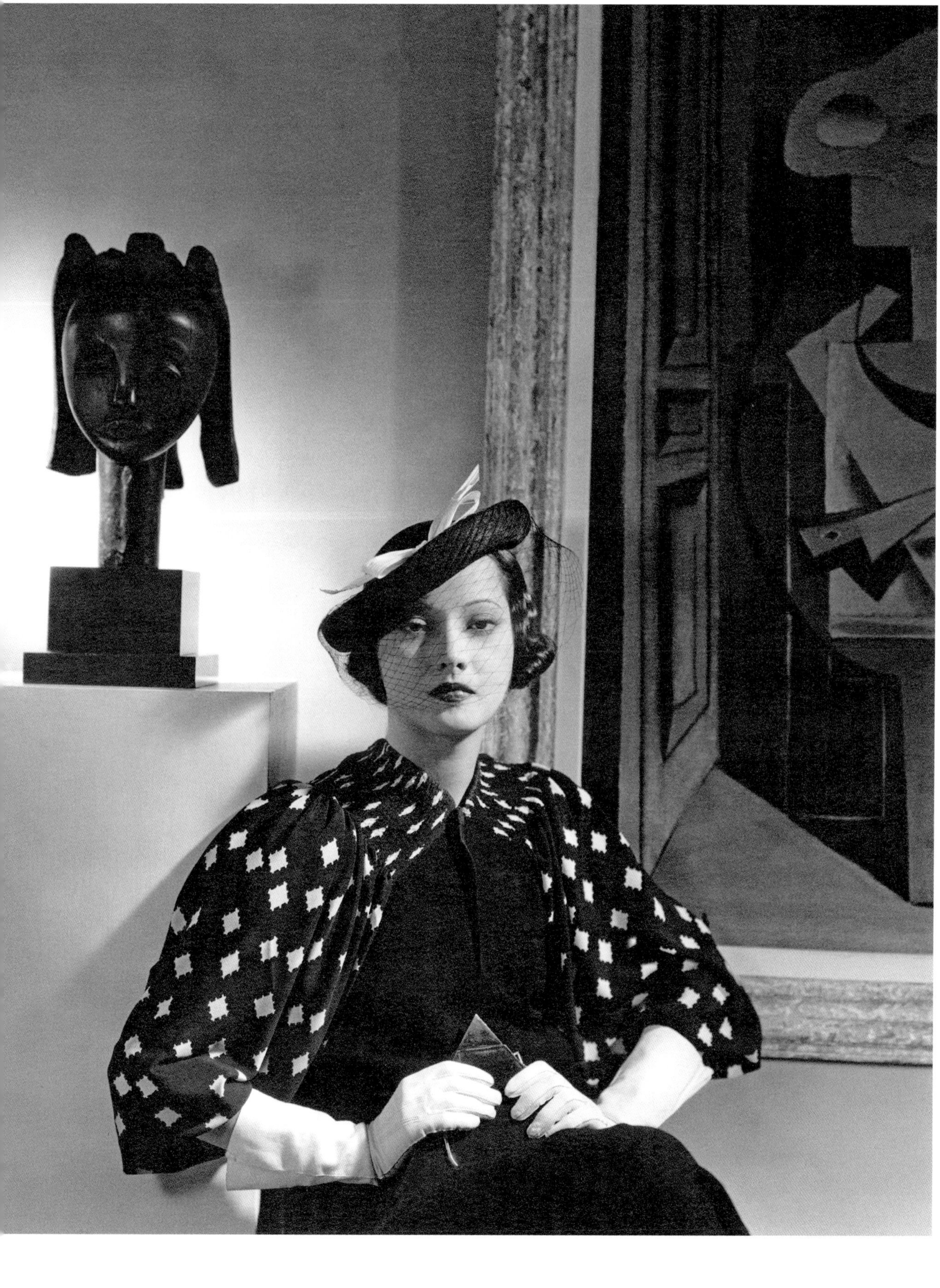

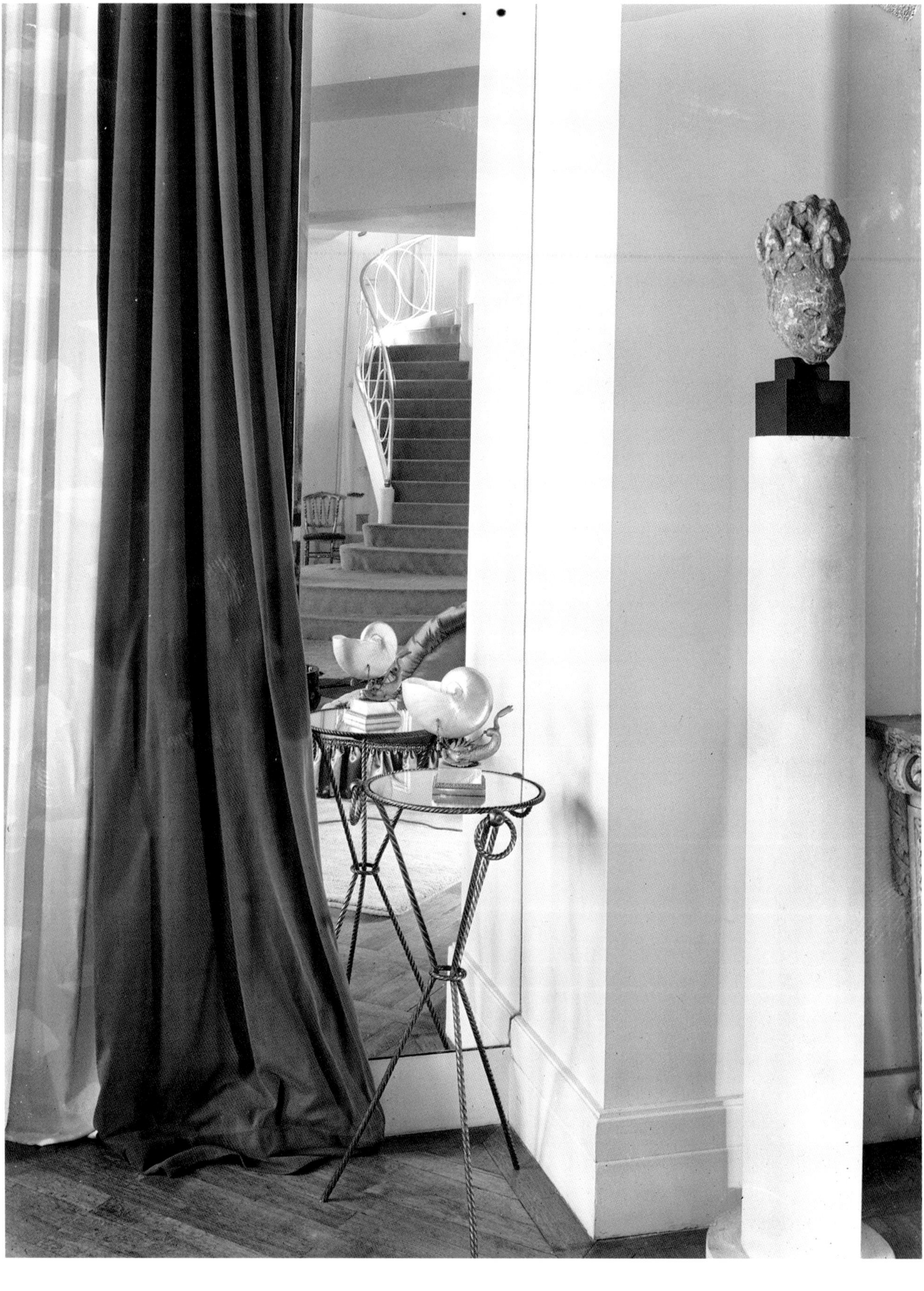

An inexhaustible treasure trove, such photographs—an amalgam of interior, portrait, and object to the point that they become inseparable, interchangeable, even—can be read in a myriad of ways. A documentary source for any understanding of the collection, the photographic corpus created around Helena Rubinstein also casts light on her relationship with her works. The frequent appearance of African and Oceanic pieces proclaims their importance in the construction of her identity. The use of such artifacts feeds into the image the collector desired to convey of herself—that of a modern woman, in the spirit of the times and with unconventional tastes. Her choices speak volumes as to the status the arts of Africa and the Pacific had attained in enlightened milieus in 1920s–30s Paris and New York.

In revealing such art to the general public, Rubinstein was instrumental in liberating it from the compartmentalized world of cognoscenti and specialists. Was this action a business risk... or a promotional masterstroke? Coming from one of the few women in the male universe of the African and Pacific art market, the choices she made were certainly strategic. As a patron, she afforded a deliberately feminine touch to her activity, if more through the image she presented of it than by her selection of objects, which remained essentially tributary to the canons of the time. Since it was Rubinstein who stage-managed her image, it is easy to forget the interpretative role of the photographer in the visual expression of the dialog between artist and model in the photo portrait. While other voices remain permanently silent: those of the African and Pacific artists themselves. As with the photographs she practically created herself, Rubinstein shapes the image of the African and Oceanic objects she owned. Divorced from their original context, they are reinvented and inserted into a completely different narrative structure linked to Western modernism and the world of fashion. Images of them thus become witnesses to the reinvention orchestrated by Rubinstein.

ILL. 61

The apartment at 24, Quai de Béthune, Paris, 1937, photograph by Dora Maar. On the column, a Yoruba head (lot 175)

Exhibited works of Madame's collection

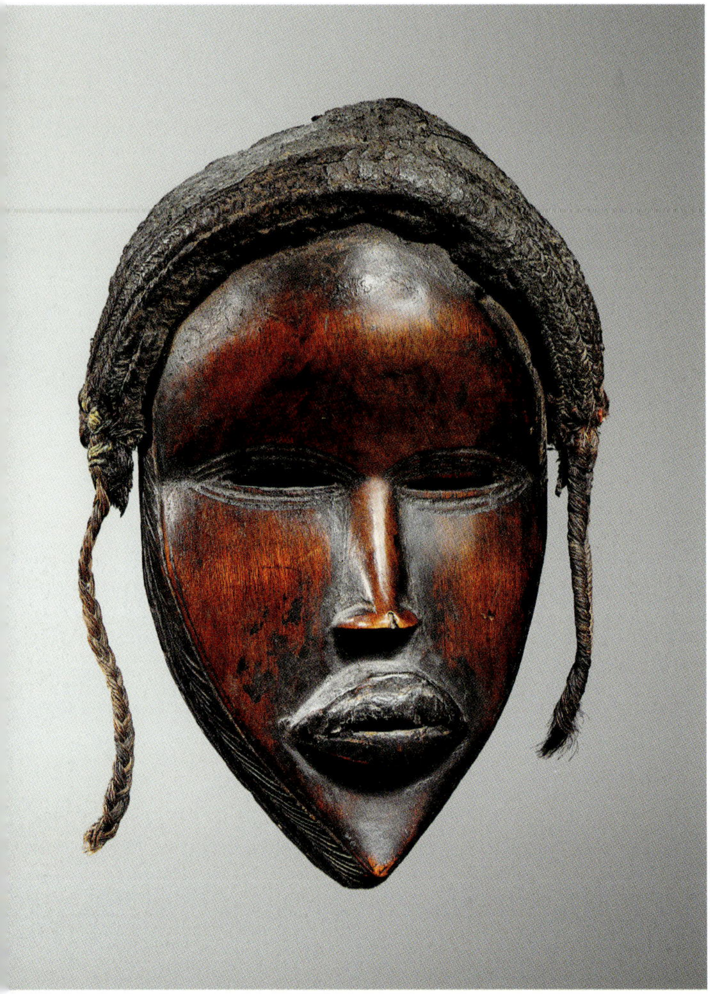

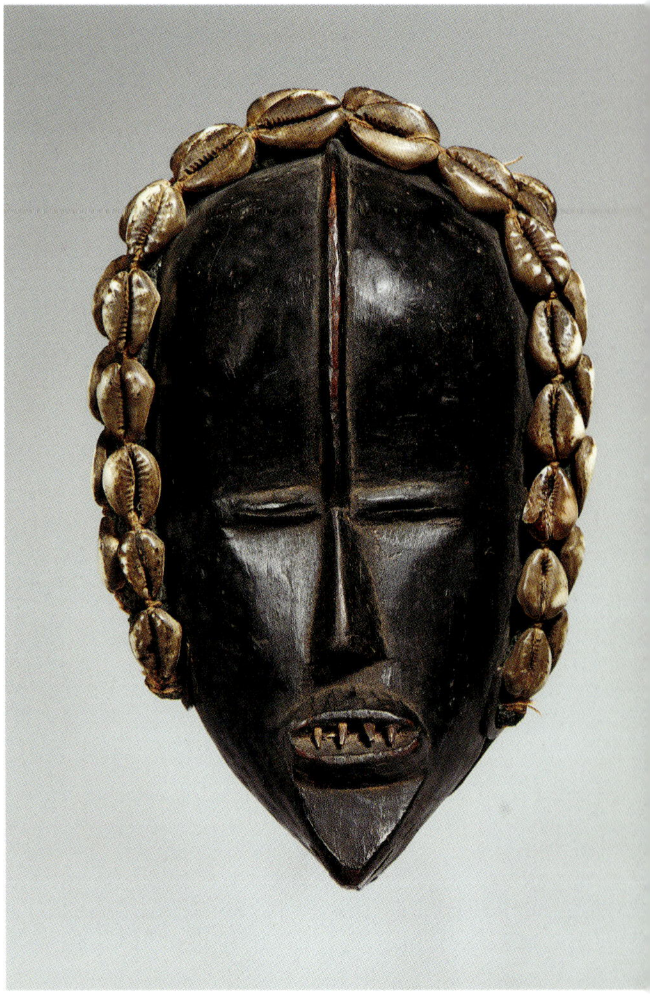

ILL. 62 [LOT 13]

Female initiation mask
Dan, Ivory Coast,
Man region
19th cent.
Wood, plant fibers, metal, pigments
20.3 × 14 × 8 cm
Paris, Private collection
(cat. 3)

ILL. 63 [LOT 8]

Miniature protection mask
Bete, Ivory Coast
19th–early 20th cent.
Wood, cowries, metal
16.5 × 10.5 cm
Paris, Private collection
(cat. 1)

ILL. 64 [LOT 10]

Protection mask
Dan-Ngere, Ivory Coast,
Danané region
19th cent.
Wood, plant fibers,
animal hair
47 × 21.5 cm
Paris, Marc Ladreit
de Lacharrière collection
(cat. 2)

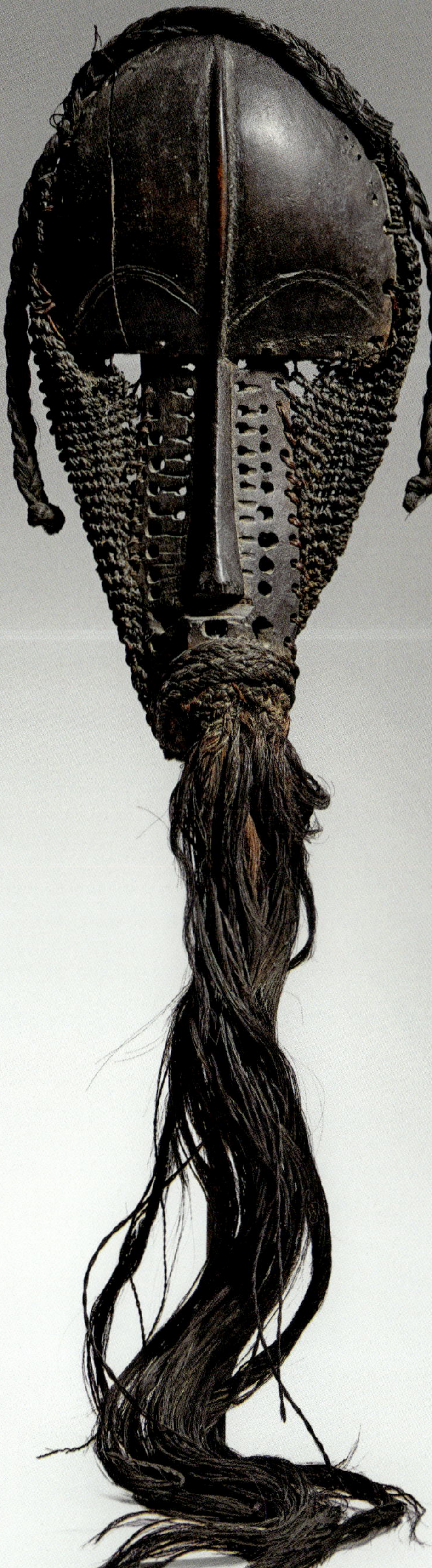

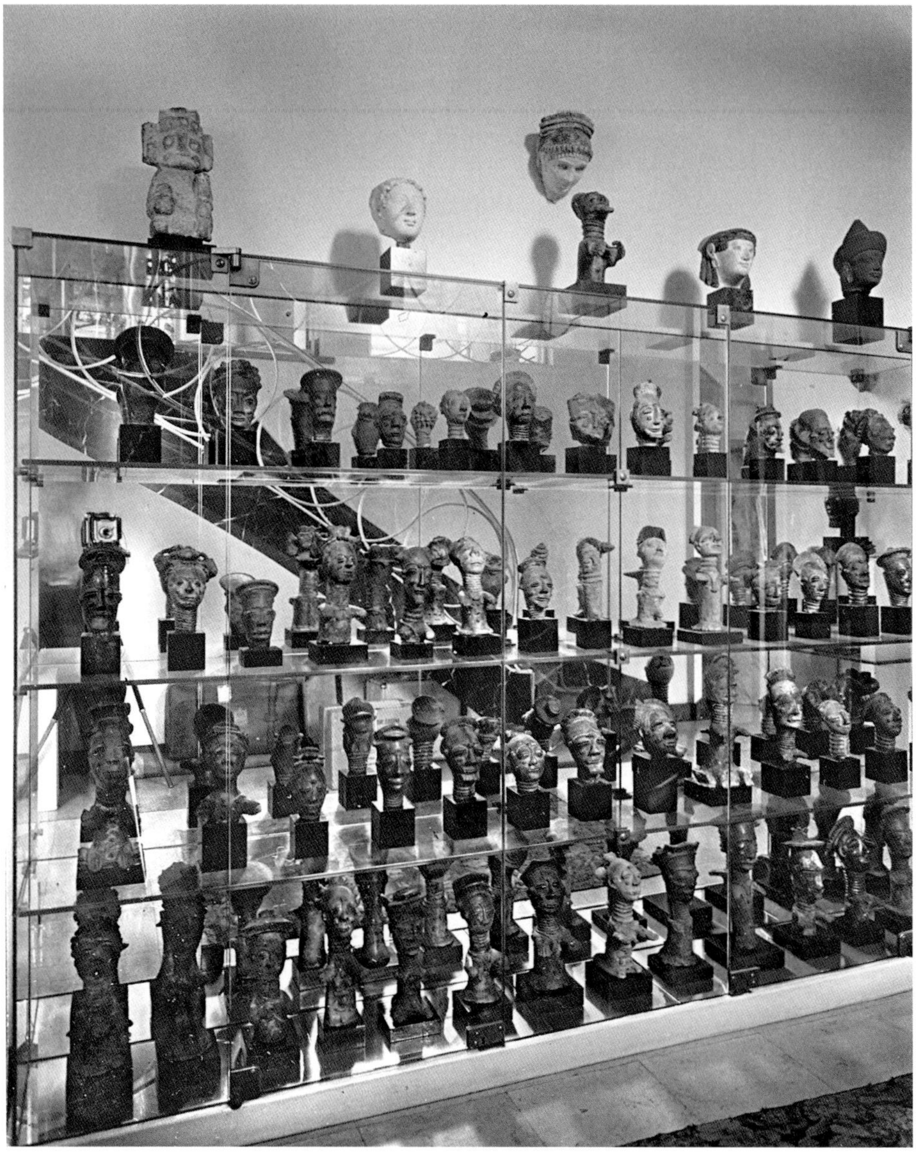

Ill. 65

Display case containing
Agni heads,
24 Quai de Béthune,
after 1952

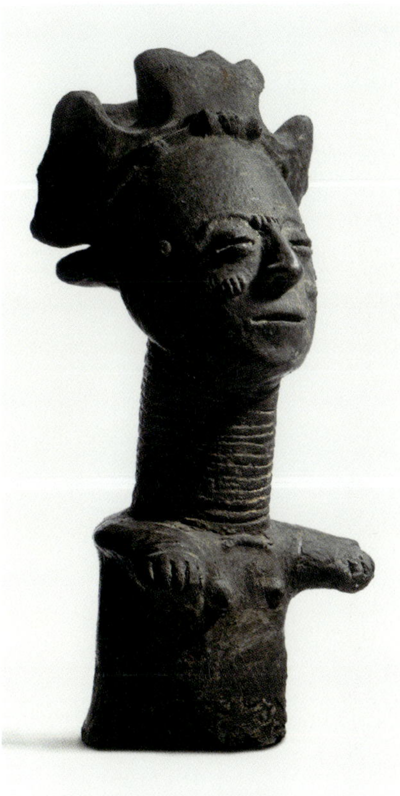

Ill. 66 [lot 149]

Mma funerary figure
Agni, Ivory Coast,
Krinjabo region
18th–19th cent.
Terracotta
31.5 × 13.8 × 13.8 cm
United States,
Africarium Collection
(cat. 5)

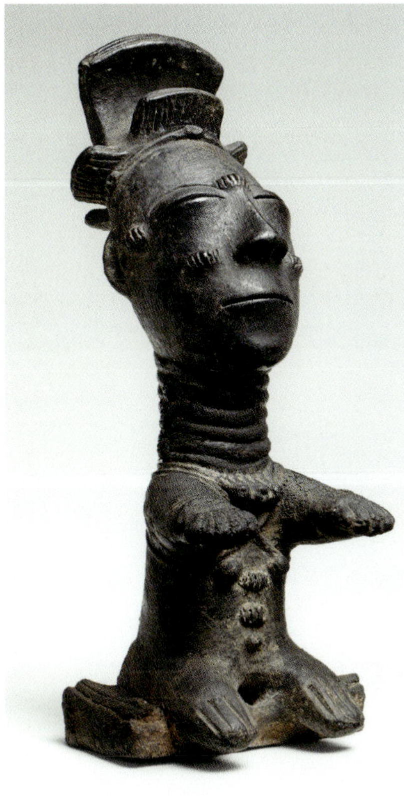

Ill. 67

Mma funerary figure
Agni, Ivory Coast,
Krinjabo region
18th–19th cent.
Terracotta, glass beads
37.5 × 14 × 13 cm
Paris, Musée du Quai
Branly – Jacques Chirac
(cat. 7)

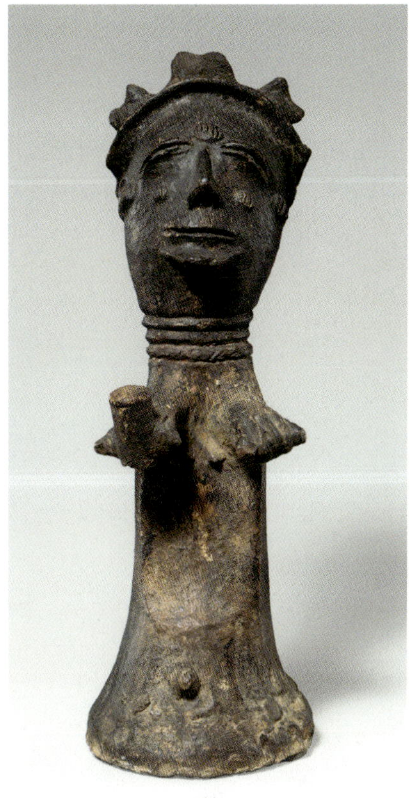

Ill. 68 [lot 157]

Mma funerary figure
Agni, Ivory Coast,
Krinjabo region
18th–19th cent.
Terracotta
36.8 × 12.7 × 14.6 cm
New York, Metropolitan
Museum of Art
(cat. 4)

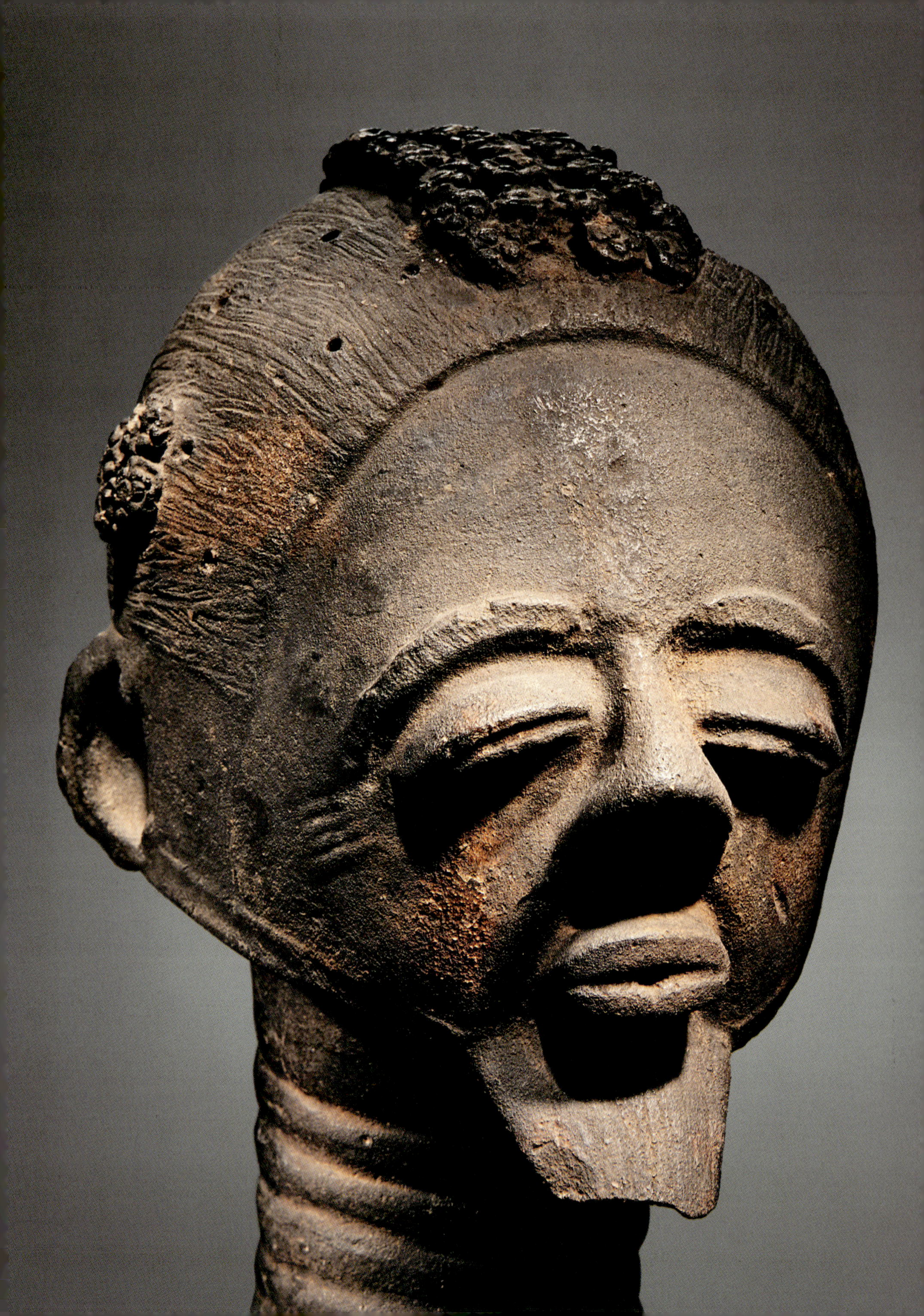

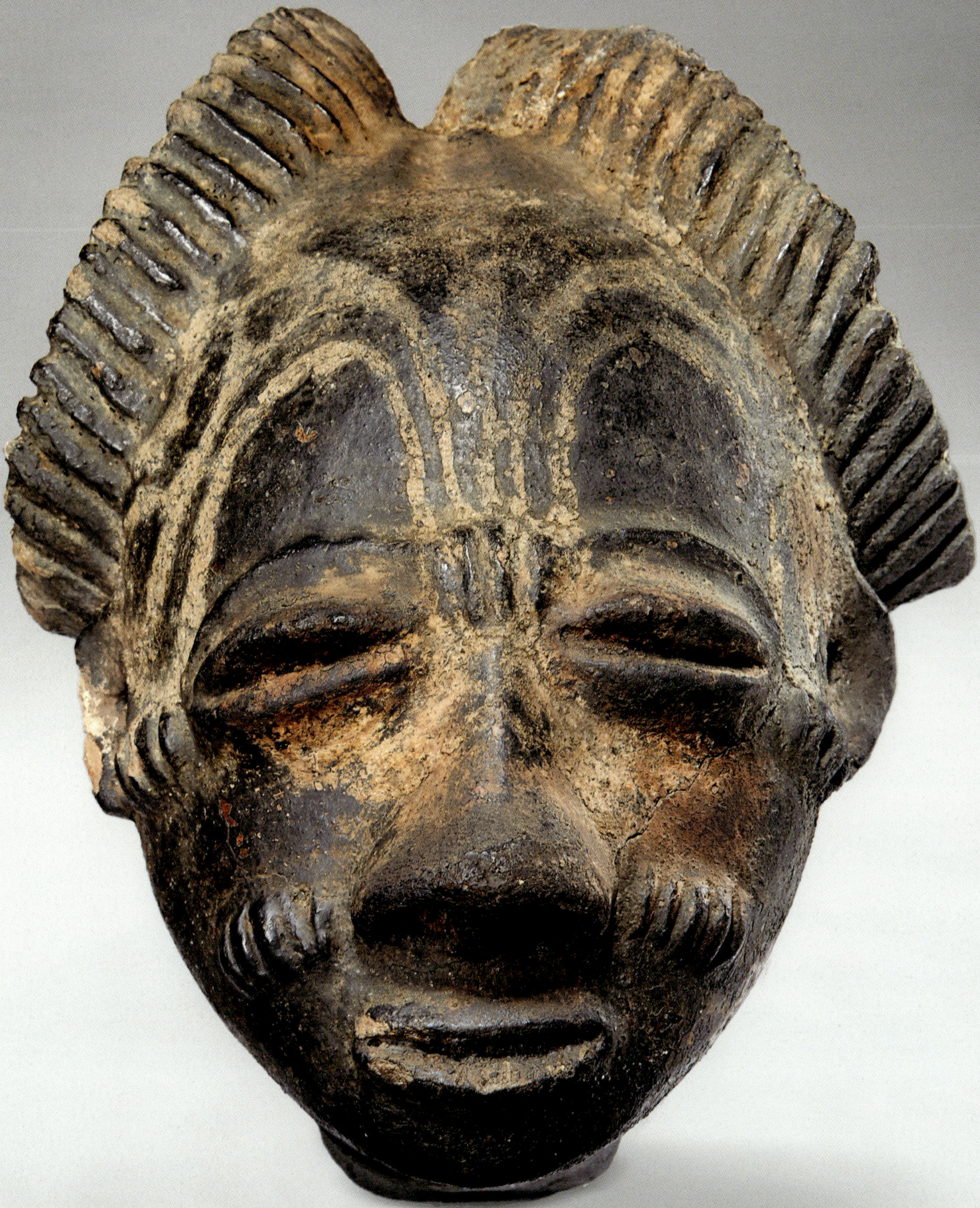

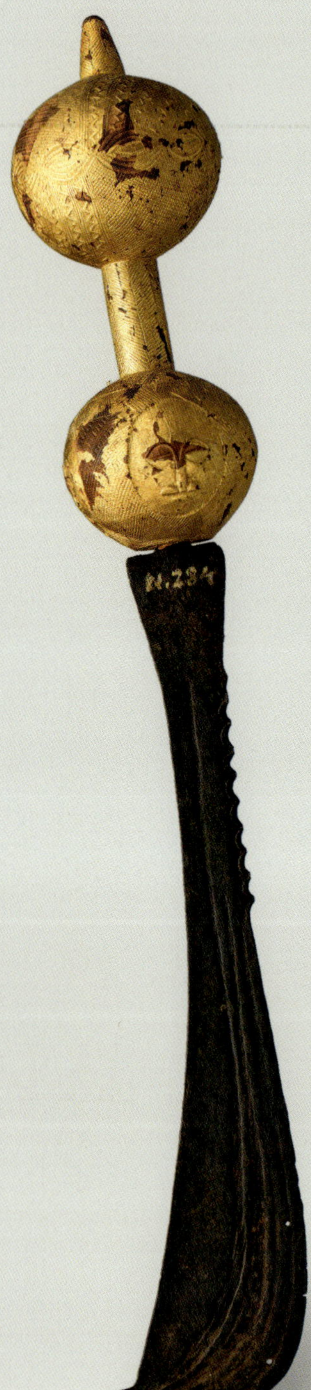

Previous pages
ILL. 69 [LOT 173]

Nsodie male funerary head
Akan, Fomera, Ghana, Adansi region
17th cent.
Terracotta
23 × 18 × 20 cm
Paris, Lilane and Michel Durand-Dessert Collection
(cat. 6)

ILL. 70

Mma funerary head
Agni, Ivory Coast, Krinjabo region
18th–19th cent.
Terracotta
16.1 × 15.5 × 16.7 cm
Paris, Musée du Quai Branly – Jacques Chirac
(cat. 8)

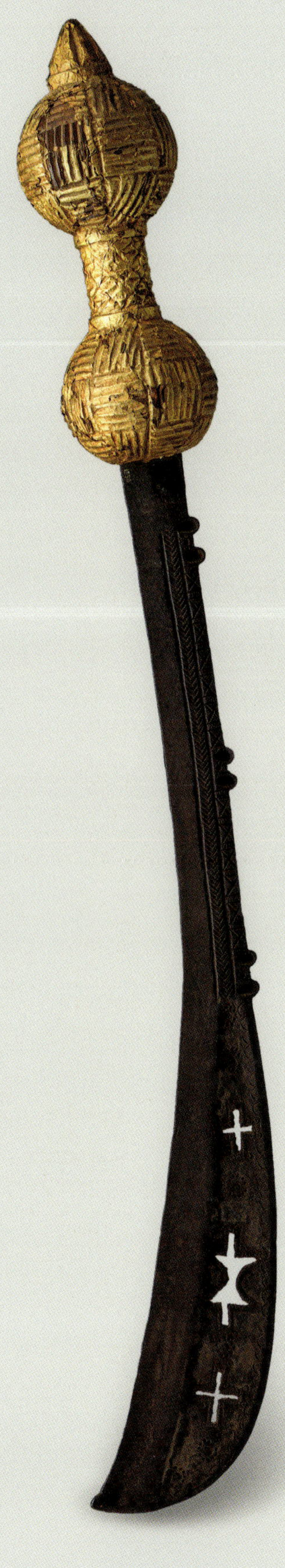

Left
ILL. 71 [LOT 170]

Afena sword
Akan, Ivory Coast, Agnibilékrou region
First half of 20th cent.
Iron, wood, gilded aluminum
61.5 × 9.2 × 9.8 cm
Washington D.C., National Museum of African Art – Smithsonian Institution
(cat. 10)

Right
ILL. 72 [LOT 171]

Afena sword
Akan, Ivory Coast, Agnibilékrou region
First half of 20th cent.
Iron, wood, gilded aluminum
71.1 × 9.8 × 7.5 cm
Washington D.C., National Museum of African Art – Smithsonian Institution
(cat. 9)

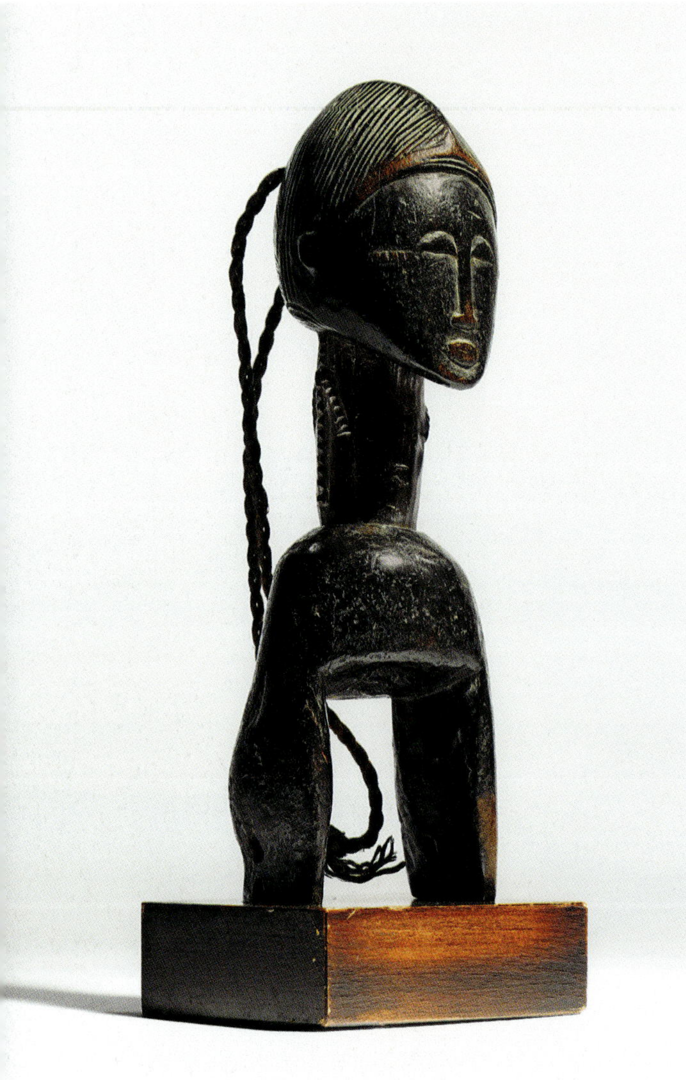

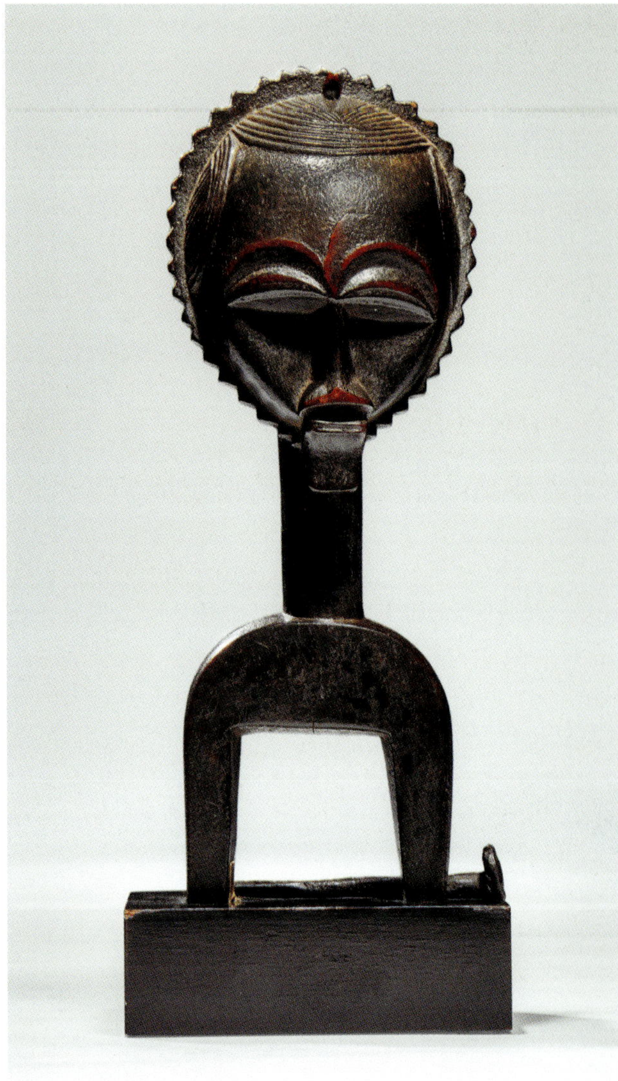

ILL. 73 [LOT 22]

Heddle pulley
Baule, Ivory Coast
19th cent.
Wood, plant fibers
18.4 × 10 × 10 cm
Private collection
(cat. 11)

ILL. 74 [LOT 38]

Heddle pulley
Baule, Ivory Coast
19th cent.
Wood, iron
22.9 × 5.1 × 8.3 cm
Diane and Brian Leyden
collection (cat. 12)

ILL. 75 [LOT 72*]

Pair of female and male anthropomorphic combs
Bete/Guro, Ivory Coast
19th–early 20th cent
Wood
H. 22.9 and 24.8 cm
Private collection (cat. 13)

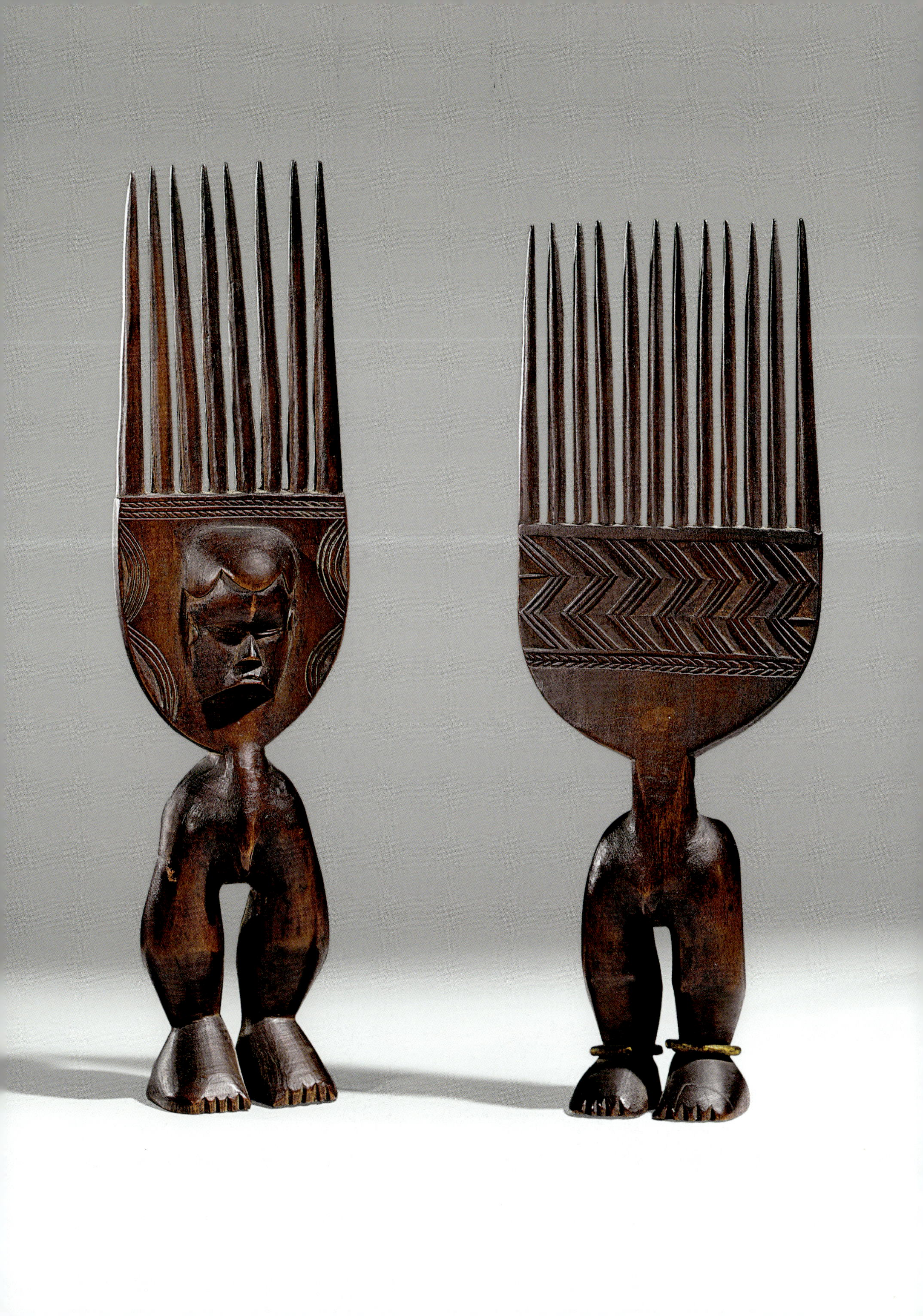

Ill. 76 [lot 40]

Blolo bian male statue
Baule, Ivory Coast,
Bouaké region
19th cent.
Wood
44.5 × 9 × 8 cm
Canada, private collection
(cat. 16)

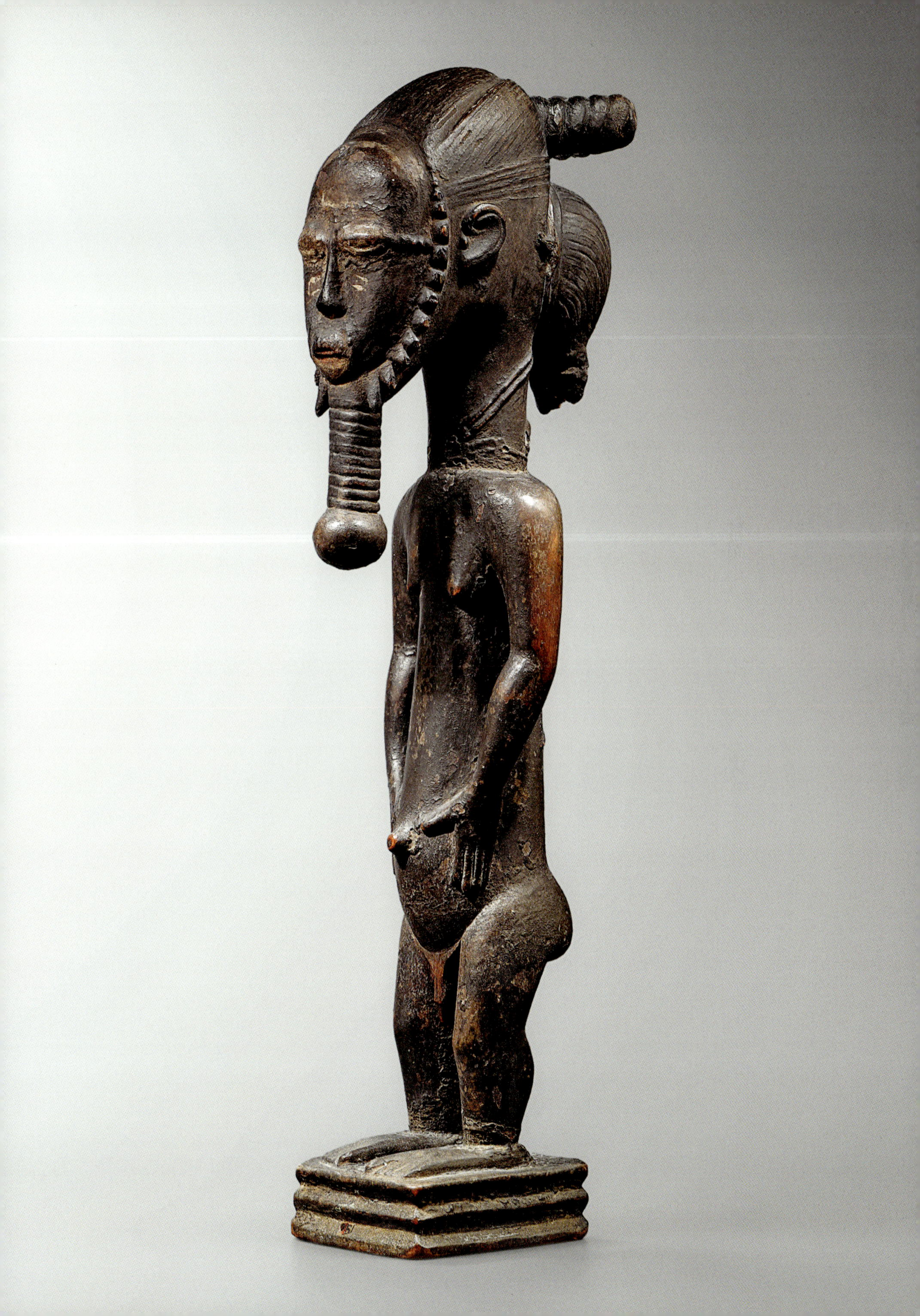

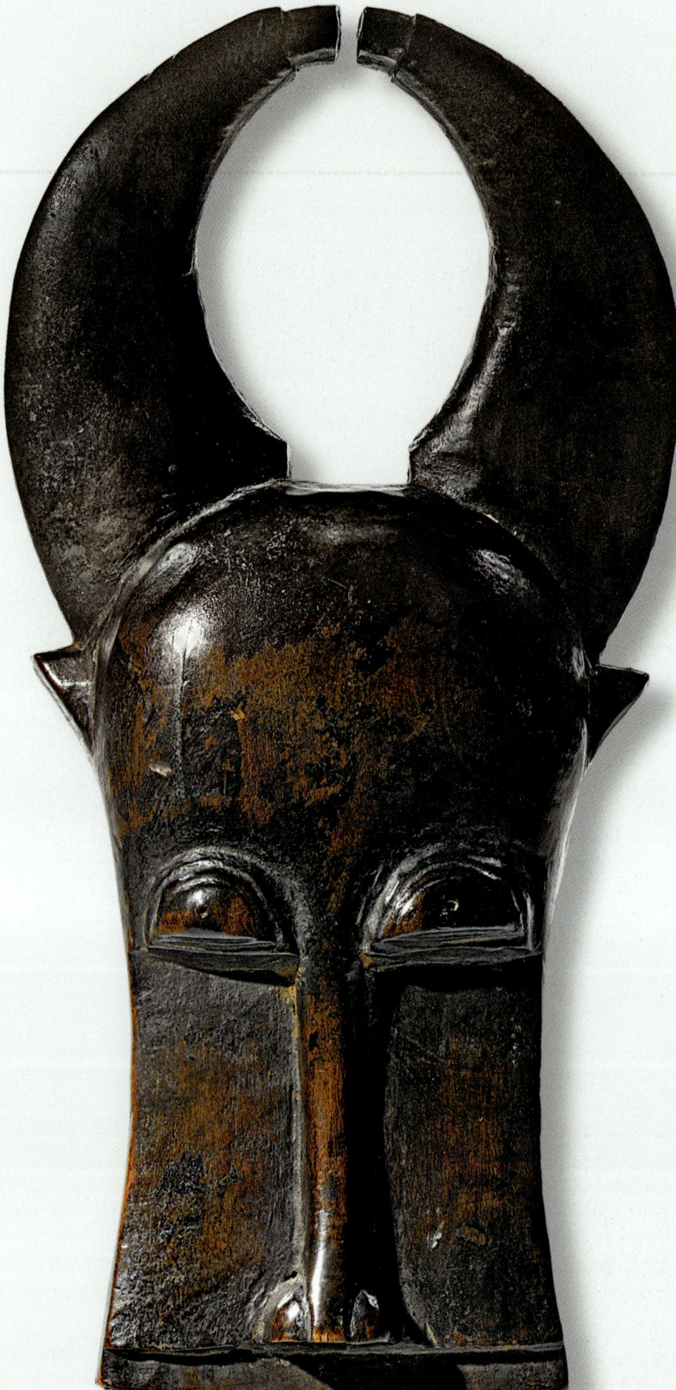

ILL. 77 [LOT 37]

Small, *bonu amwin* type water-buffalo mask
Baule, Ivory Coast
19th–early 20th cent.
Wood
25 × 15 × 15 cm
Private collection (cat. 15)

ILL. 78 [LOT 29*]

Door shutter
Baule, Ivory Coast
19th–early 20th cent.
Wood, pigments
54.6 × 27.9 cm
The Netherlands, private collection (cat. 14)

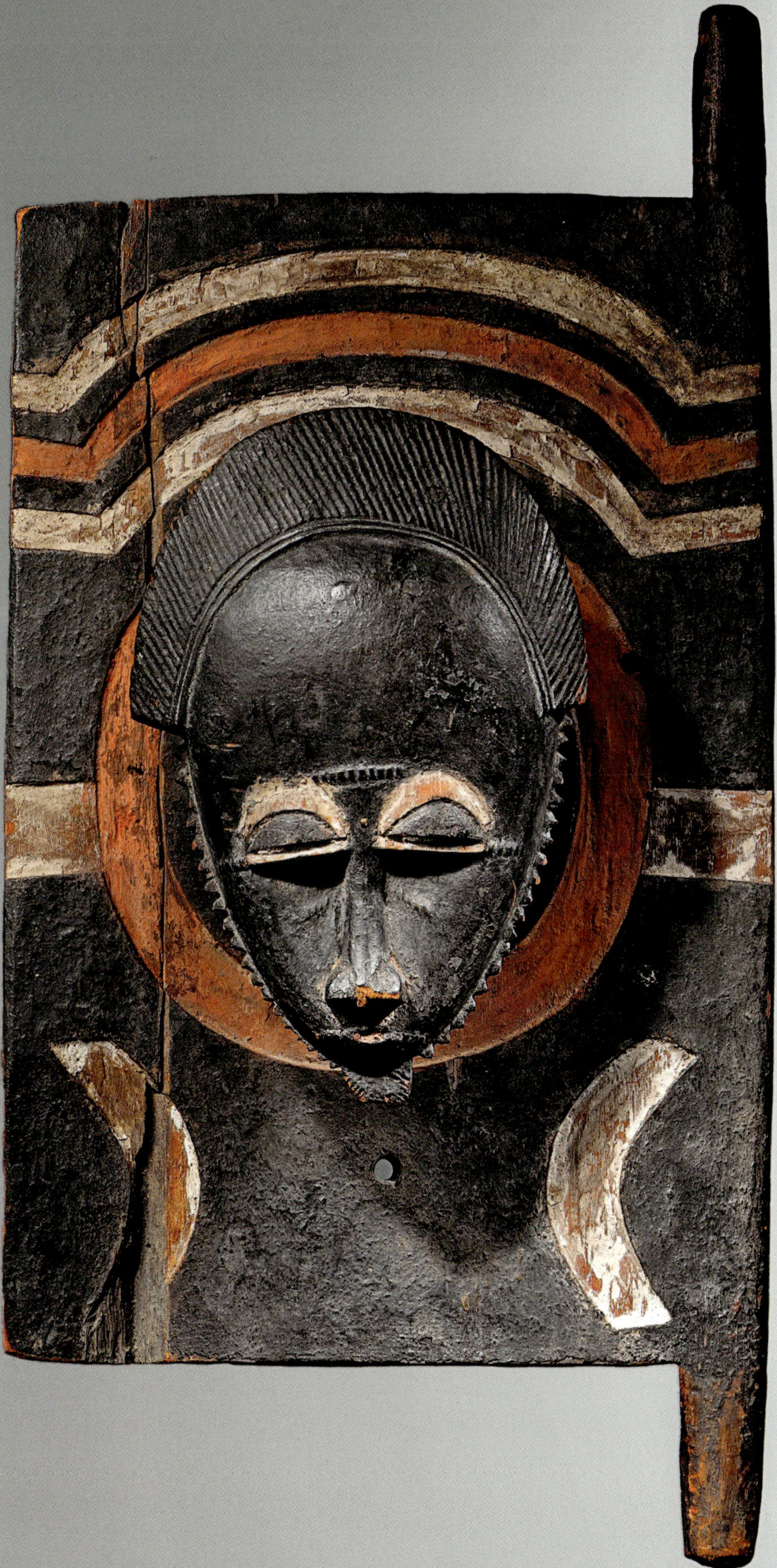

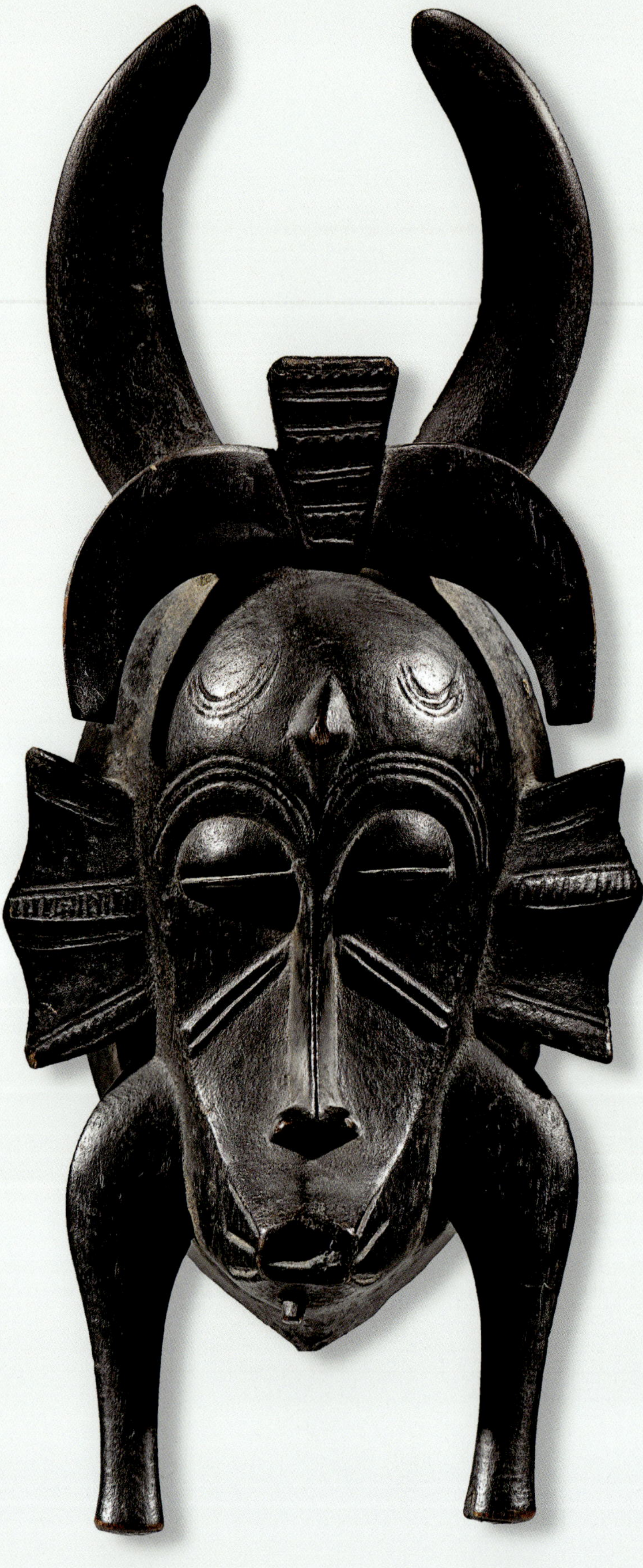

Ill. 79 [lot 108]

Face mask
Senufo, Ivory Coast,
Korhogo region
19th–early 20th cent.
Wood
37.5 × 17 × 8.8 cm
France, Private collection
(cat. 18)

Ill. 80 [lot 35*]

Gu Female mask
Guro, Ivory Coast
19th cent.
Wood
49 × 15 × 16 cm
Paris, Marceau Rivière
collection (cat. 19)

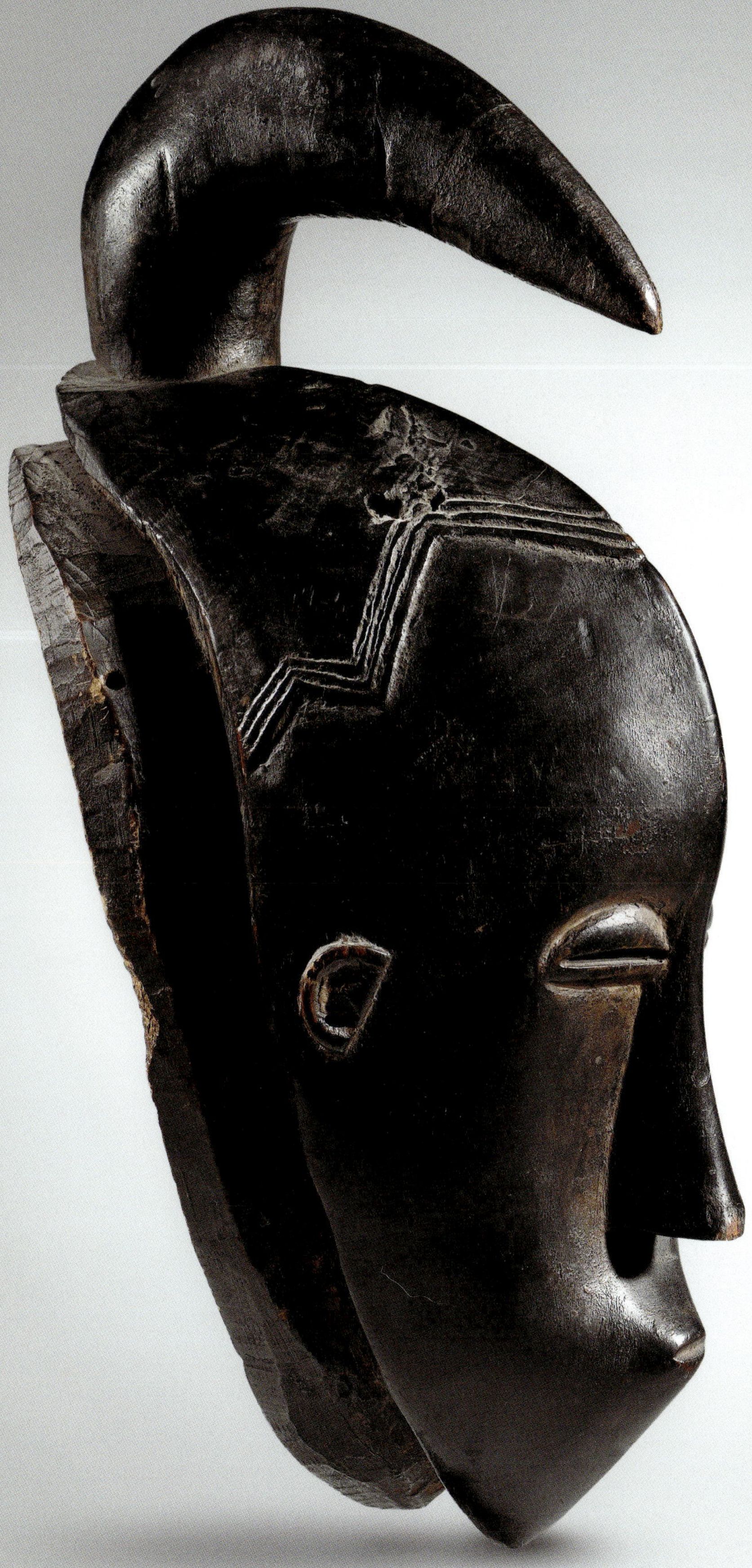

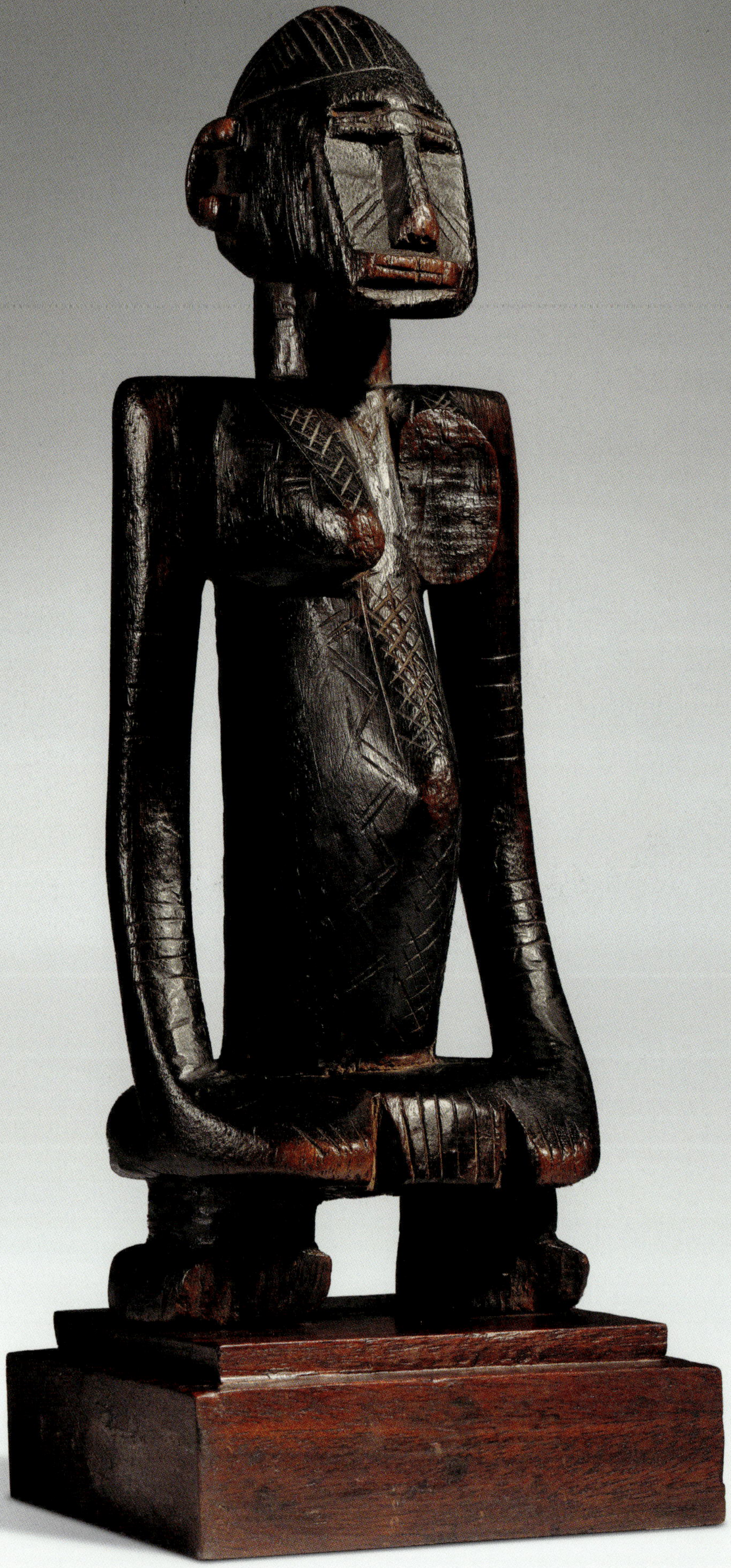

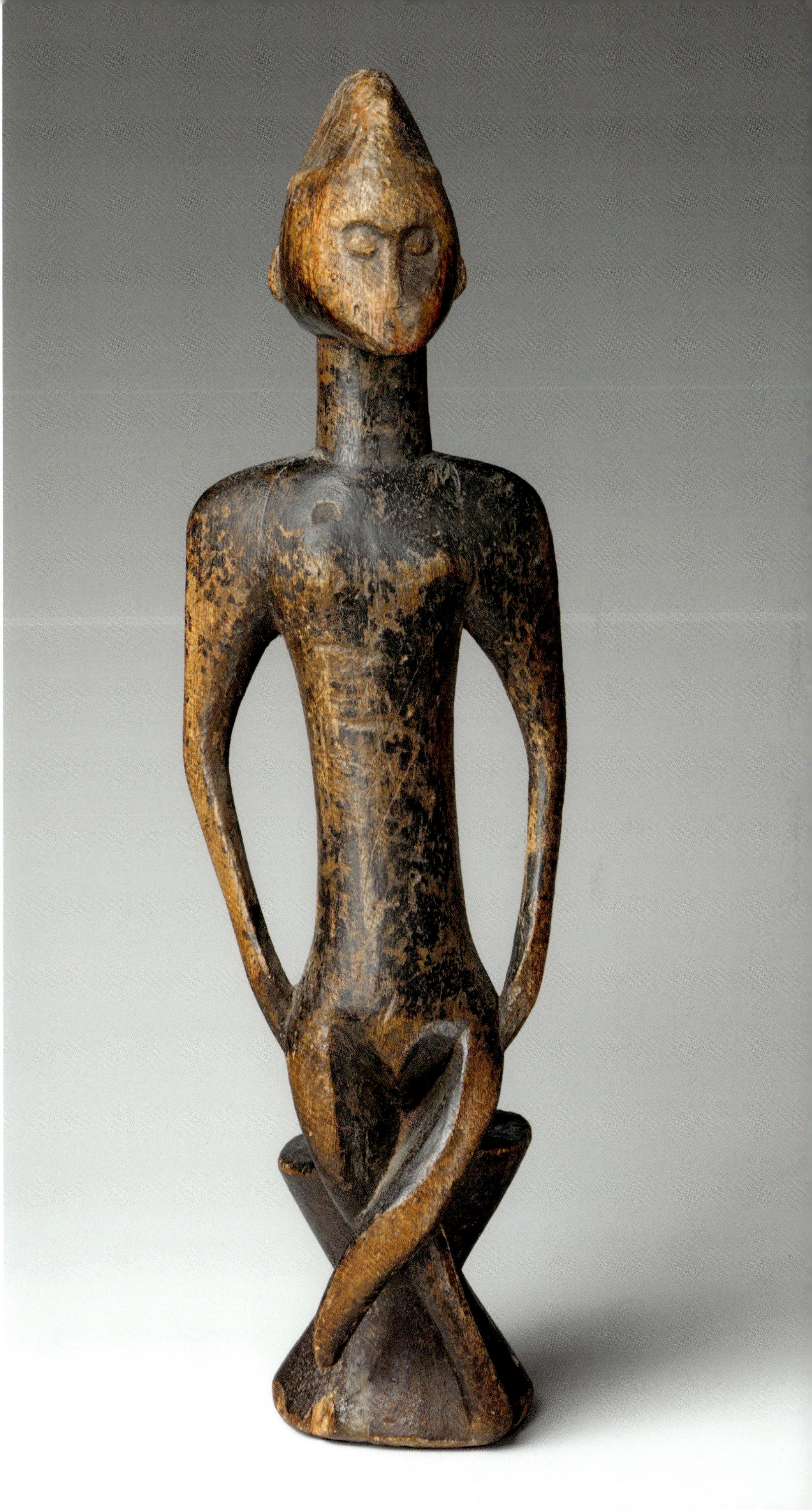

ILL. 81 [LOT 98]

Female figure
Senufo/Turka/Bobo (?)
Mali/Ivory Coast,
Sikasso region
19th–early 20th cent.
Wood
27.5 × 20 × 15 cm
Private collection (cat. 17)

ILL. 82 [LOT 134]

Seated female figure
Senufo/Bamana (?), Mali,
Folona region
19th–early 20th cent.
Wood
31.8 × 8.9 × 7 cm
New York, Metropolitan
Museum of Art (cat. 20)

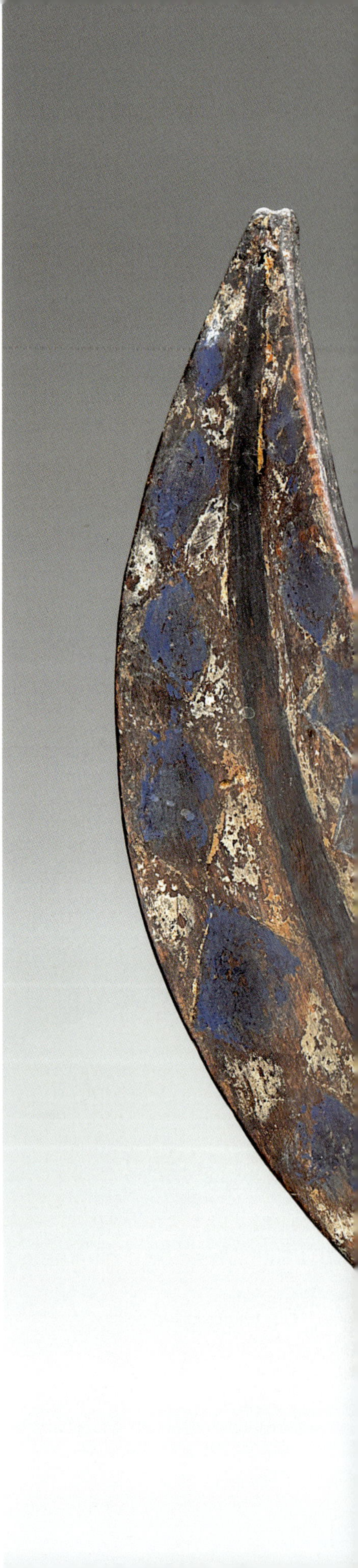

Ill. 83 [lot 135]

Helmet mask
Senufo/Bamana (?), Mali, Sikasso region
19th–early 20th cent.
Wood, metal, pigments
52 × 44.5 × 25.4 cm
Newark, Newark Museum
(cat. 21)

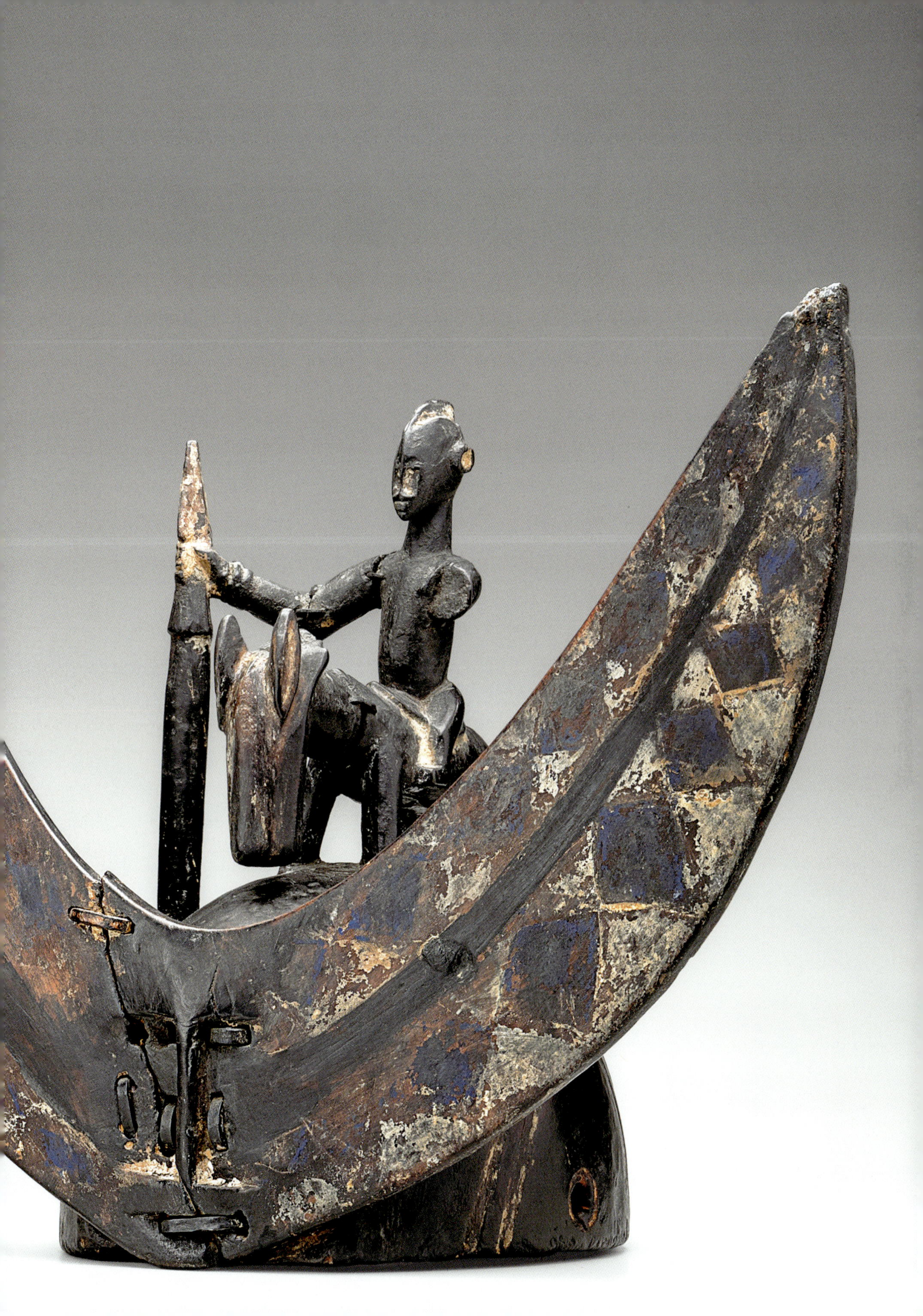

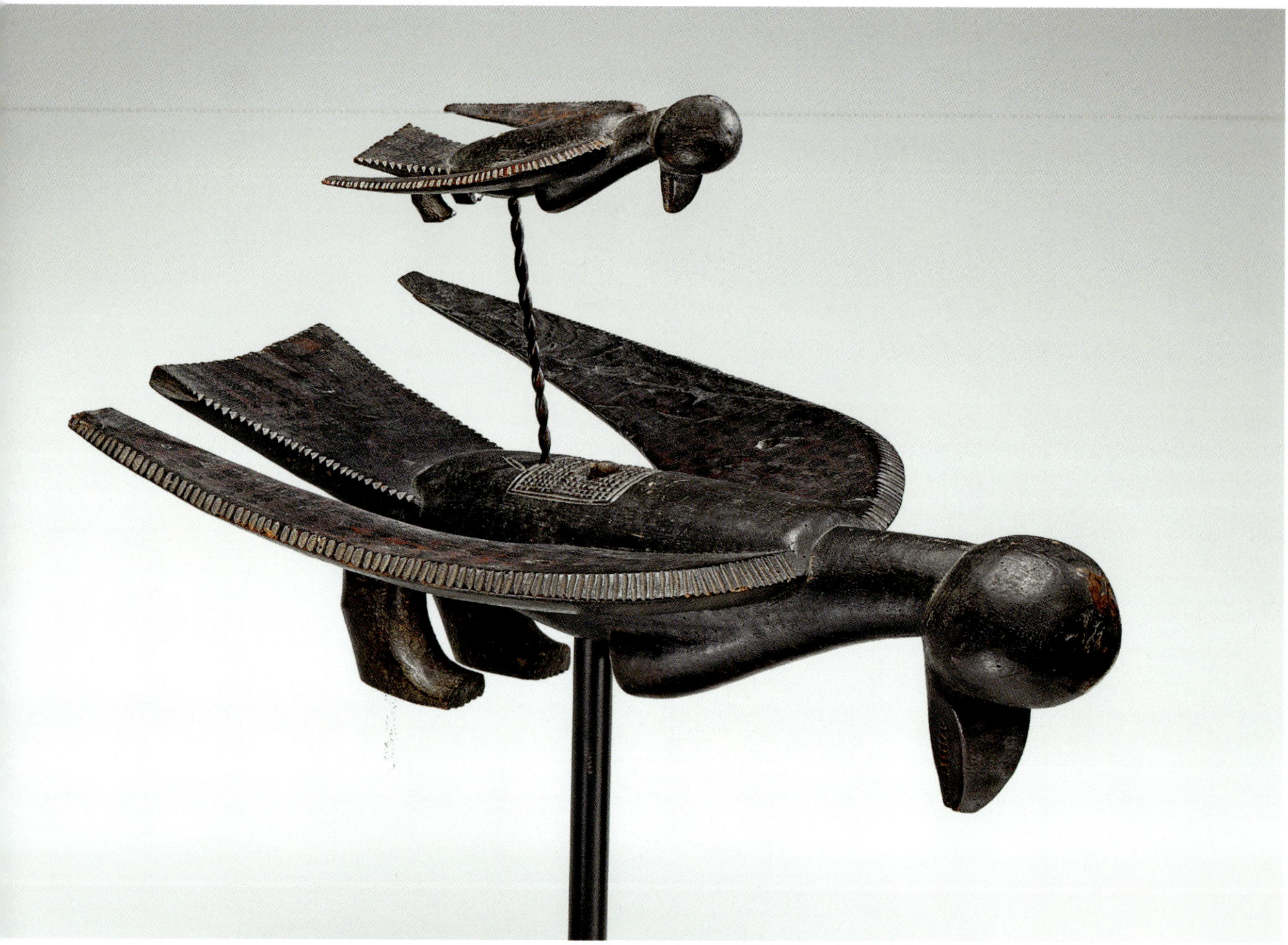

ILL. 84 [LOT 96]

Tefala sejen farmer's staff finial
Senufo, Burkina Faso, Fourou region
1900–35
Wood, metal
27 × 47 cm
Newark, Newark Museum (cat. 22)

ILL. 85 [LOT 100]

Tefalipitya farmer's staff
Senufo, Ivory Coast, Korhogo region
19th cent.
Wood
138.4 × 7 × 7.6 cm
New York, Private collection (cat. 23)

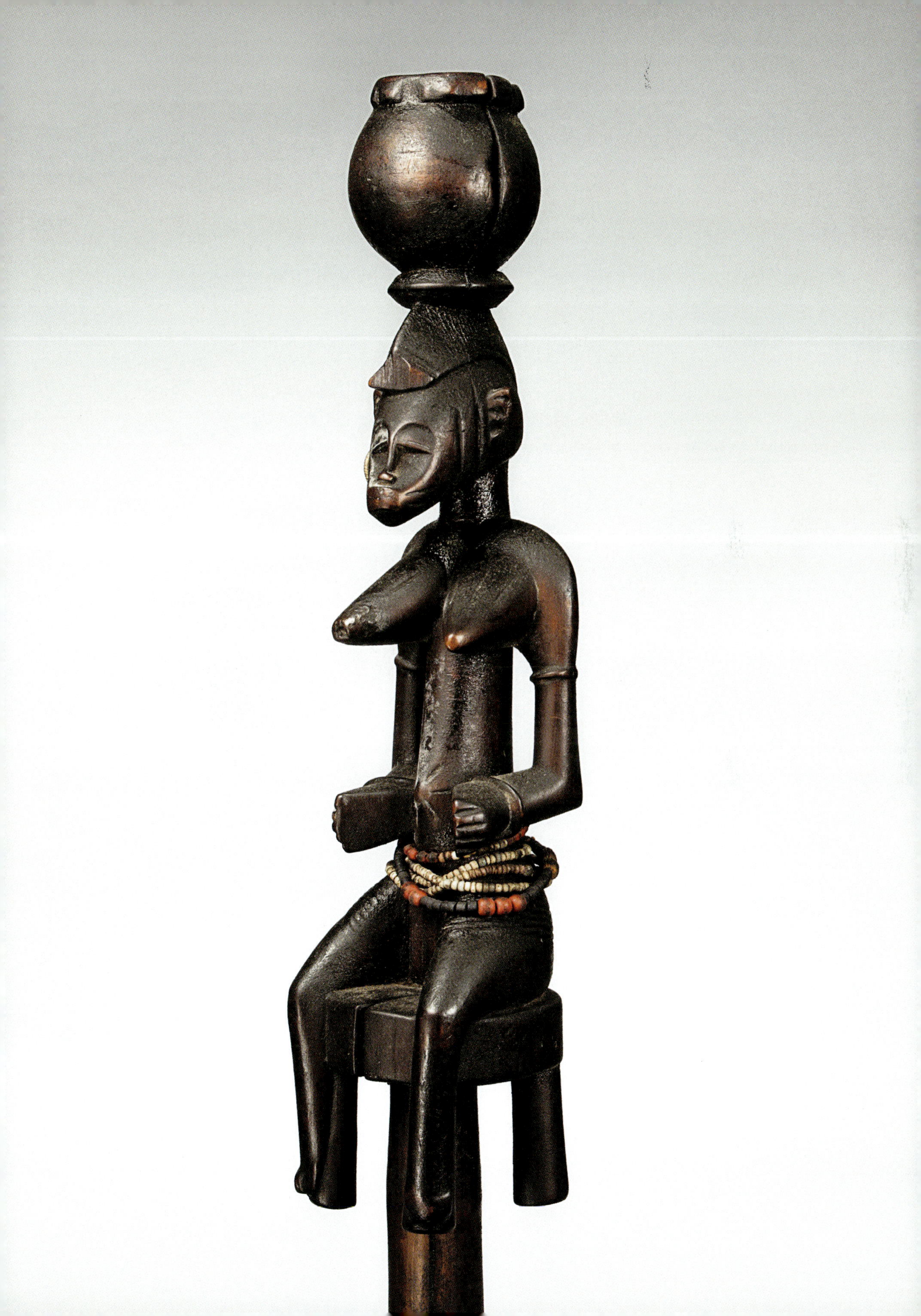

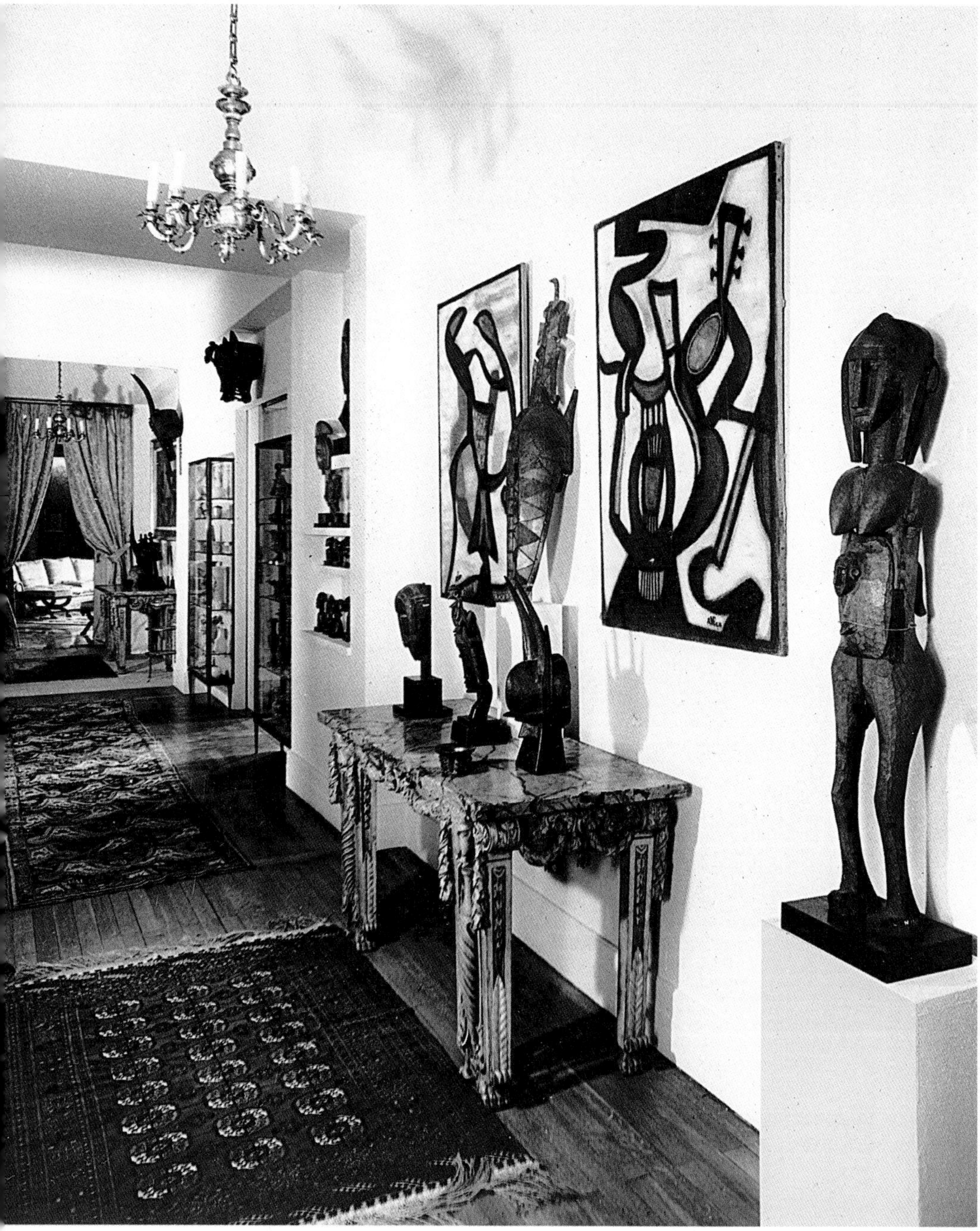

ILL. 86

The hall
at 24, Quai de Béthune,
decorated with African
artifacts, Paris,
c. 1940–60

ILL. 87 [LOT 55]

Anthropo-zoomorphic initiation mask
Bamana, Mali,
Koulikoro region (?)
19th cent.
Wood, metal plates
28 × 20 × 5 cm
Private collection (cat. 24)

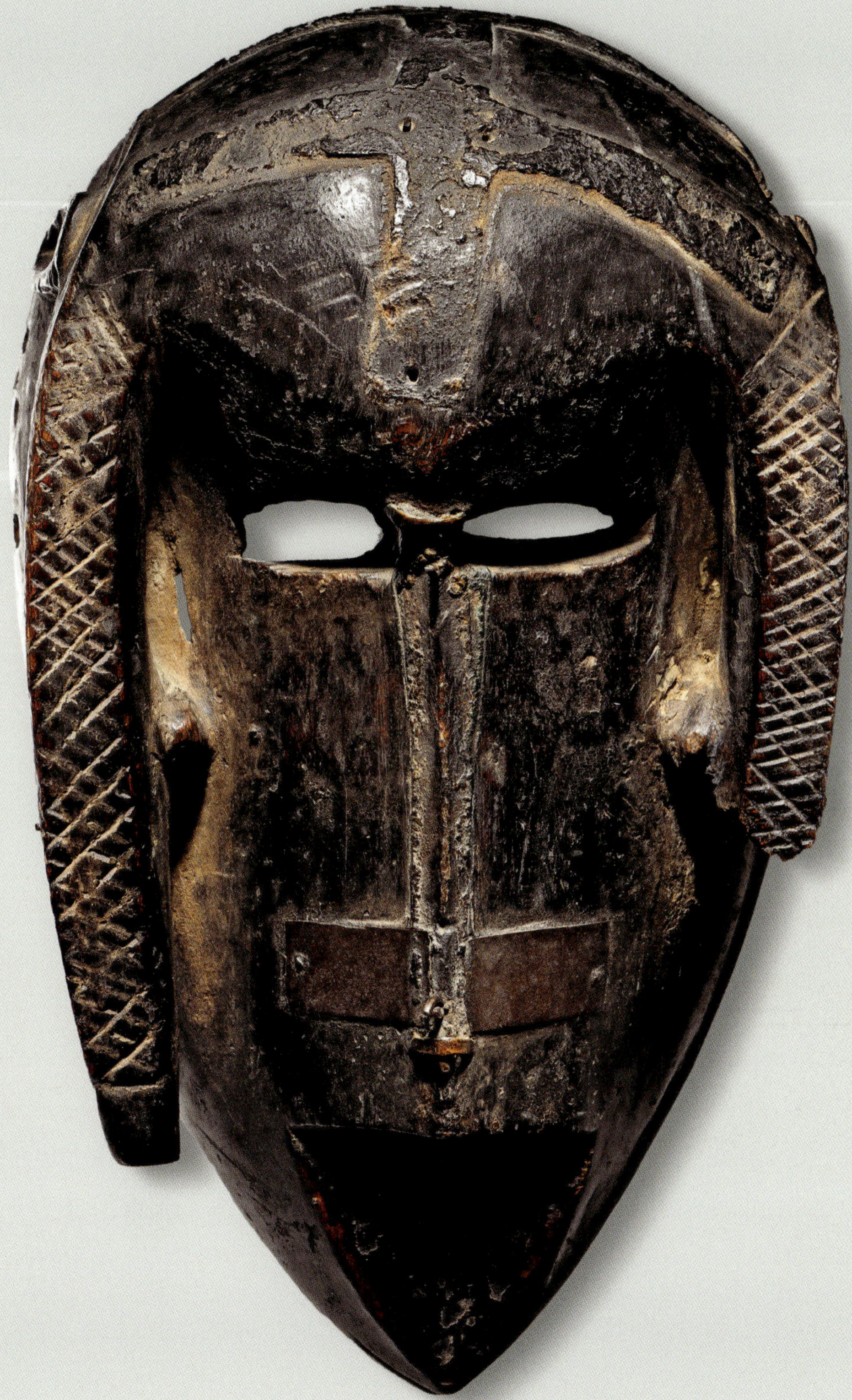

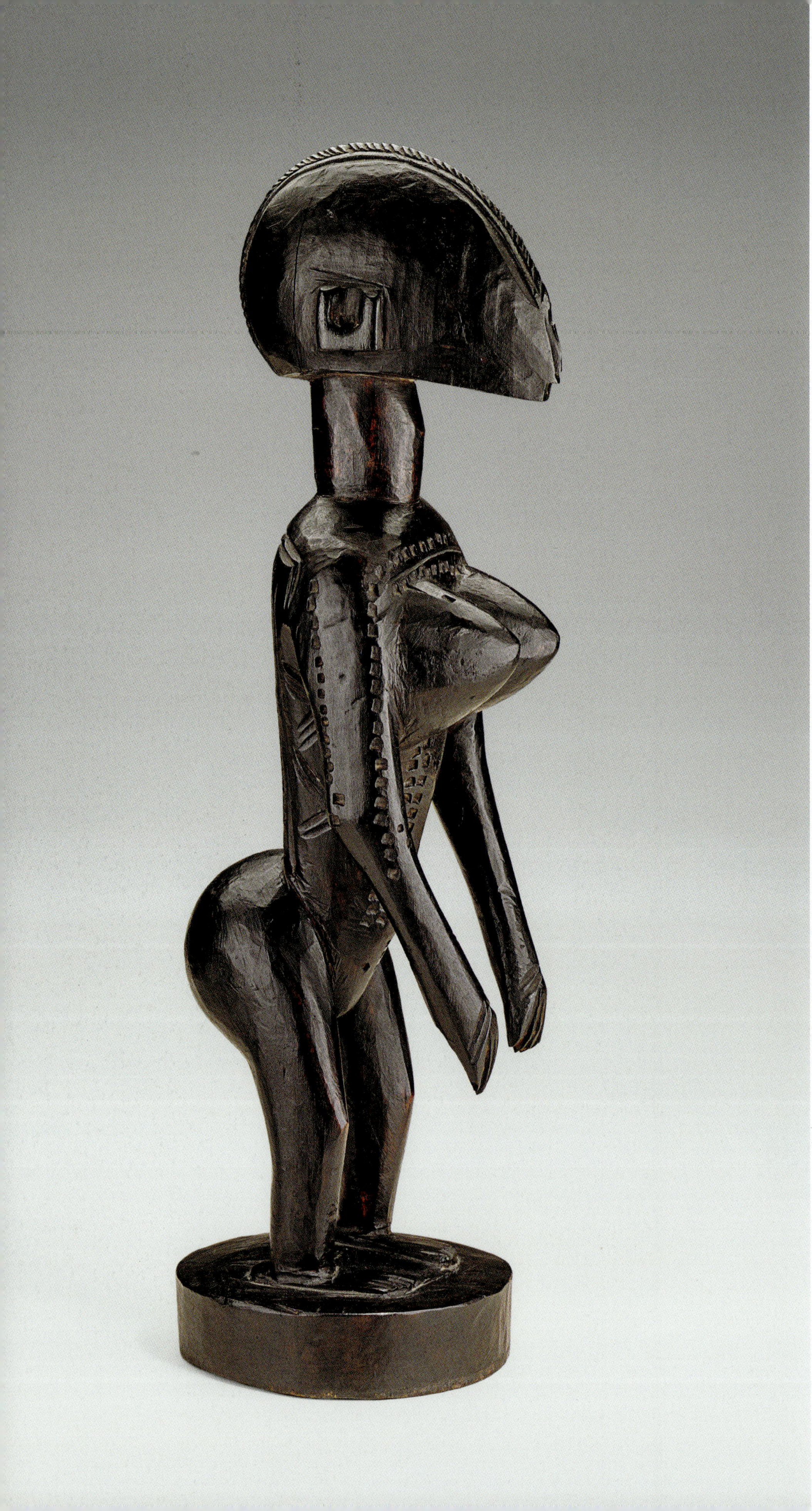

Ill. 88 [lot 62]

Nyeleni female figure
Bamana, Mali
19th–early 20th cent.
Wood
40.4 × 11.8 × 12.5 cm
Washington D.C., National Museum of African Art – Smithsonian Institution
(cat. 26)

Ill. 89 [lot 58]

Nyeleni female figure
Bamana, Mali,
Sikasso region
19th–early 20th cent.
Wood
42 × 13.5 × 14 cm
Célestin Clamra collection
(cat. 25)

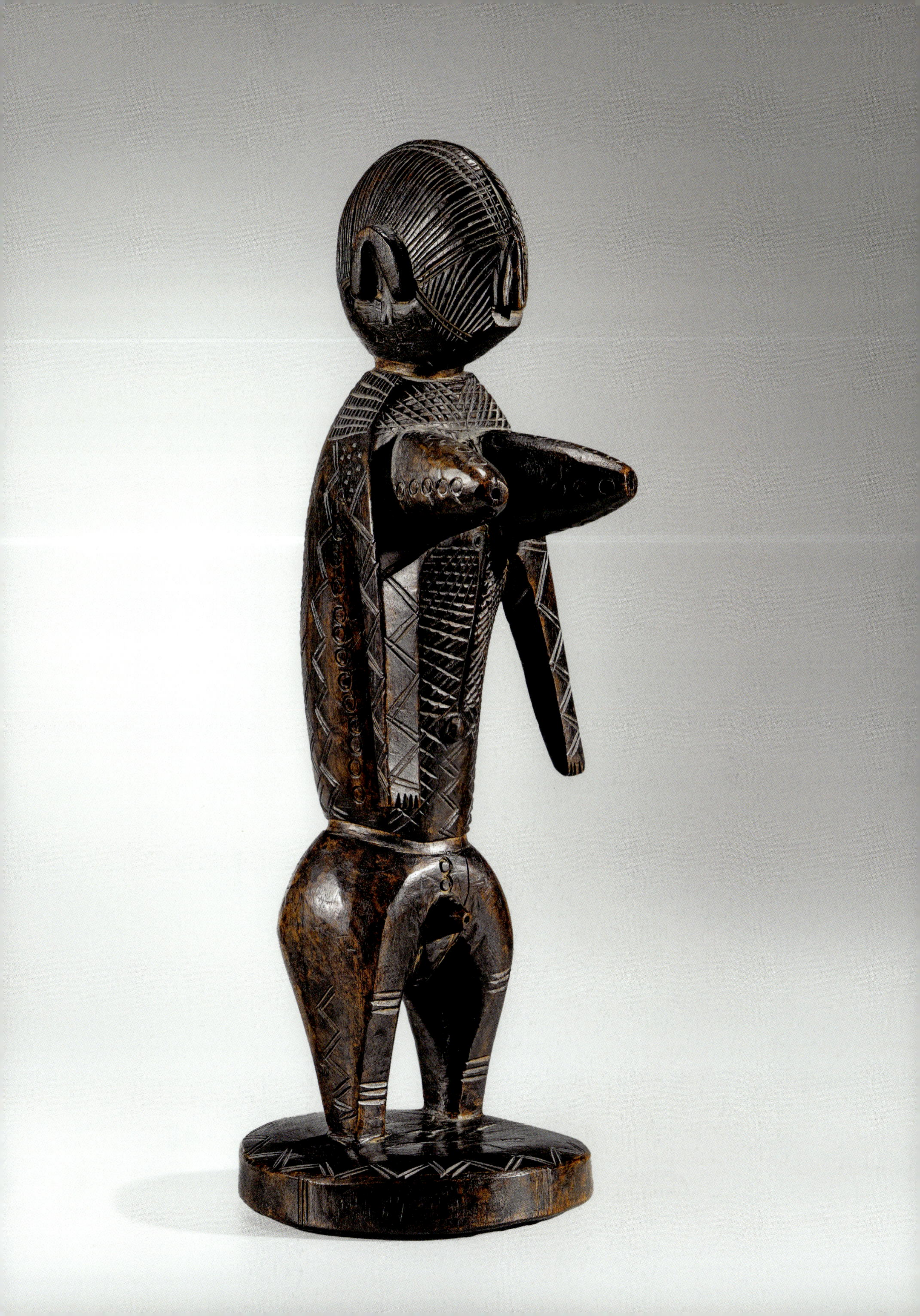

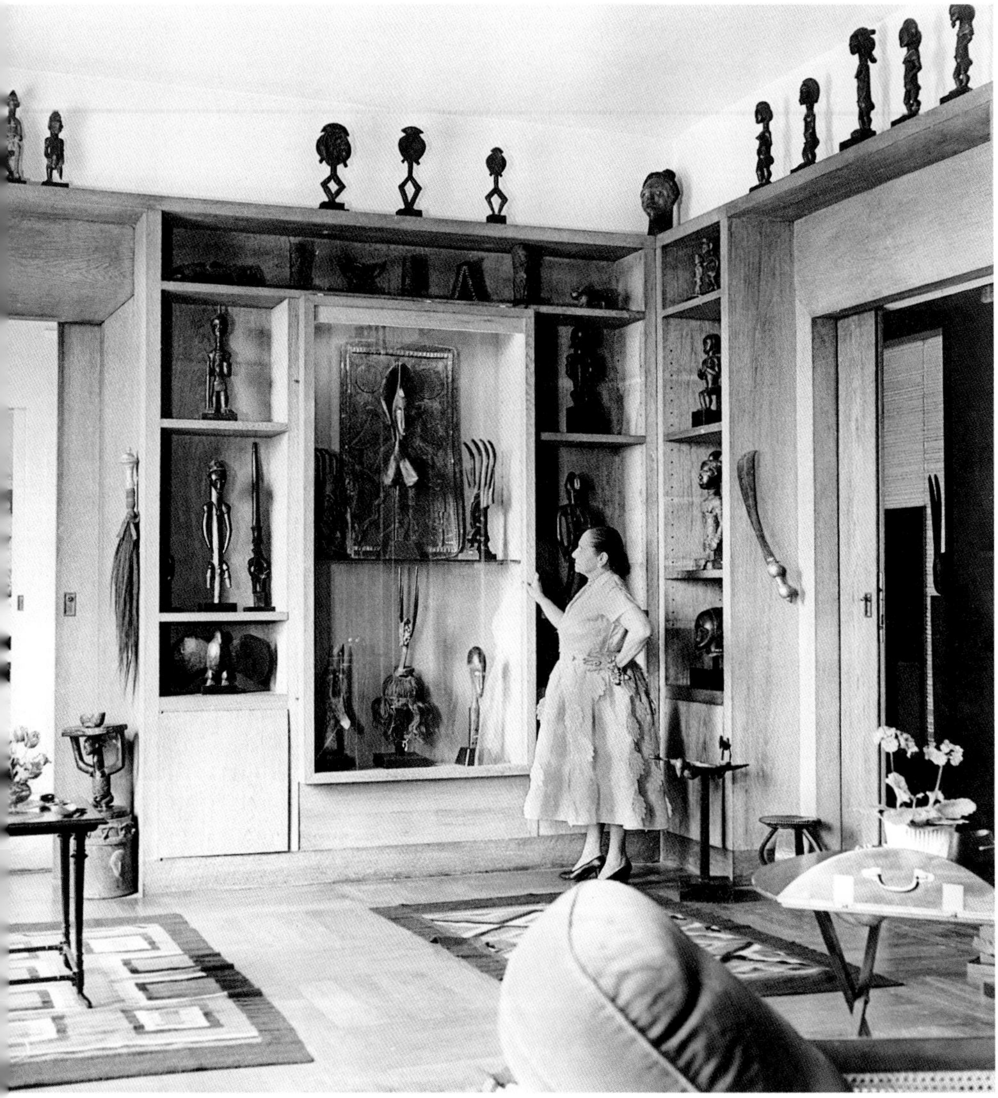

ILL. 90

Helena Rubinstein
in the African room,
24, Quai de Béthune,
Paris, 1951

ILL. 91 [LOT 66]

Sogo bo female
marionette
Bamana, Mali,
Koutiala region
19th–early 20th cent.
Wood, cowries, pigments
H. 80 cm
Tenafly, Malcolm
collection (cat. 27)

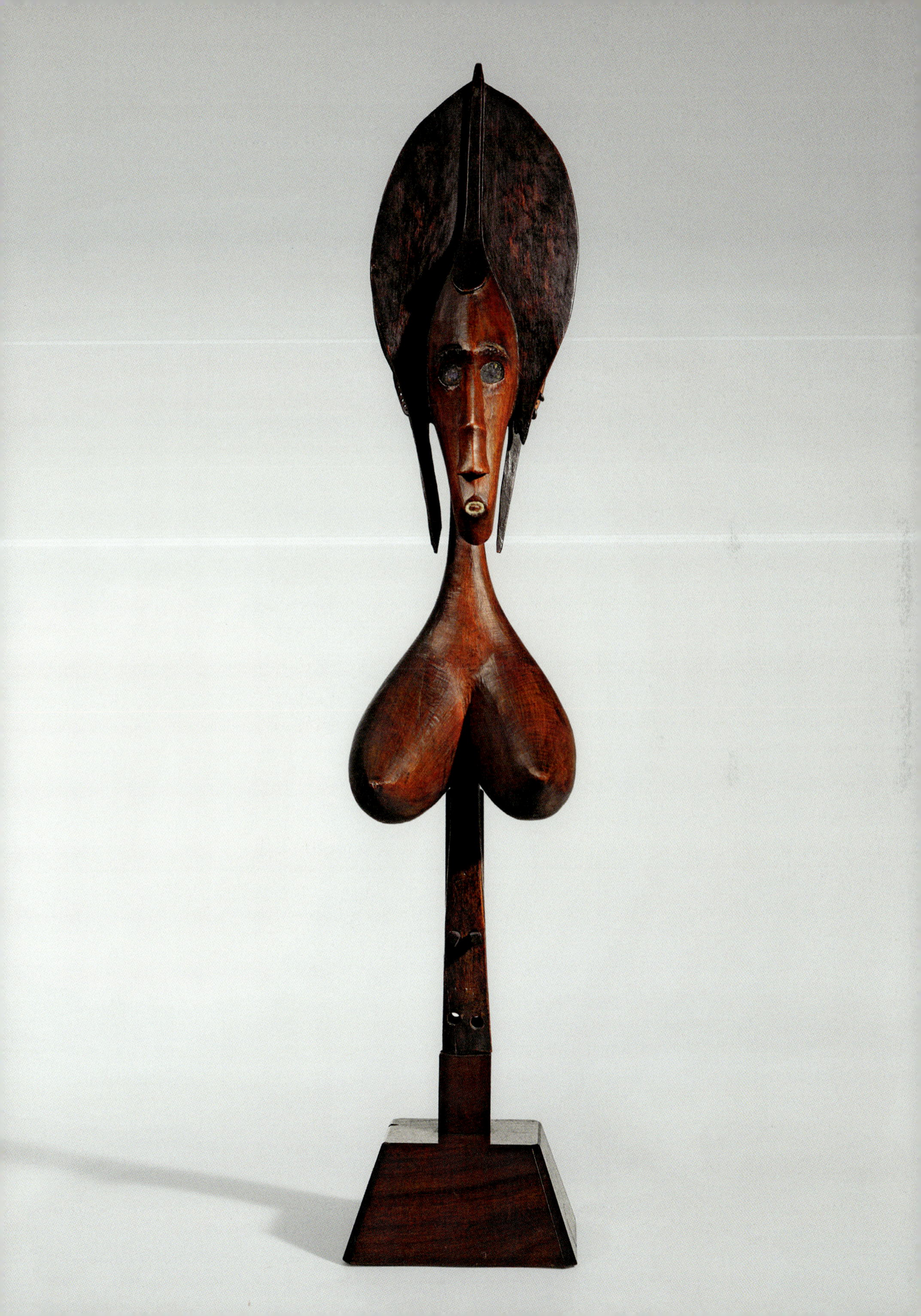

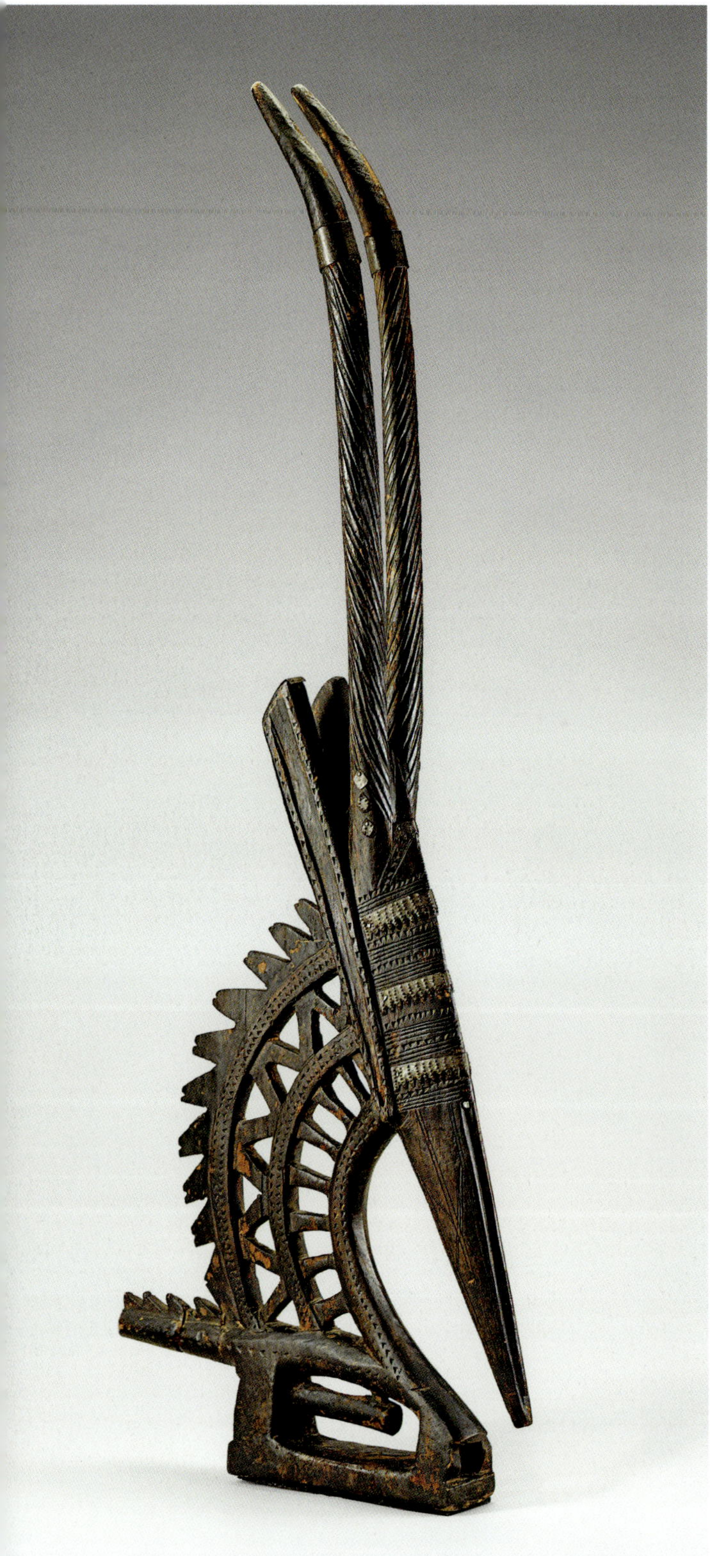

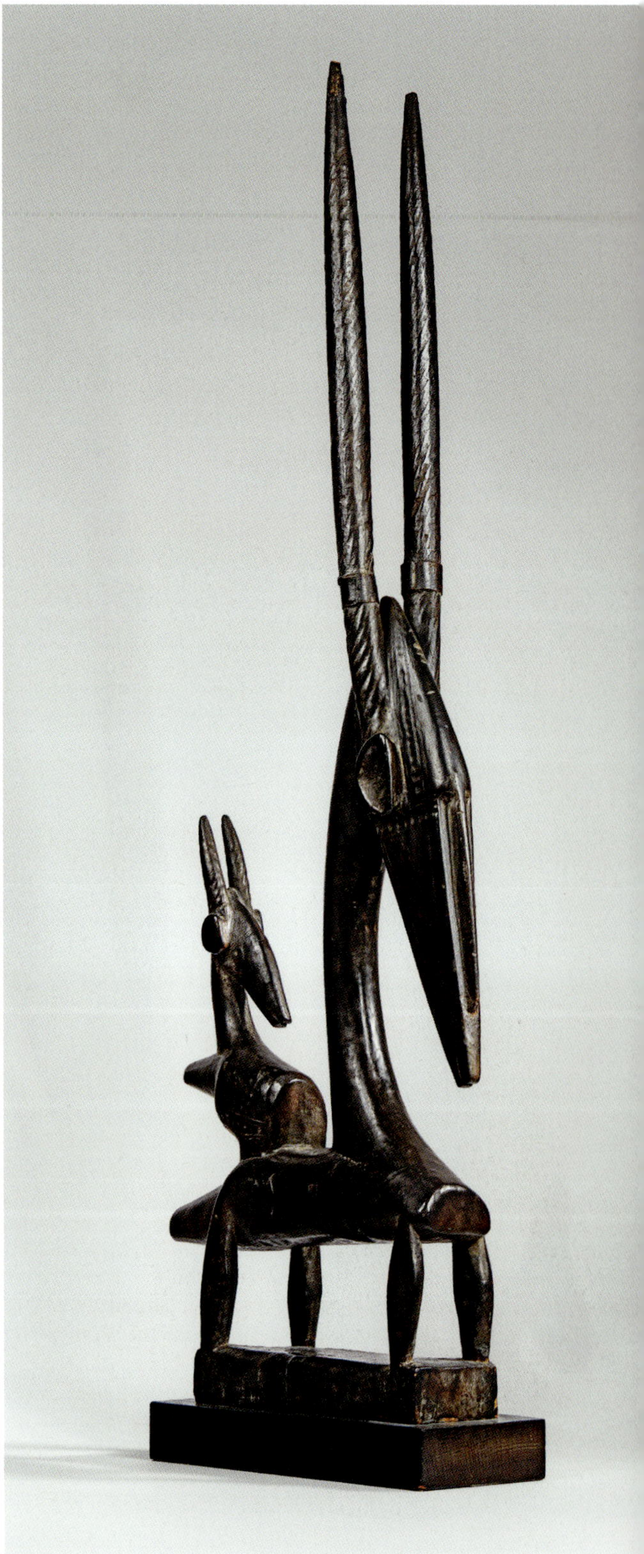

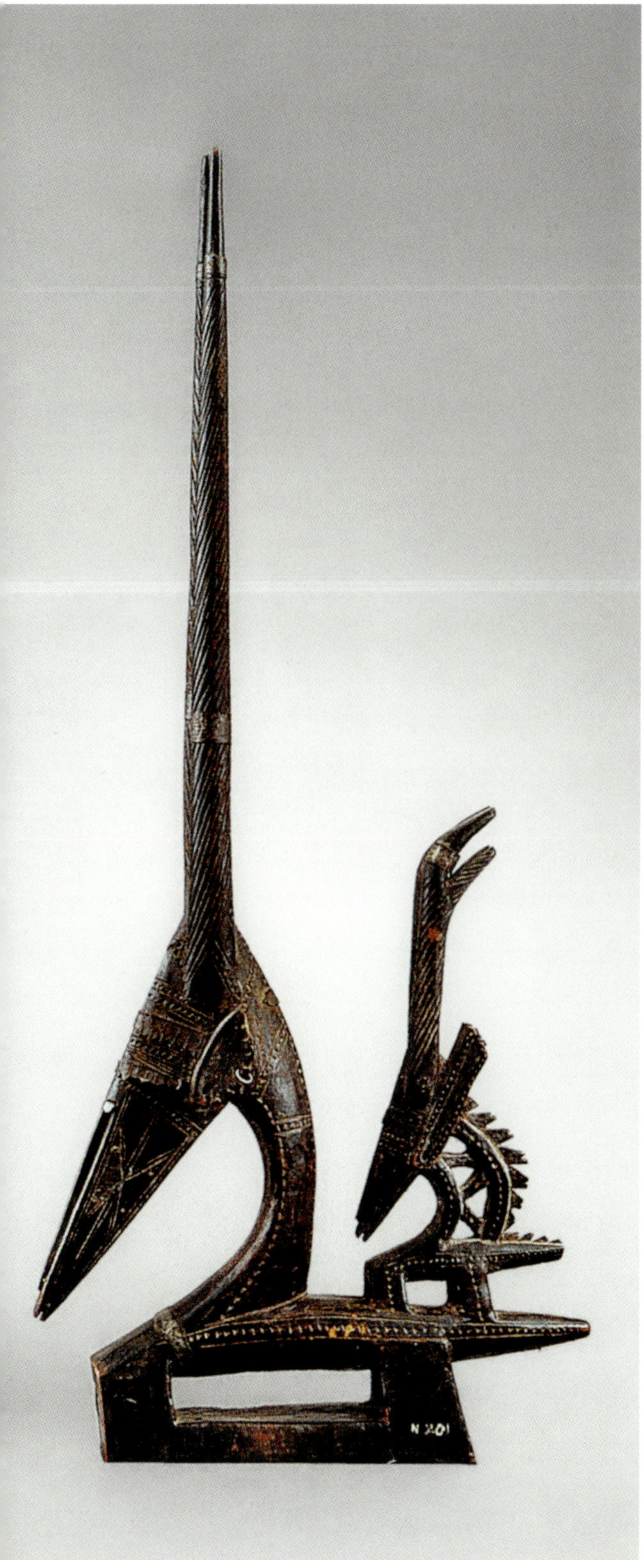
N.201

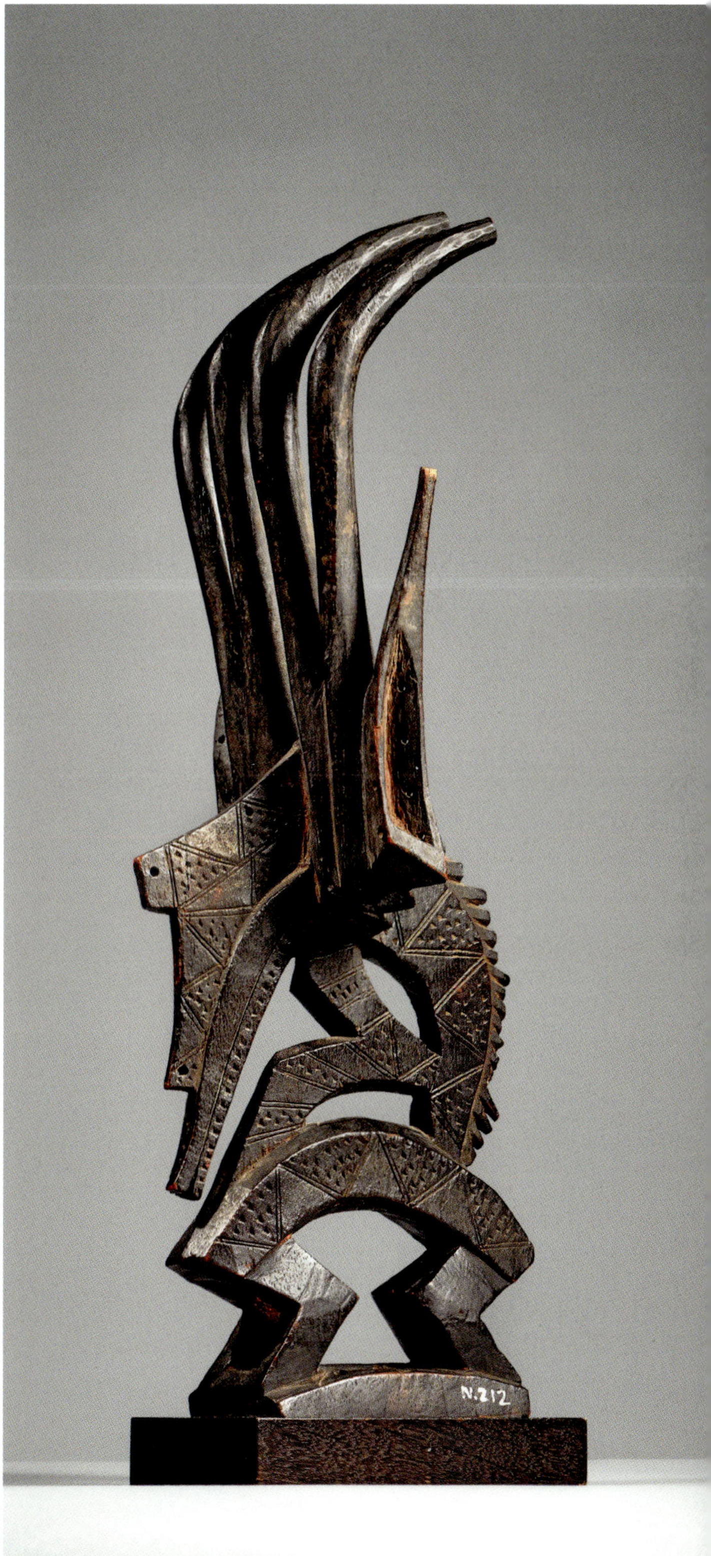
N.212

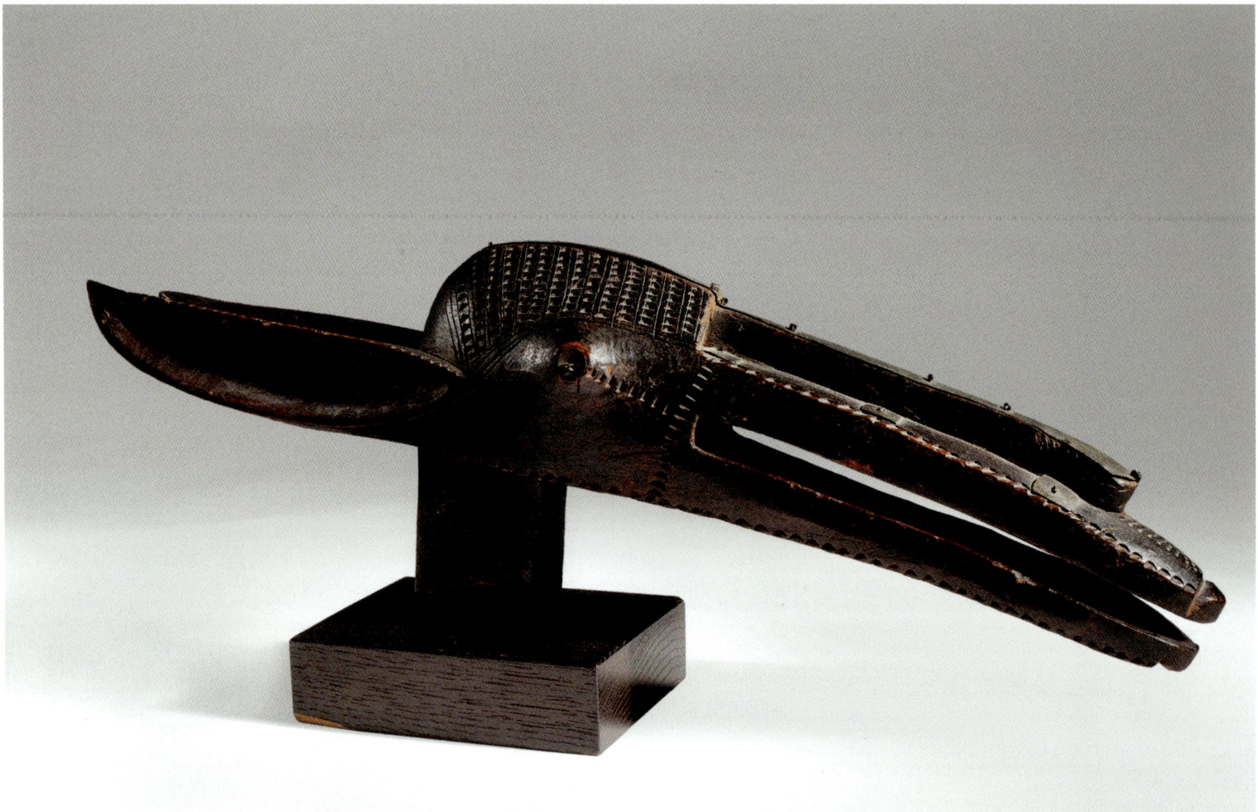

Previous pages
ILL. 92 [LOT 68]

Male *ciwara* crest (antelope)
Bamana, Mali,
Minianka region
19th–early 20th cent.
Wood, metal
93.3 × 7.5 × 35.8 cm
Washington D.C., National Museum of African Art – Smithsonian Institution
(cat. 30)

ILL. 93 [LOT 70]

Female *ciwara* crest (antelope and fawn)
Bamana, Mali,
Ségou region
19th cent.
Wood, metal
H. 78 cm
Paris, Marc Ladreit de Lacharrière collection
(cat. 29)

ILL. 94 [LOT 69]

Female *ciwara* crest (antelope and fawn)
Bamana, Mali,
Ségou region
19th cent.
Wood, metal
71.6 × 30.5 × 6 cm
New York, Laura and James J. Ross collection
(cat. 31)

ILL. 95 [LOT 75]

***Sogoni koun* crest**
Bamana, Mali,
Wassoulou region
19th–early 20th cent.
Wood
H. 54.5 cm
The Arman Marital Trust, Corice Arman Trustee
(cat. 32)

P. 118
ILL. 96 [LOT 83]

Head of zoomorphic marionette
Bamana, Mali, San region
19th–early 20th cent.
Wood
11.6 × 11.4× 48 cm
St. Louis, James C. Jamieson III collection
(cat. 28)

P. 119
ILL. 97 [LOT 38*]

***Ciwara* crest**
Bamana, Mali,
Kenedougou region
19th–early 20th cent.
Wood
53.4 × 8.9 × 9.5 cm
The Jerome Kenney Family Collection
(cat. 33)

ILL. 98 [LOT 40*]

***Ciwara* crest**
Bamana, Mali,
eastern Bamana country
19th–early 20th cent.
Wood
43 × 7.5 × 10.5 cm
Michigan,
Private collection
(cat. 34)

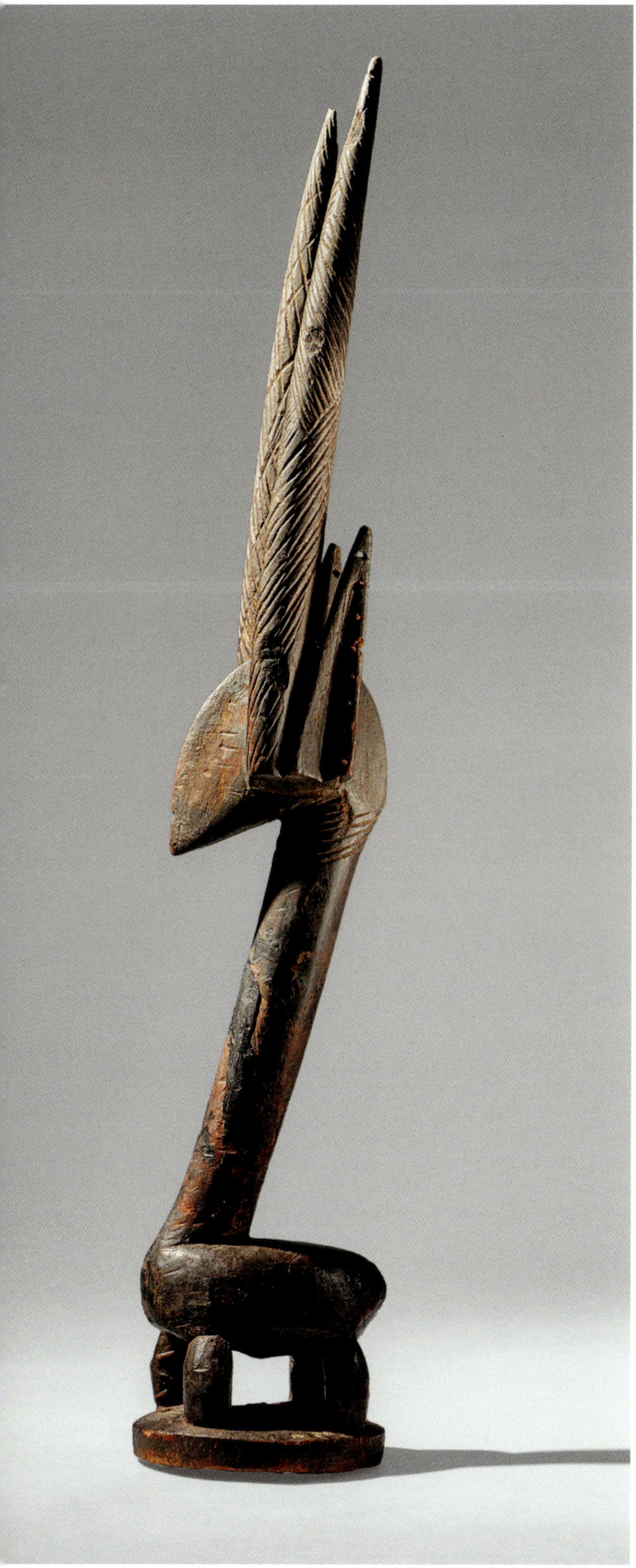

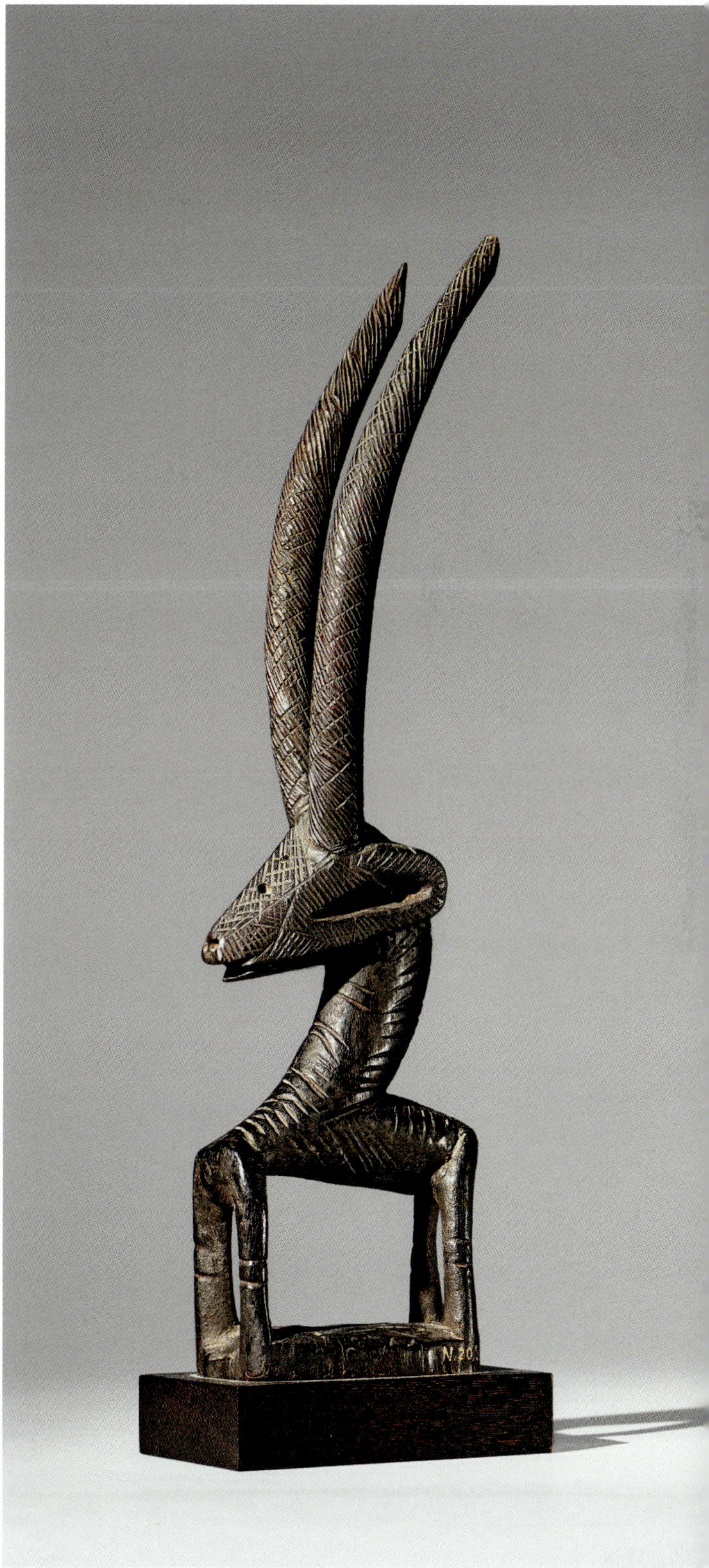

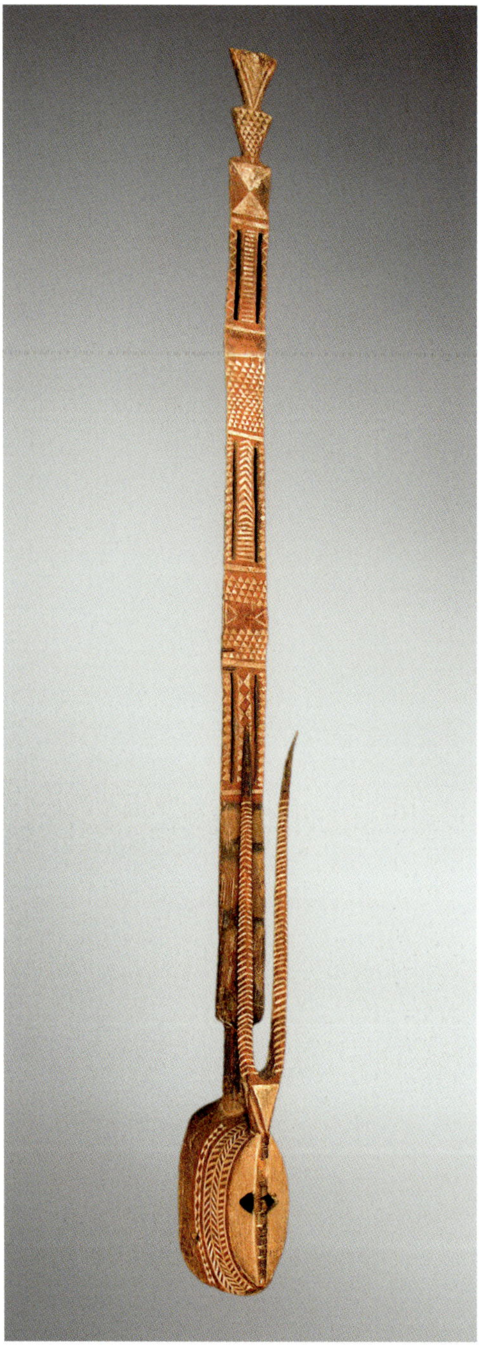

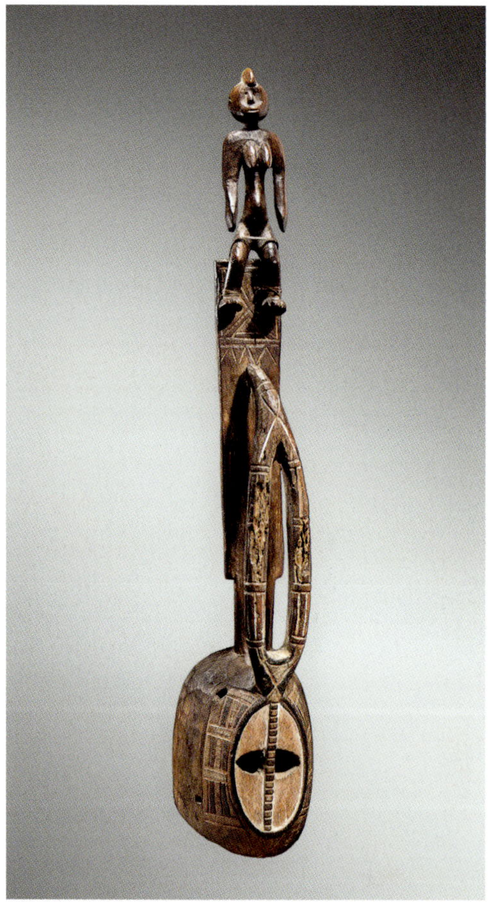

Ill. 99

Karanga mask
Mossi, Burkina Faso,
Yatenga region
Late 19th–early 20th cent.
Wood, pigments
216 × 18.5 × 17.5 cm
Paris, Musée du Quai
Branly – Jacques Chirac
(cat. 36)

Ill. 100 [Lot 88]

Karan wemba dance mask
Mossi, Burkina Faso,
Yatenga region,
Upper Volta
19th cent.
Kapok wood, pigments,
vegetable fibers
117 × 20 × 18 cm
Paris, Private collection
(cat. 35)

Right
Ill. 101

View down the corridor,
24, Quai de Béthune, Paris,
c. 1954–55, colorized
photograph taken from
the album composed
by Jean Vincent (cat. 91)

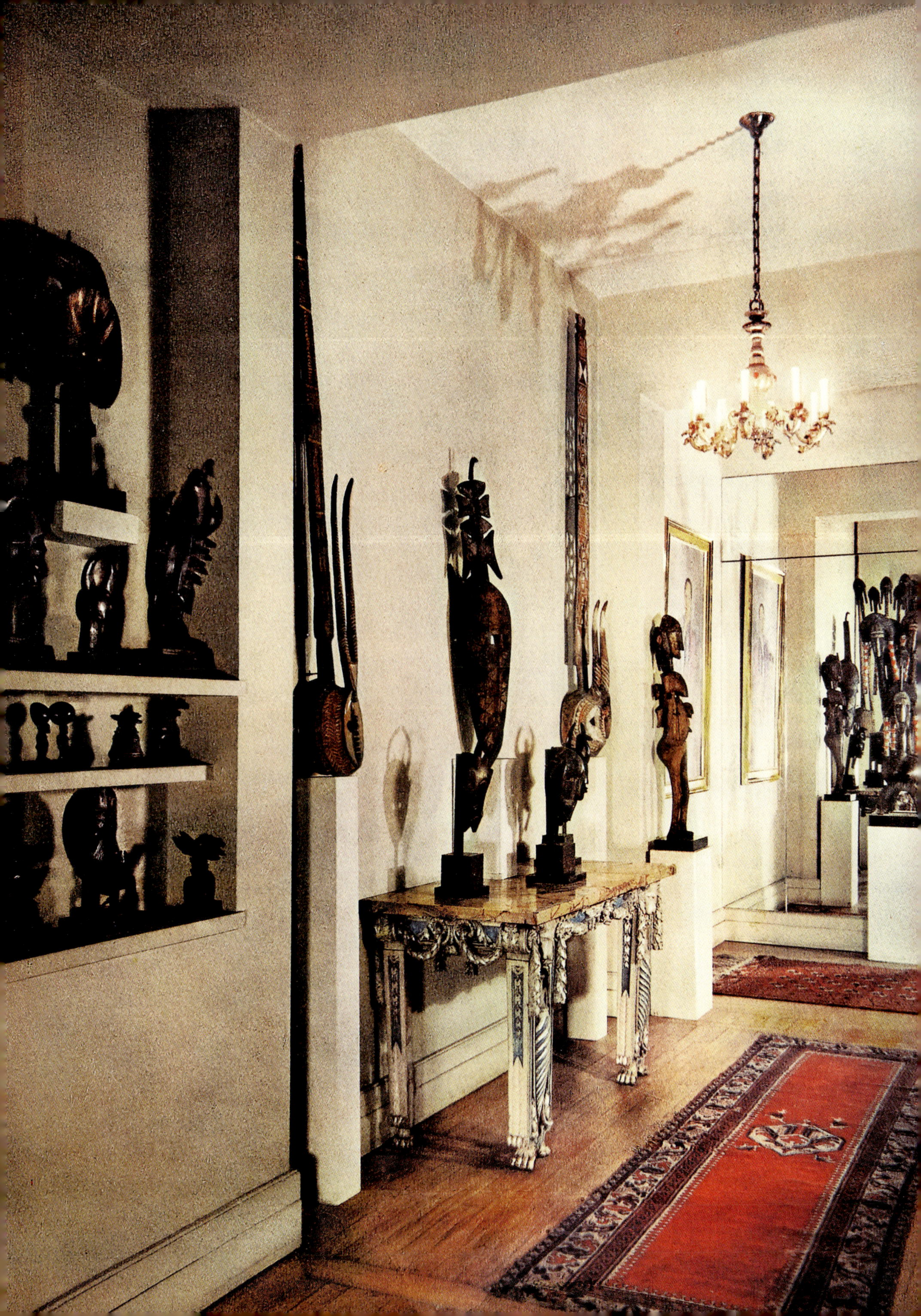

Ill. 102

Female figure
Mossi, Burkina Faso,
Yatenga region
Late 19th–early 20th cent.
Wood
66 × 18.6 × 15.7 cm
Paris, Musée du Quai
Branly – Jacques Chirac
(cat. 37)

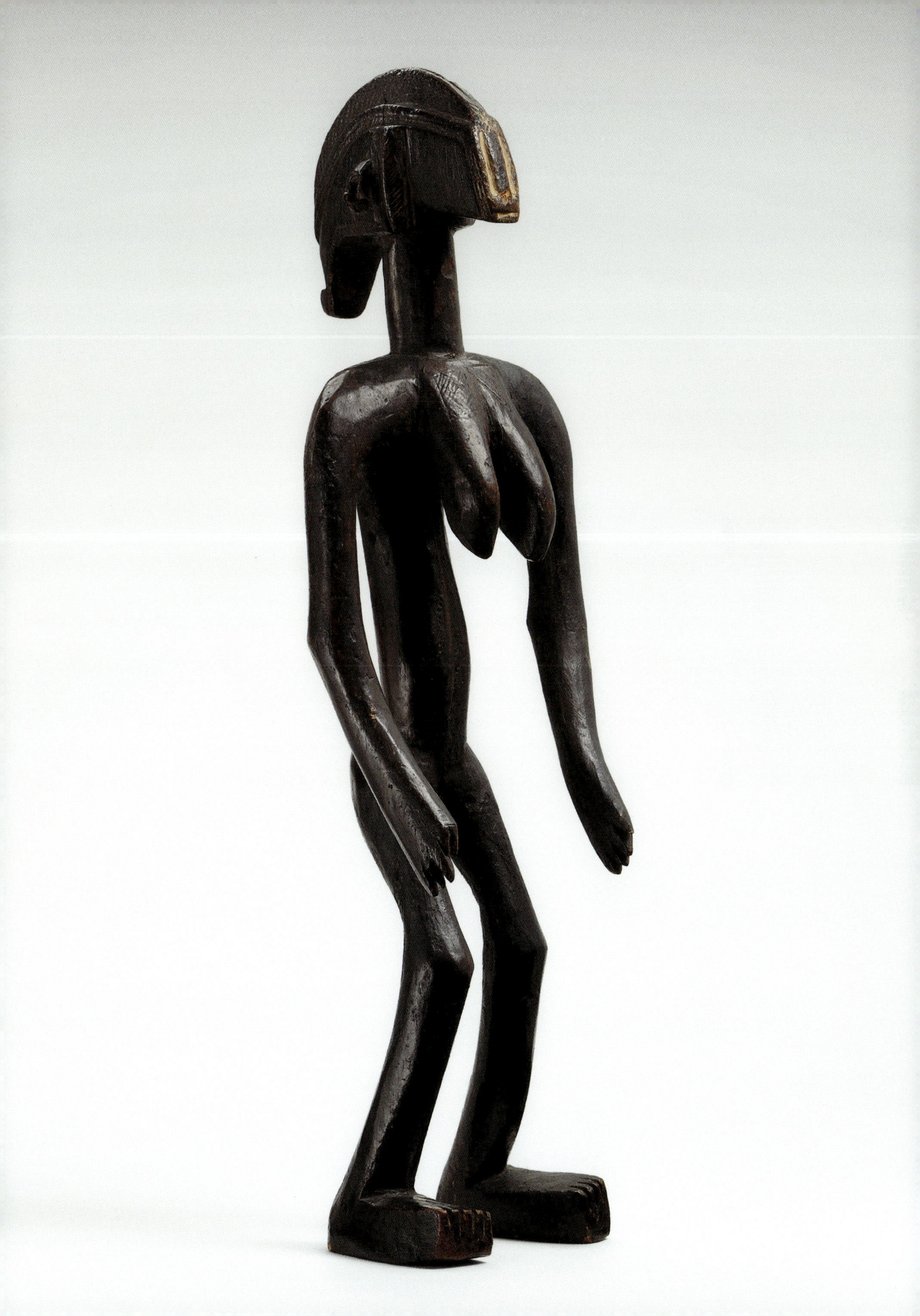

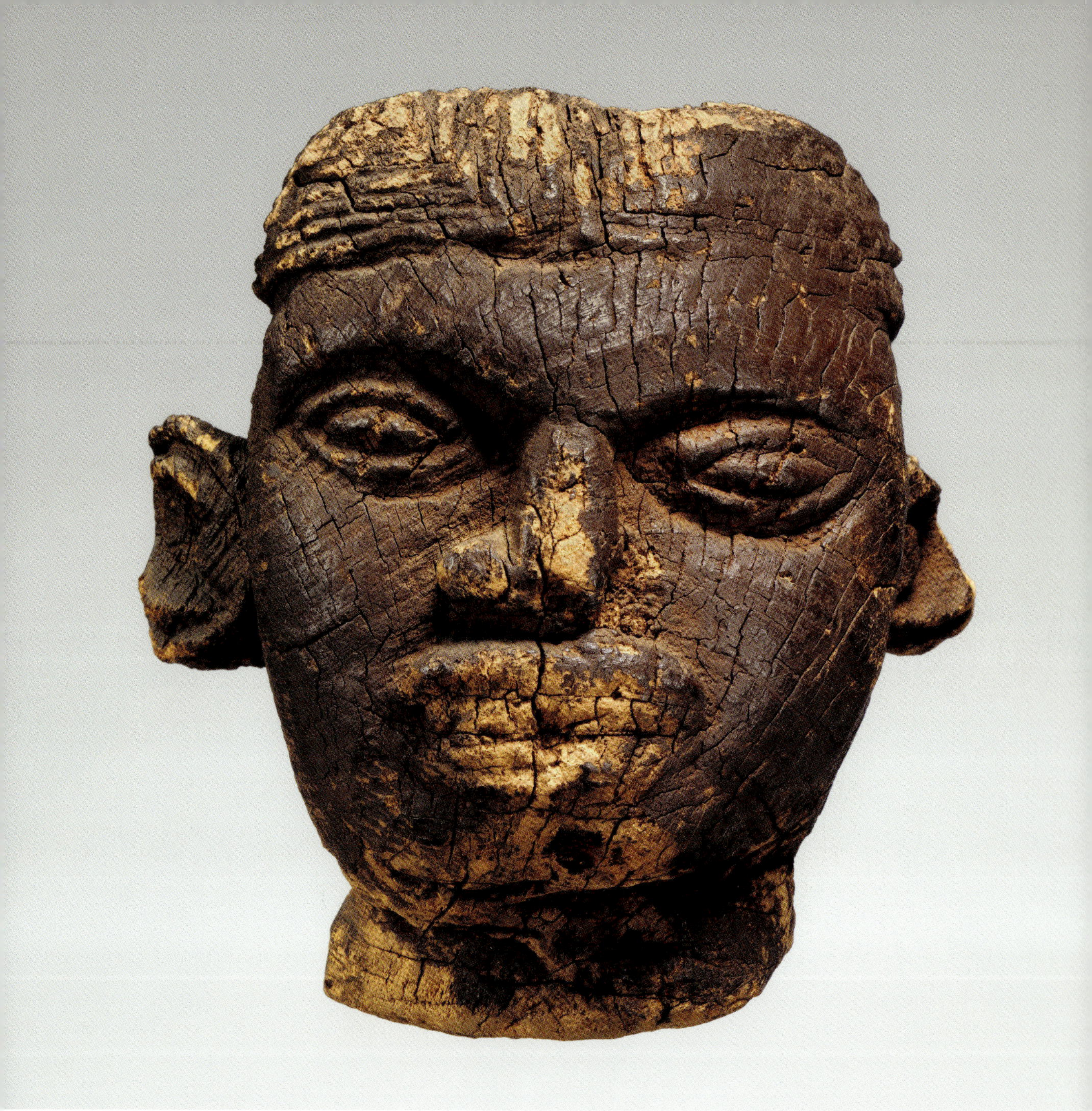

Ill. 103 [lot 186]

Element from figurative drum
Bamileke, Cameroon,
Bansoa kingdom,
treasury of King Foméné
19th cent.
Wood
18.4 × 15.9 × 25.4 cm
New York, Metropolitan
Museum of Art (cat. 41)

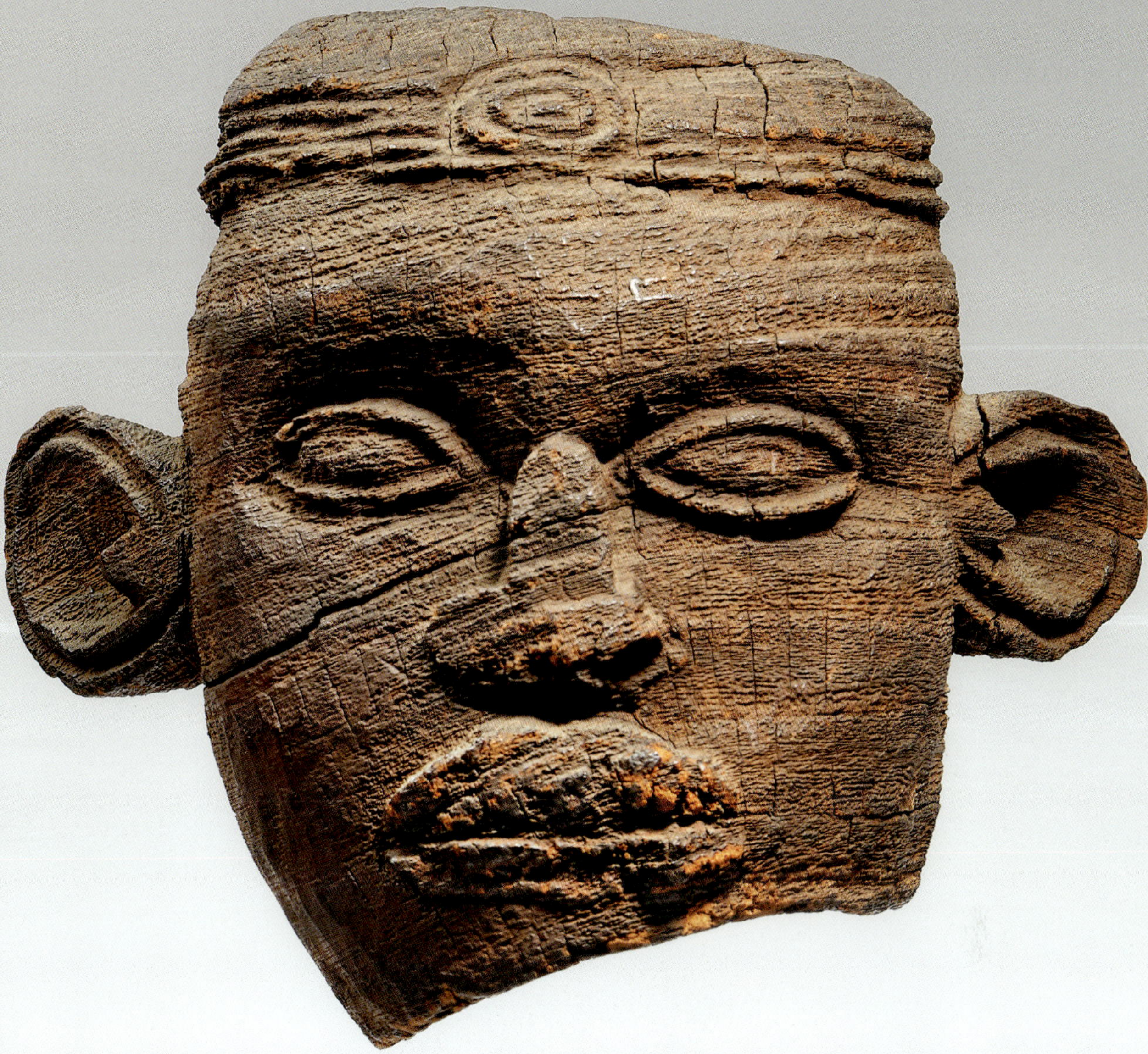

Ill. 104 [lot 187]

Element from figurative drum
Bamileke, Cameroon, Bansoa kingdom, treasury of King Foméné
19th cent.
Wood
20.3 × 21 × 23 cm
Paris, Private collection
(cat. 42)

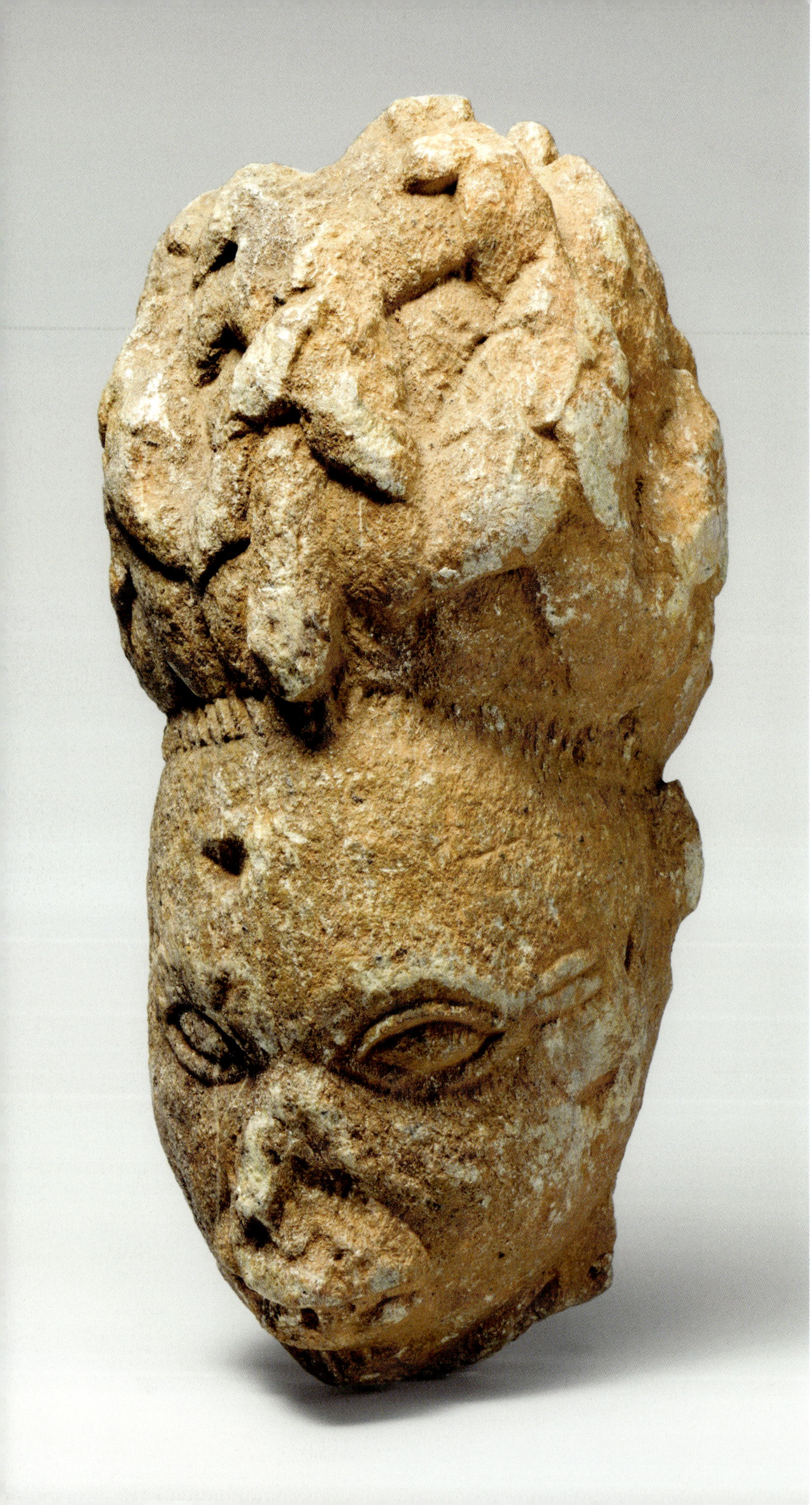

Ill. 105 [lot 175]

Head,
statuary fragment
Yoruba, Nigeria,
Esie region, Offa
12th–15th cent.
Steatite
29.8 × 9.2 × 15.2 cm
New York, Metropolitan
Museum of Art
(cat. 39)

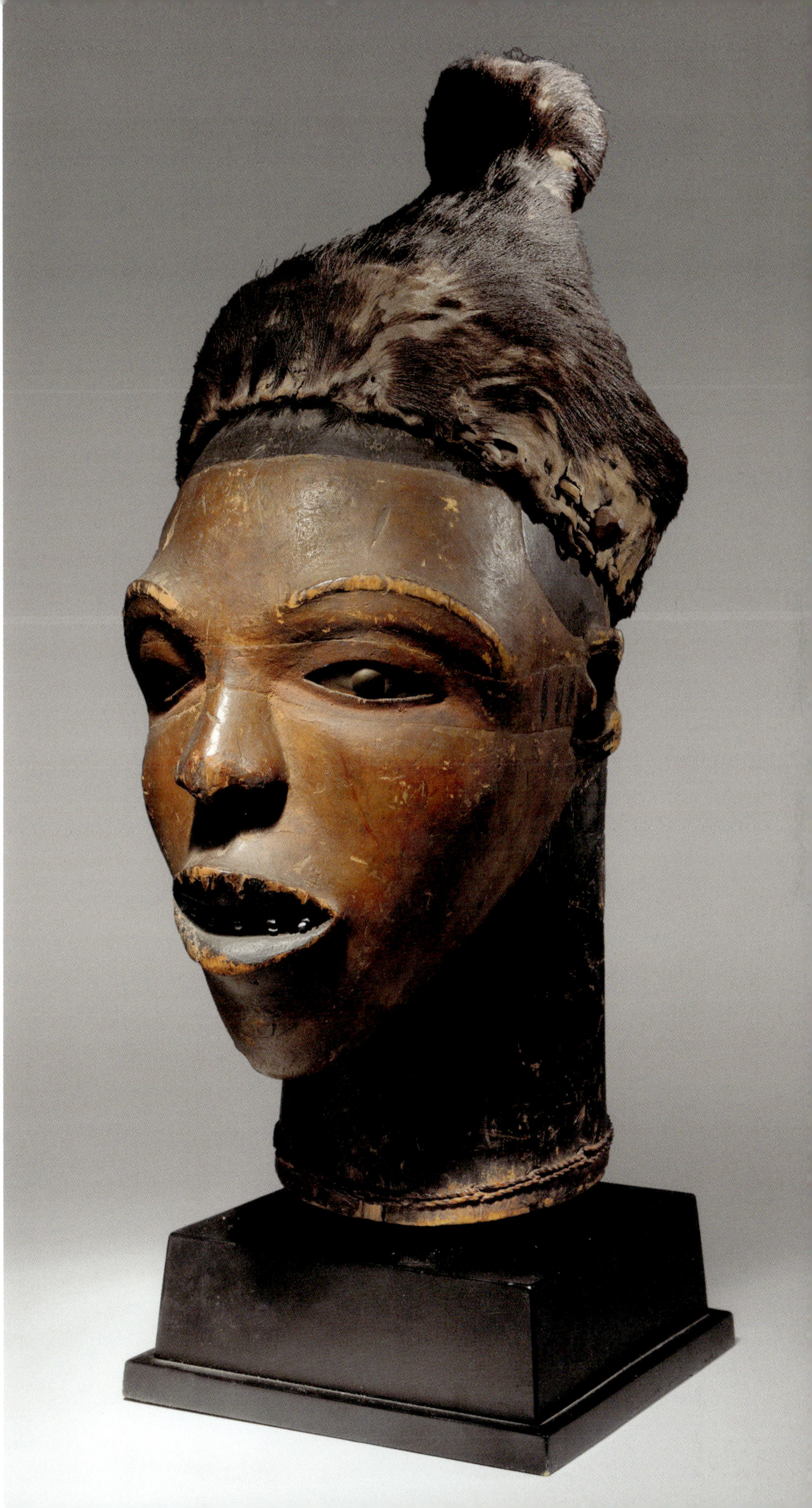

ILL. 106 [LOT 181]

Anthropomorphic crest mask
Ejagham, Nigeria,
Cross River region
19th cent.
Wood, tin, brass, iron,
African buffalo skin,
plant fibers, pigments
H. 35.5 cm
Private collection
(cat. 40)

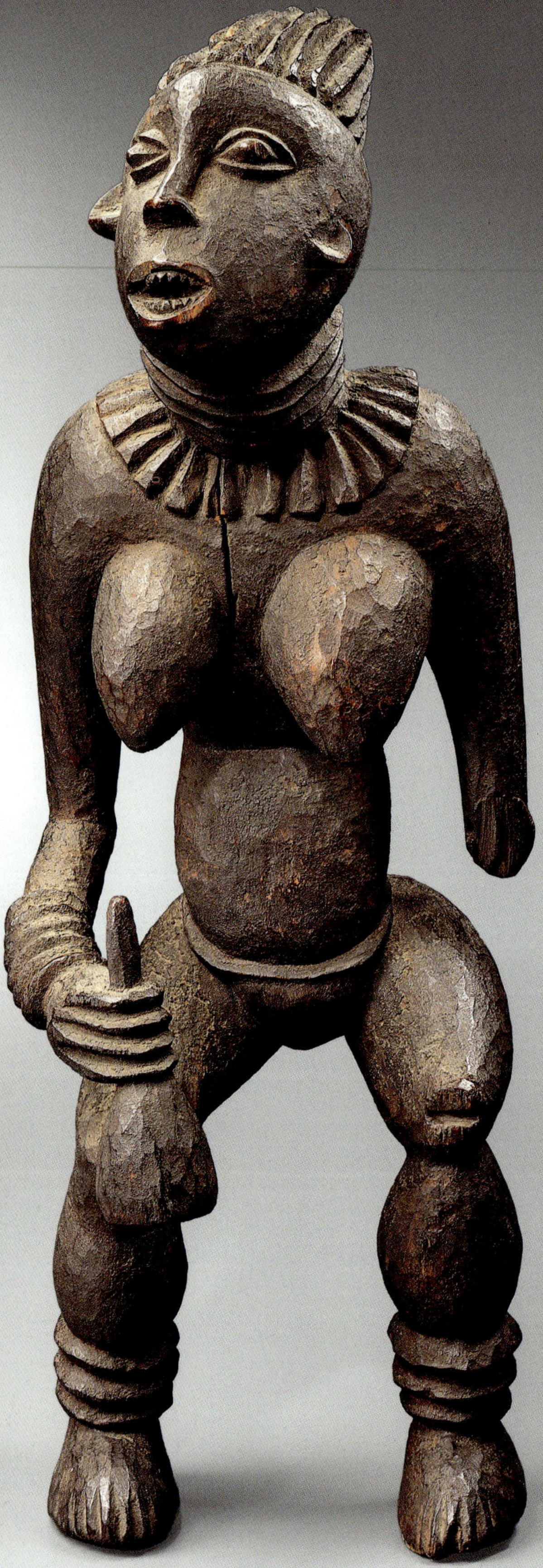

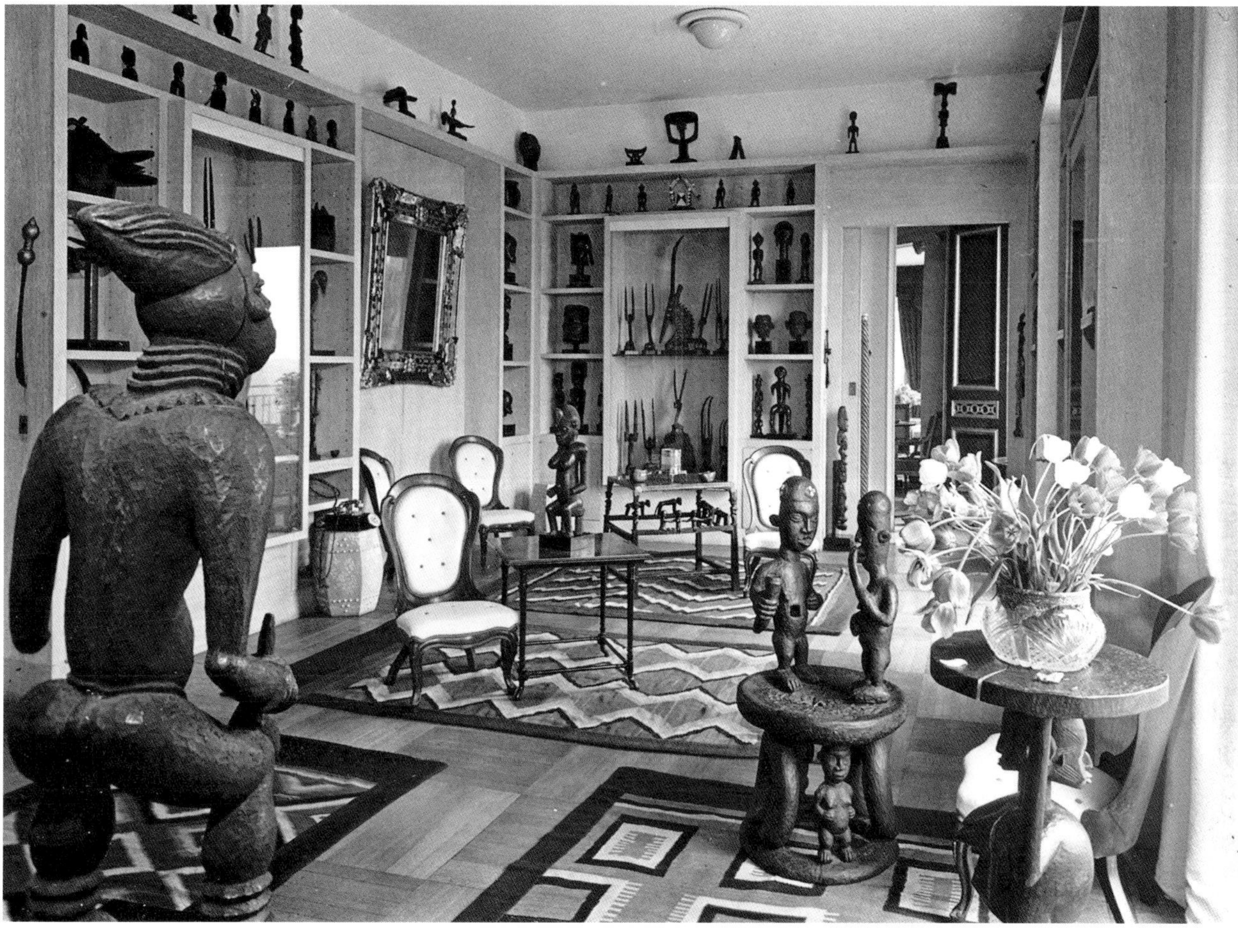

Ill. 107 [lot 189]

Lefem female figure
Bamileke,
Bangwa chiefdom
Cameroon,
Grassland region, Fontem
Before 1897
Wood, pigments
81.5 × 35 × 20 cm
Paris, Fondation Dapper
(cat. 38)

Ill. 108

The African room,
24, Quai de Béthune, Paris,
after 1947

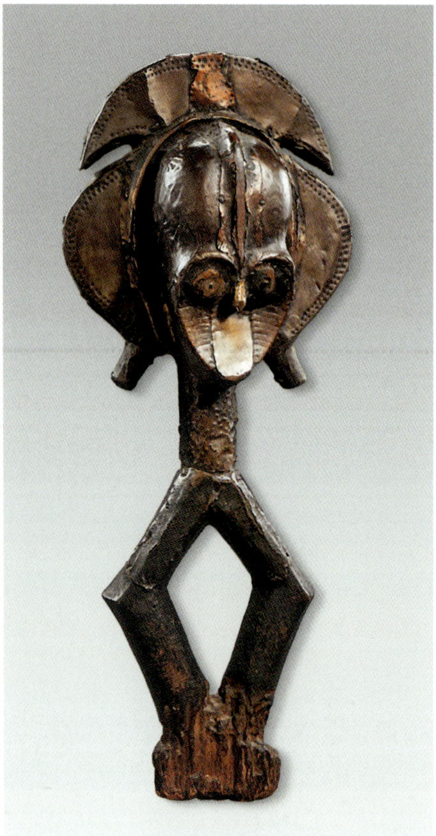

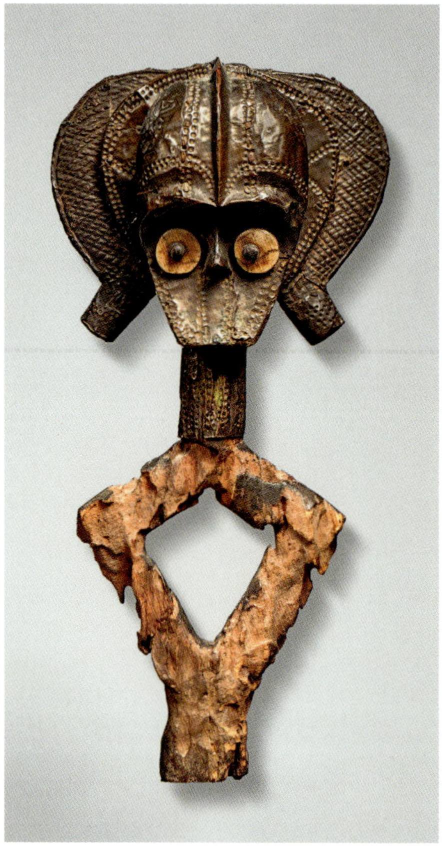

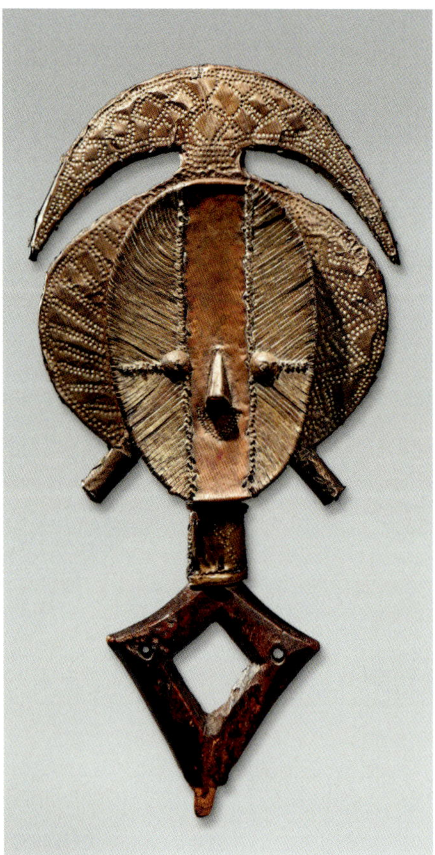

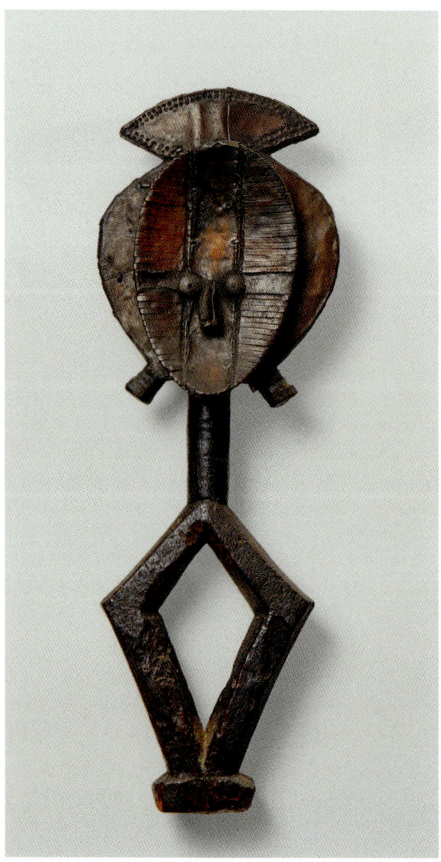

Above left
Ill. 109 [lot 202]

Ancestor figure, reliquary guardian
Kota, Obamba, Gabon, banks of the Sébé River
19th cent.
Wood, brass, copper
52 × 20 × 20 cm
Paris, Fondation Dapper (cat. 46)

Above right
Ill. 110 [lot 203]

Ancestor figure, reliquary guardian
Kota, Gabon, Makokou region
19th cent.
Wood, brass, copper
52.1 × 20 × 20 cm
New York, The Arman Marital Trust, Corice Arman Trustee (cat. 47)

Below left
Ill. 111 [lot 200]

Ancestor figure, reliquary guardian
Kota, Gabon, Makokou region
19th cent.
Wood, brass, copper
55 × 22 × 22 cm
New York, The Arman Marital Trust, Corice Arman Trustee (cat. 45)

Below right
Ill. 112 [lot 195]

Ancestor figure, reliquary guardian
Kota, Gabon
19th cent.
Wood, brass, copper
39.4 × 13.5 × 7.6 cm
Private collection (cat. 44)

P. 131
Ill. 113 [lot 192]

Ancestor figure, reliquary guardian
Kota, Gabon
19th cent.
Wood, brass, copper, iron
66 × 32.5 × 20 cm
Private collection (cat. 43)

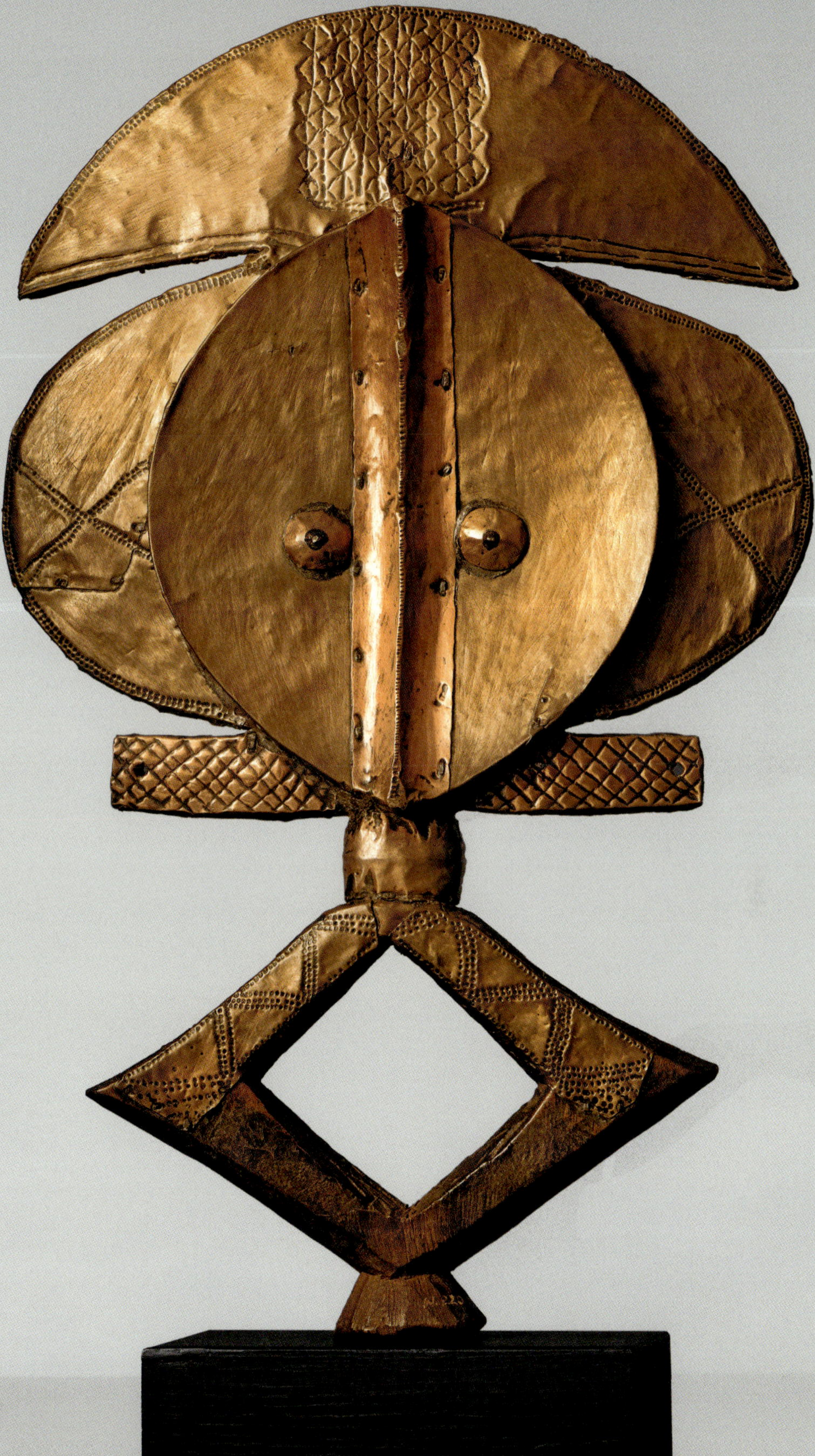

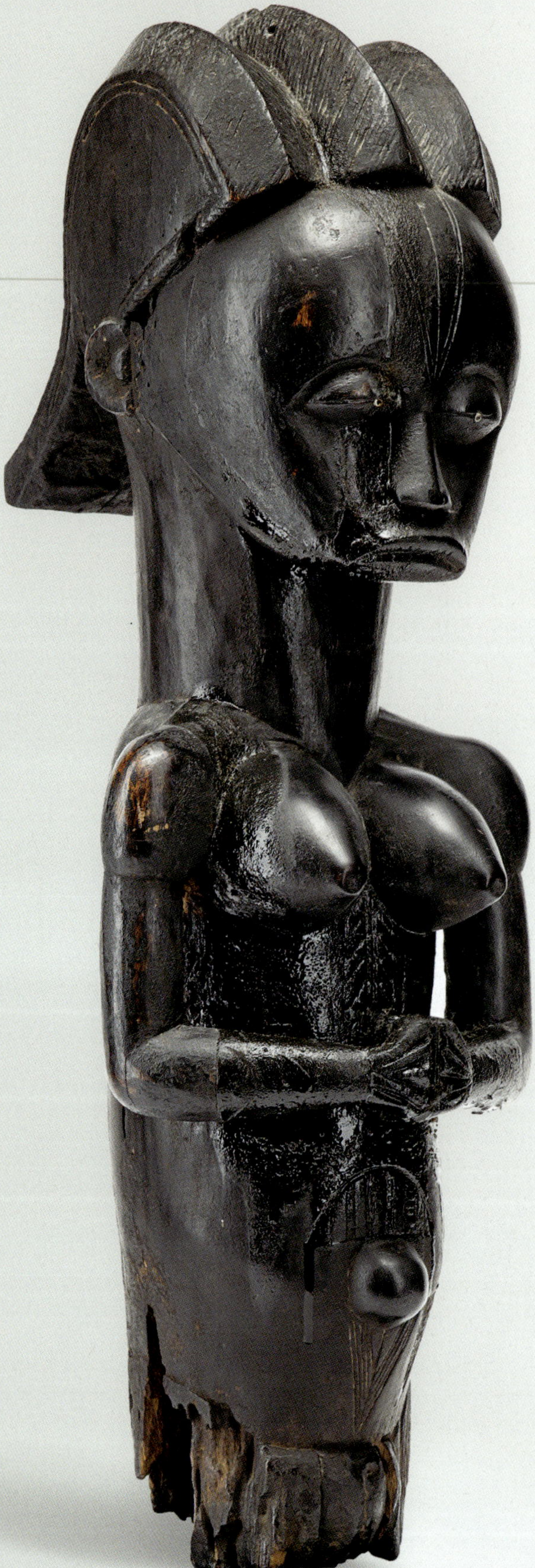

Ill. 114 [lot 209]

Eyema byeri ancestor figure, reliquary guardian
Fang Mvai, Gabon,
Minvoul region
19th cent.
Wood
35 × 15 × 15 cm
Paris, Q. Laurens collection
(cat. 50)

Ill. 115 [lot 215]

Ancestor head, _byeri_ reliquary guardian
Fang Betsi, Gabon,
Okano Valley region
19th cent.
Wood, metal
35.5 × 13 × 13 cm
Paris, Private collection
(cat. 48)

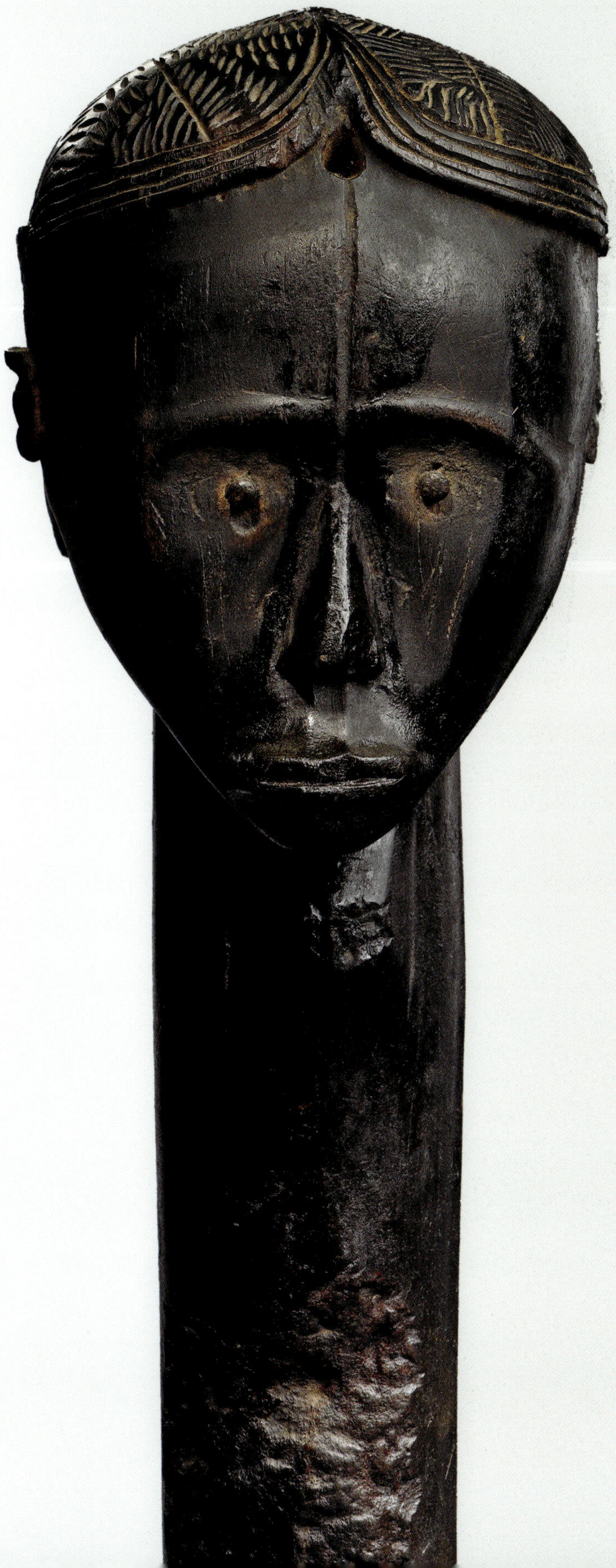

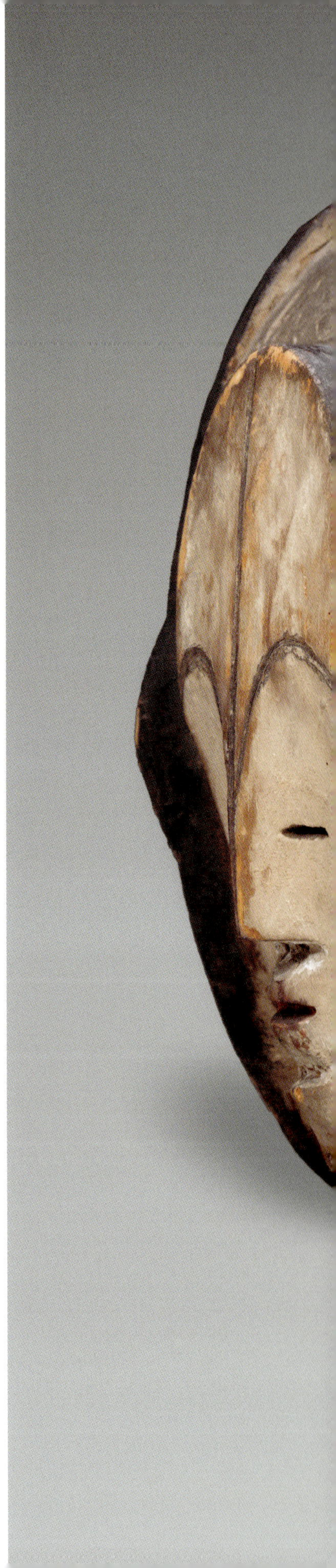

ILL. 116 [LOT 221]

Ngontang helmet-mask
Fang, Gabon,
Komo River region
19th cent.
Wood, kaolin
35.6 × 25.4 × 31.1 cm
Detroit, Detroit Institute
of Arts (cat. 49)

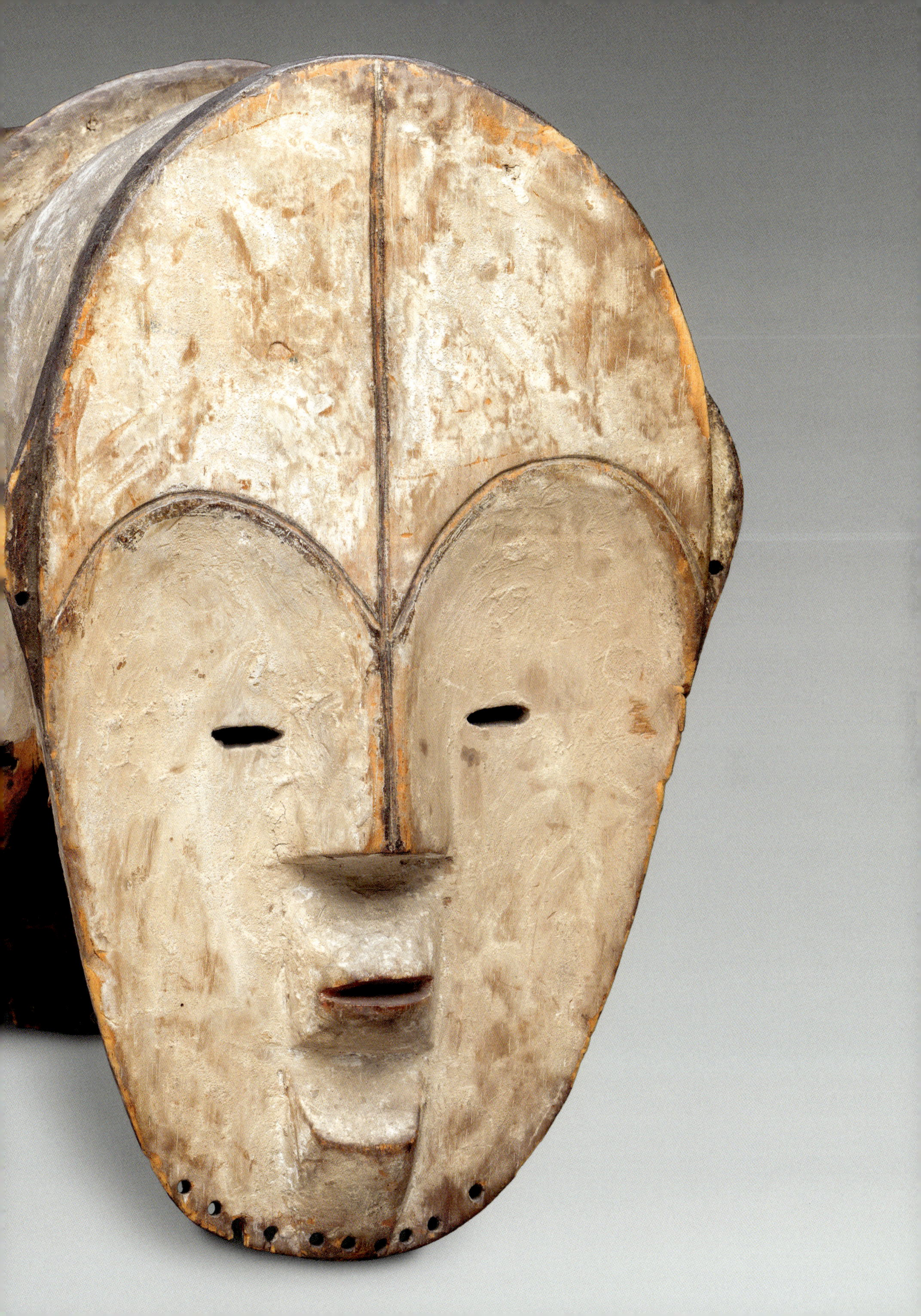

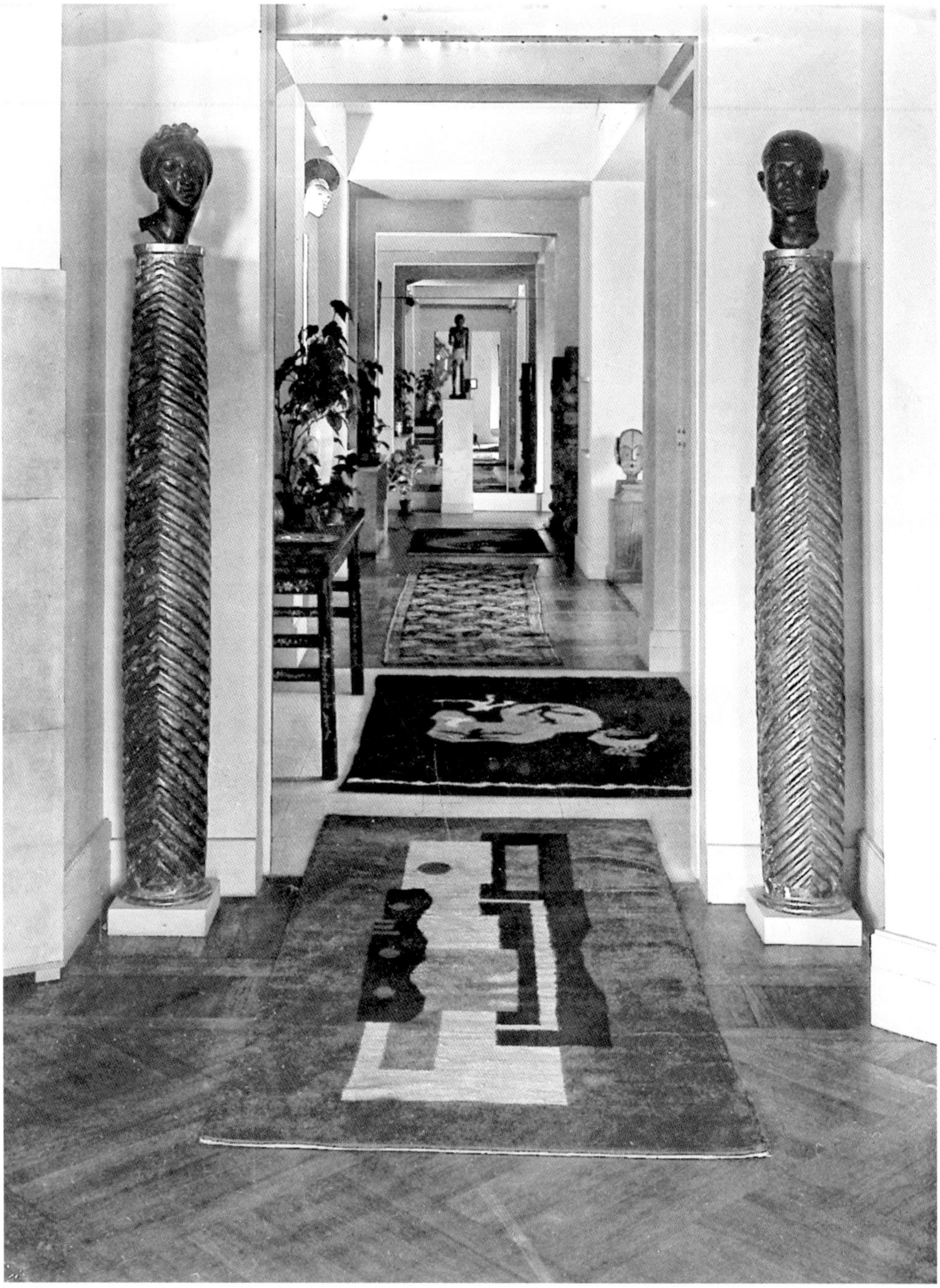

Ill. 117

The corridor
in the apartment
at 24, Quai de Béthune,
Paris, c. 1937,
photograph by Dora Maar

Ill. 118

The future music room
in 24, Quai de Béthune,
c. 1937, photograph
by Dora Maar (cat. 87)

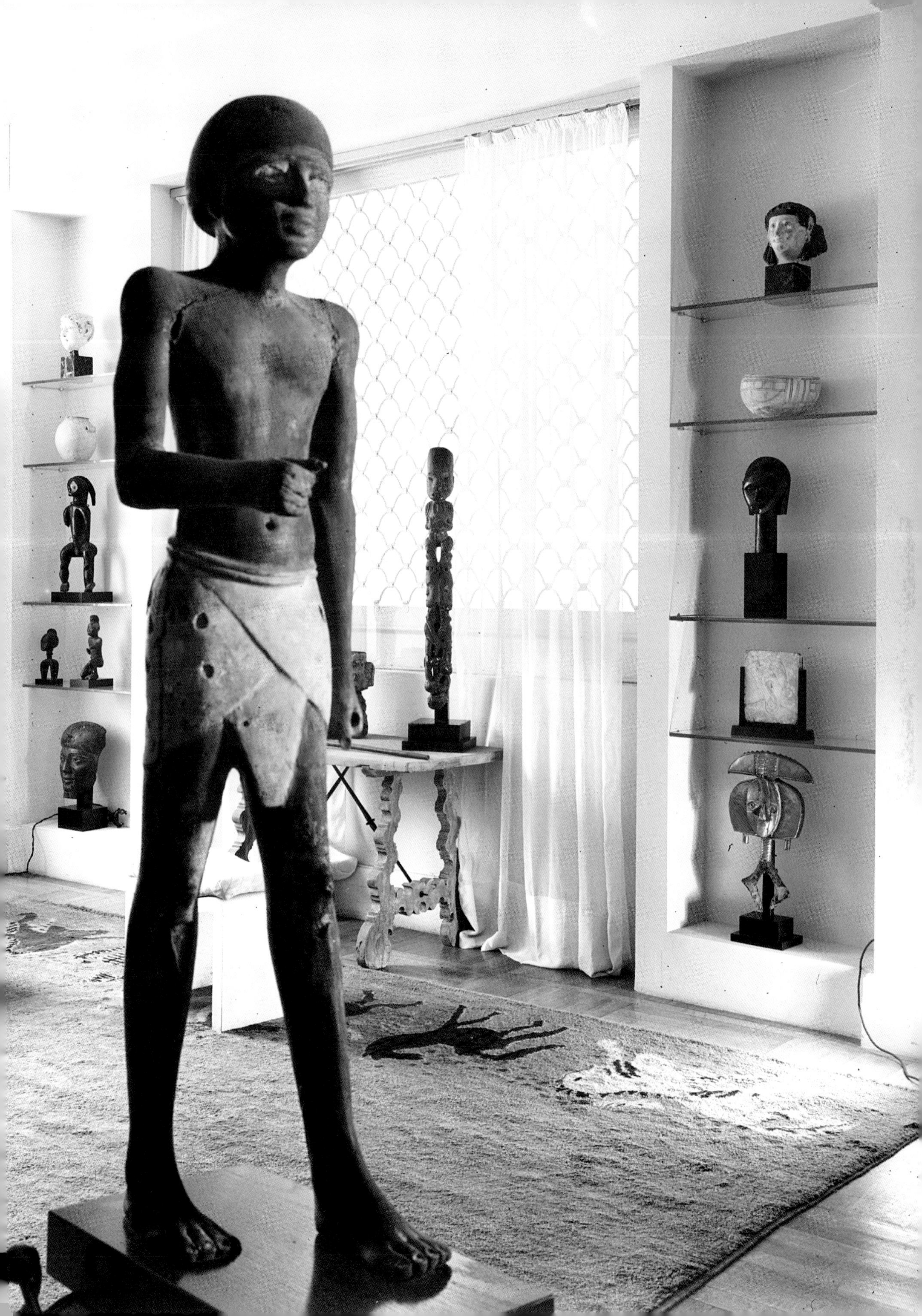

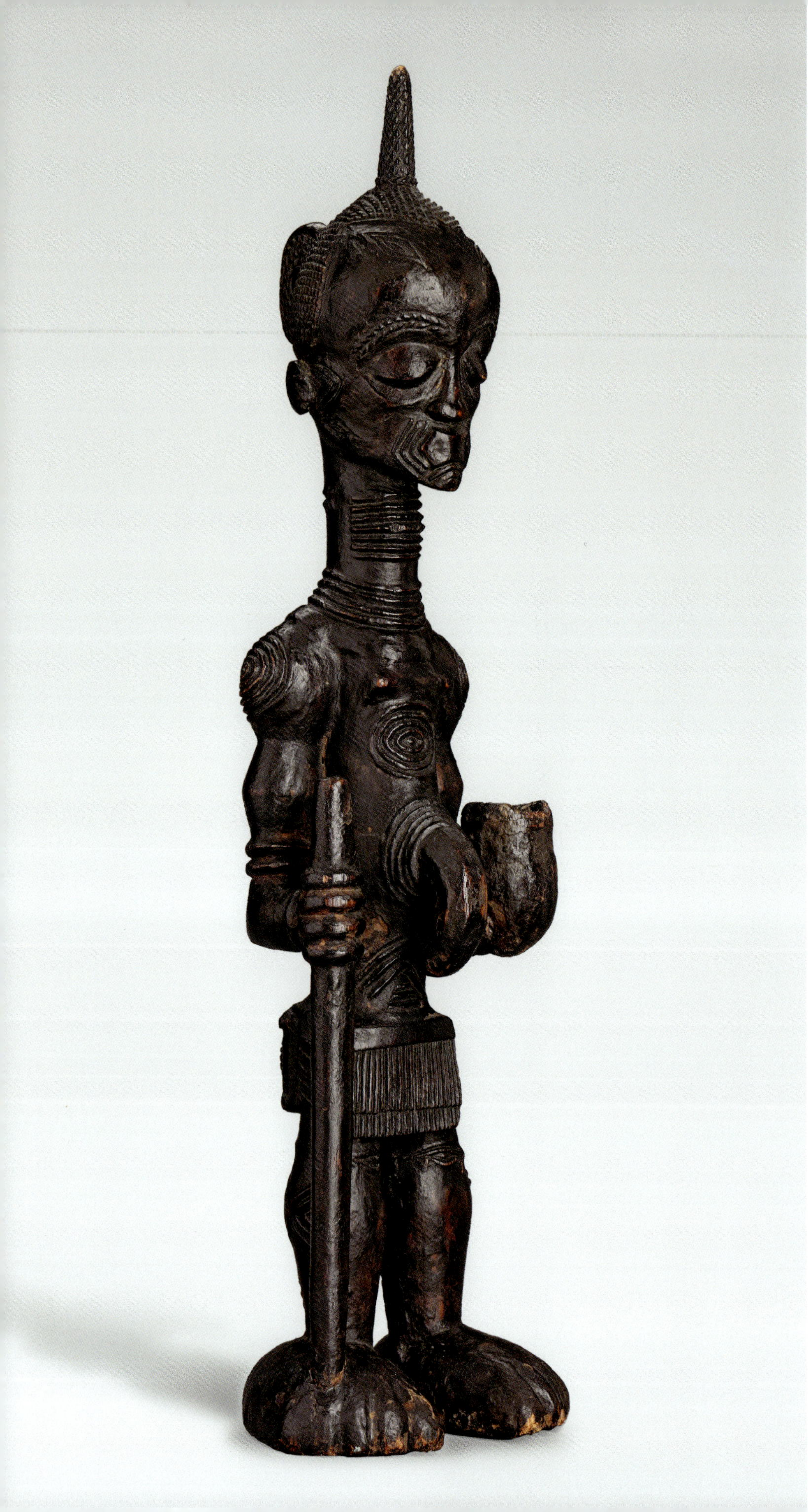

ILL. 119 [LOT 227]

Chief figure
Luluwa, Democratic Republic of the Congo, Kasaï Occidental region
1875–1900
Wood
50.5 × 13.3 × 14 cm
Detroit, Detroit Institute of Arts (cat. 51)

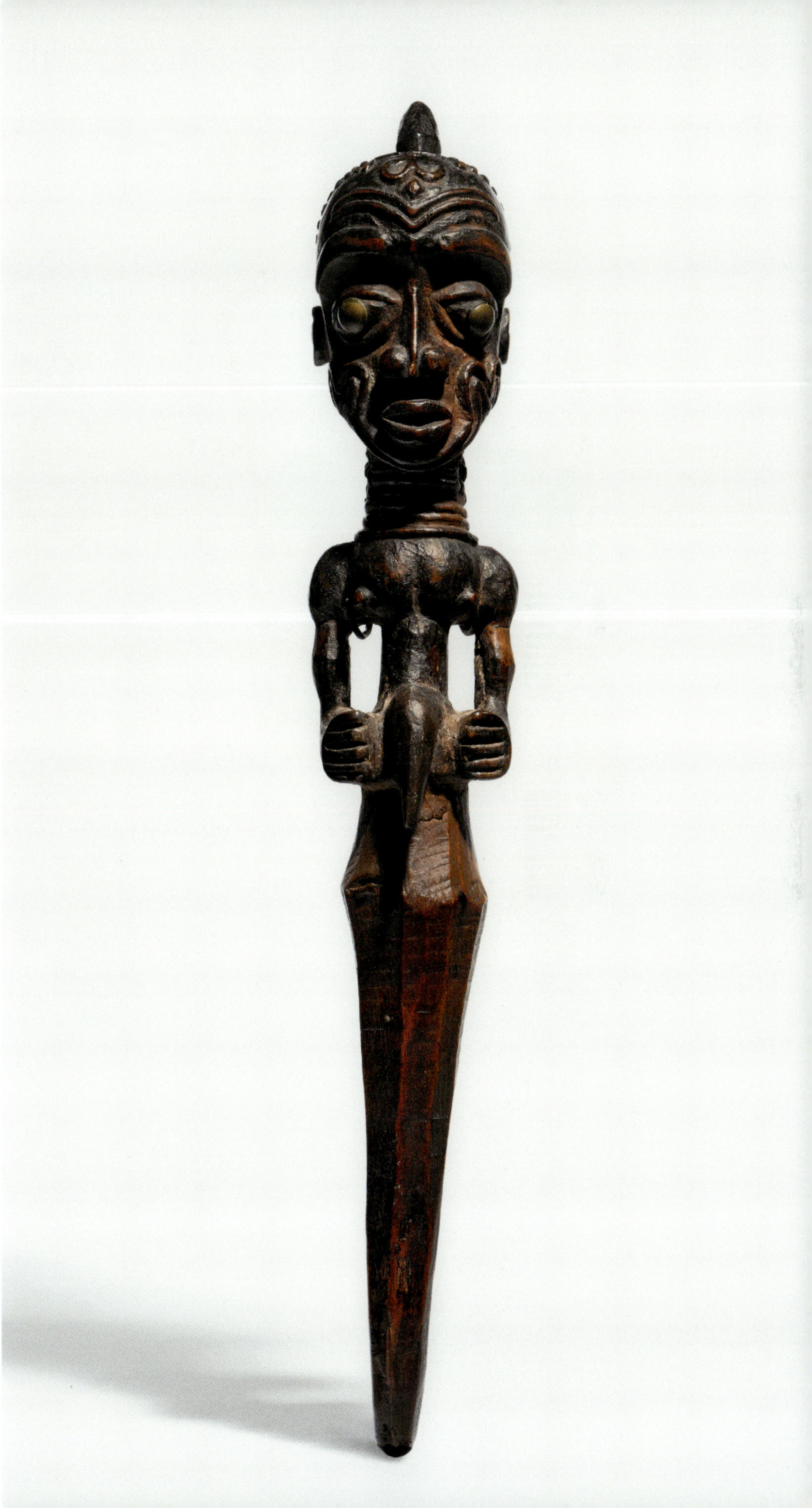

Ill. 120 [lot 228]

Bust
Luluwa, Democratic Republic of the Congo, Kasaï Occidental region
19th cent.
Wood, brass nail
H. 30.5 cm
Tenafly, Malcolm collection (cat. 52)

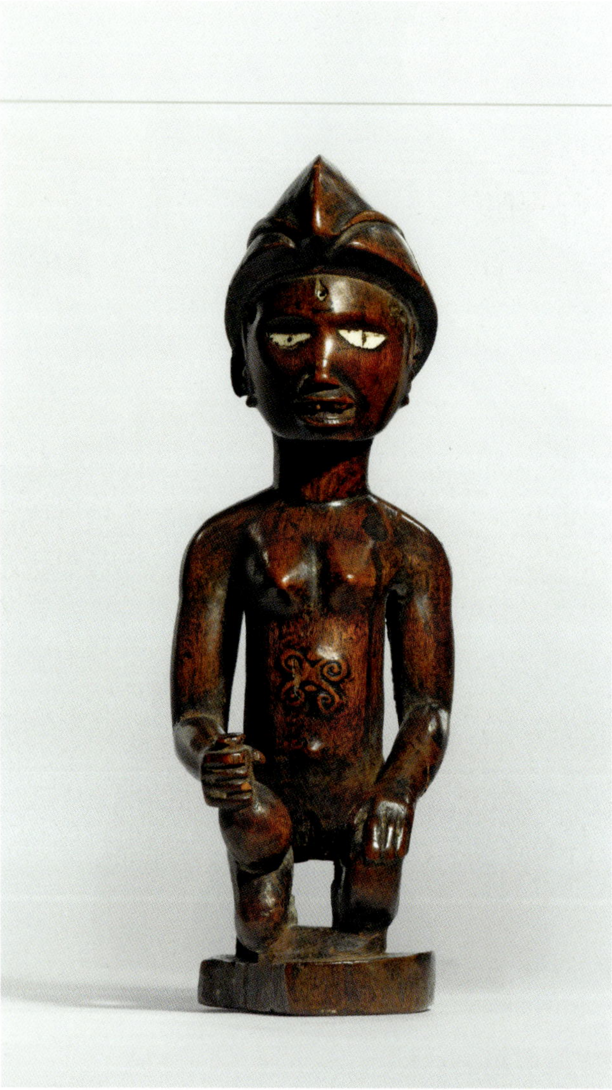

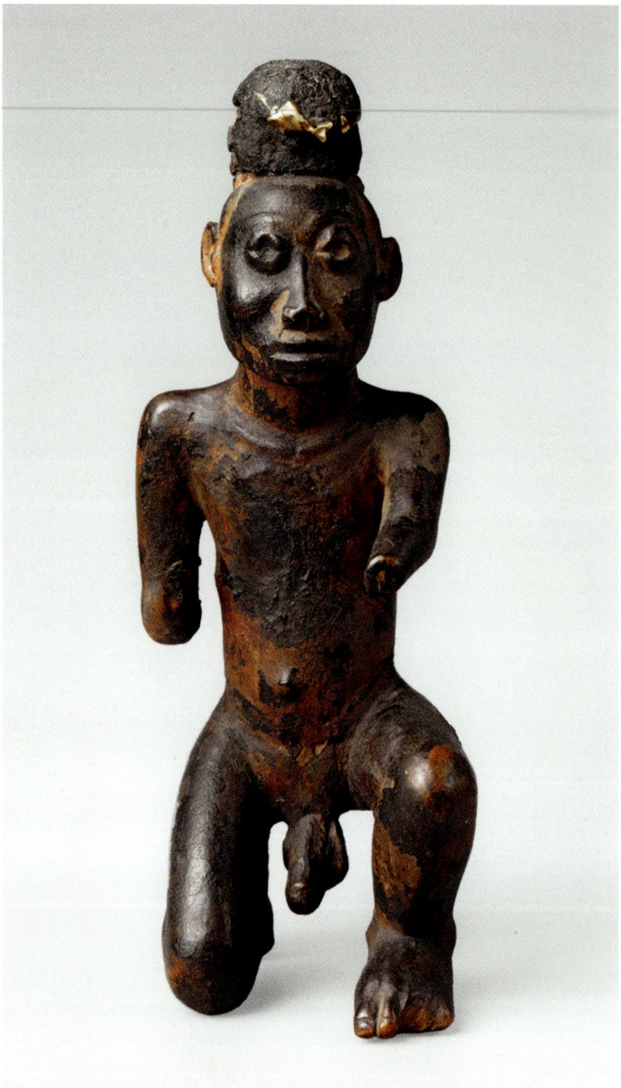

ILL. 121 [LOT 237]

Ancestor figure
Punu Lumbu, Gabon/
Republic of the Congo
19th cent.
Wood, porcelain
18.4 × 5.6 × 5.6 cm
United States, Africarium
Collection (cat. 54)

ILL. 122 [LOT 233]

Nkisi figure
of a kneeling man
Kongo, Democratic
Republic of the Congo
19th cent.
Wood, organic materials,
pigments, bone
28.5 × 8.5 × 10.2 cm
New York, Metropolitan
Museum of Art (cat. 53)

ILL. 123 [LOT 232]

Figure of a seated man
Dengese, Democratic
Republic of the Congo,
Kasaï Occidental region
19th cent.
Wood, metal staples,
pigments
55.2 × 20 × 15.2 cm
New York, Metropolitan
Museum of Art (cat. 55)

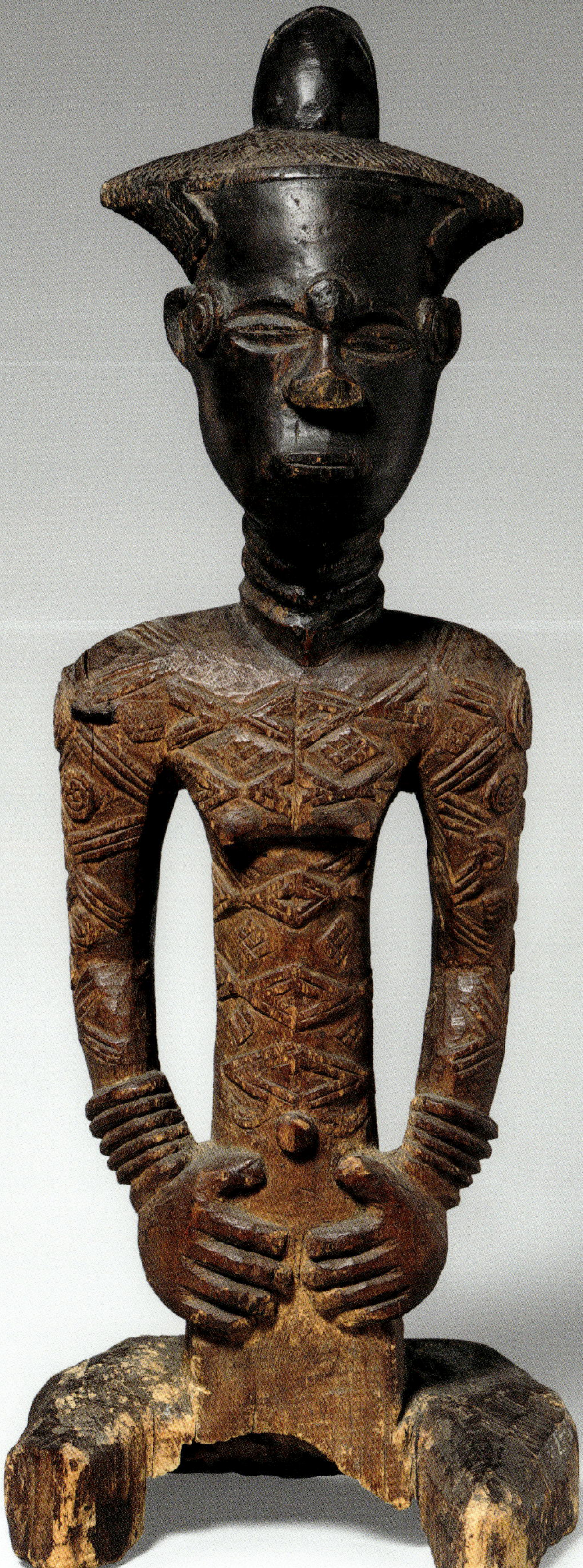

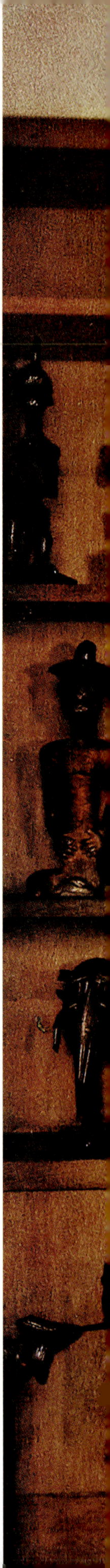

Ill. 124

View of link between
the African room
and the music room,
24, Quai de Béthune, Paris,
c. 1954–55, colorized
photograph taken from
the album composed
by Jean Vincent (cat. 91)

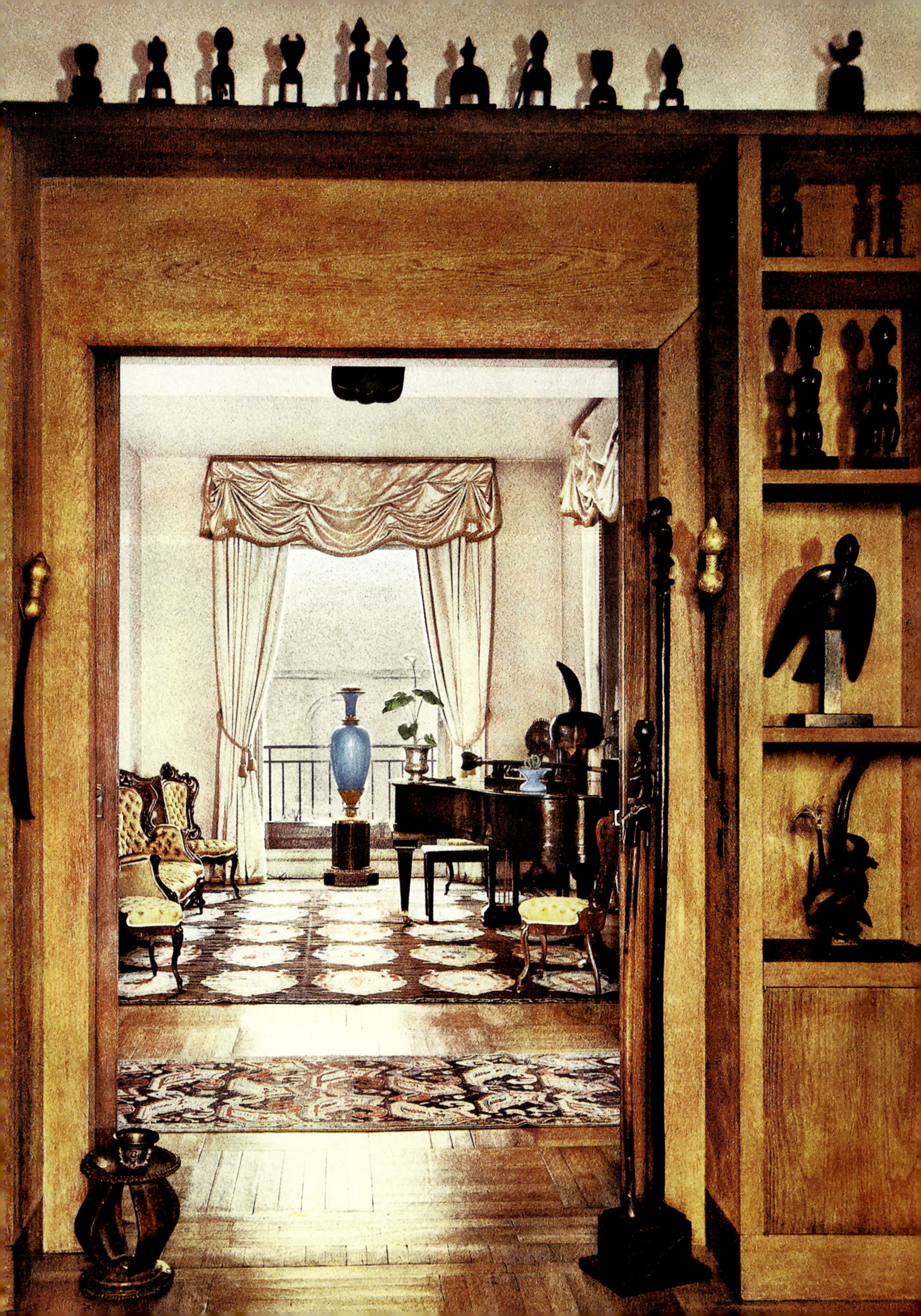

ILL. 125 [LOT 32*]

Drum
Attié, Ivory Coast
19th cent.
Wood, pigments
183 × 29 × 29 cm
Paris, Nicolas Hug
collection (cat. 56)

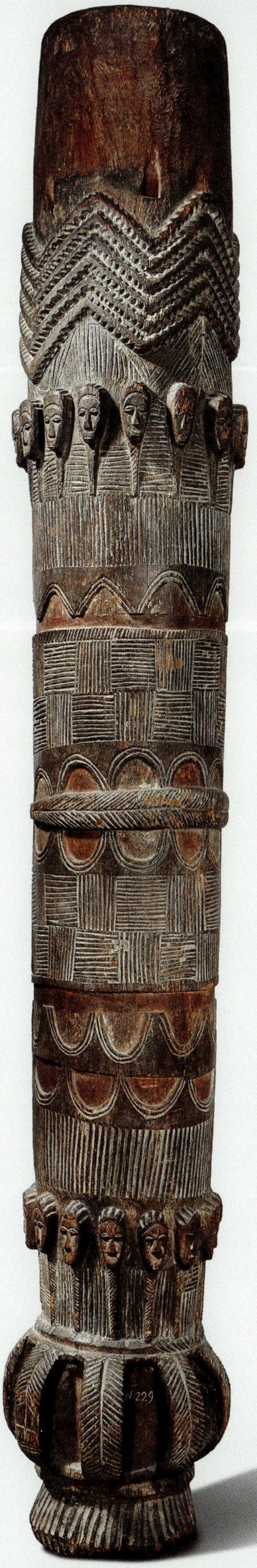

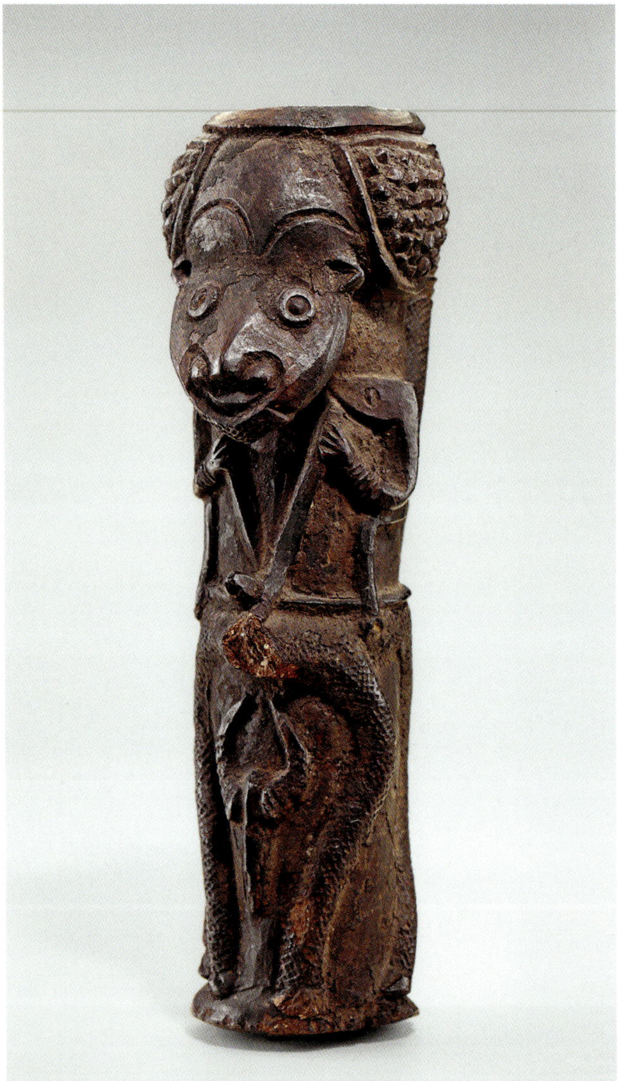

ILL. 126 [LOT 184]

Anthropomorphic pipe bowl
Bamun, Cameroon
19th–early 20th cent.
Terracotta
28 × 8.2 × 13.3 cm
Washington D.C., National Museum of African Art – Smithsonian Institution
(cat. 58)

ILL. 127 [LOT 243]

Chief's chair
Tchokwe,
Democratic Republic of the Congo/Angola
19th cent.
Wood, metal, hide
60.1 × 29.9 × 35.7 cm
Washington D.C., National Museum of African Art – Smithsonian Institution
(cat. 57)

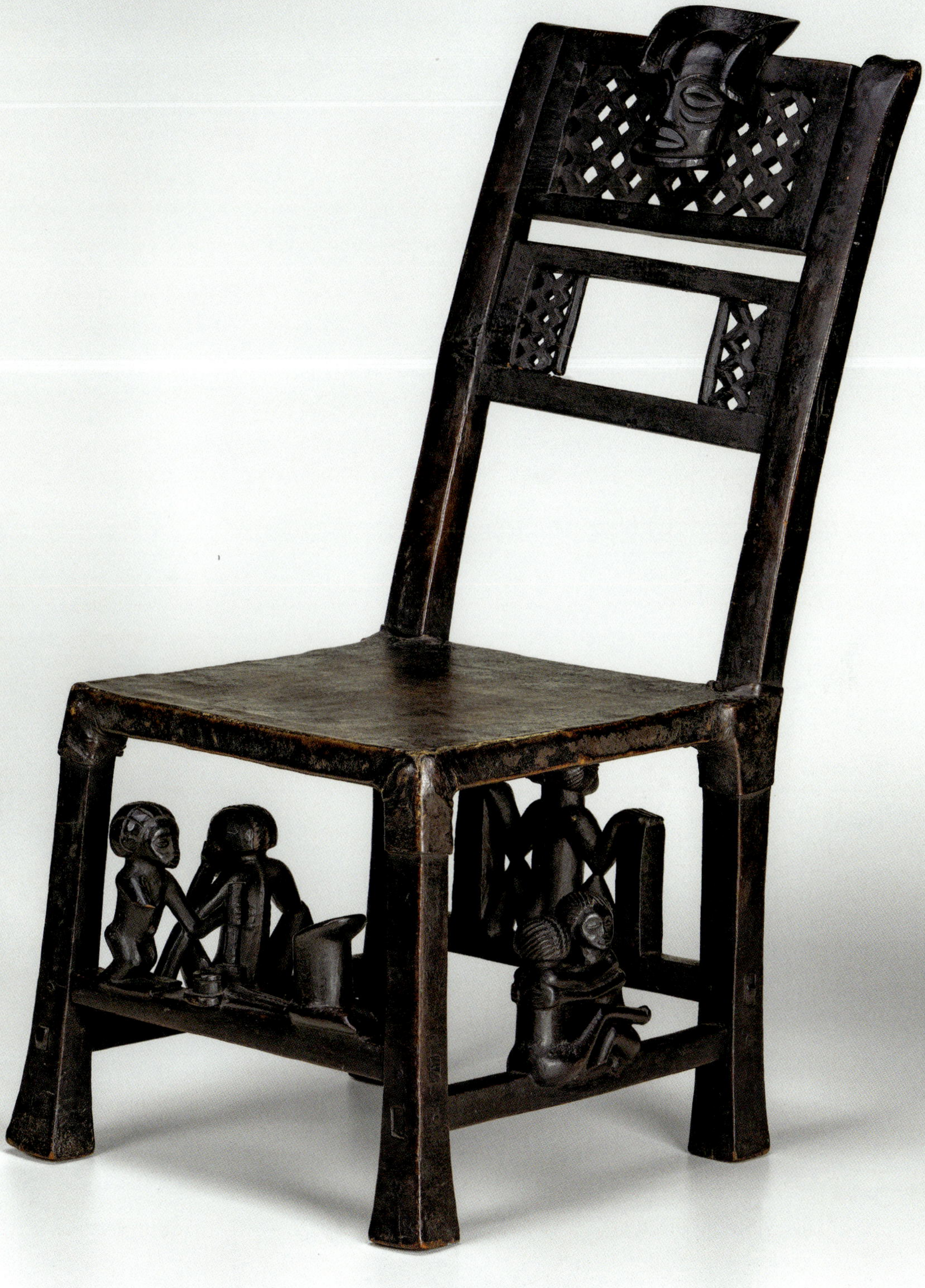

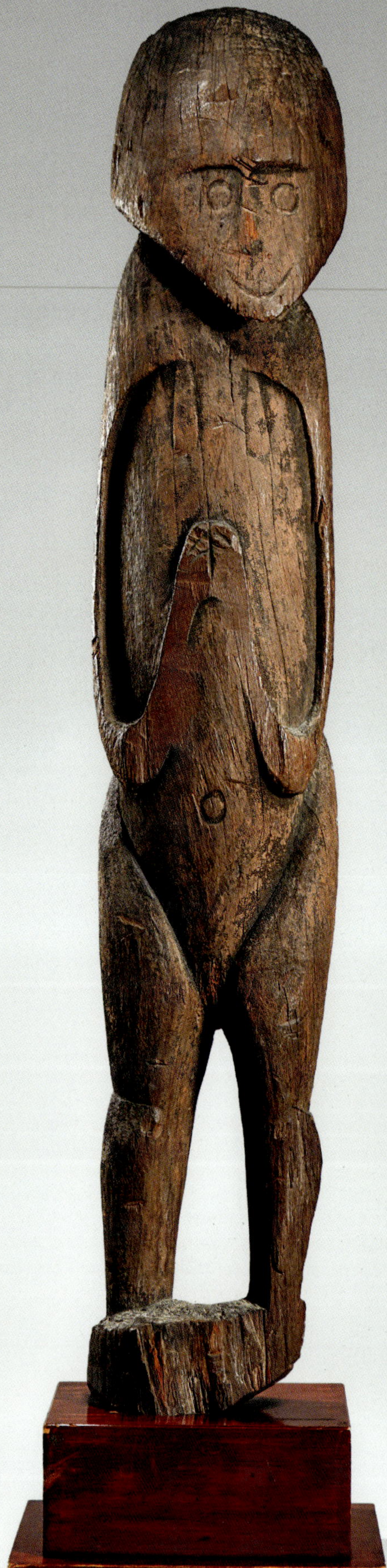

Ill. 128 [lot 260]

Anthropomorphic sculpture
Sentani, Irian Jaya, northeast New Guinea, Lake Sentani
19th cent.
Wood
120.7 × 20 × 20 cm
Gordon Sze MD collection
(cat. 60)

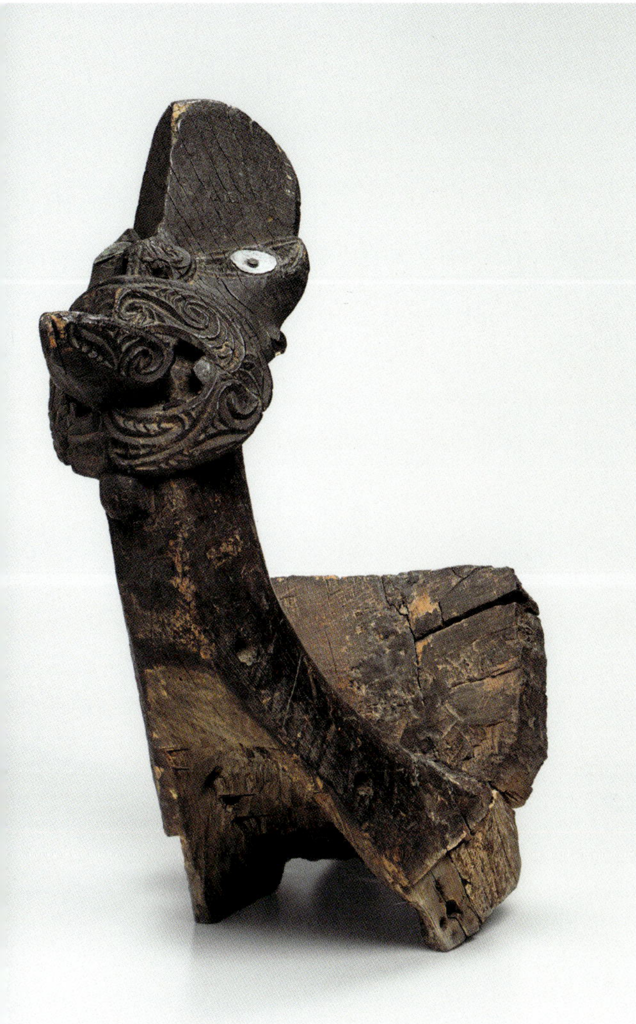

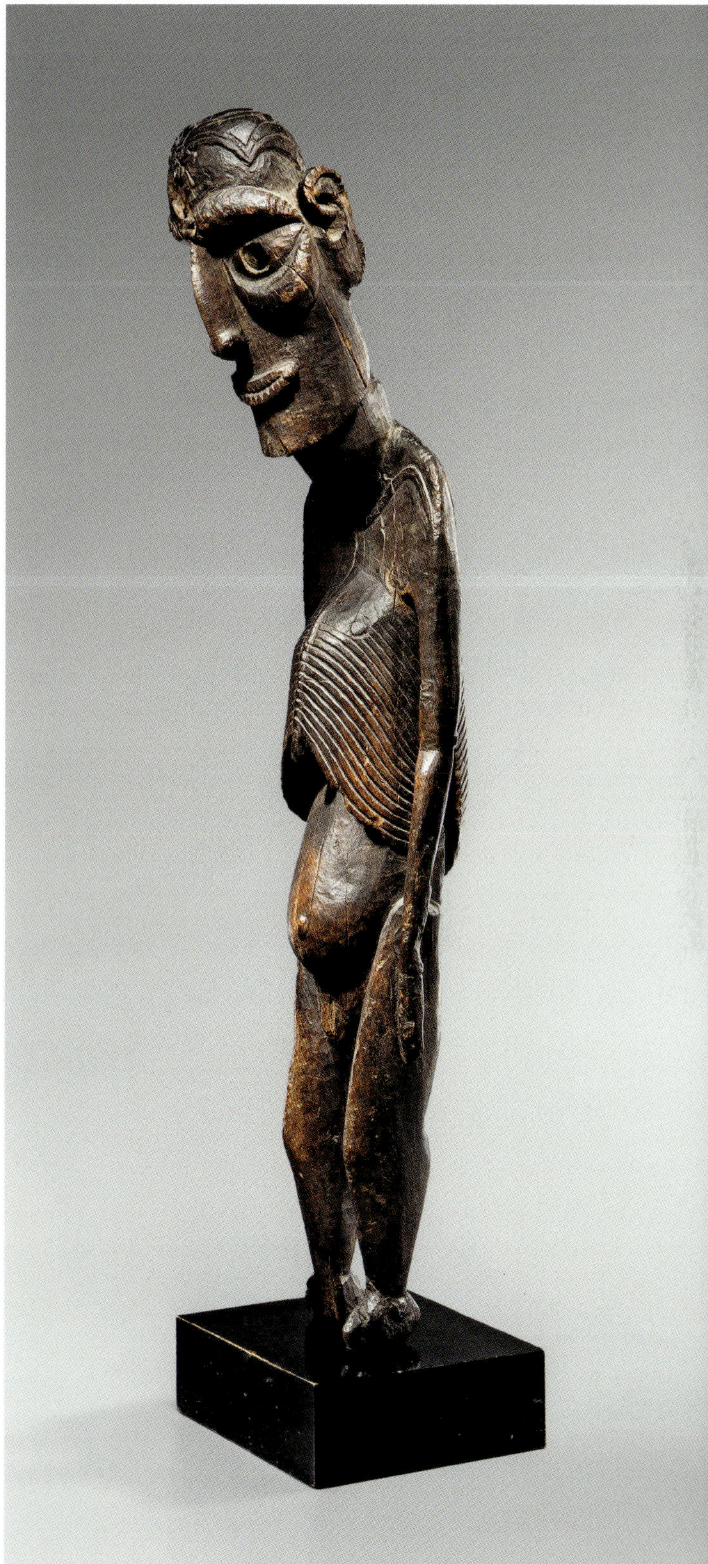

ILL. 129

Tauihu canoe prow
Maori, northern
New Zealand, east coast,
Gisborne
1850–70
Wood, pāua shell
33.5 × 28 × 71 cm
New York,
Brooklyn Museum (cat. 61)

ILL. 130 [LOT 261]

Moai kava kava male figure
Rapa Nui, Easter Island
Late 19th cent.
Toromiro wood, pigments
60 × 13 × 14 cm
Jean-François Schmitt
collection (cat. 59)

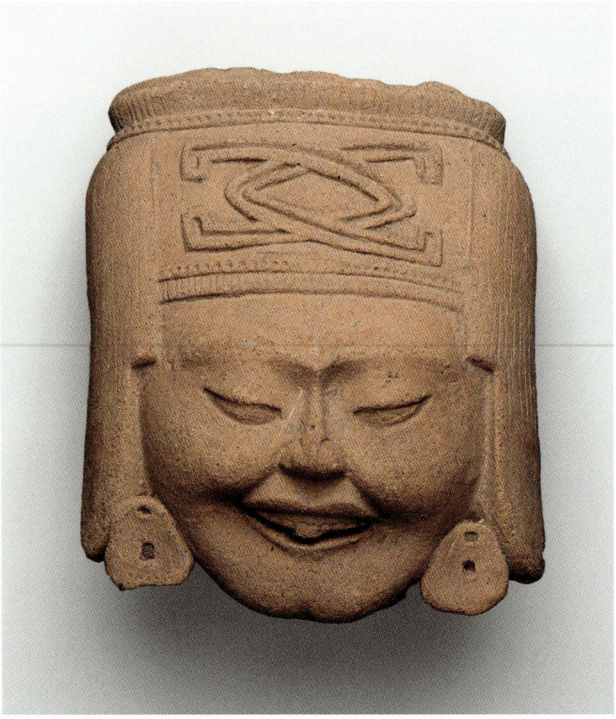

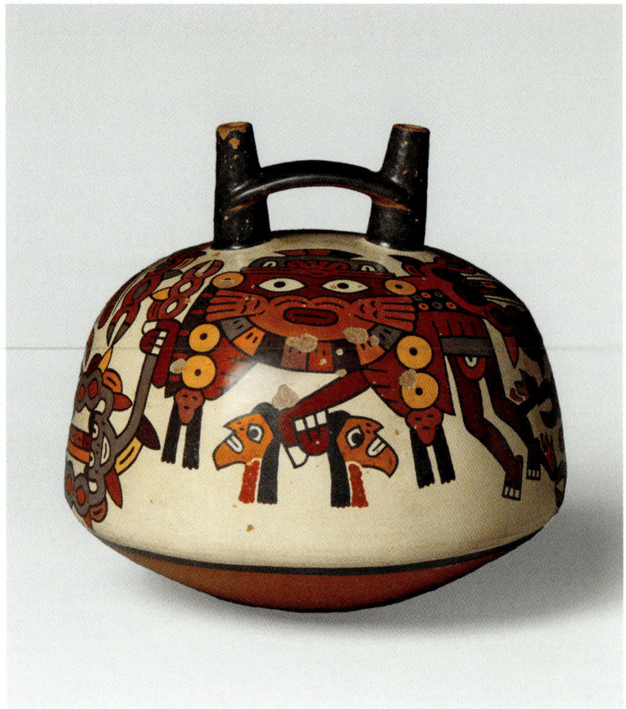

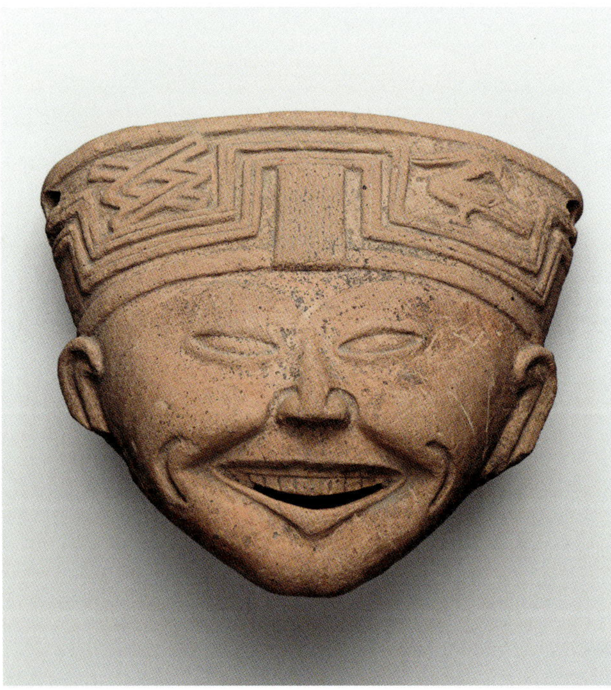

ILL. 131

Head of a smiling woman
Totonaque, Mexico,
Veracruz
C. 600–900
Terracotta
15.9 × 13.3 × 10.2 cm
New York,
Brooklyn Museum (cat. 62)

ILL. 132

Head of a smiling man
Totonaque, Mexico,
Veracruz
C. 600–900
Terracotta
15.2 × 17.1 × 10.8 cm
New York,
Brooklyn Museum (cat. 63)

ILL. 133

Vase representing a mythical anthropomorphic being
Nasca, Peru,
southern coast
100 BCE–100
Polychrome terracotta
15.5 × 16 × 15 cm
Paris, Musée
du Quai Branly – Jacques
Chirac (cat. 65)

ILL. 134

Front section of a crest
Charles Edenshaw
(1834–1924), Haida artist
Canada, British Columbia
End of 19th cent.
Maple wood, pigments,
abalone shell
15.6 × 14 × 7.6 cm
New York,
Brooklyn Museum (cat. 64)

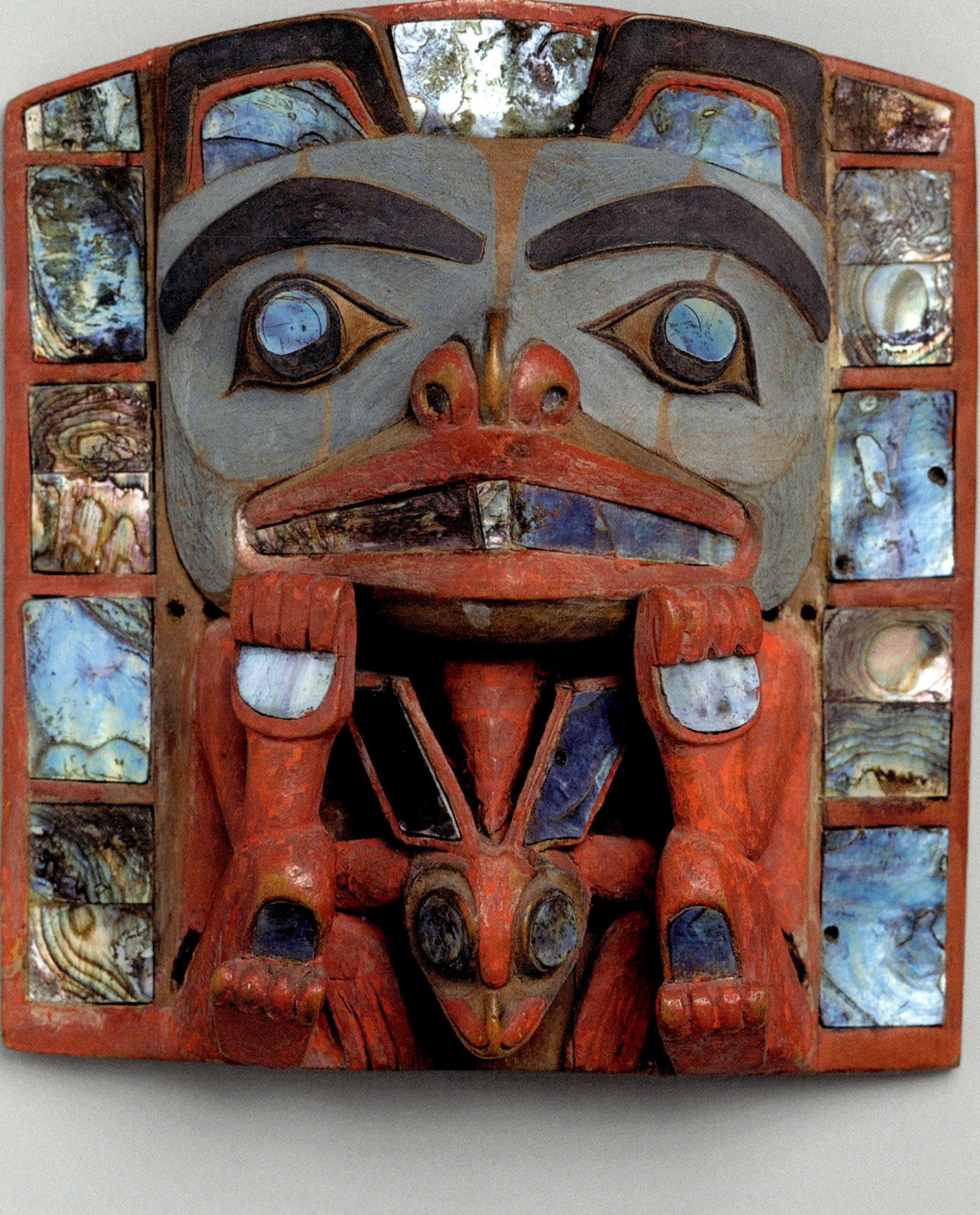

Being a collector and patroness

Madame and Me

Suzanne Slesin

On December 18, 1960, my mother, Niuta, married Roy Valentine Titus. He was the elder son of cosmetic and beauty expert Helena Rubinstein Titus Gourielli. It was my mother's third marriage and Roy's fourth. Rubinstein was almost 90 years old. The ceremony took place in the black-and-white checkered marble floor foyer of Rubinstein's magnificent 36-room triplex penthouse [ill. 135] at 625 Park Avenue in Manhattan. "I have fallen in love with a castle in the air," she had written to Roy. Refused the rental—supposedly because she was Jewish—she bought the entire building and lived there until her death.

I was quite a bohemian, usually dressed-all-in-black, teenager when Madame, as she was called both professionally and in her personal life, become my step-grandmother. My twice-widowed mother who had emigrated from Lithuania to Palestine, then Paris, before arriving in New York in 1940, with my father Beno, was beautiful, charming, and vivacious, and had captured the Polish-born Helena's heart—in part because they came from the same part of the world and spoke similar languages.

But I was barely aware of my new step-grandmother's legendary career or that she was considered the most successful and richest businesswoman of her time. I knew that she had left her native Poland at the age of 18 in defiance of her traditional Jewish family and fled to Australia. Her unblemished, pale skin fascinated the women there and the cream she had brought with her became the much sought-after Crème Valaze—the perfect treatment for their weather-beaten faces. Within a few years, she was living in London, where, in 1927, she had commissioned the architect Erno Goldfinger to design her the façade of the building; then in Paris, where the couturier Paul Poiret created her salon on the Rue du Faubourg Saint-Honoré; then on to New York—where the salon boasted art by the Polish-born sculptor Elie Nadelman, furniture by the French designer Jean

ILL. 135
The atrium in the apartment at 625 Park Avenue, New York, 1951

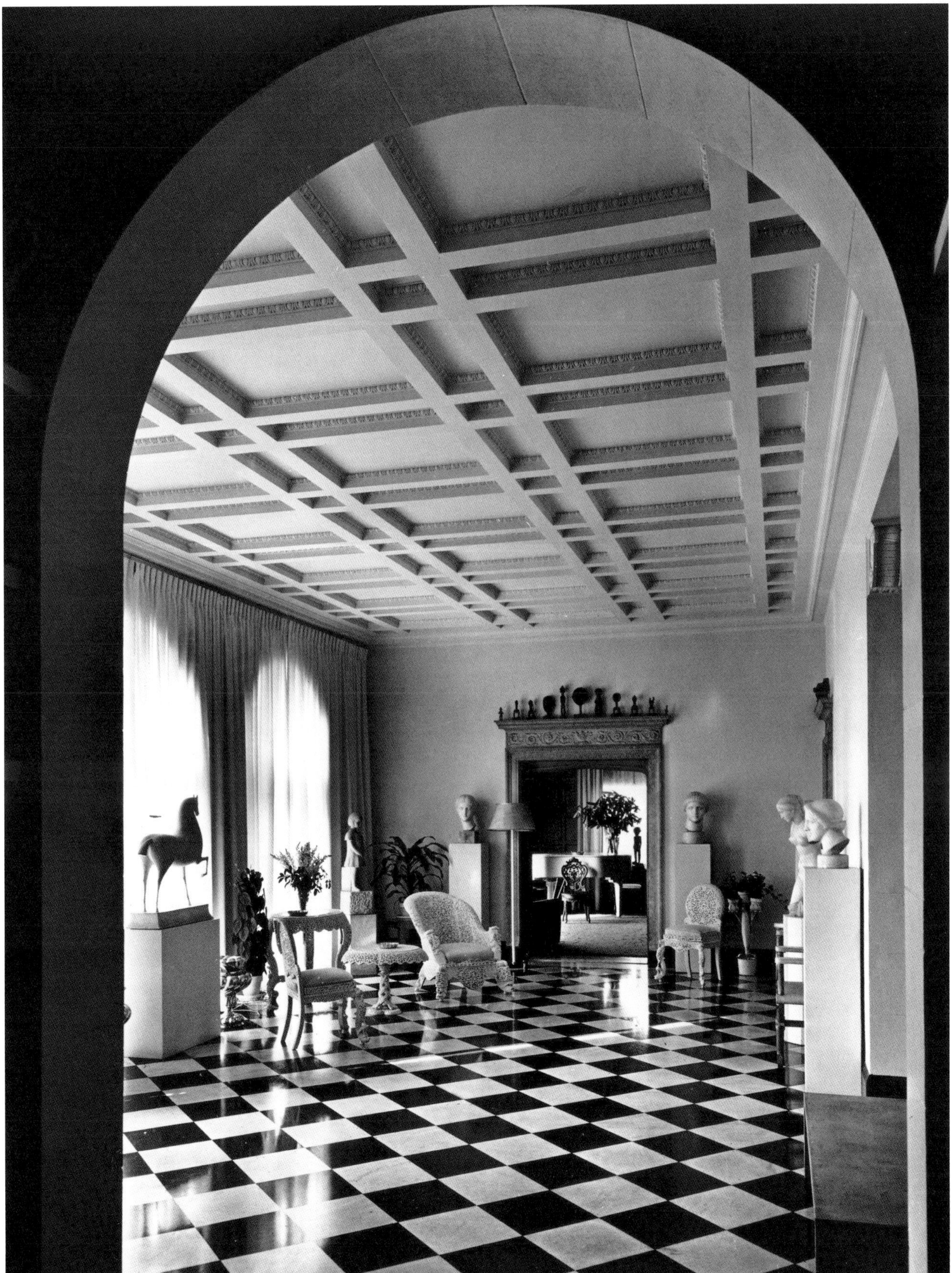

Michel Frank, and drawings by Amadeo Modigliani. The idea was for the cultivated and elegant environment to promote not only her products but her philosophy about beauty.

Soon after the wedding, I went off to university, and after graduation, continued my studies in art history with a Master's degree program in London. Madame died in New York on April 1, 1965 at the age of 93. A year later, all her collections, her jewelry, and her real estate were sold at auction. Over the ensuing years, I often thought of asking my stepfather to explain the huge dichotomy between Madame's celebration of her obsessive collecting and his total lack of interest in acquisitions of any kind. But I feared that this would stir up too many memories of their difficult relationship, and I suspected a need to distance himself from what I gathered was an unhappy and peripatetic childhood.

My new stepfather—tall, elegant and very cultured—had moved into my mother's modest apartment with only his bespoke English suits and his beloved stamp albums—nothing that would hint that he was the offspring of a woman who covered herself in exotic jewels to be photographed by the famous Cecil Beaton or who surrounded herself with extraordinary works by Joan Miró, including the artist's 1927 *Portrait* or Constantin Brancusi's—he was a countryman of hers, so to speak—*Négresse Blanche* of 1928. And there was, of course, much more.

She had met the Spanish artist Salvador Dalí in 1942 who painted her portrait as a bejeweled sphinx-like Madame at one with the craggy landscape—depicting her both as a lover and a destroyer of men.

Madame's relationship with Picasso was not nearly as affable. Meeting in 1955 in the South of France, Picasso did a sketch of her, focusing more on her hands than on her already famous face, and every detail of her outfit—from the seashell motifs on her skirt to her signature bangles. The ensuing sketches tell a harsher story. Madame never saw them, but Picasso did not hide his hostility toward his subject, even depicting her in the last ones as wizened and cross-eyed [ill. 136 and 137].

Meanwhile, my professional journey did not develop as I had planned. Returning to New York, Roy told me to "get a job" rather than pursuing a doctorate in art history. Lasting less than a day in secretarial school, I somehow, a few years later, became an editor, writer, and reporter for *New York* magazine, and by 1980, for the Home Section of the *New York Times*. My focus was on contemporary design, decorating, and architecture—and I introduced the French designers Andree Putman, Charlotte Perriand, and Philippe Starck to an American audience.

As a confirmed modernist, I was really only interested in cutting edge design. My first apartment had a bedroom lined with metal filing cabinets and my second was a space age, minimal, industrial-carpeting covered environment—both rebellions against my mother's Fine French Furniture.

That was all worlds away from Madame's lifestyle. In all her homes, the lavish bedroom was a particularly important room, where, in her later years, she held business meetings, surrounded by her executives, including my stepfather, of course.

Her other bedrooms reinforced that our worlds—and lifestyles—could not have been further apart. I considered her Lucite bed with its embedded lighting a bit silly and her luxurious bedroom in Paris by Jansen was a Hollywood fantasy that I could not relate to at all.

And I considered the portrait of her in an embroidered jacket, sitting in a room with glistening red draperies, a blackamoor, African sculpture, and the requisite Dalí, to be in really bad taste.

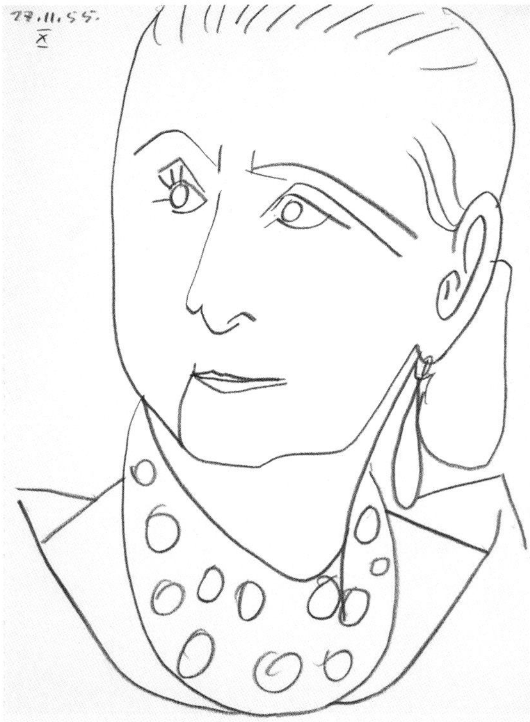

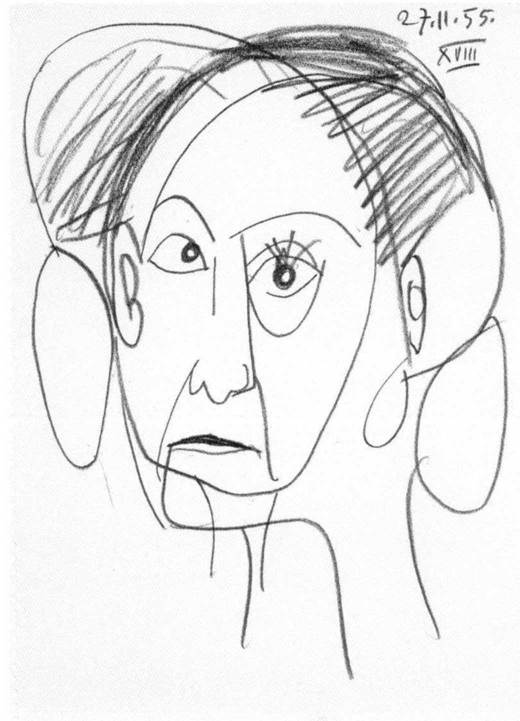

I ran off in a completely different direction.

In 1978, with Joan Kron, I co-authored the revolutionary *High-Tech, the Industrial Style and Sourcebook for the Home*. The designers we were interested in were mavericks like Ward Bennett who thought it was a good idea to place a barrier from a Con Edison construction site as a towel rack around a hospital tub, or the iconoclastic Joseph D'Urso who installed a rotating dry cleaner's rack in a New York apartment. Now those, in my opinion, were sexy ideas!

Paris' Centre Georges Pompidou by Richard Rogers and Renzo Piano of the 1970s, and Pierre Chareau's 1932 Maison de Verre in Paris, were the architectural monuments in my life.

But walking around Paris and looking across the Seine to the impressive modernist building at 24 Quai de Bethune on the Ile Saint-Louis, I would immediately be taken back to my exposure to Madame and her spectacular duplex on its two top floors. I remembered that the richly-carved *porte cochere*—photographed by the legendary Eugene Atget—with its rams' heads and garlands was all that remained of a 17th-century building by Louis Le Vau that had fallen into disrepair. Madame had it torn down and replaced with a modern structure by Louis Süe. The red suede-covered book of hand-colored photographs of that apartment, with its extraordinary panoramic view from its rooftop terrace of the Seine and the Cathedral of Notre Dame, was one of the gifts from Roy I treasured the most. It was because of that apartment that I came to realize that Madame was truly an original—and where her eclectic taste and mix of so many different works of art and objects took on a life of their own.

Advised by the famous sculptor Jacob Epstein, she became an early collector of African sculpture. But, to me, what was even more remarkable was the way she had paired the African and Oceanic pieces with Native American Navajo rugs in the wood-paneled

Ill. 136
Pablo Picasso
Portrait of Helena Rubinstein XI, 1955
Pencil on paper,
44 × 32 cm
Japan, Himeji City Museum of Art

Ill. 137
Pablo Picasso
Portrait of Helena Rubinstein XVIII, 1955
Pencil on paper,
44 × 32 cm
Japan, Himeji City Museum of Art

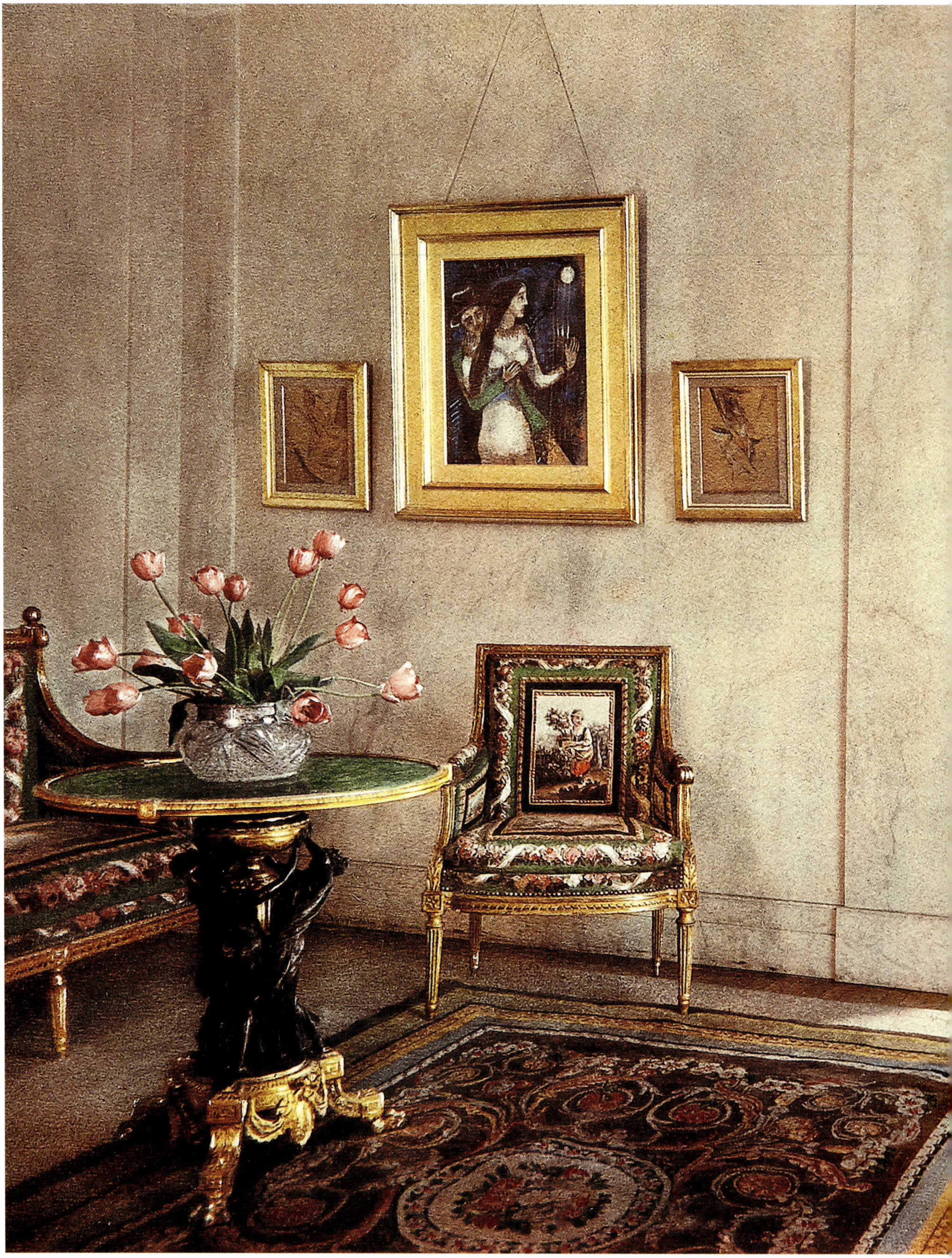

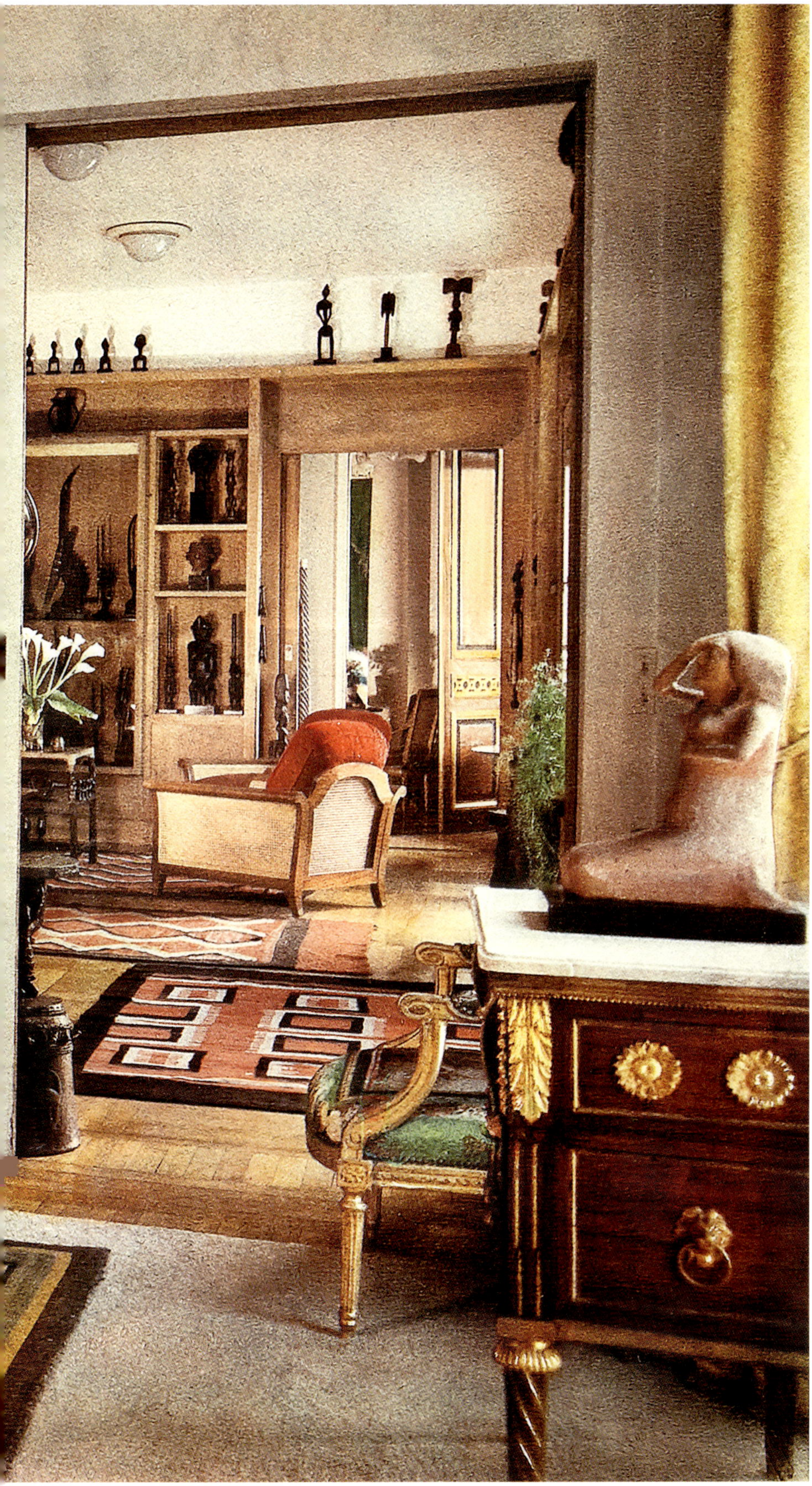

ILL. 138

The African room from one of the lounges, 24, Quai de Béthune, Paris, c. 1954–55, colorized photograph taken from the album composed by Jean Vincent (cat. 91)

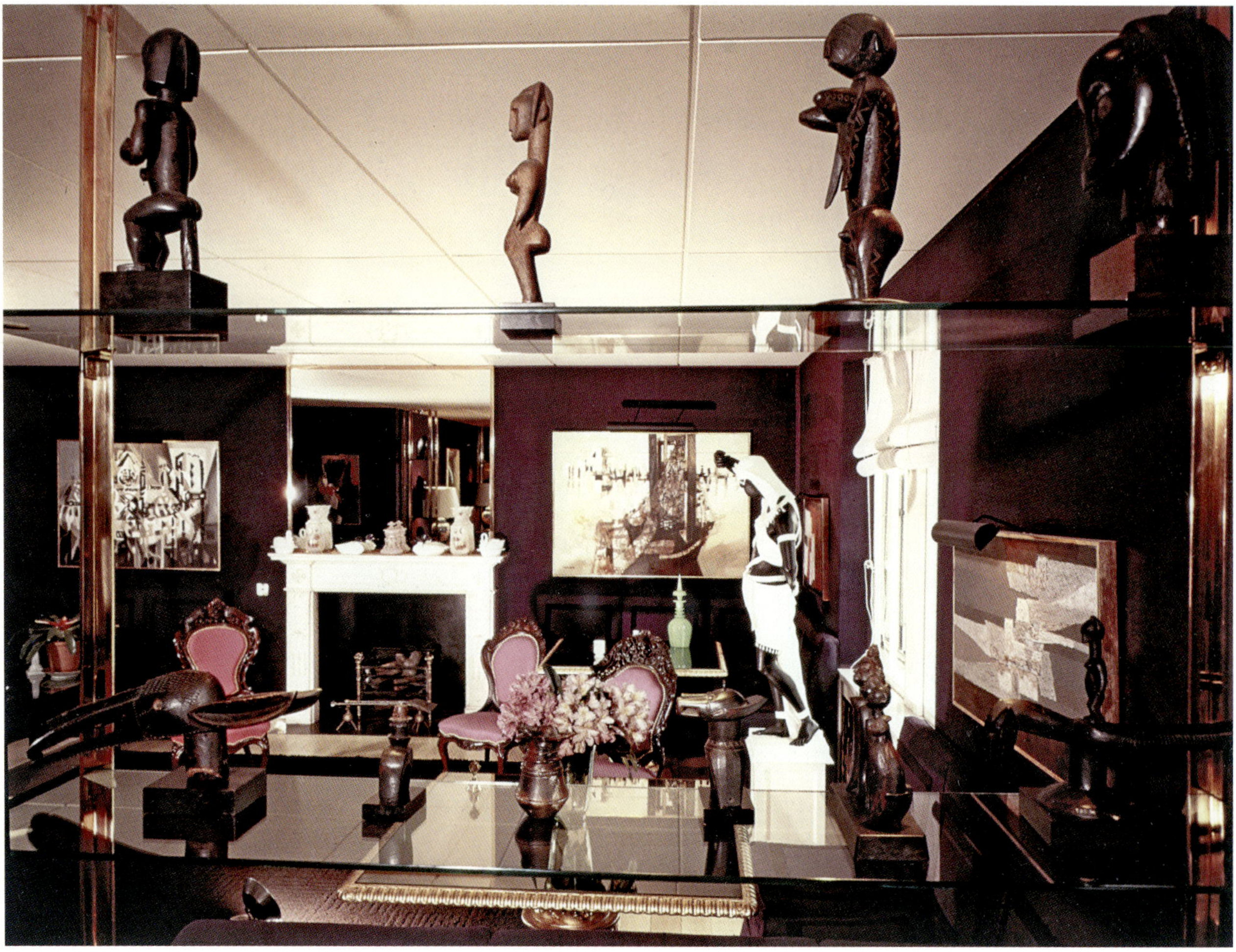

room of her Paris apartment. That room with its extraordinary mix of cultures—so surprising, so original, so truly unthinkable before she did it—was what piqued my interest in all the interiors she had lived in throughout her long life. Her vision, her eclecticism, her boldness—those were the hallmarks of the modern interiors I so admired.

I discovered that Madame had championed such designers as Donald Deskey in New York, when he was young and relatively unknown, where he had deployed a chic minimalism for her master bedroom, covering the floor in linoleum and hanging cellophane draperies. I began looking more closely at her other interiors and appreciating the luxurious restraint popular in Paris in the 1930s, such as the decor of her apartment at 216 Boulevard Raspail by Bruno Elkuken, a fellow Polish countryman who had arrived in Paris in the 1920s.

In the mid 1990s, when I wrote about the French designer Jacques Grange in *House & Garden*, I found surprising parallels between a living room he created in Provence and Madame's sensibility of the 1930s. Even more intriguing were the parallels between such rooms as the one Grange designed for Yves Saint Laurent and Pierre Bergé in Paris and Madame's more eccentric rooms—such as the living room of her New York triplex, with its mix of Victorian furniture, modern paintings, and arcane accessories.

ILL. 139

The drawing-room in the Knightsbridge apartment, London, 1962

I quickly became immersed in a world not of *Less is More* but of *More is More*—seduced by the work of interior designers who had rather extreme points of view. It was only later that I realized that maybe it had something to do with Madame influencing me on a subliminal or maybe not so subliminal level. Writing about a house by New York decorators Edward Zajac and Richard Callahan, I could not take my eyes off a fantastic Portuguese bed. *Voila!* I remembered Madame's late 1950s London pied-a-terre by the-very-young-at the time British designer David Hicks [ill. 139], whose style, even early on, displayed the verve, color, and drama for which he later became famous. The more houses I visited the more I realized that Madame's style bravura and all-round chutzpah had become an underlying barometer not only for me as a reporter and editor but for what was evolving as my own personal style.

I was drawn to her mix of high and low, to her choices of colorful and unusual pieces, and to an excess that came from a lively openness to the myriad possibilities of what the world of art and objects can offer. Madame loved to buy *en masse*—from dozens of Primitive Mexican paintings to hundreds of turquoise and candy-pink pieces of Opaline glass. Soon, dozens of yellow ware bowls filled the shelves of our country house and later, the multi-colored, vividly-patterned pieces by the Vallauris ceramicist Robert Picault became a full-blown obsession.

In 1993, my husband, Michael Steinberg, and I moved into a big wreck of an apartment on the Upper East Side of Manhattan and my antiques market forays became more frequent. Seventeen years later, we moved downtown to a loft in Chinatown that we thought would be our minimalistic dream of a home. However, as my husband masterfully hung his myriad small art works salon style and our collections of French pottery and revolutionary Chinese ceramics grew day by day, I knew I was really channeling Madame.

But it was only after everyone had gone —Roy died in 1989, my mother in 1995—that I felt I had the confidence to define Madame's style. Everything she had collected so passionately had been dispersed. I decided to try and put it all back together. The result was *Over the Top: Extraordinary Style in Beauty, Art, Fashion, and Design.*[1] When appraisers came to Madame's apartment after her death to tag the hundreds of artworks, pieces of furniture, and objects to be auctioned, one of them noted that some things were "bizarre, rather than beautiful." I especially loved that comment. It made me hope that, even though decades had past, Madame would have liked my deep appreciation for her love of things, both precious and ordinary, in good and not-so-good taste, that made up her truly singular style.

Helena Rubinstein: the power of an art collection

Julie Verlaine

For all those interested in the history of women art collectors in the 20th century, Helena Rubinstein is an essential figure who seems to combine two different models and eras. Firstly, she clearly inherited many of the practices and values of the preceding century—that of the Industrial Revolution and the development of capitalism, particularly in English-speaking countries. For Rubinstein, as for the American industrial and financial magnates of the 19th century—the Corcorans, Fricks, Morgans, Vanderbilts, and Rockefellers—collecting was a way of socially signaling economic success and of indicating her position among the elite. Yet Helena Rubinstein, when she began collecting in around 1908–9, was also a pioneer in two distinct ways: firstly by her gender—she was one of the first women to acquire works of art paid for out of her own earnings and not out of her family's or her husband's fortune—and then through her particularly eclectic and unconventional taste, which was directed towards objects then considered worthless—such as dolls—or at odds with Western aesthetic norms, such as African statuettes. In this dual capacity, by the middle of the 20th century she had come to embody a new archetype of the collector: an active and autonomous woman with an assured and individual personal taste.

Helena Rubinstein's journey as a collector and patron of the arts offers an exceptional opportunity to consider the social significance of an art collection, as well as the relationship between wealth, power, and self-affirmation. When articulated with the question of gender—how, for instance, did her identity as a woman affect her life choices?—a study of her discourse and practice reveals not only the complexity of the processes that lead to the constitution and diversification of a collection, but also the profoundly liberating impact, symbolically at least, such activities had on the woman they called "Madame."[1]

Ill. 140

Helena Rubinstein in her apartment at 895 Park Avenue, New York, photograph by Herbert Gehr published in *Life*, July 21, 1941; in the background, on the left, an Alaskan rattle (lot 257) and on the right, behind the armchair, a Kota reliquary guardian (lot 203)

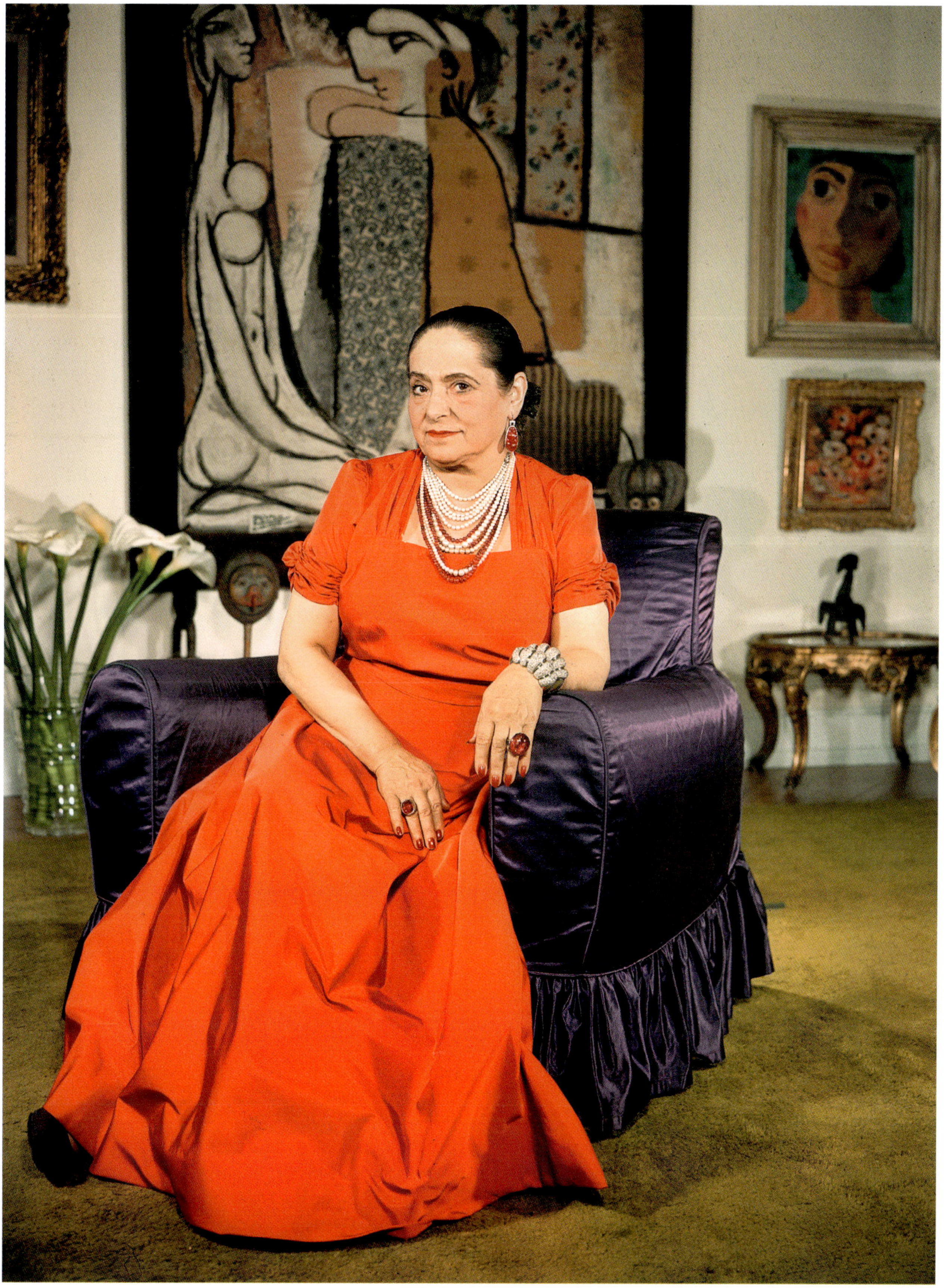

Helena Rubinstein, a 19th-century collector?

Helena Rubinstein's conception of art collecting as a preeminent social practice closely resembles that of her male predecessors, who had established the capitalist collecting norm in the second half of the 19th century. The extraordinary upheavals occasioned by the democratic (r)evolution and the Industrial Revolution proper on Western politics, economics, and culture are a matter of record. Some fortunes were lost (by the dethroned aristocratic elite), others were amassed (by those industrial and banking magnates soon dubbed "Robber Barons"). In the United States particularly, these new elites were convinced that art collecting, by proclaiming wealth and, therefore, power, acted as an effective symbol of their professional success. Art constitutes a proof of refinement, moreover, and thus expresses the cultural and social distinction of its owner—a distinction that their occasionally modest background and meteoric rise up the social ladder made difficult to assert.

Helena Rubinstein saw her collection as just one of the ostensible signs of her success. But it was also an act of revenge on a childhood spent in poverty, on a strict upbringing short on fun and games, and on an overbearing father who never permitted her to have personal possessions. One of her greatest pleasures in being rich was therefore being able to buy all those things she had been deprived of in her youth—not only clothes and jewelry, furniture and works of art, but also dolls and dolls' houses. Her intention was to assert the authentic power that wealth accrues, by acquiring the superfluous, the beautiful, and the useless, so as to dispel the frustrations and restrictions that clouded her early years. Following her dazzling professional triumph after opening the first "Beauty Salon" in Melbourne in 1902, from 1906 to 1909 compulsive shopping became a way of experiencing wealth directly. Settling first in London (1908), then in Paris (1909), and finally in New York (1914), the businesswoman felt duty bound to assert her upward mobility: initially her purchases of gowns by great couturiers (Charles Frederick Worth, Paul Poiret), as well as her first works of art, originated in what was a professional obligation. The expense incurred was therefore thought of as an investment and formed part of a career and communication strategy in which Helena Rubinstein herself was expected to "embody" her cosmetics and beauty businesses. The special care she lavished on both her physical appearance and on the environment in which she entertained was one consequence. It was then in the course of decorating her homes—which were both a place to live and, as for so many rich industrialists in the previous century, a showcase for her social position—that she truly became a collector. Was it really a coincidence that Solna, the London house she bought in 1909, had previously belonged to one of America's greatest collectors and patrons, John Pierpont Morgan?[2] In our eyes it seems more likely that the magnate—together with his house—played a decisive role as a template for Helena Rubinstein when she came to renovate and decorate the property's twenty rooms. The refurbishment of Solna proved crucial in several respects: firstly, it allowed Rubinstein to explore various aesthetics, consciously choosing eclecticism as the rule (or non-rule) that would govern her collection; secondly, because it was for here that she placed her first orders with the Polish sculptor Elie Nadelman, who carved its marble bas-reliefs; and, finally, because it coincided with her discovery of African art in the home of a neighbor, Jacob Epstein.

A new phase in her professional career (the profitable repurchase of her company after the stock market crash of 1929 and the accelerating industrialization and diversification of cosmetics production) and in her personal life (divorcing her first husband,

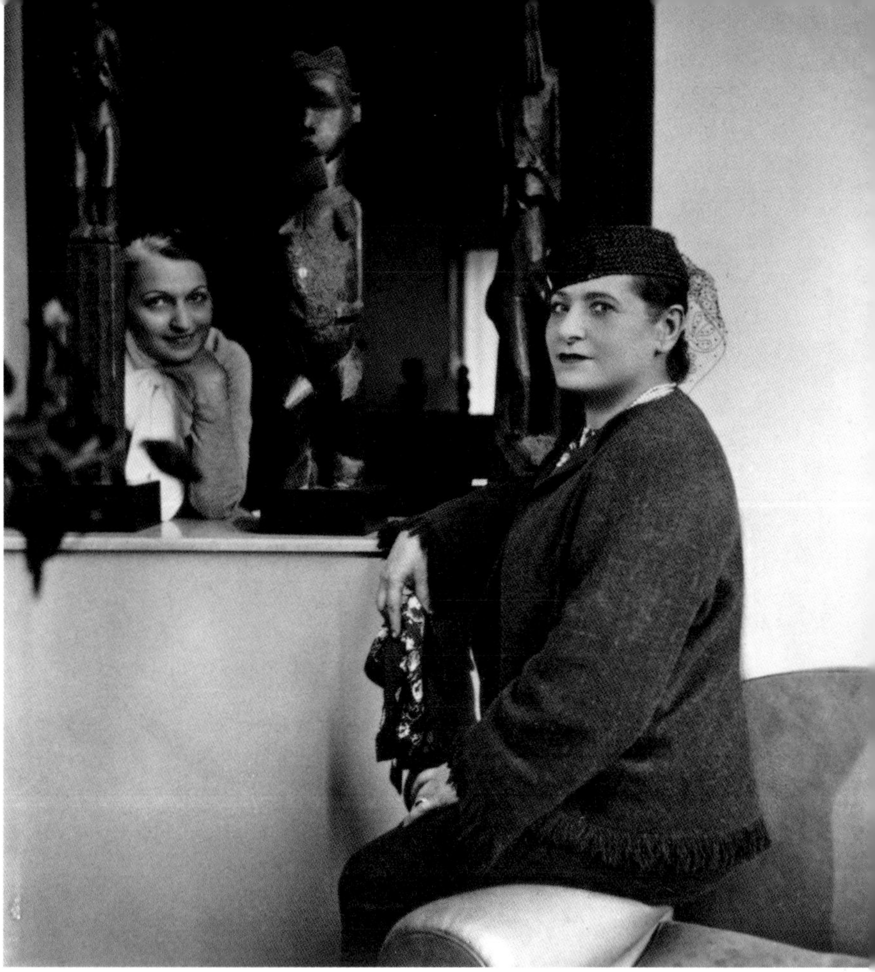

Edward William Titus, she married the Georgian Prince Artchil Gourielli-Tchkonia in 1938) coincided with a turning-point in her collecting practice marked by the purchase of a penthouse triplex at 625 Park Avenue in New York, an apartment boasting thirty-six rooms and eight bathrooms.

Helena Rubinstein seized the chance to commission Salvador Dalí to paint a series of frescoes depicting Morning, Noon and Night under the title *Fantastic Landscape* for the games room, and to decorate the main lounge with an assortment of African and Oceanic masks, Impressionist and Cubist paintings, and some period furniture. It was there that she received journalists from all over the world and many photographs show her seated in front of the large tapestry designed by Picasso and flanked by two smaller ones by Georges Rouault. Other spaces were reserved for private use, such as the "chintz room," where she would play bridge and talk shop surrounded by Native American art and, in a pair of vitrines, a collection of silver Mexican and South American artifacts for which she had acquired a liking through her friendship with Diego Rivera and Frida Kahlo, whose New York studio she visited.

Ill. 141
Marie Cuttoli and Helena Rubinstein, 216, Boulevard Raspail, Paris, 1934, photograph by Boris Lipnitzki; in the center a Teke statue (lot 245) and to either side statues from Borneo (lot 254 and 255)

Another practice—one rooted in a centuries-old tradition of patronage in the West and reactivated by the great American tycoons of the 19th century—was the commissioning of a portrait from an artist. Once again Rubinstein's are remarkable in terms of

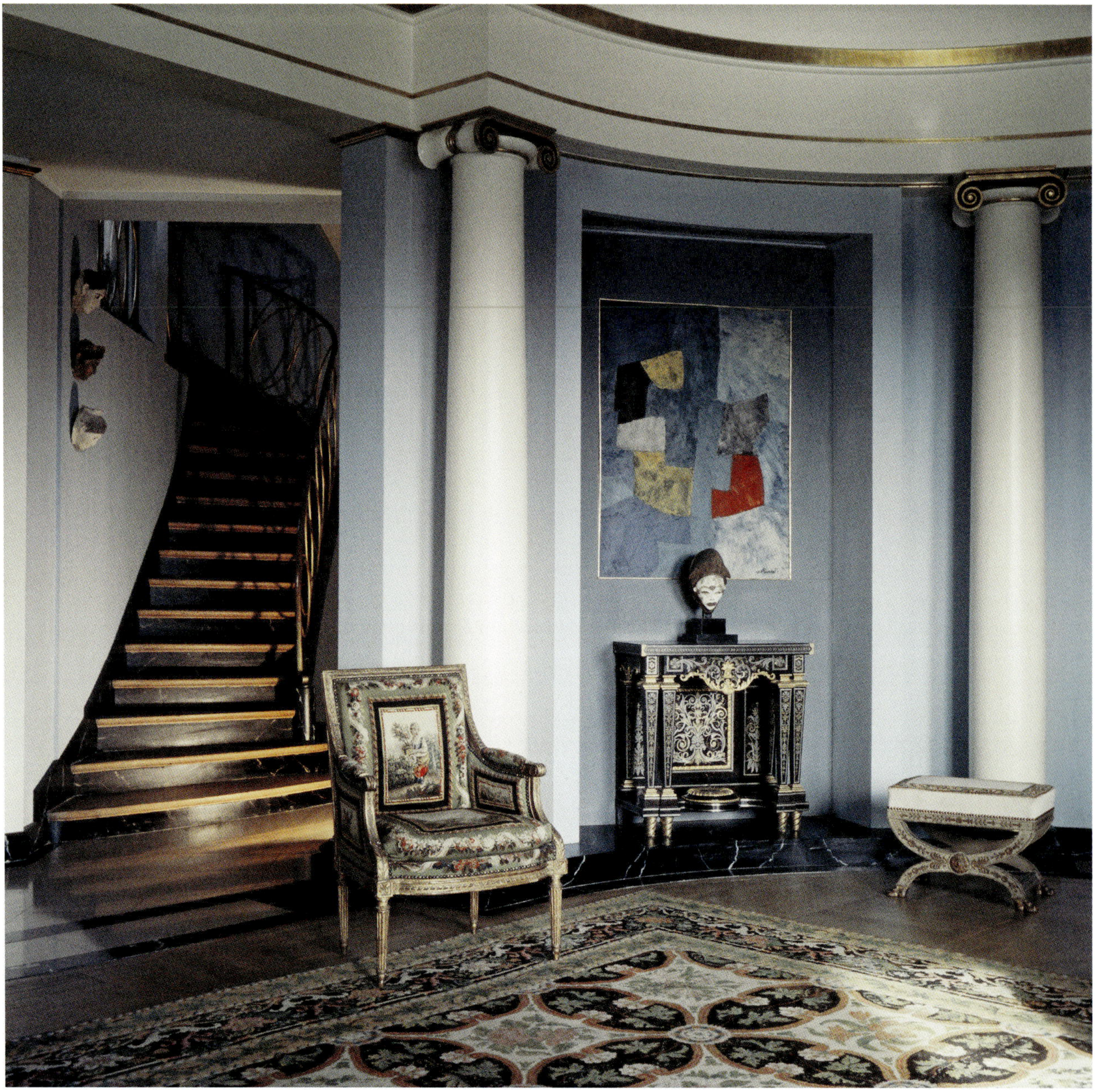

sheer quantity: between 1935 and 1965 no less than twenty-seven artists were commissioned to paint the businesswoman in a patronage opportunity that, on the symbolic level, enhanced her status further.[3] These portraits formed part of a larger body of images of the entrepreneur produced to promote the company that were designed to let clients—avid magazine readers—enjoy a glimpse of her fantasy world. These images were calculated to present a confident, wealthy, and powerful woman, who was made more approachable by her fondness for works of art. As with her contemporary[4] "Mademoiselle" Gabrielle Chanel, the media circus orchestrated by "Madame" Helena Rubinstein consisted in seeming to lift a corner of the veil over her existence. By exhibiting

ILL. 142

The rotunda in the apartment at 24, Quai de Béthune, Paris, c. 1960, photograph by Willy Maywald; on the console table, a Punu mask (lot 191)

the objects she owned and that formed part of her everyday life, she asserted her success, her power, and her femininity.

Collecting and women's liberation

Neither a man, nor even the wife (or widow, or daughter) of a man, Helena Rubinstein reconfigured and subverted the accepted practice of 19th-century collecting. Attuned to the developments of her epoch, she was a pioneer who foreshadowed the growth of work among women and heralded their capacity to become entrepreneurs or business leaders and thus follow brilliant careers. In so doing she spawned a new paradigm of the female collector—that of an active, modern, financially and artistically independent woman, free of the patriarchal shackles that then still weighed so heavily on the majority of her sisters.

A wholly different form of power, collecting became a vector for channeling this sense of liberation. Each acquisition was an expression of free will—something that could be viewed as provocative in conservative circles at a time when women in the US were not yet even full citizens (the right to vote was only granted in 1920). Helena Rubinstein could buy whatever she wanted, when she wanted... and as much as she wanted. As early as 1909, she started what she herself dubbed "buying in bulk," readily snapping up individual lots (sculptures, engravings, statuettes) or purchasing entire collections (e.g. those of F.-H. Lem and Dr. Lheureux). For her, it seems to have been part and parcel of living the high life.

The influence of several close friends was crucial to this doggedly won freedom. Helena Rubinstein always relied on her family and friends in developing her artistic tastes and in selecting acquisitions. It was Misia Sert—like Rubinstein born into a poor family in Poland—widow of a financier who left her a fortune and remarried to the artist José Maria Sert, who opened the doors of the glamorous world of the arts and the theater in Paris. Convincing Rubinstein of the "profound significance of the artistic revolution" undertaken by the Fauves and Cubists, Misia provided a remarkable model of women as both patrons and muses.[5]

The sculptor Jacob Epstein, whose Polish parents had emigrated to the United States before he was born, taught her to "love the expressive intensity" of the African sculptures he collected in his London home close to Solna.[6] What makes Helena Rubinstein so modern and distinguishes her from collectors of earlier generations, attracted more by specific periods (such as the Italian Renaissance) or exotic pieces (chiefly Japanese), is precisely her openness to so-called "primitive," and, in particular, African art, with which Parisians were becoming more familiar at that time. Her artistic sensibility was such that she felt in phase with the Cubist then the Surrealist avant-gardes, both fascinated by the impact and forms of these statuettes and masks. Helena Rubinstein, like several other notable women of her generation (Gabrielle Chanel, Marie Cuttoli, Jacqueline Delubac, Ima Hoog), was also attracted by the artistic experiments of Matisse, Chagall, and Marcoussis, as well as by the Surrealist schools in Paris and New York. Claiming to have one foot in the arts and the other in business, her ambition was to draw the two worlds closer or even to unite them.

Beauty: a constant theme in life and art

Since, especially for women like Helena Rubinstein, art collecting occurred at the intersection of her social and private life, her activity offers a prime example of the growing osmosis between the personal and public spheres. Above all, for her, collecting was a tool for asserting her femininity otherwise than through physical appearance. Her individual, atypical range of tastes may be said to articulate a basic theory of universal beauty.

Over the course of her life Helena Rubinstein did not just amass one, but several very diverse collections. In addition to African, Oceanic, and Mesoamerican pieces, avant-garde Parisian art of the years 1910–30, and rare furniture (the three areas best known during her lifetime[7]), she also collected dolls and dolls' houses. Most of the latter collection, which she started as a child in Krakow, vanished during WWII, since it had been left behind in her Paris apartment on the Quai de Béthune or in the mill at Combs-la-Ville, both looted by the Germans.[8] Following the Liberation, Helena Rubinstein started constituting a new collection of some 20,000 pieces of toy furniture, some dating back to the 17th century. A room in her apartment on Park Avenue was dedicated to this collection displayed in miniature houses, carefully lit, and protected in display cases; one is a replica of Modigliani's studio as the collector saw it on a visit shortly after WWI.

Rubinstein did not simply concede that her tastes and collections were eclectic: she positively proclaimed it. For instance, the living-room interior in the Quai de Béthune apartment designed by Louis Süe in 1930 intentionally adopts a mixture of styles and periods: paintings by Modigliani, Bonnard, and Miró on walls with yellow hangings, together with dozens of African sculptures, dialog with French Regency and Louis-Philippe furniture. A similar philosophy was evident a few years later in the lounge in the Park Avenue penthouse furnished with Victorian chairs, Chinese tables, and Turkish lamps dotted about an acid green carpet signed by Miró. The walls were lined with the serried ranks of an extraordinary panoply of paintings by the foremost artists of the period that included Matisse, Braque, Chagall, Derain, Gris, Rouault, Picasso, and Dalí.

Helena Rubinstein was the target of numerous and sometimes virulent attacks against, in turn, her volatile temperament, the unevenness of her collection, her proclivity for the ugly and the bizarre, even accusing her of a total lack of taste. Her defense, with respect to both her collecting and her life choices, was to keep faith with a personal conception of beauty, defined as something irreducibly subjective, and therefore individual, conveyed by the character or strength of a face, an expression, or an object: "the unspoken connection between the works that move and inspire me exercises a kind of lyrical power in the service of happiness," she wrote in one of her autobiographies.[9] As noted above, Helena Rubinstein cared not one iota for the frontier between art and non-art, between the "worthy" and the "unworthy." The eclecticism of her collections resulted, on the one hand, from how she acquired the objects—instinctively, without forethought or rationalization—and, on the other, from a very personal quest for beauty and the primacy afforded to the "emotional pull" a given artifact might exert over her. "Being surrounded by art objects serves as a counterbalance to the concern I recommend with external appearance. This time we are dealing with health in our external life. Thus are the two poles of the aspiration to the ideal set up."[10] It is, she explained in 1957, a "kind of aesthetic fatality."

Helena Rubinstein's journey as a collector shattered the overly rigid typologies that sought to pigeonhole her practice into pre-established categories. A daughter of the flamboyant American capitalism of the 19th century, she was above all a 20th-century woman who reveled in a freedom and autonomy gained by dint of hard work.

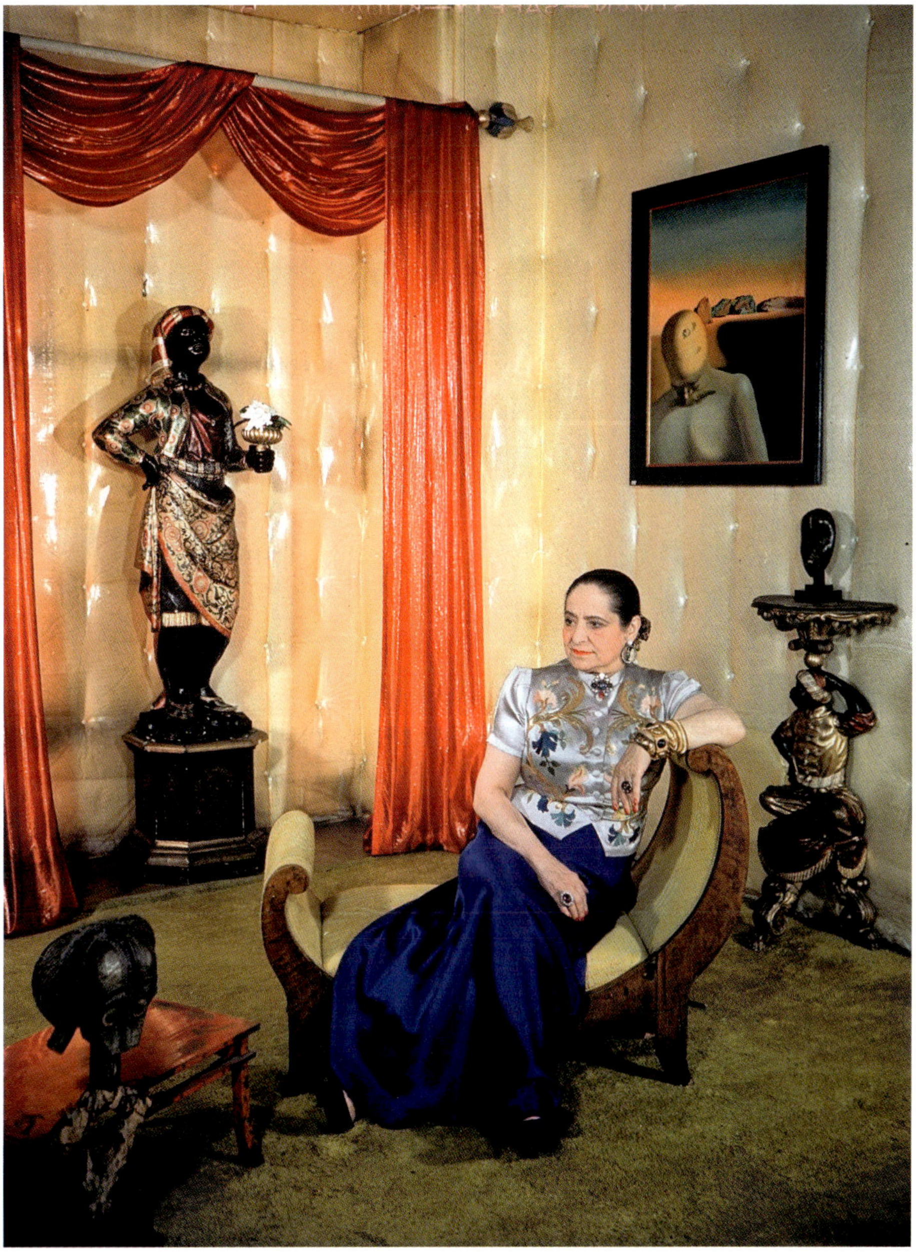

Ill. 143

Helena Rubinstein in her apartment at 895, Park Avenue, New York, 1941, photograph by Herbert Gehr, published in *Life*, May 15, 1964; in the foreground a Kota reliquary guardian (lot 203), in the background a Dan mask (lot 7)

Her art collection was but one aspect of an existence founded on self-assertion, grandeur, and generosity—an important, if secondary activity, which answered her personal quest for emotional enrichment and media recognition. Different from, yet complementary to, Peggy Guggenheim—the other trailblazing woman collector of the era—Helena Rubinstein embodied a new archetype of the mid 20th-century art lover and patron. For her fellow women and subsequent generations, she is also the incarnation of a new, inspiring female role model.

To Collect "au Féminin"

Susan Kloman

The present exhibition and catalog will remind those who already know, the cognoscenti, of the importance of the Helena Rubinstein Collection of African and Oceanic art. For those yet to be acquainted with her, it will serve as a history lesson about the woman behind the famous eponymous cosmetic brand, and her life as an art collector. Among collectors of African and Oceanic art, she is considered to be among the greatest, for what she achieved, both in terms of scope and quality, was no small feat. Moreover, she collected in a field that even today, irrespective of the collector's gender, is reserved for the brave of heart. The present study contemplates what it meant to be a woman, a female art collector, in the early part of the 20th century. It raises questions that may remain just that—questions—while nevertheless considering that she was a unique individual who did not follow the usual trails—she blazed them.

Parallel Histories: Helena Rubinstein and Catherine the Great

Catherine the Great of Russia (1729–1796) is often cited as the first female to have built a vast and important collection of art.[1] Her story sets the stage, in overarching terms, for certain recurring themes regarding women as art collectors, and there are distinct parallels between these two women, even though they lived two hundred years apart.

Perhaps to state the obvious, economics play a key role in art collecting. Independent access to money and wealth today remains a topical issue with regard to gender bias in the workplace. This applies to all levels of society, and men today continue to hold the vast majority of wealth, which is one reason why such a disproportionate number of significant women collectors are known. In the case of Catherine the Great, she held total power and was able to access funds through the state. It is important to bear in

Ill. 144
Madame
in the music room at
24, Quai de Béthune, Paris,
c. 1963; on the piano
a Punu mask (lot 191)
and in the background,
a Kota reliquary guardian
(lot 194)

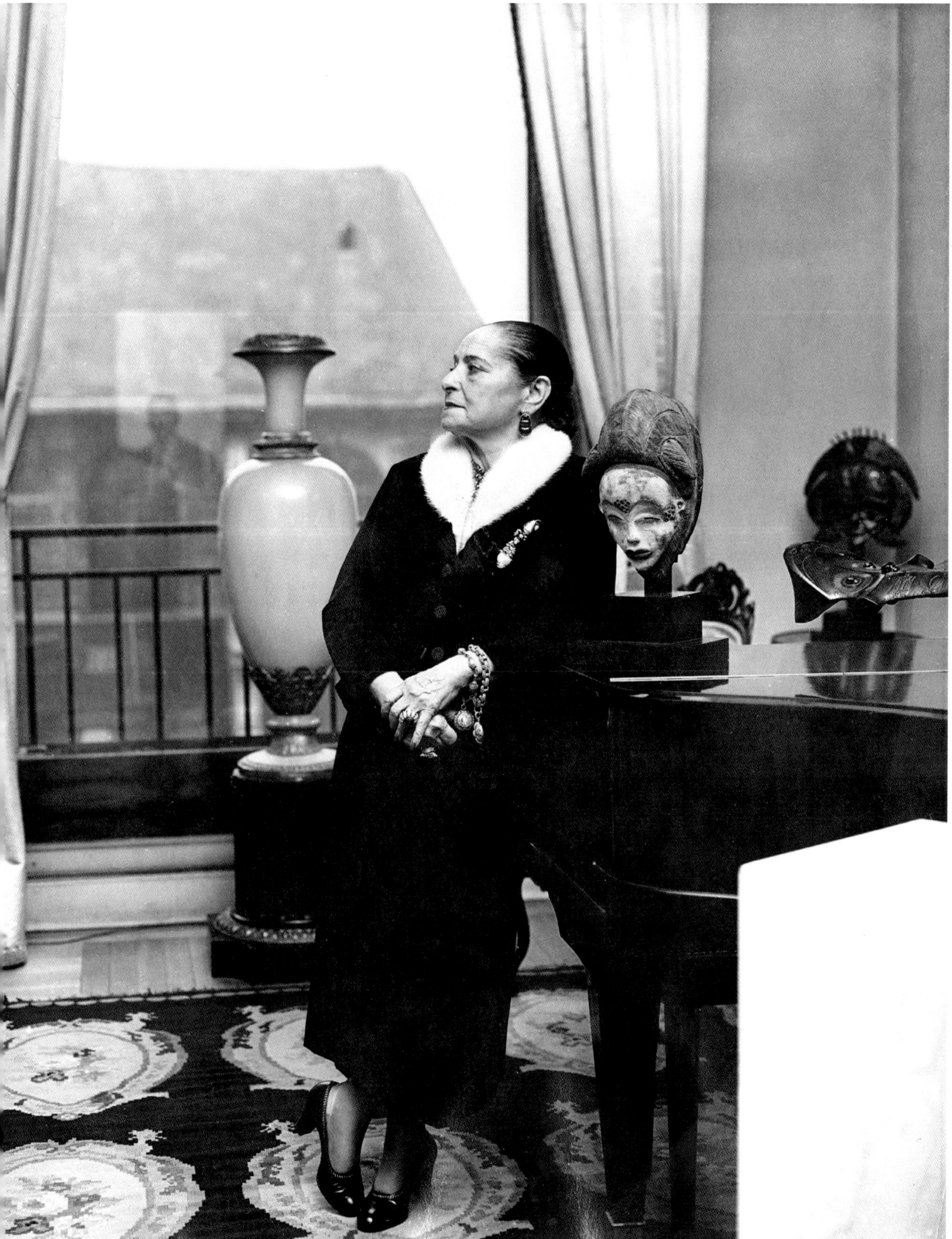

mind that she did not blithely inherit her position. She was ambitious and acquired her status by positioning powerful and savvy allies to overthrow her husband, Peter III, a foreign and unpopular leader. In Helena Rubinstein's case, as a self-made woman in business, she had vast wealth from her cosmetics company, as well as other well-conceived financial and real estate ventures. These were both exceptional women who transcended societal norms.[2]

Despite the wealth and power each ultimately acquired, they, nevertheless came from modest backgrounds. Catherine the Great, while of noble heritage, was raised unostentatiously in a small town in what is today Poland. Similarly, as other authors will have noted in this catalog, Rubinstein also lived meagerly in her formative years, coincidentally also in Poland.[3]

Empress Catherine tended to acquire collections in total, and she was therefore sought both for her patronage by artists and for her benevolence by collectors or estates that had fallen upon hard times. In 1764, the Hermitage Collection was effectively born with the Empress's acquisition of 225 paintings, initially gathered for Frederick the Great, who then could not commit to buying the collection. This is today the State Hermitage Museum in St. Petersberg, and the second-largest art museum in the world. For her part, Rubinstein also acquired entire collections in benevolent, through seemingly though not completely altruistic gestures. For example, she bought almost the entirety of the collection that F.-H. Lem had assembled during his journey to Africa in 1934–35.

An enlightened despot, Empress Catherine carried a view that art was a means of instruction and served the betterment of humanity. At the same time, she used art to promote another kind of political agenda for a new Russia—one that had an international scope and would be better for incorporating this vision. She therefore tailored her collecting across a spectrum of cultures and periods. While this can be viewed as a type of propaganda—today we might call it "marketing for the state"—leaders before her had held provincial views of art and collecting, and promoted only Russian art of former times to bolster the country's greatness. In a parallel vein, Rubinstein also promoted her own collection as a marketing tool to advance herself and her business.

"Quality's Nice, but Quantity Makes a Show!": African Art Collecting as Beauty Marketing

One of the keys to Rubinstein's success in business was her marketing genius. On the one hand, she portrayed herself as a scientist to legitimize her products, often posing in white lab coats surrounded by beakers. On the other hand, she emphasized the association of makeup with fashion, and she further distinguished her salons as the ultimate in luxury through innovative thinking in artistic terms by adopting art historical language. The application of her cosmetics was an "art form" and her products touted as "masterpieces."

Rubinstein started collecting art early in her career. It is believed that as early as 1908, she started acquiring African art at the encouragement of her friend the artist Jacob Epstein when she was residing in London.[4] She increasingly displayed works of art from her collection in her salons to create an atmosphere that would associate herself (it was, after all, an eponymous brand) and, by extension, her clients, with high culture and sophistication. Knowing that African art was a primary inspiration for Modernist artists, she viewed both the art itself and her pursuit of it as cutting-edge. It reflected precisely where she always wanted to be in business—at the forefront, the avant-garde. She turned something that was her natural inclination and pleasure into a tool to advance her business. She also associated her art collecting with her extensive travels and tireless hunt for new ingredients. Though she didn't travel to Africa, the natural association, as she eloquently framed it, was that by obtaining African sculptures and studying their exotic character, she was unearthing their secret and unknown magic for her beauty potions.

"[The] collection of these weird objects which appeal to this beauty expert because of their 'strange charm and beauty of expression,' was gathered by Helena Rubinstein with infinite pains during the past fifteen years of her traveling about the world in search of new ingredients and formulas for her well-known beauty products [. . .]. They have a strange beauty all their own. Such well-known modern artists as Picasso, Matisse, Modigliani, Epstein, Zadkine, and others owe an admitted debt to the newly discovered sculpture of darkest Africa, having been inspired by the original arrangement of lines, masses, colors, light and shades to be found in these carvings of bygone eras."[5]

Considering the Female Perspective: Case Study of Helena Rubinstein and African Negro Art at the Museum of Modern Art, 1935

Like any good business person, Rubinstein kept an inventory of the art in her collection. She inextricably intertwined her collection with her self-image and the branding of her business, and the collection, including her African art, was viewed as an asset. She shared this inventory via her then secretary, Sara Fox, with James Johnson Sweeney as he was preparing for the 1935 landmark exhibition *African Negro Art* at The Museum of Modern Art in New York, to which she was a significant lender [ill. 147]. With the exception of Charles Ratton, for whom dealing in African art was his chief occupation, no other lender to the exhibition seems to have had such an organized account of their material. Rubinstein's notes included where the works had been published or reproduced, and she annotated the list with qualifying language in which some works are noted as "celebrated," "fine," or "magnificent." In particular, two works of art from her collection that today are acknowledged as some of the greatest examples known are given special annotations. The Bangwa commemorative figure [ill. 145]—the so-called "Bangwa Queen"—from Cameroon is listed as "Large figure of standing woman apparently singing—remarkable tragic expression." For the Fang head for a reliquary [ill. 5], she notes, "Great Bieri Head from Gabun [sic]. One of the largest heads in existence."[6]

No other correspondence from lenders to this important exhibition make the same qualitative statements. The quality of the works of art she lent was recognized at the time as extremely high, and time has cemented the fact that her contribution made the show a memorable and highly noteworthy *tour de force*. A few other women are noted as lenders to the exhibition, associated with interesting but relatively minor works of art, and others are listed as the wives of collectors. In the listing of lenders to the exhibition, Rubinstein is unquestionably noted as the collector: Collection Madame Helena Rubinstein, New York.

Something else that makes her unique amongst other collectors in this context is that she created a press release timed to correspond with MoMA's press release of *African Negro Art*. For it, she commissioned a now-famous photograph by George Maillard Kesslere of herself in a business suit holding a stylized African mask [ill. 146], and in the text she discusses her interest in and pursuit of African art.[7]

Perhaps her closest counterpart who also lent to the exhibitions was Frank Crowninshield, the tastemaker and famed editor of *Vanity Fair* magazine. Who else could be better poised for self-promotion? He had the vehicle of *Vanity Fair* and, like Rubinstein, collected Modern and African art. While he did publish four short articles about African art at the time[8], there do not appear to be any photographs of him with his African sculptures. Indeed, there are surprisingly few photographs of him with his collection at all, especially compared to Rubinstein. The correspondence he had relating to the MoMA exhibition was perfunctory, suggesting he had a very different relationship to his collection than Rubinstein.

During this period of the 1930s, the Parisian art dealer Charles Ratton was very active in the New York art scene. In addition to his participation with MoMA for the *African Negro Art* exhibition, he also worked with important Modern art gallerists such as Pierre Matisse for the promotion of African art. As dynamic as he was, he and Matisse complained to each other at the time about slow sales and the lack of appreciation for the field.[9] While their efforts are noteworthy historically, perhaps they would have been recognized contemporaneously had they followed Rubinstein's examples in publicity.

"Au Feminin" for Further Consideration

The world still undervalues what it defines as "feminine." Helena Rubinstein built an important collection of African art, and today her accomplishments are recognized in their full value, as testified by this major exhibition at the Musée du Quai Branly and others in her name. As such, one could argue her endeavors were neither trivialized nor "feminized." Forming an important art collection is something that in and of itself is characterized as "masculine," as is African art collecting.[10] One way to distinguish what makes the Rubinstein collection "feminine" is not her predilection for collecting or the subject of her interests, but rather to consider how her process was unlike that of her male counterparts. The case study of her participation in the exhibition of *African Negro Art* at The Museum of Modern Art provides the most telling snapshot. Rubinstein's collection was an extension of herself. With her careful lists and the way she lived with artwork, she pampered and valorized her collection as part of her own image. What also sets her apart is her modernism. The ways in which she portrayed herself both with and through her collection and its pursuit seems normal to us today in our culture of social media and "selfies." At the time, however, she was audacious and cutting edge.

Above left
Ill. 145
"Commemorative figure" [lefem bangwa female statue, Cameroon], photograph by Walker Evans taken from the *African Negro Art* portfolio, New York, Museum of Modern Art, 1935 (cat. 75)

Above right
Ill. 146
Helena Rubinstein holding a Guro mask, 1934, photograph by George Maillard Kesslere

Bas
Ill. 147
View of the *African Negro Art* exhibition at MoMa, 1935, photograph by Soichi Sunami; on the right a Bamileke seat from the Rubinstein collection

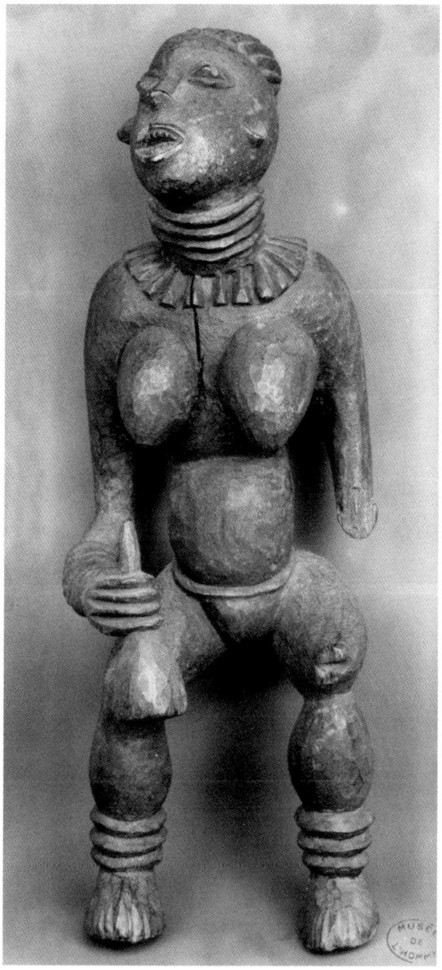

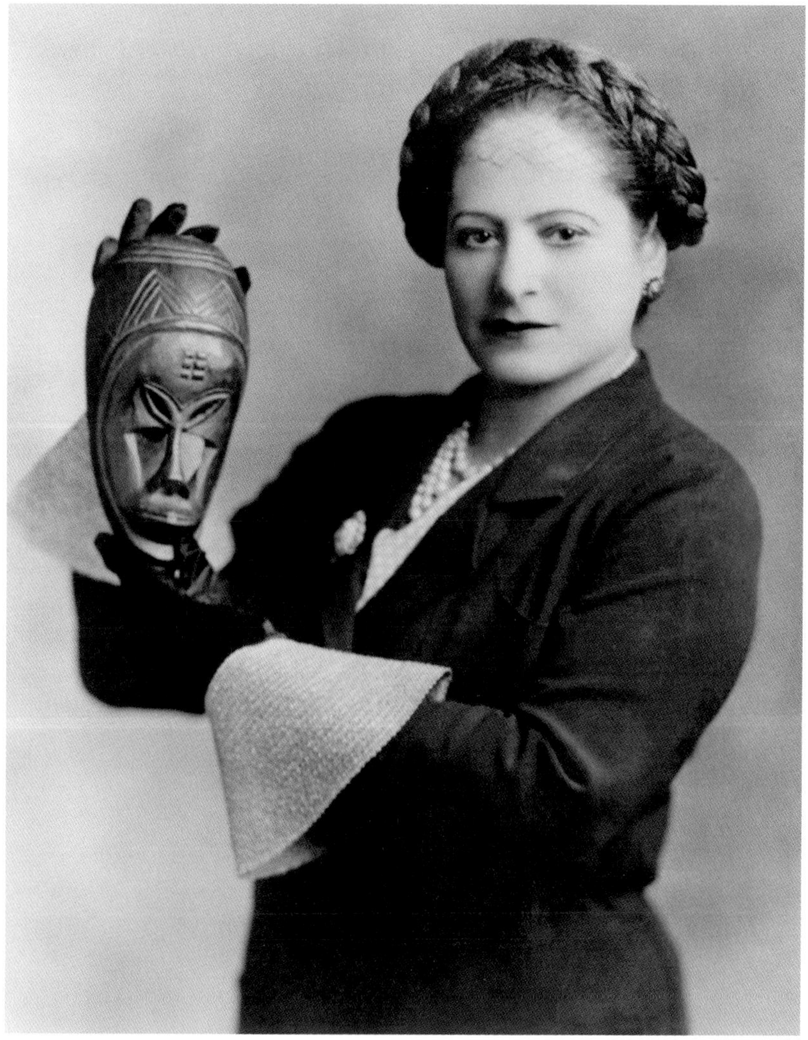

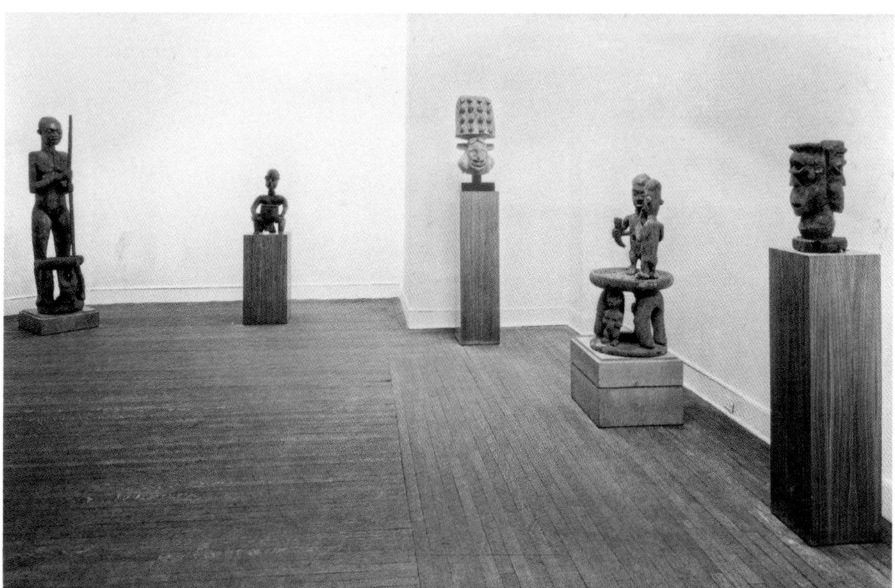

A conversation with Estrellita B. Brodsky

Catherine Grenier

Estrellita B. Brodsky is an art historian and a major collector and patron. Her efforts focus particularly on the recognition of Latin American art in the United States and Europe.

C.G.: One of the leading patrons of modern and contemporary art, your profile is intriguing. Not only are you a philanthropist, in the tradition of those great, cultured patrons who strive to increase public awareness of art, you are also a woman with firm convictions. Could you start by reminding us of the origins of your love of art. How did you learn about art and what was your first artistic revelation?

E.B.: I think it was back when I began studying art at Sarah Lawrence College in New York, with the idea of becoming an artist. I quickly realized that I didn't have an artistic gift as such, but that I was passionate about art and art history. The first artist to really fascinate me was Picasso. But, after leaving university I was more and more attracted to Latin American art. Both my parents came from Latin America. My father had arrived in Venezuela from Eastern Europe in the 1920s and adored the country that gave him his freedom. My mother was born into an old Uruguayan family. It was in Uruguay that my parents met. After their marriage they moved to Venezuela, but my mother was a little disappointed by a country whose culture was so different from hers. Modernity had not developed there in the same way: Uruguay was very close to European culture, while Venezuela had remained far more tropical in character. My parents decided to continue farther north, first to Mexico City, then on to New York. For a time, they considered leaving for Europe, but were deterred by the difficulties of the postwar situation. My father often thought about going back to Venezuela, but my mother loved living in New York. So that's where I grew up, though I went on many trips to both Venezuela and Uruguay. I soon realized that the term "Latin America" as employed by North Americans is misleading:

they actually had no idea of the diversity and richness of the diverse cultures of South America. Over time, I've suffered a lot from this. Because of my origins people used to imagine I came from a family of poor immigrant workers. They had no inkling that my great-grandfather had been president of Uruguay, that he owned an art collection, and that his family was highly educated. My father also had a cultured background; he was a music lover and an occasional collector. Art was highly thought of at home. When we went to Venezuela, I came into contact with works by kinetic artists, which for me represented a true breath of fresh air. These artists taught us that art could change life: in the 1960s we were brought up with the idea that we could change the world. That's when my interest in Latin American art was born. Later, I studied art history at Hunter College in New York, where I did a master's degree in Impressionism. Then I embarked on a thesis on two Latin American artists, the Venezuelan Jesús Rafael Soto and the Argentine Julio Le Parc, who had settled in Paris after the war. Ever since then, I have tried my utmost to improve the understanding of Latin American art among the public, especially in the United States and Europe.

C.G.: So you made your way into the museum world to encourage it to do more in this field.

E.B.: Yes. First of all, I presided as co-chair on the Board of Trustees of the Museo del Barrio in New York. In 1998 I also participated, on a technical level, in the exhibition *Taino. Pre-Columbian art and Caribbean culture.* I was a member of the selection committee that appointed Julian Zugazagoitia director. Finding the trustees well set up, I quit my position on the Board to resume and finish my PhD. I went back to museums a little later. I tried to urge them to create curatorial positions so as to alter their vision of Latin American art and help develop knowledge in that field. I was involved in setting up a specialized post at Tate Modern in London, then, round about the same time, in 2006, at the Museum of Modern Art, New York—and today I'm doing the same for the Metropolitan Museum. I think it's worked out rather well, as there have since been many exhibitions dedicated to Latin American artists that have turned the spotlight onto their work. Of course, there remains much to be done, because institutions always tend to follow the same artists, whereas there are so many others to discover.

C.G.: Would you define yourself more as a philanthropist or a collector?

E.B.: I don't know if philanthropist is the right word. I consider myself more of an activist. I offer support wherever I think change is needed. Philanthropy can sometimes seem passive. I'm an active collector, though I think that if tomorrow my activity no longer had any impact, I'd stop. I'd tell myself, that's enough, I've enough works as it is. But, as long as I see Latin American art insufficiently recognized and incorrectly contextualized, I won't feel fulfilled. So, I think in that sense I'm more of a philanthropist than a collector: let's say I'm an activist philanthropist.

C.G.: Why did you choose to help existing museums rather than open one of your own?

E.B.: Because I think that all this is not about ego. What's important is to transform museums from the inside. To open up museums to other perspectives that are not mine alone. For a museum it's not healthy for a collector to become over prescriptive. It's essential to cater for different voices and different narratives, to maintain openness, to accept the challenge of different ways of thinking about certain artists, so as to be urged to reconsider one's own. So, having my own museum would be the opposite of what I want.

C.G.: How did you build up your collection? Do you collect artists from different generations?

E.B.: Yes. I've just acquired some very beautiful works by Xul Solar, a modern Argentine artist. I also have pieces by Uruguayan artists from the same period, including Joaquín Torres-García. But I also buy works by contemporary artists, including young talents, because I think it's important to support their work. They need encouragement. That's why I now use my office space to hold exhibitions. I'm backing the work of two artists in the next one, which will be dedicated to the effects of drug trafficking on societies in both Americas.

C.G.: Do you also give support to museums in Latin America? Or do you prefer funding American museums to help them improve the recognition of artists from those countries?

E.B.: I have offered support to several for specific exhibition projects, but not on a regular basis. I also try to help North American museums outside New York. But there's so much to do....

C.G.: Does your collection also include artists who are not Latin American?

E.B.: Yes, I sometimes venture off the beaten path, but in general that's the remit of my husband, Daniel. For example, he loves Calder and Le Corbusier, and also Moholy-Nagy, and we've acquired works by these artists. Calder was one of my early favorites, before I devoted myself to Latin America. We have also purchased works by personalities who rubbed shoulders with Latin American artists in Paris in the 1950s and 1960s, such as Vasarely, who was very important for the artists I collect, such as Takis, Arman, and artists in the Zero group... What interests me most about Latin American artists is that they seek to interact with society; they articulate a social and political message, even when practicing abstraction. They make art for everyone. Many European artists share in this desire to democratize art. I've helped produce works of this type, such as The Academy of Failure, by the Argentine visual artist Marta Minujín, and work by the Guatemalan artist, Aníbal López, for the 2012 Documenta show, which involved the presence on site of a young contract killer.

C.G.: Your husband, Daniel Brodsky, is also a collector and a major patron. Do you encourage one another?

E.B.: Daniel keeps away from my personal collection, but he encourages me. In the same way, I offer him encouragement. At first, we tried to collect together, but it didn't work out. We often disagreed.

C.G.: You don't share the same artists because your own personal commitment is deeply linked to your family's origins and your roots?...

E.B.: Yes, in a positive sense. And because, in 1960s Latin America, the engagement with art was a profound one. You could see art in the streets, there were commissions for universities, a lot of large-scale public art. More than in New York, art was part and parcel of the landscape. As for Daniel, he was raised in New York in the 1950s, at a time when it was not uncommon to find yourself in a milieu with artists and collectors. We both have the impression of having grown up surrounded by art, by the theater, music, galleries...

C.G.: Philanthropy has played a major part in developing modern culture in the United States. Do you think that's still the case today?

E.B.: I hope so, but I think it will be difficult for institutions to attract the new generation. I don't want to generalize, but I notice, for example, that my own children are more interested in philanthropy in favor of social causes. They are aware of their responsibility in how society evolves. The whole atmosphere has changed.

C.G.: You are today one of the most important patrons of the arts. There have been great women philanthropists in the history of modernity to whom we owe museums such as MoMA, the Whitney, and the Guggenheim... Have these models been important to you?

E.B.: Absolutely, I've been very affected by several of them! They gave an immense impetus to art by creating all these museums. I can't compare myself to such leading lights. On the artistic level there have indeed been women who've played a major role. They're especially inspiring. They were really driven by their love of art and perhaps less guided by their personal interests than some men.

C.G.: Do you consider it important to give backing to works from outside the mainstream?

E.B.: Very much so. And that's why, for example, I helped produce Aníbal López's piece for the 2012 Documenta show. It's not an art form you can stick in your home; it made a huge impact, but it was neither mainstream nor commercial. It's necessary to take risks, by supporting events and performances, and by trying to reach out to audiences beyond the elite. Public museums are very important, but so are universities. I fund university scholarships for students from Hunter College and New York University who wish to study Latin American art. I put great store in these programs, which really do make a difference. Of course, large institutions, such as the MET, are the ones that appeal to the widest audience, in number terms as well as across the generations. But smaller institutions, such as the Museo del Barrio, attract families who are proud to see their culture feted. It's important that in the United States, where communities of so many different backgrounds live, it is difference, rather than exclusion, that is cultivated and celebrated. That's what I hope to make happen.

June 2018

Madame's collection: Africa at its heart, Hélène Joubert

1. "I *am* the business," in O'Higgins 1972, p. 318. The course of her life is indeed inseparable from the development of the cosmetics company she founded in Australia at the beginning of the 20th century (1903) and gradually expanded into Europe and the United States.
2. See bibliography.
3. 2,000 lots were sold, for a record total of $5 million; the African and Oceanic art pieces (catalogs 1 and 2, for the auctions on April 21 and 29, 1966) brought in $470,000. On October 15, 1966, at 11.00 am, Parke-Bernet organized the "African and Oceanic Art, Part Three" auction, with 100 lots. Considered less important, it included the articles housed in New York.
4. Her favorite couturiers from the beginning of the century were Worth, Poiret, Chanel, Molyneux, Lanvin, Balenciaga, Schiaparelli, and Dior, who had once been an antique dealer, an experience that meant they had much in common.
5. Eugénie Merz, housekeeper at the Quai Béthune residence, told Patrick O'Higgins on the occasion of his first trip to Paris in 1951: "There are two wings...In the wing facing us, Madame has her bedroom. It is linked with this side of the apartment by *les salles de reception*, a salon, a library, a card room, a music room, the main dining room. There's a lot for me to dust! *Pensez*, just think, *six cent vingt-deux nègres...* six hundred and twenty-two blacks for a start!" quoted in O'Higgins 1972, p. 107.
6. See the essay by Susan Kloman, p. 170, in the present volume.
7. Numerous objects in the collection bear numbers and letters inscribed in white ink comparable to the marks used by museums. In 1956 a list of Madame's art collections (L'Oréal Archives) provided some interesting clues that coincide with the white ink markings observed on a majority of objects: the list records forty-four "African" objects, including objects from Oceania and Insular Southeast Asia, scattered about various rooms and levels in the apartment at 625 Park Avenue in New York, the numbers opposite hinting at a collection chronology.
8. Patrick O'Higgins mentions the purchase in Paris of a painting by Van Dongen negotiated for one million French francs at the time and paid cash on the nail, O'Higgins 1972, p. 173.
9. 216, Boulevard Raspail (architecture and interior design by Bruno Elkouken and Louis Marcoussis, 1932); 24, Quai de Béthune, île Saint-Louis (acquired in 1934; architecture and interior design by Louis Süe, Louis Marcoussis, and Paule Marot, 1937).
10. 895 Park Avenue (interior design by Donald Deskey, 1934); 625 Park Avenue (interior design by Max Weschler, 1940), a 36-room triplex.
11. 247 Knightsbridge (interior design by David Hicks, 1961).
12. "The best pieces are in Paris. The French appreciate such things more than they do here in America," she said of her collection of African art, in O'Higgins 1972, p. 86.
13. O'Higgins 1972, p. 352.
14. Jazdzewski 1999, p. 4.
15. Idem.
16. Idem.
17. Rubinstein 1965.
18. O'Higgins 1972.
19. O'Higgins 1972, p. 83.
20. Real name Arthur Ameisen (1870–1951), he was born in Krakow and raised in Louisiana, marrying an American woman from Pennsylvania, Helen J. Anthony (1879–1942), with whom he had two sons, Richard Anthony Ameisen (June 21, 1900–1925) and Herbert Ameisen (c. 1904–?), before abandoning her sometime after 1904 and starting a new life under the name Edward William Titus. Divorcing from Helena Rubinstein in 1937, he married the daughter of a Swiss banker of Polish Jewish origin, Erica de Meuronurech, some 38 years his junior, whom he had met at Jacob Epstein's in London.
21. Sources are at odds as to the date and place of their wedding: London, 1907 or 1908? Sydney, July 1908?
22. With Dr. Mathilde Pokitonoff, who had published *La Beauté par l'hygiène* in 1894 (Paris: E. Dentu). In her memoirs she alludes to a fictional dermatologist from Saint-Louis Hospital, Professor Berthelot, thereby confirming that she had no memory for names whatsoever.
23. Rubinstein 1965, p. 51.
24. "So, so he told me what to buy for him, adding, 'I'll spend up to three pounds for each object.' That was fifteen dollars, then! If the price went higher, I bought it for myself," in O'Higgins 1972, pp. 85–86.
25. Rubinstein 1965, p. 50.
26. O'Higgins 1972, p. 85.
27. Christie's London, "Egyptian, Greek and Roman Antiquities and Primitives Works of Africa, from the Epstein Collection", December 15, 1961.
28. According to Malcolm McLeod (*Jacob Epstein, il collezionista* in Bologna 2019, pp. 134–35), Epstein reportedly stated in 1930 that he had begun collecting in Paris in 1905; at the end of his life, however, he placed his encounter with the "les arts nègres" in 1902. It seems that he owned about a hundred objects in 1925, more than two hundred in 1931, and more than a thousand by the time he passed away in 1959.
29. Working out of 16, Rue de Miromesnil, then, from 1916, Avenue de Villiers, and, before the end of the war, Rue du Faubourg-Saint-Honoré.
30. In the 1910s, Joseph Brummer, particularly interested in African art, opened a gallery with his brother Ernest on Boulevard Raspail, with another in New York in 1914.
31. Before 1914, Anthony Innocent Morris (1866–1951), in association with Marie Barberger, had opened a store at 10 Rue Victor-Massé (9th arr.) benefitting from windows onto the street. Close to Émile Heyman, through him he had met the African art collectors of the time (including Paul Rupalley and Josef Mueller). Picasso and Paul Guillaume, who lived in the same neighborhood, became customers, followed, in the 1920s, by Charles Ratton and Pierre Vérité.
32. Graduating from the École du Louvre in 1923, Charles Ratton (1895–1986) became a dealer in medieval and Renaissance antiquities and the "*arts nègres*" in 1927. He seems to have met Helena Rubinstein at a sale of some major private collections in 1931, for which he worked as

a consultant. Ratton's photographic archives provide a record of some of the objects that ended up with Helena Rubinstein, including the Yoruba *gelede* mask (lot 179, sold April 29, 1966) and the Yoruba head from Esie (lot 175, sold April 29, 1966), previously acquired from the Hamburg Museum of Ethnography in 1936 (original label on the Esie head at the museum, entitled "N. Yoruba," bearing the number 13: 209: 145, in the Ratton/Ladrière archives, Paris).

33. Probably in around 1935 Helena Rubinstein acquired from the Galerie Pierre (P. Loeb) the two Bansoa heads adorning a Grassland drum (lots 186 and 187, sold April 29, 1966) brought to Europe by the pastor Franck Christol, one of which had been acquired in around 1926 by the great collector Henry Solomon Wellcome, as well as the *moai kava kava* from Easter Island and the statues from Lake Sentani, collected by Jacques Viot after 1929. Albert Loeb recounted how Rubinstein would buy up lots of items from his father's gallery, stuffing a bag with objects—some of uneven quality—as gifts for those close to her in the hope of making them more aware of her admiration of art from distant lands.
34. O'Higgins 1972, p. 117.
35. "This is where I bought some of my best bargains!" in O'Higgins 1972, p. 351.
36. Her 1908 portrait by Paul-César Helleu, a fashionable society portraitist in Paris, London, and New York, shows that she was firmly established in high society by that date; see O'Higgins 1972, p. 109.
37. In 1909 Helena Rubinstein opened the Valaze beauty salon at 255, Rue du Faubourg-Saint-Honoré, after buying up a line of cosmetics developed in the 1880s by Georgine de Champbaron, whose hygiene and beauty firm was located at no. 364 on the same street.
38. Paris became the family residence in autumn 1912.
39. "When in Paris in her younger days, Madame Rubinstein has always lived 'over the shop,'" in O'Higgins 1972, p. 118.
40. Lot 207, in Parke-Bernet Galleries 1966b, p. 178.
41. Slesin 2003, p. 39.
42. In the wake of an exhibition in Paris in 1909 at the Druet gallery, Nadelman aroused interest in the circles frequented by Rubinstein and in 1914–15 she took him under her wing in New York, where he was to exhibit in Alfred Stieglitz's 291 gallery (1915).
43. Slesin 2003, pp. 50–51.
44. Lot 193, sold April 29, 1966
45. Lot 190, sold April 29, 1966
46. K. Inagaki made the stands for practically all the artifacts Madame acquired before 1930. Perhaps indicative of a provenance (Paul Guillaume), this also suggests that she was attentive to the quality of pedestals by Inagaki, who worked for the foremost dealers, artists, and collectors of the time, and that she was keen to present her acquisitions in the best light.
47. Rubinstein 1930.
48. O'Higgins 1972, p. 86.
49. Lem's sister, Jeanne, was the wife of a painter, Jacques Boussard, who had also assembled a collection of African art. The latter's father rented an apartment on the 4th floor of 24, Quai de Béthune, from Helena Rubinstein, which was later occupied by Claude and Georges Pompidou (see the memoirs of Hélène Leloup; working document in progress: interview with Hélène Leloup, January 22, 2018).
50. It was offered in 1936 to the Directorate of the Information and Document Service of the Ministry of Colonies, on the condition it be exhibited in Paris before being deposited in the museum of the French Institute of Black Africa (IFAN) in Dakar.
51. Upon his return, Lem compiled a handbook for the French Secretary of State for the Navy and the Colonies, *Carrières coloniales* (1943). From 1942 onwards, he published a few specialized articles in the *Bulletin de l'Institut français d'Afrique noire* and in the magazine *Soleils*, volume I, reproducing five Bamana and Kurumba crest masks, which later entered the Rubinstein collection. In 1948 he wrote an introduction to the catalog for the *Océanie* exhibition held at the Andrée Olive gallery, in which some previously unpublished poems by André Breton appeared. For the special issue *L'Art nègre* (nos. 10–11) of *Présence africaine*, published in 1951 with art direction by Charles Ratton, he penned an essay entitled *Variété et unité des traditions plastiques africaines*. This number formed a springboard for the documentary by Chris Marker and Alain Resnais *Les statues meurent aussi* (1953) featuring outstanding pieces from the Rubinstein collection, notably the Bangwa statue and the Senufo *deble*. Lem pursued a career as an eclectic art historian with texts on Théodore Géricault (1962), the "theme of the Negro in Géricault's art" (1962), Paul Cézanne (1969), Pont-Aven and the Nabis (exhibition at the Grand Palais, Paris, in 1971).
52. Of the two hundred and twenty-five items collected, she acquired at least sixty-seven, according to the "Lem" provenance notes in the 1966 auction catalog. Thirty-four are reproduced in Lem's study (1948–49). Other objects from Lem may have entered the Rubinstein collection but their provenance has been mislaid over time, thereby perhaps explaining the absence of any mention of this source in the auction catalog.
53. The volume also mentions other objects owned by Lem coming from other collections: the Barnes Foundation, the collections P.C. (Pierre Chadourne), Pierre Vérité, Charles Ratton, Gimond, André Lhôte, the Musée de l'Homme, the Musée de la France d'Outre-Mer, and the crafts center in Bamako.
54. Lem 1948; translated into English, Lem 1949. On this subject, see the essay by Susan Gagliardi, p. 50 in the present volume.
55. In 1938, Helena Rubinstein married the Georgian-born Prince Artchil Gourielli-Tchkonia, whom she met in Paris through the Countess de Polignac, daughter of Jeanne Lanvin.
56. Lem, "The Art of the Sudan in 'Masterpieces of African Art,'" in New York 1954, p. 17 and 21.
57. Fifty-six funerary terracottas collected in the Krinjabo region in June 1928 by Dr. Lheureux had been on display since November 15, 1935

at the Musée de la France d'Outre-Mer. Dissatisfied with the conditions of their display after the war, Lheureux informed Marcel Lucain on July 26, 1952, that he wished to recover the artifacts. On August 20, 1952, he delegated Lem to return the forty-eight terracotta pieces inventoried by the museum (Musée du Quai Branly archives, DA000657/59486). One series was sold at Drouot's on March 5, 1958, presided over by auctioneer Maître Alphonse Bellier, with Jean Roudillon acting as expert. The remaining part of the collection, twenty-nine terracottas in all, was sold at Drouot's on December 11, 1990.

58. "Thirty sculptures from the Sudan" coming from the collection of Helena Rubinstein, Princess Gourielli, were exhibited in 1951 by the decorator Jules Leleu, at 65, Avenue Franklin D. Roosevelt, along with six loans of African pieces from Dr. Paul Chadourne, Jacques Lipchitz, Pierre Vérité, and the Musée de la France d'Outre-Mer, as well as "several paintings by contemporary masters."
59. Madame acquired a set of four Yaka idiophones at the sale of the Roland Tual collection at the Hôtel Drouot, Paris, on February 10 and 11, 1930 (lot 86 in the Tual sale; lot 247 in the Parke-Bernet sale).
60. An article in *Vogue* on November 15, 1933, "New Paris Apartment of Madame Helena Rubinstein" (pp. 52–53), published views of her collection in the apartment on Boulevard Raspail. A January 1938 reportage in the American magazine *House and Garden* entitled "Helena Rubinstein in her Paris Home" (pp. 50–51) reconstitutes the prewar appearance of the mythical apartment on Quai de Béthune, recently completed. On July 21, 1941, Elaine Brown Keiffer's piece in *Life Magazine* was illustrated with a photograph of a sumptuously dressed Helena Rubinstein in a baroque universe including a Kota reliquary guardian and a Dan mask. In 1943, the journal *Arts et industrie*, vol. XVI, published an article on "*Le musée d'art nègre d'Helena Rubinstein.*" All these publications deal with the collection in Paris, a city that then seemed the natural place to amass and preserve her works.
61. Fang seated male statue, Gabon, reproduced plate III, in Breton-Éluard 1931.
62. Chokwe scepter, Angola.
63. The list of auction results, with the names and addresses of the purchasers as recorded by Charles Ratton, the expert, and Alphonse Bellier, the auctioneer, mentions the contact details of "M. Titus, 4, Rue Delambre;" Charles Ratton-Guy Ladrière archives, Paris, Breton-Éluard sale file. "At the Sign of the Black Manikin" at 4, Rue Delambre, in the Montparnasse district, was the name of the bookstore opened by Helena Rubinstein's husband, Edward Titus, in 1924; it subsequently became the name of his publishing house until ceasing operations in spring 1932.
64. Published in Bassani and McLeod 1989, no. 269, p. 113.
65. Musée du Quai Branly – Jacques Chirac, inv. 70.1999.3.1.
66. An indication, perhaps, that Paul Chadourne arranged purchases for Helena Rubinstein.
67. He was to appear as a member of the inaugural jury for the Helena Rubinstein Prize for modern art funded by the collector in June 1937.
68. Probably lot 213 at the April 29, 1966, sale. The inventory register of the Musée des Colonies et de la France Extérieure indicates, at number 8029, the deposit on 15 November 1931 of this head at a cost of 20,000 francs. At that time Fang statues incurred the highest insurance values.
69. Musée du Quai Branly archives, DA000745/59144.
70. February 27–end of April 1930.
71. Hourdé and Rolland 2018, no. 7, p. 179.
72. Hourdé and Rolland 2018, no. 71, p. 198; lot 128, Parke-Bernet sale, New York, April 29, 1966.
73. Hourdé and Rolland 2018, nos. 142, 143, and 144, p. 227–228; lots 187, 186, and 188, Parke-Bernet sale, New York, April 29, 1966.
74. Hourdé and Rolland 2018, no. 417, p. 319; lot 261, Parke-Bernet sale, New York, October 15, 1966.
75. Hourdé and Rolland 2018, no. 165, p. 234; lot 213, Parke-Bernet sale, New York, April 29, 1966.
76. Hourdé and Rolland 2018, no. 166, p. 234; lot 214, Parke-Bernet sale, New York, April 29, 1966.
77. Hourdé and Rolland 2018, no. 176, p. 241; lot 211, Parke-Bernet sale, New York, April 29, 1966.
78. Hourdé and Rolland 2018, no. 186, p. 243; lot 192, Parke-Bernet sale, New York, April 29, 1966.
79. Hourdé and Rolland 2018, no. 196, p. 246; lot 234, Parke-Bernet sale, New York, April 29, 1966.
80. Einstein 1915; Einstein 1998.
81. "Première exposition d'art nègre et d'art océanien," Galerie Devambez, Paris, 1919; "Indigenous art from the French colonies and the Belgian Congo," Musée des Arts Décoratifs, Paris, 1923.
82. Listed as nineteen numbers in the catalog. *The Bulletin of the Museum of Modern Art*, no. 6–7, vol. 2, March–April 1935, writes of more than 30,000 visitors and publishes a photograph of the Cameroon pipe (formerly de Miré collection) owned by Rubinstein.
83. Lot 179 at the sale on April 29, 1966.
84. The selection of works for this exhibition lives on in the memory through Walker Evans's photograph portfolio.
85. Lot 232 at the sale on April 29, 1966.
86. Lot 189 at the sale on April 29, 1966.
87. It is rather a Lefem ancestral guardian figure.
88. It was to be published by Carl Kjersmeier in 1938, with the note "Helena Rubinstein Collection, New York."
89. Lots 193 and 194 at the sale on April 29, 1966.
90. Lot 228 at the sale on April 21, 1966.
91. Lot 176 at the sale on April 29, 1966.
92. "[...] some two hundred pieces [...] displayed [...] in her New-York apartment there was quantity; in her Paris apartment there were both quantity and quality. This wasn't just a home, but a mausoleum in the guise of a museum." In O'Higgins 1972, p. 120.
93. Transcription from a lecture, New York, Archives of the Fashion Institute of Technology, special collection Helena Rubinstein Foundation.
94. Idem.
95. Idem.
96. Dossier US.NNFIT.284.1.3.1.
97. New York 1935, nos. 14, 61, 62, 63, 88, 133, 317, 318, 319, 370, 371, 372, 379, 397, 398, 424–427; Paris 1937, hall on the right, rooms X, XI, and XII; Champigneulle and Lem 1951; "*L'Art nègre*," special number of *Présence africaine*, nos. 10–11, Paris, 1951, p. 16; documentary film

by Chris Marker and Alain Resnais, art consultancy, Charles Ratton, *Les statues meurent aussi*, a Tadie Cinéma production, 1953; New York 1954, plates 11, 19, 21, 24, 40, 43; New York 1958, nos. 34, 36, 37; Elisofon and Fagg 1958, p. 41–43, 49, 51, 53, 56, 74, 80–81, 84, 86–87, 150, 152–153, 164–165, 194; Paris 1964, plates 22, 24, 54, 64, 68.
98. "John Marion [...] officiated in a marathon that lasted ten days and reaped close to five million dollars." In O'Higgins 1972, p. 363.
99. Jean Roudillon, in "*Notes personnelles*," dossier no. 147, dated January 15, 2018, observes: "Several sculptures, such as number 64, an eight-headed Bambara puppet that went for $24,000, would have made only 2,000 or 3,000 francs in France. On the other hand, the Senufo statue no. 95 at 27,000 dollars was worth much more in France."
100. With the help of Hélène and Henri Kamer.
101. On the 1966 sale, consult the essay by David Nash, p. 20 in the present volume.
102. Chatwin 2005.
103. Chatwin and Shakespeare 2012, p. 74.
104. Purchased for $29,000 by Harry Franklin in 1966 and sold at Sotheby's, New York, April 21, 1990, for $3.4 m. to the Dapper Foundation.
105. Notably Harry Franklin, Los Angeles; Merton Simpson, New York; Helene and Henri Kamer, New York; the Pierre Matisse Gallery, New York, for Nelson Rockefeller; John Friede, New York; Aaron Furman, New York; Klejman, New York; Louis Carré, Paris; Jean Roudillon, Paris.
106. Milton Rosenthal, Jay C. Leff, Morris Pinto, Allan Stone, Herbert Baker, Norman Dinhofer, Paul Tishman, Gaston de Havenon, Hy Klebanov, etc.
107. Helena Rubinstein's nephew, Oscar Kolin.
108. Max Granick, picture framer in New York.
109. Letter from Henri Kamer to Charles Ratton, November 28, 1966, Ratton-Ladrière archives.

Frederic-Henri Lem's mid-twentieth-century case for African Art and its study, Susan Elizabeth Gagliardi

1. Lem 1949: 8.
2. 1949: 7-8.
3. Lem 1949: 8.
4. Lem 1949: 8.
5. Lem 1948: 39, 1949: 37.
6. Lem 1948: 9, 1949: 9.
7. Lem 1938a.
8. Lem 1938c.
9. Lem 1938c; see also Lem 1948: 8-9, 1949: 8-9.
10. Lem 1938c.
11. Lem 1938a, 1938b, 1938c.
12. Lem 1948: 10-15, 1949: 10-14.
13. Lem 1948: 11, 1949: 11.
14. e.g. Lem 1948: 11, 17, 23, 24-5, Lem 1949: 11, 16, 21, 23.
15. e.g. Appadurai 1988, Amselle 1990, Trouillot 2003.
16. Lem 1948: 13, 1949: 13.
17. Lem 1948: 43, 1949: 42; see also Kjersmeier 1935, Vol. 1: Fig. 32.
18. see also Goldwater 1964: 25.
19. Lem 1948: 43, 1949: 41-2.
20. Goldwater 1964: ill. 67.
21. Binger 1892: 223, 225.
22. Parke-Bernet Galleries: 116, lot 135.
23. Binger 1892: 221-25.
24. Binger 1892: 225.
25. see also Gagliardi 2014, 2015, 2017.
26. e.g. Lem 1948: 13, 30, 32, 1949: 13, 28, 30.
27. Lem 1948: 13, 1949: 13.
28. Lem 1948: 31, 1949: 29.
29. Lem 1948: 8, 1949: 8; see also Lem 1938c.
30. Lem 1948: 8, 1949: 8.
31. Lem 1948: 28, 1949: 26.
32. Lem 1948: 44, Pl. 45, 1949: 42, Pl. 45.
33. Lem 1948: 42, Pl. 25, 1949: 40, Pl. 25.
34. e.g. Lem 1948: 13, 1949: 12-13.
35. Lem 1948: 38, 1949: 36.
36. Kjersmeier 1935: 29.
37. Veirman 2001: 279-80; cf. Förster 2015: 78-82.
38. Lem 1948: 26, 1949: 24-5.
39. Lem 1948: 45, 1949: 43.
40. see also Lem 1948: 38, 1949: 36.
41. Lem 1948: 45, Pl. 57, 1949: 44, Pl. 57; cf. Lem 1942.
42. Lem 1948: 7, 1949: 7.
43. Lem 1948: 44, Pl. 47, 1949: 43, Pl. 47.
44. Lem 1948: 25-6, 1949: 24.
45. cf. Parke-Bernet Galleries 1966: 114, Lot 134.
46. cf. Palmié 2013.
47. Lem 1938c.
48. Lem 1938.
49. Lem 1948: 38, 1949: 36.
50. Lem 1948: 45, Pl. 64, 1949: 46, Pl. 64.

Equatorial African treasures from the Rubinstein collection, Charlotte Grand-Dufay

1. English, *Negro Sculpture* (translated by Patrick Healy, Amsterdam: November Editions, 2016); French *La Sculpture nègre* (translated by Lilian Meffre), in Einstein 2015.
2. Gréber 2003, p. 143.
3. Tessmann 1913, vol. 2, p. 119, fig. 44.
4. Perrois 1972, p. 86, and Perrois 2001, pp. 135–39.
5. Paris 2017, p. 199.
6. Marseille 1996, no. 28.
7. Schweizer 2014, p. 140.
9. Vérité 2006, p. 227, no. 201.
10. Paris 2017, p. 246.
11. New York 2017, p. 31.
12. Marseille 1992, p. 160.
13. Balandier and Maquet 1968.
14. Lehuard 1983.
15. Inv. 73.1963.0.727
16. Chaffin 1979.
17. Inv. 73.1976.3.4.
18. Ibid., piece 134.
19. Andersson 1953, p. 345.
20. Inv. BMG 1019-54.
21. Inv. A263.
22. Perrois 2001, p. 149.
23. Apollinaire and Guillaume 1917.
24. Grand-Dufay 2016, p. 37–38.
25. Ibid., p. 104–5.
26. Paris 2010, fig. 77.
27. Cornet 1972, p. 164.
28. Petridis 2018, nos. 56 and 53.
29. Paris 1993, p. 104.

Masks, mirrors, and *mise en scène*. The collection and the image, Yaëlle Biro

1. The girl in the center of the picture can be identified either as Helena Rubinstein (see New York 2014, p. 53, and Vienna 2017, p. 29) or else as her sister Regina, of whom no other portrait is known (Paris 2019, p. 17, following Rubinstein 1965). She closely resembles portraits of Helena from the same period.
2. New York 2014, p. 52.
3. New York 2000.
4. Derlon and Jeudy-Ballini 2006, p. 359.
5. Henri Cueco, quoted ibid.
6. Du Crest 2015, p. 9.
7. Ellen Chesler, in Slesin 2003, p. 62.
8. Cole 1985.
9. Grossman and Manford 2006, p. 134.
10. Grossman 2009, p. 141.
11. Clifford 2003, p. 103.
12. For Rubinstein's ingenious blend of collecting, fashion, cosmetics, and commercial acumen, see Clifford 2003.
13. Piasa auction house, *Les Photographies de Dora Maar. Une histoire, des œuvres [succession de Mme Dora Markowitch, 1907–1997], vente, Paris, hôtel Drouot, salles 1 et 7, 20 novembre 1998, commissaires-priseurs, Mes PIASA et J. J. Mathias*, Paris, 1998, lots 60, 61, 62.
14. A question of date arises here: the photographs bear the stamp "Kefer Dora Maar," which suggests they were taken before 1934. The building on Quai de Béthune, however, was not completed until 1937, by which time Dora Maar and Pierre Kefer were no longer sharing a studio in Neuilly-sur-Seine. Perhaps, by affixing this stamp on the Rubinstein photographs, Maar was intent on differentiating her commercial work from her artistic oeuvre. Moreover, these pictures no longer corresponded to the artist's concerns at this period of her career, since, after her relationship

Madame and Me, Suzanne Slesin

1. Slesin 2006

Helena Rubinstein: the power of an art collection, Julie Verlaine

1. Although Rubinstein has been the subject of many biographies—older ones in English (O'Higgins 1971; Fabe 1972), and more recent examples in French (Leveau-Fernandez 2003; Fitoussi 2010)—the space devoted to her activities as collector and patron tends to be limited. For a long view of the history of women art collectors and patrons, we refer readers to our own book: Verlaine 2014.
2. See Kraatz 2016.
3. Paris 1977.
4. Leymarie 2010; La Haye and Tobin 1995.
5. Rubinstein 1957, p. 101.
6. Ibid., p. 167.
7. As an example, we refer to the lavishly illustrated article, "Milestone for Helena Rubinstein. A tiny, tireless tycoon of beauty celebrates a 60th anniversary", published in *Life Magazine* on May 15, 1964.
8. See her own remarks on this in Rubinstein 1965, p. 15.
9. Rubinstein 1957, p. 167.
10. Ibid., p. 53.

To Collect "au Féminin", Susan Kloman

1. It should be noted that the timeline for collecting is here placed within a "modern" context, not from an art historical definition—e.g., 20th century—but from a historiographical one—e.g., 16th–19th century, following the post-classical era. How we define collecting and the codifications around such a discussion are beyond the scope of the present essay. However, two important landmarks in the shift to a so-called modern way of collecting and the institutionalization of collecting are the opening of the British Museum in 1759 and of the Louvre Museum in 1792.
2. Other notable women collectors of the 20th century often came into their wealth through inheritance. These include as Peggy Guggenheim, Isabella Stewart Gardener, and Gertrude Vanderbilt Whitney. However, we can note that it is only in modern times that these same women could be the stewards of their own wealth. Interestingly, these three women went on to create institutions for their collections, where, like a familial lineage, the art lives in perpetuity associated with their names. Prior to the twentieth century, in most instances, any money a woman might have from her family would have been relinquished, or direct access to it denied, as a kind of dowry in marriage. In earlier times, access to funds might exceptionally be used to collect art by women in non-traditional female roles and non-traditional marital roles, such as royal mistress or consort. In this context are collectors such as Madame de Pompadour and Empress Josephine.
3. For a study on a psychological analysis of what it means to collect, including childhood proclivities, environment, and development, see Werner Muensterberger, *Collecting: An Unruly Passion – Psychological Perspectives*, Princeton University Press, 1994
4. Gere, Charlotte and Vaizey, Marina, Great Women Collectors, London, 1999, p. 160
5. Typescript of undated press release (ca. 1935) in the archives of the Helena Rubinstein Foundation, New York in Marie J. Clifford, "Helena Rubinstein's Beauty Salons, Fashion, and Modernist Display," *Winterthur Portfolio*, Vol. 38, No. 2/3 (Summer/Autumn 2003), p 104.
6. The Museum of Modern Art archives, Collection: MoMA Exhs., Series Folder: 39.4. For reproductions of these two works, see Parke-Bernet Galleries, New York, *The Collection of Helena Rubinstein: African and Oceanic Art*, Part One, April 21, 1966, lots 189 and 213, respectively. These two works of art ultimately went on to achieve the two highest prices of the auction $29,000 and $24,000 (hammer). The Bangwa 'Queen' achieved another record price for a work of African art at auction when it was offered again in New York in 1990, selling for $3.4million; a record that stood for 16 years.
7. Clifford, ibid.
8. Christa Clarke, 'John Graham and the Crowninshield Collection of African Art', *Winterthur Portfolio*, Vol. 30, No. 1 (Spring, 1995), pp. 28
9. Pierre Matisse Gallery, African Sculptures from The Ratton Collection, New York, 1935
10. Rubinstein was a voracious collector and had collections that otherwise could be characterized as "feminine," including her collection of jewelry and of miniature interiors, resembling doll houses.

A conversation with Estrellita B. Brodsky, Catherine Grenier

1. "Comfortably Numb: A Critical Investigation into the Cultural Impact of Drugs and Narcotics," Another Space, New York, November 15, 2018, – May 5, 2019.

CATALOGS OF THE HELENA RUBINSTEIN COLLECTION SALES

PARKE-BERNET GALLERIES 1965
Parke-Bernet Galleries, *Precious-Stones Jewels from the Unique Collection of the Late Helena Rubinstein*, New York: Parke-Bernet Galleries, October 12, 1965.

PARKE-BERNET GALLERIES 1966A
Parke-Bernet Galleries, *Modern Paintings and Sculptures, Part One*, New York: Parke-Bernet Galleries, April 20, 1966.

PARKE-BERNET GALLERIES 1966B
Parke-Bernet Galleries, *African and Oceanic Art, Parts One and Two. The Collection of Helena Rubinstein (Princess Gourielli), New York, Paris, and London, Sold by Order of the Executors of Her Estate*, New York: Parke-Bernet Galleries, April 21 and 29, 1966.

PARKE-BERNET GALLERIES 1966C
Parke-Bernet Galleries, *French Furniture and Decorations, Russian Icons, Other Paintings*, New York: Parke-Bernet Galleries, April 22 and 23, 1966.

PARKE-BERNET GALLERIES 1966D
Parke-Bernet Galleries, *Modern Paintings and Sculptures, Part Two*, New York: Parke-Bernet Galleries, April 27, 1966.

PARKE-BERNET GALLERIES 1966E
Parke-Bernet Galleries, *Modern Drawings and Prints*, New York: Parke-Bernet Galleries, April 28, 1966.

PARKE-BERNET GALLERIES 1966F
Parke-Bernet Galleries, *African and Oceanic Art, Part Three*, New York: Parke-Bernet Galleries, October 15, 1966.

SELECTIVE BIBLIOGRAPHY PER ESSAY

"Madame's collection. Africa at its heart", Hélène Joubert

BASSANI AND MCLEOD 1989
Ezio Bassani and Malcolm D. McLeod, *Jacob Epstein Collector*, Milan: Associazione Poro, 1989.

BOURGOIN 2019
Philippe Bourgoin, "Helena Rubinstein. L'aventure de la beauté", https://philippebourgoinarttribal.com/2019/06/10/helena-rubinstein-laventure-de-la-beaute/.

BRANDON 2011
Ruth Brandon, *Ugly Beauty. Helena Rubinstein, L'Oréal and the Blemished History of Looking Good*, New York: Harper Collins, 2011.

CAMERON 1960
Roderick Cameron, "Terrasses et balcons à Paris", *L'Œil*, no. 66, juin 1960, p. 70-74.

CARRÉ-RATTON 1931
Louis Carré, Charles Ratton, *Sculptures d'Afrique, d'Amérique, d'Océanie. Collection André Breton et Paul Éluard*, Paris: Hôtel Drouot, July 2-3, 1931.

CHATWIN 2005
Bruce Chatwin, *Œuvres complètes*, Paris: Grasset, 2005.

CHATWIN AND SHAKESPEARE 2012
Elizabeth Chatwin and Nicholas Shakespeare (eds.), *Bruce Chatwin. La Sagesse du nomade. Correspondance*, Paris: Grasset, 2012.

CLIFFORD 1999
Marie J. Clifford, *Brand Name Modernism. Helena Rubinstein Art Collection, Feminity and the Marketing of Modern Style, 1925-1940*, PhD dissertation, UCLA, 1999.

EINSTEIN 1915
Carl Einstein, *Negerplastik*, Leipzig: Verlag der Weissen Bücher, 1915.

EINSTEIN 1998
Carl Einstein, *La Sculpture nègre*, Paris: L'Harmattan, "L'Art en bref", 1998.

EKLUND 1968
Hans Eklund, *Kongo-Niger. Afrikans Skulptur ur Samling Nathhorst*, Stockholm: Etnografiska Museets Vanner, no. 6, 1968.

ELISOFON AND FAGG 1958
Eliot Elisofon and William Fagg (eds.), *The Sculpture of Africa*, London: Thames & Hudson, 1958.

FABE 1972
Maxene Fabe, *Beauty Millionaire. The Life of Helena Rubinstein*, New York: Crowell, 1972.

FITOUSSI 2010
Michèle Fitoussi, *Helena Rubinstein. La femme qui inventa la beauté*, Paris: Grasset, 2010.

FITOUSSI 2016
Michèle Fitoussi (preface), *Madame Avant-Garde*, Paris: Le Cherche-Midi, 2016.

FLANNER 1957
Janet Flanner, "De diverses formes de beauté", *L'Œil*, no. 34, October 1957, p. 25-30.

FULTER 1937
Jean Fulter, "Une maison, un appartement, par M. Louis Süe", *Art et décoration*, 1937, vol. LXVI, p. 176-183.

GOLL 1976
Claire Goll, *La Poursuite du vent*, Paris: Olivier Orban, 1976.

HOURDÉ AND ROLLAND 2018
Charles-Wesley Hourdé and Nicolas Rolland (eds.), *Galerie Pigalle. Afrique, Océanie, 1930. Une exposition mythique*, Paris: Somogy, 2018.

***HOUSE AND GARDEN* 1938**
"Helena Rubinstein in her Paris Home", *House & Garden*, 73, no. 1, January 1938, p. 50-51.

JAZDZEWSKI 1999
Catherine Jazdzewski, *Helena Rubinstein. Mémoire de la beauté*, Paris: Assouline, 1999.

KJERSMEIER 1938
Carl Kjersmeier, *Centres de style de la sculpture nègre africaine*, vol. 4, Paris: Albert Morancé; Copenhaguen: Illums Bog-Afdeling, 1938.

LAJER-BURCHARTH AND SÖNTGEN 2016
Ewa Lajer-Burcharth and Beate Söntgen (eds.), *Interiors and Interiority*, Berlin: De Gruyter, 2016.

LEM 1947
F.-H. Lem, "Magie soudanaise", *Soleils*, vol. I, Paris: Arts et métiers graphiques, 1947, p. 85-90.

LEM 1948
F.-H. Lem, *Sculptures soudanaises*, Paris: Arts et métiers graphiques, 1948.

LEM 1949
F.-H. Lem, *Sudanese Sculpture*, Paris: Arts et métiers graphiques, 1949.

LEVEAU-FERNANDEZ 2003
Madeleine Leveau-Fernandez, *Helena Rubinstein*, Paris: Flammarion, "Grandes biographies", 2003.

MANNES 1929
Marya Mannes, "African Art in the Rubinstein Collection", *International Studio*, no. 384, May 1929, p. 55-56.

O'HIGGINS 1972
Patrick O'Higgins, *Madame. The Very Intimate Biography of the Despot of Beauty, Helena Rubinstein*, New York: Dell Publishing Company, 1972.

***PRÉSENCE AFRICAINE* 1951**
"L'Art nègre", special edition of *Présence africaine*, nos. 10-11, 1951, p. 16.

RUBINSTEIN 1930
Helena Rubinstein, *The Art of Feminine Beauty*, New York: Horace Liveright, 1930.

RUBINSTEIN 1957
Helena Rubinstein, *Je suis esthéticienne*, Paris: Éditions du Conquistador, 1957.

RUBINSTEIN 1965
Helena Rubinstein, *My Life for Beauty*, New York: Simon and Schuster, 1965.

SLESIN 2003
Suzanne Slesin, *Over the Top. Helena Rubinstein. Extraordinary Style, Beauty, Art, Fashion, Design*, New York: Pointed Leaf Press, 2003.

SWERLING 1928
Jo Swerling, "Beauty in Jars and Vials", *The New Yorker*, June 30, 1928.

***VOGUE* 1933**
"New Paris Apartment of Madame Helena Rubinstein", *Vogue*, 82, no. 10, 15 November 1933, pp.52–53.

WOODHEAD 2003
Lindy Woodhead, *War Paint. Madame Helena Rubinstein and Miss Elizabeth Arden. Their Lives, their Times, their Rivalry*, London, Virago Press, 2003.

EXHIBITION CATALOGS

BOLOGNA 2019
Ezio Bassani and Gigi Pezzoli (eds.), *Ex Africa. Storie e identità di un'arte universale*, exh. cat., Bologna, Museo civico archeologico, 2019.

NEW YORK 1935A
James Johnson Sweeney (eds.), *African Negro Art*, exh. cat., New York: The Museum of Modern Art, 1935.

NEW YORK 1954
Federick R. Pleasants, *Masterpieces of African Art*, exh. cat., New York: The Brooklyn Museum, 1954.

NEW YORK 1958
African Sculpture Lent by New York Collectors, exh. cat., New York: The Museum of Primitive Art, 1958.

NEW YORK 2014
Mason Klein, *Helena Rubinstein. Beauty is Power*, exh. cat., New York: The Jewish Museum, 2014.

PARIS 1937
Origines et développement de l'art international indépendant, exh. cat., Paris: Musée du Jeu de paume, 1937.

PARIS 1964
William Fagg and Margaret Plass (eds.), *Afrique. Cent tribus, cent chefs-d'œuvre*, Paris: Musée des Arts décoratifs, palais du Louvre, pavillon de Marsan, 1964.

PARIS 2013
Philippe Dagen (eds.), *Charles Ratton. L'invention des arts "primitifs"*, exh. cat., Paris: Musée du quai Branly, 2013.

PARIS 2019
Michèle Fitoussi (eds.), *Helena Rubinstein. L'aventure de la beauté*, exh. cat., Paris: Musée d'Art et d'Histoire du judaïsme, 2019.

VIENNA 2017
Iris Meder and Danielle Spera (eds.), *Helena Rubinstein. Die Schönheitserfinderin / Pioneer of Beauty*, exh. cat., Vienna, Judisches Museum, 2017.

WASHINGTON 1940
Exhibition of Modern Paintings, Drawings and Primitive African Sculpture from the Collection of Helena Rubinstein, Washington D.C., Mayflower Hotel, March 5–6, 1940.

DOCUMENTARIES

Chris Marker and Alain Resnais, art advisor, Charles Ratton, *Les statues meurent aussi*, Tadie Cinéma Production, 1953.

Ann-Carol Grossman and Arnie Reisman, *The Powder and the Glory*, PBS Home Edition, 2007.

Eila Herschon and Roberto Guerra, *Beauty Queens. Helena Rubinstein*, Arthaus, 2012.

"F.-H. Lem's mid-twentieth-century case for African art and its study", Susan Gagliardi

AMSELLE 2010
Jean-Loup Amselle, *Logiques métisses* (1990), Paris: Payot, "Petite bibliothèque", 2010.

APPADURAI 1988
Arjun Appadurai, "Putting Hierarchy in its Place", *Cultural Anthropology*, vol. 3, no. 1, 1988, pp.36–49.

BINGER 1892
Louis-Gustave Binger, *Du Niger au golfe de Guinée par le pays de Kong et le Mossi, 1887-1889*, Paris: Hachette, 1892.

FÖRSTER 2015
Till Förster, "New Markets, New Patrons. Work-Trade Relationships in a West African Art Market", in Silvia Forni and Christopher B. Steiner (eds.), *Africa in the Market. Twentieth-Century Art from the Amrad African Art Collection*, Toronto: Royal Ontario Museum, 2015, pp. 75–101.

GAGLIARDI 2014
Susan Elizabeth Gagliardi, *Senufo Unbound. Dynamics of Art and Identity in West Africa*, Cleveland: The Cleveland Museum of Art; Milan: 5 Continents, 2014.

GAGLIARDI 2015
Susan Elizabeth Gagliardi, *Senufo sans frontières. La dynamique des arts et des identités en Afrique de l'Ouest*, translated by Anne-Marie Bouttiaux, Cleveland: The Cleveland Museum of Art; Milan: 5 Continents, 2015.

GAGLIARDI 2017
Susan Elizabeth Gagliardi, "Helmet, before 1934 or 1935 (66.619)", in Christa Clarke (eds.), *Arts of Global Africa. The Newark Museum Collection*, Newark: Newark Museum; Seattle: Lucia Marquand, 2017, p. 174-176.

GOLDWATER 1964
Robert Goldwater, *Senufo Sculpture from West Africa*, New York: The Museum of Primitive Art; Greenwich: New York Graphic Society, 1964.

KJERSMEIER 1935
Carl Kjersmeier, *Centres de style de la sculpture nègre africaine*, vol. 1, Paris: Albert Morancé; et Copenhague, Illums Bog-Afdeling, 1935.

LEM 1938A
F.-H. Lem, "Pour un musée d'art africain", *Les Annales coloniales*, September 26, 1938.

LEM 1938B
F.-H. Lem, "Pour un musée d'art africain", *Les Annales coloniales*, October 3, 1938.

LEM 1938C
F.-H. Lem, "Pour un musée d'art africain", *Les Annales coloniales*, October 10, 1938.

LEM 1942
F.-H. Lem, "Au sujet d'une statuette sénoufo", *Bulletin de l'Institut français d'Afrique noire*, no. 4, 1942, pp. 175–181

LEM 1948
F.-H. Lem, *Sculptures soudanaises*, Paris: Arts et métiers graphiques, 1948.

LEM 1949
F.-H. Lem, *Sudanese Sculpture*, Paris: Arts et métiers graphiques, 1949.

LEM 1952
F.-H. Lem, "Afrique noire, Afrique occidentale, statuettes funéraires", *Encyclopaedia universalis*, 1952, pp.110-114

PALMIÉ 2013
Stephan Palmié, *The Cooking of History. How Not to Study Afro-Cuban Religion*, Chicago: The University of Chicago Press, 2013.

TROUILLOT 2003
Michel-Rolph Trouillot, "Anthropology and the Savage Slot. The Poetics and Politics of Otherness", in *Global Transformations. Anthropology and the Modern World*, New York: Palgrave Macmillan, 2003, pp. 7–28.

VEIRMAN 2001
Anja Veirman, "'Here a Boy Always Becomes a Sculptor, Like His Father': Albert Maesen and the Study of the Art of the Senufo", dans Constantine Petridis (ed.), *Frans M. Olbrechts 1899-1958. In Search of Art*

in Africa, Antwerp: Antwerp Ethnographic Museum, 2001, pp. 268–287.

"The enigmatic F.-H. Lem (1902-1991)", Bertrand Goy

GOY 2019
Bertrand Goy, "Les Mondes de Lem", *Tribal Arts*, hiver 2019, forthcoming.

"Equatorial African treasures from the Rubinstein collection", Charlotte Grand-Dufay

ANDERSSON 1953
Efraim Andersson, *Contribution à l'ethnographie des Kuta*, I, Studia Ethnographica Upsaliensa VI, Uppsala: Almqvist & Wiksell, 1953.

ANDERSSON 1974
Efraim Andersson, *Contribution à l'ethnographie des Kuta*, II, Studia Ethnographica Upsaliensa XXXVIII, Uppsala: Almqvist & Wiksell, 1974.

APOLLINAIRE AND GUILLAUME 1917
Guillaume Apollinaire and Paul Guillaume, *Sculptures nègres: vingt-quatre photographies précédées d'une avertissement de Guillaume Apollinaire et d'un exposé de Paul Guillaume*, Paris: Paul Guillaume, 1917.

BALANDIER AND MAQUET 1968
Georges Balandier and Jacques Maquet, *Dictionnaire des civilisations africaines*, Paris: Hazan, 1968.

BIRO 2018
Yaëlle Biro, *Fabriquer le regard. Marchands, réseaux et objets d'art africains à l'aube du xxe siècle*, Dijon: Les Presses du réel, 2018.

CHAFFIN 1979
Alain and Françoise Chaffin, *L'Art kota: les figures de reliquaires*, Meudon: Chaffin, 1979.

CHRISTIE'S 2015
Art d'Afrique, d'Océanie et d'Amérique du Nord, Paris: June 23, 2015.

CORNET 1972
Joseph Cornet, *Art de l'Afrique noire. Au pays du fleuve Zaïre*, Brussels: Arcade, 1972.

EINSTEIN 2015
Carl Einstein, *Les Arts de l'Afrique*, Arles: Jacqueline Chambon-Actes Sud, 2015.

GRAND-DUFAY 2015
Charlotte Grand-Dufay, "La statuaire lumbu. Un art tout en finesse révélé au début du xxe siècle", *Art tribal*, no. 77 (XIX: 4), Fall 2015, pp. 114–127.

GRAND-DUFAY 2016
Charlotte Grand-Dufay, *Les Lumbu. Un art sacré*, Paris: Gourcuff Gradenigo, Paris: 2016.

GRÉBERT 2003
Fernand Grébert, *Le Gabon de Fernand Grébert*, 1913-1932, Geneva: Éditions D and musée d'Ethnographie de Genève, 2003.

LAGAMMA 2007
Alisa LaGamma (ed.) *Eternal Ancestors. The Art of the Central African Reliquary*, New York: The Metropolitan Museum of Art, 2007.

LEHUARD 1983
Raoul Lehuard, "La collection du père Morris", *Arts d'Afrique noire*, 1983, no. 46, pp. 36–42.

PERROIS 1972
Louis Perrois, *Statuaire fan*, Gabon, Paris: Mémoires ORSTOM, no. 59, 1972.

PERROIS AND GRAND-DUFAY 2008
Louis Perrois and Charlotte Grand-Dufay, *Punu*, Milan: 5 Continents, 2008.

PETRIDIS 2018
Constantine Petridis, *Luluwa*, Brussels: Fonds Mercator, 2018.

SCHWEIZER 2014
Heinrich Schweizer, *Visions of Grace. 100 Masterpieces from the Collection of Daniel and Marian Malcolm*, Milan: 5 Continents, 2014.

SOTHEBY'S 2008
The Collection of Frieda and Milton Rosenthal. African and Oceanic Art, New York: November 14, 2008.

SOTHEBY'S 2014
In Pursuit of Beauty. The Myron Kunin Collection of African Art, New York: November 11, 2014.

SOTHEBY'S 2017
The Collection of Edwin & Cherie Silver. Art of Africa, Oceania and the Americas, New York: November 13, 2017.

TESSMANN 1913
Günter Tessmann, *Die Pangwe. Völkerkundliche Monographie eines westafrikanischen Negerstammes. Ergebnisse der Lübecker Pangwe-Expedition 1907-1909 und früherer Forschungen 1904-1907*, Berlin: Wasmuth Verlag, 1913, 2 vol.

VALLUET 2018
Christine Valluet, *Regards visionnaires: Arts d'Afrique, d'Amérique, d'Asie du Sud-Est et d'Océanie*, Milan: 5 Continents, 2018.

VÉRITÉ 2006
Arts primitifs. Collection Vérité 2006, Paris: Hôtel Drouot, June 17-18, 2006.

EXHIBITION CATALOGS

BRUSSELS 2001
Louis Perrois, "Les Maîtres du Ntem: les sculpteurs fang mvaï du Nord-Gabon", "Le Maître de la Sébé: les figures de reliquaires kota 'à tête de mort' de l'est du Gabon", dans Bernard de Grunne (eds.) *Mains de maîtres. À la découverte des sculpteurs d'Afrique*, exh. cat., Brussels: Espace culturel BBL, 2001.

MARSEILLE 1992
Louis Perrois, *Byeri fang. Sculptures d'ancêtres en Afrique*, exh. cat., Marseille: musée d'Arts africains, océaniens, amérindiens, Centre de la Vieille-Charité, 1992.

MARSEILLE 1996
Arman & l'art africain, exh. cat., Marseille,: Musée d'Arts africains, océaniens, amérindiens, Centre de la Vieille-Charité, 1996.

NEW YORK 2017
Bernard de Grunne, *Imaginary Ancestors*, exh. cat., New York: Amine Rech Gallery, 2017.

PARIS 1993
François Neyt, *Luba. Aux sources du Zaïre*, exh. cat., Paris: Musée Dapper, 1993.

PARIS 2010
François Neyt, *Fleuve Congo. Arts d'Afrique centrale*, exh. cat., Paris: Musée du quai Branly, 2010.

PARIS 2017
Yves Le Fur and Louis Perrois, *Les Forêts natales. Arts d'Afrique équatoriale atlantique*, exh. cat., Paris: Musée du quai Branly – Jacques Chirac, 2017.

"Masks, mirrors, and mise en scène. The collection and the image", Yaëlle Biro

CLIFFORD 2003
Marie J. Clifford, "Helena Rubinstein's Beauty Salons, Fashion and Modernist Display", *Winthertur Portfolio*, vol. 38, no. 2-3, Summer-Fall 2003, p. 83–108.

COLE 1985
Herbert M. Cole, *I Am Not Myself. The Art of African Masquerade*, Los Angeles: Museum of Cultural History, University of California, "Monograph Series", no. 26, 1985.

DERLON AND J EUDY-BALLINI 2006
Brigitte Derlon and Monique Jeudy-Ballini, "Collectionneur/ collectionné. L'art primitif, le discours de la passion

et la traversée imaginaire des frontières", *L'Homme. Revue française d'anthropologie*, 2006/1-2, no. 177–178, pp. 349–372.

DU CREST 2015
Sabine du Crest (eds.), *Si loin si proche. Objets d'ailleurs dans les intérieurs européens. Photographies, 1870-2015*, Rome, Gangemi Editore, "Objets frontière", 2015.

GROSSMAN 2009
Wendy A. Grossman, *Man Ray, African Art, and the Modernist Lens*, Washington: International Arts and Artists, 2009.

GROSSMAN AND MANFORD 2006
Wendy A. Grossman and Steven Manford, "Unmasking Man Ray's *Noire et Blanche*", *American Art*, no. 20, Summer 2006, pp. 134–147.

SLESIN 2003
Suzanne Slesin, *Over the Top. Helena Rubinstein. Extraordinary Style, Beauty, Art, Fashion, Design*, New York: Pointed Leaf Press, 2003.

EXHIBITION CATALOGS

NEW YORK 2000
Pierre Apraxine and Xavier Demange (eds.), *"La Divine Comtesse". Photographs of the Countess de Castiglione*, exh. cat., New York: The Metropolitan Museum of Art, 2000.

NEW YORK 2014
Mason Klein, *Helena Rubinstein. Beauty is Power*, exh. cat., New York: The Jewish Museum, 2014.

"Madame and Me", Suzanne Slesin

SLESIN 2003
Suzanne Slesin, *Over the Top. Helena Rubinstein. Extraordinary Style, Beauty, Art, Fashion, Design*, New York: Pointed Leaf Press, 2003.

"Helena Rubinstein: the power of an art collection", Julie Verlaine

FABE 1972
Maxene Fabe, *Beauty Millionaire. The Life of Helena Rubinstein*, New York: Crowell, 1972.

FITOUSSI 2010
Michèle Fitoussi, *Helena Rubinstein. La femme qui inventa la beauté*, Paris: Grasset, 2010.

KRAATZ 2016
Anne Kraatz, *John Pierpont Morgan. Un capitaliste américain*, Paris: Les Belles Lettres, 2016.

LA HAYE AND TOBIN 1995
Amy de La Haye and Shelley Tobin, *Chanel. The Couturiere at Work*, New York: Overlook Books, 1995.

LEVEAU-FERNANDEZ 2003
Madeleine Leveau-Fernandez, *Helena Rubinstein*, Paris: Flammarion, "Grandes biographies", 2003.

LEYMARIE 2010
Jean Leymarie, *Chanel*, Paris: La Martinière, 2010.

O'HIGGINS 1971
Patrick O'Higgins, *Madame. An Intimate Biography of Helena Rubinstein*, New York: Viking Press, 1971.

RUBINSTEIN 1957
Helena Rubinstein, *Je suis esthéticienne*, Paris: Éditions du Conquistador, 1957.

RUBINSTEIN 1965
Helena Rubinstein, My Life for Beauty, New York: Simon and Schuster, 1965.

VERLAINE 2014
Julie Verlaine, *Femmes collectionneuses d'art et mécènes, de 1880 à nos jours*, Paris: Hazan, 2014.

EXHIBITION CATALOGS

PARIS 1977
Portraits d'Helena Rubinstein, exh. cat., Paris: Musée des Arts décoratifs, 1977.

"To collect 'au féminin'", Susan Kloman

CLARKE 1995
Christa Clarke, "John Graham and the Crowninshield Collection of African Art", *Winterthur Portfolio*, vol. 30, no. 1, Spring 1995, p. 28.

CLIFFORD 2003
Marie J. Clifford, "Helena Rubinstein's Beauty Salons, Fashion and Modernist Display", *Winthertur Portfolio*, vol. 38, nos. 2-3, Summer-Fall 2003, p. 83–108.

GERE AND VAIZEY 1999
Charlotte Gere and Marina Vaizey, *Great Women Collectors*, London, Harry N. Abrams, 1999.

MUENSTERBERGER 1996
Werner Muensterberger, *Le Collectionneur. Anatomie d'une passion*, Paris: Payot, 1996.

EXHIBITION CATALOG

NEW YORK 1935B
African Sculptures from the Ratton Collection, exh. cat., New York: Pierre Matisse Gallery, 1935.

Chronology

In writings and interviews throughout her life Helena Rubinstein reinvented her story ceaselessly, even altering her date of birth.
In the absence of absolutely reliable sources, some dates in this chronology may be subject to revision in the future.

The chronology below mentions various seminal references, exhibitions, and publications instrumental in improving knowledge of the "primitive arts" during the first half of the 20th century.

Circa 1869 Helena Rubinstein's future parents, Augusta Silberfeld, known as "Gittel," and Naftali Herzel Rubinstein, marry.

1872 (or 1870?) December 25: Birth of Chaja Rubinstein in Kazimierz, the Jewish quarter of Krakow, Poland, at 14, Szeroka Street. The couple's eldest daughter, she will have seven sisters: Paulina, Rosa, Regina, Stella, Ceska, Manka, and Erna. Her father runs a small business at 13, Jozefas Street, where she will work keeping the store's accounts.

Circa 1893 Rejecting various marriage offers arranged by her parents, she is sent to Vienna, where her maternal aunt Helena Silberfeld-Splitter and her husband take her on in their store selling furs.

Summer 1896 Sails for Australia aboard the *Prinz-Regent Luitpold* taking with her jars of Dr. Jacob Lykusky's cream given to her by her mother. She decides to change her first name, and is henceforth known as Helena Juliet Rubinstein.

1896-1899 Joins two uncles on her mother's side, Louis and Bernhard Silberfeld, in Coleraine to work with them. In 1899 she enters service with the Fairbairn family in Melham as housekeeper.

1901 Takes up a post as assistant governess to the children of Lord Lamington in Toowoomba. Moving to Melbourne, she works as a waitress at the "Maison Doré" café in the morning and at the "Winter Garden" teahouse in the afternoon. She develops the formula for her first skin cream that she christens "Valaze."

1902 The launch of her brand, Helena Rubinstein & Co., meets with immediate success and she opens a "Valaze" salon in Melbourne, at 138 Elizabeth Street, the first of the many beauty salons she would go on to set up in other cities, first in Australia, then in Europe and the United States.

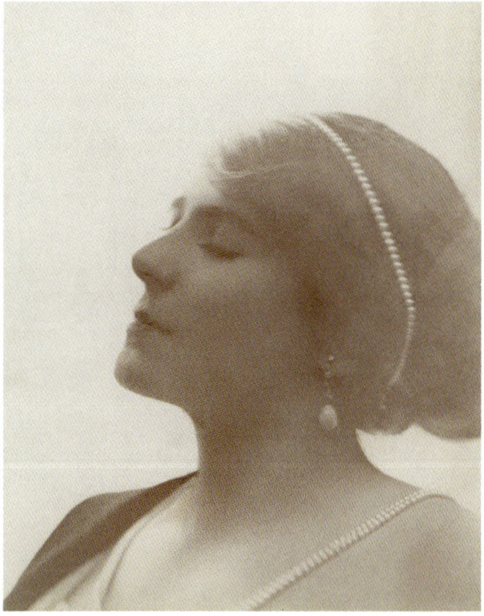

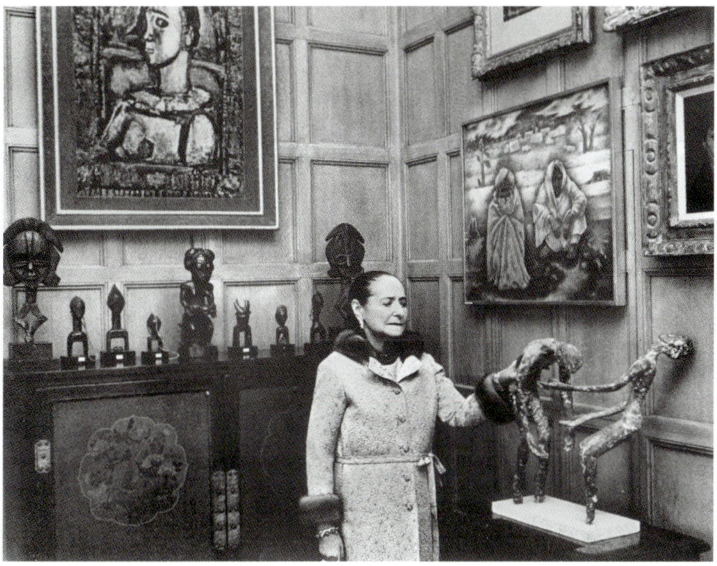

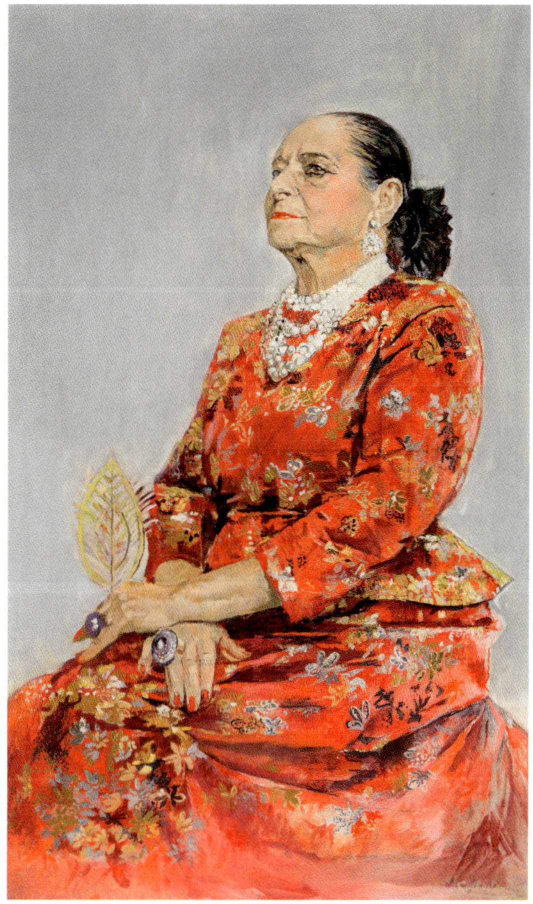

Ill. 148

Helena Rubinstein, c. 1919, photograph Lallie Charles

Ill. 149

Helena Rubinstein in her drawing-room at 625, Park Avenue, New York, 1964

Ill. 150

Graham Sutherland
Helena Rubinstein in a red brocade Balenciaga gown
1957
Oil on canvas
156.9 × 92.7 cm
National Portrait Gallery, Canberra

Throughout her life she will ensure that her company prospers.

1904 Coins her slogan: "Beauty is Power."

1905 Makes a study tour of Europe, meeting many dieticians and dermatologists. Visiting her parents in Krakow for the last time, she returns to Australia with her cousin and her sister Ceska, to whom she hands over part of the Melbourne business.
Maurice de Vlaminck, André Derain, and Henri Matisse discover the *"Arts nègres."* Guillaume Apollinaire and Paul Guillaume, as well as Pablo Picasso and many other artists follow their cue and start collecting non-European art.
October 18 – November 25: The painters Matisse, Derain, Vlaminck, and Raoul Dufy unveil works undertaken that summer at the *Salon d'automne* exhibition in Paris that ushers in Fauvism.

Late 1906 Meets her husband to-be, Edward William Titus, an American journalist of Polish origin.

1907 Opens a beauty salon in Sydney.

Obtaining Australian citizenship, on her passport she reduces her age by eight years.
Summer: Settles in London.
Discovers Serge Diaghilev's *Ballets Russes*, whose stage sets will go on to inspire the design of both her apartments and institutes.

1908 February: Rents the Marquis de Salisbury's mansion at 26, Grafton Street and establishes the first "Valaze" salon in London, opening another in Paris, at 255, Rue du Faubourg-Saint-Honoré, which is decorated by André Groult.

The move to Paris and London brings her into contact with several key influences: the couturier Paul Poiret, Misia Sert, and Flame d'Erlanger, among others, awaken in her a taste for collecting and for entertaining. In particular, her neighbor in London, the sculptor Jacob Epstein, a friend of her husband's and a significant collector of non-European artifacts, opens her mind to art and trains her eye.

July 28 Marries Edward Titus in London. The honeymoon takes place in Nice on the French Riviera.

1909 Paul César Helleu paints her portrait, the first of a long series of artists that she will sit for: Pavel Tchelitchew (1934), Marie Laurencin (1934), Raoul Dufy (c. 1935), Christian Bérard (1938), Salvador Dalí (1942-1943), Graham Sutherland (spring 1958), and René Boucher (1960). She was to collect portraits of herself throughout her life.
Visits a solo exhibition by the sculptor Elie Nadelman at the Galerie Druet in Paris.
December 12: Birth in London of her first son, Roy Titus.

1911 Buys up all Elie Nadelman's works displayed at the Patterson Gallery in London.

1912 Changes the name of her Paris salon from *Maison de beauté Valaze* to *Maison de beauté Helena Rubinstein* and builds a factory at Saint-Cloud (1911–1913).
April 23: Birth in London of a second son, Horace Titus.
Moves to Paris.

1914 October: On the outbreak of the First World War, Helena Rubinstein emigrates to New York.
November 3 – December 8: Marius de Zayas and Paul Guillaume stage the *Statuary in Wood by African Savages. The Root of Modern Art* exhibition at the 291 Gallery, New York.

1915 Opens a "Valaze" beauty salon in New York at 15 East 49th Street.
May: She is joined by her sister Manka.
Carl Einstein publishes *Negerplastik* (Leipzig, Verlag der Weissen Bücher).

1917 Together with Guillaume Apollinaire, Paul Guillaume publishes the album, *Sculptures nègres: vingt-quatre photographies précédées d'un avertissement de Guillaume Apollinaire et d'un exposé de Paul Guillaume* (Paris, Paul Guillaume).

1918 Returns to Paris as soon as the war is over.
The Paris salon moves to 126, Rue du Faubourg-Saint-Honoré, with an interior by Paul Poiret.

1919
May 10-31: Paul Guillaume holds a *Première exposition d'art nègre et d'art océanien* at the Galerie Devambez, in Paris. The catalog is compiled by Paul Guillaume, Guillaume Apollinaire, André Level, and Henri Clouzot.
June 10: Paul Guillaume stages a *Fête nègre* in Paris's Théâtre des Champs-Élysées.
Felix von Luschan publishes *Die Altertümer von Benin* (Berlin, Walter de Gruyter).

1922 The Myrbor gallery and design house opens in Paris, where a friend of Helena Rubinstein's, Marie Cuttoli, introduces the art of modern tapestry, with models by Pablo Picasso and Joan Miró.

1923 November – December: The *L'Art indigène des colonies françaises et du Congo belge* exhibition at the Pavilion de Marsan in Paris. The catalog is written in 1924 by Stephen Chauvet.

1924 Purchases the building at 52, Rue du Faubourg-Saint-Honoré, where she sets up her beauty salon and fits out the apartment above to live in it.
Edward Titus opens a bookstore, "At the Sign of the Black Manikin," at 4, Rue Delambre, which closes down in spring 1932 following the couple's separation.

1925 Visits the International Exhibition of Modern Decorative and Industrial Arts in Paris.

1927 Buys a plot of land at 216, Boulevard Raspail. Creates the holding company Franc-Am Ltd. and hires architect Bruno Elkouken to build a seven-story building.
Georges Hardy brings out *L'Art nègre. L'art animiste des Noirs d'Afrique* (Paris, Henri Laurens).
Christian Zervos publishes an article entitled *"L'Art nègre"* in *Cahiers d'art*, no. 7–8.

1928 June 30:

> *The New Yorker* publishes an article on Helena Rubinstein presenting her as a collector of African masks.

December 11: Sells off her U.S. shares in the company to Lehman Brothers for $8 million, retaining the remaining 25%.
Travels to Algeria with Jean Lurçat and Marie Cuttoli (and/or Tunisia according to an advertisement published in *Vu*, May 28, 1928).

1929 Following the Wall Street Crash, she makes a vast profit by buying back her shares from Lehman Brothers for less than $2 million.
Georges-Henri Rivière publishes the article *"Le Musée d'Ethnographie du Trocadéro,"* in the first issue of *Documents*.
Cahiers d'art no. 2-3 comes out with an article by Eckart von Sydow, *"Art primitif et psychanalyse."*
Paul Guillaume and Thomas Munro publish *La Sculpture nègre primitive* (Paris, G. Crès & Cie).

1930 Publishes *The Art of Feminine Beauty.*
February 27: Inauguration of the *Afrique/Océanie* exhibition at the Théâtre Pigalle gallery in Paris. A number of the artifacts on display from the collections of Charles Ratton, Paul Chadourne, Louis Marcoussis, Stephen Chauvet, Patrick-Henry Bruce, Joseph Hessel, and Pierre Loeb will be acquired by Helena Rubinstein.
November 15 – December 31: Joseph Maes and Henri Lavachery organize the *L'Art nègre* show at the Palais des Beaux-Arts, Brussels.
André Portier and François Poncetton publish *Les Arts sauvages: Afrique* (Paris, Albert Morancé).

1931 July 2–3 and December 16: Bids at two auctions held at the Hôtel Drouot of the collections of André Breton-Paul Éluard and Georges de Miré, with Charles Ratton and Louis Carré acting as consultants.
Man Ray photographs the model Ady (Adrienne Fidelin) alongside a Bangwa female sculpture from the Cameroon.
May 6 – November 15: The International Colonial Exhibition in the Bois de Vincennes, Paris.
Jacques Viot publishes the article *"Beauté du monde. La baie de Geelvink,"* in *L'Art vivant*, no. 147.
Charles Ratton publishes *Masques africains* (Paris, Librairie des Arts décoratifs).

1932 Completion of the building at 216, Boulevard Raspail, and of the theater on the ground floor, the Studio Raspail, by architects Bruno Elkouken and Ernö Goldfinger.

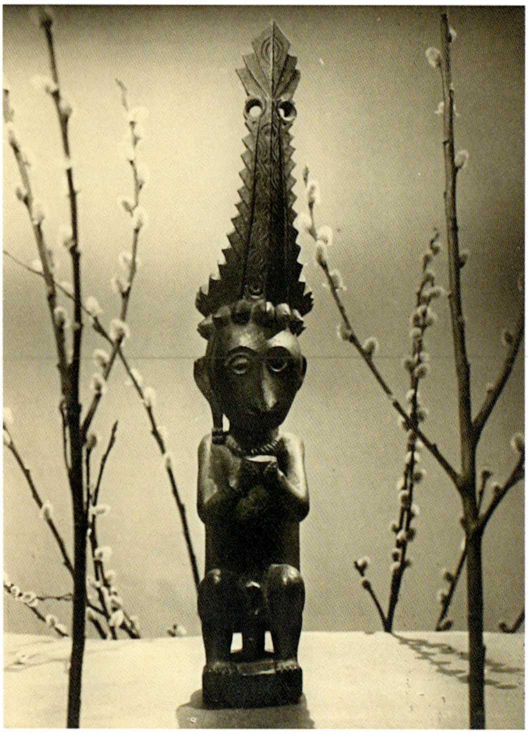

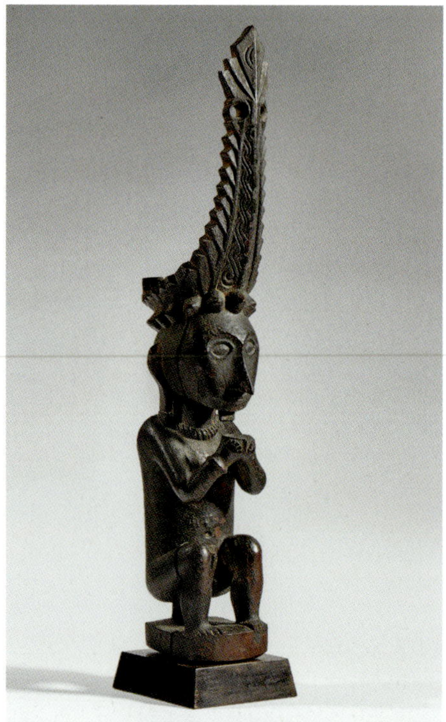

Acquires the Hotel d'Hesselin, at 24, Quai de Béthune, on the Ile Saint-Louis, from the painter José María Sert, through Misia. Commissions Louis Süe to erect a new building on the site at the top of which she reserves for herself a fifty-room duplex with a terrace; the interior is by Louis Marcoussis, one of her mentors for painting acquisitions, with Paule Marrot, Max Ingrand, and Richard Desvallières.

1934 June 1: Opening of the *L'Art des Marquises* exhibition at the Musée d'Ethnographie du Trocadéro, Paris. October 29 – November 17: *The Oceanic Art: Polynesia-Melanesia* exhibition at the Pierre Matisse Gallery, New York.

1935 Meets the Georgian prince Artchil Gourielli-Tchkonia at a soirée thrown by the Countess de Polignac, Jeanne Lanvin's daughter.
Publishes her book *This Way to Beauty*.
Undertakes a professional tour of the United States, shipping part of her collection over with her.
January: *The Oceanic Art: Polynesia-Melanesia* exhibition takes place at the Arts Club, Chicago.
March 18 – May 19: James Johnson Sweeney organizes the *African Negro Art* exhibition at the Museum of Modern Art, New York; Helena Rubinstein lends nineteen objects from her collection. One of her Bamun pipes features in an illustrated article in the *Bulletin of the Museum of Modern Art* (no. 6–7, vol. 2, March–April 1935) under the title "Extraordinary Resemblance."
March 20 – April 20: Charles Ratton arranges the *African Sculptures from the Ratton Collection* exhibition at the Pierre Matisse Gallery, New York.

1935–1938 Carl Kjersmeier publishes *Centres de style de la sculpture nègre africaine* in four volumes (Paris,

Ill. 151
Ancestor statue from Nias Island (lot 256), 1926, photograph Man Ray

Ill. 152 [lot 256]
Ancestor figure
Nias Island, Indonesia
19th century
Wood
55.7 × 10.5 × 13 cm
Musée du quai Branly – Jacques Chirac, Paris

Albert Morancé/Copenhagen, Illums Bog-Afduling). An artifact from the Rubinstein collection is reproduced in the fourth volume.

1936 Acquires the Breuil mill in Combs-la-Ville (Seine-et-Marne).
January 4–22: Exhibition of Sculptures of Old African Civilizations at the Jacques Seligmann Gallery in New York.

1936–1937 December 15 – January 17: Charles Ratton organizes the *La Sculpture des Noirs de l'Afrique* exhibition at the Théâtre Édouard-VII in Paris.

1937 Opens a new beauty salon at 715, Fifth Avenue, New York, showing some African pieces. In the fall, she is the subject of an illustrated article in *Town & Country* magazine.

> She moves with her various collections (antique furniture, opalines, miniatures, modern paintings, ancient arts, primal arts) into the apartment on Quai de Béthune. The "African room" is a lounge cum library specifically dedicated to her collection of African and Oceanic art.

July: Joins Marie Cuttoli and Pablo Picasso in Antibes.
Commissions Dora Maar to photograph her Quai de Béthune apartment.
August: Acquires F.-H. Lem's collection.
July 30–October 31: The *Origines et développement de l'art international indépendant* exhibition at the Musée du Jeu de Paume in Paris. Helena Rubinstein figures among the lenders.

1938 Divorces Edward Titus and marries Prince Artchil Gourielli-Tchkonia in Paris.

1939 Following the declaration of war, she leaves Europe and settles in New York, taking with her part of her collection. Her two sons and her nephew, Oscar Kolin, enlist.

1940 Lectures at the Brooklyn Museum, New York, as part of the *Glamour Secrets of the Ancient World* exhibition (February 3–May 5). Lends the museum books from her private library.

1941 Purchases the building at 625, Park Avenue in New York, reserving for herself a thirty-room penthouse triplex with terrace. Dalí paints a mural triptych for the bridge room the following year, and in 1943 paints her portrait.

1943 The review *Arts et Industrie*, vol. XVI, publishes the article *"Le Musée d'art nègre d'Helena Rubinstein."*

1945 September: Returns to Europe. As her first salon has been destroyed, in London she rents 3, Grafton Street. In Paris, she returns to her apartment on Quai de Béthune and her salon in Faubourg-Saint-Honoré, both ransacked by the Nazi occupiers. She embarks on a general rebuilding program.
René Gaffé publishes *La Sculpture au Congo belge* (Brussels and Paris, Éditions du Cercle d'art).

1946 Frans M. Olbrechts publishes *Plastiek van Kongo* (Antwerp, Standaard).

1947 June 11 and 13: Takes part in the auction of the Félix Fénéon collection entitled *Afrique, Océanie, Amériques* held at the Hôtel Drouot, whose consultants are Charles Ratton and Guy and André Portier. Helena Rubinstein purchases a Yoruba *oshe shango* (lot 176, Rubinstein sale, April 29, 1966).

1948 F.-H. Lem publishes *Sculptures soudanaises* (Paris, Arts et métiers graphiques). Many of the pieces he collected in situ during 1934–35 are identified as coming from the "Helena Rubinstein Collection."

Circa 1948 Launches the Gourielli men's cosmetics line at East 55th Street

in New York. Inaugurates the renovated salon at 52, Rue du Faubourg-Saint-Honoré in Paris.
April: Opens a salon at 655 Fifth Avenue in New York.

1948-1949 December 20 - January 29: W.G. Archer and Robert Melville stage the *40,000 Years of Modern Art. A Comparison of Primitive Art and Modern*, exhibition at the Institute of Contemporary Art, London.

1950 June 8–24: The Paris gallery Leleu organizes the *Sculptures du Soudan et quelques peintures de maîtres contemporains* exhibition. Helena Rubinstein appears among the lenders.

Circa 1951 Meets Patrick O'Higgins, who will act as her personal assistant until her death, before writing a biography.
The journal *Présence africaine* brings out a special number entitled *"L'Art nègre"* (no. 10–11), reproducing an object from Helena Rubinstein's collection.

After 1952 Acquires an important group of Agni terracotta funerary figures collected in 1928 by Dr. Lheureux from Krinjabo (Ivory Coast).

1953 January: Opens a new factory on Long Island.
Establishes the Helena Rubinstein Foundation that awards scholarships to encourage the education of women.
Many objects from Helena Rubinstein's collection appear in the documentary by Alain Resnais and Chris Marker *Les statues meurent aussi* (Tadié Cinéma Production) commissioned by the magazine *Présence africaine*, with artistic consultancy from Charles Ratton.

1954 Inauguration of a beauty salon for men "The House of Gourielli," in New York.

1954–1955 October 21 – January 2: Frederic R. Pleasants organizes the *Masterpieces of African Art* exhibition at the Brooklyn Museum in New York. Helena Rubinstein lends six objects from her collection.

1955 Georges and Claude Pompidou become Helena Rubinstein's tenants at 24, Quai de Béthune.
November 21: Death of Prince Artchil Gourielli-Tchkonia.
Stays in Cannes to pose for Pablo Picasso at his house: a series of sketches results, but the planned portrait never materializes.

1955–1956
Werner Muensterberger publishes *Sculpture of Primitive Man* (New York, Harry N. Abrams).

1956
Denise Paulme publishes *Les Sculptures de l'Afrique noire* (Paris, Presses Universitaires de France).

1957
April – September: Margaret Webster-Plass organizes the *African Tribal Sculpture* exhibition at the University Museum in Philadelphia.
July 6 – September 29: Hélène and Henri Kamer hold the *First International Retrospective Exhibition of the Arts of Africa and Oceania* at the Palais Miramar in Cannes.
Claude Roy brings out *Arts sauvages* (Paris, Robert Delpire).

1958 Spring: Horace Titus is killed in a car accident at the age of forty-six.
Summer: Robert Goldwater organizes the *African Sculpture lent* by New York Collectors exhibition at the Museum of Primitive Art, New York. Helena Rubinstein lends four objects from her collection.
Winter: Starts a long voyage to the Orient with Patrick O'Higgins, taking in Japan, Hong Kong, and Australia.
William Fagg and Eliot Elisofon publish *The Sculpture of Africa* (London, Thames & Hudson).

1959 Cecil Beaton decorates the art gallery in the apartment at 625, Park Avenue.
Travels to Israel where the Helena

Rubinstein Pavilion for contemporary art is inaugurated in Tel Aviv.
Graham Sutherland completes her double portrait begun in 1958.
Represents the US cosmetics industry at the US National Exhibition in Moscow.

1960 February 17 – May 8: Robert Goldwater organizes the *Bambara Sculpture from Western Sudan* exhibition at the Museum of Primitive Art in New York.
March 25 – April 23: *The Epstein Collection of Primitive and Exotic Sculpture* exhibition is held at the Arts Council of Great Britain, London.
May 18 – September 11: *The Lipchitz Collection* exhibition takes place at the Museum of Primitive Art, New York.

1960–1961 Buys an apartment at 247, Knightsbridge, in London, which she has decorated by David Hicks following a color code inspired by the lining in one of her Balenciaga suits; it will be occupied by her sister Ceska.

1962 Jacques Maquet publishes *Afrique. Les civilisations noires* (Paris, Marabout).

1963 July 12 – August 11: Robert Goldwater organizes the *Senufo Sculpture from West Africa* exhibition at the Museum of Primitive Art in New York; it will then move on to the Art Institute in Chicago and the Baltimore Museum of Art. Helena Rubinstein lends a number of objects from her collection.
Elsy Leuzinger publishes *Afrikanische Skulpturen. African Sculptures* (Zurich, Museum Rietberg-Atlantis Verlag).

1964 Publishes her autobiography *My Life for Beauty.*
28 October – 30 November: William Fagg organizes the *Afrique. Cent tribus, cent chefs-d'œuvre* exhibition at the Musée des Arts Décoratifs in Paris. Helena Rubinstein lends several items from her collection.

1965 April 1: Death of Helena Rubinstein in New York. News of her death hits the headlines, including *The New York Times.* Following three days of public viewing, her body is buried at the Mount Olivet Cemetery (Queens) next to Prince Gourielli.
October 12: First auction of the Rubinstein collection by the Parke-Bernet Galleries in New York (jewelry).
Robert Goldwater publishes *Masterpieces in the Museum of Primitive Art: Africa, Oceania, North America, Mexico, Central South America, Peru* (New York, Museum of Primitive Art).

1966 21–29 April and October 15:

> Auction sales of Helena Rubinstein's collection of African and Oceanic art at the Parke-Bernet Galleries in New York.

Her collections of art are sold off in accordance with her express wish.
Her portraits remained in her foundation until they too are auctioned by Sotheby's New York in May and October 2011.
Warren Robbins publishes *African Art in American Collections* (New York, Praeger) with a piece from the Helena Rubinstein Estate.

1967 Jacqueline Delange and Michel Leiris publish *Afrique noire. La création plastique* (Paris, Gallimard).

1976–1977 The Helena Rubinstein company is bought by Colgate-Palmolive.

1977 26 October – 12 December: *The Portraits of Helena Rubinstein* exhibition is held at the Musée des Arts Décoratifs, Paris; it subsequently travels to the Metropolitan Museum of Art, New York.

1984–1988 Colgate-Palmolive sells Helena Rubinstein to Albi International. L'Oréal buys the entire conglomerate.

* Interview with Bertrand Goy, May 15, 2019

Sales catalogs of Helena Rubinstein's collection of African and Oceanic art and List of exhibited works

Held on April 21 and 29, and October 15, 1966, in New York, the sales at which the majority of Helena Rubinstein's collection of non-European art was sold were events of international scope.

The list below outlines a history of the collection following its disposal. As well as noting the presence of major dealers—Harry A. Franklin—and collectors—E. Nathhorst and Frieda and Milton Rosenthal—it demonstrates how certain artifacts resurfaced more than once at auction, while others stayed put or "temporarily disappeared" from the art market after 1966.

To date, approximately a third of the objects from this prestigious collection have been localized. Consultation of the material available reveals, in addition to the names of major dealers and collectors in the field, those of acquaintances and relatives of Helena Rubinstein, and of several women and passing buyers attracted by the collector's reputation.

While the lack of exhaustive archives makes it very difficult to reconstruct the entire collection at the present time, the photographs in the catalogs of the three African and Oceanic art sales, and the first volume, presenting the April 1966 sales and featuring reports by Jacques Millot—the director of the Musée de l'Homme at that time—remain a helpful basis for identification.

Catalogs were sold by Parke-Bernet for between $1.50 and $3.50 each, or $10 for the set covering all sales of the Rubinstein collection. Scarce, if not impossible to find today, their value is inestimable.

The list below is identical to the technical descriptions and reproductions in the two sales catalogs (April and October 1966). Additions in italics indicate the history of the objects since their sale. When known, the collection in which they are currently held is identified by a bullet point.

For the works on display, solely the buyer at the 1966 sale, if identifiable, as well as the current collection, are mentioned. A detailed provenance can be found in the list of works exhibited, p. 230.

The present volume reproduces every object illustrated in the 1966 sales catalogs.

African and Oceanic Art
Parts One and Two

FIRST SESSION

Thursday, April 21, 1966
at 8:30 p.m.

SHERBRO

1

Sherbro Figure (Nomoli)
Soapstone
Height 6¾ inches; 17 cms
Sierra Leone
John J. Klejman, New York (1966)
Repr. p. 201

2

Sherbro Figure
Soapstone
Height 7¾ inches; 19 cms
Sierra Leone
John J. Klejman, New York (1966)
Repr. p. 201

MENDE

3

Mende Helmet Mask
Wood
(Has stand) Height
12 inches; 30.5 cms
Repr. p. 201

DAN

4

Dan Human Mask
Wood
Height 8½ inches;
21.6 cms
From the region of Man,
Ivory Coast

5

Dan Mask
Wood
Height 9 inches; 23.5 cms
Gan sub-tribe
(Gan village),
West Dan area; Ivory Coast

6

Dan Mask
Wood
Height 9½ inches;
24.1 cms
Gan sub-tribe; Ivory Coast

7

Dan Mask
Wood
Height 7½ inches; 19 cms
Possibly from the village of
Kogma, Gan sub-tribe;
Ivory Coast
Repr. p. 201

8

Dan Reliquary Mask
Wood
Height 6½ inches;
16.5 cms
Region of Toulepleu,
Cavally River district;
Ivory Coast
Jay C. Leff collection, Uniontown (1966)
• Private collection, Paris
Cat. 1, repr. p. 88

9

Dan Mask
Wood
(Has stand) Height 10¼ inches; 26 cms
Northern Dan, Yakuba region; Ivory Coast
Merton Simpson (1966)
Morris J. Pinto collection
Hubert Goldet collection
• Private collection, Paris
Repr. p. 201

10

Dan-Ngere Mask
Wood with Hair and Fibre
(Has stand) Height of mask 8½ inches; 21.5 cms / Overall length 18½ inches; 47 cms
District of Danane, Ivory Coast
Morris J. Pinto, Geneva/ New York/Paris (1966)
• Marc Ladreit de Lacharrière collection, Paris
Cat. 2, repr. p. 89

11

Dan Mask
Wood
(Has stand)
Height 5½ inches; 14 cms
Probably from Gepleu. Blomé sub-tribe; Ivory Coast
Frieda and Milton Rosenthal collection, New York (1966)
Sotheby's sale, New York, November 14, 2008, lot no. 5
Repr. p. 201

12

Dan Mask
Wood and Fibre with Cloth
(Has stand) Lenght of mask 5½ inches; 14 cms / Overall length 8 inches; 20 cms
Cavally River area, district of Toulepleu; Ivory Coast
E. Nathhorst collection, Stockholm (1966)
Sotheby's sale, Parke-Bernet New York, 14 October, 1977, lot no. 493
Repr. p. 201

13

Dan Mask
Wood and Fibre
(Has stand) Height 8 inches; 20.3 cms
Gan sub-division, region of Man; Ivory Coast
• Private collection, Paris
Cat. 3, repr. p. 88

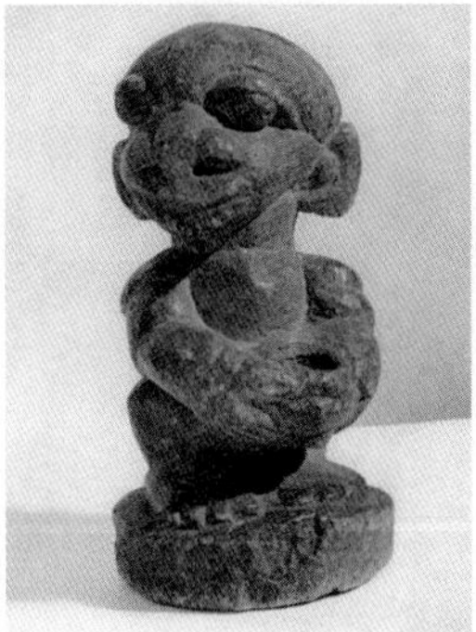

Lot 1

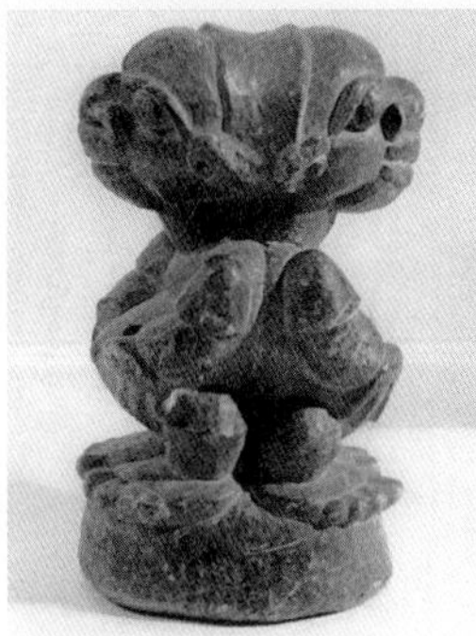

Lot 2

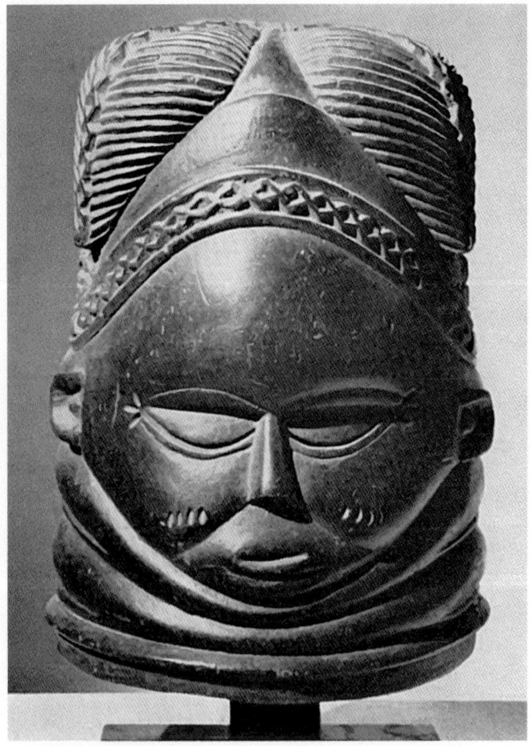

Lot 3

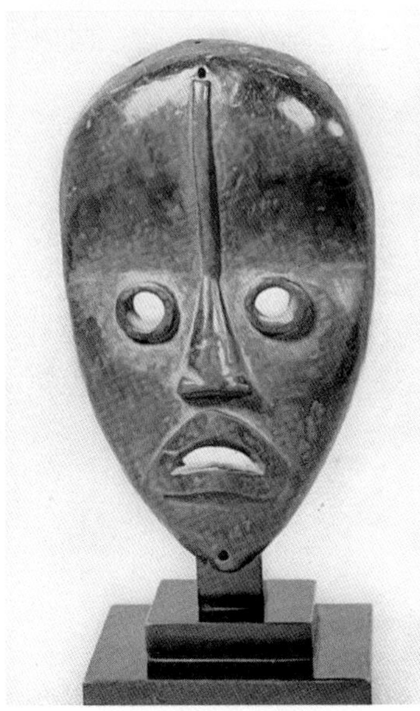

Lot 7

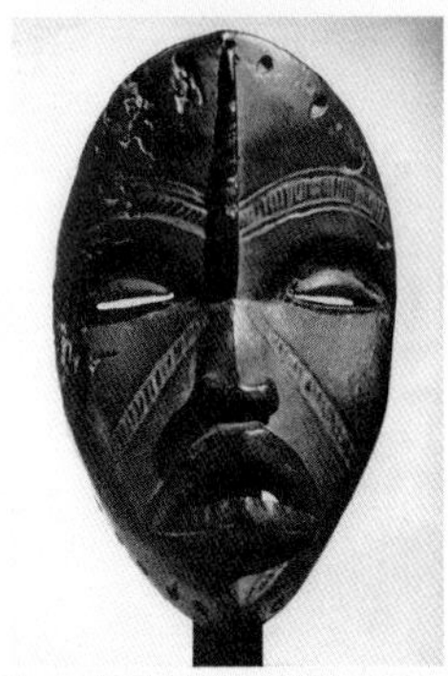

Lot 9

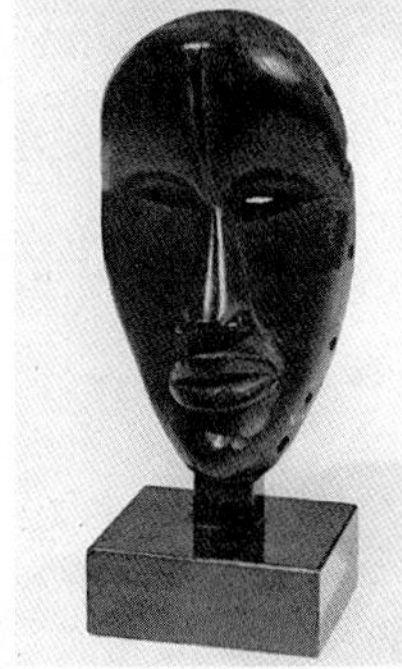

Lot 11

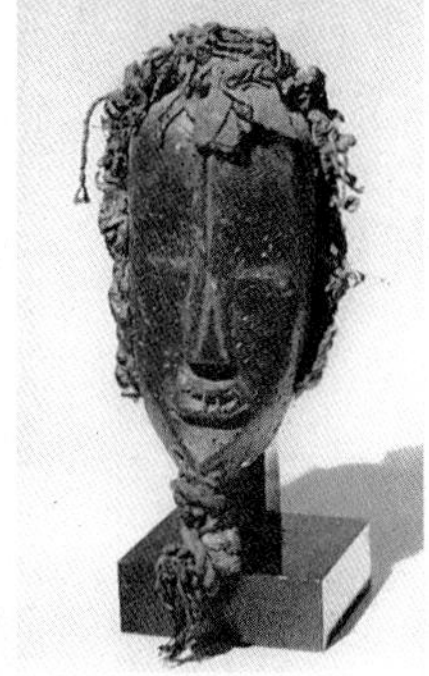

Lot 12

GREBO

14

Grebo Mask
Wood
Height 13 1/4 inches;
33.6 cms
Liberia
• *Private collection, United States*
Repr. p. 203

WOBE

15

Wobe Dance Mask
Wood
Height 12 inches; 30.5 cms
Around the village of Bangro (between the Duekue and Sassandra rivers), Zanya sub-tribe
Repr. p. 203

BAULE

16

Baule Heddle Pulley
Wood
(Has stand) Height
7½ inches; 19 cms
Harry A. Franklin collection, Los Angeles (1966)
Sotheby's sale, New York, April 21, 1990, lot no. 77

17

Baule Heddle Pulley
Wood
(Has stand) Height
6¼ inches; 16 cms

18

Baule Heddle Pulley
Wood
(Has stand) Height
8 inches; 26.2 cms
Frieda and Milton Rosenthal collection, New York (1966)
Sotheby's sale, New York, November 14, 2008, lot no. 8

19

Baule Heddle Pulley
Wood
(Has stand) Height
5 inches; 13 cms
Sotheby's sale, New York, May 12, 2005, lot no. 61

20

Baule Heddle Pulley
Wood
(Has stand) Height
5½ inches; 14 cms

21

Baule Heddle Pulley
Wood
(Has stand) Height
5 inches; 12.5 cms
Sotheby's sale, Parke-Bernet New York, October 14, 1977, lot no. 519

22

Baule Heddle Pulley
Wood
(Has stand) Height
7 inches; 18 cms
Frieda and Milton Rosenthal collection, New York (1966)
• *Private collection, Long Island*
Cat. 11, repr. p. 96

23

Baule Heddle Pulley
Wood
(Has stand) Height
6¼ inches; 16 cms

24

Baule Heddle Pulley
Wood
(Has stand) Height
7 inches; 18 cms

25

Baule Heddle Pulley
Wood
(Has stand) Height
8¾ inches; 22.2 cms

26

Baule Heddle Pulley
Wood
(Has stand) Height
7½ inches; 19 cms
Frieda and Milton Rosenthal collection, New York (1966)
Sotheby's sale, New York, November 14, 2008, lot no. 10

27

Baule Figures
Wood
(Has stand) Height
7 inches; 17.8 cms
Harry A. Franklin collection, Los Angeles (1966)
Sotheby's sale, New York, April 21, 1990, lot no. 117
Sotheby's sale, New York, November 16, 2001, lot no. 12

28

Baule Heddle Pulley
Wood
Height 9 inches; 23 cms

29

Baule Fly Whisk
Wood, Gold Leaf and Animal Hair
Length of handle 10¼ inches; 26 cms / Overall length approx. 43 inches; 109 cms
Region of Bouaké
Repr. p. 203

30

Baule Tambourine Beater (Lahouré)
Wood with Brass Studs
Height 10 inches; 25.5 cms
Harry A. Franklin collection, Los Angeles (1966)
Sotheby's sale, New York, April 21, 1990, lot no. 109
• *Musée Barbier-Mueller, Geneva, inv. 1007.219*
Repr. p. 203

31

Baule Female Figure
Wood
(Has stand) Height
15 inches; 38 cms
Region of Bouaké
Oscar Kolin collection (1966)
• *Private collection, New York*
Repr. p. 203

32

Baule Male Figure
Region of Bouaké
Wood
(Has stand) Height 14¾ inches; 37.5 cms
Oscar Kolin collection (1966)
• *Private collection, New York*
Repr. p. 203

33

Baule Heddle Pulley
Wood
(Has stand) Height
7 ½ inches; 19 cms
Herman Jarvis collection (1966)
Sotheby's sale, New York, May 12, 2005, lot no. 63
• *Private collection, New York*
Repr. p. 203

34

Baule Heddle Pulley
Wood
(Has stand) Height
8½ inches; 21.5 cms
Oscar Kolin collection (1966)
Repr. p. 203

35

Baule Heddle Pulley
Wood
(Has stand) Height
7 inches; 18 cms
Frieda and Milton Rosenthal collection, New York (1966)
Sotheby's sale, New York, November 14, 2008, lot no. 6
Repr. p. 203

36

Baule Heddle Pulley
Wood
(Has stand) Height
8 inches; 20 cms
• *National Museum of African Art – Smithsonian Institution, Washington, inv. 96.7.1*
Repr. p. 203

37

Baule Zooanthropomorphic Mask
Wood
(Has stand) Height
9¾ inches. 25 cms
Region of Bouaflé
Frieda and Milton Rosenthal collection, New York (1966)
• *Private collection*
Cat. 15, repr. p. 100

38

Baule Heddle Pulley
Wood
Height 9 inches; 23 cms
Region of Dimbokro
Oscar Kolin collection (1966)
• *Brian and Diane Leyden collection, Long Island*
Cat. 12, repr. p. 96

39

Baule Female Figure
Wood
Height 13½ inches;
34.3 cms
Region of Dimbokro
Repr. p. 203

40

Baule Standing Figure of a Chief
Wood
Height 17½ inches;
44.5 cms
Region of Bouaké
E. Nathhorst collection, Stockholm (1966)
• *Private collection, Canada*
Cat. 16, repr. p. 99

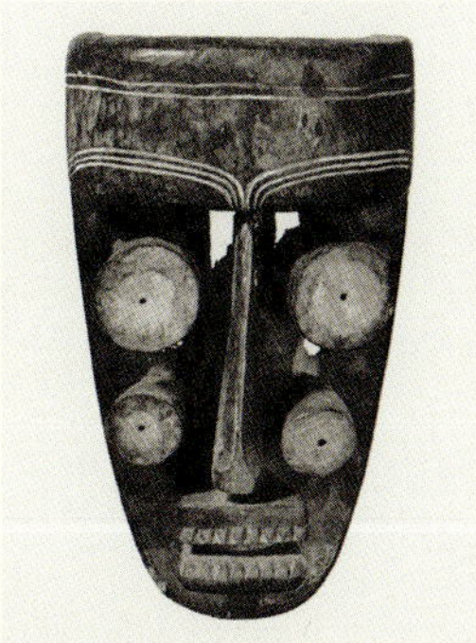

Lot 14

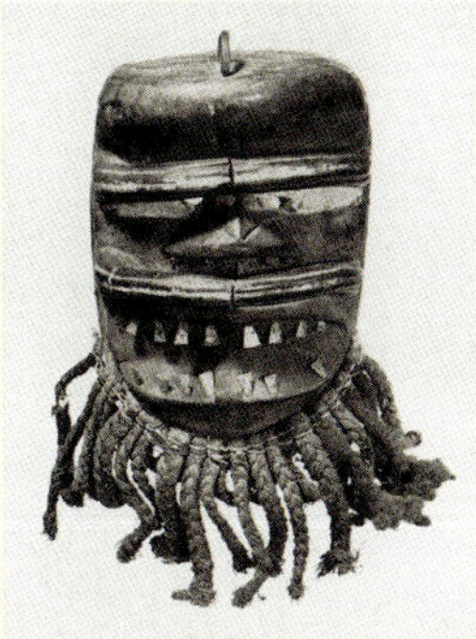

Lot 15

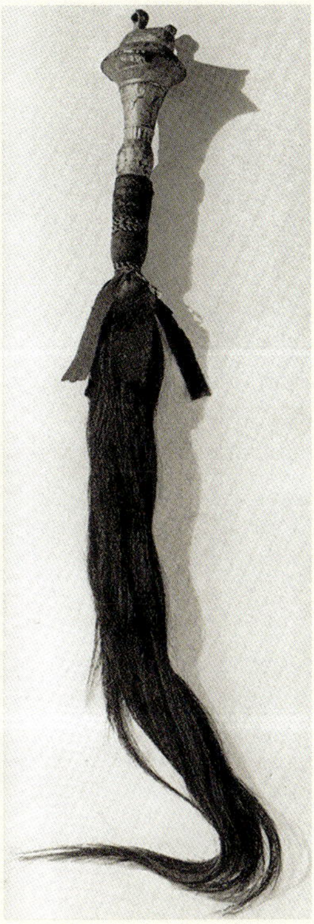

Lot 29

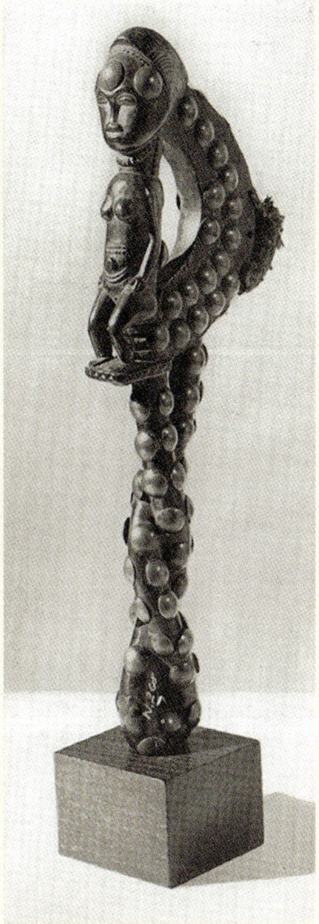

Lot 30

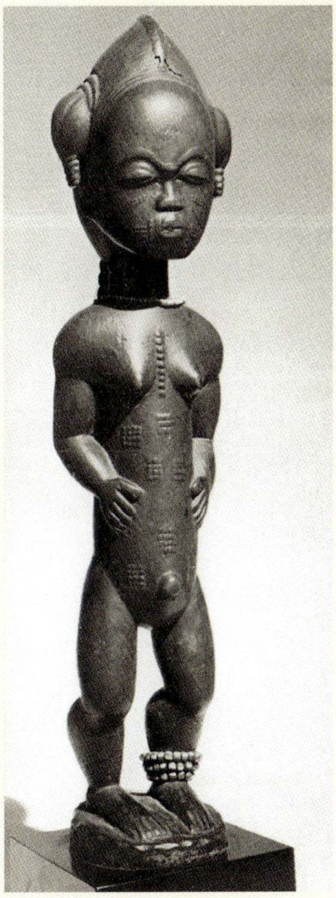

Lot 31

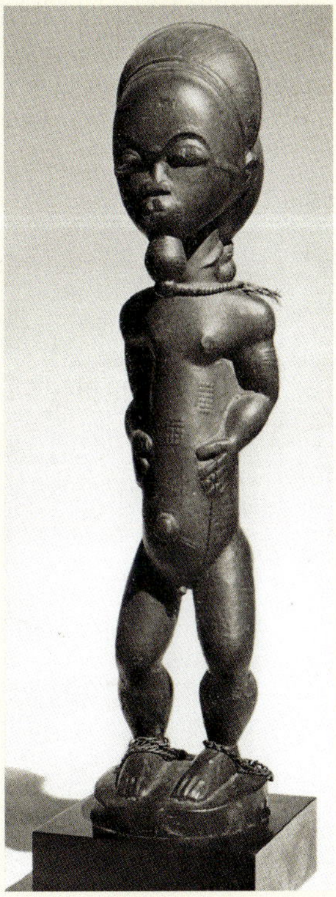

Lot 32

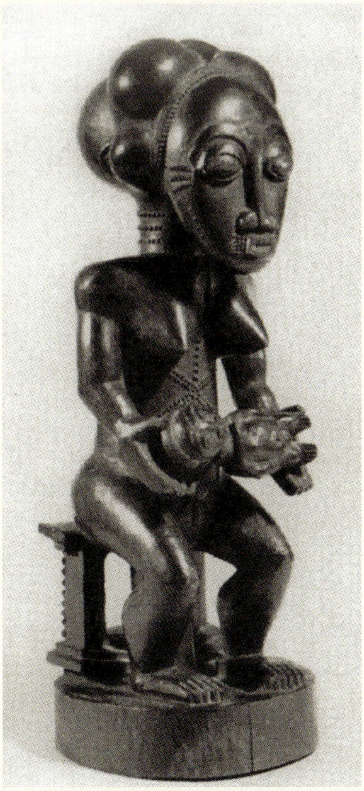

Lot 39

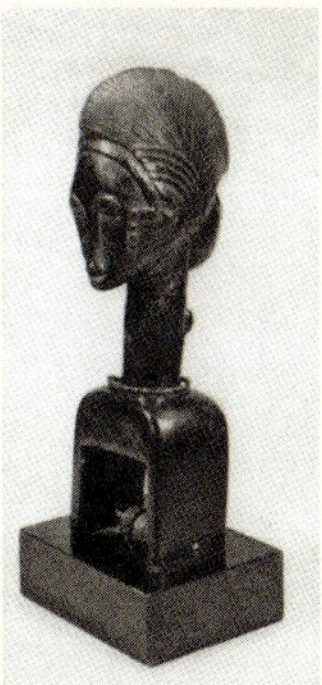

Lot [??]

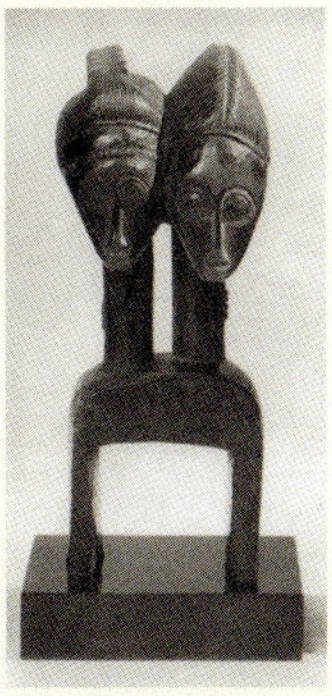

Lot 33

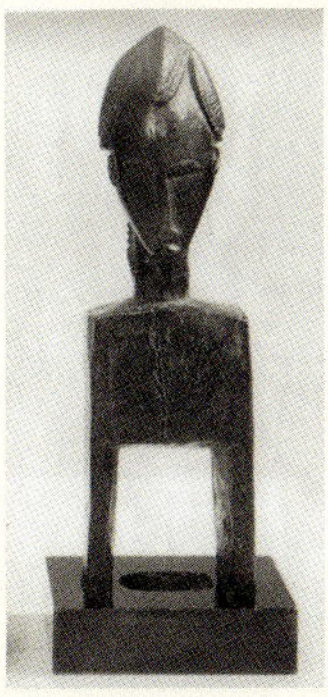

Lot 34

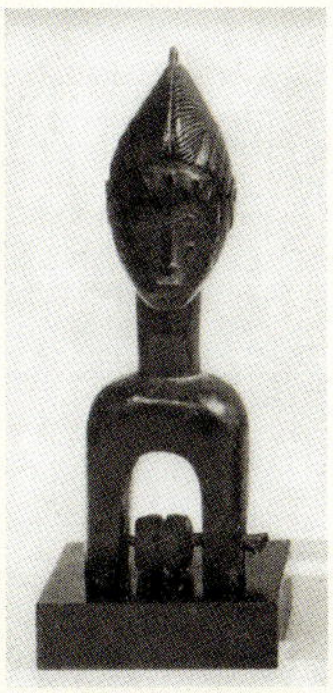

Lot 35

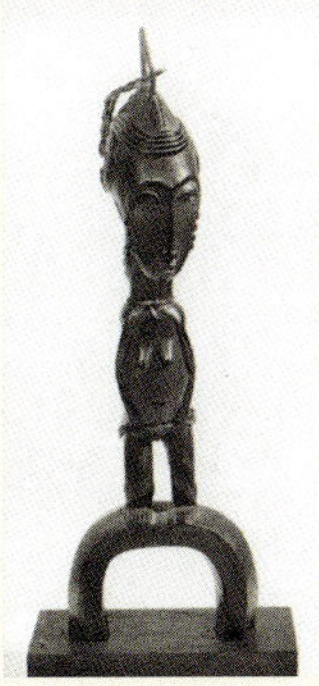

Lot 36

41
Baule Female Figure
Wood
Height 18 inches; 46 cms
Region of Bouaké

42
Baule Male Figure
Wood
Height 15 inches; 38 cms
Warren Robbins collection, Washington (1966)

43
Baule Hand Drum
Wood and Skin
Diam 9½ inches; 24 cms / Height 13 inches; 33 cms
Region of Bouaké
Allan Stone collection, New York (1966)
Sotheby's sale, New York, May 4, 1995, lot no. 161
Repr. p. 205

44
Baule Female Figure
Wood
Height 14¾ inches; 37.5 cms
Repr. p. 205

45
Baule Human Mask
Wood
Height 9¼ inches; 23.5 cms
Region of Bouaké
Harry A. Franklin collection, Los Angeles (1966)
Sotheby's sale, New York, April 21, 1990, lot no. 107
Christie's sale, Paris, "Paris avant-garde" October 17, 2019, lot 26
Repr. p. 205

46
Baule Elephant Mask
Region of Bouaké
Wood
Height 14¼ inches; 36.2 cms
Repr. p. 205

47
Baule Drum
Wood
(Has stand) Height 66 inches; 167.7 cms
Harry A. Franklin collection, Los Angeles (1966)
• The Metropolitan Museum of Art, New York, inv. 1995.64.10
Repr. p. 205

48
Baule Drum
Wood
(Has stand) Height 64 inches; 162.7 cms
Harry A. Franklin collection, Los Angeles (1966)
• The Metropolitan Museum of Art, New York, inv. 1995.64.9
Repr. p. 205

GURO

49
Guro Heddle Pulley
Wood
Height 7½ inches; 19 cms
Elsa Rogo collection, New York (1966)

50
Guro Horned Human Mask
Wood
Height 12¾ inches; 32.7 cms
Harold Rome collection, New York (1966)

51
Guro (Zamle) Dance Mask
Wood
Height 17 inches; 43.2 cms
Region of Daloa
Elsa Rogo collection, New York (1966)
• Private collection, United States
Repr. p. 205

MALINKE

52
Malinke Dance Mask
Wood
Height 22½ inches; 57 cms
Guinea
E. Nathhorst collection, Stockholm (1966)
Sotheby's sale, Parke-Bernet New York, October 14, 1977, lot no. 489
Repr. p. 205

BAMBARA

53
Bambara Dance Mask
Wood and Cowrie Shells
(Has stand) Height 20½ inches; 52 cms
Village of Neguena
Provenance F.-H. Lem, Paris
• Private collection, New York
Repr. p. 205

54
Bambara Dance Mask
Wood
Height 23¾ inches; 60.2 cms
Found in the region of Kenedougou, Eastern Bambaraland
Provenance F.-H. Lem, Paris
E. Nathhorst collection, Stockholm (1966)
Sotheby's sale, Parke-Bernet New York, October 14, 1977, lot no. 465
Harry A. Franklin collection, Los Angeles
Sotheby's sale, New York, April 21, 1990, lot no. 16
• Private collection, New York
Repr. p. 205

55
Bambara Dance Mask
Wood with Metal Sheets
(Has stand) Height 11 inches; 28 cms
E. Nathhorst collection, Stockholm (1966)
• Private collection, New York
Cat. 24, repr. p. 111

56
Bambara Mask
Wood
(Has stand) Height 11¾ inches; 30 cms
Region of Koutiala
Provenance F.-H. Lem, Paris
Aimée W. Hirschberg collection, New York (1966)
Repr. p. 205

57
Bambara Female Figure
Wood
(Has stand) Height 14¾ inches; 37.4 cms
Region of Segou, Northeastern Bambaraland
Provenance F.-H. Lem, Paris
Frieda and Milton Rosenthal collection, New York (1966)
Sotheby's sale, New York, November 14, 2008, lot no. 3
• Gilbert and Doreen Bassin collection, New York
Repr. p. 205

58
Bambara Female Fertility Figure
Wood
(Has stand) Height 16½ inches; 42 cms
From Ganadougou
Provenance F.-H. Lem, Paris
Oscar Kolin collection, New York (1966)
• Celestin Clamra collection, New York
Cat. 25, repr. p. 113

59
Bambara Fertility Figure
Wood
Height 12 ½ inches; 32 cms
Central Bambaraland

60
Bambara Figure
Wood
(Has stand) Height 7¾ inches; 19.5 cms
From the Kenedougou district, Eastern Bambaraland
Provenance F.-H. Lem, Paris
Elsa Rogo collection, New York (1966)

61
Bambara Figure
Wood
(Has stand) Height 13½ inches; 34.2 cms
Found at Sanzama in the Sikasso region of Bambaraland, bordering on the Senufo
Provenance F.-H. Lem, Paris
Jay C. Leff collection, Uniontown (1966)
Repr. p. 205

62
Bambara Figure
Wood
(Has stand) Height 15½ inches; 39.3 cms
Eastern Bambaraland
Provenance F.-H. Lem, Paris
Abe Siegal collection (1966)
• National Museum of African Art – Smithsonian Institution, Washington, inv. 96.7.2
Cat. 26, repr. p. 112

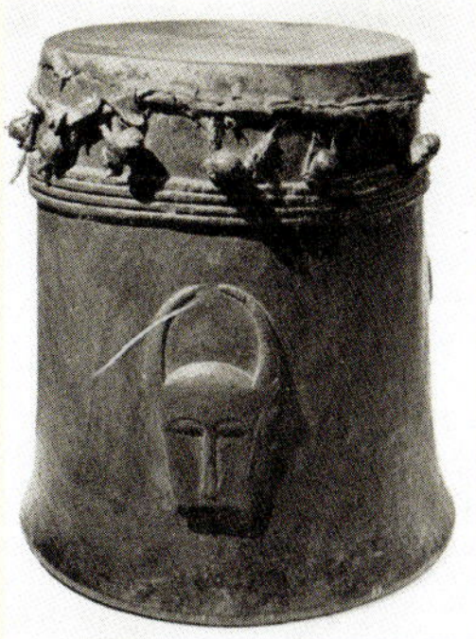

Lot 43

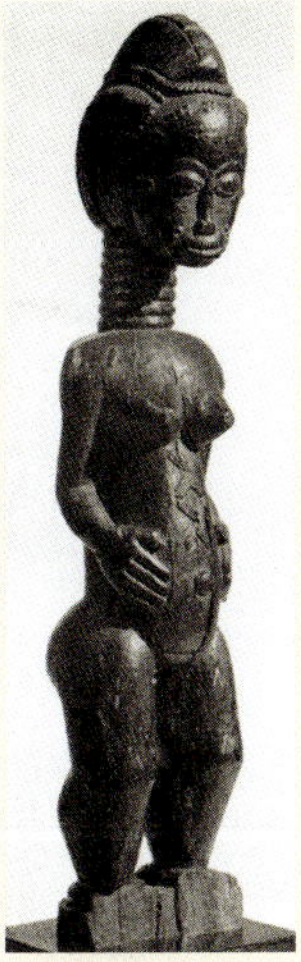

Lot 44

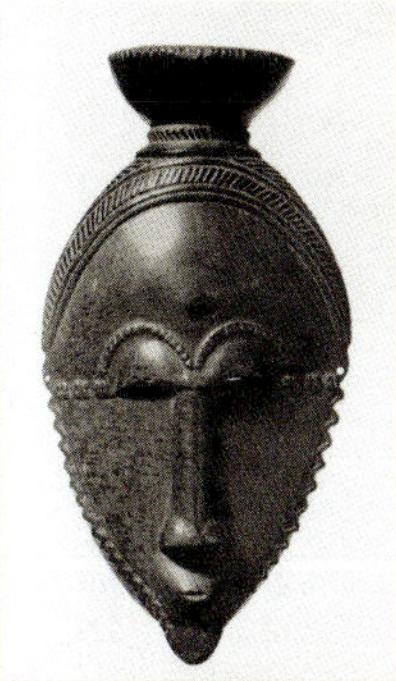

Lot 45

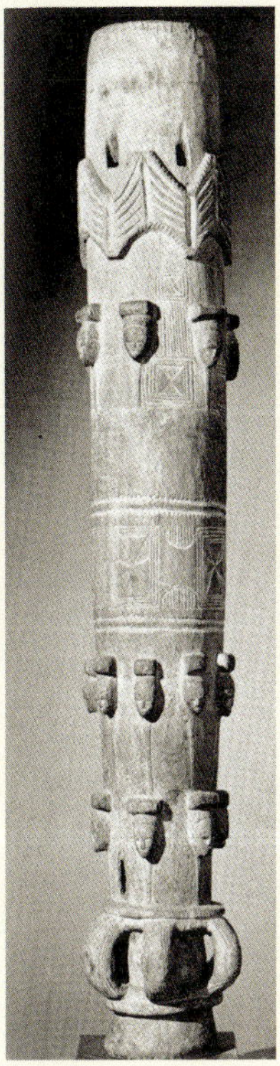

Lot 47

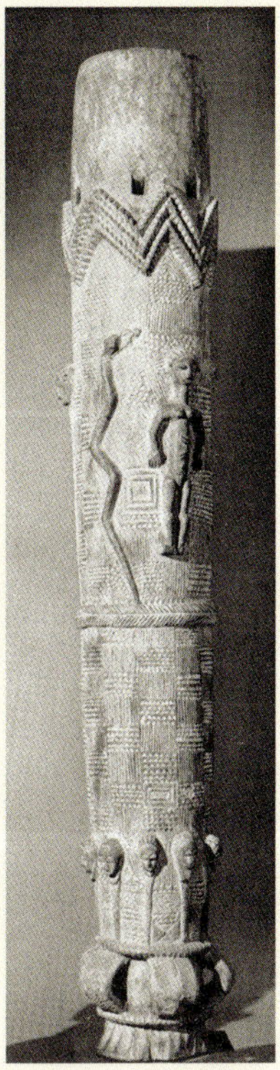

Lot 48

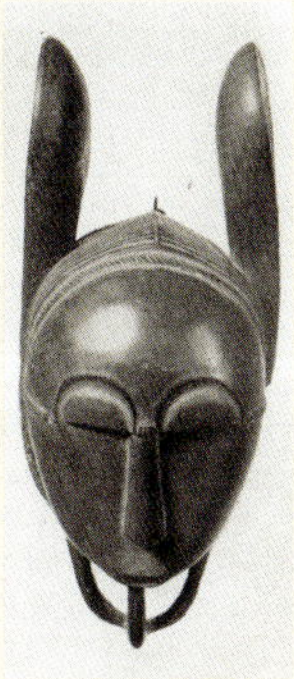

Lot 46

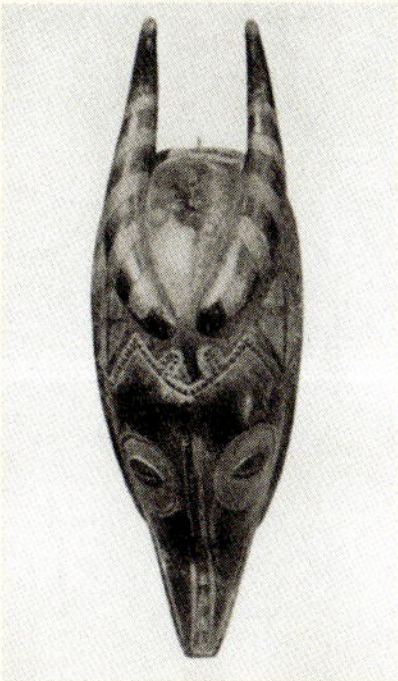

Lot 51

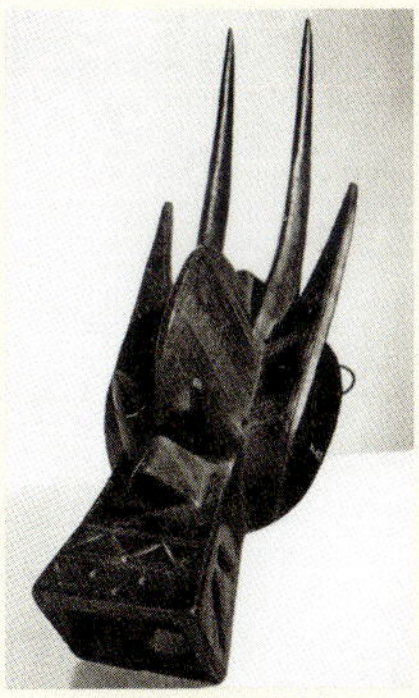

Lot 52

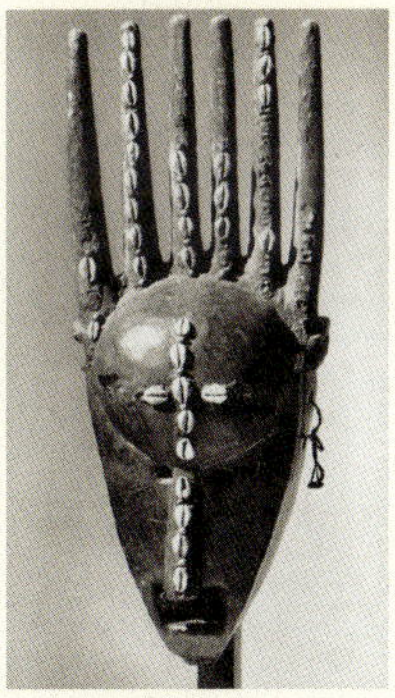

Lot 53

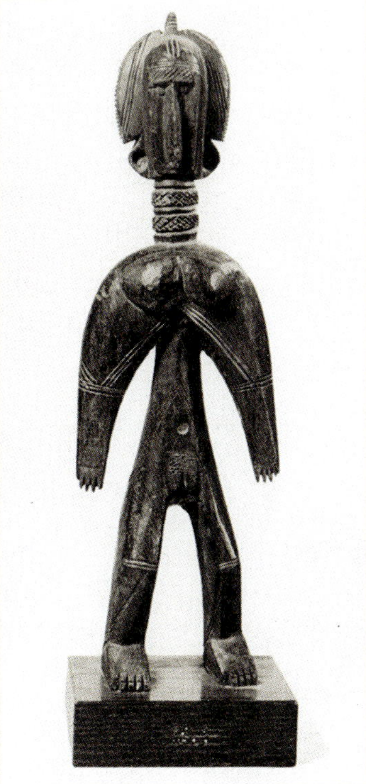

Lot 57

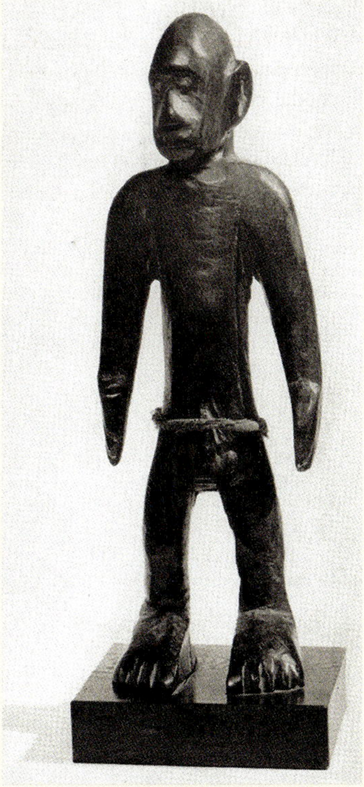

Lot 61

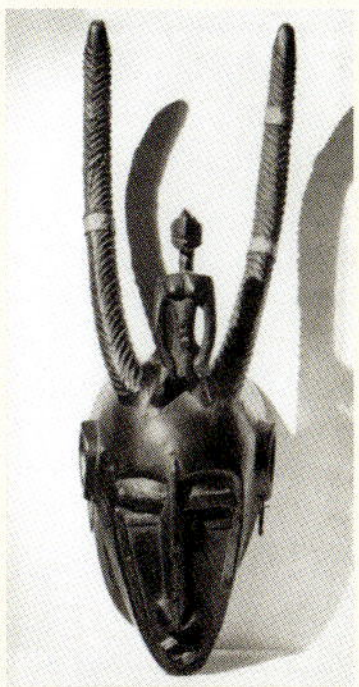

Lot 54

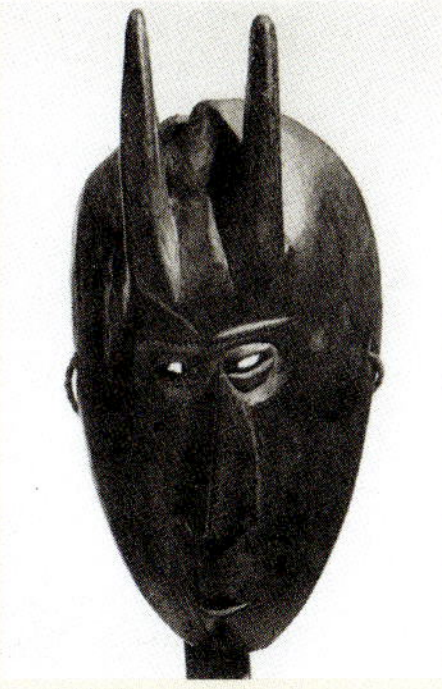

Lot 56

63

Bambara Female Reliquary Figure
Wood with Metal Sheeting
(Has stand) Height 51 inches; 129.5 cms
From the region of Touna-Neguena
Provenance F.-H. Lem, Paris
E. Nathhorst collection, Stockholm (1966)
Sotheby's sale, New York, October 14, 1977, lot no. 470
Repr. p. 207

64

Bambara Dance Headdress
Wood with Metal Strips
(Has stand) Height 57 ½ inches; 146 cms
From the village of Sela, in the region of San, Northeastern Bambaraland
Provenance F.-H. Lem, Paris
E. Nathhorst collection, Stockholm (1966)
Sotheby's sale, New York, October 14, 1977, lot no. 477
• Indiana University Museum of Art, Bloomington, inv. 77.87
Repr. p. 24

65

Bambara Male Marionette
Wood
(Has stand) Height 19 inches; 48 cms
From Niena, Kenedougou
Provenance F.-H. Lem, Paris
Repr. p. 207

66

Bambara Female Marionette
Wood
(Has stand) Height 31½ inches; 80 cms
From Niena, region of Kenedougou
Provenance F.-H. Lem, Paris
Allan Frumkin, Chicago/New York (1966)
• Dr Marian Malcolm collection, Tenafly
Cat. 27, repr. p. 115

67

Bambara Dance Headdress
Wood
(Has stand) Height 41 inches; 104 cms
From the region of Segou, Northeastern Bambaraland
Provenance F.-H. Lem, Paris
Repr. p. 207

68

Bambara Dance Headdress
Wood
(Has stand) Height 36½ inches; 93.7 cms
From the region of Segou, Northeastern Bambaraland
Provenance F.-H. Lem, Paris
Ruth and Paul Tishman collection, New York (1966)
• National Museum of African Art – Smithsonian Institution, Washington, inv. 2005.6.12
Cat. 30, repr. p. 116

69

Bambara Dance Headdress
Wood
(Has stand) Height 28 inches; 71 cms
From the region of Segou, Northeastern Bambaraland
Provenance F.-H. Lem, Paris
E. Nathhorst collection, Stockholm (1966)
• Laura and James J. Ross collection, New York
Cat. 31, repr. p. 117

70

Bambara Dance Headdress
Wood
(Has stand) Height 30¾ inches; 78 cms
From the region of Segou, Northeastern Bambaraland
Provenance F.-H. Lem, Paris
Harry A. Franklin collection, Los Angeles (1966)
• Marc Ladreit de Lacharrière collection, Paris
Cat. 29, repr. p. 116

71

Bambara Dance Headdress
Wood and Fibre
Length of headdress 19¾ inches; 50 cms / (Has stand) Overall length 33 inches; 84 cms
From the region of Kinian, Kenedougou area, Eastern Bambaraland
Provenance F.-H. Lem, Paris
Morton Lipkin collection, New York/Londres/Phoenix/Munich
Faletti Family collection, Chicago
Sotheby's sale, New York, November 16, 2001, lot no. 21
Sotheby's sale, New York, November 16, 2002, lot no. 17
• Private collection, New York
Repr. p. 207

72

Bambara Dance Headdress
Wood and Fibre
Height of antelope 21¾ inches; 55.2 cms / (Has stand) Overall height 33½ inches; 85 cms
From the region of Kinian, Kenedougou area, Eastern Bambaraland
Provenance F.-H. Lem, Paris
Aimée W. Hirschberg collection, New York (1966)
• Neuberger Museum of Art, State University of New York, Eliot Hirshberg donation, Aimée W. Hirschberg collection (1966), inv. 1984.11.01
Repr. p. 207

73

Bambara Dance Headdress
Wood and Basketwork
Height of antelope 16 inches; 40.5 cms / Overall height 22 ¾ inches; 52.5 cms
From Eastern Bambaraland
Provenance F.-H. Lem, Paris
Repr. p. 207

73A

Bambara Dance Headdress
Wood with Metal and Cowrie Shells
(Has stand) Height 22¾ inches; 57.8 cms
From the region of Segou, Northeastern Bambaraland
Provenance F.-H. Lem, Paris
• National Museum of African Art – Smithsonian Institution, Washington, inv. 2005.6.156
Repr. p. 207

74

Bambara Dance Headdress
Wood
(Has stand) Height 21¼ inches; 54 cms
From the region of Kenedougou, Eastern Bambaraland
Provenance F.-H. Lem, Paris
Repr. p. 207

75

Bambara Dance Headdress
Wood
(Has stand) Height 21½ inches; 54.5 cms
From the region of Ouassoulou, near Bougouni, West-Central Bambaraland
Provenance F.-H. Lem, Paris
Harry A. Franklin collection, Los Angeles (1966)
• The Arman Marital Trust, Corice Arman Trustee, New York
Cat. 32, repr. p. 117

76

Bambara Dance Headdress
Wood
(Has stand) Height 19 inches; 48 cms
From the region of Ouassoulou, near Bougouni, West-Central Bambaraland
Provenance F.-H. Lem, Paris
E. Nathhorst collection, Stockholm (1966)
Sotheby's sale, Parke-Bernet New York, October 14, 1977, lot no. 472
Sotheby's sale, New York, May 17, 2002, lot no. 58

77

Bambara Dance Headdress
Wood
(Has stand) Height 21¾ inches; 55.2 cms
From the region of Kenedougou, Eastern Bambaraland
Provenance F.-H. Lem, Paris

78

Bambara Dance Headdress
Wood with Tufts of Hair
(Has stand) Height 20½ inches; 52 cms
From the Bougouni region, West-Central Bambaraland
Provenance F.-H. Lem, Paris
Jay C. Leff collection, Uniontown (1966)
• The Schorr Family Collection, United States
Repr. p. 207

79

Bambara Dance Headdress
Wood
(Has stand) Height 21 inches; 53 cms
From the Bougouni region, West-Central Bambaraland
Provenance F.-H. Lem, Paris
• Herbert and Paula Molner Collection, Chicago
Repr. p. 58

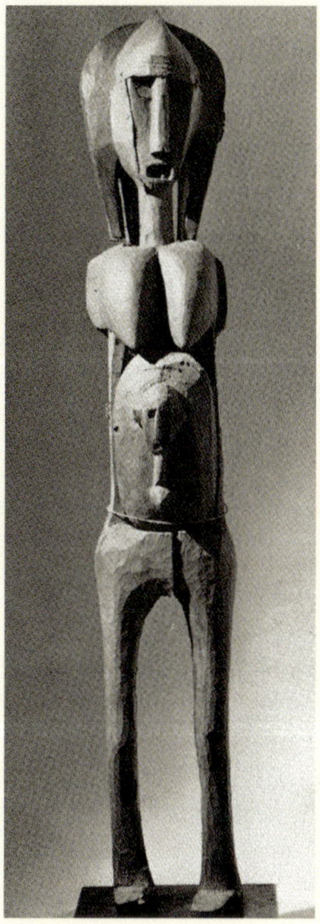
Lot 63

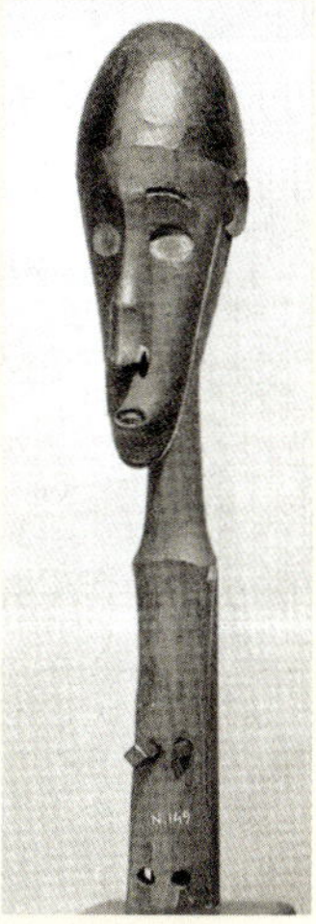
Lot 65

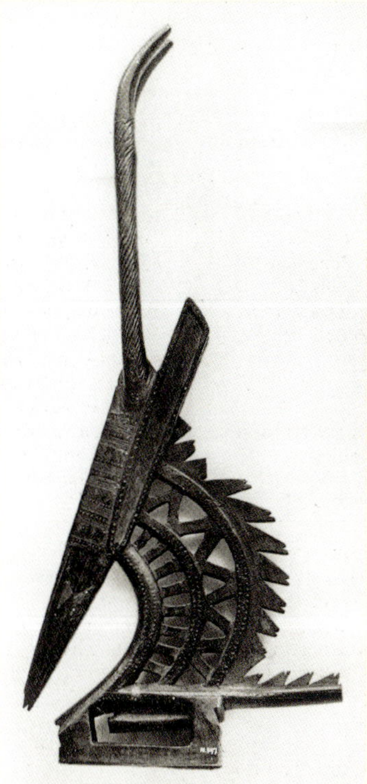
Lot 67

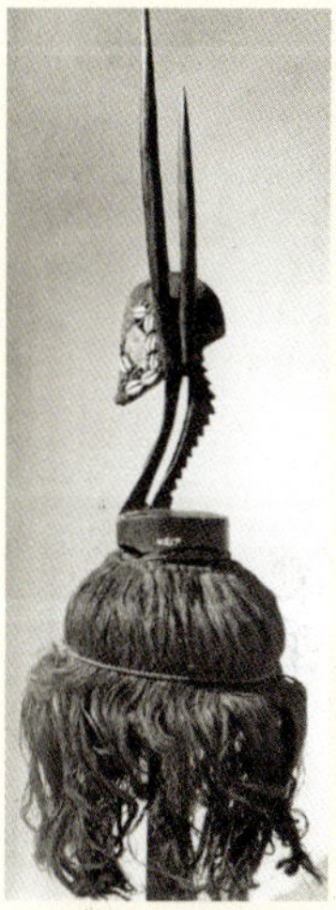
Lot 71

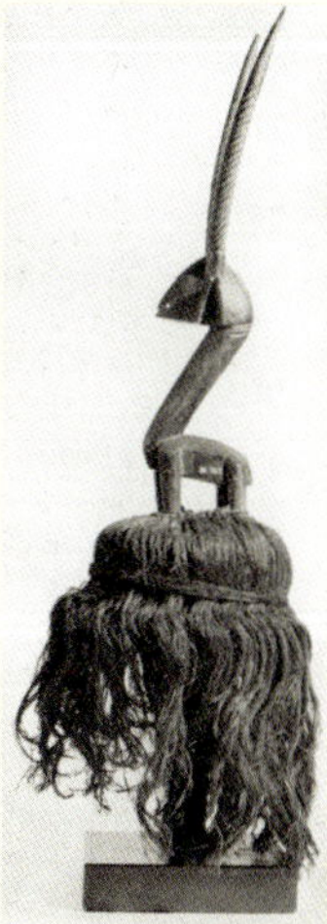
Lot 72

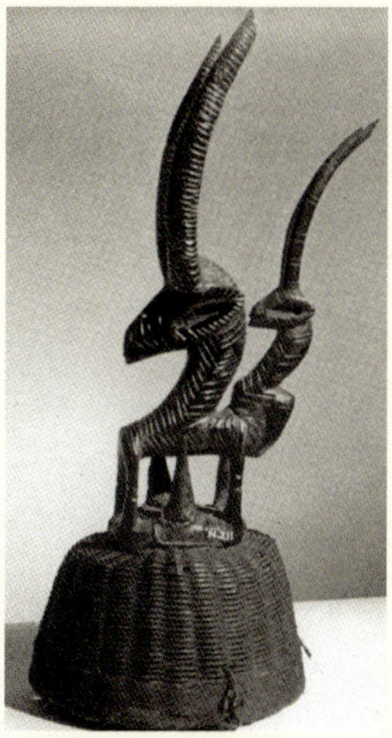
Lot 73

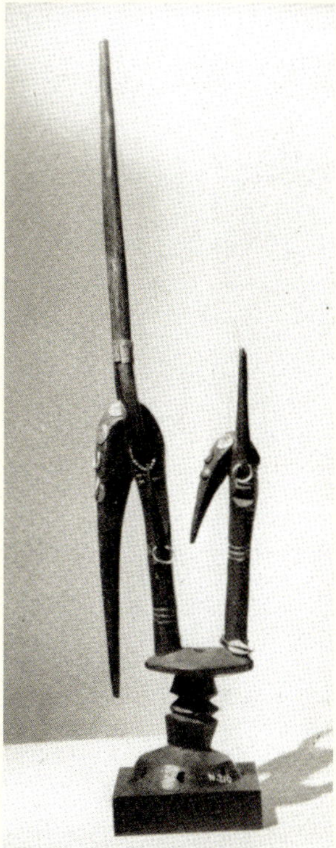
Lot 73a

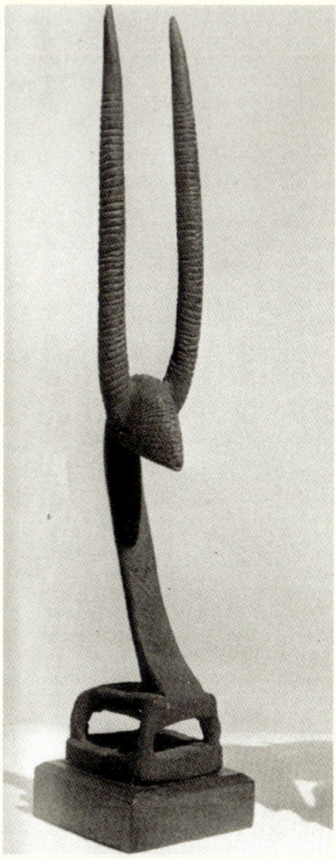
Lot 74

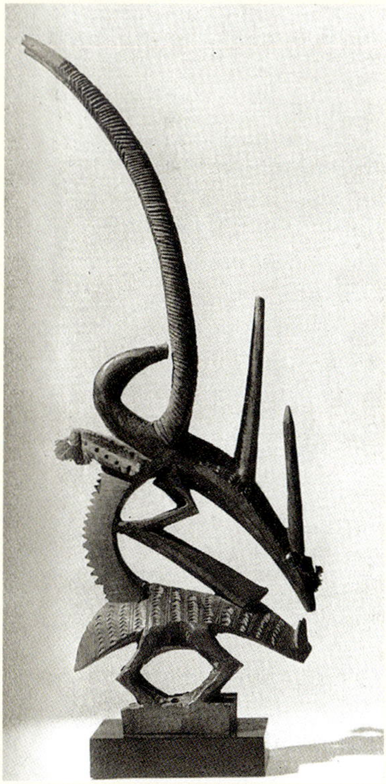
Lot 78

80

Bambara Dance Headdress
Wood
(Has stand) Height
26¾ inches; 68 cms
From the region of Segou,
From Eastern Bambaraland
Provenance F.-H. Lem, Paris
Repr. p. 209

81

Bambara Dance Headdress
Wood
(Has stand) Height
21 inches; 53 cms
From Eastern Bambaraland
Provenance F.-H. Lem, Paris
Frieda and Milton Rosenthal collection, New York (1966)
Repr. p. 209

82

Bambara Dance Headdress
Wood
(Has stand) Height
23 inches; 59 cms
From Eastern Bambaraland
Provenance F.-H. Lem, Paris
Repr. p. 209

83

Bambara Antelope Head
Wood, with Metal Sheet
Height 19 inches; 48 cms
From the region of San
Provenance F.-H. Lem, Paris
Shelly et Norman Dinhofer collection, New York (1966)
• James C. Jamieson III collection, Saint-Louis
Cat. 28, repr. p. 118

84

Bambara Dance Headdress
Wood
Length 15¾ inches;
40 cms / Height 10 inches;
26.5 cms
Region of Segou,
Northeastern Bambaraland
Provenance F.-H. Lem, Paris
Repr. p. 209

85

Dogon Mask
Wood
Height 16½ inches; 42 cms
Region of Sanga
Private collection, New York (1966)
Bonhams sale,, New York, November 13, 2018, lot no. 64
• Entwistle gallery collection, Paris
Repr. p. 209

KURUMBA

86

Kurumba Dance
Headdress Finial
Wood
Height 18½ inches; 47 cms
From the region of
Aribindia, Upper Volta/Mali
Provenance F.-H. Lem, Paris
• Private collection, Geneva (since 1966)
Repr. p. 209

MOSSI

87

Mossi Dance Mask
Kapok Wood
Height 42 inches; 117 cms
From the Yatenga area,
around Ouahigouya,
Upper Volta
Provenance F.-H. Lem, Paris
Aimée W. Hirshberg collection, New York (1966)
• Donald Hall collection, Kansas City
Repr. p. 209

88

Mossi Dance Mask
Kapok Wood
Height 46 inches; 117 cms
From the Yatenga area,
Upper Volta
Provenance F.-H. Lem, Paris
• Private collection, Paris
Cat. 35, repr. p. 120

89

Mossi Totemic Dance Mask
Kapok Wood
Height 77 inches; 195.5 cms
From the Yatenga area,
Upper Volta
Provenance F.-H. Lem, Paris
Warren Robbins collection, Washington (1966)
• Brooklyn Museum, inv. 2092.74.1
Repr. p. 209

90

Mossi Dance Mask
Kapok Wood
Height 62½ inches; 164 cms
From the Yatenga area,
Upper Volta
Provenance F.-H. Lem, Paris
Frieda and Milton Rosenthal collection, New York (1966)
Repr. p. 209

91

Bobo Totemic Mask
Wood
Height 45 inches; 114 cms
Bobo-Fing, from the area
of Bobo-Dioulasso,
Upper Volta
Provenance F.-H. Lem, Paris
Arthur H. Barth collection, Los Angeles (1966)
George F. and Hope Wick collection, San Diego
Christie's sale New York, May 18, 1993, lot no. 73
Repr. p. 209

92

Bobo Dance Headdress
Finial
Wood
Height 10 inches; 25.5 cms
Provenance F.-H. Lem, Paris
Private collection, New York (1966)
• The Schorr Family Collection, United States
Repr. p. 209

LOBI

93

Lobi Stool
Wood
Length: 21½ inches; 54.5 cms
Region of Bouna
Repr. p. 209

94

Lobi Stool
Wood
Length: 23½ inches: 59.6 cms
Region of Bouna
Frieda and Milton Rosenthal collection, New York (1966)
Repr. p. 209

SENUFO

95

Senufo Female Figure
Wood
Height 36 inches; 91.5 cms
From Sikasso in the Folona
district, Pomporo
sub-tribe; Northern
Senufo area
Provenance F.-H. Lem, Paris
Sydney Janis collection, New York (1966)
William A. M. Burden collection
Christie's sale New York, May 5, 1995, lot no. 49
Private collection, United States
• Private collection, Paris
Repr. p. 34

96

Senufo Bird Finial
Hardwood
Height 10½ inches; 27 cms
Length 16½ inches; 42 cms
Probably from Fourou
in the Kenedougou region
Provenance F.-H. Lem, Paris
Newark Museum purchase, Louis Bamberger Bequest Fund (1966)
• Newark Museum, New Jersey, inv. 66.618 A and B
Cat. 22, repr. p. 108

97

Senufo Bird Finial
Hardwood
Length 18½ inches; 47 cms
From Fourou in
the Kenedougou area
Provenance F.-H. Lem, Paris
Repr. p. 209

98

Senufo Figure
Wood
Height 10¾ inches; 27.5 cms
Collected in the region
of Sikasso
Provenance F.-H. Lem, Paris
• Private collection, New York
Cat. 17, repr. p. 104

99

Senufo Figure
Wood
Height 11½ inches; 29 cms
Found in the Sikasso region
Provenance F.-H. Lem, Paris
Sotheby's sale, New York, November 16, 2001, lot no. 10
Repr. p. 209

100

Senufo Staff
Wood
Height of figure 17 inches;
43 cms / Overall length of
staff 54½ inches; 138.5 cms
From the region of
Korhogo
Dr Alexander S. Honig collection, Bronxville (1966)
• Private collection, New York
Cat. 23, repr. p. 109

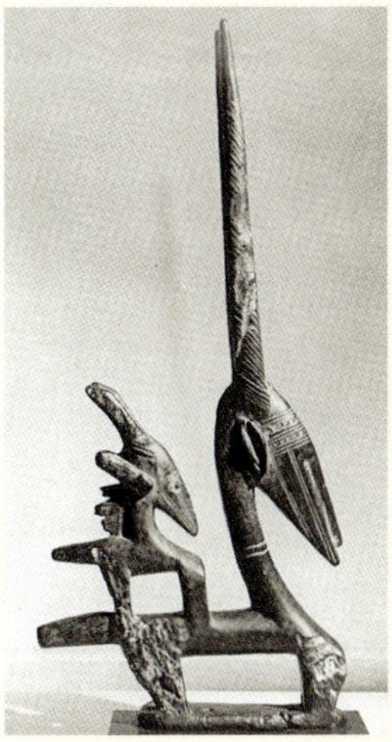

Lot 80

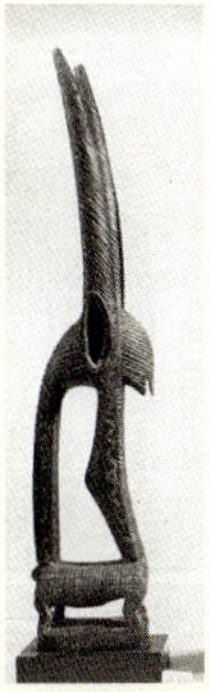

Lot 81

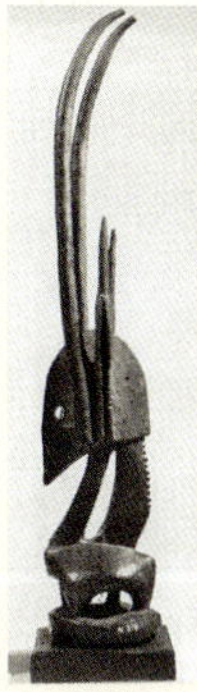

Lot 82

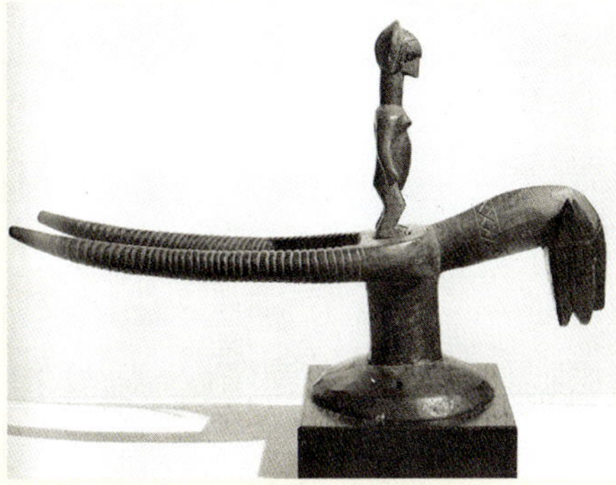

Lot 84

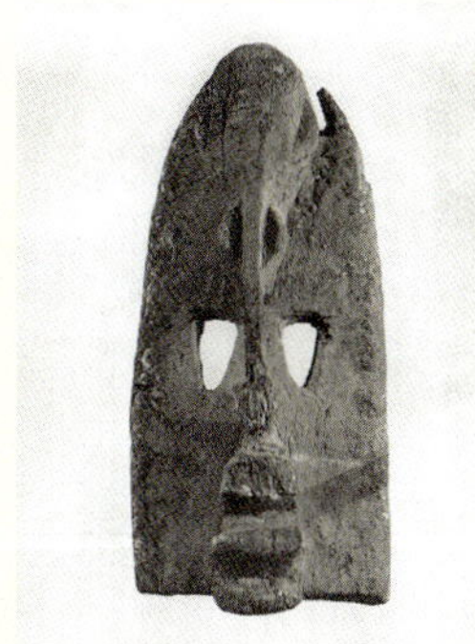

Lot 85

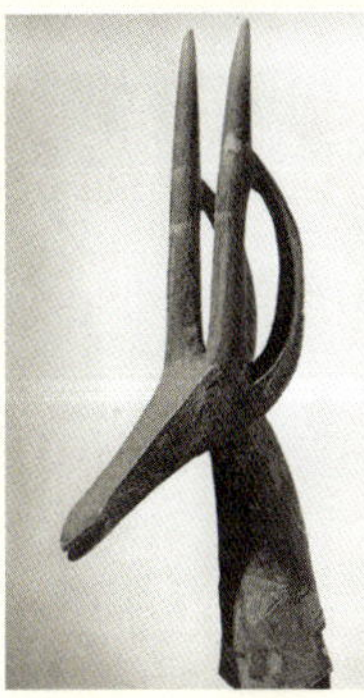

Lot 86

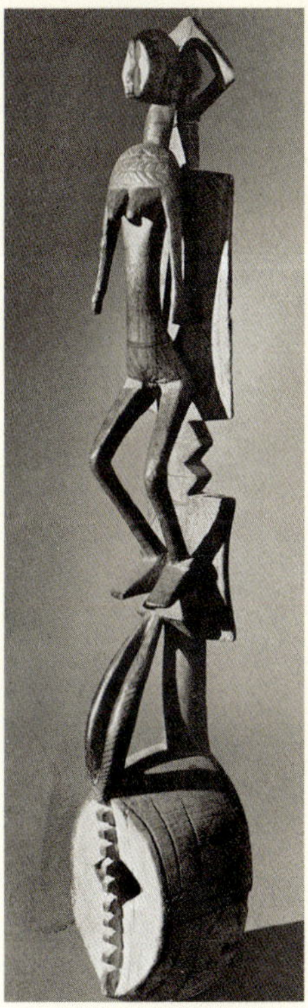

Lot 87

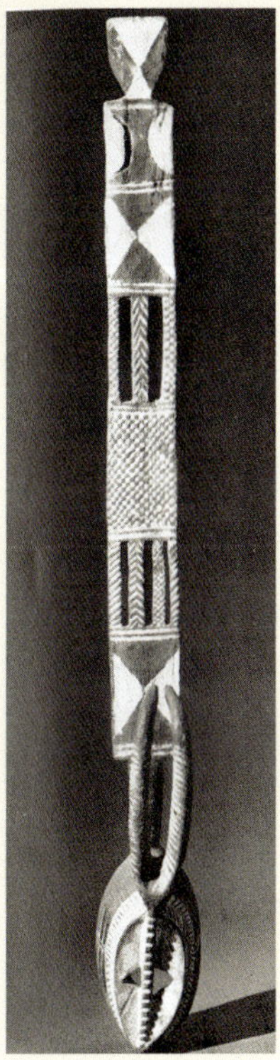

Lot 89

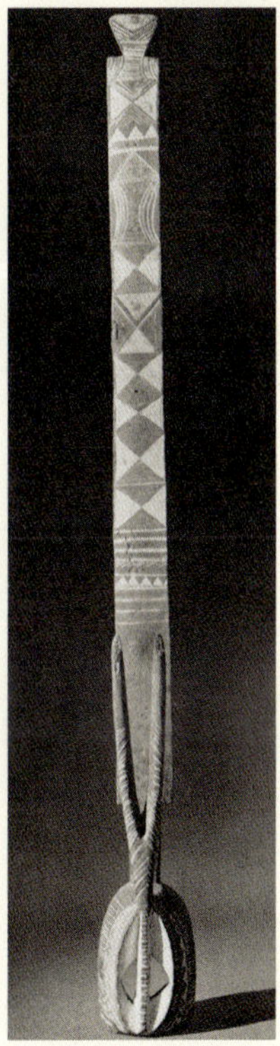

Lot 90

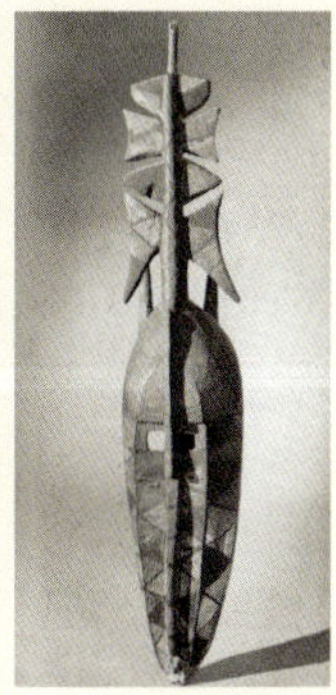

Lot 91

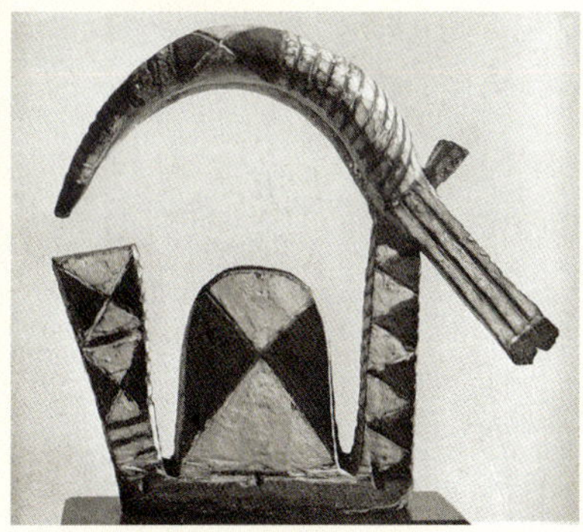

Lot 92

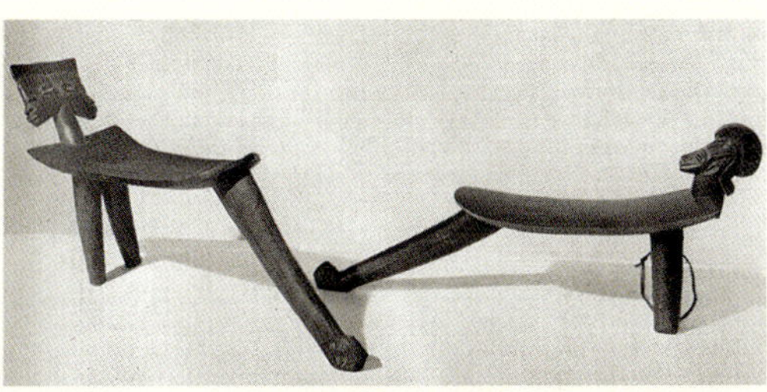

Lot 93

Lot 94

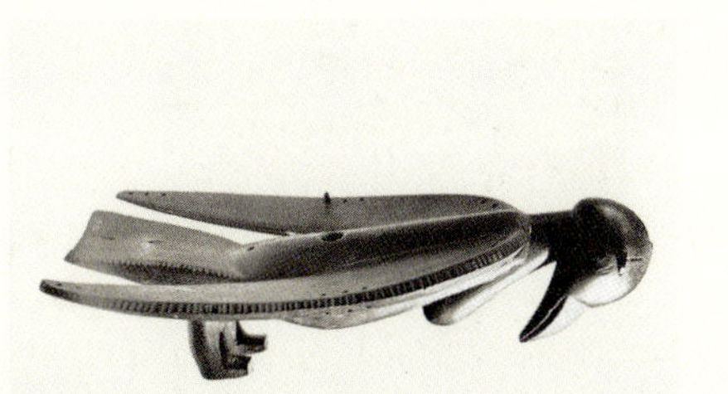

Lot 97

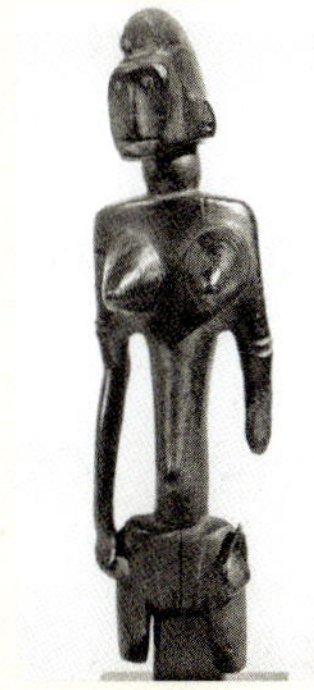

Lot 99

101

Senufo Helmet Mask
Wood
Length 19 inches; 48 cms / Height 13¾ inches; 35 cms
From the village of Siené in the Folona district, Northern Senufo area
Provenance F.-H. Lem, Paris
Jay C. Leff collection, Uniontown (1966)
• Private collection, New York
Repr. p. 211

102

Senufo Helmet Mask
Wood
Length 17½ inches; 44.5 cms
Height 11½ inches; 28 cms
From the Folona region
Provenance F.-H. Lem, Paris
Repr. p. 211

103

Senufo Dance Mask
Wood
Overall length 39½ inches; 100.3 cms
From the Korhogo area
Provenance F.-H. Lem, Paris
• Baltimore Museum of Art, inv. BMA 1966.17
Repr. p. 211

104

Senufo Dance Mask
Wood
Overall length 17 inches; 43 cms
From the Korogho district
Provenance F.-H. Lem, Paris
Repr. p. 211

105

Senufo Dance Mask
Wood
Overall length 17 inches; 43 cms
From the Korogho district
Provenance F.-H. Lem, Paris
Repr. p. 211

106

Senufo Dance Mask
Wood
Overall length 20 inches; 51 cms
From Faidonga, Korhogo district, Central Senufo area
Provenance F.-H. Lem, Paris
Repr. p. 211

107

Senufo Dance Mask
Wood
Height 14 inches; 35.5 cms
From the Folona region
Provenance F.-H. Lem, Paris
Robert and Jean Schoenberg collection, Westmoreland (1966)
Christie's sale New York, November 14, 2008, lot no. 14
Repr. p. 58

108

Senufo Dance Mask
Wood
Height 14¾ inches; 37.5 cms
From the Korhogo area
Provenance F.-H. Lem, Paris
• Private collection, France
Cat. 18, repr. p. 102

109

Senufo Heddle Pulley
Wood
Height 4 inches; 10 cms

110

Animal Mask
Wood
Height 15 inches; 38 cms
From the region of Katiola, Southern Senufo area
Provenance F.-H. Lem, Paris
Guy Loudmer sale, Paris, June 28, 1990, lot no. 73
Christie's sale Paris, June 15, 2002, lot no. 268
• Private collection, Santa Barbara
Repr. p. 211

111

Senufo Face Mask
Wood
Height 16½ inches; 42 cms
From the Korhogo district
Provenance F.-H. Lem, Paris
Collection Warren Robins, Washington (1966)
Repr. p. 211

112

Senufo Face Mask
Wood
Height 15¼ inches; 39 cms
From the Korhogo district
Provenance F.-H. Lem, Paris
Hyman Klebanov collection, New York (1966)
Repr. p. 211

113

Pair of Senufo Figures
Wood
Height (male) 23¾ inches; 60.2 cms / (female) 23 inches; 58.5 cms
From the region of Tengrela
Provenance F.-H. Lem, Paris
Repr. p. 211

114

Senufo Table
Wood
Height 29 inches; 73.8 cms
Diameter at top 17¾ inches; 45 cms
Region of Korhogo
Frieda and Milton Rosenthal collection, New York (1966)
Repr. p. 211

115

Senufo Heddle Pulley
Wood
Height 9½ inches; 24 cms
Korhogo area
Collection Max Granick, New York (1966)
Repr. p. 211

116

Senufo Bird Finial
Wood
Height 9¾ inches; 25 cms
Korhogo area
Repr. p. 211

117

Senufo Covered Vessel
Wood
Height 5½ inches; 14 cms
Korhogo area
Repr. p. 211

118

Pair of Senufo Figures
Wood
Height (man) 7 inches; 17.8 cms / (woman) 6¾ inches; 17.1 cms
Found in the region of Kenedougou but probably made in the Korhogo district
Provenance F.-H. Lem, Paris
Christie's sale Paris, December 3, 2015, lot no. 39
Repr. p. 211

119

Senufo Lock Figure
Wood
Height 16½ inches; 42 cms
From the Kenedougou area, showing strong Bambara influence
Provenance F.-H. Lem, Paris

120

Senufo Heddle Pulley
Wood
(Has stand) Height 8 inches; 20 cms
Central Senufo area

121

Senufo Covered Cup
Wood
Height 12½ inches; 31.8 cms
Korhogo area

122

Senufo Trophy Staff
Wood
Height 76 inches; 193 cms
Northern Senufo area
Collection Richard L. Feigen, New York (1966)
Sotheby's sale, New York, November 19, 1999, lot no. 77

123

Senufo Heddle Pulley
Wood
Height 6¾ inches; 17 cms

124

Senufo Figure
Wood
(Has stand) Height 22 inches; 55.7 cms
From the region of Tengrela
Repr. p. 211

125

Senufo Female Trophy Figure
Wood
(Has stand) Height 15½ inches; 39 cms
From the region of Korhogo, possibly Lataha, Central Senufo area
Hyman Klebanov collection, New York (1966)
Repr. p. 211

126

Senufo Covered Cup
Wood
Height 9 inches; 23 cms
Region of Korhogo

127

Senufo Heddle Pulley
Wood
(Has stand) Height 6¼ inches; 16 cms
Frieda and Milton Rosenthal collection, New York (1966)
Sotheby's sale, New York, November 14, 2008, lot no. 7

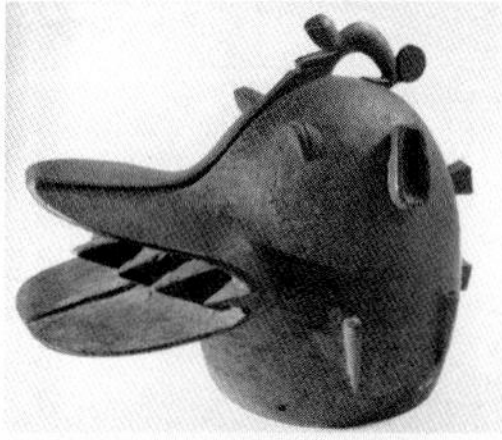
Lot 101

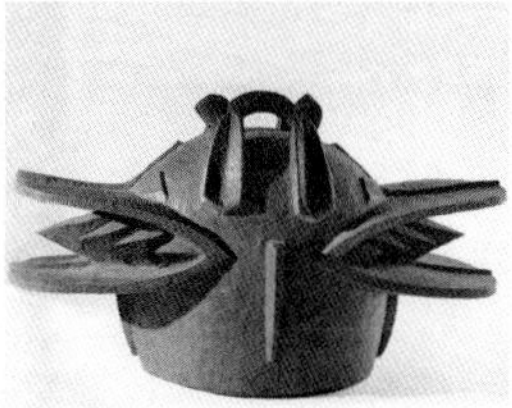
Lot 102

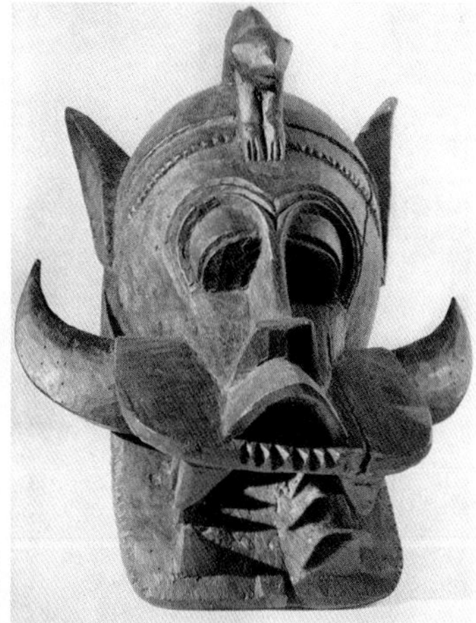

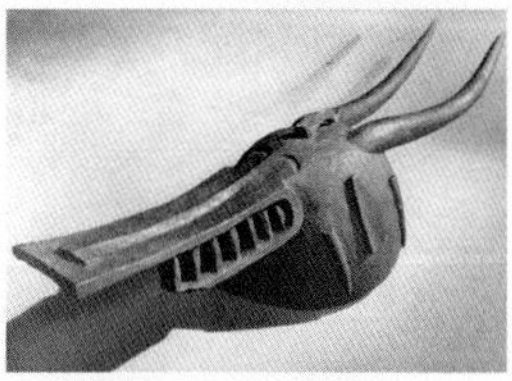
Lot 103

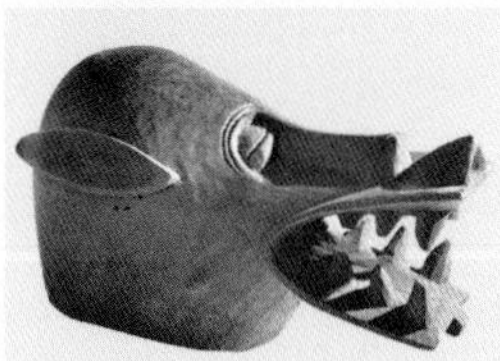
Lot 104

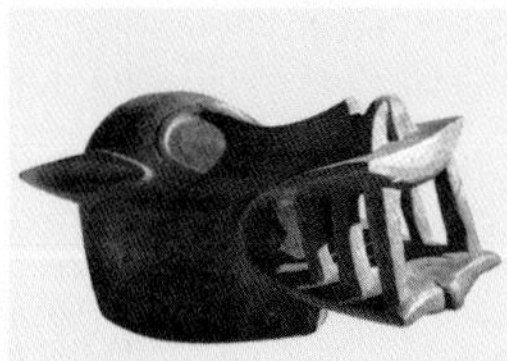
Lot 105

Lot 106

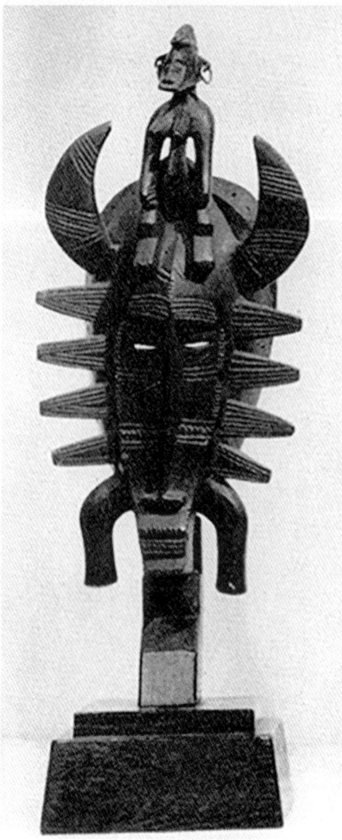

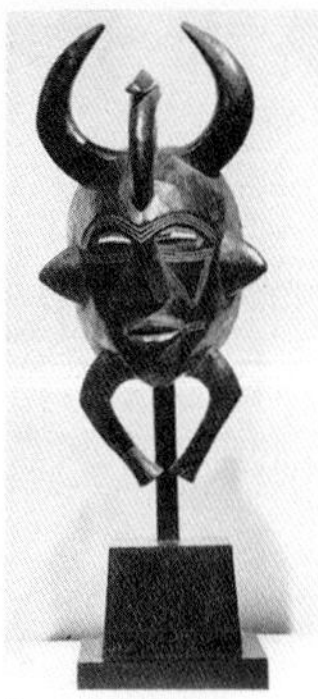
Lot 111

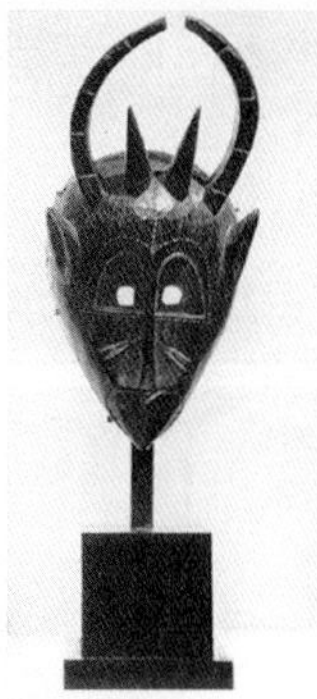
Lot 112

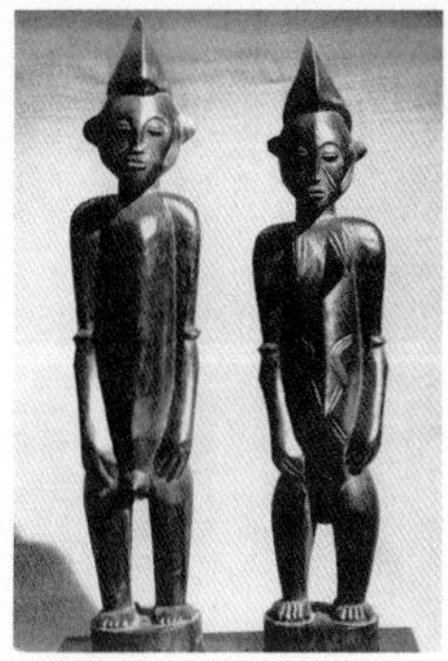
Lot 113

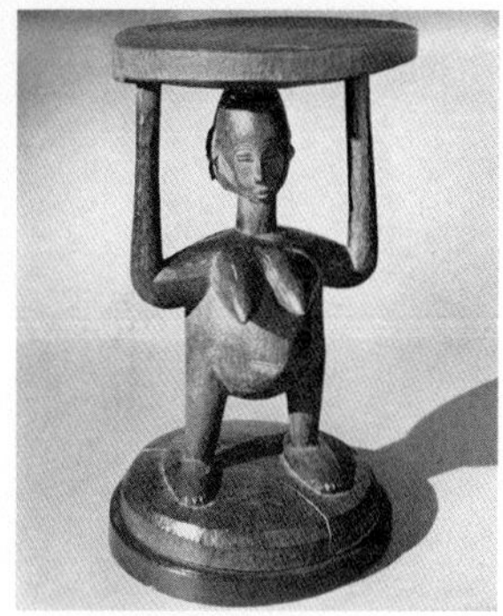
Lot 114

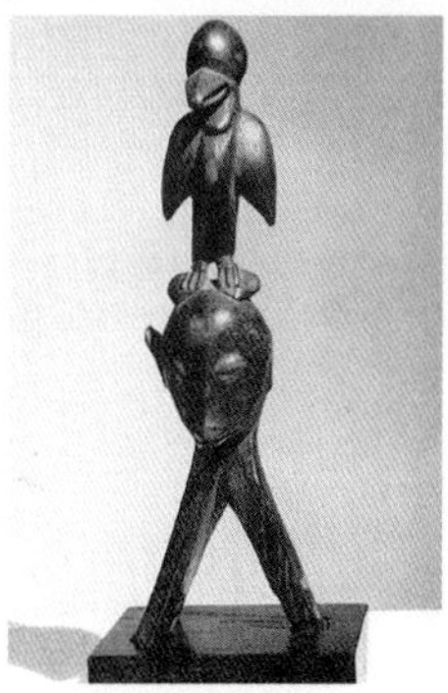
Lot 115

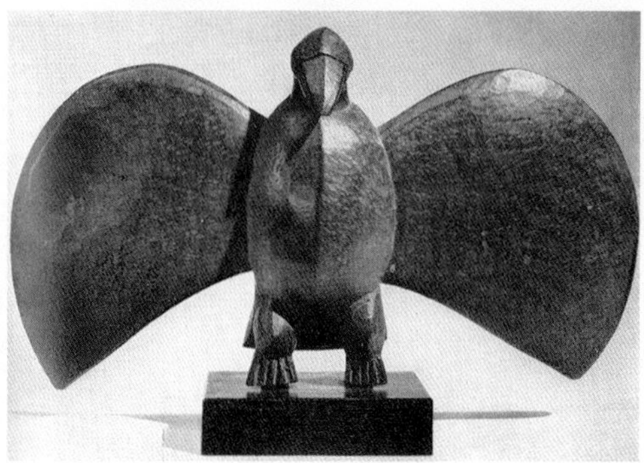
Lot 116

Lot 110

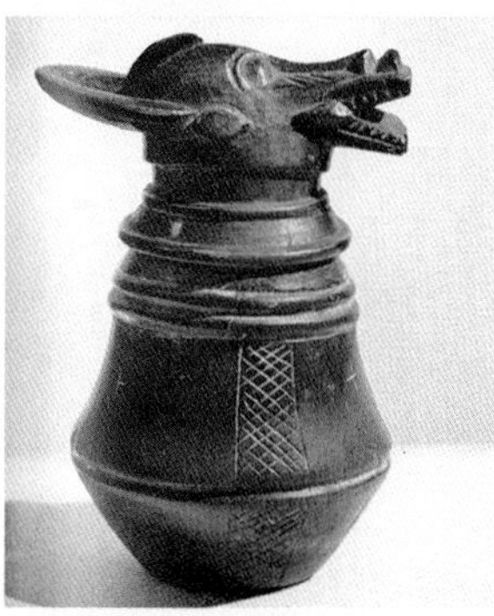
Lot 117

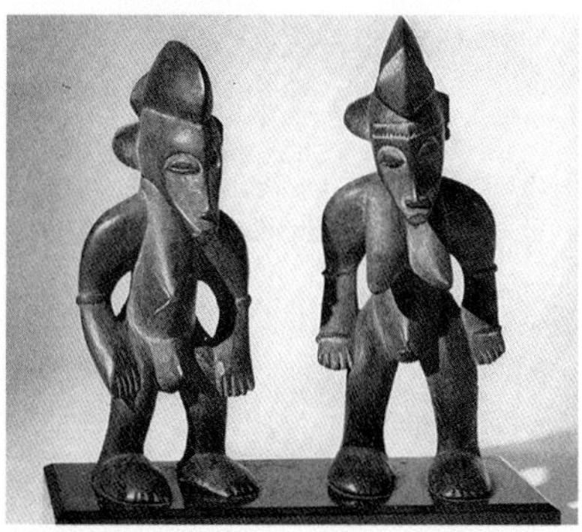
Lot 118

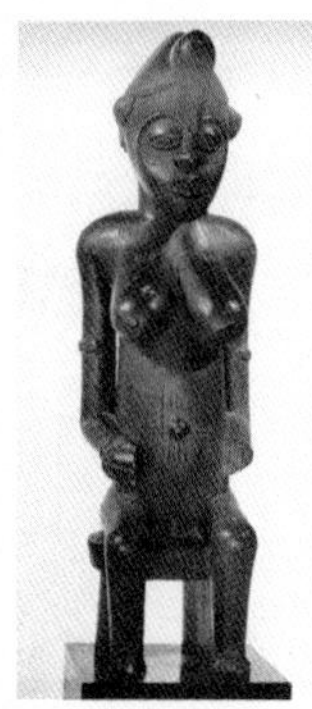
Lot 124

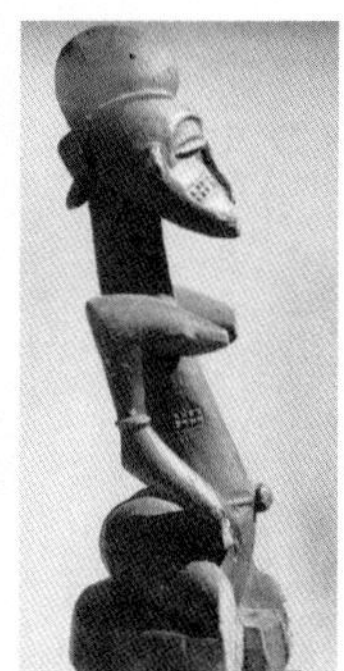
Lot 125

128
Senufo Heddle Pulley
Wood
(Has stand) Height
6¼ inches; 16 cms
Region of Korhogo
Private collection, Antwerp (1989)

129
Senufo Door
Wood
Height 40½ inches;
103 cms, Width 22 inches;
56 cms
Elsa Rogo collection, New York (1966)

130
Senufo Figure
Wood
Height 26 inches; 66 cms
From the Korhogo district
Allan M. Gordon collection, New York (1966)

131
Senufo Figure
Wood
Height 22¾ inches; 57.8 cms
From the Korhogo district

132
Senufo Seated Figures
Wood
Length: 7 inches; 17.8 cms /
Height 12¾ inches;
32.4 cms
Found near Kenedougou
Provenance F.-H. Lem, Paris
Mathias Komor, New York (1966)
• Detroit Institute of Arts, inv. DIA 66-26
Repr. p. 213

133
Senufo Figure
Wood
Height 11 inches; 28 cms
Probably originating
in the Korhogo area
Provenance F.-H. Lem, Paris
Jay C. Leff collection, Uniontown (1966)
Guy Loudmer sale, Paris, December 8, 1990, lot no. 304
Vente Guy Loudmer, Paris, December 7, 1991, lot no. 60
Repr. p. 213

134
Senufo Fertility Doll
Wood
Height 12 inches; 30.5 cms
Found in the Folona
district, Sikasso, Northern
Senufo area
Provenance F.-H. Lem, Paris
Nelson A. Rockefeller collection, New York (1966)
• The Metropolitan Museum of Art, New York, inv. 1978.412.519
Cat. 20, repr. p. 105

135
Dance Helmet
Wood
Height 19½ inches; 49.5 cms
From the village of Fenkolo
in the region of Sikasso,
North Senufo area
Provenance F.-H. Lem, Paris
Newark Museum purchase, The Member's Fund (1966)
• Newark Museum, New Jersey, inv. 66.619
Cat. 21, repr. p. 106-107

136
Senufo Figure
Wood
(Has stand) Height
12½ inches; 33.8 cms
From the Korhogo district
• Deborah Glasser collection, Zurich

137
Senufo Bird Figure
Wood
(Has stand) Height
8½ inches; 21.5 cms
From Sikasso, north
Senufo area
Provenance F.-H. Lem, Paris

END OF FIRST SESSION

SECOND AND LAST SESSION

Friday, April 29, 1966
at 8:30 p.m.

AGNI

138
Agni Head of a Man
Reddish-Brown Terra Cotta
(Has stand) Height 7
inches; 18 cms
Krinjabo
Provenance Dr. Lheureux
Christie's sale Paris, June 12, 2003, lot no. 347

139
Agni Figure of a Woman
Dark Grey Terra Cotta
(Has stand) Height
14¾ inches; 37.5 cms
Krinjabo
Provenance Dr. Lheureux
Berkeley University purchase (1966)
• Phoebe Hearst Museum, Berkeley University, inv. 5.52.87

140
Agni Head of a Man
Grey Terra Cotta
(Has stand) Height
9 ½ inches; 24 cms
Krinjabo
Provenance Dr. Lheureux
Jerome M. Eisenberg collection, New York (1966)
Repr. p. 213

141
Agni Bearded Male Head
Grey Terra Cotta
(Has stand) Height
7 inches; 18 cms
Krinjabo
Provenance Dr. Lheureux
Christie's sale Paris, June 12, 2003, lot no. 349
Lempertz sale, Brussels, June 11, 2011, lot no. 32
Zemanek-Münster sale, March 9, 2019, lot no. 118

142
Agni Head of a Woman
Grey Terra Cotta
(Has stand) Height
11 inches; 28 cms
Provenance Dr. Lheureux
Dr Alexander S. Honing collection, Bronxville (1966)
Sotheby's sale, New York, May 18, 1993, lot no. 108
Repr. p. 213

143
Agni Bust of a Woman
Terra Cotta
(Has stand) Height
9½ inches; 24 cms
Krinjabo
Provenance Dr. Lheureux

144
Agni Head of a Woman
Dark Grey Terra Cotta
(Has stand) Height 7 inches;
18 cms
Krinjabo
Provenance Dr. Lheureux

145
Fine Agni Figure of a Man
Grey Terra Cotta
(Has stand) Height 17 inches;
43 cms
Krinjabo
Provenance Dr. Lheureux
Jean Roudillon (1966)
Sotheby's sale, New York, 10 mai 1988, lot no. 48
Repr. p. 213

146
Agni Statuette of a Woman
Terra Cotta
(Has stand) Height 13 inches;
33 cms
Krinjabo
Provenance Dr. Lheureux
Christie's sale Paris, 12 juin 2003, lot no. 351

147
Agni Bearded Male Head
Terra Cotta
(Has stand) Height
8½ inches; 21.5 cms
Krinjabo
Provenance Dr. Lheureux
Frieda and Milton Rosenthal collection, New York (1966)
Sotheby's sale, New York, 14 November 2008, lot no. 11
• Private collection, Canada

148
Agni Head of a Woman
Reddish Terra Cotta
(Has stand) Height 5 inches;
13 cms
Krinjabo
Provenance Dr. Lheureux
Christie's sale Paris, 12 juin 2003, lot no. 344
Repr. p. 213

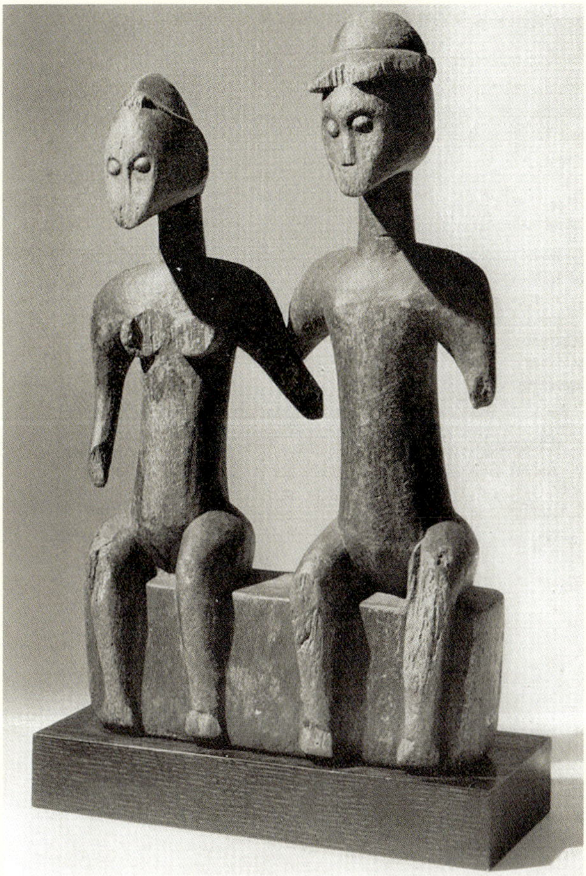

Lot 132

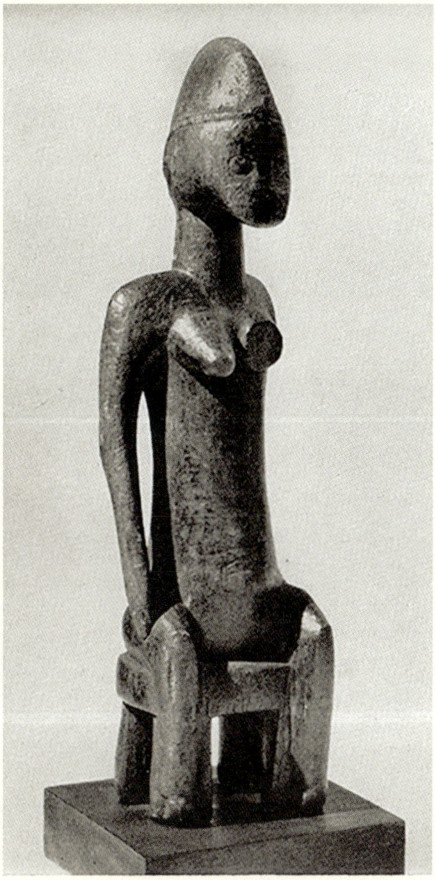

Lot 133

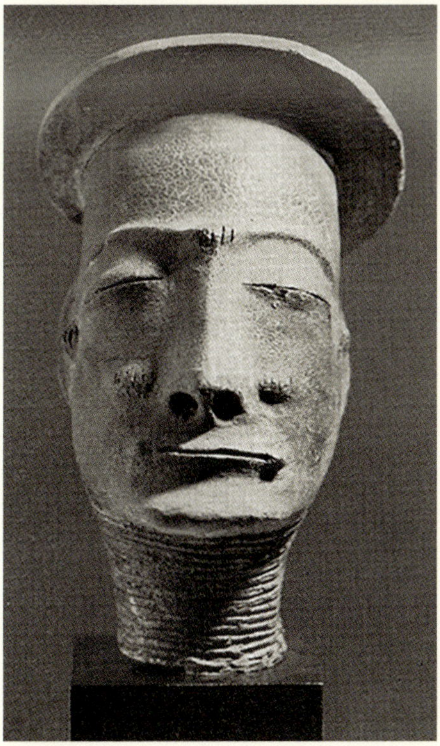

Lot 140

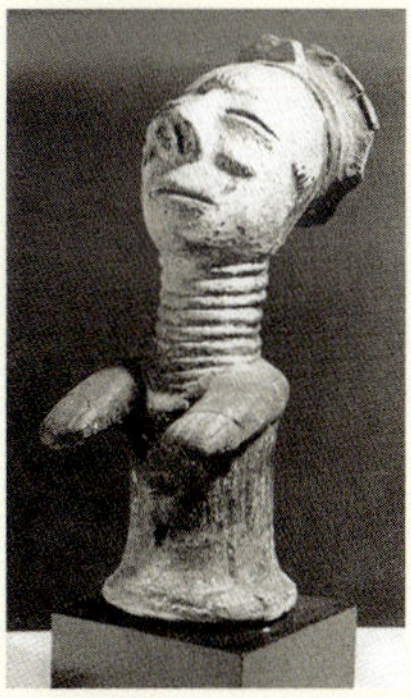

Lot 142

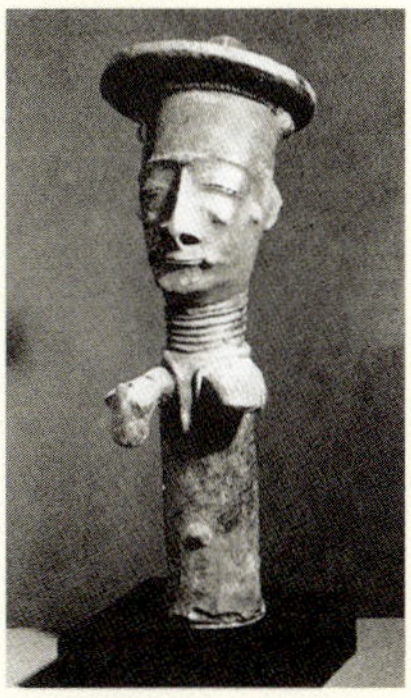

Lot 145

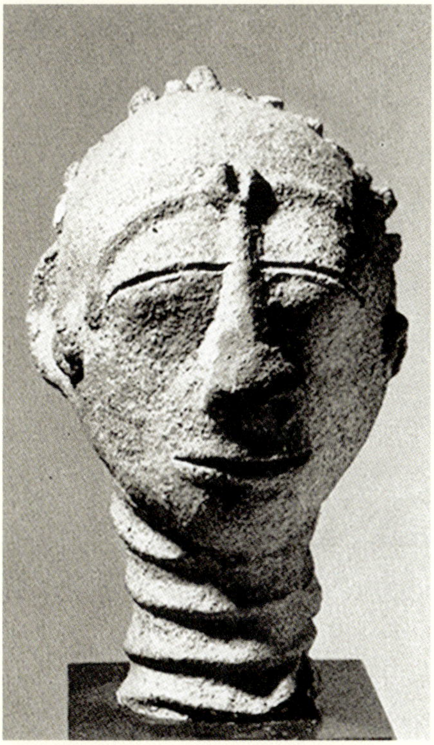

Lot 148

149

Agni Statuette of a Woman
Grey-Black Terra Cotta
(Has stand) Height
12½ inches; 32 cms
Krinjabo
Provenance Dr. Lheureux
Frieda and Milton Rosenthal collection, New York (1966)
• Africarium Collection, United States
Cat. 5, repr. p. 91

150

Agni Statuette of a Woman
Grey Terra Cotta
(Has stand) Height
14½ inches; 37 cms
Krinjabo
Provenance Dr. Lheureux
Herbert Baker collection, Chicago (1966)

151

Agni Head of a Woman
Dark Grey Terra Cotta
(Has stand) Height
8½ inches; 22 cms
Krinjabo
Provenance Dr. Lheureux
Sotheby's sale, New York, March 24, 1979, lot no. 66

152

Agni Head of a Man
Terra Cotta
(Has stand) Height
10½ inches; 27 cms
Krinjabo
Provenance Dr. Lheureux
Aimée W. Hirshberg collection, New York (1966)

153

Agni Head of a Man
Terra Cotta
(Has stand) Height
8½ inches; 22 cms
Krinjabo
Provenance Dr. Lheureux
Frida and Milton Rosenthal collection, New York (1966)
Sotheby's sale, New York, November 14, 2008, lot no. 13

154

Agni Head of a Man
Grey Terra Cotta
(Has stand) Height
8 ½ inches; 22 cms
Krinjabo
Provenance Dr. Lheureux
• Private collection, New York
Repr. p. 215

155

Agni Head of a Man
Grey-Brown Terra Cotta
(Has stand) Height
7½ inches; 19 cms
Krinjabo
Provenance Dr. Lheureux

156

Agni Statue of a Woman
Grey Terra Cotta
(Has stand) Height
13 ¾ inches; 35 cms
Krinjabo
Provenance Dr. Lheureux
Shelly and Norman Dinhofer collection, New York (1966)
Sotheby's sale, New York, May 16, 2008, lot no. 50

157

Agni Statuette of a Woman
Terra Cotta
(Has stand) Height
12¾ inches; 32.5 cms
Krinjabo
Provenance Dr. Lheureux
• The Metropolitan Museum of Art, New York, inv. 1995.64.22
Cat. 4, repr. p. 91

158

Agni Head of a Man
Grey Terra Cotta
(Has stand) Height
12½ inches; 32 cms
Krinjabo
Provenance Dr. Lheureux
• Private collection, New York

159

Agni Head of a Man
Grey Terra Cotta
(Has stand) Height 7 inches;
18 cms
Krinjabo
Provenance Dr. Lheureux
Ruth and Ernst Anspach collection, New York (1966)
Sotheby's sale, New York, October 31, 1994, lot no. 40
Sotheby's sale, New York, May 15, 2003, lot no. 119

160

Agni Bust of a Man
Grey Terra Cotta
(Has stand) Height
13½ inches; 34.2 cms
Krinjabo
Provenance Dr. Lheureux
• Private collection, New York
Repr. p. 215

161

Agni Head of a Man
Dark Grey Terra Cotta
(Has stand) Height 8 inches;
20 cms
Krinjabo
Provenance Dr. Lheureux
Dr Saul Tuttman collection, New York (1966)
• Private collection, Michigan

162

Agni Head of a Woman
Brown-Grey Terra Cotta
(Has stand) Height 8 inches;
20 cms
Krinjabo
Provenance Dr. Lheureux
Private collection, New York (1966)
Christie's sale Paris, June 12, 2003, lot no. 348

163

Agni Head of a Woman
Grey Terra Cotta
(Has stand) Height
8½ inches; 22 cms
Krinjabo
Provenance Dr. Lheureux
Private collection, New York (1966)
Sotheby's sale, New York, March 24, 1979, lot no. 65

164

Agni Head of a Woman
Grey-Brown Terra Cotta
(Has stand) Height 8 inches;
20 cms
Krinjabo
Provenance Dr. Lheureux

165

Agni Bust of a Woman
Grey-Brown Terra Cotta
(Has stand) Height
12½ inches; 32 cms
Krinjabo
Provenance Dr. Lheureux
Dr Saul Tuttman collection, New York (1966)
• Private collection, Michigan

166

Fine Agni Head
of a Bearded Man
Grey-Brown Terra Cotta
(Has stand) Height 8 inches;
20 cms
Krinjabo
Provenance Dr. Lheureux
Private collection, New York (1966)
Christie's sale Paris, June 12, 2003, lot no. 350
Repr. p. 215

167

Agni Male Figure
Grey Terra Cotta
(Has stand) Height
12¼ inches; 31 cms
Krinjabo
Provenance Dr. Lheureux
Private collection, New York (1966)
Repr. p. 215

168

Agni Male Head
Grey Terra Cotta
(Has stand) Height 8 inches;
20 cms
Krinjabo
Provenance Dr. Lheureux

169

Agni Figure of a Woman
Reddish Terra Cotta
(Has stand) Height 13 inches;
33 cms
Krinjabo
Provenance Dr. Lheureux
Sotheby's sale, New York, May 14, 2004, lot no. 52
Sotheby's sale, Paris, December 7, 2005, lot no. 58
Vente Bonhams, New York, May 13, 2010, lot no. 2101
Repr. p. 215

170

Agni Ceremonial Sword
Iron, Wood and Gold Sheet
Length 23 ¼ inches; 59 cms
Region of Agnibelikrou,
Ivory Coast
William W. Brill collection, New York (1966)
• National Museum of African Art – Smithsonian Institution, Washington, inv. 2015.16.2
Cat. 10, repr. p. 94

171

Agni Ceremonial Sword
Iron, Wood and Gold Sheet
Lengt: 27½ inches; 70 cms
Region of Agnibelikrou,
Ivory Coast
William W. Brill collection, New York (1966)
• National Museum of African Art – Smithsonian Institution, Washington, inv. 2015.16.1
Cat. 9, repr. p. 95

172

Agni Ceremonial Sword
Iron, Wood and Gold Sheet
Lengt: 27½ inches; 70 cms
Region of Agnibelikrou,
Ivory Coast
Herbert Baker collection, Chicago (1966)

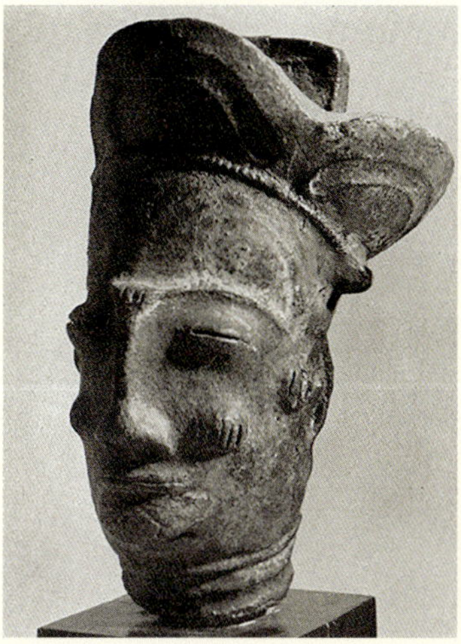

Lot 154

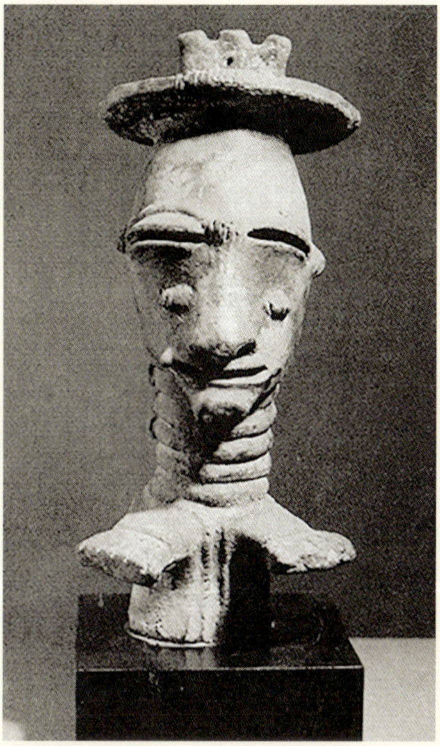

Lot 160

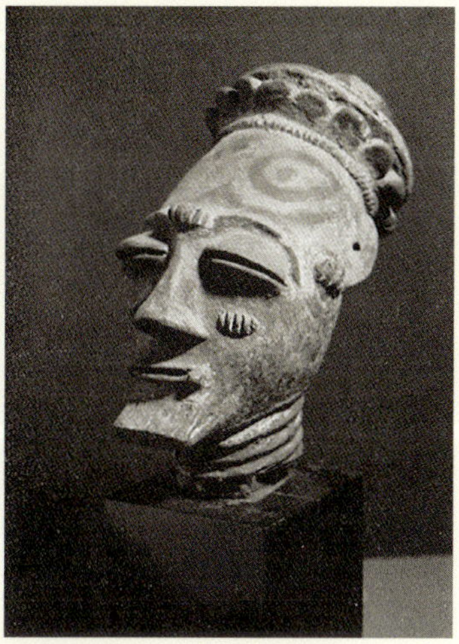

Lot 166

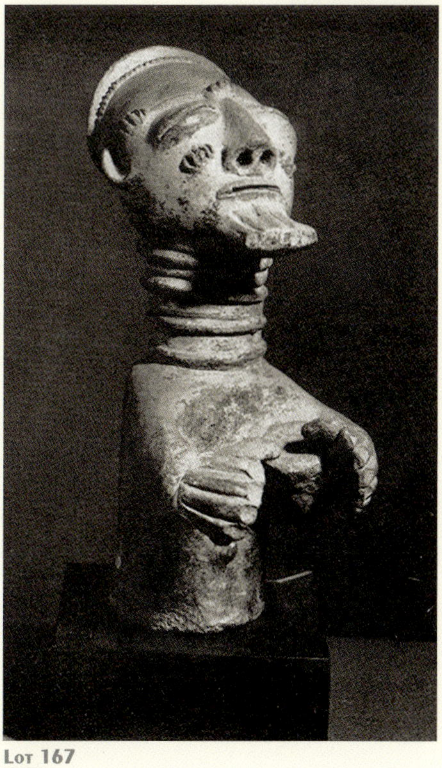

Lot 167

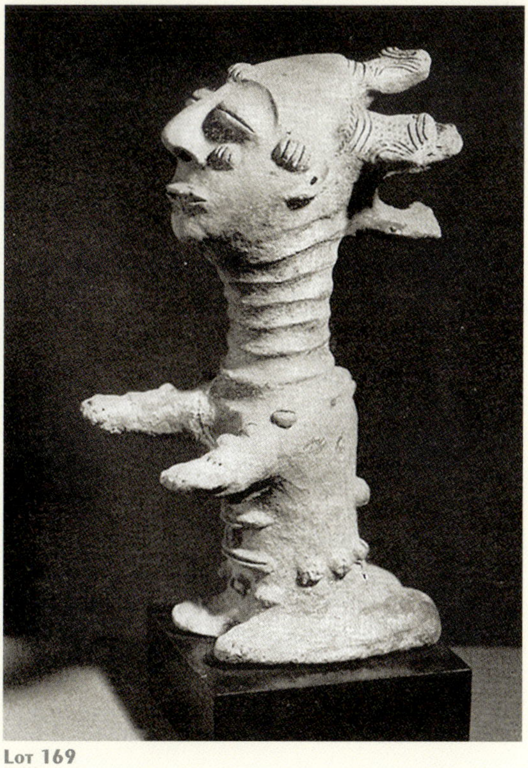

Lot 169

ASHANTI

173

Ashanti Head
Grey-Brown Terra Cotta
Height 9 inches; 23 cms
Ghana
Max Granick collection, New York (1966)
• Liliane and Michel Durand-Dessert collection, Paris
Cat. 6, repr. p. 92

174

Ashanti Stool
Wood
Height 10¾ inches; 27.4 cms / Length 16½ inches; 42 cms
Ghana
Christie's sale New York, November 20, 1997, lot no. 298

ESIE

175

Esie Head
Soapstone
(Has stand) Height 11 inches; 28 cms
Nigeria
Nelson A. Rockefeller collection, New York (1966)
• The Metropolitan Museum of Art, New York, inv. 1979.206.296
Cat. 39, repr. p. 126

YORUBA

176

Yoruba Shango Figure
Wood
Height 15¾ inches; 40 cms
Northwest Yorubaland
Provenance Félix Fénéon, Paris
Private collection, New York (1966)
• Private collection, Santa Barbara
Repr. p. 217

177

Yoruba (Ibeji) Female Figure
Wood
Height 8¾ inches; 22.2 cms
Central Yorubaland
Repr. p. 217

178

Yoruba Figurine
Wood with Cowrie Shells
Height of figure 11½ inches; 29 cms / Length overall 36 inches; 91.5 cms
Nigeria
Allan Stone collection, New York (1966)
Rago Lambertville sale, October 19, 2018, lot no. 81
Repr. p. 217

179

Yoruba (Gelede) Helmet Mask
Wood
Height 14½ inches; 37 cms
Henry Bresky, New York (1966)
Repr. p. 217

IBIBIO

180

Ibibio Group
Wood
Height 30 inches; 72.2 cms
Repr. p. 217

ANYANG

181

Anyang Head
Wood and Skin
Height 14 inches; 35.5 cms
Cross River
Allan Stone collection, New York (1966)
• Private collection, New York
Cat. 40, repr. p. 127

EKOI

182

Ekoi Human Head
Wood with Human Skin and Basketwork
Height 13 ½ inches; 34.2 cms
Cross River
Allan Stone collection, New York (1966)
Rago Lambertville sale, October 19, 2018, lot no. 43
• Private collection, Antwerp
Repr. p. 217

CAMEROONS

183

Cameroons Grasslands Head
Wood, Overlaid with Copper Sheeting
Height 17 inches; 43 cms
Cameroons
• Private collection, New York (1966)
Repr. p. 217

184

Bamum Pipe
Grey-Brown Clay
(Has stand) Height 10 inches; 25.5 cms
Ruth and Paul Tishman collection, New York (1966)
• National Museum of African Art – Smithsonian Institution, Washington, inv. 2005.6.373
Cat. 58, repr. p. 146

185

Bamum Pipe
Grey-Brown Clay
(Has stand) Height 8 inches; 20.3 cms
Al Hirschfeld collection, New York (1966)
Repr. p. 217

186

Cameroons Grasslands Head
Wood
(Has stand) Height 7 inches; 18 cms / Depth 10 inches; 25.4 cms
Nelson A. Rockefeller collection, New York (1966)
• The Metropolitan Museum of Art, New York, inv. 1979.206.297
Cat. 41, repr. p. 124

187

Cameroons Grasslands Head
Wood
(Has stand) Height 8 inches; 20.3 cms / Depth 9 inches; 23 cms
Provenance Pierre Loeb, Paris
Jay C. Leff collection, Uniontown (1966)
• Private collection, Paris
Cat. 42, repr. p. 125

BAMILÉKÉ

188

Bamiléké Seat
Wood
Height 41½ inches; 105.5 cms / diameter 20 inches; 51 cms
Ruth and Paul Tishman collection, New York (1966)
• High Museum, Atlanta, inv. 2015.271
Repr. p. 217

BAMILÉKÉ – BANGWA CHIEFDOM

189

Bangwa Figure of a Woman
Wood
Height 33 ½ inches; 85 cms
Provenance Berlin, Museum für Völkerkunde / Charles Ratton, Paris (by exchange)
Harry A. Franklin collection, Los Angeles (1966)
• Fondation Dapper, Paris, inv. 3343
Cat. 38, repr. p. 128

GABON

190

Gabon Mask
Wood
Height 12 ½ inches; 31.7 cms
Bapunu
David Lloyd Kreeger collection, Washington D.C. (1966)
• The Kreeger Museum, Washington
Repr. p. 68

191

Gabon Mask
Softwood
(Has stand) Height 12¼ inches; 31 cms
Probably from Chipanga
David Lloyd Kreeger collection, Washington D.C. (1966)
• The Kreeger Museum, Washington
Repr. p. 69

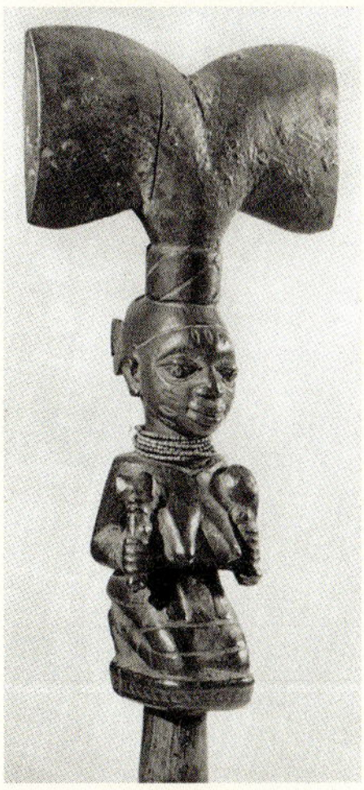

Lot 176

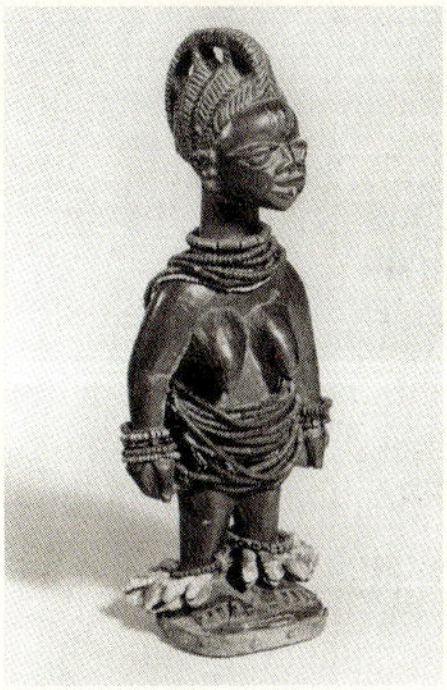

Lot 177

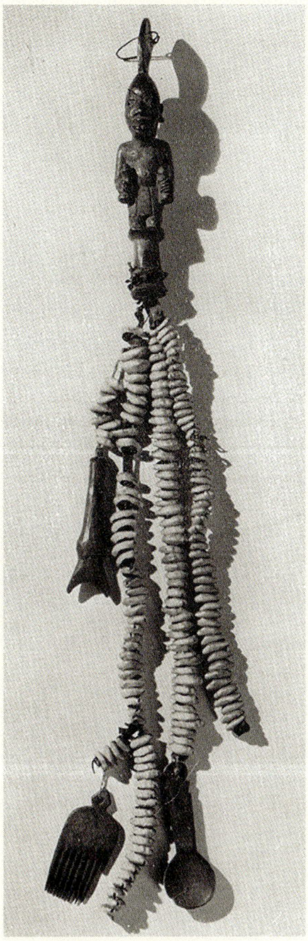

Lot 178

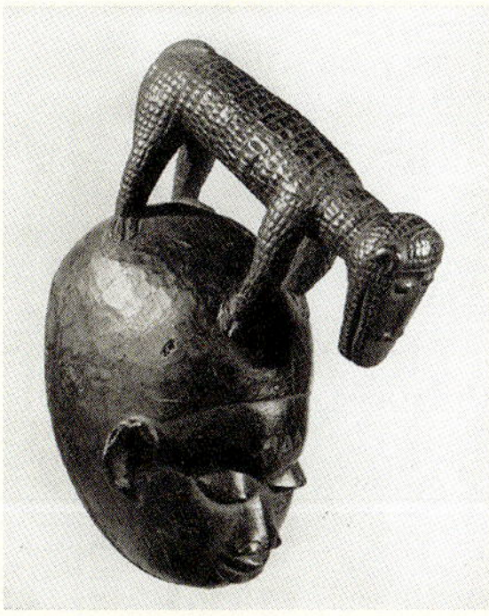

Lot 179

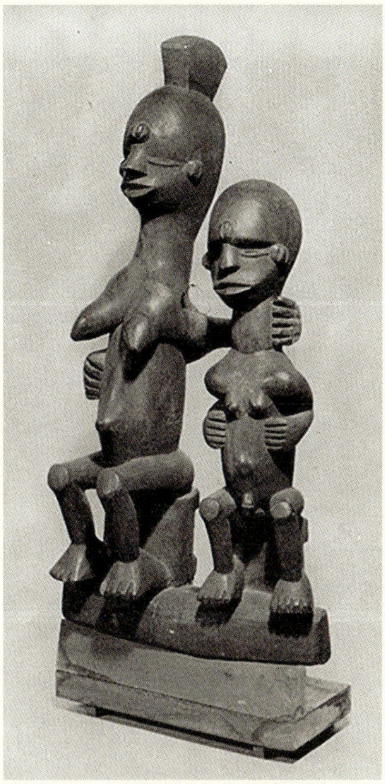

Lot 180

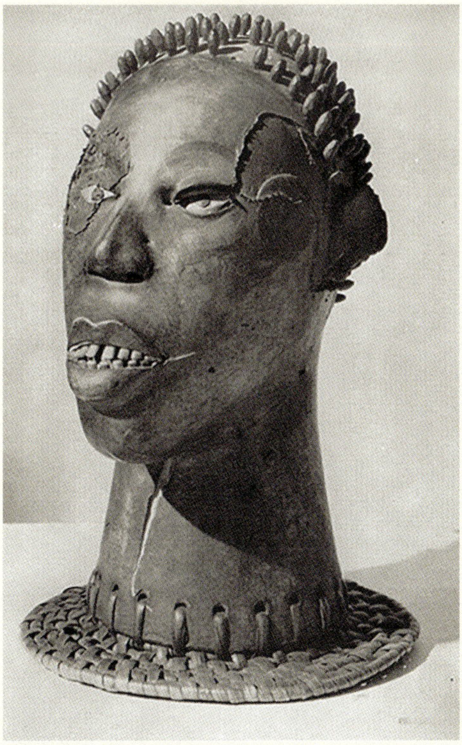

Lot 182

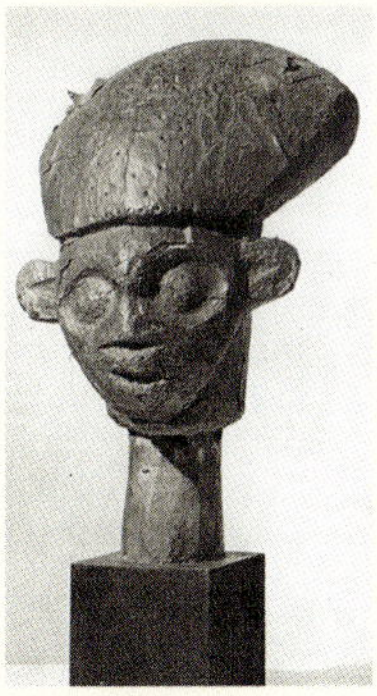

Lot 183

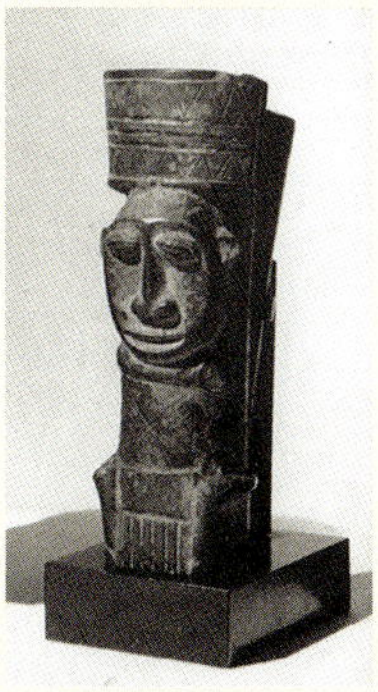

Lot 185

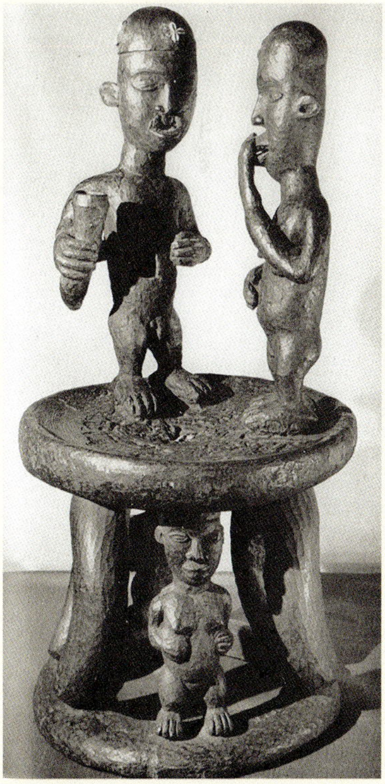

Lot 188

BAKOTA

192

Bakota Reliquary Figure
Wood with Brass and Copper
(Has stand) Height
25½ inches; 65 cms
Gabon
David Lloyd Kreeger collection, Washington D.C. (1966)
• Private collection
Cat. 43, repr. p. 131

193

Bakota Reliquary Figure
Wood with Copper and Brass Sheeting
(Has stand) Height 22 inches; 56 cms
Sotheby's sale, New York, May 17, 2002, lot no. 35
Repr. p. 219

194

Bakota Reliquary Figure
Wood, Copper and Brass
Height 20 inches; 50.8 cms
Chalette Gallery, New York (1966)
• John Fishel collection, Los Angeles
Repr. p. 219

195

Bakota Reliquary Figure
Wood with Glass and Copper
(Has stand) Height
15½ inches; 39.4 cms
Probably region of Makoku
Gaston de Havenon collection, New York (1966)
• Private collection
Cat. 44, repr. p. 130

196

Bakota Reliquary Figure
Wood with Brass and Copper Sheeting
(Has stand) Height
19½ inches; 49.5 cms
Probably region of Makoku
Harry A. Franklin collection, Los Angeles (1966)
Sotheby's sale, New York, November 13, 2017, lot no. 15
Repr. p. 65

197

Bakota Reliquary Figure
Wood, Brass and Copper
(Has stand) Height 19 inches; 48.2 cms
Probably region of Makoku
Aaron Furman, New York (1966)
• Private collection, New York
Repr. p. 219

198

Bakota Reliquary Figure
Wood with Metal Sheeting
(Has stand) Height 19 inches; 48 cms
Region of Makoku
Michael W. de Rothschild collection (1966)
Sotheby's sale, New York, May 12, 2005, lot no. 80
Repr. p. 219

199

Bakota Reliquary Figure
Wood with Copper, Brass Sheeting
(Has stand) Height 22 inches; 56 cms
Probably region of Makoku
Harry A. Franklin collection, Los Angeles (1966)
Repr. p. 219

200

Bakota Reliquary Figure
Wood with Brass and Copper
(Has stand) Height
21¾ inches; 55 cms
Region of Makoku
Gaston de Havenon collection, New York (1966)
• The Arman Marital Trust, Corice Arman Trustee, New York
Cat. 45, repr. p. 130

201

Bakota Reliquary Figure
Wood, Brass and Copper
(Has stand) Height
23¼ inches; 59 cms
Region of Makoku
David Lloyd Kreeger collection, Washington D.C. (1966)
• The Kreeger Museum, Washington
Repr. p. 219

202

Bakota Male Reliquary Figure
Wood and Copper
(Has stand) Height
20½ inches; 52 cms
Region of Makoku
• Fondation Dapper, Paris, inv. 6623
Cat. 46, repr. p. 130

203

Bakota Male Reliquary Figure
Wood Overlaid with Copper Sheeting
(Has stand) Height
19¼ inches; 48.9 cms
Region of Makoku
Gaston de Havenon collection, New York (1966)
• The Arman Marital Trust, Corice Arman Trustee, New York
Cat. 47, repr. p. 130

204

Bakota Reliquary Figure
Wood and Brass Sheeting
Heigth 13 inches; 33 cms
Region of Makoku
Gaston de Havenon collection, New York (1966)
• Private collection, Munich
Repr. p. 219

205

Bakota Reliquary Figure
Wood with Brass Sheeting
(Has stand) Height
9½ inches; 24 cms
Region of Makoku
John Friede, New York (1966)

206

Bakota Reliquary Figure
Wood and Brass
Height 14¼ inches; 36.3 cms

FANG

207

Large Fang Reliquary Head
Wood
(Has stand) Height
12½ inches; 32 cms
Region of Oyem
Alice M. Kaplan collection, New York (1966)
Sotheby's sale, New York, November 20, 1990, lot no. 117
Murray and Barbara Frum, Toronto
Sotheby's sale, New York, May 8, 1996, lot no. 114
• Private collection, New York
Repr. p. 219

208

Fang Reliquary Head
Softwood
(Has stand) Height
10 ½ inches; 27 cms
Region of Oyem
Repr. p. 219

219

Fang Female Figure
Wood
(Has stand) Height 21½ inches; 54.5 cms
From Southern Fang territory around Kango
Henri Laurens collection, Paris (1966)
• Quentin Laurens collection, Paris
Cat. 50, repr. p. 132

210

Fang Reliquary Figure
Wood
(Has stand) Overall height
20½ inches; 52 cms
Region of Oyem
John Friede, New York (1966)
Arman collection, New York
Repr. p. 219

211

Fang Reliquary Figure
Wood
(Has stand) Overall height
17¼ inches; 44 cms
Region of Oyem
Al Hirschfeld collection, New York (1966)
Repr. p. 219

212

Fang Male Figure
Wood
(Has stand) Height
20¾ inches; 52.8 cms
Region of Oyem
• Private collection, New York
Repr. p. 219

213

Fang Reliquary Head
Wood
(Has stand) Height
13¾ inches; 35 cms
Region of Oyem
David Rockefeller collection, New York (1966)
Private collection, France
Simone de Monbrison
Jean-Jacques de Launoit collection
Entwistle gallery collection, Paris
• Private collection, New York
Repr. p. 26

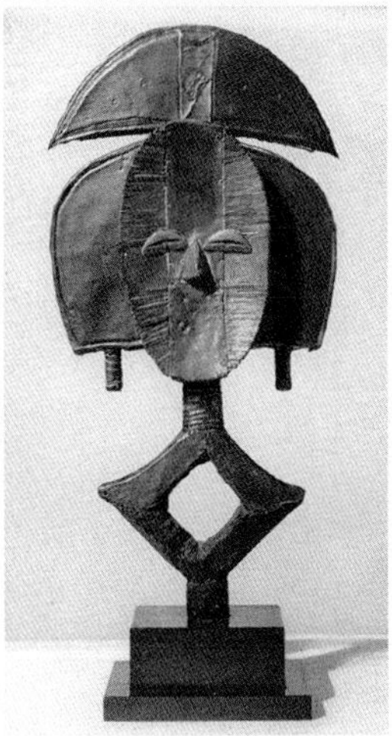
Lot 193

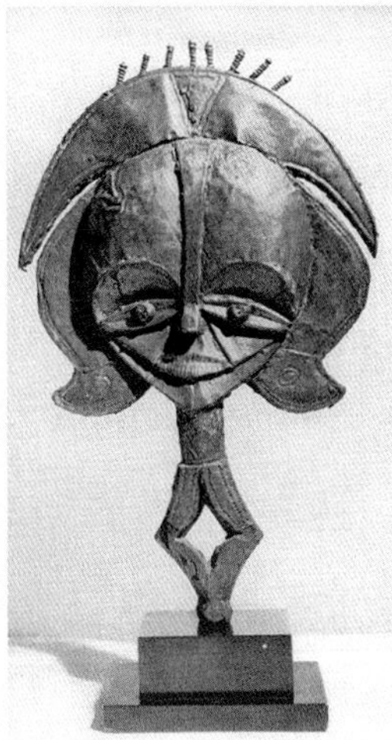
Lot 194

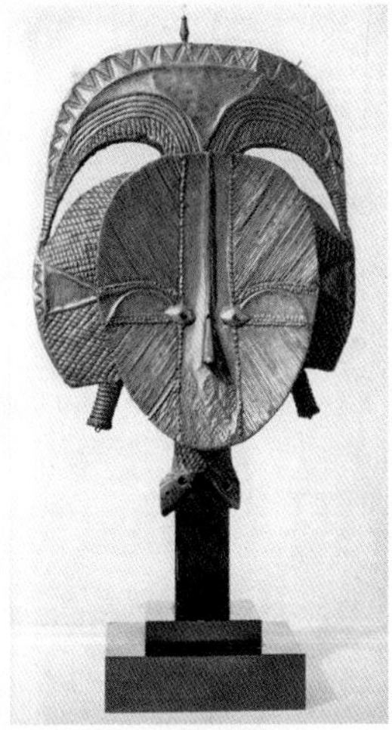
Lot 197

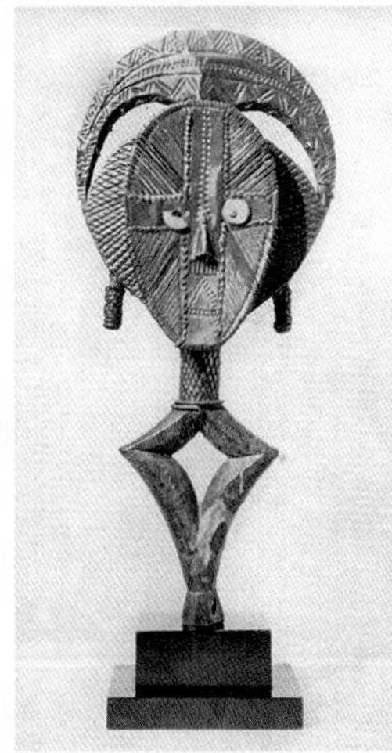
Lot 198

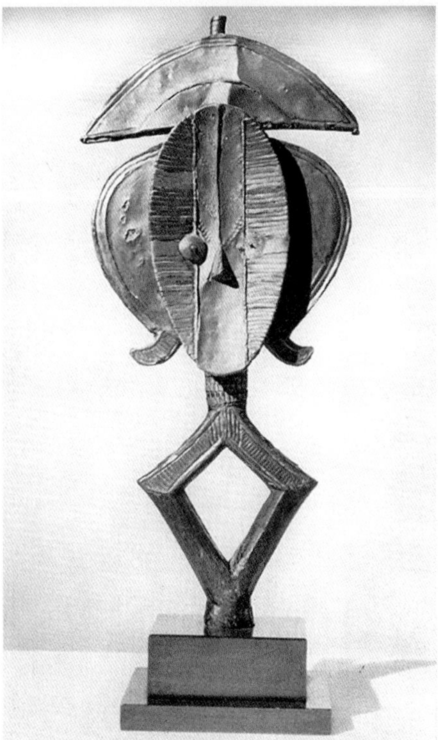
Lot 199

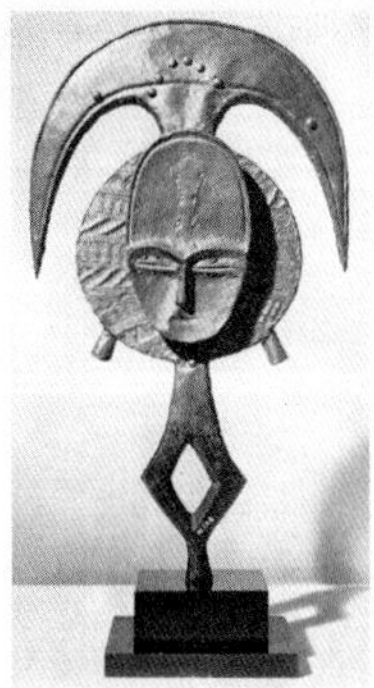
Lot 201

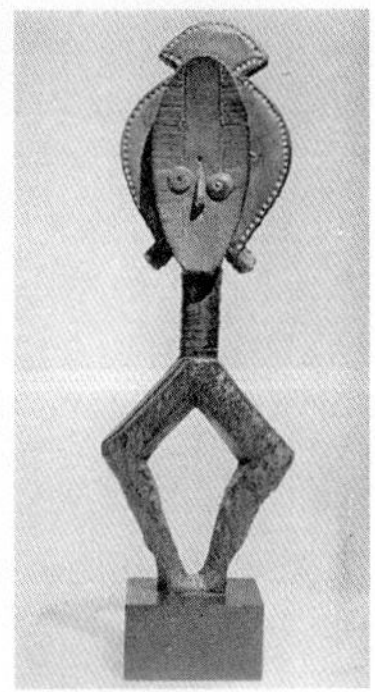
Lot 204

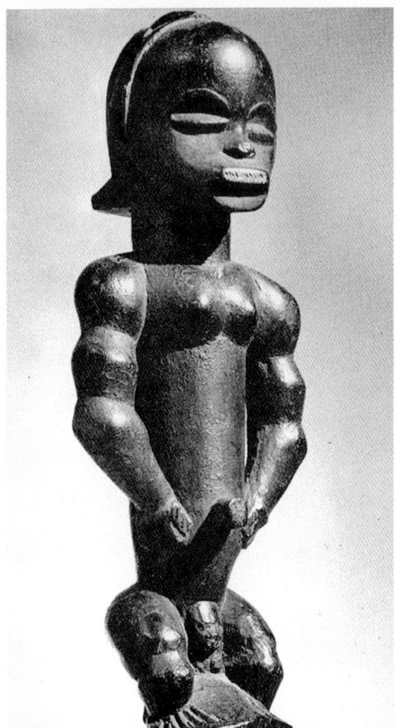
Lot 210

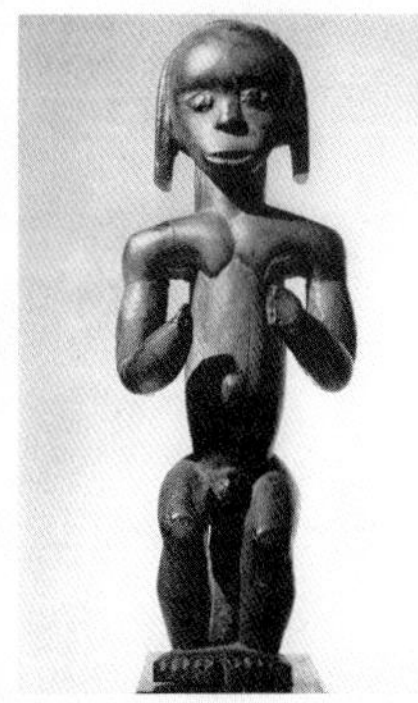
Lot 211

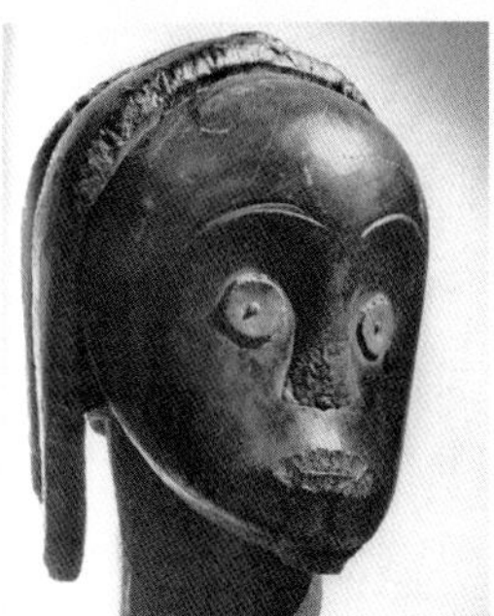
Lot 207

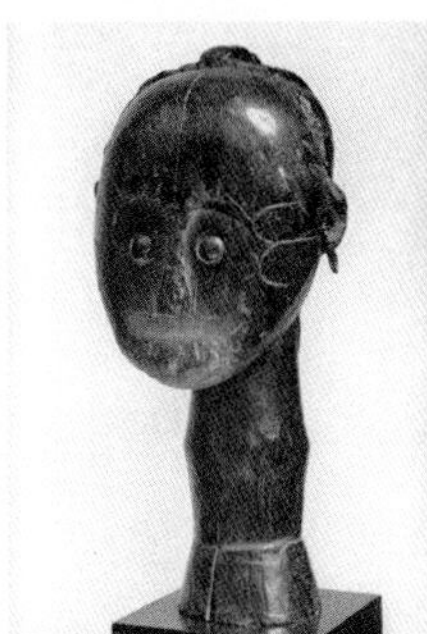
Lot 208

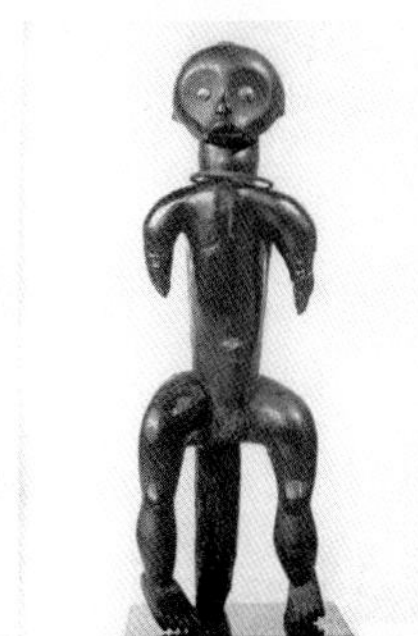
Lot 212

214

Fang Reliquary Head
Wood
(Has stand) Height
8¼ inches; 21 cms
Region of M'bdonzok
Aaron Furman, New York (1966)
Christie's sale Paris, June 15, 2002, lot no. 266
Calmels-Cohen sale, Paris December 4, 2006, lot no. 73
• Private collection, Italy
Repr. p. 221

215

Fang Reliquary Head
Wood
(Has stand) Height
14 inches; 35.5 cms
Region of Oyem
Henri and Hélène Kamer, New York (1966)
• Private collection, Paris
Cat. 48, repr. p. 133

216

Fang Head for a Reliquary
Wood
Height 23 inches; 51.2 cms
Region of Oyem
Aaron Furman, New York (1966)
• Private collection, Europe
Repr. p. 221

217

Fang Figure for a Reliquary
Wood
(Has stand) Height
24½ inches; 62.2 cms
• New Orleans Museum of Art, inv. 77.154
Repr. p. 61

218

Fang Tambourine
Wood with Brass Strips
Height 15½ inches; 38 cms
Region of M'bdonzok
Louis Carré collection (1966)
Olga Carré collection
Artcurial sale, Paris, December 11, 2002, lot no. 119
• Private collection
Repr. p. 221

219

Fang Reliquary Head
Wood
(Has stand) Height
11¾ inches; 30 cms
Region of Oyem
Henri and Hélène Kamer, New York (1966)
• Detroit Institute of Arts, inv. 77.29
Repr. p. 62

220

Fang Human Mask
Wood
Height 9 inches; 22.8 cms
Region of Oyem
David Lloyd Kreeger collection, Washington D.C. (1966)
• The Kreeger Museum, Washington
Repr. p. 221

221

Fang Helmet Mask
Wood
(Has stand) Dimensions of masks 8¼ inches; 21 cms / 13½ inches; 34.3 cms / 11½ inches; 29.2 cms / 8½ inches; 21.5 cms
Komo River area, Southern Fang territory
Provenance Paul Guillaume, Paris
Harry A. Franklin collection, Los Angeles (1966)
• Detroit Institute of Arts, inv. 1983.24
Cat. 49, repr. p. 134-135

BALUBA

222

Baluba Figure
Wood
(Has stand) Height
10¾ inches; 27.3 cms
Provenance Paul Éluard, Paris
Warren Robbins collection, Washington (1966)
• National Museum of African Art – Smithsonian Institution, Washington, inv. 68.30.8
Repr. p. 221

223

Baluba Witch Doctor Figure
Wood
Height 20 inches; 50.8 cms
Region of Kasai, Katanga
Harry A. Franklin collection, Los Angeles (1966)
• Valérie Franklin loan at the Dallas Museum of Arts
Repr. p. 221

224

Baluba Stool
Wood
Height 15½ inches; 39.5 cms / diameter 10¾ inches; 27.3 cms
Provenance Galerie Percier, Paris
Berkeley University puchase (1966)
• Phoebe Hearst Museum, Berkeley University, inv. 5.52.88
Repr. p. 221

225

Baluba Figure
Wood
Height 8 inches; 20.3 cms
Katanga
Edward Klejman, New York (1966)
Repr. p. 221

226

Baluba Amuletic Figure
Hippopotamus Ivory
(Has stand) Height
4 1/8 inches; 10.5 cms
Provenance G. Dehondt, Brussels
Edward Klejman, New York (1966)
Repr. p. 221

BENA-LULUA

227

Bena-Lulua Figure
Wood
(Has stand) Height 20 inches; 51 cms
Provenance Leo Frobenius / Hamburg Museum für Völkerkunde / Charles Ratton, Paris (by exchange)
Jay C. Leff collection, Uniontown (1966)
• Detroit Institute of Arts, inv. 82.49
Cat. 51, repr. p. 138

228

Bena-Lulua Figure
Wood
Height 12 inches; 30.5 cms
Region of Luluabourg, Kasai province
Provenance G. Dehondt, Brussels
Frieda and Milton Rosenthal collection, New York (1966)
• Dr Marian Malcolm collection, Tenafly
Cat. 52, repr. p. 139

BAKUBA

229

Bakuba Stool
Wood and Copper
Height 12½ inches; 32 cms / Diameter 9½ inches; 24 cms
Region of Kasai, Katanga
Repr. p. 221

230

Bakuba Cup
Wood
Height 8½ inches; 21 cms
Region of Kasai, Katanga
Berkeley University puchase (1966)
• Phoebe Hearst Museum, Berkeley University, inv. 5.52.89
Repr. p. 221

231

Bakuba Spoon
Wood
Length: 9½ inches; 24 cms
Region of Kasai, Katanga
Provenance Charles Ratton, Paris

DENGESE

232

Dengese Figure of a Sovereign
Wood
Height 21½ inches; 55 cms
Middle Lukenye River
Provenance Charles Ratton, Paris
Nelson A. Rockefeller collection, New York (1966)
• The Metropolitan Museum of Art, New York, inv. 1978.412.520
Cat. 55, repr. p. 141

BAKONGO

233

Bakongo Figure
Wood
(Has stand) Height
11½ inches; 29 cms
West Kongo group
Provenance Charles Ratton, Paris
Nelson A. Rockefeller collection, New York (1966)
• The Metropolitan Museum of Art, New York, inv. 1978.412.521
Cat. 53, repr. p. 140

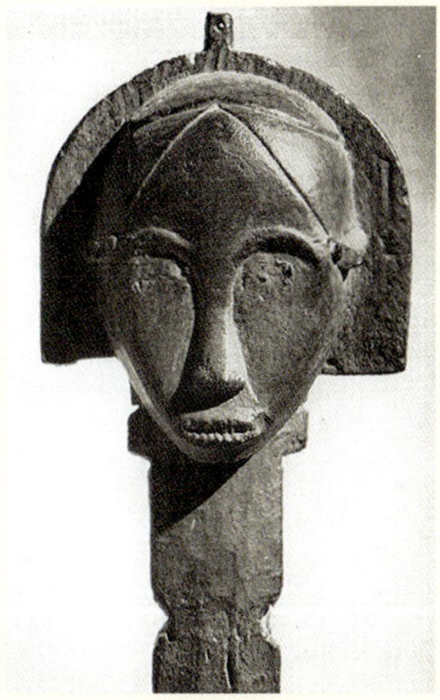

Lot 216

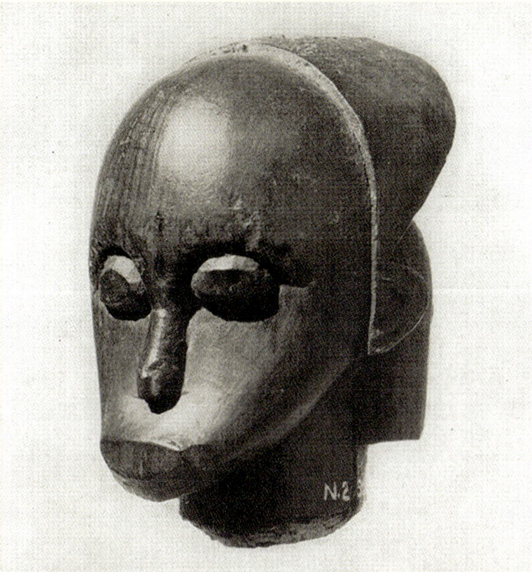

Lot 214

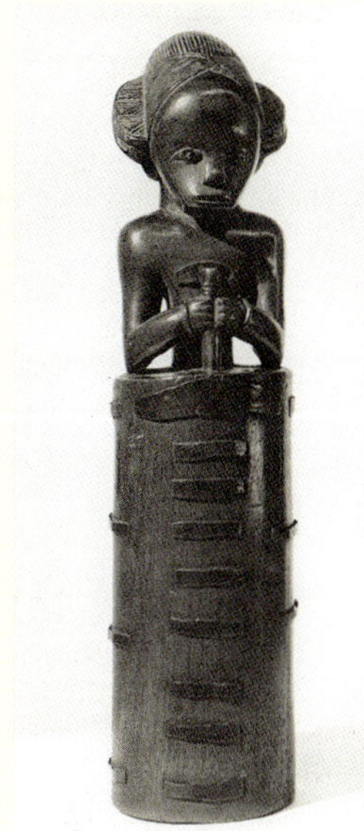

Lot 218

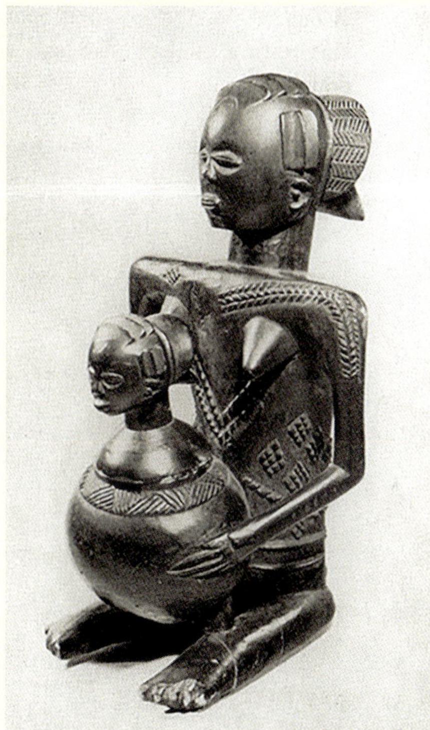

Lot 223

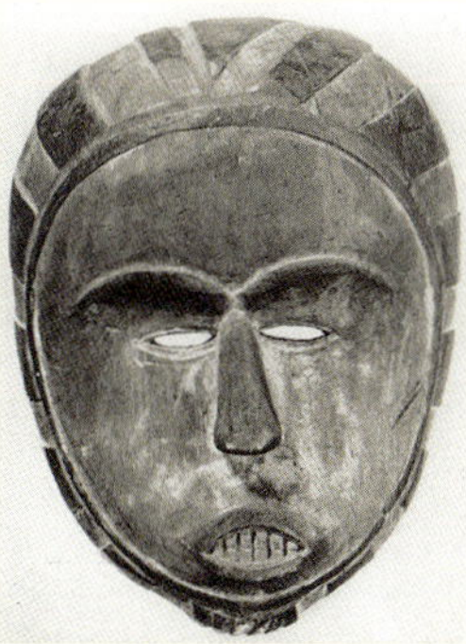

Lot 220

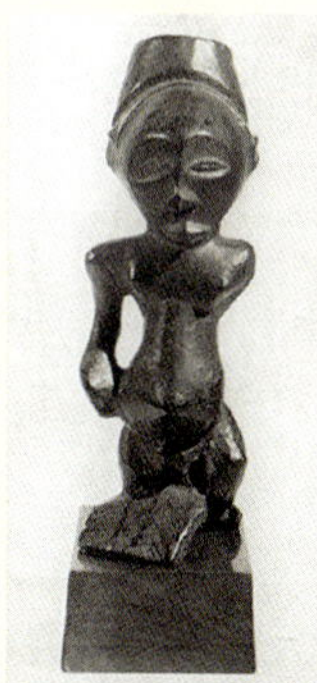

Lot 222

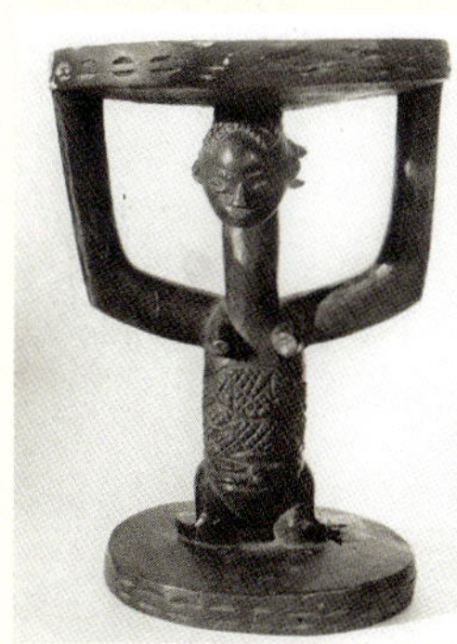

Lot 224

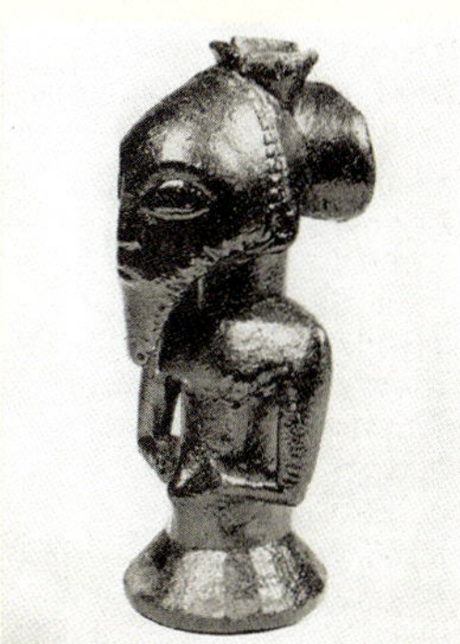

Lot 225

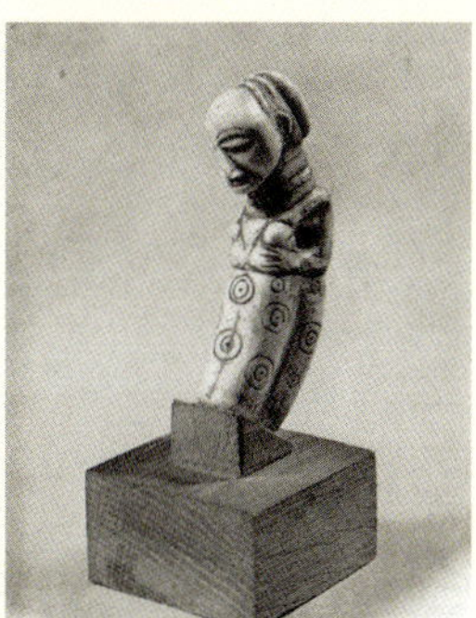

Lot 226

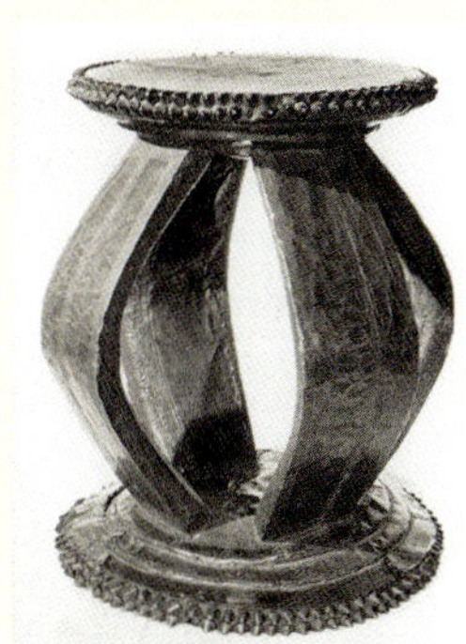

Lot 229

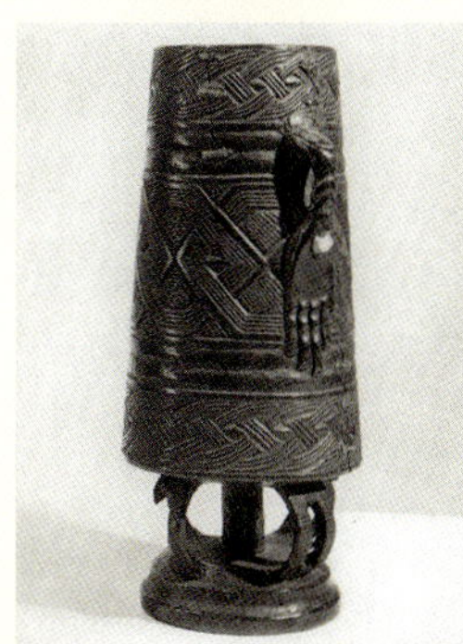

Lot 230

234

Bakongo Fetish Figure
Wood
Height 20¾ inches; 53 cms
Provenance Pierre Chadourne, Paris
Berkeley University puchase (1966)
• Phoebe Hearst Museum, Berkeley University, inv. 5.52.5290
Repr. p. 66

BABEMBE

235

Babembe Figure of a Man
Wood
Height 6¾ inches; 17.1 cms
Region of Mouyondzi-Mayama
Christie's sale Paris, June 23, 2016, lot no. 264
Repr. p. 223

236

Babembe Male Figure
Wood
Height 6½ inches; 16.5 cms
Region of Mouyondzi-Mayama
Berkeley University puchase (1966)
• Phoebe Hearst Museum, Berkeley University, inv. 5.52.5291
Repr. p. 223

237

Babembe Ancestor Figure
Wood
Height 7¼ inches; 18.4 cms
Region of Mouyondzi-Mayama
Frieda and Milton Rosenthal collection, New York (1966)
• Africarium Collection, United States
Cat. 54, repr. p. 140

238

Babembe Figure
Wood
Height 5½ inches; 14 cms
Region of Mouyondzi-Mayama
Al Hirschfeld collection, New York (1966)
Repr. p. 223

239

Babembe Figure
Wood
Height 6¼ inches; 15.9 cms
Region of Mouyondzi-Mayama
Repr. p. 223

240

Babembe Female Figure
Wood
Height 7 inches; 17.8 cms
Region of Mouyondzi-Mayama
Repr. p. 223

BASONGE

241

Basonge Fetish Figure
Wood with Brass
Height 30 inches; 76.3 cms
Region of Lamami
Morris J. Pinto Geneva/New York/Paris (1966)
Donald Morris Gallery, Detroit
George Schwelinger collection, Detroit
Sotheby's sale, New York, November 19, 1999, lot no. 300
Sotheby's sale, New York, May 19, 2001, lot no. 212
Repr. p. 223

BAJOKWE

242

Bajokwe Chief's Chair
Wood with Skin Seat
Height 14 inches; 35.5 cms
Katanga-North, Angola region
Dr Alexander S. Honig collection, Bronxville (1966)
Sotheby's sale, New York, May 18, 1993, lot no. 203
Repr. p. 223

243

Bajokwe Chief's Chair
Wood
Height 23¼ inches; 59 cms
Katanga-North, Angola region
Paul and Ruth Tishman collection, New York (1966)
• National Museum of African Art – Smithsonian Institution, Washington, inv. 81.23.3
Cat. 57, repr. p. 147

244

Bajokwe Table
Wood with Skin Top
Top 25 × 28 inches; 63.5 × 71 cms / Height 26 inches; 66 cms
Katanga-North, Angola region
Warren Robbins collection, Washington (1966)
Repr. p. 223

BATEKE

245

Bateke Fetish Figure
Wood
(Has stand) Height 28 inches; 71.1 cms
Region of Brazzaville
Hyman Klebanov collection, New York (1966)
Sotheby's sale, New York, November 11, 2014, lot no. 114
• Private collection, Hildesheim
Repr. p. 66

246

Bateke Male Figure
Wood
(Has stand) Height 21½ inches; 59.6 cms
Shelly and Norman Dinhofer collection, New York (1966)
Sotheby's sale, New York, May 16, 2008, lot no. 57
• Private collection, Hildesheim
Repr. p. 223

BAYAKA

247

Bayaka Slit-Gongs
Wood
(Has stand) Height of tallest 8½ inches; 22 cms
Al Hirschfeld collection, New York (1966)
Repr. p. 223

OCEANIA AND REGIONS OTHER THAN AFRICA

SOLOMON ISLANDS

248

Solomon Islands Canoe Prow
Wood with Shell
(Has stand) Height 5 inches; 13 cms
Repr. p. 223

249

Solomon Islands Canoe Prow
Wood with Shell
(Has stand) Height 9 inches; 23 cms
Ernest Rassiga, New York (1966)
Repr. p. 223

MARQUESAS ISLANDS

250

Marquesas Islands Club
Wood
Height 52 inches; 132 cms
Harry A. Franklin collection, Los Angeles (1966)
Sotheby's sale, New York, May 13, 2019, lot no. 9
• Private collection, New York
Repr. p. 223

251

Marquesas Islands Stilt Step
Wood
(Has stand) Height 13 inches; 33 cms
Christie's sale Paris, June 23, 2016, lot no. 206
• Collection Marshall and Caroline Mount
Repr. p. 223

251A

Marquesas Islands Stilt Step
Wood
(Has stand) Height 14 inches; 35.5 cms
Repr. p. 223

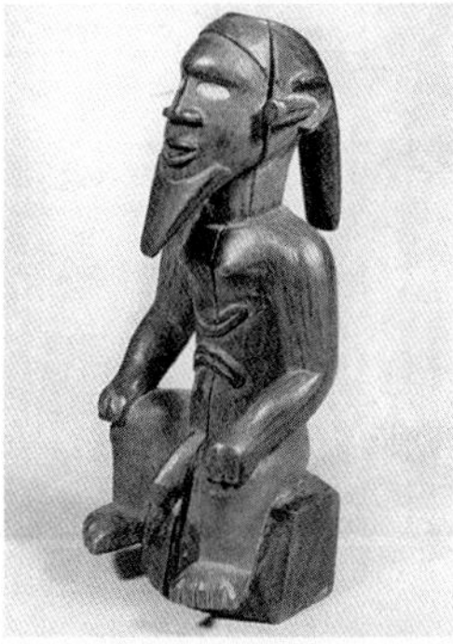
Lot 235

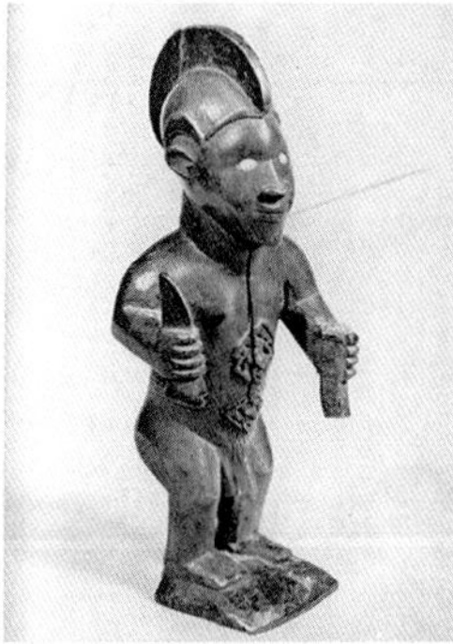
Lot 236

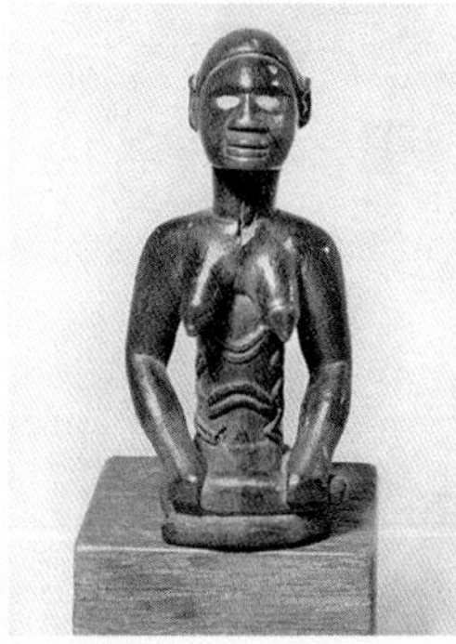
Lot 238

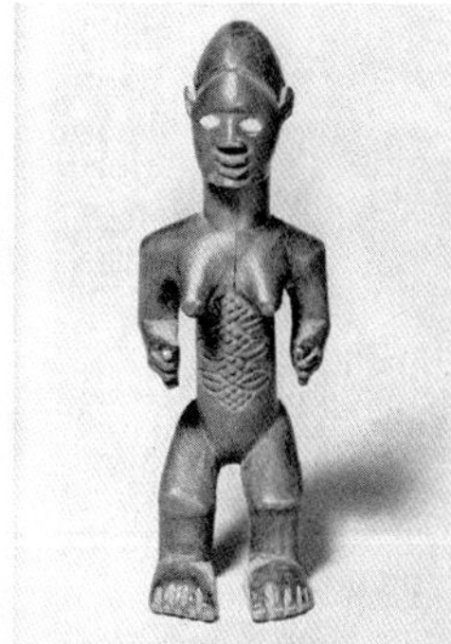
Lot 239

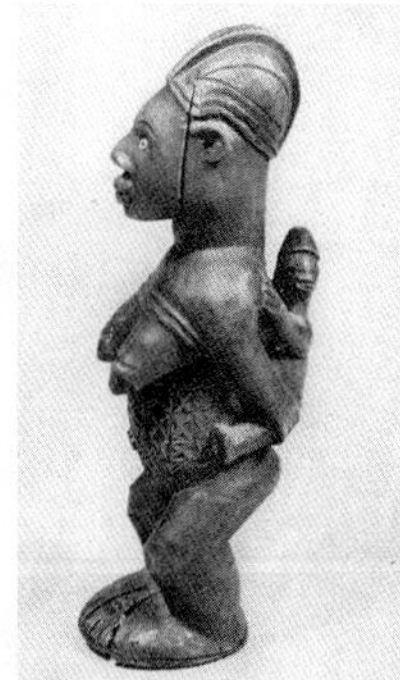
Lot 240

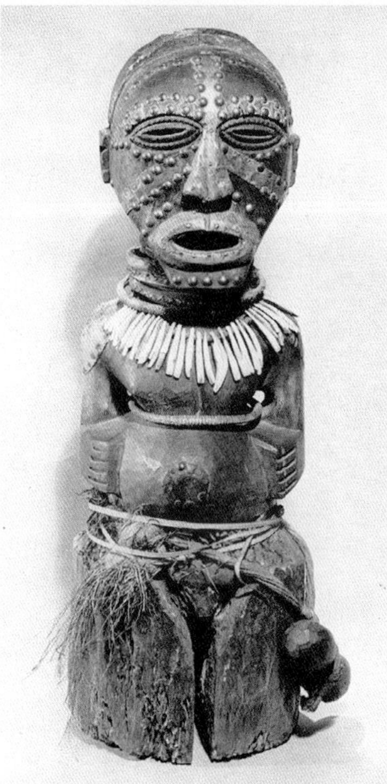
Lot 241

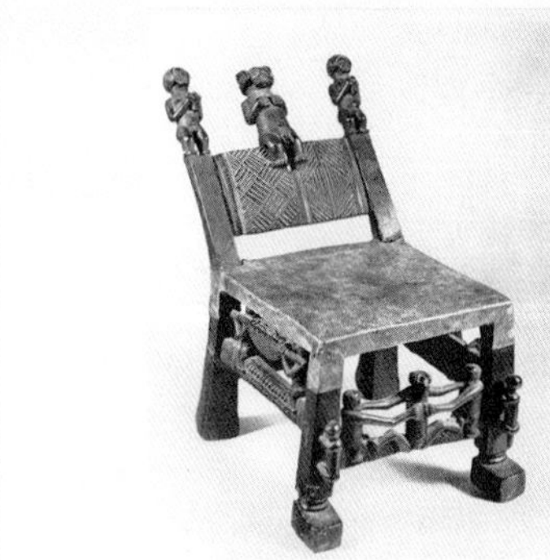
Lot 242

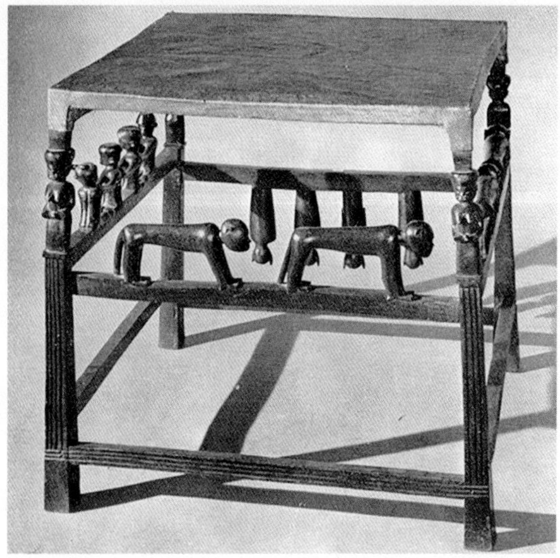
Lot 244

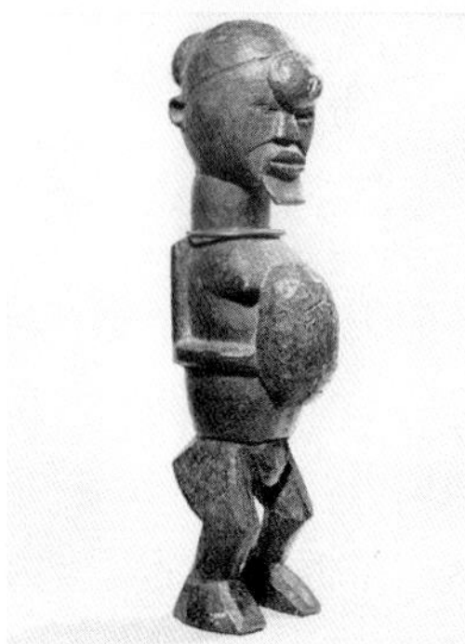
Lot 246

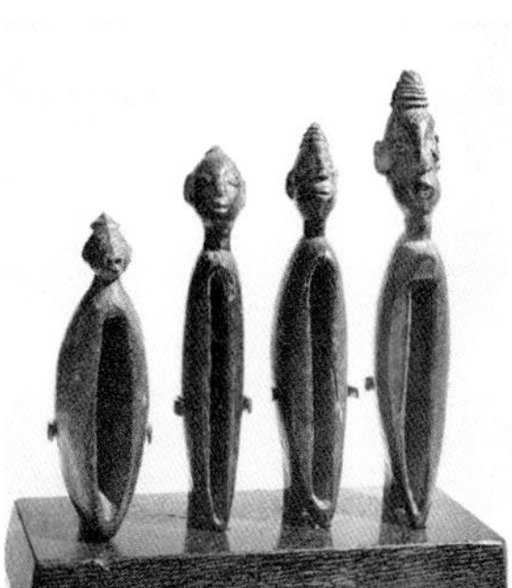
Lot 247

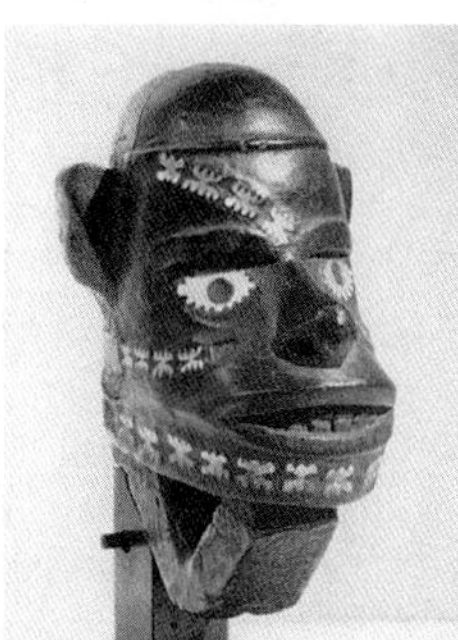
Lot 248

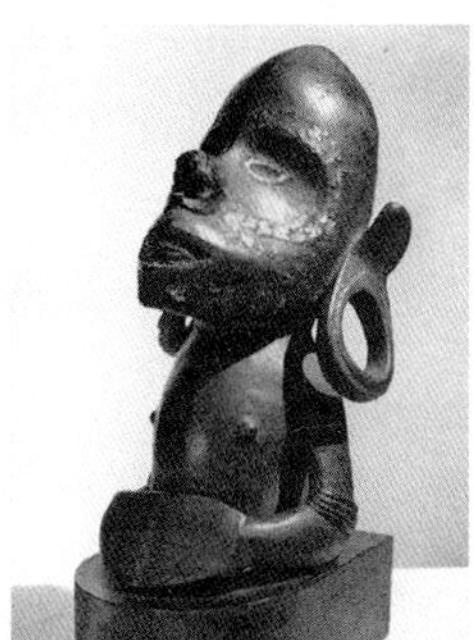
Lot 249

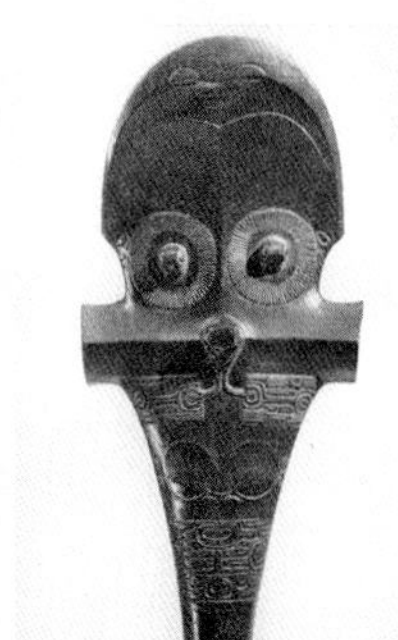
Lot 250

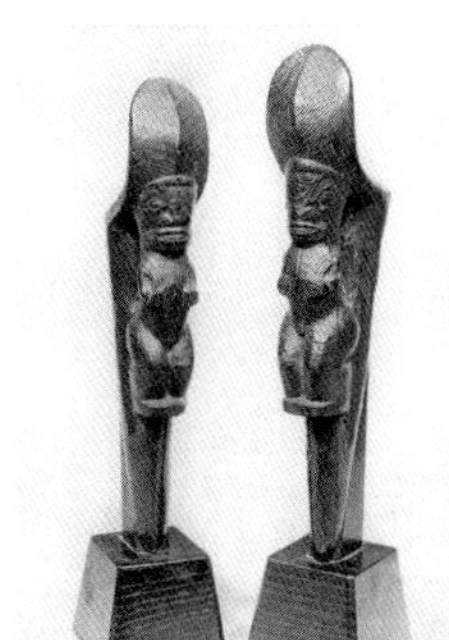
Lot 251a Lot 251

NEW ZEALAND

252

Maori Head
Wood
(Has stand) Height
8½ inches; 21.5 cms
New Zealand
Private collection, New York (1966)
Repr. p. 225

253

Maori House Post
Wood
(Has stand) Height 37 inches; 94 cms
New Zealand
Provenance André Breton-Paul Éluard, sale Hôtel Drouot, Paris, July 1931, cat. no. 142, illus.
Harry A. Franklin collection, Los Angeles (1966)
Sotheby's sale, New York, May 13, 2019, lot no. 42
Repr. p. 225

BORNEO

254

D[a]yak Figure
Wood
(Has stand) Height
39¼ inches; 99 cms
Borneo
Repr. p. 225

255

D[a]yak Figure
Wood
(Has stand) Height
40½ inches; 103 cms
Borneo
Repr. p. 225

NIAS ISLANDS

256

Nias Islands Ancestor Figure
Wood
Height 21¾ inches; 55.2 cms
Sumatra
Provenance André Breton-Paul Éluard, Sale Hôtel Drouot, Paris, 1931, cat. no. 173, illus.
Henri and Hélène Kamer, and Charles Ratton, New York-Paris (1966)
Alain Schoffel collection, France
• Musée du Quai Branly – Jacques Chirac, inv. 70.1999.3.1
Repr. p. 194

ALASKA

257

Pacific Northwest Coast Rattle
Wood
(Has stand) Height 12 inches; 30.5 cms
Tlingit
Ernest Rassiga, New York (1966)
Repr. p. 225

NEW HEBRIDES

258

New Hebrides Mask
Wood
Height 14½ inches; 36.7 cms
Vao or Rano Island, off Malekula
Harry A. Franklin collection, Los Angeles (1966)
Sotheby's sale, New York, May 13, 2019, lot no. 33
• Private collection, New York
Repr. p. 225

NEW GUINEA

259

Lake Sentani Figure
Wood
(Has stand) Height
28¾ inches; 73 cms
Northwestern New Guinea
Provenance Dr. J. Viot (collected by him in 1929)
Aaron Furman, New York (1966)
• Musée Barbier-Mueller, Geneva, inv. 4051
Repr. p. 225

260

Lake Sentani Standing Figure
Wood
(Has stand) Height
47½ inches; 120.7 cms
Northwestern New Guinea
Provenance Dr. J. Viot (collected by him in 1929)
• Gordon Sze collection, New York
Cat. 60, repr. p. 148

261

Easter Island Figure
Toromiro Wood
Height 23 ½ inches; 60 cms
• Jean-François Schmitt collection, Paris
Cat. 59, repr. p. 149

African and Oceanic Art
Part Three

Saturday, October 15, 1966 at 11 a.m.

MENDE

1

Mende Figure
Sierra Leone
Pink soapstone
(Has stand) Height
10½ inches

2

Mende Helmet Mask
Sierra Leone
Wood
Height 16½ inches

DAN

3

Dan Mask
Ivory Coast
Wood
Height 9 inches
Repr. p. 229

4

Dan Mask
Ivory Coast
Wood
Height 8 inches
Repr. p. 229

BAULE

5

Three Baule Heddle Pullies
Ivory Coast
Wood
(With stands) Heights
6¾ to 7½ inches

6

Three Baule Heddle Pullies
Ivory Coast
Wood
(With stands) Heights 6½ to 7¾ inches

7

Three Baule Heddle Pullies
Ivory Coast
Wood
(With stands) Heights 6½ to 8¾ inches

8

Three Baule Heddle Pullies
Ivory Coast
Wood
(With stands) Heights 5½ to 7 ¾ inches

9

Four Baule Heddle Pullies
Ivory Coast
Wood
(With stands) Heights 7 to 7½ inches

10

Two Baule Heddle Pullies
Ivory Coast
Wood
(With stands) Heights 8½ and 9 inches
Rothschild Family collection, London (1966)
Sotheby's sale, New York, May 12, 2005, lot no.59

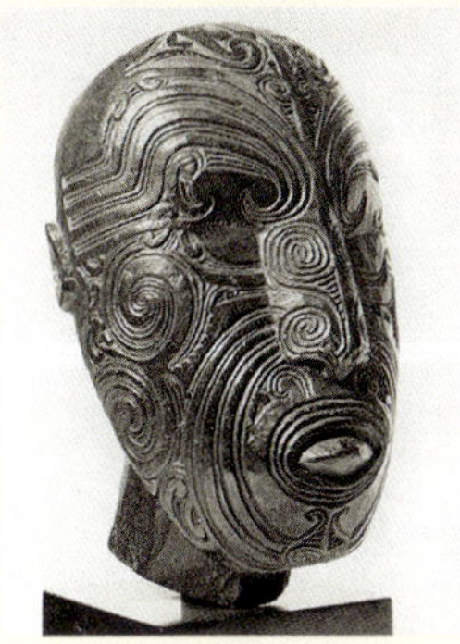
Lot 252

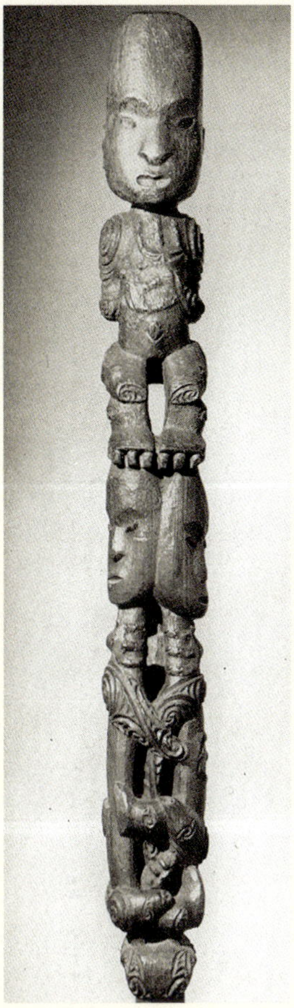
Lot 253

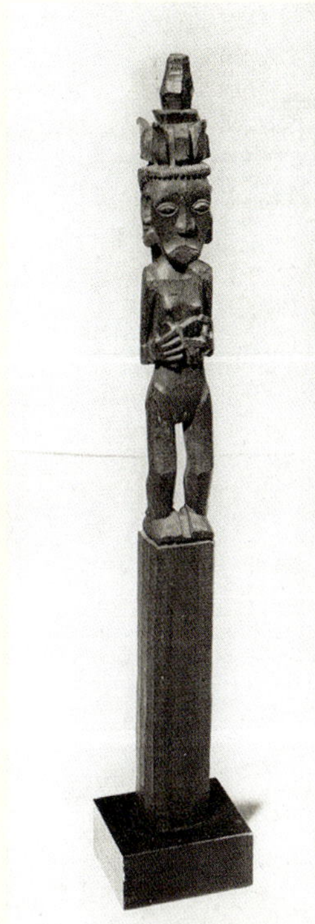
Lot 254

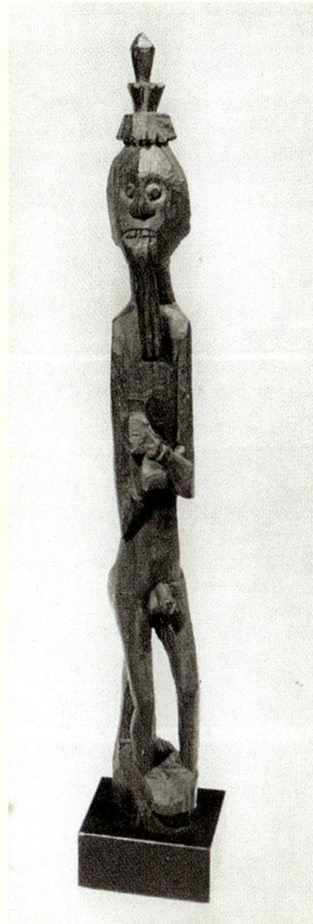
Lot 255

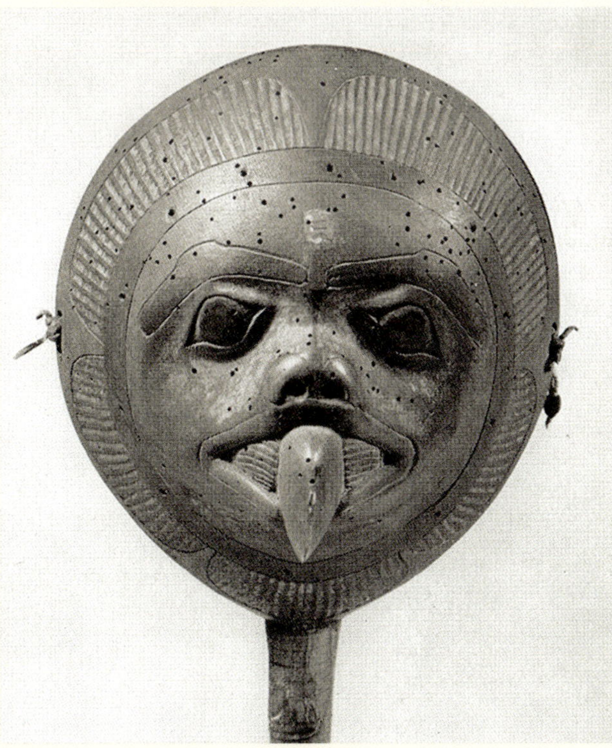
Lot 257

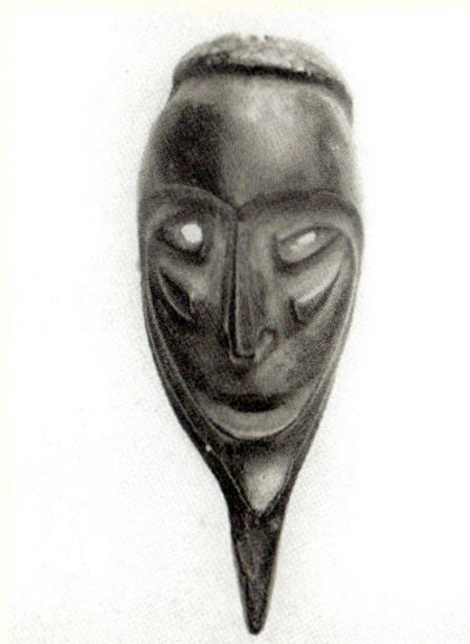
Lot 258

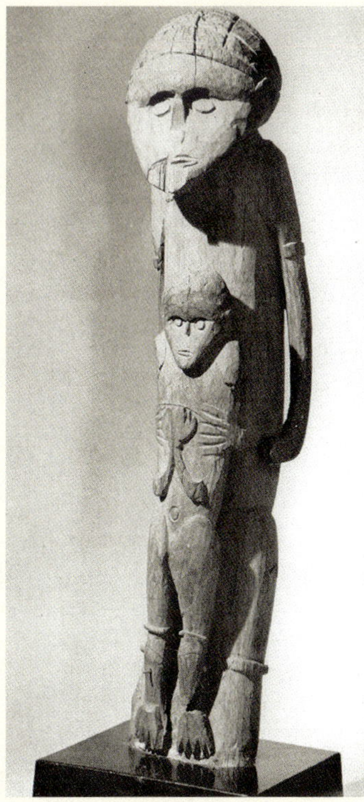
Lot 259

11

Four Baule Heddle Pullies
Ivory Coast
Wood
(With stands) Heights 6½ to 8½ inches

12

Three Baule Heddle Pullies
Ivory Coast
Wood
(With stands) Heights 6 to 7 inches

13

Two Baule Heddle Pullies
Ivory Coast
Wood
(With stands) Heights 10½ and 10¾ inches

14

Four Baule Heddle Pullies
Ivory Coast
Wood
(With stands) Heights 6¾ to 7½ inches

15

Two Baule Heddle Pullies
Ivory Coast
Wood
(With stands) Heights 7¼ and 8¼ inches

16

Two Baule Heddle Pullies
Ivory Coast
Wood
(With stands) Heights 7 and 7¾ inches

17

Three Baule Heddle Pullies
Ivory Coast
Wood
(With stands) Heights 6 to 7 inches

18

Two Baule Heddle Pullies
Ivory Coast
Wood
(With stands) Heights 5 ½ and 6 inches

19

Baule Heddle Pulley
Ivory Coast
Wood
(Has stand) Height 9 inches

20

Baule Heddle Pulley
Ivory Coast
Wood
(Has stand) Height 7¾ inches

21

Baule Heddle Pulley
Ivory Coast
Wood
(Has stand) Height 7¼ inches

22

Pair of Baule Figures
Yamassoukro region, Ivory Coast
Wood
(With stands) Height 19 inches

23

Baule Standing Figure
Bouaké region, Ivory Coast
Wood
Height 14 inches
Sotheby's sale, New York, November 9, 1979, lot no.22

24

Baule Ancestor Figure
Bouaké region, Ivory Coast
Wood
Height 15¼ inches

25

Baule Standing Figure
Bouaké region, Ivory Coast
Wood
Height 13½ inches
Marceau Rivière collection, France
• Private collection, Germany

26

Baule Female Figure
Bouaké region, Ivory Coast
Wood
Height 17 inches

27

Baule Standing Group
Bouaké region, Ivory Coast
Wood
Height 18½ inches

28

Baule Standing Figure
Bouafflé/Daloa region, Ivory Coast
Wood
Height 24½ inches

29

Baule Miniature Door
Ivory Coast
Wood
Height 21½ inches; Width 11 inches
• Private collection, Paris
Cat. 14, repr. 101

30

Baule Miniature Door
Ivory Coast
Wood
Height 18¼ inches; Width 9 inches
• Private collection, Geneva

31

Baule Miniature Door
Ivory Coast
Wood
Height 21½ inches; Width 10¾ inches
William W. Brill collection, New York (1966)
Sotheby's sale, New York, November 17, 2006, lot no.43

32

Baule Drum
Ivory Coast
Wood
Height 71½ inches
Freda and Harry Schaeffer collection, New York (1966)
• Nicolas Hug collection, Paris
Cat. 56, repr. p. 145

YAURE

33

Yaure Mask
Bouaflé region, Ivory Coast
Wood
(Has stand) Height 13 inches

GURO

34

Two Guro Heddle Pullies
Ivory Coast
Wood
(With stands) Heights 7 and 8 inches

35

Guro Mask
Ivory Coast
Wood
Height 12¾ inches
• Marceau Rivière collection, France
Sotheby's sale, Paris, June 18, 2019, lot no.57
Cat. 19, repr. p. 103

BAMBARA

36

Bambara Dance Headdress
Probably Ouassoulou region, near Bougouni, West-Central Bambaraland
Wood
Height 19¼ inches
Provenance F.-H. Lem, Paris

37

Bambara Dance Headdress
Segou region, North-East Bambaraland
Wood
Height 17¾ inches
Provenance F.-H. Lem, Paris
Sotheby's sale, New York, May 12, 2005, lot no.44

38

Bambara Dance Headdress
Kenedougou region, Eastern Bambaraland
Wood
(Has Stand) Height 20¾ inches
Provenance F.-H. Lem, Paris
• The Jerome Kenney Family collection, New York
Cat. 33, repr. p. 119

39

Bambara Dance Headdress
Eastern Bambaraland
Wood
(Has stand) Height 24 inches
Provenance F.-H. Lem, Paris

40

Three Bambara Dance Headdresses
Wood
Heights 16¾ to 19¼ inches
Provenance F.-H. Lem, Paris
• Private collection, Michigan
Cat. 34, repr. p. 119

SENUFO

41

Three Senufo Heddle Pullies
Wood
(With stands) Heights 5¼ to 6½ inches
Harold Rome collection, New York (1966)
Sotheby's sale, New York, May 15, 2017, lot no.18

42

Two Senufo Heddle Pullies
Wood
(With stands) Heights 6¾ and 7¼ inches

43

Three Senufo Heddle Pullies
Wood
(With stands) Heights 6 to 7 inches

44

Four Senufo Heddle Pullies
Wood
(Three with stands)
Heights 5¼ to 7 inches

45

Two Senufo Spoons
Wood
(Has stand) Heights 5¼ inches

46

Senufo Figure
Korhogo region
Wood
(Has stand) Height 8¾ inches

47

Senufo Mask
Wood
Height 12½ inches

LOBI

48

Four Lobi Head-Rests
Bouna region
Wood
Lenghts 11¾ inches to 13¼ inches

49

Lobi Figure
Ivory Coast
Wood
Height 48¾ inches

AGNI

50

Agni Figure of a Woman
Krinjabo
Grey Terra Cotta
(Has stand) Height 14 ½ inches
Provenance Dr. Lheureux
Sotheby's sale, New York, 24 November 1992, lot no.86

51

Agni Figure of a Woman
Krinjabo
Grey Terra Cotta
(Has stand) Height 14 inches
Provenance Dr. Lheureux

52

Agni Head of a Man
Krinjabo
Grey Terra Cotta
(Has stand) Height 8 inches
Provenance Dr. Lheureux

53

Agni Head of a Man
Krinjabo
Grey Terra Cotta
(Has stand) Height 8¼ inches
Provenance Dr. Lheureux

54

Agni Male Figure
Krinjabo
Reddish Terra Cotta
(Has stand) Height 8¾ inches
Provenance Dr. Lheureux

55

Agni Head of a Man
Krinjabo
Grey Terra Cotta
(Has stand) Height 7 inches
Provenance Dr. Lheureux

56

Agni Head of a Man
Krinjabo
Grey Terra Cotta
(Has stand) Height 8½ inches
Provenance Dr. Lheureux

57

Agni Head of a Man
Krinjabo
Grey Terra Cotta
(Has stand) Height 8½ inches
Provenance Dr. Lheureux

58

Agni Head of a Man
Krinjabo
Light Grey Terra Cotta
(Has stand) Height 6½ inches
Provenance Dr. Lheureux

59

Agni Male Figure
Krinjabo
Reddish Terra Cotta
(Has stand) Height 13 inches
Provenance Dr. Lheureux

60

Agni Head of a Woman
Krinjabo
Reddish Terra Cotta
(Has stand) Height 7¼ inches
Provenance Dr. Lheureux
Christie's sale Paris, 12 juin 2003, lot no. 346

61

Agni Head of a Woman
Krinjabo
Grey Terra Cotta
(Has stand) Height 6 inches
Provenance Dr. Lheureux

62

Agni Head of a Man
Krinjabo
Grey Terra Cotta
(Has stand) Height 6½ inches
Provenance Dr. Lheureux

63

Agni Head of a Man
Krinjabo
Grey Terra Cotta
(Has stand) Height 6½ inches
Provenance Dr. Lheureux

64

Agni Head of a Man
Krinjabo
Grey Terra Cotta
(Has stand) Height 6½ inches
Provenance Dr. Lheureux

65

Agni Head of a Man
Krinjabo
Grey Terra Cotta
(Has stand) Height 7½ inches
Provenance Dr. Lheureux

66

Agni Head of a Man
Krinjabo
Grey Terra Cotta
(Has stand) Height 6½ inches
Provenance Dr. Lheureux
Collection Dr Alexander S. Honig, New York (1966)
Sotheby's sale, New York, 18 mai 1993, lot no. 109

67

Agni Figure of a Woman
Krinjabo
Buff Terra Cotta
(Has stand) Height 10½ inches
Provenance Dr. Lheureux

68

Agni Figure of a Woman
Krinjabo
Grey Terra Cotta
(Has stand) Height 13¼ inches
Provenance Dr. Lheureux

69

Agni Figure of a Man
Krinjabo
Grey Terra Cotta
(Has stand) Height 13½ inches
Provenance Dr. Lheureux

70

Agni Figure of a Man
Krinjabo
Grey Terra Cotta
(Has stand) Height 14½ inches
Provenance Dr. Lheureux
Repr. p. 229

71

Agni Figure of a Woman
Krinjabo
Grey Terra Cotta
(Has stand) Height 13½ inches
Provenance Dr. Lheureux
Repr. p. 229

ASHANTI

72

Two Ashanti Combs
Kumasi region, Ghana
Wood
Heights 9 and 9¾ inches
Collection William W. Brill, New York (1966)
• Private collection, Long Island
Cat. 13, repr. p. 97

73

Ashanti Stool
Ghana
Wood
Length 15¼ inches

BAKOTA

74

Bakota Reliquary Figure
Makokou region, Gabon
Wood and Brass
Height 12¾ inches

75

Bakota Reliquary Figure
Gabon
Wood, Copper and Brass
Height 15 inches

76

Bakota Reliquary Figure
Gabon
Wood, Copper and Brass
Height 24½ inches

77

Bakota Reliquary Figure
Makokou region, Gabon
Wood and Brass
Height 18 inches

78

Bakota Reliquary Figure
Gabon
Wood and Brass
Height 19½ inches
• Anne and René Vanderstraete collection, Belgium

79

Bakota Reliquary Figure
Gabon
Wood and Brass
Height 14½ inches

80

Bakota Reliquary Figure
Gabon
Wood and Brass
Height 12¼ inches

81

Bakota Reliquary Figure
Makokou region, Gabon
Wood and Copper
(Has stand) Height
15¼ inches
Repr. p. 229

82

Bakota Reliquary Figure
Makokou region, Gabon
Wood and Copper
(Has stand) Height 15 inches
Repr. p. 229

83

Bakota Reliquary Figure
Makokou region, Gabon
Wood, Copper and Brass
(Has stand) Height 23 inches
• The Heard Museum, Phoenix, Arizona, United States, inv no.00.205.09
Repr. p. 229

BALUBA

84

Baluba Stool
Kasai-Katanga region
Wood
Height 16¼ inches

85

Baluba Stool
Kasai-Katanga region
Wood
Height 20¼ inches

86

Baluba Stool
Bazala Sub-tribe,
Kasai-Katanga region
Wood
Height 21½ inches
Repr. p. 229

87

Baluba Stool
Bazala sub-tribe,
Kasai-Katanga region
Wood
Height 21¾ inches
Repr. p. 229

BAKONGO

88

Bakongo Fetish Figure
Wood
Height 10½ inches

89

Congo Fetish Figure
West Mayombe region
Wood
Height 26¼ inches
James Willis, San Francisco (1966)
Sotheby's sale, New York, November 29, 1984, lot no.322
Myron Kunin collection, Minneapolis
Sotheby's sale, New York, November 11, 2014, lot no.104
• Private collection, Italy
Repr. p. 229

BABEMBE

90

Babembe Male Figure
Mouyondzi-Mayama region
Wood
Height 8 inches

91

Babembe Female Figure
Mouyondzi-Mayama region
Wood
Height 7½ inches

BASONGE

92

Two Basonge Ceremonial Axes
Wood, Copper and Iron
Heights 18 and 19 inches
Arthur A. Cohen collection, New York (1966-1967)
• National Museum of African Art – Smithsonian Institution, Washington, inv. nmafa-67-25-7 et 67.25.8

BATEKE

93

Bateke Fetish Figure
Franceville, Plateau region,
Southern Gabon
Wood
(Has stand) Height
9¼ inches

OCEANIA

94

Polynesian Bowl
Wood
Diameter 25¼ inches

95

Polynesian Bowl
Wood
Diameter 31 inches

96

New-Caledonian Figure
Wood
(Has stand) Height
12½ inches

97

Easter Island Head of a Man
Wood
(Has stand) Height
18 inches
Sotheby's sale, New York, July 14, 1970, lot no.75
Harry A. Franklin collection, Los Angeles
Sotheby's sale, New York, May 13, 2019, lot no.44

98

Tahitian Pestle
Volcanic Stone
(Has stand) Height
6¼ inches

99

Marquesas Islands Figure
Volcanic Stone
(Has stand) Height
6¾ inches
• Anthony Meyer collection, Paris

100

Marquesas Islands Group
Volcanic stone
(Has stand) Height
6 inches

END OF SALE

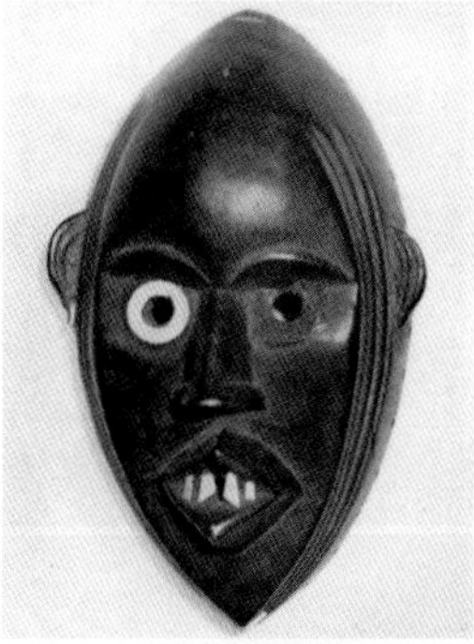
Lot 3

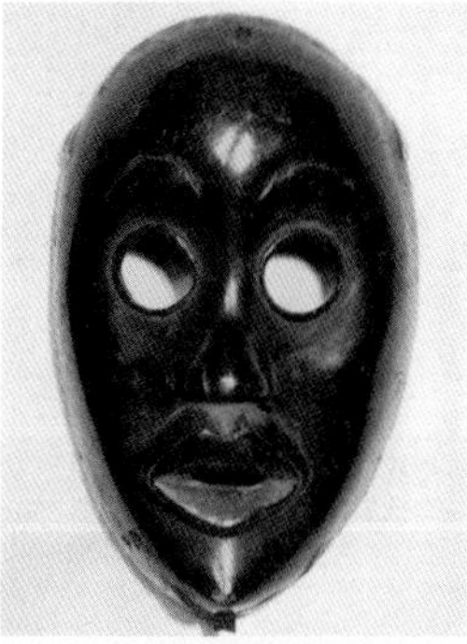
Lot 4

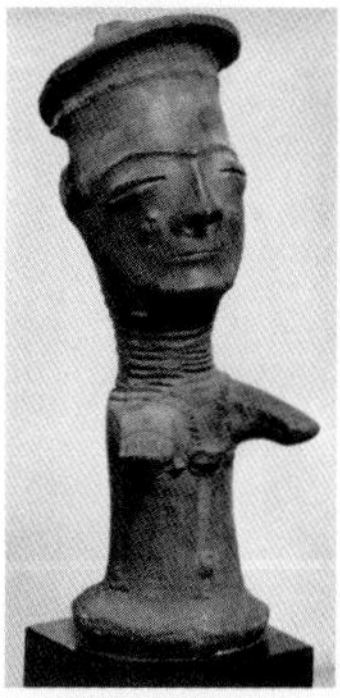
Lot 70

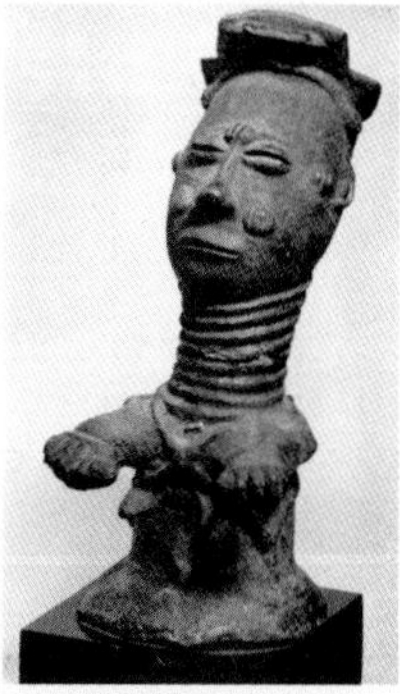
Lot 71

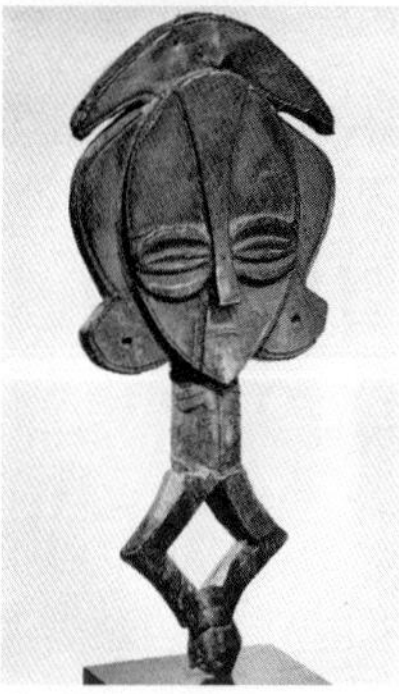
Lot 81

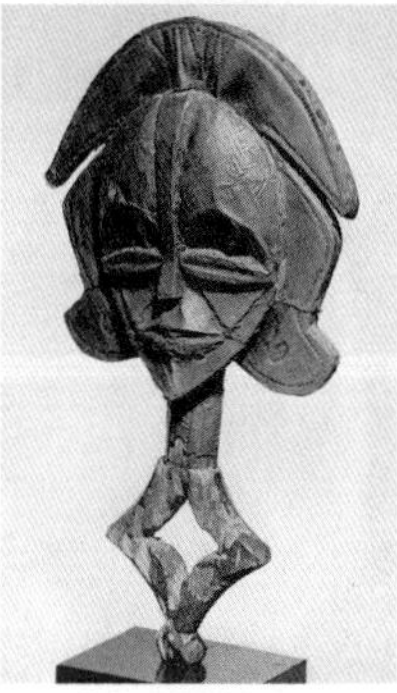
Lot 82

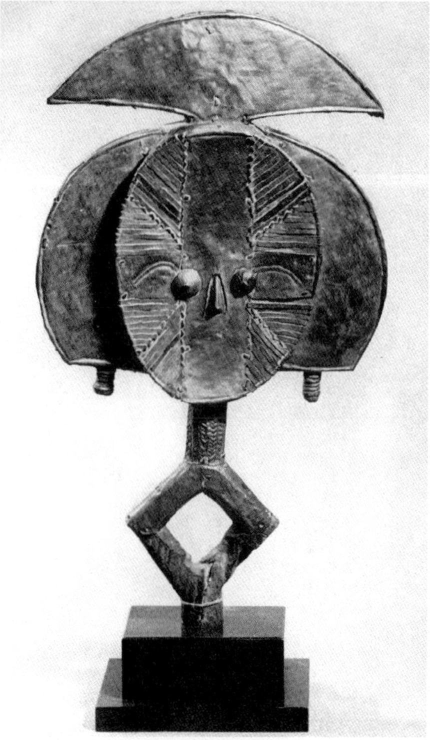
Lot 83

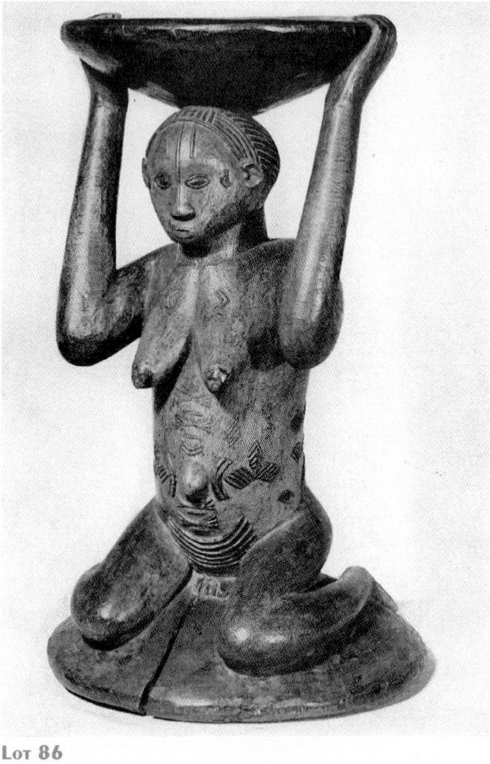
Lot 86

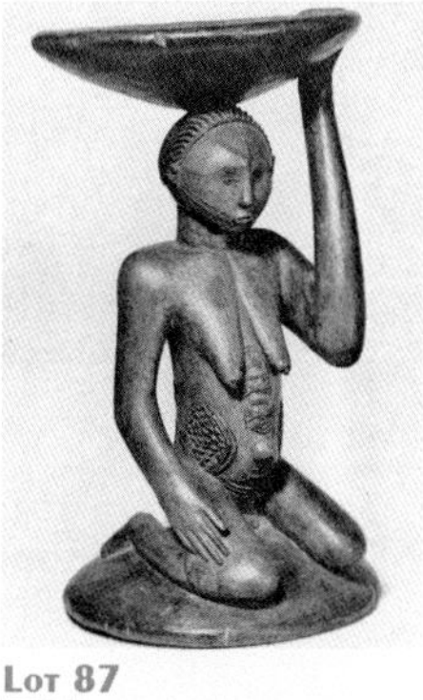
Lot 87

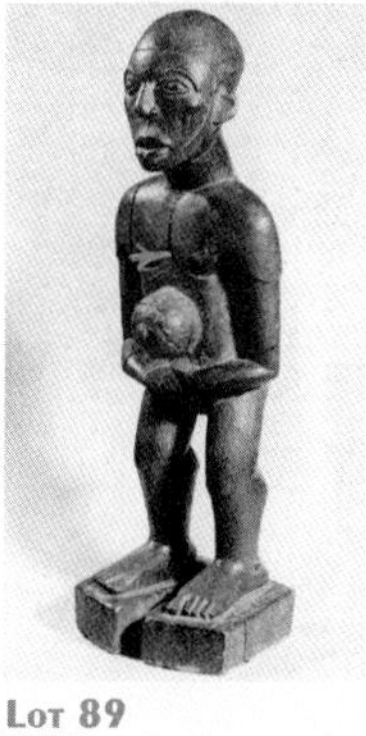
Lot 89

Works are listed in exhibition order. Unless otherwise stated they belonged to Helena Rubinstein until her death in 1965 and appear in the Parke-Bernet sale catalogs of April and October 1966 (see pp. 200–229).

The sometimes numerous published references for certain objects have not been fully mentioned for reasons of space.

AFRICA

Cat. 1, repr. p. 88

Miniature protection mask
Bete, Ivory Coast
19th – early 20th cent.
Wood, cowries, metal
16.5 × 10.5 cm
Paris, Private collection

Helena Rubinstein collection, New York/Paris (before 1965); Parke-Bernet sale, New York, April 21, 1966, lot no. 8, Jay Leff collection, Uniontown (1966).

Cat. 2, repr. p. 89

Protection mask
Dan-Ngere, Ivory Coast, Danane region
19th cent.
Wood, plant fibers, animal hair
47 × 21.5 cm
Paris, Marc Ladreit de Lacharrière collection

Helena Rubinstein collection, New York/Paris (before 1937); Parke-Bernet sale, New York, April 21, 1966, lot no. 10; Morris J. Pinto collection, Geneva/New York/Paris (1966); received as a gift from a member of the Pinto family in 1969; Christie's sale, New York, May 12, 2016, lot 603.

Photographed in 1937 by Dora Maar in the music room in (repr. p. 76) and in 1938 in the lounge that became the African room at 24, Quai de Béthune, Paris.

Cat. 3, repr. p. 88

Female initiation mask
Dan, Ivory Coast, Man region
19th cent.
Wood, vegetable fiber, metal, pigments
20.3 × 14 × 8 cm
Paris, Private collection

Helena Rubinstein collection, New York/Paris (before 1965); Parke-Bernet sale, New York, April 21, 1966, lot no. 13; Léon Karchmer collection, New York; Christie's sale, London, June 17, 1980, lot no. 225; (probably) Morris J. Pinto collection, Geneva/New York/Paris.

Cat. 4, repr. p. 91

Mma funerary figure
Agni, Ivory Coast, Krinjabo region
18th – 19th cent.
Terracotta
36.8 × 12.7 × 14.6 cm
New York, The Metropolitan Museum of Art, inv. 1995.64.22

Marked 157.

Collected by Dr. Marcel Lheureux from the Sanwi kingdom in 1928.

Dr. Marcel Lheureux collection (1928–1950); Helena Rubinstein collection, New York/Paris (c. 1950); Parke-Bernet sale, New York, April 21, 1966, lot no. 157; Nina and Gordon Bunshaft collection, New York; gift of Nina Bunshaft in 1994.

Photographed in 1962 in the corridor at 24, Quai de Béthune, Paris (repr. p. 44).

Cat. 5, repr. p. 91

Mma funerary figure
Agni, Ivory Coast, Krinjabo region
18th – 19th cent.
Terracotta
31.5 × 13.8 × 13.8 cm
United States, Africarium Collection

Collected by Dr. Marcel Lheureux from the Sanwi kingdom in 1928.

Dr. Marcel Lheureux collection (1928–1950); Helena Rubinstein collection, New York/Paris (c. 1950); Parke-Bernet sale, New York, April 21, 1966, lot no. 149; Frieda and Milton Rosenthal collection, New York (1966); Sotheby's sale, New York, November 14, 2008, lot no. 12.

Photographed in 1962 in the corridor at 24, Quai de Béthune, Paris (repr. p. 44).

Cat. 6, repr. p. 92

Nsodie male funerary head
Akan, Fomena
Ghana, Adansi region
17th cent.
Terracotta
23 × 18 × 20 cm
Liliane and Michel Durand-Dessert collection

Helena Rubinstein collection, New York/Paris (before 1965); Parke-Bernet sale, New York, April 21, 1966, lot no. 173; Max Granick, New York; Sotheby's sale, New York, November 15, 1988, lot no. 51; Hélène and Philippe Leloup, Paris; Durand-Dessert collection, Paris; Christie's sale, Paris, June 27, 2018, lot no. 51.

Cat. 7, repr. p. 91

Mma funerary figure
Agni, Ivory Coast, Krinjabo region
18th – 19th cent.
Terracotta, glass beads
37.5 × 14 × 13 cm
Paris, Musée du Quai Branly – Jacques Chirac, inv. 73.1966.1.2

Collected by Dr. Marcel Lheureux from the Sanwi kingdom in 1928.

Dr. Marcel Lheureux collection (1928–1950); Helena Rubinstein collection, New York/Paris (c. 1950); gift of the Helena Rubinstein Estate to the Musée National des Arts d'Afrique et d'Océanie (February 4, 1966); Musée national des Arts d'Afrique et d'Océanie (1966–January 31, 2003)

Photographed in 1962 in the corridor at 24, Quai de Béthune, Paris (repr. p. 44).

Cat. 8, repr. p. 93

Mma funerary head
Agni, Ivory Coast, Krinjabo region
18th – 19th cent.
Terracotta
16.1 × 15.5 × 16.7 cm
Paris, Musée du Quai Branly – Jacques Chirac, inv. 73.1966.1.1

Collected by Dr. Marcel Lheureux from the Sanwi kingdom in 1928.

Dr. Marcel Lheureux collection (1928–1950); Helena Rubinstein collection, New York/Paris (c. 1950); gift of the Helena Rubinstein Estate to the Musée National des Arts d'Afrique et d'Océanie (February 4, 1966); Musée national des Arts d'Afrique et d'Océanie (1966–Jan. 31, 2003).

Published in J. Delange and M. Leiris, Afrique noire, la création plastique, Paris: Gallimard (L'univers des Formes), 1967, no. 343, p. 299.

Photographed in 1962 in the corridor at 24, Quai de Béthune, Paris (repr. p. 44).

Cat. 9, repr. p. 95

Afena ceremonial sword
Akan, Ivory Coast, Agnibilékrou region
First half of the 20th cent.
Iron, wood, gilded aluminum
71.1 × 9.8 × 7.5 cm
Washington D.C., National Museum of African Art – Smithsonian Institution, inv. 2015-16-1

Helena Rubinstein collection, New York/Paris (before 1951); Parke-Bernet sale, New York, April 29, 1966, lot no. 171; William W. Brill collection, New York (1966); Sotheby's sale, New York, November 17, 2006, lot no. 48; Steven Morris Fine Arts, LLC Michigan; museum purchase in 2015.

Photographed in 1951 in the African room at 24, Quai de Béthune, Paris (repr. p. 114).

Cat. 10, repr. p. 94

Afena ceremonial sword
Akan, Ivory Coast,
Agnibilékrou region
First half of the 20th cent.
Iron, wood, gilded aluminum
61.5 × 9.2 × 9.8 cm
Washington D.C., National Museum of African Art – Smithsonian Institution, inv. 2015-16-2

Helena Rubinstein collection, New York/Paris (before 1951); ***Parke-Bernet sale, New York, April 29, 1966, lot no. 170;*** *William W. Brill collection, New York (1966); Sotheby's sale, New York, November 17, 2006, lot no. 48; Steven Morris Fine Arts, LLC Michigan; museum purchase in 2015.*

Photographed in 1951 in the African room at 24, Quai de Béthune, Paris (repr. p. 143).

Cat. 11, repr. p. 96

Heddle pulley
Baule, Ivory Coast
19th cent.
Wood, plant fiber
18.4 × 10 × 10 cm
Private collection, with kind permission from Schweizer Premodern, New York

Helena Rubinstein collection, New York/Paris (before 1946); ***Parke-Bernet sale, New York, April 29, 1966, lot no. 22;*** *Frieda and Milton Rosenthal (1966–2008); Sotheby's sale, New York, November 14, 2008, lot no. 9.*

Photographed after 1946 in the music room at 24, Quai de Béthune, Paris (repr. pp. 8–9).

Cat. 12, repr. p. 96

Heddle pulley
Baule, Ivory Coast
19th cent.
Wood, iron
22.9 × 5.1 × 8.3 cm
Long Island, Diane and Brian Leyden collection

Plinth K. Inagaki; marked in white ink HR 59.

Paul Guillaume; Helena Rubinstein collection, New York/Paris (before 1932); ***Parke-Bernet sale, New York, April 29, 1966, lot no. 38;*** *Oscar Kolin collection, New York (1966–1995); Pace Primitive, New York (1995).*

Published and exhibited in J. J. Sweeney, African Negro Art, *New York, MOMA, 1935, no. 63.*

Photographed c. 1932–1934 on the table in the drawing-room at 216, Boulevard Raspail, Paris (repr. pp. 2–3); in 1944 in the foyer of 625 Park Avenue, New York.

Cat. 13, repr. p. 97

Pair of female and male anthropomorphic combs
Bete/Guro, Ivory Coast
19th – early 20th cent.
Wood
H. 22.9 and 24.8 cm
Private collection, with kind permission from Schweizer Premodern, New York

Helena Rubinstein collection, New York/Paris (before 1965); ***Parke-Bernet sale, New York, October 15, 1966, lot no. 72;*** *William W. Brill collection, New York (after 1966–2006); Sotheby's sale, New York, November 17, 2006, lot no. 140.*

Published in Selections from the William W. Brill Collection, *Milwaukee Public Museum, 1969, pl. 25.*

Cat. 14, repr. p. 101

Door shutter
Baule, Ivory Coast
19th – early 20th cent.
Wood, pigments
54.6 × 27.9 cm
The Netherlands, Private collection

Helena Rubinstein collection, New York/Paris (before 1965); ***Parke-Bernet sale, New York, October 15, 1966, lot no. 29.***

Cat. 15, repr. p. 100

Small *bonu amwin* type water-buffalo mask
Baule, Ivory Coast
19th – early 20th cent.
Wood
25 × 15 × 15 cm
Private collection, with kind permission from Schweizer Premodern, New York

Helena Rubinstein collection, New York/Paris (before 1949); ***Parke-Bernet sale, New York, April 21, 1966, lot no. 37;*** *Frieda and Milton Rosenthal collection, New York (1966–2008); Sotheby's sale, New York, November 14, 2008, lot no. 4.*

Photographed in 1949 in the corridor at 24, Quai de Béthune, Paris (repr. p. 121).

Cat. 16, repr. p. 99

Blolo bian male statue
Baule, Ivory Coast,
Bouaké region
19th cent.
Wood
44.5 × 9 × 8 cm
Canada, Private collection

Georges de Miré collection, Paris; auction Hôtel Drouot, Paris, December 16, 1931, lot no. 25; Helena Rubinstein collection, New York/Paris (after 1931); ***Parke-Bernet sale, New York, April 21, 1966, lot no. 40;*** *E. Nathhorst collection, Stockholm (1966–1977); Sotheby's sale, October 14/15, 1977, lot no. 527.*

Cat. 17, repr. p. 104

Female figure
Senufo/Turka/Bobo (?)
Mali/Ivory Coast,
Sikasso region
(according to F.-H. Lem)
19th – early 20th cent.
Wood
27.5 × 20 × 15 cm
Private collection, with kind permission from Schweizer Premodern, New York

Collected by F.-H. Lem, c. 1934–1935.

F.-H. Lem collection, Paris; Helena Rubinstein collection, New York/Paris (after 1935); ***Parke-Bernet sale, New York, April 21, 1966, lot no. 98;*** *Abe Segal collection, New York.*

Published in F.-H Lem, Sculptures soudanaises, *Paris: Arts et métiers graphiques, 1948, pp. 86–87, pl. 40–41.*

Photographed in 1949 in the music room at 24, Quai de Béthune, Paris.

Cat. 18, repr. p. 102

Face mask
Senufo, Ivory Coast,
Korhogo region
(according to F.-H. Lem)
19th – early 20th cent.
Wood
37.5 × 17 × 8.8 cm
France, Private collection

Collected by F.-H. Lem, c. 1934–1935.

F.-H. Lem collection, Paris; Helena Rubinstein collection, New York/Paris (after 1935); ***Parke-Bernet sale, New York, April 21, 1966, lot no. 108;*** *Private collection (1966–2011); Sotheby's sale, Paris, December 14, 2011, lot no. 21; Private collection (2011–2014); Sotheby's sale, Paris, December 10, 2014, lot no. 53.*

Published in F.-H Lem, "Le musée d'art nègre d'Helena Rubinstein," Art et Industrie, *vol. 16, October, 1949, pp. 9–12*

Photographed after 1937 in the corridor at 24, Quai de Béthune, Paris (repr. p. 121).

Cat. 19, repr. p. 103

Gu Female mask
Guro, Ivory Coast
19th cent.
Wood
49 × 15 × 16 cm
Paris, Marceau Rivière collection

Helena Rubinstein collection, New York/Paris (before 1965); ***Parke-Bernet sale, New York, October 15, 1966, lot no. 35;*** *Armand Arman collection, Paris/New York; Thomas Alexander III collection, St. Louis; Pace Primitive, New York; Sale Cornette de Saint-Cyr,*

Paris, March 13, 1981, lot no. 17; Merton Simpson, New York; Marceau Rivière collection, Paris (1995).

Cat. 20, repr. p. 105

Seated female figure
Senufo/Bamana?
Mali, Folona region
(according to F.-H. Lem)
19th – early 20th cent.
Wood
31.8 × 8.9 × 7 cm
New York,
The Metropolitan Museum of Art,
The Michael C. Rockefeller Memorial Collection,
inv. 1978.412.519

Marked in white ink (Rubinstein number) N116.

Collected by F.-H. Lem in the Folona region, Mali, c. 1934–1935.

F.-H. Lem collection, Paris; Helena Rubinstein collection, New York/Paris (after 1935);* Parke-Bernet sale, New York, April 21, 1966, lot no. 134; *Nelson Rockefeller collection, New York, on deposit at Museum of Primitive Art, New York (1966–1969); Gift from Nelson A. Rockefeller to the Museum of Primitive Art, New York (1969-1978).

Published in F.-H. Lem,* Sculptures soudanaises, *Paris: Arts et métiers graphiques, 1948, p. 93, pl. 47.

Photographed in 1949 in the music room at 24, Quai de Béthune, Paris.

Cat. 21, repr. p. 106-107

Helmet mask
Senufo/Bamana (?)
Mali, Sikasso region
(according to F.-H. Lem)
19th – early 20th cent.
Wood, metal, pigments
52 × 44.5 × 25.4 cm
Newark NJ,
Newark Museum,
inv. 66.619 A, B

Collected by F.-H. Lem in Fenkolo, Mali, c. 1934–1935.

F.-H. Lem collection, Paris; Helena Rubinstein collection, New York/Paris (after 1935);* Parke-Bernet sale, New York, April 21, 1966, lot no. 135; *purchase Newark Museum, the Members' Fund in 1966.

Published in F.-H Lem,* Sculptures soudanaises, *Paris: Arts et métiers graphiques, 1948, p. 82, pl. 36; published and exhibited in Robert Goldwater,* Senufo sculpture from West Africa, *New York: The Museum of Primitive Art, 1964, no. 67.

Cat. 22, repr. p. 108

Tefala sejen farmer's cane finial
Senufo, Burkina Faso,
Fourou region
(according to F.-H. Lem)
1900–1935
Wood, metal
27 × 47 cm
Newark NJ, Newark Museum, inv. 66.618 A, B

Collected by F.-H. Lem in Fourou, in the Kenedougou region, Burkina Faso, c. 1934–1935.

F.-H. Lem collection, Paris; Helena Rubinstein collection, New York/Paris (after 1935);* Parke-Bernet sale, New York, April 21, 1966, lot no. 96; *purchase Newark Museum, Louis Bamberger Bequest Fund in 1966.

Photographed in 1951 in the African room at 24, Quai de Béthune, Paris (repr. p. 114).

Cat. 23, repr. p. 109

Tefalipitya farmer's cane
Senufo, Ivory Coast,
Korhogo region
19th cent.
Wood, beads
138.4 × 7 × 7.6 cm
New York,
Private collection

Helena Rubinstein collection, New York/Paris (before 1965);* Parke-Bernet sale, New York, April 21, 1966, lot no. 100; *Dr Alexander S. Honig collection, Bronxville (1966–1993); Sotheby's sale, New York, May 18, 1993, lot no. 55.

Photographed after 1946 in the African room at 24, Quai de Béthune, Paris (repr. p. 143).

Cat. 24, repr. p. 111

Anthropo-zoomorphic initiation mask
Bamana, Mali, Koulikoro region (?)
19th cent.
Wood, metal plates
28 × 20 × 5 cm
Private collection,
with kind permission from Schweizer Premodern,
New York

Marked in white ink (Rubinstein number) N244.

Helena Rubinstein collection, New York/Paris (before 1965);* Parke-Bernet sale, New York, April 21, 1966, lot no. 55; *E. Nathhorst collection, Stockholm (1966–1977); Sotheby's sale, New York, October 14/15, 1977, lot no. 466; Hyman Klebanow, New York (1977); Alan Brandt, New York; Bernard Dulon, Paris; Béatrice and Patrick Caput collection, Paris; Alain de Monbrison, Paris; Stephan Herzog collection, Munich; Sotheby's sale Paris, June 15, 2011, lot no. 75; Leslie Sacks collection, Los Angeles (2011–2016); Sotheby's sale New York, May 7, 2016, lot no. 71.

Photographed after 1937 in the corridor at 24, Quai de Béthune, Paris (repr. p. 110).

Cat. 25, repr. p. 113

Nyeleni female figure
Bamana, Mali,
Sikasso region
(according to F.-H. Lem)
19th – early 20th cent.
Wood
42 × 13.5 × 14 cm
Célestin Clamra collection

Marked in white ink (Rubinstein number) 7.

Collected by F.-H. Lem in Ganadougou in the Sikasso region, Mali, c. 1934–1935.

F.-H. Lem collection, Paris; Helena Rubinstein collection, New York/Paris (after 1935);* Parke-Bernet sale, New York, April 21, 1966, lot no. 58; *Oscar Kolin, New York (1966–1995); Pace Primitive, New York (1996); private collection; Sotheby's sale, Paris, December 11, 2013, lot no. 41.

Published in F.H. Lem,* Sculptures soudanaises, *Paris: Arts et métiers graphiques, 1948, p. 80, pl. 34.

Photographed c. 1951 in the African room at 24, Quai de Béthune, Paris; c. 1960 in the drawing-room in Knightsbridge, London (repr. p. 160).

Cat. 26, repr. p. 112

Nyeleni female figure
Bamana, Mali
19th – early 20th cent.
Wood
40.4 × 11.8 × 12.5 cm
Washington D. C.,
National Museum of African Art – Smithsonian Institution, inv. 96-7-2

Collected by F.-H. Lem c. 1934–1935.

F.-H. Lem collection, Paris; Helena Rubinstein collection, New York/Paris (after 1935);* Parke-Bernet sale, New York, April 21, 1966, lot no. 62; *Abe Siegal collection (1966–1995); Pace Primitive, New York (1995–1996); museum purchase in 1996.

Photographed in 1951 in the African room at 24, Quai de Béthune, Paris (repr. p. 114).

Cat. 27, repr. p. 115

Sogo bo female marionette
Bamana, Mali,
Koutiala region
(according to F.-H. Lem)
19th – early 20th cent.
Wood, cowries, pigments
H. 80 cm
Tenafly, Malcolm collection, with kind permission from Schweizer Premodern,
New York

Plinth K. Inagaki.

Collected by F.-H. Lem in Niéna, Mali, c. 1934–1935.

F.-H. Lem collection, Paris; Helena Rubinstein collection, New York/Paris (after 1935); ***Parke-Bernet sale, New York, April 21, 1966, lot no. 66;*** *Allan Frumkin, Chicago/ New York (1966); Noma Copley, New York; Lance and Roberta Entwistle, London.*

Published in F.-H. Lem, **Sculptures soudanaises,** *Paris: Arts et métiers graphiques, 1948, p. 59, pl. 13.*

Photographed in 1951 in the African room at 24, Quai de Béthune, Paris (repr. p. 114).

Cat. 28, repr. p. 118

Head of zoomorphic marionette
Bamana, Mali, San region
19th – early 20th cent.
Wood
11.6 × 11.4 × 48 cm
St. Louis, James C. Jamieson III collection, with kind permission from Schweizer Premodern, New York

Collected by F.-H. Lem in Mali c. 1934–1935.

F.-H. Lem collection, Paris; Helena Rubinstein collection, New York/Paris (after 1935); ***Parke-Bernet sale, New York, April 21, 1966, lot no. 83;*** *Shelly and Norman Dinhofer, New York (1966–2008); Sotheby's sale, New York, May 16, 2008, lot no. 52.*

Photographed in 1951 in the African room at 24, Quai de Béthune, Paris (repr. p. 114); c. 1960 in the drawing-room in Knightsbridge, London (repr. p.160).

Cat. 29, repr. p. 116

Female *ciwara* crest (antelope and fawn)
Bamana, Mali, Ségou region (according to F.-H. Lem)
19th cent.
Wood, metal
H. 78 cm
Paris, Marc Ladreit de Lacharrière collection

Plinth K. Inagaki; marked in white ink (Rubinstein number) N 199.

Collected by F.-H. Lem in Minianka country, Mali, c. 1934–1935.

F.-H. Lem collection; Helena Rubinstein collection, New York/Paris (after 1935); ***Parke-Bernet sale, New York, April 21, 1966, lot no. 70;*** *Harry A. Franklin collection, Los Angeles (1966–1990); Sotheby's sale, New York, April 21, 1990, lot no. 22; Edwin and Cherie Silver, Los Angeles (1990–2017); Sotheby's sale, New York, November 16, 2017, lot 16.*

Published in F.H. Lem, **Sculptures soudanaises,** *Paris: Arts et métiers graphiques, 1948, p. 74, pl. 28.*

Photographed in 1949 in the African room at 24, Quai de Béthune, Paris.

Cat. 30, repr. p. 116

Male ciwara crest (antelope)
Bamana, Mali, Minianka region (according to F.-H. Lem)
Early 20th cent.
Wood, metal
93.3 × 7.5 × 35.8 cm
Washington D. C., National Museum of African Art – Smithsonian Institution, inv. 2005-6-12

Collected by F.-H. Lem in Minianka country, Mali, c. 1934–1935.

F.-H. Lem collection, Paris; Helena Rubinstein collection, New York/Paris (after 1935); ***Parke-Bernet sale, New York, April 21, 1966, lot no. 68;*** *Ruth and Paul Tishman collection, New York (1966–1984); The Walt Disney Company, Burbank (1984–2005); gift of Walt Disney World Co., subsidiary of the Walt Disney Company in 2005.*

Published in F.H. Lem, **Sculptures soudanaises,** *Paris: Arts et métiers graphiques, 1948, p. 73, pl. 27*

Photographed in 1962 in the African room at 24, Quai de Béthune, Paris (repr. p. 43).

Cat. 31, repr. p. 116

Female *ciwara* crest (antelope and male fawn)
Bamana, Mali, Ségou region (according to F.-H. Lem)
19th cent.
Wood, metal
71.6 × 30.5 × 6 cm
New York, Laura andJames J. Ross collection

Marked in white ink (Rubinstein number) N 201.

Collected by F.-H. Lem in Kignan, Mali, c. 1934–1935.

F.-H. Lem collection; Helena Rubinstein collection, New York/Paris (after 1935); ***Parke-Bernet sale, New York, April 21, 1966, lot no. 69;*** *E. Nathhorst collection, Stockholm (1966–1977); Sotheby's sale, New York, October 14/15, 1977, lot no. 471.*

Published in: F.-H Lem, **"Magie soudanaise,"** *Soleils, Paris: Arts et métiers graphiques, 1947; F. H. Lem,* **Sculptures soudanaises,** *Paris: Arts et métiers graphiques, 1948, p. 68, pl. 22; Jean-Paul Colleyn (ed.),* **Bamana, un art et un savoir-vivre au Mali,** *Musée Rietberg, 2001, p. 209, no. 186; Alisa La Gamma,* **Genesis,** *"Ideas of Origin in African Sculpture", New York: Metropolitan Museum of Art, 2003, p. 86, no. 40*

Photographed in 1949 in the African room at 24, Quai de Béthune, Paris.

Cat. 32, repr. p. 117

Sogoni koun crest
Bamana, Mali, Wassoulou region (according to F.-H. Lem)
19th – early 20th cent.
Wood
H. 54.5 cm
New York, The Arman Marital Trust, Corice Arman Trustee

Marked in white ink (Rubinstein number) N 212.

Collected by F.-H. Lem in the Bougouni region, Mali, c. 1934–1935.

F.-H. Lem collection, Paris; Helena Rubinstein collection, New York/Paris (after 1935); ***Parke-Bernet sale, New York, April 21, 1966, lot no. 75;*** *Harry A. Franklin collection, Los Angeles (1966–1990); Sotheby's sale, New York, April 21, 1990, lot no. 21.*

Published in: F.-H. Lem, **Sculptures soudanaises,** *Paris: Arts et métiers graphiques, 1948, p. 70, pl. 24; W. Rubin, '"Primitivism" in 20th-Century Art. Affinity of the Tribal and the Modern, New York': MOMA, 1987, p. 272.*

Photographed in 1951 in the African room at 24, Quai de Béthune, Paris (repr. p. 114).

Cat. 33, repr. p. 119

Ciwara crest
Bamana, Mali, Kenedougou region
19th – early 20th cent.
Wood
53.4 × 8.9 × 9.5 cm
New York, The Jerome Kenney Family collection

Collected by F.-H. Lem in Mali, c. 1934–1935.

F.-H. Lem collection, Paris; Helena Rubinstein collection, New York/Paris (after 1935); ***Parke-Bernet sale, New York, October 15, 1966, lot no. 38;*** *Ernst Anspach collection, New York.*

Photographed in 1951 in the African room at 24, Quai de Béthune, Paris.

Cat. 34, repr. p. 119

Ciwara crest
Bamana, Mali, west Bamana country (according to F.-H. Lem)
19th – early 20th cent.
Wood
43 × 7.5 × 10.5 cm
Michigan, Private collection

Plinth K. Inagaki; Marked in white ink (Rubinstein number) N 205.

Collected by F.-H. Lem in Mali, c. 1934–1935.

F.-H. Lem collection, Paris; Helena Rubinstein

collection, New York/Paris (after 1935); **Parke-Bernet sale, New York, October 15, 1966, lot no. 40 (no. 3 as lot 40)**; Michael Rhodes, New York

Photographed c. 1960 in the drawing-room in Knightsbridge, London.

Cat. 35, repr. p. 120

Karan wemba dance mask
Mossi, Burkina Faso, Yatenga region, Upper Volta (according to F.-H. Lem)
19th – early 20th cent.
Kapok wood, pigments, wicker loop, vegetable fibers
117 × 20 × 18 cm
Paris, Private collection

Collected by F.-H. Lem in the Ouahigouya region, Burkina Faso, c. 1934–1935.

*F.-H. Lem collection, Paris; Helena Rubinstein collection, New York/Paris (after 1935); **Parke-Bernet sale, New York, April 21, 1966, lot no. 88.***

Published in C. Roy, Art of the Upper Volta Rivers, Meudon: Alain et Françoise Chaffin, 1987, no. 94, p. 126.

Photographed after 1946 in the music room at 24, Quai de Béthune, Paris (repr. p. 77).

Cat. 36, repr. p. 120

Karanga
Mossi, Burkina Faso, Yatenga region
Late 19th – early 20th cent.
Wood, pigments
216 × 18.5 × 17.5 cm
Paris, Musée du Quai Branly – Jacques Chirac, inv. 71.1966.34.1

Marked in white ink (Rubinstein number) 179.

Collected by F.-H. Lem in Burkina Faso, c. 1934–1935.

F.-H. Lem collection, Paris; Helena Rubinstein collection, New York/Paris (before 1965); gift of the Helena Rubinstein Estate to the Musée de l'Homme, Paris, in 1966; Musée de l'Homme collection (1966–2003).

Published in: F. H. Lem, Sculptures soudanaises, Paris, Arts et métiers graphiques, 1948, p. 57, pl. 11; Christopher Roy, Art of the Upper Volta Rivers, Meudon: Alain and Françoise Chaffin, 1987, no. 317 p. 126, p. 370

Photographed after 1946 in the music room at 24, Quai de Béthune, Paris (repr. p. 77).

Cat. 37, repr. p. 123

Female figure
Mossi, Burkina Faso, Yatenga region (according to F.-H. Lem)
19th cent.
Wood
66 × 18.6 × 15.7 cm
Paris, Musée du Quai Branly – Jacques Chirac, inv. 71.1966.34.3

Marked in white ink (Rubinstein number) 12 or 92.

Collected by F.-H. Lem in Burkina Faso c. 1934–1935.

F.-H. Lem collection, Paris; Helena Rubinstein collection, New York/Paris (after 1935); gift of the Helena Rubinstein Estate to the Musée de l'Homme, Paris, in 1966; Musée de l'Homme collection (1966–2003).

Published in F.-H. Lem, Sculptures soudanaises, Paris, Arts et métiers graphiques, 1948, p. 55, pl. 9.

Photographed in 1951 in the African room at 24, Quai de Béthune, Paris (repr. p. 114).

Cat. 38, repr. p. 128

Lefem female figure
Bamileke, Bangwa chiefdom
Cameroon, Grassland region, Fontem
Before 1897
Wood, pigments
81.5 × 35 × 20 cm
Paris, Fondation Dapper

Collected by Gustav Conrau in Bangwa country, c. 1897–1898. Brought back to Europe in 1899.

*Königliches Museum für Völkerkunde, Berlin, collection (1899–1926); Arthur Speyer, Berlin (1926); Charles Ratton, Paris; Helena Rubinstein collection, New York/ Paris (by exchange c. 1928–1929); **Parke-Bernet sale, New York, April 29, 1966, lot no. 189;** Harry A. Franklin collection, Los Angeles (1966–1990); Sotheby's sale, New York, April 21, 1990, lot no. 127.*

Published and exhibited in J. J. Sweeney, African Negro Art, New York: MOMA, 1935, no. 319; published in C. Kjersmeier, Centres de style de la sculpture nègre africaine, Paris: Albert Morancé, vol. 4, 1938, no. 8; exhibited in "Masterpieces of African Art," Brooklyn Museum, October 18, 1954/January 2, 1955; published in J. Delange and M. Leiris, Afrique noire, la création plastique, Paris: Gallimard (L'univers des Formes), 1967, no. 372, p. 322.

Photographed in the drawing-room at 985, Park Avenue, in 1934 and in the African room at 24, Quai de Béthune, Paris, c. 1937 (repr. p. 129).

Cat. 39, repr. p. 126

Head, statuary fragment
Yoruba, Nigeria, Esie region, Offa
12th – 15th cent.
Steatite
29.8 × 9.2 × 15.2 cm
New York, The Metropolitan Museum of Art, The Michael C. Rockefeller Memorial Collection, inv. 1979. 206. 296

Collected by Leo Frobenius in the town of Offa, Nigeria, in 1912.

*Museum für Völkerkunde collection, Hamburg, no. inv 13.209.145 (1913–1936); Charles Ratton, Paris (1936); Helena Rubinstein collection, Paris/New York (before 1937); **Parke-Bernet sale, New York, April 29, 1966, lot no. 175;** Nelson A. Rockefeller collection, New York, on deposit at the Museum of Primitive Art (1966–1978); bequest to the Metropolitan Museum of Art, New York, in 1979.*

Photographed by Dora Maar, c. 1937 au 24, Quai de Béthune, Paris (repr. p. 84).

Cat. 40, repr. p. 127

Anthropomorphic crest mask
Ejagham, Nigeria, Cross River region
19th cent.
Wood, tin, brass, iron, African buffalo skin, vegetable fiber, pigments
H. 35.5 cm
Private collection, with kind permission from Schweizer Premodern, New York

*Helena Rubinstein collection, New York/Paris (before 1951); **Parke-Bernet sale, New York, April 29, 1966, lot no. 181;** Henri and Hélène Kamer, New York; Nicole and John Dintenfass collection, New York.*

Photographed in 1951 in the African room at 24, Quai de Béthune, Paris.

Cat. 41, repr. p. 124

Element from a figurative drum
Bamileke, Cameroon, Bansoa kingdom, treasury of King Foméné
19th cent.
Wood
18.4 × 15.9 × 25.4 cm
New York, The Metropolitan Museum of Art, The Michael C. Rockefeller Memorial Collection, inv. 1979.206.297

Collected from the grandson of King Foméné by the pastor, Frank Christol, c. 1925–1926.

*Henry Solomon Wellcome collection, London (c. 1926–1935); Galerie Pierre (P. Loeb), Paris; Helena Rubinstein collection, New York/Paris (c. 1935); **Parke-Bernet sale, New York, April 29,***

1966, lot no. 186;
Nelson A. Rockefeller collection (1966); on deposit at the Museum of Primitive Art, New York (1966–1978); Nelson A. Rockefeller bequest in 1979.

Photographed in 1951 in the African room at 24, Quai de Béthune, Paris (repr. pp. 42–43).

Cat. 42, repr. p. 125

Element from a figurative drum
Bamileke, Cameroon, Bansoa kingdom, treasury of King Foméné
19th cent.
Wood
20.3 × 21 × 23 cm
Paris, Private collection

Collected from the grandson of King Foméné by the pastor, Frank Christol, c. 1925–1926.

Henry Solomon Wellcome collection, London (after 1926); Galerie Pierre (P. Loeb), Paris (before 1935); Helena Rubinstein collection, New York/Paris (c. 1935); ***Parke-Bernet sale, New York, April 29, 1966, lot no. 187;*** *Jay C. Leff collection, Uniontown; Alan Brandt, New York; Hyman Klebanow collection, New York; Dr Daniel and Marian Malcolm collection, Tenafly; Sotheby's sale New York, May 7, 2016, Malcolm Part One, lot no. 2.*

Published and exhibited in J. J Sweeney, African Negro Art, *New York: MOMA, 1935, no. 317.*

Photographed in 1951 in the African room at 24, Quai de Béthune, Paris (repr. pp. 42–43).

Cat. 43, repr. p. 131

Ancestor figure, reliquary guardian
Kota, Gabon
19th cent.
Wood, brass, copper, iron
66 × 32.5 × 20 cm
Private collection

Plinth K. Inagaki.

Georges de Miré collection, Paris (after 1923); Hôtel Drouot sale, Paris, December 15, 1931, lot 57; Helena Rubinstein collection, Paris/New York (1931); ***Parke-Bernet sale, New York, April 29, 1966, lot no. 192;*** *David Lloyd Kreeger collection, Washington (1966); Richard Feigen collection, New York (by exchange); Warren Robbins collection, Washington D.C.; William Rubin collection, New York, (c. 1981–2015); Christie's sale, Paris, June 23, 2015, lot 37.*

Published and exhibited in: V. Marquetty, Afrique/Océanie, *Paris, Galerie Pigalle, 1930, no. 186, p. 16; J. J. Sweeney,* African Negro Art, *New York, MOMA, 1935, no. 379; W. Rubin, "Primitivism" in 20th-century Art. Affinity of the Tribal and the Modern, New York: MOMA, 1984 and 1987, p. 268.*

Photographed after 1932 on the mantelpiece in the drawing-room at 216, Boulevard Raspail, Paris.

Cat. 44, repr. p. 130

Ancestor figure, reliquary guardian
Kota, Gabon
19th – 20th cent.
Wood, brass, copper
39.4 × 13.5 × 7.6 cm
Private collection

Helena Rubinstein collection, Paris/New York (before 1965); ***Parke-Bernet sale, New York, April 29, 1966, lot no. 195,*** *Gaston de Havenon collection, New York.*

Published on the cover of Alain and Françoise Chaffin, L'Art kota, les figures de reliquaire, *Meudon: Chaffin, 1979.*

Photographed in 1951 in the African room at 24, Quai de Béthune, Paris (repr. p. 114).

Cat. 45, repr. p. 130

Ancestor figure, reliquary guardian
Kota, Gabon, Makokou region
19th cent.
Wood, brass, copper
55 × 22 × 22 cm
New York, The Arman Marital Trust, Corice Arman Trustee

Formerly Helena Rubinstein collection, Paris/New York (before 1965); ***Parke-Bernet sale, New York, April 29, 1966, lot no. 200;*** *Gaston de Havenon, New York; Christie's sale, London, June 17, 1980, lot no. 261; Loudmer sale, Paris, May 31, 1983, lot 172; Arman, New York/Paris/Nice (1980–2005).*

Cat. 46, repr. p. 130

Ancestor figure, reliquary guardian
Kota Obamba, Gabon, banks of the Sebe River
19th cent.
Wood, brass, copper
52 × 20 × 20 cm
Paris, Fondation Dapper, inv. 6623

Paul Eluard collection, Paris (before 1929); Baron Lambert collection, Brussels (before 1933); Helena Rubinstein collection, Paris/New York (c. 1933); ***Parke-Bernet sale, New York, April 29, 1966, lot no. 202;*** *Private collection; Sotheby's sale, New York, May 10, 1983, lot no. 66.*

Photographed after 1941 in the drawing-room at 625, Park Avenue, New York.

Cat. 47, repr. p. 130

Ancestor figure, reliquary guardian
Kota, Gabon, Makokou region
19th cent.
Wood, brass, copper
52.1 × 20 × 20 cm
New York, The Arman Marital Trust, Corice Arman Trustee

Helena Rubinstein collection, Paris/New York (before 1938); ***Parke-Bernet sale, New York, April 29, 1966, lot no. 203;*** *Gaston de Havenon collection, New York; Christie's sale, London, June 17, 1980, lot no. 260; Arman, New York/Paris/Nice (1980–2005).*

Published in Vogue, *August 1938, in the apartment on 895, Park Avenue, New York.*

Photographed in the apartment on 625, Park Avenue, New York, after 1941 (repr. p. 163).

Cat. 48, repr. p. 133

Ancestor head, *byeri* reliquary guardian
Fang, Betsi group
Gabon, Okano Valley region
19th cent.
Wood, metal
35.5 × 13 × 13 cm
Paris, Private collection

Marked in white ink (Rubinstein number): N.255

Helena Rubinstein collection, Paris/New York (before 1937); ***Parke-Bernet sale, New York, April 29, 1966, lot no. 215;*** *Henri and Hélène Kamer, New York (1966).*

Photographed in 1937 in the African room at 24, Quai de Béthune, Paris (repr. p. 40).

Cat. 49, repr. p. 134-135

Ngontang helmet-mask
Fang, Gabon, River Komo region
19th cent.
Wood, kaolin
35.6 × 25.4 × 31.1 cm
Detroit, Detroit Institute of Art, inv. 1983.24

Paul Guillaume collection, Paris; Helena Rubinstein collection, Paris/New York (c. 1930); ***Parke-Bernet sale, New York, April 29, 1966, lot no. 221;*** *Harry A. Franklin collection, Los Angeles (1966–1983); purchase by the DIA Founders Society, with the help of the New Endowment Fund, General Endowment Fund, Benson and Edith Ford Fund, Henry Ford II Fund, Conrad H. Smith Fund in 1983.*

Published in G. Apollinaire and P. Guillaume,* Sculptures nègres*, Paris: Paul Guillaume, 1917, pl. XXIII; published and exhibited in J. J. Sweeney,* African Negro Art*, New York: MOMA, 1935; published in P. Radin,* African folktales and sculpture*, 1952, no. 20.

Photographed in 1937 in the beauty salon at 715, Fifth Avenue, New York; in 1937, by Dora Maar in the corridor at 24, Quai de Béthune, Paris (repr. p. 136).; after 1941 in the drawing-room at 625, Park Avenue, New York (repr. pp. 4–5).

Cat. 50, repr. p. 132

Eyema byeri ancestor figure, reliquary guardian
Fang, Mvai, Gabon, Minvoul region
19th cent.
Wood
35 × 15 × 15 cm
Paris, Collection Q. Laurens

Helena Rubinstein collection, Paris/New York (before 1951);* Parke-Bernet sale, New York, April 29, 1966, lot no. 209*; Henri Laurens collection (1966).

Photographed in 1951 in the African room at 24, Quai de Béthune, Paris (repr. p. 42–43).

Cat. 51, repr. p. 138

Chief figure
Luluwa, Democratic Republic of the Congo, Kasaï Occidental region
1875–1900
Wood
50.5 × 13.3 × 14 cm
Detroit, Detroit Institute of Art, inv. 82.49

Collected by Leo Frobenius c. 1905–1906.

Leo Frobenius collection, Munich/Frankfurt; Museum für Völkerkunde collection, Hamburg; Charles Ratton, Paris (by exchange); Helena Rubinstein collection, Paris/New York (before 1949);* Parke-Bernet sale, New York, April 29, 1966, lot no. 227*; Jay C. Leff collection, Uniontown; Sotheby's sale, London, June 23, 1981, lot 205.

Purchase by the DIA Founders Society, with assistance from L & R Entwistle and Co., Ralph Harman Booth Bequest Fund, Abraham Borman Family Fund, Joseph H. Boyer Memorial Fund, Joseph M. de Grimme Memorial Fund, General Endowment Fund, New Endowment Fund, Benson and Edith Ford Fund, K. T. Keller Fund, Laura H. Murphy Fund, Mary Martin Semmes Fund, Barbara L. Scripps Fund, Edna Burian Skelton Fund, Mr. and Mrs. Conrad H. Smith Memorial Fund, Henry E. and Consuelo S. Wenger Foundation Fund, and Matilda R. Wilson Fund.

Photographed in 1951 in the African room at 24, Quai de Béthune, Paris.

Cat. 52, repr. p. 139

Bust
Luluwa, Democratic Republic of the Congo, Kasaï Occidental region
19th cent.
Wood, brass nail
H. 30.5 cm
Tenafly, Collection Malcolm, with kind permission from Schweizer Premodern, New York

Gustave De Hondt collection, Brussels (c. 1938); Helena Rubinstein collection, Paris/New York (after 1938);* Parke-Bernet sale, New York, April 29, 1966, lot no. 228*; Collection Frieda and Milton Rosenthal collection, New York; Sotheby's sale, New York, November 14, 2008, lot 15.

Exhibited in "Tentoonstelling van Kongo-kunst", Stadsfeestzaal aan de Mair, Antwerp, December 24, 1937–January 16, 1938.

Published in F. Olbrechts,* Les arts plastiques du Congo belge*, Brussels: Erasme, 1959, pl. XVIII.

Cat. 53, repr. p. 140

Nkisi figure of a kneeling man
Kongo, Democratic Republic of the Congo
19th cent.
Wood, organic material, pigments, bone
28.5 × 8.5 × 10.2 cm
New York, Metropolitan Museum of Art, the Michael C. Rockefeller Memorial Collection, inv. 1978. 412. 521

Charles Ratton, Paris; Helena Rubinstein collection, Paris/New York (before 1965);* Parke-Bernet sale, New York, April 29, 1966, lot no. 233*; Nelson A. Rockefeller collection, New York (1966); on deposit at the Museum of Primitive Art, New York (1966–1969); gift to the Museum of Primitive Art, New York, in 1969.

Exhibited and published in* Afrique, cent tribus, cent chefs-d'œuvre*, Paris: Musée des Arts Décoratifs, 1964.

Cat. 54, repr. p. 140

Ancestor figure
Punu Lumbo, Gabon / Republic of the Congo
19th cent.
Wood, porcelain
18.4, × 5.6 × 5.6 cm
United States, Africarium Collection

Helena Rubinstein collection, Paris/New York (before 1965);* Parke-Bernet sale, New York, April 29, 1966, lot no. 237*; Frieda and Milton Rosenthal, New York (1966–2008); Sotheby's sale, New York, November 14, 2008, lot no. 14.

Cat. 55, repr. p. 141

Figure of a seated man
Dengese, Democratic Republic of the Congo, Kasaï Occidental region
19th cent.
Wood, metal staples, pigments
55.2, × 20 × 15.2 cm
New York, The Metropolitan Museum of Art, the Michael C. Rockefeller Memorial Collection, inv. 1978.412.520

Marked in white ink (Rubinstein number) N 155.

Belgian (?) private collection (before 1930); Charles Ratton, Paris (1935); Helena Rubinstein collection, Paris/New York (after 1935);* Parke-Bernet sale, New York, April 29, 1966, lot no. 232*; Nelson A. Rockefeller collection (1966); on deposit at the Museum of Primitive Art, New York (1966–1969); gift from Nelson A. Rockefeller to the Museum of Primitive Art, New York (1969).

Published in J. Maes and H. Lavachery,* L'art nègre au palais des Beaux-Arts de Bruxelles*, 1930, pl. 7; published and exhibited in J. J. Sweeney,* African Negro Art*, New York: MOMA, 1935, no. 445.

Photographed in 1951 in the African room at 24, Quai de Béthune, Paris (repr. p. 114).

Cat. 56, repr. p. 145

Drum
Attie, Ivory Coast
19th cent.
Wood
183 × 29 × 29 cm
Paris, Nicolas Hug collection

Plinth K. Inagaki; marked in white ink (Rubinstein number) N229.

Paul Guillaume, Paris (before 1932); Helena Rubinstein collection, Paris/New York (before 1932);* Parke-Bernet sale, New York, October 15, 1966, lot no. 32*; Freda and Harry Schaeffer collection, New York (1966–1999); Sotheby's sale, New York, May 25, 1999, lot no. 180; private collection, (1999–2013); Sotheby's sale, Paris, December 11, 2013, lot no. 45.

Cat. 57, repr. p. 147

Chief's chair
Chokwe,
Democratic Republic of the Congo / Angola
19th cent.
Wood, metal, skin
60.1 × 29.9 × 35.7 cm
Washington D.C., National Museum of African Art – Smithsonian Institution, inv. 81-23-3

Helena Rubinstein collection, Paris/New York (before 1965); ***Parke-Bernet sale, New York, April 29, 1966, lot no. 243;*** *Ruth and Paul Tishman collection, New York (1966–1981); gift Ruth and Paul Tishman in 1981.*

Cat. 58, repr. p. 146

Anthropomorphic pipe bowl
Bamun, Cameroon
19th – early 20th cent.
Terracotta
28 × 8.2 × 13.3 cm
Washington D. C., National Museum of African Art – Smithsonian Institution, inv. 2005-6-373

Helena Rubinstein collection, Paris/New York (before 1937); ***Parke-Bernet sale, New York, April 29, 1966, lot no. 184;*** *Ruth and Paul Tishman collection, New York (1966–1981); The Walt Disney Company, Burbank (1984–2005); gift from Walt Disney World Co., subsidiary of The Walt Disney Company, in 2005.*

Photographed c. 1937 in the lounge library, which will later become the African room, at 24, Quai de Béthune, Paris (repr. p. 40).

OCEANIA

Cat. 59, repr. p. 149

Moai kava kava male figure
Rapa Nui, Easter Island
Late 19th cent.
Toromiro wood, pigments
60 × 13 × 14 cm
Paris, Jean-François Schmitt collection

Marked in white ink (Rubinstein number) 103 or 105.

Galerie Pierre (P. Loeb), Paris; Helena Rubinstein collection, Paris/New York (before 1965); ***Parke-Bernet sale, New York, April 29, 1966, lot no. 261;*** *Jean Roudillon, Paris; Simon Spierer collection, Geneva; Galerie Patrik Fröhlich, Zurich (2009).*

Exhibited and published in V. Marquetty, Afrique/Océanie, Paris: Galerie Pigalle, 1930, no. 417, p 29; Published in A. Portier and F. Poncetton, Les arts sauvages, Océanie, Paris, Albert Morancé 1931, pl. Ic.

Cat. 60, repr. p. 148

Anthropomorphic sculpture
Sentani, Irian Jaya, northeastern New Guinea, Lake Sentani
19th cent.
Wood
120.7 × 20 × 20 cm
Gordon Sze MD collection

Marked in white ink (Rubinstein number) 272.

Collected by Jacques Viot in 1929.

Galerie Pierre Loeb, Paris; Helena Rubinstein collection, Paris/New York (c. 1930); ***Parke-Bernet sale, New York, April 29, 1966, lot no. 260;*** *Count Baudoin de Grunne collection, Brussels.*

Photographed after 1941 at 625, Park Avenue, New York.

Cat. 61, repr. p. 149

Tauihu canoe prow
Maori, North New Zealand, east coast, Gisborne
1850–1870
Wood, pāua shell
33.5 × 28 × 71 cm
New York, Brooklyn Museum, inv. 53.149.1

Helena Rubinstein collection, Paris/New York (before 1953); gift from Princess Gourielli (Helena Rubinstein) to the Brooklyn Museum in 1953.

AMERICAS

Cat. 62, repr. p. 150

Head of a smiling woman
Totonac, Mexico, Veracruz
c. 600–900
Terracotta
15.9 × 13.3 × 10.2 cm
New York, Brooklyn Museum, inv. 53.149.3

Formerly Helena Rubinstein collection, Paris/New York (before 1953); gift from Princess Gourielli (Helena Rubinstein) to the Brooklyn Museum in 1953.

Cat. 63, repr. p. 150

Head of a smiling man
Totonac, Mexico, Veracruz
c. 600–900
Terracotta
15.2 × 17,1 × 10,8 cm
New York, Brooklyn Museum, inv. 53.149.2

Formerly Helena Rubinstein collection, Paris/New York (before 1953); gift from Princess Gourielli (Helena Rubinstein) to the Brooklyn Museum in 1953.

Cat. 64, repr. p. 151

Front section of crest
Charles Edenshaw (1834–1924), Haida artist
Canada, British Columbia
Late 19th cent.
Maple wood, pigments, abalone shell
15.6 × 14 × 7.6 cm
New York, Brooklyn Museum, inv. 50.158

Formerly Helena Rubinstein collection, Paris/New York (before 1950); gift from Princess Gourielli (Helena Rubinstein) to the Brooklyn Museum in 1950.

Cat. 65, repr. p. 150

Vase representing a mythical anthropomorphic being
Nasca, Peru, southern coast
100 BCE – 700 CE
Polychrome terracotta
15.5 × 16 × 15 cm
Paris, Musée du Quai Branly – Jacques Chirac, inv. 71.1931.91.1

Georges de Miré collection, Paris (1920–1931); ***Hôtel Drouot sale, Paris, December 15, 1931, lot 139;*** *Helena Rubinstein collection, Paris/New York (1931), gift from Helena Rubinstein and Edward Titus to the Musée d'Ethnographie du Trocadero, Paris, in 1931.*

SALE CATALOGS

Cat. 66, repr. p. 27

The Helena Rubinstein collection, African and Oceanic art, parts One and Two, Parke-Bernet Galleries Inc., New York, sale number 2429
April 21, 1966, April 29, 1966
Paris, Musée du Quai Branly – Jacques Chirac, MH-L-B-007399

Cat. 67, repr. p. 27

The Helena Rubinstein collection, African and Oceanic art, part Three, Parke-Bernet Galleries Inc., New York, sale number 2460
October 15, 1966
Paris, Musée du Quai Branly – Jacques Chirac, F-K-Z-000004

Cat. 68

The Helena Rubinstein collection, Modern drawings and prints, Parke-Bernet Galleries Inc., New York, sale number 2432,
April 28, 1966
Paris, Musée du Quai Branly – Jacques Chirac, RA 5047

Cat. 69

The Helena Rubinstein collection, Modern painting and sculpture. Part One: including Italian, French and other works, Parke-Bernet Galleries Inc., New York, sale number 2428
April 20, 1966
Paris, Musée du Quai Branly – Jacques Chirac, RA 5045

Cat. 70

The Helena Rubinstein collection, Modern painting and sculpture. Part two: including Italian, French and other works, Parke-Bernet Galleries Inc., New York, sale number 2431
April 27, 1966
Paris, Musée du Quai Branly – Jacques Chirac, RA 5046

PHOTOGRAPHS

Walker Evans (1903-1975)

African Negro Art, portfolio presenting 477 photographs of objects in the *African Negro Art* exhibition curated by James Johnson Sweeney, New York, The Museum of Modern Art, March 18–May 19, 1935
Print on baryta paper mounted onto cardboard
25.9 × 31.4 cm
Paris, Musée du Quai Branly – Jacques Chirac

Cat. 71

"Figure (catalog no. 14). French Sudan. Wood, 14 3/4 inches high. Collection of Mme Helena Rubinstein, New York," PA000037.17

Cat. 72

"Two bobbins (left to right, catalog no. 126, 63). Ivory Coast. Baule. Wood, 7 and 9 inches high. Collection Galerie Percier, Paris, and Mme Helena Rubinstein, New York," PA000038.129

Cat. 73

"Mask in form of bird's head (catalog no. 88). Ivory Coast. Toma. Wood, 8 inches high (photograph slightly over actual size). Collection Mme Helena Rubinstein, New York," PA000037.86

Cat. 74

"Head (catalog no. 318). Cameroon. Wood with traces of polychrome, 6½ inches high (photograph actual size). Collection Mme Helena Rubinstein, New York. Possibly an architectural ornament," PA000039.270

Cat. 75, repr. p. 175 ; Cat. 176

"Commemorative figure (catalog no. 319). Cameroon, region of Duchang. Bangwa. Wood, 32 inches high. Collection Mme Helena Rubinstein, New York. Mortuary figure holding calabash," PA000039.255 and PA000039.256

Cat. 77

"Pipe bowl (catalog no. 341). Cameroon, Bamum (?). Bronze, 9½ inches high (photograph nearly actual size). Collection Mme Helena Rubinstein, New York. Chief's pipe (?)," PA000039.295

Cat. 78, repr. p. 26

"Ancestral figure, head (catalog no. 370). Gabun. Pahouin (Fan). Wood, 13½ inches high. Collection Mme Helena Rubinstein, New York," PA000039.321

Cat. 79

"Ancestral figure, head (catalog. no. 372). Gabun. Pahouin (Fan). Wood with metal eyes, 12½ inches high. Collection Mme Helena Rubinstein, New York," PA000039.323

Cat. 80, repr. p. 65

"Ancestral figure (catalog no. 379). Gabun, Ogowe River. Bakota. Copper over wood, 22½ inches high. Collection Mme Helena Rubinstein, New York. See note on plate 325," PA000039.328

Cat. 81

"Two Figures (left to right, catalog no. 397, 398). Ivory coast (?). Wood, 6¾ inches high (photograph about actual size). Collection Mme. Helena Rubinstein, New York," PA000037.75

Cat. 82

"Kneeling figure (catalog no. 243). Dahomey. Yoruba. Wood, 17 inches high. Collection Félix Fénéon, Paris. Possibly top of a sceptre. Represents priestess of 'Shango', god of thunder," PA000038.176

Cat. 83

"Seat with figures (catalog no. 335). Cameroon. Bafout. Wood, 39½ inches high. Collection Pierre Loeb, Paris," PA000039.291

Cat. 84

"Four-faced casque (catalog no. 418). French Congo, Mpongwe. Wood, whitened, 13⅜ inches high. The Paul Guillaume Collection, Paris," PA000039.361

Cat. 85

"Commemorative figure, profile view (catalog no. 445). Belgian Congo, Bena Lulua. Wood, 21⅝ inches high. Collection Charles Ratton, Paris," PA000040.368

Cat. 86, repr. p. 84; Cat. 87, repr. p. 137; Cat. 88

Dora Maar (1907-1997)
Three photographs from the series taken in Helena Rubinstein's apartment at 24, Quai de Béthune, Paris
c. 1937
Silver print
29.5 × 23 cm
New York, private collection

Cat. 89, repr p. 73

George Maillard Kesslere (1894–1979)
Helena Rubinstein in her apartment at 895, Park Avenue, New York
1934
Silver print
29.5 × 23 cm
New York, private collection

Cat. 90, repr. p. 73

Man Ray (1890-1976)
Portrait of Helena Rubinstein
c. 1924
Silver print
29,5 × 23 cm
New York, private collection

Cat. 91, repr. p. 35, 42, 81, 121, 143, 158-159

Jean Vincent (1858-1963)
Colorized album
Helena Rubinstein's apartment at
24, Quai de Béthune, Paris
1955
Photographs mounted in an album,
with a velvet cover
74 × 59 × 7.5 cm
New York, private collection

Photographic credits

© 2019. Digital image, The Museum of Modern Art, New York/Scala Florence: p. 175 below

Archives Fondation Dapper/Photo Hughes Dubois: pp. 128, 130 above left

© Art Institute of Chicago, Dist. RMN-Grand Palais/Image The Art Institute of Chicago: p. 24 left

Association Musée Air France/ Commission Histoire et Patrimoine: p. 65 above left

Association Willy Maywald: p. 166

© BAMW Photography: pp. 34, 109

Bibliothèque de l'Institut National d'Histoire de l'Art, Paris, cote Per N2 Œil 1966 (1) / © Courtesy of Sotheby's, Inc. © 2019: pp. 28–29

Brooklyn Museum, Gift of Helena Rubinstein, 50.158.: p. 151; Brooklyn Museum, Gift of Princess Gourielli (Mme Helena Rubinstein), 53.149.1: p. 149 left; Brooklyn Museum, Gift of Princess Gourielli (Mme Helena Rubinstein), 53.149.2.: p. 150 below; Brooklyn Museum, Gift of Princess Gourielli (Mme Helena Rubinstein), 53.149.3.: p. 150 above left

Centre Pompidou, Paris -MNAM - CCI, Dist. RMN-Grand Palais/image Centre Pompidou, MNAM-CCI: pp. 40, 84, 136–37

© Christie's LTD/Photo Visko Hatfield: p. 131

Collection James C. Jamieson III, Saint-Louis, with kind permission from Schweizer Premodern, New York: p. 118; Tenafly, Malcolm collection, with kind permission from Schweizer Premodern: p. 115; private collection, with kind permission from Schweizer Premodern, New York: pp. 96 left, 97, 100, 104, 111, 127

Collection of the Newark Museum, 66.619. Purchase 1966 The Members's Fund 66.619/Photo by Richard Goodbody: p. 106–107; collection of the Newark Museum, 66.618. Purchase 1966 Louis Bamberger Bequest Fund Fund 66.618/Photo by Richard Goodbody: p. 108

Collezioni d'Arte Fondazione Cariparma, donazione Carlo Bavagnoli, inv. FF 3039.21.016: p. 78

© Courtesy of the Phoebe A. Hearst Museum of Anthropology and the Regents of the University of California, (Catalog no. 5-5290): p. 66 right

David Hicks Archives © Estate of David Hicks: pp. 10–11

Detroit Institute of Art, Founders Society Purchase, Eleanor Clay Ford Fund for African Art and Mr. and Mrs. Walter Buhl Ford II Fund: p. 62; Detroit Institute of Arts, Founders Society Purchase, New Endowment Fund, General Endowment Fund et al., 1983.24.: pp. 134–35; Detroit Institute of Arts, Founders Society Purchase, with funds from L & R Entwistle and Co., Ralph Harman Booth Bequest Fund, Abraham Borman Family Fund et al., 82.49: p. 138

Eskenazi Museum of Art, Indiana University, Bloomington, inv. 77.87/ Photo Kevin Montague: p. 24 right

Gamma-Rapho/Photo Giancarlo Botti: pp. 43, 44

Getty Images/Condé Nast Collection/ Photo Edward Steichen: p. 83; Getty Images/The Life Images Collection/ Photo Herbert Gehr: pp. 23, 163, 169

Himeji City Museum of Art: p. 157

Image courtesy of Fashion Institute of Technology / SUNY, FIT Library Unit of Special Collections and College Archives: pp. 33, 36 above left and right, 47 below left, 74, 114, 171, 175 above right, 191 above left

© Leiris / Laurens, Paris: p. 132

Man Ray Trust / Telimage: p. 45 right

© Musée du quai Branly – Jacques Chirac: pp. 26, 65 below left and right, 120 left, 175 above left, 194 left; © Musée du quai Branly – Jacques Chirac / © Courtesy of Sotheby's, Inc. ©: 2019: pp. 27, 201–29; © Musée du quai Branly – Jacques Chirac, photo Patrick Gries, Valérie Torre: p. 150 above right; © Musée du quai Branly – Jacques Chirac, photo Pauline Guyon: couverture (left), pp. 1, 35, 42, 51–59, 81, 88 right, 89, 93, 102, 116 right, 121, 125, 130 below right, 142-143, 145, 158-159, 194 right; © Musée du quai Branly – Jacques Chirac, photo Thierry Ollivier, Michel Urtado: pp. 91 milieu, 123; © Musée du quai Branly – Jacques Chirac/ Pauline Shapiro: pp. 117 right, 119, 130 above right, 130 below left, 148

National Museum of African Art Smithsonian Institution/Photo Brad Simpson: pp. 94–95, 147; National Museum of African Art Smithsonian Institution/Photo Franko Khoury: pp. 112, 116 left, 146

National Portrait Gallery, Canberra: p. 191 right

New York, private collection: pp. 73 below left and right, 76

© Paris, archives Helena Rubinstein – L'Oréal: couverture (right), pp. 2–3, 4–5, 6–7, 8–9, 21, 36 below left and right, 39, 45 left, 47 above right, 73 above left, 77, 90, 110, 129, 155, 160, 191 below; © Paris, archives Helena Rubinstein – L'Oréal, photo Brian Brake: p. 47 above left; © Paris, archives Helena Rubinstein – L'Oréal, photo Alfred Eisenstaedt: p. 80; © Paris, archives Helena Rubinstein – L'Oréal, photo Boris Lipnitzki: pp. 36 below right, 73 above right, 165; © Paris, archives Helena Rubinstein - L'Oréal, photo Francis Thompson: p. 47 below right

The New Orleans Museum of Art, Bequest of Victor K. Kiam, 77.154: p. 61

© Photograph Courtesy of Sotheby's, Inc. © 2019: pp. 65 above right, 66 left, 91 left, 113, 139, 140 left

Photo Hughes Dubois: pp. 88 left, 92, 99, 101, 133

Photo Vincent Girier Dufournier: pp. 120 right, 149 right

Photo Pauline Shapiro: p. 96 right

Photo Courtesy Laura and James J. Ross: p. 117 left

Sotheby's/Art Digital Studio: p. 103

The Kreeger Museum, Washington, DC: pp. 68–69

The Metropolitan Museum of Art, Dist. RMN-Grand Palais/image MMA: pp. 91 right, 105, 140 right, 141

The Metropolitan Museum of Art, New York, The Michael C. Rockefeller Memorial Collection, Bequest of Nelson A. Rockefeller, 1979, www.metmuseum.org: pp. 124, 126

Copyrights

© Adagp Paris 2019 for the works by: Jean Atlan, *Harlem*, 1957 and *Jamaica*, 1956: p. 110; *Lilith*: pp. 10–11; Marc Chagall, *Les Amoureux et la lune*, 1927: pp. 158–59; Raoul Dufy, *Les Courses*: pp. 4–5; *Portrait d'Helena Rubinstein*, 1934: p. 44; Jacques-Nathan Garamond: p. 65 above left; Fernand Léger, *Tapis*: p. 136; Dora Maar: pp. 40, 76, 84, 136, 137; Chana Orloff, *Jeune Fille*, 1940s: p. 155; Serge Poliakoff, *Composition - fond bleu*: pp. 21, 166; Candido Portinari, *Tête de femme*, 1936, p. 163; Georges Rouault, *Tête de Clown*: p. 191 below; Ossip Zadkine, *Tête d'homme*, 1924: pp. 2–3

Association Willy Maywald © Adagp, Paris 2019: p. 166

© Boris Lipnitski/Roger-Viollet: pp. 36 below right, 73 above right, 165

© Brian Brake Estate/Museum of New Zealand Te Papa Tongarewa: p. 47 above left

© Estate of George Biddle, courtesy D. Wigmore Fine Art, Inc: p. 191 below

© Estate of Helene Sardeau, courtesy D. Wigmore Fine Art, Inc.: p. 191 below

© Fondation Foujita/Adagp, Paris 2019 for: Marie Laurencin, *La Famille du poète*, 1909: pp. 4–5

Fondation Lurçat/Adagp, Paris, 2019 for *Cavalcade*, vers 1930: pp. 76, 137

Getty Images/The Life Images Collection/ Photo Alfred Eisenstaedt: p. 80

© Graham Sutherland Estate: p. 191 right

© Man Ray 2015 Trust/Adagp, Paris 2019: pp. 45 right, 73 below right, 194 left

© Salvador Dalí, Fundació Gala-Salvador Dalí/Adagp, Paris 2019 for *Le Reflet crânien*, 1930: p. 169

© Succession Picasso 2019: p. 157; for *Confidence* (tapisserie), 1934: pp. 47 below left, 163; *Étude pour nu à la draperie*, watercolors and pencil, 1907 and *Étude pour nu à la draperie*, gouache, 1907: pp. 158–159

© Succession Brancusi, Adagp, 2019 for *Négresse blanche II*, 1928: pp. 2–3, 21; 24 left, p. 76

© Successió Miró/Adagp, Paris, 2019, for *Femmes et oiseaux dans la nuit*, vers 1944: p. 21; *Portrait*, 1927: p. 39

Walker Evans Archive, The Metropolitan Museum of Art: pp. 26, 65 below left, 175 above left

All rights reserved for the works by: © George Maillard Kesslere: pp. 73 below left, 175 above right; © Studio Granere: p. 74; © Pavel Tchelitchew: p. 73 below left; © Francis Thompson: p. 47 below right; © Jean Vincent: pp. 35, 42, 81, 121, 142–43, 158–59

The image reproduction rights are reserved for the photographers for whom we did not find any contact information despite our research or if their references were not specified.

The publishers would moreover like to thank for their help and contribution to the iconography research for this volume: Meghan Finch, Detroit Institute of Arts; Francis Grylls, David Hicks Archive; Heather A. Hales, Eskenazi Museum of Art, Indiana University, Bloomington; Robert Karrer; Susan Kloman and Remy Magusteiro, Christie's Paris; Francesca Magri, Fondazione Cariparma; Gaïa Lettere, Sotheby's New York; Charlotte Lidon, Sotheby's Paris; Jutta Nieman, Association Willy Maywald; Monica Park, Brooklyn Museum; Constantine Petridis, Art Institute of Chicago, and Ben Watkins; Jean Signoret, Association Musée Air France; Hannah Storch, Washington, Smithsonian – National Museum of African Art; Yoriko Taniguchi, Himeji City Museum of Art; Laura Teigman, Schweizer Premodern

ISBN musée du quai Branly – Jacques Chirac: 978-2-35744-124-8

ISBN Skira Paris: 978-2-37074-128-8

Printed and bound in October 2019 by Graphius in Ghent, Belgium

Legal deposit November 2019